MANAGEMENT CONSULTING

MANAGEMENT CONSULTING

A GUIDE TO THE PROFESSION

Third (revised) edition

Edited by MILAN KUBR

INTERNATIONAL LABOUR OFFICE   GENEVA

Kubr, M. (ed.)
Management consulting: A guide to the profession (third edition)
Geneva, International Labour Office, 1996

/Guide/, /Management consultancy/, /Management consultant/. 12.04.1
ISBN 92-2-109449-9

ILO Cataloguing in Publication Data

ILO publications can be obtained through major booksellers or ILO local offices in many countries, or direct from ILO Publications, International Labour Office, CH-1211 Geneva 22, Switzerland. A catalogue or list of new publications will be sent free of charge from the above address.

CONTENTS

V

Appendices

Figures

Management consulting

Tables

Boxes

AUTHORS AND ACKNOWLEDGEMENTS

This book is the result of a collective effort and reflects collective experience of the international consulting profession.

The first edition (1976) was written by the following team: James Dey, George Kanawaty, Milan Kubr, Frederic Latham, Philip Neck and J. Geoffrey Rawlinson, with contributions from Derek Bowland, Gerry Y. Elliot, Alan Gladstone, Colin Guthrie, W. J. C. McEwan, Alan C. Popham, Edgar H. Schein, P. W. Shay and W. Trevor Utting.

The second edition (1986) had the the following co-authors: Alan Gladstone, Colin Guthrie, John Heptonstall, George Kanawaty, Milan Kubr, Gordon Lippitt, Leonard Nadler, Philip Neck and John Wallace. Valuable material, ideas or comments were provided by Maurice C. Ashill, Daniel Bas, Bengt Björklund, Kenneth L. Block, George Boulden, Joseph J. Brady, Praxy Fernandes, Stelan Friberg, S. R. Ganesh, John F. Hartshorne, James H. Kennedy, Emile Laboureau, Lauri K. Leppänen, Hans-Åke Lilja, William J. McGinnis, Klaus Molenaar, Lewis S. Moore, Alex Morley-Smith, M. S. S. El Namaki, Robert Nelson, Graham Perkins, Edgar H. Schein, Howard L. Shenson, Carl S. Sloane, Sten Söderman, Fritz Steele, Arthur B. Toan, and Arthur N. Turner.

The list of authors who are responsible for the current (1996) revised and expanded edition includes several new names together with the names of co-authors already involved in the previous edition: Michael Bauer, Roland Berger, George Boulden, Chris Brewster, Chris Cooper, George Cox, Alan Gladstone, Colin Guthrie, Malcolm Harper, John Heptonstall, Hari Johri, George Kanawaty, James H. Kennedy, Milan Kubr, David Maister, Rebecca Morgan, Philip Neck, Klaus North, Joseph Prokopenko, Edward A. Stone, John Syme and Denis Tindley.

Furthermore, short contributions (most presented in box form) and other valuable materials and comments used in the book were provided by Moïse Allal, William J. Altier, Ole Bovin, Ken Dawson, Takeyuki Furuhashi, Ed Hendricks, Michael Henriques, Shozo Hibino, Pierre Hidalgo, Geert Hofstede, Kate Hook, Jean-Marie van Houwe, Osamu Ida, Václav Klaus, Eiji Mizutani, Gerald Nadler,

Brian O' Rorke, Jean-François Poncet, John Roethle, Steven E. Sacks, Emmanuel S. Savas, Edgar H. Schein, Karl Scholz, E.Michael Shays, Marko Simoneti and Hedley Thomas.

Milan Kubr served as team leader and technical editor for the three editions of the book.

There are many colleagues in consulting firms and their associations, management institutes and business companies, and in the ILO, whose experience, ideas and constructive suggestions made the publication of this book possible. The ILO extends its sincere thanks to all co-authors and contributors, including those who could not be mentioned by name.

FOREWORD

Management consulting has long been recognized as a useful professional service that helps managers to analyse and solve practical problems faced by their organizations, improve organizational performance and learn from the experience of other managers and organizations. Hundreds of thousands of private businesses and public organizations in both industrialized and less developed countries have used the services of management consultants, separately or in combination with training, project management, information technology consulting, financial advice, accounting, engineering consulting and other professional services.

The Entrepreneurship and Management Development Programme of the ILO has therefore from its inception in the early 1950s paid considerable attention to the development of management consulting and the promotion of effective consulting practices in member States. Through its technical cooperation projects, the ILO has assisted many of its member States in establishing local consulting services for the various sectors of the economy, and in developing management consultants and trainers.

To respond to a pressing demand for a comprehensive, practically oriented guide to management consulting, two editions of this book were published in 1976 and 1986. The book quickly became a basic reference work and learning text on management consulting, published in 12 different language editions in addition to the English original and used worldwide by management consultants and educators, and by many clients of consultants.

However, management consulting is a dynamic and rapidly changing sector of professional services. To be relevant and useful to clients, consultants have to keep abreast of economic and social trends, anticipate changes that may affect their clients' businesses, and offer advice that helps the client to achieve and maintain high performance in an increasingly complex, competitive and difficult environment.

A fundamental reference text on consulting has to take the same approach. Therefore the third edition of our guide aims to describe state-of-the-art consulting practices, issues of major concern to consultants and clients alike, current and emerging trends, and approaches likely to enhance the value of the services provided by consultants. The text of the second edition underwent a major revision. A number of new topics of growing concern to consultants were added. Several recognized authorities, including experienced consulting practitioners, were invited to join the author team. A consistently international perspective was maintained: as in the past, this third edition of the guide aims to give a balanced picture of consulting as it is known and practised in various parts of the world, including the developing countries.

The concept of consulting

In this book management consulting is treated as a *method* for improving management practices first of all. This method can be used by an independent private firm, an internal consulting (or similar) unit in a private or public organization, a management development, productivity or small enterprise development institute, an extension service, or an individual (e.g. a sole consulting practitioner or a university professor). Even a manager can act as a consultant if he or she provides advice to peers or subordinates.

At the same time, however, management consulting has been developing into a *profession*. Thousands of individuals and organizations make consulting their full-time occupation, striving for professional standards in the quality of the advice provided, methods of intervention and ethical principles. Even individuals who do some consulting without being full-time members of the profession can comply with the profession's standards and principles, and should be helped to do so.

There is no conflict between these two ways of viewing consulting. Indeed, consulting as a method and consulting as a profession constitute two sides of one coin, and a guide such as ours has to deal with both these sides of consulting.

Management consulting is practised in many different ways. These reflect the diversity of the business and management contexts in which consultants operate, the different personalities of clients and consultants, and the various conceptual approaches and intervention methods developed by consultants. Therefore to generalize about consulting and recommend a best way of approaching it is difficult and risky. In our book we have opted for an eclectic approach, providing the reader with a comprehensive and balanced picture of the consulting scene, including the different methods, styles, modes or techniques applied, and pointing out their advantages and shortcomings. Thus the reader can make his or her own choice, consistent with the technical, organizational and human context of the given organization.

However, to say that the authors of this book have no bias whatsoever for any approach to consulting would not be correct. We do have a bias, and a strong one, for a form of consulting in which: (i) the consultant shares expertise with the client instead of trying to hide it; (ii) the client participates as closely and intensively as possible in the assignment; and (iii) both parties spare no effort to make the assignment a valuable learning experience. Many different methods and techniques can apply within this broad concept.

Purpose of the book

The main purpose of the book is to contribute to the upgrading of professional standards and practices in management consulting and to provide information and guidance to individuals and organizations wishing to start or improve consulting activities. The book is an introduction to professional consulting, its nature, methods, organizational principles, behavioural rules, and training and development practices. It also suggests guidelines to consultants for operating in various areas of management. However, it is not intended to replace handbooks and manuals which deal in depth and detail with various management functions and techniques: for this the reader is referred to special sources, some of which are suggested in our selected bibliography. The same point applies to certain special areas of consulting, such as executive search, market studies, advertising or information technology, which are mentioned briefly in this book, but can be studied in detail from special publications.

In summary, the book is intended for:

— new entrants to the consulting profession;

— independent management consultants and consulting firms, companies and services;

— consulting departments of productivity, management and small business development institutes and centres;

— departments and divisions performing internal management consulting and advisory functions in large private and public organizations, including management services, organization and methods services, and so on, in governments;

— management teachers, trainers and researchers who may be part-time consultants, and whose work is closely related to that of consultants;

— students of management and business administration taking courses in management consulting or involved in in-plant projects where they can use some consulting techniques;

— managers, business people and administrators wishing to use consultants more effectively, or to apply some consulting skills in problem solving and in improving productivity, quality and performance.

Finally, many principles and techniques described in the book apply to *consulting in general*; hence consultants operating in areas other than management and business may also find it useful and inspiring.

Terminology

The most common terms used in management consulting in various countries are explained in the text of the book. But the meaning and use of two basic terms warrant a definition at this early point:

— the term *management consultant* is used in the book as a generic term and applies to those persons who perform all or some of the typical consulting functions in the field of management on either a full-time or a part-time basis;

— the term *client* is also used as a generic term and applies to any manager, administrator or organization using the services of management consultants in private businesses, public enterprises, government agencies or elsewhere.

The two terms relate to consultants and clients in general, regardless of their sex, sectoral, ethnic, country or other characteristics. Both terms are sometimes used in the masculine gender for the sake of style, although it is fully appreciated that in practice there are more and more women among business people, managers and consultants.

Unless specified otherwise, the term *consulting firm* applies to any type of organizational unit whose function is to provide consulting services. This term is sometimes used interchangeably with the terms *consulting unit* or *consulting organization*.

The term *consulting process* is used as a generic term to describe the range of activities and the consultant-client interaction in solving the client's problems. A particular job done by a consultant for a particular client is normally called a *consulting assignment (project, case, engagement)*.

Plan of the book

The guide is divided into 34 chapters grouped in 5 parts. These are followed by 11 appendices.

Part I (Chapters 1-6) presents an overall view of the consulting method and profession. Emphasis is placed on the consultant-client relationship, on the role of management consultants in the process of change and on the principles of professional ethics.

Part II (Chapters 7-11) is a systematic review of the consulting process, divided into five major phases: entry, diagnosis, action planning, implementation and termination.

Part III (Chapters 12-22) provides an introduction to consulting in various areas of management. The areas covered are general management and corporate strategy, finance, marketing, production, human resources, information technology, small businesses, informal sector enterprises, privatization, public administrations and enterprises, and productivity and performance improvement.

Part IV (Chapters 23-31) deals with the management of consulting firms. The main aspects examined are the nature of management in the professions and in consulting, the strategy of consulting firms, marketing of consulting services, costs and fees, assignment management, quality management and assurance, operational and financial control, structuring of consulting firms and the use of information technology in consulting.

Part V (Chapters 32-34) focuses on careers and remuneration in consulting, the training and development of consultants, and the future perspectives of the international consulting profession.

The appendices provide information supplementing the main text, as well as material for a deeper study of consulting methods and communication techniques discussed in various parts of the book. They also include a selected bibliography intended to facilitate an in-depth study of the aspects of consulting treated in this book.

Appendix 1 is a concise memento addressed to clients who want to become more competent and effective in choosing and using consultants.

PART I

MANAGEMENT CONSULTING
IN PERSPECTIVE

NATURE AND PURPOSE OF MANAGEMENT CONSULTING

1

1.1 Definition: What is consulting?

There are many definitions of consulting, and of its application to management situations and problems, i.e. of management consulting.[1] Setting aside minor stylistic and semantic differences, two basic approaches to consulting emerge.

The first approach takes a broad functional view of consulting. Fritz Steele defines consulting in this way: "By the consulting process, I mean any form of providing help on the content, process, or structure of a task or series of tasks, where the consultant is not actually responsible for doing the task itself but is helping those who are."[2] Peter Block suggests that: "You are consulting any time you are trying to change or improve a situation but have no direct control over the implementation . . . Most people in staff roles in organizations are really consultants even if they don't officially call themselves consultants."[3] These and similar definitions emphasize that consultants are helpers, or enablers, and assume that such help can be provided by persons doing different jobs. Thus, a manager can also act as a consultant if he or she decides to give advice and help to a fellow manager, or even to subordinates rather than directing them and issuing orders to them.

The second approach views consulting as a special professional service and emphasizes a number of characteristics that such a service must possess. According to Larry Greiner and Robert Metzger, "management consulting is an advisory service contracted for and provided to organizations by specially trained and qualified persons who assist, in an objective and independent manner, the client organization to identify management problems, analyse such problems, recommend solutions to these problems, and help, when requested, in the implementation of solutions".[4] Similar more or less detailed definitions are used by other authors, and by professional associations and institutes of management consultants.

We regard the two approaches as complementary rather than conflicting. Management consulting can be viewed either as a professional service, or as a

3

method of providing practical advice and help. There is no doubt that management consulting has been developing into a specific sector of professional activity and should be treated as such. At the same time, it is also a method of assisting organizations and executives in improving management and business practices, as well as individual and organizational performance. The method can be, and is, applied by many technically competent persons whose main occupation is not consulting but teaching, training, research, systems development, project development and evaluation, technical assistance to developing countries and so on. To be effective, these persons need to master consulting tools and skills, and to observe the fundamental behavioural rules of professional consulting.

In our book, we have chosen to address the needs of both these target populations. Although it has been written primarily about and for professional management consultants, the needs of any other person who intervenes in a consulting capacity, even though he or she is not a full-time consultant, are borne in mind.

Let us start by reviewing the basic characteristics of management consulting.

Professional service

Whether practised as a full-time occupation or an ad hoc service, management consulting provides technical knowledge and skills relevant to practical management and business problems. An individual becomes a management consultant by accumulating, through study and practical experience, considerable knowledge of varying management situations, and by acquiring skills needed for solving problems, improving organizational performance and sharing experience with others: understanding the nature and goals of organizations; finding information; analysing and synthesizing; developing proposals for improvement; communicating with people; planning changes; coping with resistance to change; motivating people; helping clients to innovate and learn from experience, and so on.

It could be objected that managers, too, need to possess this range of knowledge and skills, and that each management situation is unique. What then can be gained by bringing in a newcomer who has no management responsibility and is not familiar with a given situation?

Over the years, management consultants pass through many different organizations and learn how to use experience from previous assignments in helping their new clients, or their existing clients, to face new situations. Because they are exposed to varying combinations of circumstances, consultants learn how to discern general trends and common causes of problems with a good chance of finding an appropriate solution; they also learn how to approach new challenges and opportunities. Professionals employed by consulting firms can learn from the experience of their colleagues who have worked for other clients, and use the whole firm's accumulated know-how. In addition, consultants aim continuously to keep abreast of developments in management theories, concepts, methods and systems.

4

Box 1.1   On giving and receiving advice

"Every man, however wise, needs the advice of some sagacious friend in the affairs of life."

Plautus

"To accept good advice is but to increase one's own ability."   *Goethe*

"Many receive advice: few profit by it."   *Publius Syrus*

"To profit from good advice requires more wisdom than to give it."

John C. Collins

"Men give away nothing so liberally as their advice."   *La Rochefoucauld*

"Never give advice in a crowd."   *Arabian Proverb*

"We give advice by the bucket, but take it by the grain."   *William Alger*

"Do not have the conceit to offer your advice to people who are far greater than you in every respect."

Rabindranath Tagore

"Harsh counsels have no effect; they are like hammers which are always repulsed by the anvil."

Helvetius

"Good counsellors lack no clients."   *Shakespeare*

"Advice is like mushrooms. The wrong kind can prove fatal."   *Unknown*

"Free advice is often overpriced."   *Unknown*

Selected by James H. Kennedy.

Thus, consulting can be essentially experience based, or research based, or both. Research-based consulting has become important with the development of operations research, systems theories, computer science and information technology, behavioural sciences and other scientific investigations in the functioning and behaviour of human organizations and systems in the business and social sectors. While these developments have brought a number of management professors and researchers to consulting, they have also stimulated quite a few consulting firms to start their own research programmes for developing new research-based client services.

Another key characteristic of a professional approach is professional ethics (to be discussed in detail in Chapter 6). In serving clients, management consultants observe a number of principles adopted by the profession in order to protect clients' interests and demonstrate to clients that they can rely on the consultants' integrity.

Advisory service

Consulting is essentially an advisory service. This means that consultants are not used (with certain exceptions) to run organizations or to take delicate decisions on behalf of the managers. They have no direct authority to decide on changes and implement them. Their responsibility is for the quality and integrity of their advice; the clients carry all the responsibilities that accrue from taking it.

Of course, in the practice of consulting there are many variations and degrees of "advice". Not only to give the right advice, but to give it in the right way, to the right persons and at the right time — these are the basic skills and art of a consultant. Above all, the consultant's art consists in "getting things done when you are not in charge".[5] The client in turn needs to become skilful in taking and using the consultant's advice and avoiding any misunderstanding on who is responsible for what. These points are so important that we will be returning to them many times in the text that follows.

Independent service

Consulting is an independent service. A consultant must be in a position to make an unbiased assessment of any situation, tell the truth and recommend frankly and objectively what the client organization needs to do without having any second thoughts on how this might affect his or her own interests. This detachment of the consultant has many facets and can be a very tricky matter in certain cases.

Technical independence means that the consultant is in a position to formulate a technical opinion and provide advice independently of what the client believes, or pretends or wishes to hear. Even if their collaboration is very close, the consultant is able to make and present his or her own independent conclusions and recommendations.

Financial independence means that the consultant has no interest in the course of action taken by the client, e.g. in a decision to invest in another company or to purchase a particular system. The desire to get more business from the same client in the future must not affect the objectivity of the advice provided in a current assignment.

Administrative independence implies that the consultant is not the client's subordinate and cannot be affected by his or her administrative decisions. While this does not present a problem to autonomous consulting organizations, it is a rather complex, although not insurmountable, problem in internal consulting (see section 2.5).

Political independence means that neither the client organization's management nor employees can influence the consultant informally, using political power and connections, political party membership, and similar influences.

Emotional independence means that the consultant preserves detachment, irrespective of empathy, friendship and other emotional affinities that may exist at the beginning or develop in the course of an assignment.

Temporary service

Consulting is a temporary service. Clients turn to consultants for help to be provided over a delimited period of time, in areas where they lack technical expertise, or where additional professional manpower is temporarily required. This may even be in areas where the requisite skills are available in the organization, but managers or staff specialists cannot be fully released for a major problem or project. Consultants not only provide the time and expertise required, and give undivided, 100 per cent attention to the problem at hand, but will leave the organization once the job is completed.

Commercial service

A practitioner who does consulting for a living has to charge a fee for all the work done for clients. Consulting firms are sellers of professional services and clients are buyers. In addition to being professional service organizations, consulting firms are also businesses.

Therefore a consulting assignment must be not only a technically justified activity, but also a financially feasible and profitable commercial undertaking according to both the client's and the consultant's criteria. From the client's point of view, the benefits obtained should exceed the costs incurred, including the fee paid to the consultant and other costs to the client such as staff time or the purchase of new computer programs. From the consultant's point of view, consulting must be a profitable activity measured by criteria normally applied by professional service firms. This will be examined in detail in Part IV.

In certain cases, the fee paid by the client will not cover the full cost of the consulting service provided. As we shall see later, consulting may be subsidized on account of government economic policy or for another reason, which may be economic, political or social. An institution may provide consulting in conjunction with training and subsidize it from the income earned from training. A not-for-profit social organization may provide consulting and counselling as a fully or partially subsidized service to entrepreneurs in underprivileged social groups or neglected regions.

What should not be required from consulting

There is an abundance of case histories of successful assignments carried out by some of the world's best management consultancies in order to rescue companies facing bankruptcy, or to give new life to ageing firms. They have created a reputation which implies that some consulting firms can resolve virtually any management difficulty. This reputation is not justified. There are situations where nobody can help. And even if help is still possible, it would be unrealistic and unfair to expect that consultants can work miracles.

Also, the consultant should never be expected to take a problem away from the client, on to his or her own shoulders. A consultant's presence and intervention may provide considerable relief to a troubled client, but it will not liberate the client from inherent managerial responsibility for decisions and their consequences.

To be recognized as such, consulting does not have to be a full-time occupation. If other professional criteria are met and the advice provided helps the client to make real improvements, it is not important whether the consultant is primarily (and for most of the time) a business school professor, a researcher, a retired executive or any other sort of professional worker. Also, if quality and independence are assured, consulting does not have to be an external service. Internal consultants are also consultants. Some consultants' associations may not share these views in defining membership criteria. This, however, is a different matter.

Our definition

Following this short discussion of the basic characteristics of management consulting, let us offer our definition:

> Management consulting is an independent professional advisory service assisting managers and organizations in achieving organizational purposes and objectives by solving management and business problems, identifying and seizing new opportunities, enhancing learning and implementing changes.

We have chosen a definition that omits certain characteristics which are not common to all consulting, such as "external" service, or service by "specially trained" persons. Conversely, our definition includes the fundamental, or generic, purposes of consulting that are discussed in the next section.

1.2   Why are consultants used: Five generic purposes

A manager may turn to a consultant if he or she perceives a need for help from an independent professional and feels that the consultant will be the right source of this help. But what sort of help are we talking about? What can be the purpose of using a consultant?

Consulting purposes can be looked at from several angles and described in various ways. Let us look, first, at five broad, or generic, purposes pursued by clients in using consultants, irrespective of differences in the technical area of intervention and in the specific intervention method used (figure 1.1):

— achieving organizational purposes and objectives;
— solving management and business problems;
— identifying and seizing new opportunities;
— enhancing learning;
— implementing changes.

Figure 1.1   Generic consulting purposes

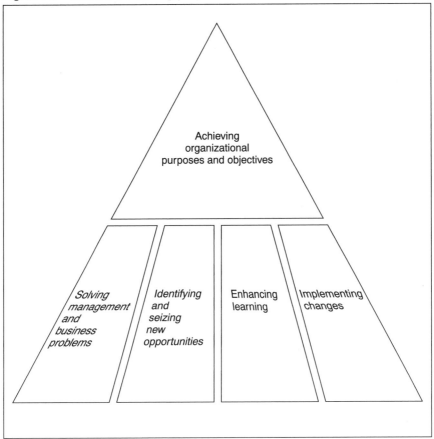

Achieving organizational purposes and objectives

All consulting to management and business tends to pursue a general and overriding purpose of helping clients to achieve their business, social or other goals. These goals may be defined in various ways: sectoral leadership, competitive advantage, customer satisfaction, total quality or total productivity, corporate excellence, high performance, profitability, improved business results, effectiveness, growth and similar. Different concepts and terms reflect the thinking and the priorities of both clients and consultants, the current state of the art of management and consulting, and even fashion. Different purposes will be stressed in commercial enterprises, public services and social organizations. The time horizon of a consultancy will differ from case to case. Yet the common denominator remains the same: consulting has to add value to the client organization, and this value should be a tangible and measurable contribution to achieving the client's principal purposes.

This global purpose of management consulting provides a rationale and a sense of direction for all consulting work. What would be the sense of organizational learning or costly and risky organizational changes if the client organization could not get closer to its principal goals? What would be the sense of successfully solving a few seemingly pressing management problems if "like the mythological hydra that grows two heads for every one cut off, the solutions we develop are often rapidly overwhelmed by a plethora of new problems"[6]?

The purpose of achieving the client organization's goals assumes that the client has defined such goals. In some organizations this is not the case, and management operates without any perspective, goal and sense of mission. The consultant's main contribution may well be in helping the client to develop a vision of the future, set ambitious but realistic goals, develop a strategy, focus on results, and start viewing current problems and opportunities in the light of longer-term and more fundamental organizational goals.

Consultants must appreciate that client organizations can pursue different sorts of goals. At times, the objective of a consultancy may be to advise the client on how to maintain the status quo or even how to get out of business.

Solving management and business problems

Helping managers and other decision makers with problem-solving is probably the most frequently mentioned purpose of consulting. The consultant's task is described as professional assistance in identifying, diagnosing and solving problems concerning various areas and aspects of management and business. The term "problem" is used to describe a situation where there is a difference or discrepancy between what is actually happening or will be happening and what should or might be happening. Therefore, a problem can only be described in relative terms, as a difference between two situations. In addition, someone has to be concerned about this difference and aim to overcome it, or to reduce it. A situation *per se* is not a problem (box 1.2).

Frequently a current situation of the client organization is compared to a situation that existed in the past. If there has been a deterioration such as plummeting sales or profits, the problem is defined as a need to restore the original condition. This explains why consultants are sometimes called "troubleshooters", "company doctors" or "business healers".

Alternatively, the current situation is compared to some standard (benchmark) and this comparison reveals that the current situation is not

Box 1.2　What do we mean by problems?

The term "problem" is probably the most used, and misused, label in the literature on management and consulting. It can mean almost anything. We tend to use it as a matter of convenience if we do not want to be, or cannot be, more precise. The risk of misunderstanding is considerable. Do you mean what I mean if both of us speak about problems?

For example, within a business firm, a "problem" justifying the use of a consultant can result from any of the following (and you can think of many other reasons):

Complaining clients	Unrealistic expectations
Poor business results	Unrealistic self-image
Unexpected loss	Lack of resources
Natural disaster	Idle resources
Lack of competence	Pressure of competition
Lack of perspective	Failure to meet targets
Obsolete control system	Lack of self-confidence
Wrong decision	Excess of self-confidence
Missed opportunity	Slowness of action
Emerging new opportunity	Disagreement over action
Rapidly changing environment	Lack of information
Reluctance to change	Excess of information
Feeling of insecurity	Internal conflicts
Feeling of frustration	Ambitious business goals

The reader should be aware of the various uses of the term "problem" and of their practical implications.

If "problem" stands only for mistake, failure, shortcoming or missed opportunity, the client's and the consultant's perspective tends to be essentially backward looking and narrow. Focus will be on corrective action (with implied criticism and determination of responsibilities). Unfortunately, in management and consulting practice this use of the term "problem" prevails.

The term "problem" is also used as a more general and global concept to describe the difference between any comparable situations (past, present or future) about which we are concerned. In this sense, even a successful and forward-looking company that has been pursuing and achieving ambitious business objectives has "problems" — a desire to further enhance its competitive advantage, to become a sector leader, not to miss a new marketing opportunity, to identify a new business partner or to explore an emerging technology, and so on. Clearly, this will be a different class of problem . . .

In our guide, the term "problem" will be used in this second way — as a generic term describing a client's dissatisfaction with the difference between any comparable situations in the client organization. Thus, some of these problems will be past errors and shortcomings that will need to be corrected. Many others will concern perspectives, opportunities and strategies for improving the business in future years.

satisfactory. The problem is then defined as the need to meet or surpass the standard, e.g. a competitor's product quality, range of models offered or after-sales service.

Consulting whose purpose is confined to corrective measures aiming to restore a past situation or attain a standard already met by other organizations may produce significant and urgently needed benefits. A crisis will be avoided, negative developments will be arrested and the client's business will survive. There may be general satisfaction and a feeling of relief. Yet ensuring a mere return to an already existing condition or catching up with competition gives the client no competitive advantage, no additional competence and strength for coping with new situations and achieving superior performance in the future.

Identifying and seizing new opportunities

For the reasons stated above, consultants are not especially happy to be called troubleshooters. After all, if a company has no trouble, it has no reason to use a troubleshooter. Yet consultants feel that they can offer much more than helping organizations to get out of difficulties. This has been perceived by many business corporations and other organizations that are well managed, successful and ambitious. At times they may also call on a consultant for tracking back the deviations that have taken place, and finding and correcting the reasons for them. However, they prefer to use consultants for identifying and taking new opportunities. They regard consulting firms as a source of valuable information and ideas that can be turned into a wide range of initiatives, innovations and improvements in any area or function of business: developing new markets and products; assessing and using state-of-the-art technologies; improving quality; becoming more useful to customers; developing and motivating staff; optimizing the use of financial resources; finding new business contacts (and contracts), and so on. Experience shows that even strong and important corporations have developed many ideas for action and have seized major business opportunities with the help of their consultants.

Enhancing learning

"The only work that is really worth doing as a consultant is that which educates — which teaches clients and their staff to manage better for themselves", said Lyndon Urwick, one of the main contributors to the development of professional management consulting. In the modern concept of consulting this dimension is omnipresent. Many clients turn to consultants, not only to find a solution to one distinct problem, but also to acquire the consultant's special technical knowledge (e.g. in environmental analysis, business re-structuring or quality management) and the methods used in assessing organizations, identifying problems and opportunities, developing improve-ments and implementing changes (interviewing, diagnosis, communication, persuasion, feedback, evaluation and similar skills).

Consulting assignments become learning assignments. The purpose is to empower the client by bringing new competence into the organization and helping managers and staff to learn from their own and the consultant's experience. It is often stressed that in this way "organizations are helped to help themselves" and become "learning organizations". This is a two-way exchange, since by helping clients to learn from experience a management consultant enhances his or her own knowledge and competence.

The learning effect of consulting is probably the most important and durable one. The choice of the consulting methods and the degree of the client's involvement can increase or reduce this effect. We shall, therefore, pay considerable attention to these questions in our guide.

Implementing changes

"Change agent" is another label frequently given to consultants. They are proud to be referred to in this way since this is a reflection of another general purpose of consulting: helping client organizations to understand change, live with change and make changes needed to survive and be successful in an environment where continuous change is the only constant. The importance of this consulting purpose has considerably increased in the current period owing to the complexity and pace of environmental changes, the need to keep informed about changes that may affect the organization and to think constantly of possible implications, the speed with which organizations have to adapt, and the increased demands on people's flexibility and ability to cope with change.

1.3 How are consultants used: Ten principal ways

In pursuing the generic purposes outlined in the previous section, consultants can intervene in many different ways. Both clients and consultants can choose among so many alternatives that trying to give an exhaustive and complete picture of these alternatives would be an impossible task. However, most of the consulting assistance to management will be given in one or more of the following ten ways:

● providing information;
● providing specialist resources;
● establishing business contacts and linkages;
● providing expert opinion;
● doing diagnostic work;
● developing action proposals;
● improving systems and methods;
● planning and managing organizational changes;
● training and developing management and staff;
● providing personal counselling.

Providing information

Better, more complete and more relevant information is often the main or only thing that a client needs to make the right decision. It can be information on markets, customers, sector trends, raw materials, suppliers, competitors, potential partners, sources of engineering expertise, government policies and regulations, or other. The consulting firm may have this information in its files, or know where and how to find it. Information gathering and analysis may be the only or the main objective of an assignment. Finally, any consulting assignment will have an information dimension and function. There is no consulting without working with information and providing better information.

In providing information, a delicate question of confidentiality may be faced. Consultants have to distinguish between information that can be provided to a client because it is publicly available or has been gathered and developed specifically for that client, and information developed for previous clients or obtained from private sources, which may need to be treated as confidential.

Providing specialist resources

A consultant can be used to supplement the client organization's staff. Usually these consultants will be specialists in areas where the client is looking for short-term expertise, or wants to avoid recruiting a new employee. Some clients, mainly in the public sector, use consultants in this way to bypass restrictive regulations preventing them from recruiting new staff and/or paying appropriate salaries to specialists. Other clients have been forced to cut down their technical departments and find it convenient to recruit short-term specialists from consulting firms.

A special case is "interim management". Recently this way of using consultants has become more widespread and some client firms may "borrow" staff members of consulting firms to occupy a position in their management hierarchy on a temporary basis.

Establishing business contacts and linkages

Many clients turn to consultants in their search for new business contacts, agents, representatives, suppliers, subcontractors, joint-venture and merger partners, companies for acquisition, sources of funding, additional investors and so forth. The consultant's task may involve identifying one or more suitable candidates (people or organizations), presenting their names to the client, assessing their suitability, recommending a choice, defining and negotiating conditions of an alliance or business deal, and acting as intermediary in implementation. Often these contacts will be in sectors or countries not sufficiently known to the client.

Providing expert opinion

Various uses fall under this heading. The consultant may be approached to provide expert opinion in cases where the client can choose among several alternatives and prefers to seek impartial and independent third party advice before taking an important decision. Consultants can be invited to act in an expert witness (testifying expert) capacity in lawsuits or arbitrations calling for specialized knowledge.

Conversely, expert opinion can be provided in a totally informal way. This is the case of decision makers who like to use their consultants as a sounding-board without asking for a formal report or expertise. It should be stressed that any consultancy involving assessment and choice will engage the consultant's expert opinion, in particular if management decisions risk being affected by shortage of information, company myopia, lack of expertise, emotions or vested interests.

Doing diagnostic work

Diagnostic skills and instruments are among the consultants' principal assets. Clients therefore use consultants for a wide range of diagnostic tasks concerning the organization's strengths and weaknesses, positive and negative trends, potential for improvement, barriers to change, competitive position, underutilized resources, technical or human problems requiring management's attention and so on. Diagnostic work can concern the entire business or its part — a department, sector, function, product line, information system, organizational structure or other.

Developing action proposals

Effectively completed diagnostic work may be followed by the development of specific action proposals in an area that was diagnosed. The consultant may be asked to do the whole job, share the task with the client or act as an adviser to a client who has chosen to develop new proposals with his or her own resources. Action proposals may involve one or more alternatives. Also, the consultant may be asked to present alternatives with or without recommendations on the course of action to be taken by the client.

Improving systems and methods

A major portion of all consulting services concerns systems and methods in areas such as management information, business planning, operations scheduling and control, business process integration and management, inventory control, client order processing, sales management, personnel records, compensation, social benefits, and other systems. Traditionally, many consulting firms have developed one or more of these areas as special lines of expertise. The systems can be custom-made or standard. The consultant can take full

15

responsibility for establishing the system's feasibility, choosing the proper system, adapting it to the client's conditions and putting it into effect in collaboration with the client's staff. Alternatively, clients can play a more active role in developing and adapting the system with the consultant's support.

Some systems are proprietary and the consultant firm holds copyright or is authorized by the holder of the copyright to sell the system as part of its services.

Many organizations prefer to retain the consultant until the system gets "debugged", becomes operational and achieves the promised parameters. In today's consulting, most of the systems provided are computerized and their development, design and application require a combination of management and information technology consulting.

Planning and managing organizational changes

A fairly common case is that of a client who possesses the technical and managerial expertise to run the organization, but has difficulties and feels insecure when organizational changes are anticipated and cannot be avoided. Often these changes will put a lot of strain on people, since deeply rooted relationships, work habits and individual or group interests will be affected. In such situations, the special expertise sought from a consultant would be in change management — in identifying the need for change, developing a change strategy and plan, choosing and applying the right approaches to encourage change and overcome barriers to change, monitoring the change process, evaluating the progress made and results obtained, and adjusting the approach taken by management at all stages of the change cycle.

The consultant may provide expertise and advice both on specific methods and techniques that are being changed, and on how to deal with interpersonal

---

Box 1.3   Should consultants justify management decisions?

From time to time consultants are approached with a request to undertake assignments and submit reports so that a manager can justify a decision by referring to an external consultant's recommendations. In other words, a manager may have determined his or her aims and have reached a personal decision, but wants to be able to say that he or she is putting into effect suggestions made or endorsed by an independent and respected professional adviser.

This can turn out to be another straightforward and correct case of providing expert opinion. It can also be a trap. A consultant who accepts such an assignment may be pulled into the hidden and intricate world of in-company politics. His or her report will have a political role in addition to the technical message it carries. This role may be constructive and useful if a manager is facing strong resistance to changes that are inevitable, and needs to refer to the consultant's authority. It can also happen that a consultant produces a report that will be misused for in-company politics and for promoting vested individual or group interests. Independent and impartial assessment of every situation will help the consultant to avoid being used as a scapegoat.

relations, conflicts, motivation, team building, and other issues in the organizational and human behaviour field. The weight given to behavioural skills will be higher in assignments where change will put a lot of strain on people, resistance to change can be expected and management feels that its own change management skills are inadequate. In addition to behavioural skills, which are sometimes referred to as "soft" skills needed for change management, the consultant's help may also concern the "hard" skills area: effective change scheduling; sequencing; coordination; redefining structures; responsibilities and relationships; reallocating resources; adjusting recording and control systems; preventing gaps and disorder caused by poor monitoring of change operations; ensuring smooth transition from old to new work arrangements, costing the project and measuring the results, and similar.

Training and developing management and staff

While learning is a general purpose inherent in all consulting, training and development of managers or staff can be a distinct client service provided in conjunction with and in support of other services, or separately.

The client and his or her staff can be trained in the new methods and techniques provided by the consultant, so that they become autonomous in using and improving them. There are many ways in which diagnosis, advice, systems development and training can be combined in consulting practice.

Training can be organized instead of the other interventions and ways of using consultants described above. It may be the client's deliberate choice. Rather than asking a consultant to work on a specific diagnostic, problem-solving or change management assignment, the client may prefer the consultant to prepare and conduct a course or a workshop for managers and/or staff specialists on the subject area where the assignment would have taken place. For example, a set of workshops on productivity diagnosis and improvement is organized instead of requesting the consultant to identify specific productivity improvement measures and present a productivity improvement programme.

Providing personal counselling

Management consultants can render an excellent service to managers and entrepreneurs who need strictly personal feedback and relaxed friendly advice on their leadership style, behaviour, work habits, relations with colleagues, weaknesses that could be damaging to the business (such as the reluctance to make decisions or the failure to seek the collaborators' advice) and personal qualities that need to be well utilized. Personal counselling is necessarily a one-to-one relationship based on trust and respect. It can be fully confidential. Despite its obvious potential, few consultants offer such a service to clients and few clients ask for it.

1.4 Fundamentals of the consulting approach

This whole book is about the consulting approaches and methods applied to various types of management and business problems, organizations and environments. Indeed, there is an extremely wide range of consulting approaches, techniques, methods, modes and styles. This diversity is one of the exciting features of management consulting. It allows even clients with very peculiar problems and characters eventually to find a consultant who fits their organization and personality.

However, consulting exhibits not only diversity but also certain common principles and methods. Some of them are quite fundamental; they are used by the vast majority of consultants. For example, every consultant must be able to use interviewing, diagnose the client's problems and purposes, structure and plan the work to be done in his or her particular area of intervention, and present proposals and conclusions to clients orally and/or in writing.

The key dimensions of consulting

In a nutshell, an effective consulting approach suggests how to deal with two critical dimensions of change in client organizations:

(1) *The technical dimension*, which concerns the nature of the management or business problem faced by the client and the way in which this problem can be analysed and resolved.

(2) *The human dimension*, i.e. interpersonal relationships in the client organization, people's feelings about the problem at hand and their interest in improving the current condition, and the relationship between the consultant and the client as persons.

For methodological reasons, our text will often deal separately with these two dimensions. In consulting practice they are not separated; technical and human issues of management and business are interlinked. In consulting, it is absolutely essential to be aware of these two sides of problems in human organizations, but mere awareness is not enough. In working for a client, the consultant must be able to choose approaches and methods needed to uncover and understand both the technical and the human issues involved, and help the client to act on both of them.

It should be noted at this point that, as regards the balancing of the technical and human aspects of management and change, three major strains can be observed in management consulting.

The first strain is essentially *technical*. Its protagonists are fine technicians competent in providing advice on structures, systems, resource allocation and utilization, and similar tangible, quantifiable and measurable issues in areas such as production, technology, finance and accounting. The consultants' backgrounds may be various — in technology, industrial engineering, computer science, statistics, mathematics, operations research, accounting, and so on. Some of them may have a strong research background, as mentioned in section 1.1. They view the client's problems as mainly technical — the client

needs a better cost control system, better information on customers' requirements and complaints, a stable network of reliable subcontractors, and similar.

The second strain focuses on *the human side of organizations*. Its roots are
in behavioural sciences and its doctrine is that, whatever the client feels and tells
the consultant, there is always a human problem behind any other organizational
problem, whether technical or financial. If human problems can be resolved in
ways that will motivate, energize and empower people, all other problems will
be resolved, or at least their solution will be greatly facilitated. Organizational
development (OD) and human resource development (HRD) consultants are the
typical representatives of this second strain. Its share of the whole consulting
industry has been relatively small, but its influence has been remarkable and out
of all proportion to its numbers. As distinct from the previous group, the
behavioural scientists have been not only practising consulting but also writing
extensively about their approaches and experiences. Most of the writing on
consulting concepts and methodologies comes from this group.

The third strain groups a wide range of *practical and pragmatic approaches*
to diagnosing organizational problems and helping clients to run their businesses
more effectively. Most consultants in this group are practitioners and their advice
is based more on experience and common sense than on behavioural science or
another theory. Many of them have been in business practice before turning to
consulting. Experience, not research, has taught them that organizational
problems and achievements are affected by a mixture of technical, financial,
human, political and other factors. They view a business as a whole and their
approach is interdisciplinary by nature. It may, however, lack depth, if it comes
to specific and complex issues of particular systems and functions.

As usual, these archetypes cannot be taken as exclusive models. We shall
see later (Chapters 3 and 33) that, thanks to general progress in consulting
methodologies and better education and training of consultants, more and more
consultants can either deal with various aspects of the client's business, or
suggest the use of other specialists when facing issues outside their main field
of competence.

Consulting and problem solving

Another basic and frequently debated issue is the consultant's approach to
problem solving. In section 1.2 we stressed that our definition of "problems"
will be a broad one — a difference between two situations (which can be past,
present or future situations) can be described as a problem if someone is
concerned about this difference and wants to overcome it, or at least to reduce
it. If this definition is accepted, all consulting can be described as problem
solving. Indeed, it is a special kind of problem solving: a consultant deals with
"other people's problems".

A correct definition of the problem to be resolved, and the purpose to be
achieved by the consultancy, is critical. Observers of consulting warn against
accepting the client's perception of the problem at face value: the problem may
be wrongly defined and the consultant will be caught in a trap. Either he or she

---

Box 1.4 Define the purpose, not the problem

The way consultants define a problem is critical to the quality of their solution. If they define the problem in terms of its origin or cause, they tend to focus on who or what is to blame. This is a fruitless exercise because fixing blame doesn't really matter. It actually gets in the way of the best solution. It also inhibits the initiative of people who will do little to risk having blame directed towards themselves in the future. Instead, management consultants can achieve breakthroughs for their clients and higher fees for themselves by focusing first on a hierarchy of incrementally larger purposes to be achieved.

Traditional consulting approaches — focusing on the problem, starting with data collection, copying others, taking the first solution that can be made to work, failing to involve others — create other problems of their own. These approaches lead to excess costs and time, early obsolescence of solutions, wasted resources and rework in the consulting process.

Breakthrough Thinking provides a more effective approach. It is not a step-by-step process but seven ways of thinking about problems and their solutions, based on the following principles:

(1) **The uniqueness principle**: Whatever the apparent similarities, each problem is unique and requires an approach that dwells initially on its own contextual needs.

(2) **The purposes principle**: Focusing on expanding purposes helps strip away non-essential aspects to avoid working on the wrong problem.

(3) **The solution-after-next principle**: Innovation can be stimulated and solutions made more effective by working backwards from an ideal target solution. Having a target solution in the future gives direction to near-term solutions and infuses them with larger purposes.

(4) **The systems principle**: Every problem is part of a larger system of problems, and solving one problem inevitably leads to another. Having a clear framework of what elements and dimensions comprise a solution assures its workability and implementation.

(5) **The limited information collection principle**: Excessive data gathering may create an expert in the problem area, but knowing too much about it will probably prevent the discovery of some excellent alternatives. Always determine expanded purposes of any proposed information collection before doing it.

(6) **The people design principle**: Those who carry out and use the solution should be intimately and continuously involved in its development by getting involved in the first five principles. Also, in designing for other people, the solution should include only the critical details in order to allow some flexibility to those who must apply the solution.

(7) **The betterment time-line principle**: The only way to preserve the vitality of a solution is to build in and then monitor a programme of continual change to achieve larger purposes and move towards target solutions.

Author: E. Michael Shays. A detailed discussion can be found in G. Nadler and S. Hibino: *Breakthrough Thinking: The seven principles of creative problem solving* (Rocklin, California, Prima Publishing, 1994).

will work on a wrong problem, or the problem may not justify the consultant's intervention and the costs incurred. To avoid this elementary flaw, the real professionals insist on making their own independent assessment of the problem presented to them by the client, and on developing a common definition in discussion and collaboration with the client.

Equally important is to clarify the purpose of the consultant's intervention (see box 1.4). It could be argued that "the purpose is to solve the client's problem", but this would be a tautology. It has been observed that "effective leaders and problem solvers always placed every problem into a larger context".[7] This implies asking and clarifying a number of questions about the purposes of the client organization and its key constituents, the focus and the significance of the proposed assignment, and the immediate and ultimate benefits to be obtained by the client if the current problem is resolved. It will be thus be possible to select the "focus purpose",[8] avoiding purposes that are too narrow and meaningless, and those that are too wide and too distant to be tackled by the client at the present time. However, these wider and future purposes ought to be kept in mind in order to place the client's problem in a proper time perspective and work on solutions that will not block the path to the future.

An overview of the consulting process

During a typical assignment, the consultant and the client undertake a set of activities required for achieving the desired purposes and changes. These activities are normally known as "the consulting process". This process has a beginning (the relationship is established and work starts) and an end (the consultant departs). Between these two points the process can be subdivided into several basic phases. This helps both the consultant and the client to be systematic and methodical, proceeding from phase to phase, and from operation to operation, as they follow each other in logic and in time.

Many different ways of subdividing the consulting process, or cycle as some authors call it, into major phases can be found in literature. Various authors suggest models ranging from three to ten phases.[9] We have chosen a simple five-phase model, including the following major phases: *entry*, *diagnosis*, *action planning*, *implementation* and *termination*. This model, shown in figure 1.2 (overleaf), will be used consistently in our book. Obviously, a universal model cannot be applied blindly to all situations, but it provides a good framework for explaining what consultants actually do and for structuring and planning particular assignments and projects.

When applying the model to a concrete situation it is possible to let some phases overlap, e.g. implementation may start before action planning is completed, or a detailed diagnosis will not be necessary or will be integrated with the development of proposals. It may be useful to cycle backwards from a later to an earlier stage. Thus evaluation serves not only for a final assessment of the results of the assignment and of benefits drawn from change (termination phase) but also for deciding whether to move back and take a different approach.

Figure 1.2   Phases of the consulting process

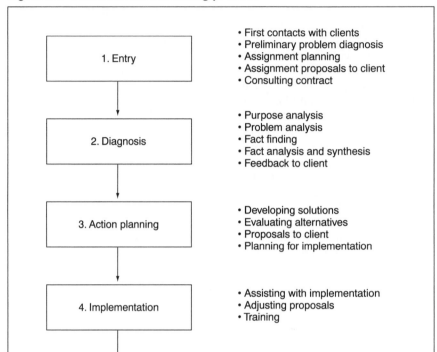

Every phase can be broken down into several sub-phases or parallel activities. The whole model has to be applied flexibly and with a great deal of imagination.

The reader may also have seen various models of planned organizational change and may be interested in comparing them with the model in figure 1.2. The consulting process can be viewed as a variant of the change process (Chapter 4), one in which the need for change is identified, the purpose of the change defined and specific change measures prepared and implemented with a consultant's help.

The consulting process will be examined in detail in Chapters 7-11, but at this point it may be helpful to have short descriptions of its five basic phases.

Entry

In this phase the consultant starts working with a client. This phase includes their first contacts, discussions on what the client would like to achieve and change in his or her organization and how the consultant might help, the clarification of their respective roles, the preparation of an assignment plan based on preliminary problem analysis, and the negotiation and agreement of a consulting contract.

It is a preparatory and planning phase. It is often emphasized that this phase lays down the foundations for everything that will follow, since the subsequent phases will be strongly influenced by the quality of conceptual work done, and by the kind of relationships that the consultant will be able to establish with the client at the very beginning.

In this initial phase it can also happen that an assignment proposal is not prepared to the client's satisfaction and no contract is agreed, or that several consultants are invited to present proposals but only one of them is selected for the assignment.

Diagnosis

The second phase is an in-depth diagnosis of the problem to be solved. During this phase the consultant and the client cooperate at identifying the sort of change that is required, defining in detail the purposes to be achieved by the assignment and assessing the client's performance, resources, needs and perspectives. Is the fundamental change problem technological, organizational, informational, psychological or other? If it has all these dimensions, which one is the crucial one? What attitudes to change prevail in the organization: is the need for change appreciated, or will it be necessary to persuade people that they will have to change? The results of the diagnostic phase are synthesized and conclusions drawn on how to orient work on action proposals so that the real problem is resolved and the desired purposes achieved. Some possible solutions may start emerging during this phase.

Fact finding and fact diagnosis often receive the least attention. Yet decisions on what data to look for, what data to omit, what aspects of the problem to examine in depth and what facts to skip, predetermine the relevance and quality of solutions that will be proposed. Also, by collecting data the consultant is already influencing the client system, and people may already start changing as a result of the consultant's presence in the organization. Conversely, fact finding has to be kept within reasonable limits, determined by the basic purpose of the consultancy.

Action planning

The third phase aims at finding the solution to the problem. It includes work on one or several alternative solutions, the evaluation of alternatives, the elaboration of a plan for implementing changes and the presentation of proposals to the client for decision. The consultant can choose from a wide range of techniques, in particular if the client's participation in this phase is active. Action planning requires imagination and creativity, as well as a rigorous and systematic approach in identifying and exploring feasible alternatives, eliminating proposals that could lead to trivial and unnecessary changes, and deciding what solution will be adopted. A significant dimension of action planning is developing strategy and tactics for implementing changes, in particular for dealing with those human problems that can be anticipated, for overcoming resistance to change and for gaining support for change.

Implementation

Implementation, the fourth phase of consulting, provides an acid test for the relevance and feasibility of the proposals developed by the consultant in collaboration with the client. The changes proposed start turning into reality. Things begin happening, either as planned, or differently. Unforeseen new problems and obstacles may arise and false assumptions or planning errors may be uncovered. Resistance to change may be quite different from what was assumed at the diagnostic and the planning stage. The original design and action plan may need to be corrected. As it is not possible to foresee exactly and in detail every relationship, event or attitude, and the reality of implementation often differs from the plan, monitoring and managing implementation is very important. This also explains why professional consultants prefer to be associated with the implementation of changes that they have helped to identify and plan.

This is an issue over which there has been much misconception and misunderstanding. Many consulting assignments end when a report with action proposals is transmitted, i.e. *before* implementation starts. Probably not more than 30 to 50 per cent of consulting assignments include implementation. If the client is fully capable of handling any phase of the change process alone, and is keen to do it, there is no reason why he or she should finance a consultant. The consultant may leave as early as after the diagnostic phase. Unfortunately, the decision to terminate the assignment after the diagnostic or action-planning phase often does not reflect the client's assessment of his or her own capabilities and determination to implement the proposals without any further help from the consultant. Rather it mirrors a widespread conception, or misconception, of consulting according to which consultants do not have to achieve more than getting their reports and proposals accepted by the clients. Some clients choose it because they do not really understand that even an excellent consulting report cannot provide a full guarantee that a new scheme will actually work and the promised results will be attained. Other clients may be happy with it because what they really wanted was a report, not a change.

Termination

The fifth and final phase in the consulting process includes several activities. The consultant's performance during the assignment, the approach taken, the changes made and the results achieved have to be evaluated by both the client and the consulting firm. Final reports are presented and discussed. Mutual commitments are settled. If there is an interest in pursuing the collaborative relationship, an agreement on follow-up and future contacts may be negotiated. Once these activities are completed, the consulting assignment or project is terminated by mutual agreement and the consultant withdraws from the client organization.

A consulting assignment

Services to clients are normally organized and delivered through particular consulting assignments (also called engagements, cases, consultancies, projects or client accounts). In a typical assignment, the consultant and the client agree on the scope of the job to be done:

— the purposes (objectives, results) to be achieved;
— the expertise to be provided by the consultant;
— the nature and sequence of tasks to be undertaken by the consultant;
— the client's participation in the assignment;
— the resources required;
— the timetable;
— the price to be paid;
— other conditions as appropriate.

This agreement is confirmed in a consulting contract, which is written in most cases, but can also be verbal (section 7.6).

A retainer

An alternative to an assignment covering a distinct task and period of time is a retainer. Under a retainer contract, the client books, or purchases in advance, a certain amount of the consultant's working time. The nature and purpose of the work to be done are defined in general terms only and will be specified at the beginning of each period covered by the contract. For example, the client may use the consultant's services for two days every month during the first week of the month to review jointly the general situation of the business, the problems and opportunities that have developed during the previous month, and the key decisions that will have to be taken.

There are various types of retainer arrangement, but from a technical viewpoint two types tend to prevail:

● *a generalist retainer*, under which the consultant follows global results and trends of the client's business, looking for improvement opportunities in various areas and feeding the client with new information and ideas;

● *a specialist retainer*, providing the client with a permanent flow of technical information and suggestions in an area where the consulting firm is particularly competent and advanced (e.g. computer systems, quality management, international financial operations, identification of new markets).

25

---

[1] Some management consultants prefer to call themselves "business consultants", or "management and business consultants", to stress that their firms are able to deal with a wide range of issues faced by business companies.

[2] F. Steele: *Consulting for organizational change* (Amherst, Massachusetts, University of Massachusetts Press, 1975), p. 3.

[3] P. Block: *Flawless consulting: A guide to getting your expertise used* (Austin, Texas, Learning Concepts, 1981), pp. v and 2.

[4] L. E. Greiner and R. O. Metzger: *Consulting to management* (Englewood Cliffs, New Jersey, Prentice-Hall, 1983), p. 7.

[5] See G. M. Bellman: *Getting things done when you are not in charge* (San Francisco, California, Berrett-Koehler, 1992).

[6] P. Stroh: "Purposeful consulting", in *Organizational Dynamics* (New York, American Management Association), Autumn 1987, pp. 49-67.

[7] G. Nadler and S. Hibino: *Breakthrough Thinking: The seven principles of creative problem solving* (Rocklin, California, Prima Publishing, 1994), p. 128. See also Stroh, op. cit.

[8] ibid., p. 149.

[9] Frequently referred to is the Kolb-Frohman model, which includes the following seven phases: scouting, entry, diagnosis, planning, action, evaluation, termination. See D. A. Kolb and A. L. Frohman: "An organization development approach to consulting", in *Sloan Management Review* (Cambridge, Massachusetts), Vol. 12, No. 1, Fall 1970.

RANGE AND SCOPE OF CONSULTING SERVICES

2

2.1 A historical perspective

A historical perspective will help us to understand the present scope, strengths and limitations of management consulting. Where does management consulting have its historical roots? How far back can they be traced? What principal events and personalities have given the consulting business its current shape?[1]

Management consulting has its origins in the Industrial Revolution, the advent of the modern factory, and the related institutional and social transformations. Its roots are identical with those of management as a distinct area of human activity and a field of learning. Consulting in or for management becomes possible when the process of generalizing and structuring management experience attains a relatively advanced stage. Methods and principles applicable to various organizations and situations have to be identified and described, and the entrepreneur must be pressed — and motivated — to seek a better way of running and controlling the business. These conditions were not fulfilled until the latter part of the nineteenth century, a period which saw the birth of the "scientific management" movement.

The pioneers of scientific management

There were a number of predecessors of scientific management. One of them was the American manufacturer Charles T. Sampson, who in 1870 reorganized the whole production process in his shoe-making factory in order to be able to staff it by unskilled Chinese labour. One year later, acting in a consulting capacity, Sampson passed on his experience to an owner of a laundry, who accepted the advice and applied the approach previously used by Sampson.

The pioneers of scientific management, including Frederick W. Taylor, Frank and Lillian Gilbreth, Henry L. Gantt and Harrington Emerson, gave a major impetus to the development of consulting. Their technical and method-ological approaches to simplifying work processes and raising workers' and plant productivity were not the same and in certain cases even conflicted with each other. However, they all believed in the application of the scientific method to solving production problems. They believed, too, in the benefit of combining several methods for disseminating their scientific approach and making sure that it would be used by the business corporations. They were tireless in lecturing, making studies, writing books and articles, organizing practical demonstrations, and providing advice in every possible way. Later in his life, Taylor chose to become a full-time management and productivity consultant.

These pioneering efforts gave rise to a very important strain in management consulting, one which has strongly marked the profession and its image. Consulting that emerged from the scientific management movement focused mainly on factory and shop-floor productivity and efficiency, rational work organization, time and motion study, eliminating waste and reducing production costs. This whole area was given the name of "industrial engineering". The practitioners, often called "efficiency experts", were admired for their drive, methodical approach and improvements achieved (which were often spectacular). But their interventions were also feared and detested by workers and trade unions because of their often ruthless approach.

The negative early image of some management consultants has changed considerably over the years. New areas of management and new types of problem were tackled and became a normal part of the consulting business, thus reducing the share of work in production and work organization. Important changes in the social and labour-relations fields tended to limit the use of techniques unacceptable to the workers; negotiation and collaboration became indispensable methods of handling many assignments affecting workers' and other employees' interests. The positive side of the efficiency expert's image has been very much preserved: consultants continue to be regarded as persons able to find new opportunities for saving resources and raising productivity even where others see none.

Towards a general management approach

The limitations of the industrial-engineering and efficiency-expert approaches have led to a broadened interest in other aspects and dimensions of business organizations, and to the birth of new areas of consulting. One of the first, perhaps the first, consulting firm of the kind known today was established in Chicago in 1914 by Edwin Booz under the name "Business Research Services".

In the 1920s, Elton Mayo, with his Hawthorne experiment, gave impetus to research and consulting in human relations. Important consulting work in human resource management and motivation was started by Mary Parker Follett. Interest in more effective selling and marketing was fostered by people such as the Englishman Harold Whitehead, the author of *Principles of salesmanship* written in 1917. A number of consulting firms were established during the 1920s. These were increasingly able to diagnose business organizations in their totality, treating manufacturing and productivity problems in a wider perspective of sales and business-expansion opportunities.

Consulting in finance, including financing the enterprise and financial control of operations, also started developing rapidly. A number of the new management consultants had a background in accountancy and experience drawn from working with firms of public accountants. One such was James O. McKinsey, a protagonist of the general management and comprehensive diagnostic approach to a business enterprise, who established his own consulting firm in 1925, and today is regarded as one of the founders of the consulting profession.[2]

In the 1920s and 1930s, management consulting was gaining ground, not only in the United States and in Great Britain, but also in France, Germany, Czechoslovakia and other industrialized countries. Yet its volume and scope remained limited. There were only a few firms, prestigious but rather small, and their services were used mainly by the larger business corporations. The consultant remained unknown to the overwhelming majority of small and medium-sized firms. On the other hand, assignment requests began coming from governments: this was the start of consulting for the public sector.

Consulting for governments, and for the army, played an important role during the Second World War. The United States in particular understood that the war was a major management challenge and that mustering the country's best management expertise was essential to winning on the battlefield. In addition, operations research and other new techniques, applied first for military purposes, rapidly found their way into business and public management, adding a new dimension to the services offered by consultants.

The golden years of consulting

Post-war reconstruction, the rapid expansion of business coupled with the acceleration of technological change, the emergence of new developing economies and the growing internationalization of the world's industry, commerce and finance, created particularly favourable opportunities and demands for management consulting. This is the period in which most consulting organizations that exist today were established and in which the consulting business has attained the power and the technical reputation it enjoys at the present time. For example, PA, the largest consulting firm based in the United Kingdom, had only six consultants in 1943 but 370 in 1963, over 1,300 based in 22 countries in 1984, and 1,700 in 1993. The total number of full-time management consultants was assessed at 100,000 in the United States by the end of the 1980s, six times the number that existed in the mid-1960s.

In this period, the expansion of management consulting has been impressive by any standard. However, significant qualitative changes have also occurred.

Service diversification. To meet their clients' needs and to attract clients from new sectors of economic and social activity, management consultants have developed varying strategies, offering new special services, specializing in particular sectors or, on the contrary, providing a broad comprehensive package of services to the most demanding clients.

At the forefront of technical progress. In doing this, most management consultants have made it their policy to be associated with the latest developments in management and related fields that can interest their clients, and to offer a new sophisticated service before anyone else can do so. The computer business, the use of information technologies in all aspects of management and accounting, and new communication technologies belong to such areas. Consultants do not hesitate to step out of the traditional limits of the management field and deal with plant automation, communication systems, quality control, equipment design, software development, economic studies, environmental protection and the like if these are of interest to clients and if they can enhance a consultant's competitive edge.

Growing competition in consulting. Competition in management consulting has greatly increased over the past 20 years. In addition to improving service quality and offering new sorts of services, management consultants have become more dynamic and even aggressive in searching for new clients and trying to convince potential clients that they can offer a better service than others. This has brought about many developments in the advertising and marketing of consulting services.

The "Big Eight" come on the scene. A major development has been the new attitude of the Big Eight public accounting firms towards management consulting. Considered for several decades as incompatible with professional accounting and auditing, management consulting started being promoted vigorously by the Big Eight in the early 1960s, producing 15-20 per cent of their income, and in some cases even more. By the end of the 1980s, the Big Eight were reduced through mergers to the Big Six. However, their management consulting services kept expanding more rapidly and generating higher profits than traditional accounting and audit work. Currently six out of the seven world's largest management consulting firms are those of the Big Six group.[3]

Continued internationalization. All larger and many smaller consulting firms continued to internationalize their operations in searching for new markets, adapting to the changes in the international economy, and taking advantage of the new opportunities for consulting in the less developed countries and, since the late 1980s, in Central and Eastern Europe. In larger consulting firms, foreign operations may contribute 30-70 per cent of income. Many new consulting firms have been established in developing and reforming economies.

Internal consulting. Consulting services provided under various names by internal units within private and public organizations are not a new phenomenon, but their volume and role increased very considerably in the 1970s and 1980s. The internal consultant has become a regular actor on the management consulting stage.

Progress in the methodology of consulting. Great efforts have been made to increase the long-term benefits derived by clients from consulting assignments, by diversifying and perfecting the intervention methods applied at all stages of the consulting process. Greater emphasis has been placed on clients' active participation in problem solving, new and more effective approaches to organizational change, the development of clients' own problem-solving skills, and the need for clients to learn from every consulting assignment generally.

Increased clients' competence in using consultants. Many organizations, private and public, have become real experts in using consultants effectively. They have developed their own criteria and methods for selecting consultants, collaborating with them during assignments, monitoring their interventions, learning from their approach and evaluating results. The progress made by the consulting profession would not have been possible without these improvements on the clients' part.

The current market

The developments described in the previous paragraphs have shaped the current market for management consulting services.

It is *a global market*, where all larger consulting firms operate internationally and have offices or daughter companies in dozens of countries. Consulting across country borders is common practice.

It is *an important market* as the figures bear witness: in 1992 management consulting revenues worldwide attained some US$28.3 billion. This included the world's largest market, the United States, with US$15.2 billion spent on consulting, Europe with US$7.6 billion, and Asia with US$3.2 billion. The rest of the world spent the remaining US$2.3 billion.[4]

It is *a competitive market*, where supply has matched and even outgrown demand. Clients can be more and more selective; service quality and innovation have become important criteria in judging consultants.

It is *an open and liberal market*. Entry, and work in foreign countries, are easy, since there are minimal legal barriers to business consulting services. Language and cultural barriers persist, but do not constitute serious obstacles to consulting across national boundaries.

It is a market with relatively high and rapidly evolving *centralization and polarization*. In 1990-92, the revenue of the 40 largest international consulting firms exceeded 60 per cent of the entire world market. At least 25 international firms employ more than 1,000 consultants (while only four law firms in the whole world employ more than 1,000 lawyers). In 1992, Andersen Consulting had 20 per cent of the whole United Kingdom consulting market. In contrast, there are thousands of sole consulting practitioners and small firms with 2-10 consultants.

It is *a professionally challenging market*. In consulting, the share of repetitive, routine and boring work is smaller than in law, accounting and auditing. Demand has not only grown, but has also changed in nature. Globalization, information and communication technologies, regional economic groupings, the fall of the communist regimes, privatization and many other developments have not only increased demand for consulting, but have also changed the content and quality of demand. In consulting, the demand side requires continuous creativity and innovation. The supply side provides unlimited opportunities for initiative and intellectually rewarding work.

2.2   Range of services provided

Today's management consulting professionals can be asked to help with any type of management problem in any sort and size of organization. If new problems appear and new needs are identified, it is more than certain that some management consultant will immediately make a special effort to become an expert in such a new field.

There have been many attempts to list and classify the areas covered by management consultants. The professional associations of consultants are interested in such lists, both to define areas from which they accept members and to be able to provide information on the types of service available from members. The publicity and information booklets of individual consulting firms normally list areas of the firm's competence. However, a generally acceptable and "user-friendly" (easy to interpret and use) classification has yet to be developed. Currently used lists and publicity brochures include many vague terms and concepts, which can be easily misinterpreted by potential clients.

Areas and functions of management

Traditionally, management consulting services were structured in accordance with the prevailing structuring of the management functions. Services were offered in production organization and management, marketing and sales, personnel management, office organization, financial management, general management and organization, and similar fields. This structuring of service offerings has been very much preserved until the present time. A consulting firm may provide services in one or more of these areas, depending on its size, specialization strategy and other factors. Conversely, a firm's or an individual consultant's specialization can be deeper and may concern only one segment of a management function, such as maintenance or stock control within production management, or job evaluation and compensation within personnel or human resource management.

Problems and challenges faced by management

Consulting services focus on particular sorts of problems and challenges developed in response to challenges cutting across several management functions and reflecting new business opportunities and constraints. Their range is extremely wide. Examples are consulting in cost cutting, productivity improvement, energy saving, joint ventures, mergers and acquisitions, technology transfer, company turnarounds, project development and management, cross-cultural management, privatization, environmental management and so on.

Systems development and improvement

Management information, reporting, planning, scheduling and decision systems have become another important strain of consulting services. This is very much linked with the developments in underlying information technologies — from manual systems, through simple but increasingly specialized mechanical office technologies, to successive generations of computerized information and communication technologies. Two key factors have triggered off the growth of specialized systems-oriented and information-technology-based consulting: the amount of special expertise temporarily needed for systems analysis and development, and the speed with which systems become obsolete and have to be modernized, or replaced by totally new systems. As mentioned, a growing amount of consulting in this area is interdisciplinary, combining assistance and advice in management, information and communication technologies and systems. The systems have become increasingly integrated, unifying data and procedures from production, sales, purchasing, cost control, quality management and other areas in one computerized system.

In this area management consulting is often provided in combination with various information technology services, which may include the development of customized software and assistance in installing the system and making it fully operational.

Approaches to organizational performance improvement and change

Other consultants emphasize that their main strength and usefulness to clients lie not in a detailed knowledge of a specific technical area or system, but in their ability to share with the client their effective work method — for diagnosing and resolving organizational problems, devising action programmes for organizational change and performance improvement, and making sure that such programmes are implemented. Their service is defined neither by the area of intervention (e.g. marketing) nor by the problem to be tackled (e.g. high production or distribution costs), but by the consulting approach or method used.

Examples are organizational development with its wide range of intervention techniques, action learning, business diagnosis, various problem-analysis and problem-solving methodologies, total quality management, creative thinking and innovation techniques, benchmarking, business process re-engineering, organizational transformation, and so on. Some of these methods and approaches are highly structured and applied as complete, often proprietary and copyright-protected, consulting and training packages. Some are passing fads or new labels for old things. Others are true innovations and their impact on organizational effectiveness and the consulting industry itself can be significant and lasting.

Consulting approaches to organizational change and performance improvement are increasingly offered in combination with special knowledge and skills in areas mentioned in the previous paragraphs.

Sectoral services

Some consultants have chosen a sectoral approach: they do their whole business for one sector, or have established sectorally specialized divisions. The reasons are both technical (the need for an intimate knowledge of sector technologies, economics, and business practices and culture) and commercial (many clients' preference for consultants who know their sector). As some practitioners put it: "If you develop a reputation as a sugar-industry consultant, you get sugar-industry clients." This is quite important in sectors that traditionally regard themselves as different from other sectors (e.g. the construction or mining industries) and are sceptical about the value of advice coming from outside the sector.

The shifts in the sectoral focus of consulting reflect the structural changes in the economy. Originally, most consultants used to work mainly for industrial and commercial enterprises. In today's consulting, work for the service sectors tends to be very important; this includes clients from banking and insurance, communications, transportation, community development, central and local government administration, education, health care, voluntary associations, leisure and entertainment.

Complementary services

Sectorally specialized consulting firms often provide their clients with a service package combining management, business and engineering consulting. Other services offered by various management consulting firms include technical and managerial training, training of supervisory and office personnel, production and distribution of audiovisual training packages, information processing services, collection and distribution of business information, book publishing, psychological testing, opinion polls for market research, consumer taste surveys, advertising, sectoral economic and market studies, management and supervision of investment projects, real estate, statistical work, and so on. Consulting firms have moved into areas such as choice and transfer of technology, patents and licences, product design and testing, design of control equipment, and similar fields.

All these are closely related to management consulting, but some of them are clearly outside its framework. By branching out into new service areas, management consultants are doing the same as other professions — looking for new markets and aiming to satisfy their clients' demand for coherent and complete service packages.

2.3   Generalists and specialists

One of the oldest issues debated by the observers of consulting is whether both generalists and specialists have the right to be called management consultants. Some contend that only an all-round generalist is a real management consultant, while a specialist can be an industrial engineer, a financial analyst, an expert in compensation techniques or an industrial psychologist, but not a management consultant. Others object to this, pointing out that generalists lack the in-depth knowledge required to solve problems in today's business; therefore to be really useful a consultant must be a specialist.

The history and the current profile of the profession indicate that both generalists and specialists have their place in management consulting. The issue is not generalists *versus* specialists, but how to combine generalist and specialist skills and perspectives to achieve a better total effect. This combination has several facets.

Specialist work viewed from a generalist perspective

To manage an organization is an interdisciplinary and multifunctional task, and measures taken in one specialist area relate to other areas. Therefore a management consultant will always try to view specific (and often narrow) problems, requiring the intervention of a specialist, in a wider context. To be a good consultant, the specialist has to be able to look at the problem from the generalist point of view. He or she must be able to apply diagnostic and other methods common to all skilled consultants, and understand organizational relationships. This is one of the main objectives of theoretical and practical training in a consulting firm.

Generalists and specialists cooperate

It would be unrealistic to require every consultant to be both a complete specialist and a generalist, although a few talented and experienced individuals do achieve this. However, in most consulting firms there is some division of work between those who are primarily specialists (and keep up to date in a special area of knowledge and its applications) and those who are generalists (and deal with several areas of management and focus on their interaction, coordination and integration).

The so-called generalists prepare and coordinate global assignments requiring combined specialist and generalist interventions. They normally take care of preliminary organizational diagnoses, negotiations with clients, assignment planning and coordination, drawing conclusions from specific observations made by specialists, presenting final proposals to clients, and so on. Supervisory and managerial functions in consulting are often in the hands of the generalists.

Some assignments are totally or primarily in the general management field and are undertaken by senior generalists. They concern issues such as corporate policy and strategy, leadership and management style, organizational structure, mergers, turnarounds and the like. Most consulting for small businesses is done by generalists, capable of advising the client on the business in its totality. Clients expect that the generalist will suggest the participation of a specialist consultant whenever such a need is identified, just as they expect that the specialist will exercise self-discipline and refrain from giving advice in areas beyond his or her special competence.

35

The trend towards specialization

In today's management consulting there is a pronounced trend towards greater specialization, which reflects the growing range and complexity of issues handled by consultants. This trend concerns the service specialization of the consulting firms (of all sizes, including individual practitioners) first of all. Increasingly, clients are interested in working with firms that do not present themselves as universal experts in solving business problems, but possess the right specialist knowledge and expertise, e.g. in the industrial sector or functional area concerned. Many firms have started rethinking their profile to comply with this requirement.

Furthermore, management consulting firms have started modifying their internal staff structure, that is, the number and the respective roles of the specialists and generalists employed. There are more and more assignments that clients wish to be undertaken by a specialist, and if a firm does not have full-time employment for such a specialist, it will employ the person part time, or borrow his or her services from another firm when necessary. However, many of these specialists, highly competent in their technical fields, urgently need to widen their outlook and improve their understanding of the functions of the total organization.

As for all-round generalists, their role in dealing with interdisciplinary and multifunctional problems will remain important. But there are various degrees of generalization, and the trend seems to be towards generalists who do not try to deal with all kinds of situation but become proven experts in certain sectors (health, transportation) or types of organizational and business problems (mergers and acquisitions, diagnosing and assisting organizations in difficulties).

2.4 Main types of consulting organization

The diversity of the clients and markets served, technical services provided, approaches taken and personalities involved, is reflected in the wide range of types of management consulting organization. Without going into details concerning their strategies and organization, which will be covered in Part IV, we will now review the main types.

Large multifunctional consulting firms

A consulting firm employing several hundred professionals can be considered as large, but there are more than 25 giants in the consulting world with over 1,000 management consultants on their staff. Most of them operate as multinational firms, with branch offices or daughter companies in 20 or more countries. Their size permits them to deal with a wide range of clients and most complex management problems; they are sometimes referred to as "full-service management consulting firms" able to provide "total service packages". They prefer to serve large and multinational clients. Many of them have also developed some special skills which make them different from each other, e.g. they may be known for possessing special sectoral expertise and have important sectorally specialized departments, or they may be strong in corporate strategy and business restructuring (the strategy consultancies), or focus on management consulting services based on information technology.

Management consulting services of major accounting firms

The management advisory services (MAS), established as divisions of major accounting firms, have in the last decade grown into large multifunctional management consultancies. Today they are the world's largest professional firms not only in accounting and audit, but also in management consulting measured separately. They have drawn considerable benefits from the environment of leading accounting firms in terms of expertise, image, contacts and assignment opportunities. Some of them used to emphasize that they were not keen to undertake just any type of assignment, but only those that "would be expected from a reputable professional accounting firm". This, however, has changed radically. At the present time, the Big Six also operate in areas such as human resource management and development, organization development, production engineering, total quality, integrated information and control systems, and small business consulting.

Small and medium-sized consulting firms

This group embraces a variety of organizations, ranging from a few to 50-100 consultants. Obviously a firm small by American standards can be extremely large in a smaller developing country. Their prevailing technical profiles include:

— general management and business development consulting for small and medium-sized client firms, as a rule in a limited geographical area;

— consulting in one or a few technical areas, such as corporate strategy (the "strategy boutiques"), personnel administration, maintenance, quality control and management, marketing, sales management, office management, environmental auditing and management, and so on;

— full sectoral specialization, e.g. in urban transport, textiles, printing industry, insurance.

Sole practitioners

The existence of thousands of sole consulting practitioners demonstrates that, despite competition and aggressive marketing by large professional firms, there is plenty of interest in working with independent individuals. These may be generalists, emphasizing their broad management experience, problem-solving and behavioural skills, or specialists working in a narrow technical area. Their strength is in a highly personalized and flexible approach, more difficult to apply consistently in a large consulting firm. The services of a senior individual practitioner can also be less expensive, because he or she can avoid many of the overhead costs of a larger organization. Before becoming independent consultants, many sole practitioners worked as business executives or spent the first part of their careers with larger consultancies.

Some clients prefer to entrust the whole assignment to a very senior person, one who in a larger firm would probably work as a project leader, supervising the work of several more junior consultants. Sole practitioners are often connected with other colleagues in informal networks and so can team up to undertake larger and more complex assignments, or can recommend another person for work outside their own area of competence. Most of them consult for smaller enterprises, but even larger enterprises sometimes use sole practitioners' services for smaller assignments and special tasks.

The problem is that, alongside highly competent and committed individuals, this group also includes mediocre consultants and it is not always easy to find out who is who.

The "consulting professors"

While a sole practitioner makes a living from consulting, there are management professors, lecturers, trainers and researchers whose only job is not consulting, but who are involved in it on a part-time, though fairly regular, basis. Most of them provide ad hoc advice on management issues which may be quite important from the client's perspective, but which do not require extensive consulting time.

Some full-time consultants do not regard the "professor" as a real management consultant. This, however, is a short-sighted view. Experience has shown that outstanding benefits can be drawn from combining research, teaching and consulting. The consulting professors' main contribution has been new perspectives and new ideas, not routine consulting work. A small group has attained the level of "guru consulting", which influences the thinking of legions of business executives and management consultants alike.

Consulting services of management institutions

To foster local management consulting capabilities and link management teachers and trainers with the world of practice, a number of business schools, management institutions and productivity centres, primarily (but not only) in developing countries, have established consulting services to private and public organizations. Often this has been done with technical assistance from international agencies and with the involvement of experienced consultancy firms from other countries. These "institutional" units enjoy some independence in choosing clients and selling services. Some of them employ full-time consultants, while others staff assignments from the institution's teaching and research personnel.

A combination of teaching/training and consulting services is highly valued by many clients. However, there are institutions where this form of consulting conflicts with individual "professor" consulting and teaching: the best individuals on the teaching staff tend to give priority to their personal clients, from whom they earn considerable income, before projets negotiated and executed through the institution, and before classroom teaching.

Non-traditional suppliers of consulting services

A new group of suppliers of management consulting services has emerged in recent years. This group is rather heterogeneous but has one common characteristic: its original and main function is something other than consulting, but consulting is viewed as a technically useful and financially profitable addendum to its products and services. The group includes, among others:

- suppliers and vendors of computer and communication equipment;
- computer software houses;
- commercial and investment banks, brokers, insurance companies and other organizations in the finance sector;
- suppliers of equipment and turnkey projects in energy, transportation, drinking-water, irrigation and other utilities;
- economic, statistical and sectoral research institutes and information centres;
- other organizations that have turned their internal management service groups into external consulting services.

A number of organizations, usually those with a strong mathematical, computer science, operations research or econometrics background, offer special consulting services in areas such as strategic studies, model building, forecasting of consumer demand, systems analysis and design, plant and office automation, and others. Some of them are also referred to as "think-tank" organizations. They may be independent, or associated with a computer firm, a technological university or a research institute. These consulting services tend to be research and/or technology based.

2.5   Internal consultants

An internal consulting unit is one which is established within an organization — a business corporation, a public utility, a government ministry or department — to provide consulting services to other units of the same organization. Definitions and delimitations are not very precise. These services are given many different names, but the term "management services" prevails. They can be found at different places in the organizational structure. Some of them are consulting services in the full sense of the term — they have a mandate to intervene in an advisory capacity at the request of a senior manager, or a unit manager within the organization. In other cases, consulting is one of the staff functions, and the units concerned are also responsible for internal audit, developing and maintaining accounting and information systems, records and reporting procedures, organizational circulars, staff development programmes and other similar functions.

The current trend

The growth of internal consulting has been impressive in recent years. Internal units undertake many types of assignment which used to be given to external consultants. To have some sort of internal management consulting service has become common practice in larger business corporations; multinational corporations have large and versatile consulting units, available both to headquarters and to foreign subsidiaries. These units are staffed with technically competent specialists and generalists, some of whom have experience with external management consulting or accounting firms. The same trend can be observed in government administrations.

Total numbers of internal consultants are not known, but most probably they are very large. Internal consultants started establishing their own professional associations, and several professional bodies of external consultants have recognized them. Already in 1976, the Institute of Management Consultants in the United Kingdom agreed that the term *independent practice* "shall include consultants engaged as in-house consultants who meet the required standards of knowledge, experience and competence and are free at all times to offer objective and independent advice".

The critics

There are many critics of internal consulting. The main criticism comes from some larger consulting firms, which contend that internal consulting can be a useful staff function, but does not deserve to be called management consulting. They challenge the internal consultants' independence and objectivity, and criticize their lack of exposure to different situations in various companies, which it is believed leads to in-breeding. Also, it is said, only a large firm or government department can really afford a sufficiently important and competent internal unit for consulting work. This criticism does not seem to be shared by organizations that continue to build up their own internal consulting services.

Why such an interest?

First of all, the rapid growth of internal consulting is a recognition of the power of the consulting approach. It is only logical that, having appreciated the technical and methodological advantages of consulting, businesses and governments want to make more use of this approach. Many of them have found that an internal consulting service is one way of achieving it. Consulting is thus made accessible to many internal units and is available for making improvements where previously consultants would not have been used.

Further reasons for retaining an internal consultant are quick availability, an intimate knowledge of the organization's internal practices, work and management style, culture and politics (hence sensitivity and a more rapid orientation in any work situation), and confidentiality. Internal consulting is often thought to be more appropriate for problems that require a deep knowledge of the highly complex internal relations and constraints in large organizations. In governments, they may be given priority for reasons of national security and interest.

The cost factor is not negligible. Because of reduced overheads, travel and other expenses, even a well-paid internal consultant will cost 30-50 per cent less than an external one — if the company has enough work for him or her.

Independence and other problems

Independence and objectivity represent a problem in some cases. This occurs if the management of the organization and the internal consultants fail to clarify the roles and mutual responsibilities of client and consultant within an organization, if consultants are used for anything that comes into an executive's mind, and if they know that they have to please top management or their direct client instead of giving an impartial view. An internal consulting service which has low status and has no access to top management (you are not a prophet in your own house!) will not be able to deal with higher-level and strategy-related problems, and its recommendations will lack credibility and authority.

If the role and status of internal consulting are properly defined and respected, the independence, objectivity and credibility of this service can be considerably enhanced.

Combining internal and external consulting

The use of internal consultants is not a passing fad, nor will it replace the use of external consultants. The latter will continue to be preferred in situations where an internal consultant does not meet the criteria of impartiality and confidentiality, or lacks expertise. However, it is difficult to contest that internal consulting has a definite role to play, and its obstinate opponents would do well to stop denigrating its potential.

In a growing number of cases, assignments are entrusted to joint teams of external and internal consultants. This is a technically interesting arrangement: it can reduce costs; it helps external consultants to learn quickly about the client organization; it facilitates implementation; and it contributes to the training of internal consultants.

Many external consultants enjoy this way of working and regard internal consultants as useful technical partners, not competitors. They have learned not to underestimate and not to ignore any internal consultant in a client organization. In many situations it is tactically better if proposals are endorsed by an internal unit, or are presented by this unit, than if they represent only an outsider's view. Internal consultants are more and more involved in defining terms of reference for external consultants, establishing short-lists for selecting consultants, making the selection, negotiating the terms of contracts, discussing recommendations, and monitoring implementation. Their use can improve the quality and reduce the costs of implementation quite considerably.

An interesting way of increasing the competence and credibility of internal consultants is to involve them in external consulting. For example, management services units in several electricity corporations, railways and other public utilities have developed performance improvement and staff training programmes that are of interest to public utilities in other sectors or countries. In-company management services units in various sectors have done a great deal of work on project and systems design, consulting and training in developing countries.

From cost centres to profit centres

The traditional way of using internal consultants prevented these units from covering their costs from their income. They were treated as cost centres, financed from the company budget as part of the general costs. Their growth was not determined by client demand, or by the consultant's ability to develop and sell better services, but by the company's budgetary process and the unit's ability to negotiate higher allocations. If the allocation to the internal consulting unit was insufficient, the demand for its services could probably not be met. The unit's staff could not really be motivated to develop and sell more and better services.

To change this set-up, many organizations have started treating their internal consulting units as profit centres. This is more than a change in budgetary procedures. A profit centre is regarded as a unit that creates value, generates income and contributes to the company's profit. It must be able to sell its services, thus demonstrating that there is demand even if the clients have to pay. Internal clients, however, must have the right to choose. If the internal consulting unit satisfies them, they buy its services. If not, they turn to external consultants.

The helping relationship within an organization

Besides the activities of internal consulting units, there are many other opportunities for making effective use of the helping relationship within organizations. Examples are advisory missions of managers and specialists to other subsidiaries and plants within a corporation, temporary task forces and project groups, short-term detachments, personal coaching and counselling, and so on. Some of these forms will be described in Chapter 4, when organizational forms and interventions for managing and assisting change are discussed. They are often used in connection with a consulting project carried out by an external or internal consulting unit.

Although this sort of helping activity is not normally referred to as consulting, it tends to produce better results if the individuals involved are familiar with the principles and methods of professional consulting.

2.6   Management consulting and other professions

On the previous pages we have made several references to two trends: firstly, management consultants have been increasingly moving into new service areas, which may be emerging areas of management consulting, but also areas outside the management consulting field; and, secondly, other providers of professional and business services have tended to do more and more management consulting. This shows that professions no longer enjoy impenetrable borders and absolute protection against intruders. The world of the professions is undergoing profound transformations, which are reshaping individual professions, shifting their borders and changing their status, relationships and methods of work.

Professional infrastructure of the market economy

To function smoothly, the market economy needs a well-developed, reliable and effective infrastructure of professional services. Management consulting is one of them. The total infrastructure comprises many other services (figure 2.1, overleaf). They all serve the same private and public sector client base, including business firms, administrations, social organizations and individuals. They also serve each other.

The structural changes through which business and governments have passed in the last decades have had a major impact on professions providing services to them. The services of lawyers, accountants, investment bankers, management consultants and others are in great demand as the pace of structural changes accelerates and as these changes become radical and complex. Mergers and acquisitions, joint ventures, privatization, trade liberalization, export development, new forms of cross-border trade and financial operations, business alliances, or new laws and agreements regulating business nationally and internationally — are all green pastures for business- and management-related professions.

Most of these business transactions and structural changes do not fall under the jurisdiction of one single profession. They involve legal, financial, accounting, organizational, managerial and other aspects, although one of these aspects may dominate in a given case. In addition, an international perspective and expertise is increasingly required from all professions.

Management consulting has grown and evolved in this context. It has been changing in interaction with other professions, which has included both competition and cooperation. This interdependence is best documented by the spectacular growth of management consulting services of international accounting firms. Within less than 20 years, these firms have been able to become world leaders in consulting in addition to having achieved a leadership position in accounting and audit.

Figure 2.1   Professional service infrastructure

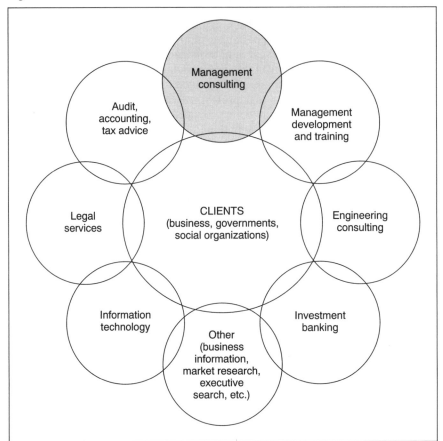

Taking a bite out of other professions' cake

Tough competition is one of the main characteristics of the current state of the professions. There is competition both within and among professions. When a new market starts emerging, several professions may claim that this market is primarily within their province. This has been the case of privatization, where accounting firms, investment bankers, management consultants and law firms have all been competing for a leadership position and a bigger market share.

If the work to be done requires *an interdisciplinary approach* — which is more and more the case — a firm in one profession may decide to establish a new service line in an area that falls under another profession from a strictly technical point of view. A management consultant would branch out into tax advice, or a computer firm decide to offer management consulting. Other examples were given in section 2.4. Thus the firm becomes multi-professional, or multidisciplinary. If there are legal or other barriers preventing a combination of certain service lines within one firm (e.g. legal advice and management consulting or accounting and audit), a solution is usually found in establishing a new sister or affiliated firm for the new service line.

In some grey areas competition is straightforward. For example, *company valuation* is not a guarded domain of any profession in many countries. Management consultants rightly emphasize their advantages: assessing potential future earnings of a manufacturing company requires an ability to analyse demand and sectoral trends, the maturity level of the technology used, emerging technologies, raw materials, local and foreign competitors, quality and cost of labour, and the like. Conversely, accountants and investment bankers also offer valuation services, stressing the accounting and financial market aspects and implications. There are, too, independent experts in property, real estate and company valuation. Thus, valuation services are available from several professions, and clients can choose which ones to use.

Cooperation among professions

Cooperation among different professions is an equally important trend. Clients are not interested in interprofessional skirmishes and jealously guarded borders between professions. They resent corporatist attitudes that put the profession's self-interest before the clients' interest. What they want is a service in which no important aspect of the problem in hand is ignored or treated unprofessionally. If a management consultant cannot deliver such a service with his or her own resources, well-organized collaboration with other professions provides a solution.

Management consultants collaborate closely with *lawyers* on many issues with legal aspects and implications. The initiative often comes from the legal side: legal counsel may feel the need for management or financial advice in dealing with a legal problem, and so turn to a management consulting firm, which may or may not already be on contract to a mutual client. However, the management consultant can also perceive the need for legal advice in a given situation, invite a lawyer to participate in a joint assignment, seek consultation with internal counsel or recommend that the client engage outside legal counsel.

Another area with numerous links to consulting is *audit*. It can be argued that auditing in the narrow sense of the term, that is, checking and certifying accounting records and financial reports, is not consulting. However, it is only a small step to consulting. Auditors who make a value judgement on the client organization's records and reports or recommend an improvement — and this is what is increasingly required in many countries — act as consultants whether they call themselves consultants or not. Auditing often prepares the ground for important management consulting projects; this was well perceived by accounting firms when they decided to enter management consulting (see also the discussion of cross-selling in Chapter 25).

Engineering consultants (consulting engineers) constitute a vast and diversified sector providing technical expertise in areas such as civil engineering, the construction industry, architecture, land and quantity surveying, town and country planning, project planning and supervision, mechanical engineering, chemical engineering, patent services, computer science and systems, and so on.

The link between management consulting and consulting in engineering has traditionally been very close and the boundaries are in many cases blurred. On the one hand, some engineering consultants also deal with organization and management questions, particularly in areas such as industrial or production engineering and control, quality management, maintenance, feasibility studies, patents and licences, plant design, or project design, implementation and supervision. On the other hand, production management consultants with an engineering background can deal with various production and productivity improvement problems that are of both a managerial and a technological nature. In many contexts the best results will be achieved if management and engineering experts work together on interdisciplinary projects.

Several remarks on the relationships between management consulting and *information technology (IT) consulting* have already been made on the previous pages. Indeed, it is in this interface that the most spectacular and most rapid changes have occurred in recent years — and will continue in the future. Computer software houses and hardware manufacturers first entered management consulting in the area of systems design, development and application, and then widened their interest and embraced general management and strategy consulting, and other areas. Management consultants' strategies have been very similar: they have been adding more and more IT services to their portfolio. On both sides firms have come up with a widening range of integrated management/systems/IT services, as well as highly specialized services. This has been achieved through numerous mergers and acquisitions, and also through authentic development of new service lines and new competencies.

It is difficult to predict how far the *rapprochement* of management and IT consulting will reach, but it is easy to see that the current situation is a transitional one and that further changes will be forthcoming.

2.7 Management consulting, training and research

There is a very special relationship, different from what was described in the previous section, between management consulting on the one hand, and management training, development and research on the other hand. It could even be argued that conceptually they constitute subsectors of the same profession, since they have the same object of study and practical intervention and the same educational background, and pursue the same ultimate purposes. What is different is methodology, and immediate purposes.

There are professions where the relationships between practical intervention, education, and training and research have been clarified and arranged long ago. In medicine, no one would think of the practitioners, the medical schools and the researchers as of different professions. In management, we have not arrived at that point. We have not been able to overcome fully the traditional dichotomy between the practically oriented consultant, committed to producing tangible results for the client, and the professor-researcher, writing and teaching about concepts and theories, but less concerned with practical applications.

Consulting and training

Fortunately, there have been signs of real progress in bridging the gap between consulting, and training and development, in the field of management:

— In modern consulting, learning is pursued as one of the main purposes. In choosing his or her work methods and collaborating with the client, the consultant aims to pass on personal know-how and experience to the client.

— Consultants view training (both informal and formal) as their key intervention tool and use it extensively.

— Some consulting firms have established management development and training centres as a special client service, which can be used in conjunction with consulting assignments, or separately.

— Many consultants collaborate with business schools and other educational and training establishments as part-time teachers or trainers.

— Conversely, more and more management teachers and trainers practise consulting alongside teaching and training (the "consulting professors" mentioned in section 2.4) and use consulting experience to make training more relevant and practically oriented.

— In some educational and training establishments, consulting has become an institutional function, organized through special consulting departments and/or projects.

— There are also hybrid firms and institutions, providing combined consulting/training services and stressing the benefits that the client can obtain from their approach.

Consulting and research

Similar comments can be made on the relationships between management consulting and management research. Many of the older-generation consultants liked to stress that they were down-to-earth practitioners who had nothing in common with the researcher. This dichotomy, however, reflected a poor theoretical preparation of the consultant and a lack of practical purpose on the side of most academics, rather than a substantive conflict between the consulting and the research approach. Despite their differences (see box 2.1 overleaf), research and consulting have a lot in common and can be very useful to each other.

In dealing with practical management problems, consultants need to know the results of research and draw from them — for example, before recommending an incentive technique it is better to know whether any research has been made into the use of that technique in conditions similar to those experienced

Box 2.1	Factors differentiating research and consulting	
Factor	**Research**	**Consulting**
Problem	Mainly fashioned by researcher; more open-ended, especially in exploratory research	Mainly fashioned by client, sometimes on joint basis
Time scale	Usually flexible	More tight and rigid
End product	New knowledge and new theories + ? better practice	Better management practice
Ownership of information	Usually publicly available	Often confidential
Decision-making	Focus may change at researcher's discretion subject to plan	Discretion limited to main task only
Academic rigour	Methodology tight	Minimum level appropriate to problem
Evaluation	External — by peers in scientific community, policy-makers	Internal — by company

by the client. Consulting organizations increasingly encourage their members not only to be informed about published results of management research, but also to keep in touch with on-going research projects and with the leading researchers.

Research, then, can only benefit from close links with consulting. The data collected in client organizations by consultants can serve wider research purposes. Data from a number of organizations can be used for drawing general conclusions on sectoral or other trends, without infringing confidentiality. On becoming aware of this, many consulting firms have also gone into research. They have their own research programme, undertake contract research, and publish books based on their own research, or they cooperate on research projects with universities and individual researchers. Some consulting firms have gained the reputation of being strongly research based. Business schools and research institutes are increasingly interested in testing and diffusing the results of their research through consulting assignments.

Methodologically, consultants learn a lot from researchers and vice versa. Action research is an example of research that is on the borders of research and consulting; it aims simultaneously at solving a meaningful practical problem and yielding new knowledge about the social system under study. Action research involves changing that which is being investigated; conventional research does not.

[1] For a fine account of the history of management consulting see H. J. Klein: *Other people's business: A primer on management consultants* (New York, Mason-Charter, 1977); and P. Tisdall: *Agents of change: The development and practice of management consultancy* (London, Heinemann, 1982).

[2] See W. B. Wolf: *Management and consulting: An introduction to James O. McKinsey* (Ithaca, New York, Cornell University, 1978).

[3] The "Big Eight" included the following international accounting firms: Arthur Andersen; Arthur Young; Coopers and Lybrand; Deloitte Haskins and Sells; Ernst and Whinney; Peat, Marwick, Mitchell; Price Waterhouse; and Touche Ross. In 1989, Ernst and Young was established by merging Ernst and Whinney with Arthur Young. Deloitte Haskins and Sells merged with Touche Ross. Peat, Marwick, Mitchell became KPMG following a 1986 merger with Klynveld Main Goerdeler.

[4] *Consultants News* (Fitzwilliam, New Hampshire), July 1993, and other sources.

THE CONSULTANT-CLIENT RELATIONSHIP

3

The consulting process involves two partners — the consultant and the client. The client has decided to purchase a professional service under certain terms — for example, for an agreed number of days and a daily fee. During this time, the consultant's expertise will be fully available to the client, and in theory it should be easy to put this expertise to work on the client's project. It is fair to assume that both parties are keen to achieve the same purpose.

The reality is infinitely more complex. The consultant remains an external person to the organization, someone who is supposed to achieve a valid result in the client organization without being part of its administrative and human system. Even an internal consultant — an organization's employee — is an external element from the viewpoint of organizational units where he or she is supposed to intervene. Quite independently of its technical relevance and quality, the consultant's advice may or may not be understood and accepted by the client. The consultant can upset people and hurt their feelings in many different ways. Rejection can take many forms. The history of consulting records thousands of excellent reports that have been buried in managers' desks and never implemented, although they were formally accepted. This underlines the critical importance of creating and maintaining *an effective consultant-client relationship*.

Experience shows that building this relationship is not easy. To achieve success, both consultants and clients ought to be aware of the human, cultural and other factors that will affect their relationship, and of the errors to be avoided when working together on the assignment. They must be prepared to make *a special effort* to build and maintain a relationship of understanding and trust that makes the effective intervention of an independent professional possible. There is no alternative.

3.1 Defining expectations and roles

To begin with, the client and the consultant may look differently at both the expected outcome and the ways of carrying out the assignment. The client may have only a vague idea of how consultants work and may be slightly suspicious — possibly he or she has heard about consultants who try to complicate every issue, require more information than they really need, ask for more time in order to justify longer assignments, and charge exorbitant fees. The client may be approaching the consultant with mixed feelings (box 3.1). But even if there is no suspicion, and no fear on the client's side, there is a risk of misunderstanding.

Box 3.1   What it feels like to be a buyer

(1)   I'm feeling **insecure**. I'm not sure I know how to detect which of the finalists is the genius, and which is just good. I've exhausted my abilities to make technical distinctions.

(2)   I'm feeling **threatened**. This is my area of responsibility, and even though intellectually I know I need outside expertise, emotionally it's not comfortable to put my affairs in the hands of others.

(3)   I'm taking a **personal risk**. By putting my affairs in the hands of someone else, I risk losing control.

(4)   I'm **impatient**. I didn't call in someone at the first sign of symptoms (or opportunity). I've been thinking about this for a while.

(5)   I'm **worried**. By the very fact of suggesting improvements or changes, these people are going to be implying that I haven't been doing it right up till now. Are these people going to be on my side?

(6)   I'm **exposed**. Whoever I hire, I'm going to reveal some proprietary secrets, not all of which are flattering. I will have to undress.

(7)   I'm feeling **ignorant**, and don't like the feeling. I don't know if I've got a simple problem or a complex one. I'm not sure I can trust them to be honest about that: it's in their interest to convince me it's complex.

(8)   I'm **sceptical**. I've been burned before by these kinds of people. You get a lot of promises: How do I know whose promise I should buy?

(9)   I'm **concerned** that they either can't or won't take the time to understand what makes my situation special. They'll try to sell me what they've got rather than what I need.

(10) I'm **suspicious**. Will they be those typical professionals who are hard to get hold of, who are patronizing, who leave you out of the loop, who befuddle you with jargon, who don't explain what they're re-doing or why, who . . . , who . . ., who . . .? In short, will these people deal with me in the way I want to be dealt with?

Source: David Maister: *Managing the professional service firm* (New York, The Free Press, 1993), p. 113.

Joint problem definition

First, the reason for which the consultant was brought in needs to be well defined. A manager who wants to call for a consultant's help should not merely recognize a need for such help, but define the problem as he or she sees it, as precisely as possible. In many organizations, top management would not even consider using consultants unless presented with a clear description of the problem and the purpose of the consultancy.

Before accepting the assignment, the consultant must be sure that he or she can subscribe to the client's definition of the problem. With the exception of the most simple and clear cases, the consultant wants to be able to reach his or her own conclusion as to what the problem is and how difficult its solution might be.

There are many reasons why the consultant's definition of the problem might differ from the client's. Frequently managers are too deeply immersed in a particular situation, or have created the problem themselves. They may perceive the symptoms but not the real issue. They may also prefer the consultant to "discover" certain significant aspects of the problem.

Comparison of the client's and the consultant's definition of the problem lays down the basis of sound working relations and mutual trust for the whole duration of the assignment. It requires discussion. Both the consultant and the client should be prepared to make corrections to their initial definition of the problem and to agree on a joint definition. But this joint definition should not be considered as final. Once the assignment has started, detailed diagnostic work may uncover new problems and new opportunities, and impose a redefinition of what was originally agreed.

Results to be achieved

Secondly, the consultant and the client should clarify what the assignment should achieve and how this achievement will be measured. This may require an exchange of views on how each party regards consulting, how far the consultant should continue working on an agreed task (possibly exceeding the scope of that task), and what his or her responsibility to the client is. As mentioned in section 1.4, there is often a misunderstanding about the consultant's role in implementation. The consultant may be keen to participate in it, but the client may be used to receiving reports with action proposals, and to deciding on implementation only after the consultant has left. If possible, the consultant will try to be involved in implementation. If cost is what worries the client, the consultant's presence during implementation can be a light one (see also Chapter 10).

The consultant's and the client's roles

Thirdly, it is important to determine how the assignment will be conducted by the two parties:

— What roles will be played by the consultant and what by the client? What will be their mutual commitments?

— Who will do what, when, and how?

— Does the client want to obtain a solution from the consultant, or does he prefer to develop his own solution with the consultant's help?

— Is the client prepared to be intensely involved throughout the assignment?

— Are there specific areas that the consultant should cover without trying to involve the client? And vice versa?

These and similar questions will clarify the client's and the consultant's conception of management consulting and of the roles that can be effectively played by consultants. The answers will define the strategy to be followed in order to make the assignment a success by both the client's and the consultant's standards.

During the assignment, many unforeseen events may occur and new facts may be uncovered so that it becomes necessary to review the original definition of expectations and roles. Both the client and the consultant should be alert to this possibility and be flexible enough to adjust their contract and work arrangements. The client's staff may find at some stage that they can easily produce information or action proposals that the consultant was originally supposed to work out, or that it would be more useful to use the consultant as a trainer than as a problem solver. Insisting on keeping to the initial definition of roles, although changed conditions require a new definition, may prove to be counter-productive.

3.2   A collaborative relationship

Different situations and client expectations lead to different definitions of the consultant's roles and intervention methods. Sections 3.4 and 3.5 will review a number of role models from which to choose. Nevertheless, whatever choice is made, the overriding objective should always be the creation and maintenance of *a true collaborative relationship*. This is a golden rule of consulting. The degree and form of client-consultant collaboration will differ from case to case, but there should always be a strong spirit of collaboration, characterized by a shared desire to make the assignment a success, by trust and respect, and by an understanding of the other partner's technical and human roles.

Some clients imagine that by actively collaborating with the consultant they would actually do the job themselves, paying the consultant a handsome fee for nothing. The consultant who insists on the client's collaboration is compared to "the guy who borrows your watch to tell you the time". Often the real will to collaborate is tested at the fact-finding stage. The client feels that he or she should not give the consultant all the data requested and even instructs the staff to withhold information. This shows that the need for active collaboration is not automatically perceived by every client and that various misconceptions may have to be dispelled.

In some countries the client's reluctance to give the consultant all information on the state of the business cannot be interpreted as a misunderstanding of consulting, or as the client's unwillingness to establish a collaborative relationship. Accounting and financial information may be regarded as strictly confidential by a local business and the consultant should not ask for it unless the assignment is in the area of finance. Clearly, it is not possible to provide advice on financial matters without having access to financial data.

The modern concept of consulting methodology assumes strong client collaboration for the following main reasons:

(1) There are many things that the consultant cannot do at all or cannot do properly, if the client is reluctant to collaborate. This happens if the consultant is refused information or cannot exchange ideas with the right people.

(2) Often higher management is unaware of all the competence existing in the organization, and important strengths may be concealed from it. Through collaboration, consultants help clients to uncover and mobilize their own resources.

(3) Collaboration is essential so that the client associates fully with the definition of the problem and with the results of the assignment. Consultants emphasize that their client must "own" the problem and its solution. The reason is that human systems often reject changes proposed or imposed from the outside. By collaborating on a solution the client is more likely to be committed to it and will not put all the responsibility onto the consultant. This commitment will be not only rational, but also emotional. We all know that we tend to have different attitudes towards projects into which we have had to put long hours of hard work and a lot of energy, and to those which we are asked to adopt without ever having been consulted on them.

(4) Most importantly, unless the client collaborates in the assignment, he or she is unlikely to learn from it. Learning is one of the basic purposes of consulting. However, it does not occur by defining terms of reference and accepting or rejecting a final report, but by joint work at all stages of the assignment, starting with problem definition and diagnosis, and ending with the implementation and the assessment of the results actually obtained.

3.3   The client system

With whom, then, and how, will the consultant collaborate? The client, in the widest sense of the term, is the organization which employs the services of a consulting firm. There we have an institutional relationship. A professional service firm works for a manufacturing enterprise, or similar. But there are also clients in a narrower sense of the term — individuals or groups of persons in the client organization who initiate the bringing in of the consultant, discuss the job with him or her, collaborate in the course of the assignment, receive reports and recommend to higher management whether or not to accept them, and so on. Often a number of managers, supervisors, staff members, workers and liaison officers will be directly involved in the assignment at its various stages, or affected by the conclusions reached. Here the consultant-client relationship is personalized and will be influenced by psychological and other factors.

In professional advisory services the consultant-client relationship is always personalized (see Chapter 23). There may be a formal contract between the consulting firm and the organization using its services. However, the delivery of the service occurs through direct contact between persons acting on behalf of the two organizations. This is fundamental. A really productive relationship cannot be fully guaranteed by any legal contract between organizations; it will depend on the abilities and attitudes of, and on the "psychological contract" between, the individuals directly involved.

Management consultants know that in working with client organizations they can discover highly complex and recondite relations. They can face conflicting expectations, hopes and fears, respect and disrespect, confidence and distrust. Information may be readily offered or deliberately concealed or distorted. Consultants refer, therefore, to "client systems", taking a systems view of the client organization and trying to map out the network of relationships in which they are going to operate. This may show that the client system embraces only a part or an aspect of the client organization. Within the client system, the consultant needs then to determine:

— who holds the real power for making decisions related to the assignment (at all stages);

— who has the main interest in the success or failure of the assignment;

— whose direct collaboration is essential.

Many consultants make the mistake of automatically considering and treating the person at the top as their main client. This upsets those people who know that they will have the main responsibility for implementing the conclusions reached, and that they — not the top manager — will be directly affected and will have to live with the results. On the other hand, it may also be a great mistake to leave out the higher-level manager. He or she should be informed and asked for support before it is too late.

During the assignment, the consultant continues to explore the client system and improve his understanding of the roles played by various persons. He does this because he cannot be sure that his original assessment of roles was correct, and also because assignments are living processes and shifts in role can occur at any moment. The appointment of a new manager can change the course of a consulting assignment dramatically.

Some situations may be particularly intricate, e.g. if the consultant does not really know who the main client is and whom he or she should try to satisfy first of all. This may happen if top management recruits the consultant, but leaves it solely to a functional department to handle the job, if a consulting assignment is recommended and sponsored by a bank as a precondition of a loan to its client, or if a ministry sends consultants to a public enterprise. In these and similar situations, the consultant needs to clarify whether he or she is supposed to act as an inspector, an auditor, an informant, or a real management consultant. He or she should find out who "owns" the problem and is keen to be helped — this person or organization will be the main client.

3.4   Behavioural roles of the consultant

This section examines the concept of the consultant's behavioural roles (consulting modes), which is very popular in literature on consulting. It tries to show, in a condensed form, the most typical and frequent consulting behaviours, and to describe how consultants relate to clients, what inputs they make, and in

---

Box 3.2   Various categories of clients within a client system

In a complex client system it is useful to think in terms of categories of clients, aiming to understand their varying motivations and roles, and deciding how to work with each category (some clients may belong to two or more categories simultaneously):

(1)   **Contact clients**: they approach the consultant initially.

(2)   **Intermediate clients**: they participate in various meetings on fact finding, assignment planning, reviewing alternatives, and so on.

(3)   **Main or primary clients**: they "own" a problem for which they need and want help and for which the consultant was brought in. They are likely to be the consultant's principal collaborators.

(4)   **Contract clients**: they play a key role in the consultant selection procedure and in negotiating and signing a consulting contract.

(5)   **Ultimate clients**: their welfare and interests will ultimately be affected by the assignment; they must be considered in planning the intervention, although they may not be directly involved with the consultant.

(6)   **Sponsoring clients**: they provide financial resources for the consultancy and may or may not wish to play a role in determining the procedure to follow, choosing the consultant and approving the proposals to be implemented.

Developed from a typology of clients originally proposed by E. Schein, in *Process consultation*, Vol. II (Reading, Massachusetts, Addison-Wesley, 1987), pp. 117-118.

---

what way and how intensively clients participate. It emphasizes that the roles assumed depend on the situation, the client's preferences and expectations, and the consultant's profile.

There is no shortage of different descriptions and typologies of consulting roles. We have found it useful to make a distinction between *basic roles*, which include the resource and the process role, and *a further refinement of the role concept*, in which many more roles or sub-roles can be visualized in order to facilitate the understanding of the various intervention modes used in consulting.

Basic roles: The resource and the process role

In *the resource role* (also referred to as an expert or content role), the consultant helps the client by providing technical expertise and doing something for and on behalf of the client: he or she supplies information, diagnoses the organization, undertakes a feasibility study, designs a new system, trains staff in a new technique, recommends organizational and other changes, comments on a new project envisaged by management, and the like.

Management does collaborate with the resource consultant, but this collaboration may be limited to providing information on request, discussing the progress made, accepting or declining proposals, and asking for further advice on implementation. Management does not expect the consultant to deal extensively with the social and behavioural aspects of the change process in the organization, although the consultant will have to be aware of these aspects.

In *the process role*, the consultant as the agent of change attempts to help the organization to solve its own problems by making it aware of organizational processes, of their likely consequences, and of intervention techniques for stimulating change. Instead of passing on technical knowledge and suggesting solutions, the process consultant is primarily concerned with passing on his or her approach, methods and values so that the client organization itself can diagnose and remedy its own problems. In various descriptions of process consulting, the organization behaviour (OD) approach comes across loud and clear.

Expressed in simpler terms, while the resource consultant tries to suggest to the client *what* to change, the process consultant suggests mainly *how* to change and helps the client to go through the change process and deal with human problems as they arise. Edgar Schein describes process consultation as "a set of activities on the part of the consultant that help the client to perceive, understand, and act upon the process events that occur in the client's environment".[1] According to Schein, "the most central premise of process consulting is that the client owns the problem and continues to own it throughout the consultation process. The consultant can help the client to deal with the problem, but the consultant never takes the problem onto his own shoulders".[2] While any consulting involves some collaboration with the client, the process approach is a collaborative approach par excellence.

Choosing between the basic roles

In past years, "pure" resource or expert consulting used to be quite common. In today's consulting practice, it tends to be confined to those situations where the client clearly wants to acquire and apply, in one way or another, special technical expertise, and does not want the consultant to become involved in human problems and organizational change. In most situations, the two roles should be seen as complementary and mutually supportive. On the one hand, this is possible thanks to progress in the competence of management consultants: today even technical specialists intervening in a relatively narrow area tend to have some training in the behavioural aspects of organizational change and of consulting, and are keen to help in implementation. On the other hand, the "pure" behavioural scientists, the traditional protagonists of process consulting, have come to the conclusion that the possibility of their helping in organizational change would remain modest if they did not improve their understanding of technical, economic, financial and other problems and processes in client organizations. Thus, more and more consultants feel comfortable in both roles.

Nevertheless, it is possible to refer to situations, or to phases in assignments, where one or the other approach predominates. A consultant may start an assignment as a resource consultant in order to become acquainted with key data on the client organization and demonstrate to the client that he is a real expert in the technical field concerned. He can then act more and more as a process consultant, trying to involve the client in looking for solutions likely to make effective use of the client's capabilities and to be internalized by the client system. Temporarily he will switch back to the role of resource consultant to provide missing technical knowledge so that the process of change does not stop.

Conversely, other consultants emphasize that they would start every assignment in the process mode in order to ensure the client's active involvement and develop a fair understanding of the organization's human problems right at the beginning. They would then switch to other roles or models when they feel that this is the right way to proceed.[3] It is also useful to see that the concept of process consulting continues to evolve (box 3.3).

Box 3.3   Soft and hard participative process consulting

William Altier and Miles Overholt have observed that Schein's concept of process consulting is appropriate for a limited range of situations calling for an intervention of an organizational development (OD) nature. They propose to use an umbrella term, "participative process consulting", which covers a wide variety of approaches and methodologies. These are described as either "soft", i.e. those focusing on people's behaviour, attitudes, values and relationships, or "hard", suitable for systematic, rigorous and disciplined problem identification and problem solving, in ways suggested by Kepner-Tregoe in *The rational manager*. As distinct from soft process consulting, in the hard sector the consultant suggests a structured process methodology likely to lead the client on the path to correct results, the intention being to limit the information used by the group to that which is deemed to be relevant. The approach is illustrated by the minicase below. In between the hard and the soft, there is an infinite range of combinations of information-oriented and people-oriented processes.

Minicase

A multinational firm was acquiring a company whose strength in a particular product area was the perfect answer to their weakness in that area. However, both companies had extensive sales and distribution organizations that were essentially carbon copies of each other. They had serious concerns about their ability to integrate these two organizations. If they were not able to accomplish this, the merger would be a disaster.

They asked a consultant to help, utilizing the consultant's "merger integration process", which is actually a composite of the fundamental processes of "situation assessment" (SA), "decision analysis" (DA), and "potential problem analysis" (PPA), operating within the environment of the specific merger situation. A merger is undertaken to accomplish certain desired change. This body of desired change also frames an unrecognized body of undesired change and resistance to change that, at worst, has the potential to destroy the merger. The merger integration process employs the tools of SA, DA and PPA within the merger's change environment to identify and remove the undesired change and the resistance to change.

The consultant's role was to lead the participants through the steps of the thinking processes by directing specific, targeted questions at them and then recording their responses on flip charts in the relevant process formats. This allowed them to see the analytical progression and conclusions that were being developed for each issue.

A vice-president of the acquiring company and the consultant, along with the Chief Executive Officer (CEO) of the company being acquired, selected four people

---

from each organization to make up the team to work on this. The vice-president wanted them to meet at his headquarters, but the consultant vetoed this idea. He suggested that the meeting be held on "neutral ground" — in a city located between the two headquarters — so that none of the participants, consciously or subconsciously, might feel that they had a "home court advantage".

The meeting started with a couple of hours devoted to SA, a tool that is concerned with uncovering and stating the relevant issues and concerns in their purest form, and then recognizing any dependent or independent relationships between them. The SA session produced a list of four critical decisions and the order in which they should be attacked. After a few minutes of discussion, the best answer to the first decision was obvious. It was therefore accepted and the group moved on.

The second situation was complex and the group proceeded to subject it to DA, a tool that is used to define the relevant objectives which should influence the choice, then to create the widest possible range of options, and finally to evaluate the options against the objectives. Shortly into the DA process, it became obvious that the statement of the second decision really embodied two separate choices; it was broken into two new decision statements and the analysis proceeded.

By the end of the second day, the team had completed decision analyses on four complex issues. The morning of the third day was spent identifying actions to be taken to accomplish the changes, and deciding who should be responsible for each. By noon, these elements had been meshed together into an implementation plan and the group was able to adjourn.

Author: William J. Altier. See also M. H. Overholt and W. J. Altier: "Participative process consulting: The hard and soft of it", in *Journal of Management Consulting* (Milwaukee, Wisconsin), Vol. 4, No. 3, 1988.

In choosing a role, the consultant must never forget that it constitutes a "communicating vessel" with the client's role. Both the consultant and the client should feel competent and comfortable in their respective roles and believe that they have made the right choice. No one should try to play a role which is alien to his or her nature and in which he or she will be less effective. Also, the client may be unaware of the various consulting roles, or may be used to a different consulting style from previous projects. This should be discussed and clarified as early as possible in starting an assignment.

3.5   Further refinement of the role concept

Reducing the various consulting processes to two basic roles or modes is a simplification that is conceptually useful, but disregards a number of situational variables. For practical purposes it is also instructive to visualize a greater number of consultative roles along *a directive and non-directive continuum*, as suggested by Gordon and Ronald Lippitt and shown in figure 3.1. By directive we mean these behaviours where the consultant assumes a position of leadership, initiates activity or tells the client what to do. In the non-directive role he or she provides data for the client to use or not to use. Here again the

Figure 3.1   Description of the consultant's role on a directive and non-directive continuum

MULTIPLE ROLES OF THE CONSULTANT

Reflector	Process specialist	Fact finder	Alternative identifier	Collaborator in problem-solving	Trainer/ educator	Technical expert	Advocate

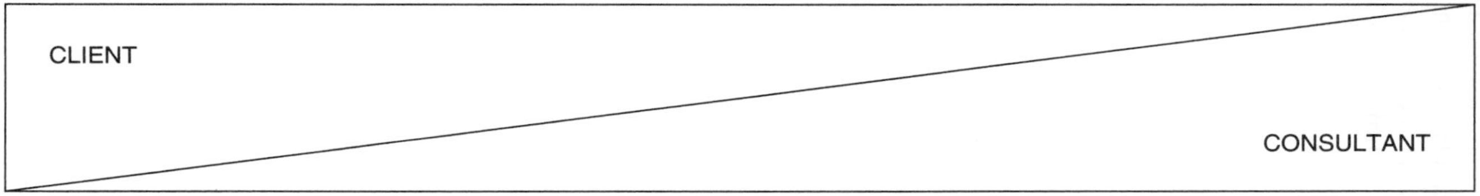

CLIENT

CONSULTANT

LEVEL OF CONSULTANT ACTIVITY IN PROBLEM-SOLVING

Non-directive   Directive

Raises questions for reflection	Observes problem-solving processes and raises issues mirroring feedback	Gathers data and stimulates thinking	Identifies alternatives and resources for client and helps assess consequences	Offers alternatives and participates in decisions	Trains the client and designs learning experiences	Provides information and suggestions for policy or practice decisions	Proposes guidelines, persuades, or directs in the problem-solving process

Source: Adapted from G. Lippitt and R. Lippitt: *The consulting process in action* (La Jolla, California, University Associates, 1979), p. 31.

situational roles are not mutually exclusive and manifest themselves in many ways in a particular consultant-client relationship. The consultant can play several roles simultaneously or consecutively, switching from role to role as the relationship evolves. These roles are "spheres of influence" rather than a static continuum of isolated behaviour. Let us examine these different role choices in response to a client's needs.

Advocate

In an advocate role, the consultant endeavours to influence the client. There are two quite different types of advocacy:

- *positional or "contact" advocacy* is a role which tries to influence the client to choose particular goods or to accept particular values;
- *methodological advocacy* is a role which tries to influence the client to become active as problem solver, and to use certain methods of problem solving, but is careful not to become an advocate for any particular solution (which would be positional advocacy).

In this role, the behaviour of the consultant is derived from a "believer" or "valuer" stance on content or a methodological matter.

Technical expert

One of the roles adopted by any consultant is that of technical specialist or expert. As mentioned above, the more traditional role of a consultant is that of an expert who, through special knowledge, skill and professional experience, is engaged to provide a unique service to the client. The client is mainly responsible for defining the objectives of the consultation. Thereafter the consultant assumes a directive role until the client is comfortable with the particular approach selected. Later in the relationship the consultant may act as a catalyst in helping to implement the recommendations he or she has made. Either the external or the internal consultant may be a resource (content) specialist in the client's problem, or a process specialist advising how to cope with a problem and how to implement change. This particular role brings out the consultant's substantive knowledge.

Trainer and educator

Innovative consultation frequently requires the consultant to initiate periodic or continuous training and education within the client system. In this aspect of the helping relationship, the consultant can play a role in bringing to bear the learning process that can best be employed, critically and creatively, depending upon the situation and the need. The consultant may design learning experiences, train or teach by imparting information and knowledge directly. This work requires the consultant to possess the skills of a training methodologist and developer of others' potential.

Collaborator in problem solving

The helping role assumed by the consultant uses a synergistic (cooperative) approach to complement and collaborate with the client in the perceptual, cognitive and action-taking processes needed to solve the problem. The consultant helps to maintain objectivity while stimulating conceptualization during the formulation of the problem. Additionally, he or she must help to isolate and define the real dependent and independent variables that influenced the problem's cause, and will ultimately influence its solution. He or she also assists in weighing alternatives, aids in sorting out salient causal relationships which may affect alternatives, and synthesizes and develops a course of action for an effective resolution. The consultant in this role is involved in decision making as a peer.

Alternative identifier

There are direct costs associated with decision making. While the value of a decision is dependent upon the attainment of a given set of objectives, in selecting an appropriate solution to a problem the consultant can normally propose several identifiable alternatives, along with their attendant risks. The alternatives, either because of economic or other identifiable implications, should be discovered jointly by the client and the consultant. In this helping relationship, the consultant establishes relevant criteria for assessing alternatives and develops cause-effect relationships for each, along with an appropriate set of strategies. In this role, however, the consultant is not a direct participant in decision making, but a retriever of appropriate alternatives facing the decision maker.

Fact finder

As we know, fact finding is an integral part of any consulting assignment, both for developing a data base and for resolving intricate client problems. But the consultant's role can be confined to fact finding. In this case he or she will assist the client system by choosing the sources of data, using a technique that will get the client more or less involved in gathering and examining data, and presenting data to the client in a way that will show where and why improvements are needed. In this role the consultant is functioning basically as a researcher.

Process specialist

This is the "pure" process role as described in section 3.4. The consultant focuses chiefly on the interpersonal and intergroup dynamics affecting the process of problem solving and change. He must bring all his role skills to bear on helping the client. He works on developing joint client-consultant diagnostic skills for addressing specific and relevant problems in order to focus on *how* things are done rather than on *what* tasks are performed. Furthermore, the

63

consultant helps the client to integrate interpersonal and group skills and events with task-oriented activities, and to observe the best match of relationships. In this role, an important function of the consultant is to provide feedback.

Reflector

When operating in the mode of a reflector, the consultant stimulates the client to make decisions by asking reflective questions which may help to clarify, modify or change a given situation. In utilizing this attribute, the consultant may be an arbitrator, an integrator or an emphatic respondent who experiences jointly with the client those blocks which provided the structure and provoked the situation initially.

3.6   Methods of influencing the client system

Whether the consultant likes to admit it or not, he or she exercises personal influence on the client system in adopting any one of the behavioural roles described in the previous sections. The consultant has to influence people in order to obtain information, gain confidence and respect, overcome passive resistance, enlist collaboration, and get proposals accepted and implemented. This section will therefore review some general methods of exercising personal influence.[4]

To exercise personal influence on the client is not in conflict with a professional approach. The consultant is committed to helping the client to achieve a particular purpose and this may be impossible without influencing certain people. The consultant will aim to energize and activate the client in the client's own interest, not to manipulate the client in the interest of the consultant. Nevertheless, the consultant must realize that his or her influence on some people may be quite strong and that by exercising this influence he or she assumes considerable technical and moral responsibility. Obviously, this is an important issue of consulting ethics (see also Chapter 6). The consultant will be able gradually to transfer this responsibility to the client by developing the latter's knowledge and problem-solving skills. This will help the client to recognize when and in what sense he or she is being influenced, and reach a judgement on whether there are any alternatives.

Various methods are available, and it is difficult to say in advance which one will produce the desired effect. These methods reflect the fact that people's attitudes and decisions have both rational and irrational (emotional) motives. In one case it may be enough to show the client a few meaningful figures and he or she will immediately draw practical conclusions from them. In another case the client will be so impressed by the consultant's personality, which inspires confidence, that he or she will blindly trust the advice received without examining the rationale behind it. Conversely, clumsy and irritating behaviour will make the client suspicious even if the consultant is absolutely right in his or her conclusions. Here again, experience is the best guide in making the right choice and combining the methods as appropriate.

Demonstrating technical expertise

The consultant should consider whether he or she enters the client organization as a technical expert enjoying prestige or, on the contrary, as someone totally unknown. Demonstration of theoretical knowledge and practical expertise appeals mainly to technically oriented individuals who are themselves experts in the consultant's field. This can be done in informal discussions, by passing on information on developments in theory, new techniques and equipment, successful firms or projects in which the consultant was personally involved, and in similar ways. Technically superior findings or proposals submitted by the consultant may speak for themselves and influence the client's stance.

Exhibiting professional integrity at work

The consultant's behaviour at work is closely observed by the client, whose attitude can be influenced by the way in which the consultant exhibits commitment, integrity, a methodical approach and efficiency. These are demonstrated at various stages and aspects of the assignment — the way of going about collecting information, self-discipline and perseverance in fact finding, the ability to discover pitfalls about which the consultant was not informed by the client, persistence in looking for a better technique, rational use of time, tact in handling delicate matters, and the like. A powerful effect can be achieved if people see that the consultant is prepared to share knowledge and work methods with them.

Demonstrating empathy with the client

The client's confidence is a condition of success in consulting. This confidence is best earned if the client can feel that the consultant cares for and enjoys working with him or her, and wants to be as helpful as possible. The consultant's interest in the client's concerns must be genuine and sincere. It must be expressed in deeds, not in nice words and promises. If the client feels that he is regarded and treated just as another income opportunity, the consultant's impact on the client will be considerably weakened even if the consultant's proposals are technically correct.

Using assertive persuasion

This widely applied method uses the force of logical argument to convince the other persons that what you want them to do is the right, correct or effective action to take. As a rule, new ideas or suggestions are put forward followed by reasons for and against, as the consultant presents arguments, facts or data to support a position. The method is most effective when the consultant is perceived as knowing what he or she is talking about and seen as relatively objective; the consultant should, too, know enough about the other person's situation to speak to specific needs. However, assertive persuasion tends to be overused in the practice of consulting and people often think of it as synonymous with influence.

Developing a common vision

A common vision is a shared picture of where you are headed, what you are trying to accomplish, and why it would be worthwhile for others to help. Articulating exciting possibilities includes generating images of what the future of the organization could be like if such and such a course were followed. In addition, the consultant can influence people by showing enthusiasm for what is to be done and where that action will take the client. The method tends to be more effective when the consultant must influence a number of people and generate collective commitment to action. It does not work if it is not clear what the other person can actually do towards achieving a common vision. In contrast to assertive persuasion, common vision tends to be the least utilized mode of influence.

Using participation and trust

This method implies recognizing and involving others by asking for their contributions and ideas, giving them credit for an idea, and building on what others have proposed. This is accompanied by sharing feelings with others and being open about one's own mistakes, shortcomings and lack of knowledge. The purpose is to develop an atmosphere of collaboration and co-responsibility for achieving a common goal. The other person involved must believe that your interest in participation and mutual trust is genuine and not just a facade, and that collaborating with you is really the right way to achieve the desired results. Attempts at one-way influence and control should be avoided. Also, participation is hard to achieve when the situation is such that it is not really in the other person's best interest to cooperate. This method is absolutely essential in collaborative consulting styles that emphasize the client's active involvement and "ownership" of the problem, as well as of the solutions representing the final outcome of the assignment.

Using rewards and punishments

Consultants normally do not control the same kinds of rewards and punishments that are available to management in the client organization.

Nevertheless, they can influence people by giving or taking away from them certain things which seem desirable. It could be a public acknowledgement (e.g. in a meeting) of a person's competence, achievement or exceptional contribution to the assignment. Enhancing someone's self-esteem is a reward. Omitting to invite someone to a meeting that he or she would probably like to attend, or withholding some information from the person, could be a punishment. Rewards and punishments which do not motivate people, which are out of proportion to the importance of the issue involved, or which are chosen arbitrarily, produce little or undesirable effect and should be avoided.

Using tensions and anxieties

Although it is not always realized, tensions and anxieties do play a role in consulting. Often, the very presence of the consultant creates tensions because there are speculations about the hidden causes of his or her presence, and about possible outcomes that could upset the status quo and affect the positions and interests of individuals or whole groups. The tensions that exist in the organization can be exploited in collecting information to obtain a true picture of the situation. Interdepartmental competition can be used when choosing the unit in which to start applying a new method in order to demonstrate its feasibility to other units.

In generating and strengthening desire for change, it may be useful to explain what would happen to the organization and/or to the individual if the necessary change were resented or delayed, thus creating a state of anxiety. It may be enough to produce data showing that the organization already is or is likely to be in trouble (see also section 4.4).

Here again, a wrongly focused and excessive use of tensions and anxieties will produce negative rather than positive effects. Also, the consultant must be careful not to become involved in internal power struggles and be perceived as their instrument.

3.7   Counselling as a tool of consulting

Counselling is a method whereby individual persons are helped to discover, understand, face and resolve their own personal problems, which may be those of education, health, employment, competence, career, relations with colleagues, family relations and so on. Counselling is often thought of as a sort of intervention that is very different from management and business consulting. Yet there is tremendous potential for using counselling as a tool of consulting, especially in helping individuals or groups to overcome personal difficulties and become more effective as managers and entrepreneurs.

Counselling is necessarily a one-to-one relationship. In the case of small businesses, the person and the business may even be the same. A counsellor is consistently concerned in a very personal way with the problems and opportunities facing a particular individual.

It is perfectly possible for the person being counselled to decide to leave the organization altogether or close down the business as the result of an effective counselling process, since the counsellor's aim is to help his or her personal client rather than the organization, if their interests do not coincide. However, a more frequent and typical result of personal counselling is a client who feels empowered, more self-confident and more independent in pursuing personal objectives, and reconciling personal and organizational objectives. It may be not too much of an exaggeration to suggest that the best evidence of an effective counselling relationship is when the client denies that the counsellor has had any role at all in the successful solution of his or her difficulties.

An effective counsellor is a good listener above all. All too often managers need most of all someone who will listen to them in an understanding way. They may be afraid of the people who are above them in the hierarchy, and those who are "beneath" them are afraid of them in their turn. In some organizations, honest admission of confusion and uncertainty is regarded as a sign of incompetence or weakness, and few managers are fortunate enough to have friends outside the organization who have the time or the ability to listen to them. A consultant who has been called into what appears to be a traditional consulting assignment often finds himself in the position of having to be a counsellor to a lonely and distressed person. It is important not to regard time spent in this way as a distraction from the main business: it may well be the most important contribution that an outsider can make.

Good listening is not as simple as it might appear, but there is more to counselling than sympathetic listening. A counsellor is clearly more of a process facilitator than a specialist resource, and whose task is to help the client to think through his or her own personal situation, difficulties, priorities, options and the advantages and disadvantages of each, and then decide to act. Not only should the counsellor not propose solutions to the client, but he or she may not even participate too actively in the process of problem identification. The counsellor should rather help the client to identify his or her own problems, and the solutions to them, by asking questions, listening, and being supportive and encouraging. At the same time he or she must be scrupulously neutral as to what the client actually decides to do, since the objective is to develop the client's ability to perform better in every way, and not merely to advise him or her what to do in a given situation. The fundamental task of the counsellor is to help clients to "think things through", to organize their own approach to thinking about their work and perhaps their life in general.

The counsellor must have a genuine desire to "put oneself out of business" by enabling the client to perform effectively without further counselling. Personal development of this sort obviously requires very different skills and, possibly, a different order of responsibility than is normally required of a consultant. A counsellor may need no particular management skills or experience, and these can even be a disadvantage, since he or she may be tempted to make technical suggestions to the client when the task is to enable the client to come up with his or her own ideas. The client will be more likely to expect such suggestions and be diffident about putting forward ideas if he or she knows that the counsellor is an expert in the topic at hand.

Because the task is so personal, and so all-embracing, it is easy for counselling sessions to devolve into unstructured chats. Like any consultancy, counselling almost always involves a series of meetings, and it is important to ensure that the client has a sense of progress being achieved from one session to another. One way of doing this is to conclude each session by agreeing on certain tasks that the client, and perhaps the counsellor as well, will complete before the next session. It is important not to allow assignments of this kind to turn into instructions which take the decision making away from the client.

Finally, it is all too easy for the client to become dependent on his or her counsellor. This is exactly what must not happen, since the objective is to enable clients to be independent. A good counsellor must "move in" and establish a trusting relationship with the client, so that he or she draws out all the client's feelings and all the information which may be relevant, but the counsellor must also learn how to "move out" and leave the client at the end of the process. At the beginning it may seem difficult to create the necessary trust, but in the end breaking away is often even more difficult. An effective counsellor is able to do both.

---

[1] E. H. Schein: *Process consultation*, Vol. II: *Lessons for managers and consultants* (Reading, Massachusetts, Addison-Wesley, 1987), p. 34.

[2] ibid., p. 29.

[3] See also ibid., p. 38.

[4] The description of assertive persuasion, common vision, participation and trust, and rewards and punishments is taken and adapted from Ch. 8 in F. Steele: *The role of the internal consultant: Effective role shaping for staff positions* (Boston, Massachusetts, CBI Publishing, 1982), which refers to a model developed by R. Harrison and D. Berlew.

CONSULTING AND CHANGE

4

Change is the *raison d'être* of management consulting. If diverse consulting assignments have any common characteristic, it is that they assist in planning and implementing change in client organizations. In Chapter 1, organizational change was mentioned as one of the fundamental and generic purposes of consulting. Organizational change, however, is full of difficulties and pitfalls. In managing change, consultants and clients tend to repeat the same mistakes. Often the very behaviour of those who strive to make changes generates resistance to change and brings the whole process to a standstill. The need for change is recognized, yet there is no change. To avoid this, every management consultant needs to be aware of the complex relationships involved in the change process, and must know how to approach varying change situations and how to help people to cope with change.

This chapter is, therefore, particularly important for understanding the nature and methods of consulting and of the consultant-client relationship. Throughout the chapter the consultant's point of view and intervention methods will be emphasized. However, they will be reviewed in the wider context of changes occurring in society, in organizations and in individuals, and related to the managers' roles in generating and managing organizational change. The chapter provides some notions of the theory of organizational change, and also practical guidelines for planning and implementing changes.

4.1   Understanding the nature of change

The concept of change implies that there is a perceptible difference in a situation, a person, a work team, an organization or a relationship, between two successive points in time. How does this difference occur, what are its causes, and what does it mean to a manager or a consultant? To answer these and similar questions, we will first look at the various levels and areas of change, and at the relations between them.

Environmental change

There is nothing new about change: it has always been a feature of the very existence and history of the human race. We all know that without change there is no life and that human efforts to obtain better living conditions imply coping with change. There is a new phenomenon, however: the unprecedented depth, complexity and pace of technological, social and other changes occurring at the present time. Today's organizations operate in an environment which is continually changing. The ability to adapt to changes in the environment has become a fundamental condition of success and survival in business.

It is not the purpose of this chapter to analyse current development trends or predict future changes in the business and social environment. Other publications are available which attempt to do this from various angles. They show that today the processes of change concern all aspects of human and social life, both nationally and internationally.

The former communist bloc is a case in point. The depth and magnitude of political, economic and social changes, as well as the pace of change in most countries of Central and Eastern Europe, have no historical precedent. The current transformation of whole national economies is marked by a radical departure from central planning, by massive privatization of state-owned and state-controlled enterprises, and by a rapid transition to a market economy. All this constitutes an exceptional challenge and work opportunity for the many consultants who are interested in assisting total company restructuring and renewal, new business creation and development, the forming of new partnerships and alliances, and a revolutionary change in managerial thinking.

In a particular business or other organization, the practical question is what to regard as its external environment. This question is increasingly difficult to answer. Often managers are totally perplexed when they realize that their organization can be affected by forces — economic, social or political — which they would previously never have considered when making business decisions. Competition can come from sectors and countries which in the past were never thought of as potential competitors. New sources of finance and new ways of mobilizing resources for business development and restructuring have required profound changes in corporate financial strategies. New information and communication technologies have enabled many new ways of doing business and running complex organizations that were unthinkable with old technologies. Environmental considerations, increased mobility of people and changing social values have created new constraints and new opportunities for decision makers responsible for running business firms.

This is where management consultants can step in to render an invaluable service to their clients. Making clients aware of the new complexity and dynamics of environmental changes and of new opportunities provided by them, and helping them to react to these changes promptly and effectively, will be the most important and forward-looking area of management consulting at the turn of the millennium.

Organizational change

Organizations do not change for the sake of change, but because they are part of a wider process of development and have to react to new environmental changes, constraints, requirements and opportunities. They are continually forced to adapt to the environment within which they exist and operate. But more than that — businesses and other organizations also generate changes in their external environment, for example by developing and marketing new products and services that capture a significant part of the market, launching and publicizing products that will change consumer taste, or pioneering new technologies that become dominant and change the shape of whole industrial and service sectors. Thus they modify the business environment, both nationally and internationally.

Change can concern any aspect or factor of an organization. Therefore it can involve products and services, technologies, systems, relationships, organizational culture, management techniques and style, strategies pursued, competences, performances and any other features of a business. It also involves changes in the basic set-up of the organization, including the nature and level of business, legal arrangements, ownership, sources of finance, international operations and impact, diversification, mergers and alliances with new partners, and similar.

Change in people

The human dimension of organizational change is a fundamental one. For it is people in the organization — its managerial and technical staff, and other workers — whose behaviour ultimately determines what organizational changes can be made and what real benefits will be drawn from them. Business firms and other organizations are human systems above all. People must understand, and be willing and able to implement, changes which at first glance may appear purely technological or structural, and an exclusive province of higher management, but will affect the working conditions, interests and satisfaction of many other people.

In coping with organizational change, people have to change, too: they must acquire new knowledge, absorb more information, tackle new tasks, upgrade their skills, give up what they would prefer to preserve and, very often, modify their work habits, values and attitudes to the way of doing things in the organization. Change in values and in attitudes is essential. There probably cannot be any real and lasting change without a change in attitudes.

It is important to recognize that in an organization this requirement relates to everyone, starting with the top manager. Those who want their subordinates and colleagues to change must be prepared to assess and change their own behaviour, work methods and attitudes! This is a golden rule of organizational change.

But how do people change? What internal processes bring about behavioural change? Many attempts have been made to describe the change process by means of models, but none of these descriptions has been exhaustive and fully satisfactory. Different people change in different ways, and every person has many unique features that influence his or her willingness and ability to change. The influence of the culture in which a person has grown up and lived is paramount, as will be explained in Chapter 5.

Social scientists tend to agree that a useful concept of change in people is one developed by Kurt Lewin.[1] It is a three-stage sequential model, whose stages are referred to as "unfreezing", "changing" and "refreezing".

Unfreezing postulates a somewhat unsettling situation as it is assumed that a certain amount of anxiety or dissatisfaction is called for — there must be a need to search for new information if learning is to take place. Conditions which enhance the unfreezing process usually include a more than normal amount of tension leading to a noticeable need for change — for example, an absence of sources of information; removal of usual contacts and accustomed routines; and a lowering of self-esteem amongst people. In some instances, these preconditions for change are present before the consultant arrives on the scene. In other instances, the need for change is not perceived and has to be explained if unfreezing is to occur — for example, by making it clear what will happen if the organization or the person does not change.

Changing, or the movement towards change, is the central stage of the model, in which both management and employees start practising new relationships, methods and behaviours. The subprocesses of changing involve two elements:

— *identification*, where the people concerned test out the proposed change, following the external motives presented to them (e.g. by management or a consultant);

— *internalization*, where individuals translate the general objectives and principles of change into specific personal goals and rules; this process may be quite difficult, usually requiring a considerable effort by the person concerned, and a great deal of patience, creativity and imagination on the part of the consultant in assisting the change, to convert the external (general) motives to internal (specific and personal) motives for accepting the change proposed.

Refreezing occurs when the person concerned verifies change through experience. The subprocesses involved require a conducive and supportive environment (e.g. approval by responsible management) and are usually accompanied by a heightening of self-esteem as a result of a sense of achievement derived from task accomplishment. During the initial stages of the refreezing step it is recommended that continuous reinforcement of the required behaviour (by means of rewards, praise, and so on) should be carried out to encourage and accelerate the learning process. At later stages, intermittent or spaced reinforcement will help to prevent extinction of the newly acquired behavioural patterns. Eventually the new behaviour and attitudes are either reinforced and internalized, or rejected and abandoned.

Change in a particular person takes place at several levels: at the knowledge level (information about change, understanding its rationale), the attitudes level

Figure 4.1   Time span and level of difficulty involved for various levels of change

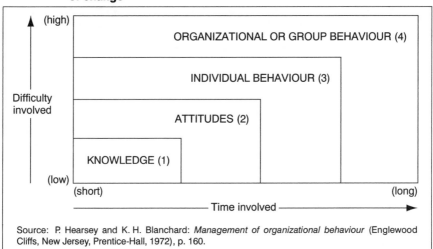

Source: P. Hearsey and K. H. Blanchard: *Management of organizational behaviour* (Englewood Cliffs, New Jersey, Prentice-Hall, 1972), p. 160.

(accepting the need for change and a particular measure of change both rationally and emotionally) and the behavioural level (acting in support of effective implementation of change). The relationship between change in people and organizational change is set out in figure 4.1. The diagram shows four levels of change: (1) knowledge changes, (2) attitude changes, (3) individual behaviour changes, and (4) organizational or group behaviour changes. The relative levels of difficulty and time relationship are also indicated in the diagram. This, however, does not imply that change must always start at a lower level and proceed to higher levels as shown in the diagram (see box 4.1, overleaf).

Change in individual persons within an organization is also directly affected by changes in the external environment. This environment is not something that "starts behind the factory gate", but permeates organizations where people are employed. People bring the environment with them and it stays with them when they come to work. Thus, changes occurring in the environment of an organization may facilitate or hamper change in people working within this organization. A frequent problem is that of individuals who are simultaneously exposed to so much change and stress, both at work and in their social and family life, that they are not able to cope and so break down. On the other hand, many environmental changes, such as an increased penetration of new information and communication technologies into all areas of human life, greatly facilitate the changes that have to be made within particular organizations.

Resistance to change

The history of the human race has taught us that, after all, people are remarkably adaptable, can cope with change and generally accept it as a natural

---

Box 4.1   Which change comes first?

The relationship between the various change levels shown in figure 4.1 is an open issue. Some behavioural scientists are consistent in suggesting that the best results will be obtained if the sequence of changing knowledge — attitudes — individual behaviour — group behaviour is fully respected. Others do not subscribe, for either conceptual or practical reasons, to this sequence of change levels. Fonviella points out that "trying to change behaviour by changing values and attitudes is unnecessarily indirect ... while attitudes influence behaviour, behaviour influences attitudes".[1] Following a study of several organizational change programmes, Beer, Eisenstat and Spector observe that "most change programmes do not work because they are guided by a theory of change that is fundamentally flawed ... The theory that changes in attitudes lead to changes in individual behaviour, and that changes in individual behaviour, repeated by many people, result in organizational change ... puts the change process exactly backward".[2] They conclude that the most effective way to change behaviour is to put people into a new organizational context, which imposes new roles, responsibilities and relationships on them.

---

1 W. Fonviella: "Behaviour vs. attitude: Which comes first in organizational change?", in *Management Review* (New York, American Management Association), Aug. 1984, p. 14.

2 M. Beer, R. A. Eisenstat and B. Spector: "Why change programmes don't produce change", in *Harvard Business Review* (Boston, Massachusetts), Nov.-Dec. 1990, p. 159.

---

fact of life. Why, then, is change in people so often the bottleneck of organizational change? Why is "change" such a frightening word for many people?

People resist and try to avoid changes that will leave them worse off than they are now in terms of job content, conditions of work, workload, income, relationships, personal power-base, lifestyle and the like. This is understandable. But a great deal of resistance may be met even if the proposed change is neutral, or beneficial to the persons concerned. While there are many reasons for this, psychological and other, the reasons listed in box 4.2 appear to be the most common.

Some of these causes of resistance to change stem from human nature. However, often they are reinforced by life experience (e.g. by negative consequences of past changes). People who have experienced a great deal of unnecessary and frustrating change, such as frequent but useless reorganizations, or to whom harm was caused by changes presented to them as beneficial, tend to become very suspicious about any further changes. This is very important. Causes of trouble are often sought in inherent resistance to change, although they lie elsewhere — for example, in wrong choice of new technology, in the failure to explain why change is necessary or in poor coordination of various change interventions. In such cases, resistance to change is only a symptom and the real problem is change management which is hectic, messy and insensitive to people's concerns and feelings.

There are then differences in the character of individuals so far as attitude to change and the ability to cope with change are concerned. In section 4.3 we shall see that some people are natural allies of managers and consultants in preparing and introducing changes in organizations. Unfortunately, but not surprisingly, those who are in greatest need of change often resist it more than anybody else, and require special attention and support. These may be individuals (both workers and managers), groups, organizations, and even whole human communities.

Change is not an end in itself

Organizational change is not an end in itself. It is only a necessary means of adjusting to new conditions and sustaining or increasing competitiveness, performance and effectiveness. If an organization can achieve its objectives without disturbing the established product and service lines, practices and relationships, there may be no need for major changes, at least in the short term. Certain changes are very costly (e.g. if a successful product is phased out and replaced by a new product at the wrong moment). Some managers suffer from chronic "reorganization disease": they feel that to be seen as dynamic, they must

---

Box 4.2   Reasons for resistance to change

Lack of conviction that change is needed. If people are not properly informed and the purpose of change not explained to them, they are likely to view the present situation as satisfactory and an effort to change as useless and upsetting.

Dislike of imposed change. In general, people do not like to be treated as passive objects. They resent changes that are imposed on them and about which they cannot express any views.

Dislike of surprises. People do not want to be kept in the dark about any change that is being prepared; organizational changes tend to be resented if they come as a surprise.

Fear of the unknown. Basically, people do not like to live in uncertainty and may prefer an imperfect present to an unknown and uncertain future.

Reluctance to deal with unpopular issues. Managers and other people often try to avoid unpleasant reality and unpopular actions, even if they realize that they will not be able to avoid these for ever.

Fear of inadequacy and failure. Many people worry about their ability to adjust to change, and maintain and improve their performance in a new work situation. Some of them may feel insecure, and doubt their ability to make a special effort to learn new skills and attain new performance levels.

Disturbed practices, habits and relations. Following organizational change, well-established and fully mastered practices and work habits may become obsolete, and familiar relationships may be altered or totally destroyed. This can lead to considerable frustration and unhappiness.

Lack of respect and trust in the person promoting change. People are suspicious about change proposed by a manager whom they do not trust and respect, or by an external person whose competence and motives are not known and understood.

---

periodically reorganize their enterprise or department. Consultants sometimes lack the courage to tell the client that the best solution is to leave things as they are, especially if the work is being done for a client who obviously is eager to make some spectacular changes.

In a world where technological, social and other changes are occurring at an unprecedented pace and frequency, people and organizations are in need not only of change, but also of relative stability and continuity. Striking the right balance between change and stability, and helping the client to maintain this balance throughout the organization, is one of the vital tasks of the consultant.

4.2 How organizations approach change

Unplanned or planned change?

It is common knowledge that in every organization a great deal of evolutionary, natural change occurs. A typical example is the ageing of equipment and people, which has both problematic aspects (e.g. the need to repair and replace equipment, or to replace managers who have lost dynamism and drive), and positive aspects (technical and managerial competence acquired by years of experience). While most of these changes cannot really be kept under full control, it is possible to anticipate preventive measures for avoiding and/or mitigating negative consequences of evolutionary change.

A great deal of unplanned change is not of an evolutionary nature. It occurs because all of a sudden organizations must react to new situations. A manufacturing firm may be compelled by competition to drastically cut its prices. A strike may force an organization to raise wages, and the like. Such a change is *adaptive* or *reactive*. The organization has not planned it and, quite often, has not foreseen its necessity until very late in the day. But the organization does make the change to avoid a crisis, or an unplanned but radical and fast change is made in order not to lose an unexpected new opportunity that has just emerged.

It is a sign of poor management if an organization confines its total change effort to inevitable unplanned changes. Where this happens, it is a demonstration of reluctance or inability to look ahead and prepare the organization for reacting to future opportunities and constraints. True, no planning will completely eliminate the need for unplanned changes. However, planning helps the organization to prepare itself for changes that can be anticipated, and minimizes the number of situations where hasty (and costly) changes have to be made in an atmosphere of panic.

More than that, the planning of change enables the organization to be proactive and "create the future", e.g. to shape its environment and its own profile and outperform competition by creating new products and services, influencing consumer taste and demand, restructuring the key organizational processes before competition does so, pushing for changes in the regulatory environment, and similar.

> **Box 4.3   What do we address in planning change?**
>
> Some typical questions addressed in planning change and choosing strategies of organizational change are:
>
> ● What changes are occurring in the environment? What will be their implications for our organization?
>
> ● What changes should we foresee in order to achieve our development objectives, improve our performance, increase our share of the market, etc.?
>
> ● What undesirable changes will occur in our organization if we do not take timely steps to prevent them?
>
> ● What sort of and how much change are we able to manage?
>
> ● What sort of and how much change will our people be able to absorb and support? How should we help them to cope with change?
>
> ● Should we implement change in stages?
>
> ● What will be the relations between various changes that we intend to make? How will they be coordinated?
>
> ● Where and how should the change process be initiated?
>
> ● How should we manage change? Do we need a consultant? What would be this consultant's role?
>
> ● What should be our time horizon and timetable for implementing change?

The last question in box 4.3 is crucial. Both organizations and individual people can absorb only a limited amount of change over a certain period of time, and this absorptive capacity is not the same in different countries, organizations and individuals. Conversely, delaying urgent changes can lead to crises and hopeless situations. The pacing of change is therefore one of the main skills needed in planning and implementing change.

Imposed or participative change?

In business practice, a great deal of change is *decided and imposed* on the organization by management. After all, by acting in this way management assumes its basic responsibility. However, change imposed from a position of authority may cause unhappiness and resentment, in particular if people affected by such changes believe that they should have been consulted, or at least informed well in advance and in a proper way.

If change is initiated from a position of power and imposed upon people, it could be inherently volatile; it could disappear with removal of the power source, or in the absence of appropriate punishments and sanctions. Yet we cannot say that every imposed change must be bad. There are emergency situations where discussion is impossible and delaying a decision would be suicidal. There are regulatory and administrative measures which will affect many people, but which are of minor importance and do not justify long discussion and consultation. Also, imposed change is considered to be more effective when dealing with dependent rather than independent persons. In general, the attitude to imposed change is very much influenced by culture, education, access to information, the existence of alternatives, and other factors.

A manager should think twice before deciding to impose a change. He or she should do it only if firmly convinced that there is no alternative — if, for example, he or she was unable to gain the support of the group, yet feels that change is inevitable. But the manager should always take the trouble to explain the reasons for choosing to impose a change.

People in different national and organizational cultures do not feel the same way about change that is presented to them as an accomplished fact, and imposed on them without prior discussion or consultation. However, *the trend towards participative change* is ever more pronounced in most parts of the world. People want to know what changes are being prepared, and to be able to influence changes that concern them. Managers and administrators are increasingly aware of this fundamental demand and react to it by adopting a participative approach to change.

In certain cases a participative change process may be slower and more time-consuming and costly than imposed change, but it is considered to be long lasting. It helps to prevent resistance and generates commitment to change. In addition, participative change helps management to draw on people's experience and creativity, which is difficult to do if change is imposed.

There are different *levels and forms of participation* in the change process, depending on the nature and complexity of the change itself, on the maturity, coherence and motivation of the group, and on the relationship between management and employees (see also box 4.4). At the *first level*, the manager or the consultant informs the staff concerned about the need for change and explains the specific measures that are being prepared. At the *second level*, consultation and discussion about change take place in the course of the change process — in identifying the need for change, proposing the specific changes to be made and checking whether people would react negatively to the measures proposed. Suggestions and criticism are solicited and management may reconsider its plan for change on the basis of these. At the *third level*, management seeks active involvement of the staff in planning and implementing change by inviting them to participate in defining what to change and how to do it, and in putting the agreed changes into effect. This is normally done through workshops, task forces, special committees and projects, staff meetings and other methods reviewed later in this chapter (section 4.5).

In many situations change requires *negotiation*. This takes place when two or more individuals or groups discuss together the changes to be made and the benefits and costs to the parties involved. This may lead to a compromise that neither party considers to be an ideal solution by its own standards. However, the probability of support by those concerned, and hence the probability of implementing the agreement reached, will be much higher.

There are, then, changes that require negotiation *between management and the representatives of employees*, who may be trade union or other representatives. These sorts of change may be determined by law, through collective bargaining, or by any other joint agreement, formal or informal. Managers and

---

Box 4.4   Ten overlapping management styles, from no participation to complete participation

(1) **None**: There is no participation and involvement. People express surprise if the "boss" asks them a problem-solving question. People are paid to "work", not "think".Managers "send down" decisions.

(2) **Persuasive autocracy**: There is some recognition that an effort to "sell" the project or the solution has been considered and will be incorporated "if there is time and money".

(3) **Consultative**: Responsible managers ask people many questions and seek to obtain as many ideas as possible, but establishing criteria, weightings and details are left entirely to managers.

(4) **Reactive control**: The organizations do involve others with measuring, comparing and assessing the performance of a satisfactory system. Citizen groups, regulatory boards, peer review, and so on, are means whereby participation is obtained. Policy formulation matters arise only occasionally.

(5) **Bargaining**: More adversarial or at least structured formal involvement is built into normal operations.

(6) **Anticipatory control**: The organization consciously scans the horizon to become aware of possible future occurrences. Groups are allowed to report intelligence that could indicate developments. They can also develop alternatives for responding and "controlling" the future.

(7) **Joint determination**: Although decisions are usually joint, there is a relatively continuous interchange of ideas among those charged with the responsibilities for operating a system and those working in it. Management operates this way because it thinks it's desirable, and workers have no assurance of its continuation. Most other stakeholders also may not be included in the participatory effort.

(8) **Supportive collaboration**: Efforts are likely to be more formalized, with some decision responsibilities spelled out (for example, advisory group, citizens' commissions).

(9) **Permanent work groups**: Employees and managers meet regularly (usually during working hours) and seek to solve all types of problems that emerge in any area of concern.

(10) **Complete self-determination**: A joint worker/management board of directors or several joint groups share key decision-making responsibility (budgets, new products, acquisition and divestiture, personnel policies and practices, and so on).

Source: G. Nadler and S. Hibino: *Breakthrough Thinking: The seven principles of creative problem solving* (Rocklin, California, Prima Publishing, 1994), pp. 283-284.

---

consultants should be particularly alert to the desirability of a dialogue with the workers' and other employees' representatives, not only in cases explicitly stipulated by laws or formal agreements, but also in preparing any changes that may affect the interests of people in the organization and where employee support may be essential.

A frequent and sincere dialogue with employees and their representatives is the best means for preventing organized large-scale resistance to change, expressed through strikes and similar forms of vigorous protest against decisions taken or planned by management. Clearly, resistance to change is not the only reason for strikes. It is, however, a frequent reason, and it can often be traced back to management's failure to consult and inform people, explain why change cannot be avoided, seek alternative solutions, and implement change in ways that minimize hardship to the people concerned.

Finally, in thinking of participative approaches our perspective is often limited to employee participation, direct or through their representatives. In managing change, this perspective may prove to be narrow and may miss important inputs. It is useful to think of *a wider circle of "stakeholders"*, i.e. organizations and people having various stakes in the organization in question. Customers are important stakeholders, and learning from them in preparing important changes is absolutely essential. Other stakeholders include people and authorities in the local community, suppliers of equipment, systems and raw materials, banks and other providers of financial services, and so on. Not only can they provide useful advice, but they have specific stakes, or interests, in the organization which is implementing a change programme. They are likely to make contributions reflecting the nature and importance of their stakes.

Managing the change process

Change requires *leadership*, and it is quite natural that this should be provided by those managers who have the principal responsibilities in operating the organization. This leadership is necessary even if an important role in the change process is assigned to a consultant and if the approach taken is highly participative. If senior management shows no interest and the handling of particular changes is relegated to lower management or a functional department, this signals to the organization that management has other priorities and does not care much about the changes that are being prepared.

It is, of course, understandable that management must cope both with restructuring, reorganization, launching new products, mergers with other companies and similar major change measures and processes, and with routine everyday activities of the organization. There may be competition for scarce resources: some key people may be wanted both for preparing a major change and for running current business. A consultant can be used to facilitate the manager's task, but not to manage change on the manager's behalf.

This being said, management has to determine the specific change measures requiring its leadership, and decide on the intensity and style of its direct involvement. The complexity of the changes that are being prepared, and their importance to the organization's future, are key criteria. In a larger organization, senior managers cannot be personally involved in all changes, but there are certain changes which they must manage personally, or they must find a suitable way, explicit or symbolic, of providing and demonstrating support. Reinforcing messages from the leaders are a key stimulus in a change effort.

The style of leadership should be consistent with the organizational culture, the approach to change that has been chosen for the given situation, the urgency of the changes to be made and the maturity of the people involved. Thus, a directive, or "telling", style of leadership will be appropriate for situations of urgency and an audience of relatively low maturity. In contrast, a low-profile delegating style can be used if responsibility can be given to mature followers who understand the framework within which the changes need to be planned and put into effect.[2]

Various change processes within the organization need to be harmonized with each other. While this may be easy in a small and simple organization, it may be quite difficult in a large and complex one. Often various departments work at similar problems (e.g. on new information systems). They may come up with proposals that do not fit general management policy and standard procedures, or present excessive resource requirements. Or one department develops superior proposals, and other departments will have to be convinced that they should give up their current system or their new proposals, and accept the best proposal developed by another unit. These are situations where higher management has to intervene with tact and an independent consultant can be of great help.

The role of innovators and change agents

A change effort requires *a successful start*. Making a correct decision on what to change and assigning responsibilities is not enough. There must be people who have critical and innovative minds, enjoy experimenting, can visualize the future, believe that change is possible, and influence others, not by talking about change, but by demonstrating what can be achieved. These "innovators", "prime movers", "champions" or "intrapreneurs", as they are sometimes called, may be in managerial jobs, but they are often design engineers, marketing specialists, project coordinators, work study technicians, experienced workers and supervisors, or other staff members.

Organizations which are keen to change must *encourage innovation, experiments and entrepreneurship*. To management this means not only tolerating departures from routine and tradition, and admitting that this is not possible without some risk, but deliberately employing innovators, giving them chances, observing their work, and referring to their example in showing what the organization is able to achieve.

Innovative and entrepreneurial individuals and teams tend to play a prominent role in successful strategies for organizational change. They are the organization's principal *change agents*. Often it is in their unit that change will start. Some of them will become managers of new units responsible for new product lines or services, coordinators of change projects, or trainers and internal consultants helping other individuals and groups in making the necessary changes.

Different roles are played by *two basic types of change agent*: those whose interest is and remains predominantly technical, and who may produce excellent technical ideas without being able to convert them into business opportunities; and those who are mainly entrepreneurs and leaders, and can help management to generate and implement changes that require the active involvement of many people, individually or in groups.

A strategy for organizational change may rely entirely on internal capabilities and on managerial and specialist staff members who can play the role of change agents. An alternative is to bring in *a change agent from outside* as a consultant. This is an important managerial decision affecting the whole approach to the change process. The consultant will not only be contributing some missing technical competence and an alternative viewpoint, but, as we know, will be influencing, by his or her presence and by action taken (or not taken), the behaviour of those concerned in change. The consultant will possibly influence the behaviour of the very person who has invited him or her. The main factors to consider are:

- the consultant's profile (knowledge, experience and personality: he or she must be acceptable to and respected by people who are being helped to change);
- the mode of consulting to choose in order to assist change (as discussed in Chapter 3, there are various modes; the question is, which mode is likely to generate the desired effects in a particular human system).

Organizational culture supportive of change

It is easier to keep pace with environmental change and generate effective changes from within if change has a prominent place in organizational culture and if it is not handled as something exceptional, requiring a special campaign and special arrangements in every single case.

High-technology companies in electronics and other fields now operate in an atmosphere of constant change. Yet people understand that this is a salient characteristic of the sector with which they have to live. The required pace of change in many other organizations is not as high. Every organization should define what is the necessary and optimum pace of change in its sector, and try to adopt it as a common value shared by management and staff. This helps to balance change and stability, minimize hectic unplanned changes and avoid change for its own sake.

People should know what preoccupies management and where they should focus efforts at individual and group performance improvement in order to avoid dispersion of resources and help the company where it needs help most. However, every interesting idea should be examined, even if it is not in an area defined as a priority.

To value change and meet the requirements of an organization where the pace of change is high, people must know that it pays to have a positive attitude to change and constantly to look for changes from which the organization can benefit. Innovation and creativity can be stimulated by financial rewards, public recognition, promotions, making the job content more interesting, offering training and self-development opportunities, and so on. Conversely, people must be able to see that it does not pay to be conservative and resist innovation and change.

Values, attitudes and collectively held norms that make up organizational culture (see Chapter 5) develop over a number of years and, once established, they are not easy to change. But it is not impossible to influence and eventually to change them. Therefore if organizational culture constitutes the main obstacle to change, or if it does not stimulate change in an environment that is rapidly changing, managers' and consultants' efforts may need to focus on organizational culture first of all.

4.3   Gaining support for change

One of the principal messages of this chapter is that effective change is best achieved if it enjoys the support of the people involved. This can be a very complex matter. Managers and consultants may feel uncertain about their ability to mobilize support for the change envisaged. Owing to errors made by management, the existing support may be lost and give way to resistance; to redress the situation may then be a delicate task.

Inviting people to participate actively in a change effort at all its stages is a useful general method for gaining support and reducing resistance. It helps to create an atmosphere in which people feel they are *the "owners" of a change proposal*: the idea comes neither from the top, nor from an external person, but from within the group. If things go wrong, the group does not seek a culprit from without, but examines the causes and willingly helps in redefining the proposals.

Arousing attention to the need for change

Undeniably there must be unlimited methods of drawing the attention of individuals and groups to the need for a change. The reader should refer to section 3.6 where various methods of influencing the client system are discussed. However, two proven methods are of particular interest to consultants.

The most effective manner of arousing immediate attention occurs when people become *anxious*. In special cases the introduction of a state of extreme anxiety is undeniably effective — for example, a building will be cleared very promptly if it is reported that a bomb has been placed in it. However, the continued use of the heightened anxiety approach tends to be self-defeating. Recipients eventually ignore such threats, especially if the alleged events do not occur.

Notwithstanding, the use of minimal anxiety is effective as an attention-arousing device which can be sustained over a long period. A particularly successful combination is to use an anxiety state to draw attention to specific needs (i.e. the unfreezing process described in section 4.1) and to follow up by providing a solution meeting these needs.

The second method is called *the two-step information process*. The underlying idea is that the acceptance and effective introduction of change occurs as the result of a multiplier effect in the flow of information.

Detailed research findings suggest that people most likely to experiment and to to be influenced by new approaches possess certain characteristics. These individuals, labelled as "isolates", are inclined to be highly technically oriented;

to read widely on their chosen subjects; to attend meetings and conferences frequently; and to travel in order to investigate new schemes. They may be considered by their group to be something akin to "cranks". Surprisingly, they are not likely to influence other members of their group directly.

Nevertheless, the activities of these technically oriented isolates are kept under constant observation by a second type of person who possesses characteristics similar to those of isolates but, usually owing to widespread interests in other fields, does not have the same amount of time available to experiment and test new methods in any considerable depth. This second type of person, identified as an "opinion-leader", has considerable influence over the group, and even beyond it. In addition to acknowledged technical expertise, this type of person usually has considerable civic and social standing.

In tracing the life-cycle of the adoption of new procedures, it seems that the new scheme is first investigated, along with other possible choices, by the isolate and is eventually chosen over other alternatives because of its proven technical superiority. At a later stage the opinion-leader adopts the new idea once he or she is convinced that the isolate has firmly decided on this new approach. Subsequently an "epidemic" phase erupts as the followers of the opinion-leader also adopt the new approach. Therefore, when introducing change a strong case can usually be made for emphasizing the highly technical aspects of the new approach in order to attract and convince both the isolates and the opinion-leaders who should under normal circumstances assist in influencing and convincing the other members of the group.

Getting support for specific proposals

Once the audience's attention has been aroused, and interest created in seeking change, then comes the time to develop a desire for the change proposal. In presenting information to enhance the selection of a given proposal in preference to alternative schemes, it is often necessary to mention some negative aspects of the proposed scheme in addition to the more beneficial ones. Similarly, the positive and negative aspects of existing or alternative schemes should also be presented. This technique of providing all aspects of the case under review is referred to as an "inoculation" effect; it weakens any counterproposals likely to arise at a later date.

Experience has shown that an effective manner of presenting information where proposal B is intended to displace proposal A is to employ the following sequence:

(1) present a complete listing of all the positive and beneficial aspects of proposal B;
(2) mention the obvious and real drawbacks associated with proposal B;
(3) describe a comprehensive listing of the deficiencies of proposal A;
(4) indicate the most pertinent positive features of proposal A.

Following this presentation of the positive and negative features of the alternate proposals, the manager or the consultant should then draw conclusions as to why the favoured proposal (B) should be employed by listing the benefits to be accrued (i.e. service provided), the effectiveness of the new proposal (i.e. technical and economic superiority) and, if applicable, instances where such a proposal has been successfully employed.

Personality composition of the audience

To maintain control when dealing with a gathering or crowd of people is difficult at the best of times. When dealing with individuals or small groups, there are sometimes opportunities to use group members as enhancers of the change process.

Individuals who are poised, confident and have a certain amount of self-esteem appear to be able to influence others who lack these characteristics. In turn, these individuals with relatively high self-esteem appear to be more influenced by information containing optimistic rather than pessimistic or negative connotations.

The consultant should use opportunities to enlist support for the change process from persons who possess such traits of high self-esteem by drawing attention to likely optimistic results. These persons are then in a position to support the consultant's proposals before the group.

The informal communication network

Communications on a highly topical issue appear to produce a greater and more rapid attitude change in an audience when the information is "accidentally overheard", or leaked through informal communication networks than when delivered through formal channels. Rumours, which flourish in the absence of formal communications ("the grapevine"), are usually confined to informal channels and can often be countered by appropriate use of the same network. Even a fundamental piece of information, such as one stating that the future of a particular programme or unit is highly uncertain, may affect people's attitudes more strongly if spread informally than if officially issued by management. Occasionally, both formal and informal channels should be combined to reinforce the message.

Handling objections to change

An essential skill for managing and assisting change is the ability to handle objections. Broadly speaking, objectors can be classified as "sharpeners" or "levellers". *Sharpeners* include those people who ask specific, detailed questions concerning the change process. They tend to be genuine objectors who want to be convinced that the change proposal is justified, and are accessible to logical argument. *Levellers* are those who generalize and broaden the issue under review. They are usually quite difficult to convince as they are often more interested in the form of their objections than in the content.

Objections and resistance to change can be expressed in many different ways. Non-verbal messages, such as gestures, facial expressions, or repeated attempts to avoid discussing the issue with the manager or the consultant, may be significant and tell more than words.

In general, experience suggests that whenever a manager or a consultant senses that people may object to the change proposed, he or she should help those concerned to express their doubts or apprehensions by formulating objections. The objections made have to be analysed: they may point to weaknesses of the proposed scheme, show that not enough information was given to people affected by a change, reflect aversion to the manager's or the consultant's behaviour, or express fear of resistance that will need to be dealt with.

When the consultant has to handle *specific objections*, it is more useful to repeat the objection, put it in writing if appropriate, break it down into component parts, and treat each component as a separate entity rather than attempt to deal with the problem as a whole. It is recommended to commence with those items on which agreement is most likely to be reached and move later to those items causing most disagreement. Should a total impasse be reached on an issue, it is better to reword the disagreement in objective terms relating to the new proposal rather than continue arguing in the often coloured and emotional words originally proposed by the objector. The consultant should frequently take the opportunity to recapitulate, and to refer to parts of the original objection on which agreement has already been reached, before continuing with new points.

If a point is reached when the consultant does not have the appropriate information to hand, this fact should be readily admitted and the objector advised that the information will be obtained and transmitted to him or her at a later date. The consultant should not fail to carry out this promise.

4.4   Managing conflict

When objections to change become a matter of *intergroup conflict*, different problems requiring special treatment may arise. This may happen if a group is to give up its work method to adopt one practised by another group. If a group sees itself threatened, there will be a closing of the ranks and more cohesive action, and the group will become more tolerant of authoritative rule by its chosen leaders. Hostility to other groups is likely to arise, especially if the situation is perceived as a "win-lose" encounter. Communication will become distorted and difficult, as each group will be prepared to admit only the positive aspects of its own argument and the negative aspects of the "enemy's".

Basic strategies to reduce intergroup conflict (box 4.5) require the establishment of goals upon which both groups can agree in order to restore valid intergroup communication. It may be useful to identify a common "enemy", thus setting a superordinate goal. Emphasis should be placed on common needs and goals of different groups rather than on partial goals. If possible, a reward system which encourages effective communication should be introduced. Groups should be exposed to numerous activities likely to enhance empathy and mutual understanding.

Box 4.5   How to manage conflict

In planning and implementing change, interpersonal or intergroup conflict may develop for a number of reasons:

- poor communication;
- disagreement on objectives and results to be pursued;
- disagreement on intervention methods used;
- differences over the pace of change;
- resistance to change;
- fear of losing influence and power;
- competition for resources;
- non-respect of commitments;
- refusal to cooperate;
- personality and culture clashes;
- poor performance and inefficiency.

The principal methods of interpersonal conflict resolution were summarized by Gordon Lippitt in the following terms:

Withdrawal: retreating from an actual or potential conflict situation.

Smoothing: emphasizing areas of agreement and de-emphasizing areas of difference over conflictual areas.

Compromising: searching for solutions that bring some degree of satisfaction to the conflicting parties.

Forcing: exerting one's viewpoint at the potential expense of another — often open competition and win-lose situation.

Confrontation: addressing a disagreement directly and in a problem-solving mode — the affected parties work through their disagreement.

As a rule, it is advisable to depersonalize conflict by ensuring that the disputants do not sit in judgement over each other, and to focus the conflict on the basic issue by concentrating disagreement on factual grounds. Withdrawal avoids the issue, but the solution may be only provisional; it may be used as a temporary strategy to buy time or allow the parties to cool off. Forcing uses authority and power and can cause considerable resentment; it may be necessary in extreme cases where agreement obviously cannot be reached amicably. Smoothing may not address the real issue, but permits the change process to continue at least in areas of agreement. Compromising helps to avoid conflict, but tends to yield less than optimum results. Confrontation is generally regarded as most effective, owing to its problem-solving approach involving an objective examination of alternatives that are available and the search for an agreement on the best alternative. Finally, adopting an attitude of one side winning and the other side losing is like pouring gasoline on the fire of conflict.

Source: Gordon Lippitt: *Organizational renewal* (Englewood Cliffs, New Jersey, Prentice-Hall, 1982), pp. 151-155.

4.5   Structural arrangements and interventions for assisting change

Since the manager bears the main responsibility for managing change in his or her organization or unit, he or she may decide to take charge of a specific change effort personally, involving direct collaborators and other staff members as necessary. In many cases, no special structural arrangements are made, and the manager and the staff work out and implement change proposals, handling their other duties simultaneously.

In the practical life of organizations, however, the use of special *structural arrangements* and *intervention techniques* for handling change may be required for certain specific reasons:

(1)   The regular organizational structure may be fully oriented towards current business and could not cope with any additional tasks, for technical reasons or owing to a high workload.

(2)   Rigidity, conservatism and resistance to change may be strongly rooted in the existing structure, and it would be unrealistic to expect that this structure would generate and manage any substantive change.

(3)   In certain cases it is desirable to introduce change in steps, or to test it on a limited scale before making a final decision.

(4)   In many cases, management has to look for a suitable formula that is easy to understand and will involve a number of individuals and/or groups in a change effort (possibly including staff from different organizational units), clearly establish a case for change, reveal objections and risks, develop and compare alternative solutions, and mobilize support for the solution that will be chosen.

Managers and consultants have access to a wide range of structural arrangements and intervention techniques for managing and facilitating change efforts of individuals, groups and whole organizations. This section will review some commonly used arrangements and techniques, which can be applied for various purposes and at various stages of the change process: to demonstrate the need for change; stimulate thinking about the direction to take and generate new ideas; develop an action programme; reduce resistance; help people to cope with new tasks and conditions; generate commitment; gear initiative and creativity towards priority goals; monitor and/or accelerate implementation, and so on.

Many of the techniques for assisting change are behavioural-science based, and focus on changes in attitudes, values and individual or group behaviour. However, as Beckhard and Harris rightly pointed out,[3] over the last decades we have witnessed a shift in the technology of planned change. This technology has moved from an emphasis on team building, intergroup relations and the like to an emphasis on diagnostic and action-planning processes for coping with the total organization and its environment, designing methods for organizational diagnosis, and implementing comprehensive programmes for business re-structuring and improving organizational performance. Essentially, there has been a growing understanding of the fact that a one-sided approach, as fostered by some behavioural scientists in the past, has limitations and should give way to a comprehensive view of the organization, embracing all organizational factors and subsystems as well as their interaction with the environment.

The experience of companies that have successfully completed challenging change programmes demonstrates the desirability of combining "soft" techniques for stimulating and assisting change (based essentially on a behavioural science approach and aiming to improve people's attitudes to change and enlist their active participation) with "hard" techniques, (aimed to ensure effective problem identification, needs assessment, sequencing, coordination, resource allocation, quality control, follow-up, and other measures without which even the best-intended and fully participative change effort can turn into total confusion).

The current panoply of approaches, methods and techniques for assisting organizational change is impressive: over 300 of them have been identified by surveys and this number keeps growing.[4] Many consultants have specific variants or packages of the "classical" change management and performance improvement approaches and techniques: some of these variants are not described in literature and are available only to clients as proprietary techniques. In other cases, the technique used is a common one, but is presented under a different name. If a consultant proposes to use a specific and not very well-known technique, the client should ask him or her to explain what is unique in the proposed technique and how it relates to the basic and commonly known techniques. In fact, the consultant should take the initiative and give such an explanation when proposing the method to the client.

This chapter is confined to a short review of selected and fairly well-known techniques. For their detailed study, the reader may wish to refer to specialized sources on change management, project management, organizational development, process consulting, or organizational behaviour and psychology. Change management approaches and techniques are also discussed in other parts of this book, especially in Chapters 3, 8, 9, 10 and 22.

Structural arrangements

Structural arrangements are used to provide a suitable (as a rule temporary) organizational setting for a particular change project or effort, and to use other change management methods within this setting rather than throughout the organization.

Special projects and assignments. This is a very popular form. A person or unit within the existing structure is given an additional special task as a temporary assignment. He or she may be given some additional resources for this purpose if resources existing within the current structure are regarded as insufficient. For mobilizing resources and taking decisions that are beyond his or her authority, the project manager or coordinator would, of course, turn to the general manager who appointed him or her. This is, in fact, a transitional arrangement between a normal and a special structure.

Temporary groups. Task forces, working parties and similar arrangements are frequently used as temporary groups, either at one stage of the change process (e.g. to establish the need for change, gather new ideas, determine priorities or develop alternatives), or throughout the whole process for its planning and coordination. The group should pursue a clearly defined purpose.

Selecting the members of a temporary group is extremely important. They should be people who can and want to do something about the problem that is the focus of the change. Often they will come from different organizational units, in particular if change efforts focus on processes cutting across boundaries between units. The group should not be too large and its members must have time to participate in group work. Task forces often fail because they are composed of extremely busy people who give priority to running current business before thinking about future change. They also fail if they are dominated by individuals who use their formal authority to impose their views on the group.

Thanks to modern telecommunication technologies, task forces and other temporary groups can also work effectively in geographically dispersed and multinational organizations. Expensive and exhausting travel can be replaced by teleconferencing and other distance communication, reserving face-to-face communication for situations where it is absolutely necessary.

The group should also have a defined life. A possibility is to introduce the use of the "sunset calendar" — that is, at a predetermined point the group will cease to exist unless there is a management decision to continue it. This avoids the possibility of the group slowly disintegrating as more and more members absent themselves from meetings.

The group may use a convener. This could be the consultant or somebody designated by management, after discussion with the consultant. The convener is not the chairperson of the group, but just the person who gets it moving initially. The group may decide that they do not want a regular chairperson and might even rotate the role of the convener.

As far as possible, the expected output of the group should be identified. It should bear a direct relationship to the problem and be amenable to review.

Meetings. Meetings or workshops, which are used for many purposes, can also be designed to bring about and manage change. The focus of the meeting, as an intervention in support of change, is to enable various individuals to work on the problem face to face. The purpose pursued must be consistent with the organization's culture: where autocratic management has prevailed and people know that at the end of the day their views will be ignored anyhow, a meeting to discuss change will probably achieve very little.

It is important that the manager or consultant involved should establish the appropriate climate. This may mean that the meeting may have to be held on "neutral ground", where none of the parties has any territorial advantage. The role that the consultant will play during the meeting should be clarified as early as possible. That role, essentially, is that of facilitator and process observer. The consultant has the advantage of distance or stranger value, and his or her comments can prevent the group from falling into the usual trap of complaining about current difficulties without trying to come up with any practical suggestions for improvement. It is also possible to use meetings as an intervention without the consultant. When this is to be done, it is even more important that the relative roles and expectations of all those attending should be made clear prior to the meeting.

Experiments. Experiments are used to test a change process or its results on a limited scale, e.g. in one or two organizational units, and/or over a short time period, say several months. For example, flexible working hours or a new scheme of bonuses may first be applied on an experimental basis in selected departments and workshops.

A true experiment involves pre- and post-test control design. Two (or more) units or groups are used. They should exhibit the same or very similar characteristics (which may be very difficult to achieve and prove scientifically). Data are collected about both groups. A change is then made in one group (experimental group) but not in the other (control group). Once the change has been made, further observations are made or data collected. The data collected before and after the change in both groups are compared. However, as the famous Hawthorne experiments illustrated, it is possible in a field experiment that some other variable is influencing performance.

Pilot projects. A pilot project may be used to check on a limited scale whether a new scheme — involving considerable (and costly) technological, organizational or social change — is feasible, and whether adjustments will be necessary before introducing the scheme on a larger scale. A great deal of experience is normally drawn from a properly prepared and properly monitored pilot project, and in this way the risks involved in an important new scheme are minimized.

In drawing conclusions from the evaluation of pilot projects, certain mistakes are made again and again. In order to demonstrate that the proposed change is justified and feasible, both managers and consultants tend to pay special attention to a pilot project (e.g. by assigning the best people to it, intensifying guidance and control or providing better maintenance services). The pilot project is thus not executed under normal, but under exceptionally favourable, conditions. Furthermore, it is assumed that the conditions under which a pilot project is undertaken can be replicated for a larger programme. Often this is not possible, for a number of reasons. For example, the organization may be unable to provide support services of the same quality to a large-scale activity. Hence, learning from a pilot project also includes an unbiased review of the conditions under which it succeeded.

New organizational units. These units are often established if management has made up its mind to go ahead with a change measure (e.g. develop and start marketing a new service) and decides that adequate resources and facilities must be fully assigned to it right at the outset. As a rule, this would be done if the need for change has been well documented, and the importance of the change envisaged justifies an underutilization of resources which may well occur in the first period after the establishment of the unit.

Organization development (OD) techniques

Below are some examples of techniques originally used by behavioural scientists in organization development (OD) approaches and programmes. As mentioned above, these techniques are now applied more and more in combination with other techniques, or within comprehensive and multidisciplinary change management programmes.

Team building. This intervention is used frequently. Indeed, there are those who contend that it has been overused and abused. In part, the tendency to use this intervention is rooted in the early days of process consultation. Coming from group dynamics, the T-group approach and the sensitivity movement, there was an assumption that the basic factor in improving individual and organizational behaviour resided in people working together in groups. Although this is important, it is by no means the only nor the chief type of intervention that should be considered. As with any other intervention, it should be based on the diagnosed need.

Although there are many variations, the team-building approach focuses on how the team functions, rather than on the content area of the team. Slowly and carefully, the problem or task can be introduced into the situation, after work on interpersonal relationships has indicated that the climate is appropriate for moving into the real world.

Team building is not a one-off activity, although some consultants treat it that way. In many organizations, there is a recurring need to engage in team-building activities.

Confrontation. Within most organizations, there is generally competition for limited resources. There are times when an organization appears to have unlimited access to resources, but these periods do not usually last too long. External influences impose limitations and restrictions. One way of dealing with internal competition for limited resources is to ignore it, but this merely forces various organizational members and units to devise ways to defeat other elements of the organization.

This brings about the need for some kind of confrontation. This is a situation where individuals must confront each other and take action. It can result either in compromise (win-win), or in a situation where one unit or individual wins points at the expense of the other (win-lose). Confrontation is not necessarily negative — rather, it depends on how individuals deal with the confrontation.

Confrontation meetings normally employ a structured approach in which selected staff are exposed to: (1) historical and conceptual ideas about change and organizations; (2) preparation of a list of significant problem-areas in their own organization or unit; (3) classification of stated problems into categories;

(4) development of plans of action to remedy problems; (5) comparison of the action proposals developed; and (6) planning for implementation.

There are cultures where confrontation is seen as negative behaviour. In these it is considered impolite and counter-cultural to force an individual into decision-making. This does not mean that decisions are not made, but rather that they are not made through confrontation. The state of economic development has little to do with this aspect of cultural behaviour. It can be found in places as divergent as Japan and Malaysia. The consultant must also determine in which areas confrontation is inadvisable, as such cultural behaviour may only be appropriate for certain situations or between certain people.

When the need for a decision exists in a non-confronting culture, the consultant can bring about the needed confrontation as an intervention. He or she must do this very cautiously. One approach is to use a third party — that is, the confronting groups or individuals in the organization do not meet face-to-face. Instead, the consultant engages in what is sometimes called "shuttle diplomacy". This can work effectively as the entry phase of a confrontation intervention, with the plan that, at a later phase, the parties will actually meet. In other situations, the entire confrontation may be dealt with indirectly.

Feedback. Feeding back data on individual, group and organizational performance can help to bring about some change in individual or group behaviour.

It is very important to provide feedback. Research and experience tell us that without feedback, data may be meaningless. Particularly when an attitude survey is used, it is important that the participants in the survey receive an analysis of the data that they have provided.

The process of feedback must be handled very cautiously, because raw data are frequently misunderstood. The analysis may prove critical or damaging to some individuals, and in such a situation the results can be anticipated. Obviously, those individuals will attempt to block any movement towards change.

On a positive note, feedback can be extremely helpful. Many people in an organization do not receive sufficient feedback to enable them to assess their own performance or the performance of the organization as a whole. The consultant should plan carefully, so that there will not be an information overload. Care should be taken with both the process and the content of the feedback.

Coaching and counselling. Commonly used change-assisting interventions are coaching and counselling (see also section 3.7). They are often used in process consultation where the client as a person seeks help in improving his or her own personal performance or interpersonal relationships. The basic method is for the consultant to observe and review individual performance, listen to the client, provide feedback on problems or behavioural patterns that hinder operating effectiveness and inhibit change, and help the individual to gain self-confidence, acquire new knowledge and skills and behave in a way required by the changing nature of the job and the organization.

Training and developing people

Training and development of managers and staff can be a powerful technique for change:

- management workshops, both external and in-house, can be used to sensitize managers and staff to the need for change, to environmental trends and opportunities, to various options available to their organizations and to them as individuals, or to performance and other standards already reached elsewhere; experience has shown that managers can learn a great deal at workshops where other managers describe and discuss specific experiences with organizational change;

- training can help people to develop the skills and abilities for coping with change effectively, such as diagnostic and problem-solving techniques, planning, project management and evaluation techniques, or communication and group work skills;

- tailor-made and paced training can assist the change process at its various stages by providing missing technical information and skills, thus helping managers and staff to proceed to the next step, and overcoming fears and resistance caused by lack of knowledge or of self-confidence;

- training of "internal" change agents increases the pool of those on whom management can rely in planning and assisting programmes of organizational change.

Training in support of organizational change can be provided by professional trainers, external or in-house, by management and OD consultants, or by the managers who are in charge of particular change programmes. The participants can themselves make significant inputs, for example by defining their needs in a participative mode, or engaging in programmes of the action-learning type as discussed below. Training can be both formal and informal. The key objective is to facilitate learning of those concepts and skills that are necessary and directly applicable to an on-going change programme.

In the current context of rapid technological, social and other changes, training and learning are more than useful change techniques: organizations where learning does not enjoy a prominent place find it increasingly difficult to keep track of significant trends in business and its environment, and to maintain their managers and staff at the necessary level of competence.

Action learning. Action learning, pioneered by Reg Revans, is based on the assumption that managers learn best by solving real problems either in their own or in other organizations, and by exchanging relevant experience with other managers. The problems tackled must be important enough to the organization concerned and should involve both technical and human aspects. Emphasis is placed on implementation — that is, on the most difficult part of the change process. Exchange of experience with other managers involved in action learning is organized as a regular part of the programme. If necessary, the participants also receive technical assistance — missing information is supplied or expert advice is given on the approach taken. The ultimate objective is to achieve changes both in individual skills and attitudes, and in organizational practices and performance.[5]

Learning company. The "learning company" concept (see section 16.6 for a detailed discussion) aims to link and integrate training and learning with change processes that have a significant impact on company strategy and performance. Emphasis is put on creating favourable conditions and incentives for continuous individual learning and on innovation in training and self-development. To turn individual learning efforts into "organizational learning", various techniques and approaches are used to share and disseminate results of individual learning, learn in teams, enhance managerial responsibility for training and learning, combine the processes of learning with organizational change processes and use learning to achieve a competitive advantage.[6]

Organizational diagnosis and problem-solving techniques

There is a wide range of such techniques; some of them are known under special names. Their main advantage is that they help to apply a systematic and methodical approach, making sure that important factors, relationships or steps are not omitted and symptoms not mistaken for their causes. In a consulting project, the diagnostic phase and the action-planning phase (see Chapters 8 and 9) can also serve as an intervention for making people aware of the need to change, involving them in identifying and analysing problems and opportunities, and developing proposals meeting the organization's needs and objectives. Box 4.6 (overleaf) provides an example of a recent technique in which comparison at operational level (individual processes, activities, units, etc.) with other organizations and units is used to identify and develop practical suggestions for change.

Campaign-type, action-oriented change programmes

A campaign-type, action-oriented programme is a major organized and planned change effort over a defined period of time to tackle a significant practical problem, mobilizing fairly large teams and often requiring considerable resources. The intervention has to be extended long enough for bottom-line results to become visible or striking. Feedback on results achieved has to be provided with a view to maintaining interest in the programme and adjusting the approach as appropriate. Also, missing information, skills, equipment and materials have to be made available when necessary. Examples of problems tackled include total business performance, corporate strategy, labour productivity, product and service quality, energy consumption, waste, accident prevention and so on. As a rule, a great deal is at stake in such a programme and demands on programme management and methodology are high. Business process re-engineering, which has become popular in the 1990s, is an example of such a comprehensive programme approach (see box 4.7, pp.100-101, and section 22.3).

Box 4.6 Benchmarking

Benchmarking has been defined by the American Productivity and Quality Center as "a process in which companies target key improvement areas within their firms, identify and study best practices by others in these areas, and implement new processes and systems to enhance their own productivity and quality", and as "the practice of being humble enough to admit that someone is better at something and being wise enough to try to learn how to match and surpass them at it". Pioneered by the Xerox Corporation in the late 1970s in response to Japanese competition, benchmarking is currently practised by managers and consultants in many different ways. Yet all benchmarking approaches tend to exhibit certain common characteristics:

(1) Why benchmark?

The purpose is to stimulate and facilitate performance improvement and organizational change by identifying and analysing specific and measurable performance gaps, and establishing and achieving performance improvement targets based on best or better practices used by others.

(2) What to benchmark?

Benchmarking deals with distinct activities, processes, services, units, etc., identified as weak points and/or areas of potential improvement.

(3) What should be the performance target?

While the current level is a logical starting-point and comparison base in any benchmarking exercise, the performance improvement target can be established at various levels, as shown in the figure below. The level chosen will reflect factors such as the quality of information and analysis, the resources and the competencies needed to achieve a higher level and, in particular, the company's vision and commitment to pursuing the "best-of-best" level of practice.

The benchmarking principle

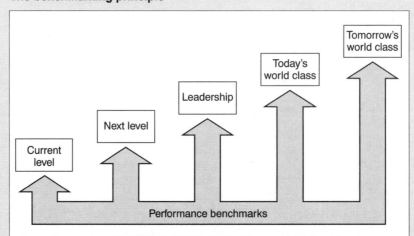

Source: Adapted from C.Y. McNair and K.H.Y. Leibfried: *Benchmarking: A tool for continuous improvement* (New York, Harper Business, 1992), p. 33. Copyright © 1992 C.J. McNair and K.H.Y. Leibfried. Reprinted by permission of HarperCollins Publishers, Inc.

(4)   With whom to benchmark?

In "external benchmarking", with sector leaders, competitors, suppliers, customers and other partners interested in comparing specific and detailed performance data and experiences and collaborating in the search for improved practices (a wrong choice of partners may make the exercise useless). In "internal benchmarking", with other departments, plants, subsidiaries, services, etc., within the same organization, multinational group or similar.

(5)   What are the main steps?

The three major steps of a typical benchmarking exercise, measurement-analysis-change, are outlined in the figure below.

Outline of benchmarking steps

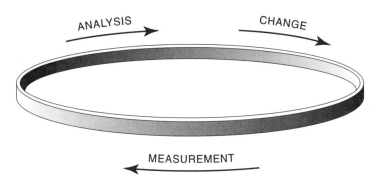

- Interview internal staff
- Gather internal information
- Prepare questionnaire
- Conduct external interviews
- Analyse and contrast data
- Report

- Establish entity goals
- Develop action plans
- Communicate results
- Implement specific actions
- Monitor programmes
- Recalibrate benchmarks

ANALYSIS ▸   CHANGE ▸

◂ MEASUREMENT

- Identify scope for benchmarking studies
- Identify appropriate drivers and performance drivers
- Identify potential external organization to benchmark

Source: W. Kreuz: *Competitive benchmarking: Will it change your strategy?*
(unpublished paper, 1992).

(6)   Who can do the work?

Benchmarking teams from participating companies, involving managers, technical experts, experienced workers, informal leaders and others who "own" or "co-own" the problems at hand, with consultants helping as facilitators and new system developers, especially if several companies team up in one benchmarking exercise.

Box 4.7   Business process re-engineering

Among the latest approaches to company productivity and overall performance improvement, business process re-engineering (BPR) appears to have aroused more interest in managers' and consultants' circles than many other techniques. Michael Hammer and James Champy define re-engineering as "the fundamental rethinking and radical redesign of business processes to achieve dramatic improvements in critical contemporary measures of performance, such as cost, quality, service and speed". They stress four terms used in this definition:

- *Rethinking must be fundamental*, therefore BPR begins with no assumptions and no givens, and takes nothing for granted. It ignores what *is* and concentrates on what *should be*. Before asking how to do an operation more effectively, it asks whether that operation needs to be done at all.

- *Redesign must be radical*. Re-engineering is about business reinvention — not business improvement, enhancement or modification.

- *Improvement should be dramatic*, therefore BPR is the opposite of systematic incremental improvements, and should be used only when dramatic improvements are needed and possible.

- *BPR focuses on processes*, not on tasks, jobs, people, structures or units. It regards a business process as "a collection of activities that takes one or more inputs and is of value to the customer". It eliminates tasks that were invented to satisfy internal demands of the company's own organization and have nothing to do with meeting customer needs.

Hammer and Champy point out that the BPR approach is of interest to three kinds of companies: companies that are in deep trouble and have no choice; companies that see trouble coming and have the vision to start re-engineering in advance of running into adversity; and those that perform very well, but their ambitious and aggressive management chooses to re-engineer in order to "raise the competitive bar even higher".

The use of *state-of-the-art information technology* is a key characteristic of BPR and can even trigger off a re-engineering effort, especially if IT professionals are invited to apply the latest IT to tasks that probably should not be performed at all, or to fragmented tasks that need radical rethinking and integration making use of the current IT capabilities. This IT dimension of re-engineering is fundamental. The "business process" concept on which BPR is built uses IT to merge separate tasks, integrate tasks physically located in different places, integrate process control and management with execution, automate choices and decisions that do not require direct human control, radically cut process lead time, make the processes highly reactive, flexible and adaptable to changing customer requirements, and make sure that identical, up-to-date and reliable information can be instantly and simultaneously used at different process stages.

The new concepts used in BPR include *"case workers"* and *"case teams"* — de-specialized individuals and groups responsible for complete processes (including coordination and management) rather than for small tasks within fragmented processes held together by paperwork and supervision. The traditional management hierarchies may undergo considerable "flattening" and "delayering".

In re-engineering, the following roles emerge in a company, either distinctly or in various combinations:

> — *Leader*: A senior executive who authorizes and motivates the overall re-engineering effort.
> — *Process owner*: A manager with responsibility for a specific process focused on it.
> — *Re-engineering team*: A group of individuals dedicated to the re-engineering of a particular process, which diagnoses the existing process and oversees its redesign and implementation.
> — *Steering committee*: A policy-making body of senior managers which develops the organization's overall re-engineering strategy and monitors its progress.
>
> A consultant may be engaged to structure and facilitate the change process without necessarily knowing too much about the existing procedures — the aim being to "reinvent".
>
> Finally, BPR advocates a *"big-bang" approach* to rethinking business processes, and a substantially more radical treatment of organizational change than any other change management approach. Managing the people side of re-engineering is therefore essential. This includes retraining, re-education, continuous communication and providing leadership.
>
> Source: Adapted from M. Hammer and J. Champy: *Re-engineering the corporation: A manifesto for business revolution* (New York, Harper Business, 1993).

Choosing among intervention techniques

We have seen that only rarely will one particular technique or approach lead to a successful implementation of all stages of a change process. In many situations, managers and consultants have to use a variety of interventions, simultaneously or successively.

A fully competent consultant is flexible in choosing intervention and change-assisting techniques, combining several interventions as appropriate and switching to a new technique if the originally chosen technique appears to be ineffective. As a rule, this choice is more effective if treated as one of the later areas of selection rather than being the subject of an early decision.[7] A trap to be avoided is choosing a wrong technique at the outset of the change process, and so rapidly creating a great deal of disenchantment and missing the target, but obstinately continuing to use the technique although it is obviously leading nowhere. Two criteria are more important than any other:

(1) The structural arrangement or intervention technique chosen should be compatible with organizational culture and, if it is not, great care should be given to explaining why the technique had to be chosen and how it will be used; also, adaptations of the technique may be required during its use.

(2) The consultant and the managers responsible for the change programme should feel comfortable with the technique and be able to use it effectively.

It is knowledge and practice of skills in choosing an appropriate approach and employing it in a life situation that set the consultant apart from the academic theoretician. The techniques may be acquired in part by studying research findings and publications, but, more particularly, they will be mastered and fine-tuned by experience.

---

[1] An American social psychologist, whose main writings on change date from the 1940s and 1950s. See, e.g., K. Levin: *Field theory in social science* (New York, Harper, 1951).

[2] See also the discussion of situational leadership, ibid., Ch. 7.

[3] R. Beckhard and R. T. Harris: *Organizational transition: Managing complex change* (Reading, Massachusetts, Addison-Wesley, 1977), p. 5.

[4] A. Huczynski: "Performance through intervention using organizational change methods", in *European Management Journal* (Oxford, United Kingdom), Vol. 5, No. 1, 1987, p. 49.

[5] See, e.g., G. Boulden and A. Lawlor: *The application of action learning: A practical guide*, MAN DEV/46 (Geneva, ILO, 1987).

[6] See also P. M. Senge: *The fifth discipline: The art and practice of the learning organization* (New York, Doubleday, 1990).

[7] Beckhard and Harris, op. cit., p. 44.

CONSULTING AND CULTURE 5

In helping clients to plan and implement change, the consultant needs to be aware of the power of culture. Culture is normally defined as a system of collectively shared values, beliefs, traditions and behavioural norms unique to a particular group of people. "Culture is the collective programming of human mind that distinguishes the members of one human group from those of another group. Culture, in this sense, is a system of collectively held values."[1] Or, in the words of the French mathematician and philosopher Blaise Pascal, "there are truths on this side of the Pyrenees that are falsehoods on the other".

Culture has its roots in basic conditions of human life, including material conditions, the natural environment, climate, and ways in which people earn their living, and in the historical experience of human communities which includes interaction with other countries and cultures. People create culture as a mechanism that helps them to cope with their environment and maintain the cohesion and identity of the community in interacting with other communities. In developing countries, in rural areas in particular, traditional cultures reflect the people's poverty and helplessness before the forces of nature. Culture tends to be deeply rooted in people's hearts and minds, and therefore cannot be easily changed.

5.1 Understanding and respecting culture

The problem with culture is that, although it is omnipresent and its influence on the functioning of organizations and whole societies is very strong, it is difficult to identify and grasp. Culture is nowhere precisely described, and it also includes taboos: values that people respect, but about which they do not normally talk and sometimes resent talking. Individuals and whole communities may be unaware of their culture because they have not learned it as a structured subject or a technical skill. Values and beliefs that make up culture evolve over generations, are transmitted from generation to generation, and are normally acquired unconsciously, early in people's lives — in the family, at school,

---

Box 5.1   What do we mean by culture?

Culture is composed of many elements, which may be classified in four categories: symbols, heroes, rituals and values.

Symbols are words, objects and gestures which derive their meaning from convention. At the level of national cultures, symbols include the entire area of language. At the level of organizational culture, symbols include abbreviations, slang, modes of address, dress codes and status symbols, all recognized by insiders only.

Heroes are real or imaginary people, dead or alive, who serve as models of behaviour within a culture. Selection processes are often based on hero models of "the ideal employee" or "the ideal manager". Founders of organizations sometimes become mythical heroes later on, and incredible deeds are ascribed to them.

Rituals are collective activities that are technically superfluous but, within a particular culture, socially essential. In organizations they include not only celebrations but also many formal activities defended on apparently rational grounds: meetings, the writing of memos, and planning systems, plus the informal ways in which these activities are performed: who can afford to be late at what meeting, who speaks to whom, and so on.

Values represent the deepest level of culture. They are broad feelings, often unconscious and not open to discussion, about what is good and what is bad, clean or dirty, beautiful or ugly, rational or irrational, normal or abnormal, natural or paradoxical, decent or indecent. These feelings are present in the majority of the members of the culture. or at least in those persons who occupy pivotal positions.

Author: Geert Hofstede.

---

through religious education, at work and by socializing with other members of the community.

A management consultant faces the same problem. His or her personality and value system have been moulded by the culture in which he or she has grown up, worked and socialized with other people. Yet the consultant may be unaware of it. For as "the last thing that a fish will discover is water", often culture will be the last thing that a management consultant, otherwise an outstanding expert in a particular technical field, will discover.

Being culture-conscious

In management consulting, a concern for culture is as important as a concern for the specific technical problem for which the consultant was brought in. But what can he do to be sure that he is culture-conscious and that neither his behaviour nor his suggestions clash with culture?

To be culture-sensitive, a management consultant does not have to become a sociologist or an anthropologist. Some knowledge of culture can be gained by reading about culture and discussing cultural issues with other people. Genuine interest in the meaning of culture and in different cultures provides a good background for understanding and correctly interpreting a particular cultural context.

However, this is only the first step. Like any other person, a consultant who has never lived and operated in a culture different from his own will find it difficult to perceive and understand the full meaning and power of another culture, and the role of various factors that may be unknown in his own culture. Experience has shown that only people who have been in contact with a different culture for some time start understanding not only that culture but also their own culture. Social and working contacts with other cultures provide us with a mirror in which we see our own culture.

Being culture-tolerant

Culture is very important to people. Their preference for fundamental cultural values is emotional, not rational. They may even regard certain social norms and traditions as eternal and sacrosanct. In contrast, a management consultant may regard the same norms as anachronistic and irrational. There may be a grain of truth in the consultant's view, since not everything is positive and progressive in cultures: they often include values that perpetuate social inequalities and inhibit development. Nevertheless, cultures reflect centuries of society's experience and help people to cope with life. Respect for different cultures and tolerance of values and beliefs alien to his or her own culture, but dear to other people, are therefore essential qualities of a good consultant.

In attitude to other cultures, a consultant is strongly influenced by his or her own culture. Tolerance towards other cultures, religions and ethnic groups is a cultural characteristic, too: some cultures are highly tolerant of different cultural values, while others are not. A consultant who has been moulded by a less tolerant cultural environment should be particularly cautious when working in other cultures.

5.2   Levels of culture

National culture

The term "national culture" is used to define the values, beliefs, behavioural norms, habits and traditions that characterize human society in a particular country. There can be one national culture in an ethnically and linguistically homogeneous country, but in many countries there are several distinct cultures and the country may be a mosaic of cultures. The question is, do these cultures mix with each other, cohabit peacefully and tolerate each other, or do they make the functioning of the State and of the economy difficult?

An important cultural phenomenon is the existence of minorities and their relationship to other ethnic groups within society. Often minorities make a special effort to preserve their particular culture in order to protect their identity and ensure survival within an environment where a majority culture dominates and tends to alter or even oppress minority cultures. Certain minorities possess attitudes, skills, historical experience and material means, thanks to which they have been extremely successful in business. The implications of this are well known in many countries. Thus, while sensitivity to cultural differences is essential in international consulting, a consultant operating within his or her own country also needs to be aware of culture.

Another increasingly important factor is the movement of people across the boundaries of countries and cultures. In many countries the workforce is international and so may be the management team in the client company. People coming from other cultures bring their cultural values and habits with them, and because they are also influenced by the culture of their country of residence, the result is an interesting and sometimes peculiar mix of cultures.

It would be impossible to review here all the factors embraced by the concept of national (or local) culture. It would be even more difficult to point to all the differences between cultures of which a consultant needs to be aware because they may be related to the work assignment. The spectrum of cultural values, norms and rituals can be extremely wide and can concern any aspect of human, economic and social life. Some cultural factors affecting management are shown in box 5.2.

Box 5.2 Cultural factors affecting management

The following factors of national cultures tend to be reflected in management structures and practices:

- the distribution of social roles and the status assigned to them;
- the criteria of success and achievement in economic and social life;
- respect for age and seniority;
- the role of traditional authorities and community leaders;
- democratic versus autocratic traditions;
- individualism versus collectivism;
- spiritual versus material values;
- responsibility and loyalty to family, community and ethnic group;
- socialization and communication patterns;
- the acceptability and the form of feedback, appraisal and criticism;
- religion, its importance in social life and its impact on economic activity;
- attitudes to other cultures, religions, ethnic groups, minorities;
- attitudes to social, technological and other changes;
- the conception of time.

Language plays a prominent role in culture. Cultural concepts are described in words, the meaning of many words is culture-bound and language is a vehicle for the functioning and interaction of cultures. Non-verbal expressions and gestures are also culture-bound and may be very important. Non-verbal communication is more difficult to control consciously than verbal communication and tends therefore to be more trustworthy. Some cultures (e.g. North American) attach importance to what is said, while in other cultures (e.g. Asian) it is essential to understand non-verbal messages.

National cultures are unique, but they are not closed systems. There are similarities between cultures for reasons such as common language or religion. Long-term interaction of cultures (e.g. between neighbouring countries or during domination of one country by another) also influences culture. In some developing countries, the social groups most exposed to the culture of the former colonial power (e.g. administrators, intellectuals and the business community) tended to adopt some of its values and behavioural patterns. Thus, strong influences of French culture can be observed in French-speaking Africa, while influences of Dutch culture are still present in Indonesia. Cultural changes occur in many countries under the influence of growing material wealth, better general education, a massive expansion of contacts with different cultures and other factors.

There is a growing interest in exploring the role played by national culture in the economic performance and development of particular countries. For many decades, North American culture has been widely regarded as a major factor in the dynamism, competitiveness and achievement of American businesses. At the present time, managers all over the world are keen to get a deeper insight into Japanese national culture (box 5.3, overleaf).

The term "culture" is also applied to values and behaviours that characterize other social groups: professions, trade groups, organizations, clubs and associations. Even small social units, such as families, may have their specific cultures. All of these are sometimes called micro-cultures.

Professional culture

Professional culture is one shared by individuals who belong to the same profession, e.g. by lawyers, medical doctors, civil engineers or accountants. It is very much related to job content and to the role played in society by the members of the profession. It is influenced by professional education and training and tends to exhibit common characteristics across organizational and national boundaries. One of the objectives of professional associations and societies is to preserve and develop professional culture. Ethical values promoted by professional associations tend to become a part of this culture.

The understanding of professional culture may help a management consultant in establishing constructive relations with clients and other professionals in foreign countries. It is useful to be informed about the background of managers and staff in a client organization and know, for example, from which universities they graduated. Some members of a client organization (e.g. accountants, internal consultants, training managers) may share common professional values with the consultant: this may be of particular help in penetrating the problems of local culture.

Box 5.3   Japanese culture and management consulting

Japanese culture, which is a historical growth of indigenous culture with the medieval influence of Chinese culture and the modern influence of Western culture, has created a unique approach to management. Two of its key characteristics have strongly influenced business management in Japan:

(1) Group orientation

The values, attitudes and behaviours of managers and workers are oriented towards the interest of the group to which they belong. The basic principle is that the personal interest of the group must be served best. In the Japanese context, the nation and the individual company are the two groups with which both managers and employees identify most closely.

(2) Long-term orientation

Japanese managers and workers view their work, as well as their life in general, from a long-term perspective and act accordingly. Time is money to them, too, primarily in the sense that the more time is spent on a plan for an activity, the greater the result of its implementation is likely to be. Typically, a Japanese employee makes work decisions on the basis of a lifetime career with the organization where he or she is employed.

Only those management techniques — be they techniques for decision making, problem solving, leadership, motivation, communication, negotiation or change — which have met these two characteristics of Japanese culture have been successfully transferred from Western culture. Now that consultants and managers worldwide are trying to reverse the historical flow and transfer Japanese management techniques to their own work environment, these characteristics are becoming critical in judging the appropriateness of such a transfer and organizing the environment for the transfer.

An additional complexity in such a transfer is the nature of Japanese language which, as compared with Western languages, is rich in context ("high context"), reflecting the nature of its cultural foundations. Therefore, particular care must be taken in correctly interpreting not only the cultural meaning but also the linguistic meaning of Japanese techniques.

As the nation is becoming affluent and international, Japanese culture is undergoing changes that go all the way down to its basic characteristics. The change is already visible with the younger generation, whose attitudes and behaviours are conspicuously less group oriented and less long-term oriented than those of their seniors. These changes are likely to lead to significant modifications of the Japanese management techniques in the coming decades.

Author: Eiji Mizutani.

Organizational culture

Organizations, too, tend to have their specific culture: a peculiar mix of values, attitudes, norms, habits, traditions, behaviours and rituals that, in their totality, are unique to the given organization (box 5.4). Some organizations are well aware of their culture and regard it as a powerful strategic tool, used to

Box 5.4 Cultural values and norms in organizations

Within organizations, the specific cultural values and behavioural norms may concern, for example:

- **the organization's mission and image** (high technology; superior quality; pride in being a sector leader; dedication to the service ethos; customer satisfaction; innovative spirit; entrepreneurial drive);
- **seniority and authority** (authority inherent in position or person; respect for seniority and authority; seniority as a criterion of authority);
- **the relative importance of different management positions and functions** (authority of personnel department; importance of different vice-presidents' positions; respective roles and authority of operations and marketing);
- **the treatment of people** (concern for people and their needs; equitable treatment or favouritism; privileges; respect for individual rights; training and development opportunities; lifetime careers; fairness in remuneration; how people are motivated);
- **the role of women in management and other jobs** (acceptance of women for positions of authority; jobs either unavailable or reserved for women; respect for women managers; equal treatment; special facilities);
- **selection criteria for managerial and supervisory positions** (seniority versus performance; priority for selection from within; political, ethnic, nationality and other criteria; influence of informal groups);
- **work organization and discipline** (voluntary versus imposed discipline; punctuality; use of time clocks; flexibility in changing roles at work; use of new forms of work organization);
- **management and leadership style** (paternalism; authoritative, consultative or participative style; use of committees and task forces; providing personal example; style flexibility and adaptability);
- **decision-making processes** (who decides; who has to be consulted; individual or collective decision making; need to reach consensus);
- **circulation and sharing of information** (employees amply or poorly informed; information readily shared or not);
- **communication patterns** (preference for oral or written communication; rigidity or flexibility in using established channels; importance attached to formal aspects; accessibility of higher management; use of meetings; who is invited to what meetings; established behaviours in the conduct of meetings);
- **socialization patterns** (who socializes with whom during and after work; existing barriers and inhibitions; special facilities such as separate dining-rooms or reserved clubs);
- **ways of handling conflict** (desire to avoid conflict and to compromise; preference for informal or formal ways; involvement of higher management);
- **performance evaluation** (substantive or formalistic; confidential or public; by whom carried out; how results used);
- **identification with the organization** (manager and staff adherence to company objectives and policies; loyalty and integrity; esprit de corps; enjoying working with the organization).

orient all units and individuals towards common goals, mobilize employee initiative, ensure loyalty and facilitate communication. They aim at creating a culture of their own and making sure that all employees understand it and adhere to it.[2]

Organizational cultures, or micro-cultures, reflect national cultures first of all. But they also include other values and norms. Recent research has provided some insight into organizational cultures of leading corporations in various countries. It has shown that many companies which have been outstanding performers over a long time exhibit a strong corporate culture. Many multi-national corporations possess certain cultural characteristics world-wide, and the parent company's culture has considerable bearing on the cultural norms and behaviour of subsidiaries in other countries. The strong personalities of the founders and of certain top managers also influence organizational culture even in very large and complex corporations. This leads to an interesting mix of cultures in the case of foreign subsidiaries, where the influence of local national culture is combined with that of the parent company's culture.

The hidden dimensions of organizational culture tend to surface during company mergers and takeovers, which in many cases fail to produce expected results mainly because management is unable to harmonize different cultures.

Many organizational cultures develop a specialized vocabulary and a wide range of symbols and rituals that staff members have to use and respect if they do not want to be regarded as outsiders by their colleagues.

A management consultant needs to learn about organizational culture as early as possible in the assignment if he or she does not want to be perceived as a stranger who does not know how things are normally done in the client organization and whose presence therefore is an irritation. But there is another much more important reason for this: the client organization's culture may be one of the causes, or the principal cause, of the problems for which the consultant was brought in. Even if changes in organizational culture are not explicitly stated among the objectives of the assignment, the consultant may have to deal with them and recommend what in his opinion needs to be changed.

Changing organizational culture may be a difficult and painful exercise, especially if it is necessary to change the values of the founders and leaders, and habits and practices that have become collective and have been widely established. Changes in leadership and management styles, and patient re-education, may be required. However, it has been pointed out that "organizational cultures reside at a more superficial level of programming than the things learned previously in the family and at school".[3] Changing organizational culture is a top management task, but the consultant's catalytic input can be essential (see also section 12.4).

The consulting firm's culture

The above-mentioned characteristics of organizational cultures are present in consulting firms as in any other organizations. Their cultures encompass values and norms concerning a wide range of issues including consulting methods and practices, commitment to clients, responsibilities and rights of junior and senior consultants, career progression, transfer of know-how to clients, the application of a code of ethics, and many others. Thus, a consulting firm's culture is a unique mix of organizational, professional and national cultural factors. It is essential to be aware of it, in particular if there is any risk of incompatibility and clash with a client's culture.

5.3   Facing culture in consulting assignments

The consultant's behaviour

A great deal of useful guidance is available on how consultants should behave when operating in other cultures. Most of it concerns interpersonal relations and manners. For example, it is good to get advice on:

- how to dress;
- how to deal with people;
- punctuality;
- when and how to start discussing business;
- written and/or oral communication with the client;
- formal and informal interpersonal relations;
- the use of go-betweens;
- display or restraint of emotions;
- what language and terms to use;
- taboos to avoid.

Such things are relatively easy to learn and remember. Also, these days it is helpful that more and more clients are becoming tolerant of other cultures. Your client may know that a first contact with an American consultant will be quite different from a contact with a Japanese consultant. However, there is no guarantee that your particular client really is "culturally literate", and culture-tolerant. It is therefore wise to find out beforehand how he or she expects a professional adviser to behave.

However important, questions such as whether to use first names and what topics must not be openly discussed represent only the tip of the iceberg in the cross-cultural consultant-client relationship. The less visible and more profound aspects of this relationship concern such issues as power and role distribution, decision making, confrontation and consensus in problem solving, use of team-work, consultation with employees, religious beliefs and practices, and any criteria whereby management will judge the consultant's work and suggestions.

Some consultants feel that they must try to identify themselves with a foreign culture, behaving as the client behaves ("when in Rome do as the Romans do!"), and sharing the client's values and beliefs in order fully to understand his or her environment and render an effective service. This may be impossible, even undesirable, to achieve. It implies no longer being authentic and genuine, thus abandoning key behavioural characteristics of a professional consultant. Understanding and respecting other people's culture does not imply giving up one's own!

How to find out

The consultant has to use all his or her experience and talent to learn enough about the cultural factors which may be relevant to the assignment. In some cases, direct questions on what values prevail, how things are normally done and what pitfalls to avoid will be perfectly acceptable, in particular if the client is keen to get a technically valid solution and is personally aware of the differences between cultures. In other cases, tactful and patient observation of the client's behaviour may produce an answer. A great deal can be learned by mixing with people and observing how they act and socialize, what symbols they use and what rituals they observe. Discussions of cultural issues should be informal; formal and structured interviews are not well suited for dealing with culture. Judgement should be suspended until the consultant has learned more. Also, the consultant should try not to be nervous and uneasy in a new situation that appears ambiguous. To detect and overcome cultural barriers, it may be useful to team up with an internal consultant or another member of the client organization who is prepared to help.

A study of the client company's history can be revealing. The roots of present corporate culture may be far back in the past: in the personality of the founder, in past successes or failures, in the growth pattern (e.g. many acquisitions or frequent changes of owners), and the like.

Establishing a climate of trust

We have already emphasized that it is important to establish as early as possible a climate of trust among all the parties in the consultant-client relationship. This can be difficult since not all cultures agree that trust of an outsider is desirable. One way of looking at these relations is by comparing high-context and low-context societies.

In *a high-context society*, relationships are based on friendship, family ties and knowing each other well. The context, the total situation, is essential to building relationships. The formation of these relationships is paced quite slowly and includes many rituals or rites of passage. This can include eating certain kinds of food, or engaging in various social activities unrelated to work.

In *a low-context society*, the relationship generally is spelled out in a written contract. The client is keen to obtain a precisely defined piece of technical work and may not care all that much about the total relationship with the consultant. What is not in the contract is not part of the relationship. Of course, there are subtle forms of interaction even in a low-context society. Generally, however, the relationship is built first on the written document; the building of trust follows.

In some cultures, developing trust takes time, but it is possible in most cultures. This need for time should be recognized and built into the plan of the assignment. Also, the concept of high- and low-context societies is a developing one. The consultant should be careful about applying it to an entire country or an entire people, since there are individual variations.

Criteria of rationality

In working for a client, a management consultant aims to find and recommend solutions which are in the client's interest. To justify the proposed measures to himself and to the client, a consultant applies criteria that are rational by his standards. For example, he may apply economic effectiveness as a criterion and judge various alternatives by their impact on the productivity and financial performance of the organization. He may use cost/benefit analysis and return on investment as the main assessment techniques.

Yet even the concept of rationality is culture bound. In Western industrial economies, where the notions of efficiency, competitiveness and profitability have not only an economic but also a strong cultural connotation, economic rationality is not always the main criterion applied by top management in evaluating alternative decisions. Personal, cultural, social or political preferences may prevail. The desire to maintain the status quo, fear of the unknown, the company owner's social image, or reluctance to make changes affecting collectively shared values, may eventually determine top management's choice even in a European or North American enterprise. In several Asian countries, certain cultural values tend to be applied as criteria of rationality: to preserve harmony, to avoid dismissing employees, to maintain status differences and to respect feelings about ethnic groups may be seen as more effective and more rational than to optimize performance in strictly economic and financial terms.

Transferring management practices

Management consultants use their past experience in working with present clients. This involves transferring management practices from one organization or country to another organizational or national environment. Other items could be substituted for "management practices". We could also speak about management techniques, technologies, methods, expertise, systems, concepts, patterns, approaches, and the like, but the question remains the same: to what extent and under what circumstances are management practices transferable?

There are factors whose influence on the choice of management techniques is evident — for example, the nature of the product, the technology used, the technical skills of the employees or the size of the organization. The influence of culture is more subtle and not so easy to perceive, but experience has shown that it tends to be very strong.

Some management techniques are *value laden*. They were developed for use in a particular culture and reflect its value systems and behavioural norms. They concern the human side of organizations: individual and group interests, interpersonal and intergroup relations, motivation and control of human behaviour. The possibility of transferring these techniques has to be carefully examined in each case. A value-laden technique may be difficult or impossible to transfer. Remuneration techniques stimulating individual performance rather than collective solidarity fail in collectivist societies; high wage differentials may not be acceptable in an egalitarian society; organization development methods based on confrontation cannot be used where harmony and conflict avoidance are strongly valued; problem-solving approaches built on democratic values are difficult to apply in a traditionally autocratic culture; matrix organization does not work effectively in cultures where people prefer the unity of command and want to receive orders from one single higher authority. Examples of failures caused by a mechanistic transfer of value-laden techniques are abundant.

Some other techniques were developed in response to organizational characteristics such as the nature and complexity of the production process, or the amount of data to be recorded and analysed; that is to say, they concern the technological, economic and financial side of organizations. Such techniques are relatively *value neutral* and their transfer across cultures is a simpler matter. However, while a technique *per se* may appear value neutral, its application creates a new situation that may be value laden. A production control or maintenance scheduling technique required by the technology used may conflict with the workers' beliefs and habits concerning punctuality, work organization and discipline, justified absence from work, accuracy and reliability of records, and the like. Every organization is unique, and the combined effects of national and organizational cultures are key factors of this uniqueness. Thus a seemingly universal and value neutral management technique may have to be modified to fit a different cultural context, or it may be even more appropriate to develop a new technique.

Culture and change

Values and beliefs concerning change have a prominent place in culture. Generally speaking, modernistic and optimistic cultures regard change as healthy; without it, business cannot flourish and society prosper. Cultures dominated by traditionalism value the status quo, stability and reverence for the past. They are suspicious about change and may perceive it as disturbing and subversive even if, in the consultant's professional view, the need for change is self-evident. To realize and appreciate this may be particularly difficult for a consultant who has been used to working with dynamic clients, keen to apply quickly any changes from which the company can derive benefits.

The presence of cultural factors impeding or retarding change does not imply that change is impossible. Even the most conservative individuals and groups are able to reconcile themselves to change if they realize its necessity, in particular if change is imposed by strong external influences, such as the deterioration of material conditions of living. Better information, education, contacts with more dynamic cultures and new technology also affect the traditionalist societies' attitude to change. However, the process of change may be slow and difficult.

When operating in an environment where resistance to change has cultural roots, a consultant will be well advised to bear in mind:

— the sort of change that is acceptable (refraining from proposals that the client will judge to be culturally undesirable or unfeasible);

— the pace of change (deciding whether to plan for a fundamental one-off change, or for gradual changes in a number of small steps; assessing the "acceptance time" needed by clients and their staff to convince themselves about the desirability of proposed changes);

— the client's readiness for change (it is unreasonable to press for change if the client is not ready to face the cultural problems that change may cause him);

— the level of management and the particular person (authority) by whom change has to be proposed and promoted in order to be accepted and implemented;

— the persuasion and educational effort needed to convince people that maintaining the status quo is not in their interest.

Consulting in social development

At the present time more and more management consulting is done for social development programmes and projects in sectors such as health, nutrition, basic education, drinking-water supply, sanitation, community development or population control. Many of these programmes requiring consulting interventions are in rural areas of developing countries. There are, too, many programmes of assistance to small entrepreneurs and micro-enterprises in the informal sector (see Chapter 19). Management consultants, including consultants who have worked in developing countries and are aware of their cultures, are as a rule familiar with the cultural setting encountered in industry and central government administration, but the informal economy, and rural and social development, are new worlds to them.

In social development, the consultant's clients are not managers operating modern enterprises or well-established administrative structures, but managers, social workers and organizers working with local communities, groups of farmers, or even individual families and persons. The technology used is simple and may be outdated. The concepts of "professional culture" or "organizational culture" do not apply. In contrast, the power of traditional social culture is very strong. Human behaviour, essentially fatalistic and conservative, is governed by deeply rooted beliefs and prejudices. Cultural characteristics reflect difficult living conditions, poverty and poor education. Passivity, resignation, lack of personal drive, fear of change and uncritical respect for traditional authorities may prevail.

In consulting, knowledge of these factors is essential, but it is not all that is needed. Consultants need to possess cultural and social work skills rather than knowledge of refined management techniques. They need to be patient, to be able to live and operate under conditions of imperfection and uncertainty, to know how to improvise using limited local resources, and to apply a great deal of imagination in proposing solutions which cannot be found in any management handbook. Personal commitment to and empathy with the underprivileged are qualities without which it is hard to succeed.

---

[1] G. Hofstede: "Culture and organizations", in *International Studies of Management and Organization*, No. 4, 1981. See also idem: *Cultures and organizations: Software of the mind* (Maidenhead, Berkshire, McGraw-Hill, 1991). The word "culture", in English and some other languages, also has another meaning. It is used when referring to the arts, literature, and so on. Obviously, this is not the meaning intended here.

[2] See, e.g., T. E. Deal and A. A. Kennedy: *Corporate cultures: The rites and rituals of corporate life* (Reading, Massachusetts, Addison-Wesley, 1982); E.H. Schein: *Organizational culture and leadership* (San Francisco, California, Jossey-Bass, 2nd ed., 1992); and Hofstede, op. cit.

[3] G. Hofstede: "Business cultures" in *Courier* (Paris, UNESCO), Vol. 47, No. 4, 1994, pp. 12-16.

PROFESSIONALISM AND ETHICS IN CONSULTING

6

The growth of management consulting has given ample evidence that at one time almost anyone could call himself or herself a consultant and set up in practice. In its early years the business attracted the good, the bad and the indifferent. The word "business" is used deliberately: "professions" seldom start as such. Professional awareness and behaviour come when the early juggling with a little knowledge gives way to skilled application of a generally accepted body of knowledge according to accepted standards of integrity. The professions of medicine, the law and the applied sciences all followed this path, and management consulting is proceeding in the same direction.

6.1 Defining a profession

Before discussing in detail how consultants can enhance their professional approach, we should mention the criteria normally used to define a profession. These criteria, about which much has been said and written, can be summarized under five headings.

Knowledge and skills

There is a defined body of knowledge proper to the profession, which can be acquired through a system of professional education and training. The necessary level of professional expertise is not reached without a certain number of years of practical experience in addition to completed higher education, preferably under the coaching of senior members of the profession. Furthermore, the practising professional has to keep continuously abreast of relevant developments in theory and practice.

The professions tend to have their own criteria and systems for verifying and assessing required knowledge and experience, including examinations on entry, assessment by professional bodies, testing the results of further training, and similar.

The concept of service and social interest

Professionals put their knowledge and experience at the disposal of clients as a service against appropriate remuneration. The real professionals are characterized by the "service ethos": they serve clients' needs and interests, to which they subordinate their own self-interest. Furthermore, they view individual client interests from a wider social perspective, and keep broader social needs and interests in mind when serving individual clients.

Ethical norms

There is a set of recognized ethical norms, shared and applied by the members of the profession. These norms define what is proper and what is improper behaviour in providing a professional service. They demand more than respecting the law: a behaviour that is perfectly legal may not always be ethical judged by the profession's norms.

Community sanction and enforcement

The community in which the profession operates and the clientele which is served recognize the social role, the status, and the ethical and behavioural norms of the profession. There may be explicit recognition (e.g. by means of a legal text governing and protecting professional practice). This may include definitions of educational or other standards required and special examinations to be passed, as well as of behaviours considered as unprofessional and illegal, and of corresponding sanctions.

Self-discipline and self-control

While serving clients, an individual member of the profession applies self-discipline and self-control in observing the profession's behavioural norms. The profession organizes itself in one or more voluntary membership institutions (associations, institutes, chambers, etc.), thus exercising collective self-regulation and self-control over the application of an accepted code of professional conduct and over the development of the profession. An equally important purpose of membership institutions is to defend the collective interests of the profession in dealing with representatives of the clients and the community.

Is management consulting a profession?

There has been a long but inconclusive debate on whether management consulting meets the criteria discussed above and deserves to be called a profession. Both scholars and leading consulting practitioners have expressed and defended diametrically different opinions (box 6.1). These opinions illustrate the current state of management consulting. While consulting exhibits

---

Box 6.1   Is management consulting a profession?

In 1993, James Kennedy interviewed a number of leading personalities in American consulting, to find out that not more than 60 per cent of the respondents regarded management consulting as a profession. He received, among others, the following answers:

"Management consulting is indeed a profession, but certification is irrelevant."

Victor Millar

"Sure it's a profession: management consultants offer professional services and get paid for it . . . and, as such, are the elite of service occupations."

Bob Hayes

"Management consulting is actually several professions."

Pete Bradshaw

"No, because we lack precise methodologies, a body of knowledge, educational link. Much of the work is professional and many consultants are professional, but we are not a profession by a long shot!"

Ken Tunnell

"Management consulting has never found its true identity as a professional field. And management consultants as a group do not meet the test of being a profession."

Phil Shay

"The clamour for professionalization is years out of date. A profession is a social construct (prestige, status, etc.), not a business construct, and it's too late to try and grab for social status."

David Maister

"The very nature of the management consulting profession argues against a clearcut definition of the term. Maybe the emphasis should not be labels or initials but an imposing quality of services."

Ed Hendricks

"We have a nucleus of a profession, but it needs another 25 years to mature."

Glen Van Doren

Source: James H. Kennedy: *Management consulting today — a look around and a look ahead* (Fitzwilliam, New Hampshire, Consultants News, 1993).

---

a number of criteria applied to professions, it does not meet some other criteria. We can call it an emerging profession, or a profession in the making, provided that we are aware of the gaps that need to be filled and improvements that need to be made.

We will comment on these issues in the following sections of the chapter, trying to show what can be done to increase the professional level and quality of management consulting.

6.2 The professional approach

What then are the salient characteristics of a professional approach in management consulting? Some of them can be found, in succinct form, in the codes of ethics or conduct adopted by the membership organizations of management consultants; others are set out in information pamphlets issued by consulting firms. These are the norms held collectively, i.e. by the members of a consultants' association or of a consulting firm that has formally declared what its ethical rules are. However, in many situations it is practically impossible to refer to a formal declaration of norms defining truly professional and ethical behaviour. In such cases the consultant will be guided by a personal code of professional ethics and behaviour — his or her own conception of what is proper and improper practice, and what is beneficial to the client and to the community and what is not.

The consultant is in a position of trust; the client most probably believes that certain behavioural norms will be respected without their even being mentioned. Many clients believe that consultants would never use false credentials, and some clients are even unable to evaluate the consultant's technical competence. The consultant may be in a position of technical superiority and possess knowledge and information denied to the client. The

---

Box 6.2   The power of the professional adviser

The "technical superiority" of the management consultant, and his or her "power" over clients, are often different from what can be observed in some other professions, e.g. in medicine. There are two main reasons for this. First, if there is a knowledge and experience gap between management consultants and their clients, this gap can be quite small. To many clients management consulting is not a "black box". Both the consultant and the client may have the same educational background and similar practical experience. The client may be quite well prepared for deciding to use or not to use a consultant and to accept or reject the consultant's advice, and for controlling the consultant's work during an assignment. Clearly, this is not the normal position of a patient who turns to a physician, or of a layman who seeks legal counsel and in certain situations must retain a lawyer even if he would prefer to avoid him. Second, management consulting is not a closed and highly protected profession. In most countries there are no barriers or only minimal barriers to entering the profession. There are no jobs that would be reserved to management consultants. The consultant's and the client's roles can even be interchangeable. He or she who is client today can be consultant tomorrow. And vice versa.

There are two typical situations where the consultant's ethics are clearly put to the test: first, if he does enjoy technical superiority because he works for an uninformed or technically weak client; and second, if he works for a client whose judgement has been diminished by distress and difficulties and who desperately needs help. Such clients may be very vulnerable yet easy to manipulate, and the choice of the terms of the consulting contract, the intervention methods and the changes proposed can be very much in the hands of the consultant. Even if participative consulting is applied, the client may be a subdued, not a self-confident and strong participant in the consultancy.

---

client, on the other hand, may be in a position of weakness, uncertainty, and even distress (box 6.2).

Any consultant whose ambition is to become a real professional must clarify his or her own conception of ethics and the norms to be observed in working for clients. This applies equally to external and internal consultants, as well as to persons who intervene in a consulting capacity although they are not full-time consultants.

The following characteristics of a professional approach are essential.

Technical competence

The consultant's technical competence is the basis of his professional approach. Above all, he must possess the sort of knowledge and skills needed by a particular client. As a general rule, the consultant must be able and willing to critically assess his own knowledge and skills when considering a new assignment or when reaching a point in a current assignment where different competences are required. A professional consultant will never misrepresent himself, pretending that he can do a job that is beyond his competence, even if he is short of work and keen to get any assignment. The consultant who wants to tackle a new sort of problem (experience cannot be increased except by trying out something new) will discuss this openly with the client.

The difficulty is that in management and business consulting there is a lack of reliable and fully objective benchmarks for assessing competence to do a particular job to the client's full satisfaction. Consulting associations have attempted to define *a common body of knowledge* of professional consultants, and *the type and minimum duration of experience* which is a condition of association or institute membership, or certification (see section 6.4). These, however, are general and rather elementary criteria of admission or certification, which cannot show whether a consultant is competent for a given task. They are not applied to consultants who are not members of associations or who do not seek certification. In addition, the work on developing a generally recognized body of knowledge for the consulting profession is far from being completed. The documents that are available from various consulting associations are useful, but cannot be regarded as authoritative texts establishing the knowledge base of the profession (see also Chapters 32 and 33 dealing with the careers and development of consultants).

The client's interest

During an assignment, the consultant makes his competence and time fully available to the client, with the objective of achieving the best possible results in the client's interest. This is a golden rule of consulting. Unfortunately, it is not always obvious what "client's interest" means and what the client really expects from the assignment. There is often a conflict between the client's short-term and long-term interests, or between interests of various groups within a client organization, but the client may not see this until the consultant brings it to his attention. In agreeing to serve a client, the consultant must be sure that his and the client's interests do not conflict. This can happen if the consultant also pursues objectives that have little in common with the client's objectives or even conflict with these objectives.

Avoiding a conflict of interests is one of the most delicate and critical issues of professionalism and ethics in current consulting. There may be many reasons for this, including the complexity of business ventures and transactions in which consultants become involved as advisers or intermediaries, to the multidisciplinary structure of many larger professional firms and the rather liberal interpretation of the very meaning of conflict of interest in some cultures and countries.

Box 6.3   Is there conflict of interest? Test your value system!

- An international consulting firm is an adviser to the government in a privatization project, although it has long-standing work relationships with a potential foreign buyer of the public enterprise to be privatized, and is actually executing, but through another branch office and a different team of consultants, an assignment for this potential buyer.

- An auditor is suggesting that the client should turn to the consulting division of his professional firm with a specific problem that surfaced during the audit, although there are probably other consultants who could do the same job better or for a lower fee.

- A consultant keeps an eye on the client's staff and does not miss an opportunity to offer a job to the most talented among the client's people, especially if there is a malaise in the client organization and the consultant can offer a better salary. Another consultant pursues the same objective but decency dictates to her to wait several months after the end of the contract before approaching any candidate.

- A client does the same in respect of the consultant working for him.

- A consultant is pursuing an assignment step by step, rigorously respecting the work plan defined in the contract, although it is almost certain that she will get nowhere and the proposals will never be implemented.

- A consultant is a leading professional expert on particular sectors — textiles, automotive industry, machine tools, etc. This implies working simultaneously or successively for competing firms, which may or may not know about it. What is the difference between providing the best sector-related expertise to every client, and leaking information from one competitor to another?

- A consultant, who has been adviser to a number of public sector companies to be privatized, participates in establishing an investment fund, or becomes adviser to an investment fund, which takes a financial interest in these companies during the privatization process.

Box 6.3 points out some situations where conflict of interest may not be obvious at first glance. Conversely, certain instances of conflict of interest are blatant and may therefore be explicitly mentioned in the codes of conduct (see Appendix 3). Thus, consultants are required to disclose, prior to assignments —

all relevant personal, financial and other business interests which could not be inferred from the description of the services offered. In particular this relates to:

- any directorship or controlling interests in any business in competition with the client;
- any financial interest in goods or services recommended or supplied to the client;
- any personal relationship with any individual in the client's employ;
- any personal investment in the client organization or in its parent or any subsidiary companies.[1]

The question whether to "empower" the client by sharing expertise, transmitting know-how, and providing training in conjunction with advice, is another complex issue in which conflict of interest may arise. In the previous chapters we have said and repeated that a truly professional consulting approach, as currently viewed by the overwhelming majority of consultants, has a strong learning dimension. To "help clients to learn to help themselves" is a fundamental objective to which consultants adhere wholeheartedly. However, a general declaration of a noble principle is not enough. The consultant must be sure that the assignment is so designed, and the client so involved, that the consultant will not retain for his or her own use the knowledge and expertise that should be passed on to the client.

Consultants who are looking to the future do not see teaching and training clients as a threat. They do not view the future as a simple replica of the present, which would permit them to continue to do the same things indefinitely. Clients will have new sorts of problems, and a consultant from whom the client has learned useful skills may be called on again. Such a client will gladly recommend the consultant to business colleagues. Other clients will come, and so on.

Impartiality and objectivity

Clients who turn to professional advisers believe that they will receive impartial and objective advice. They assume that the consultant will be free of any biases, prejudices, preconceived ideas or prefabricated and prepackaged solutions, that may have worked in other contexts but may be totally inappropriate to the given client. The true professional aims to be as impartial and objective as possible. He or she is someone who has learned to control emotions and not to let prejudices erode the value of advice. Yet experience has shown that absolute impartiality and objectivity are an ideal that is difficult, if not impossible, to attain.

In addition to conflicting interests, other factors may affect impartiality and objectivity. Every consultant is influenced by his or her cultural background and personal value system which may include political, racial, religious or other beliefs and prejudices. In addition, consultants tend to have personalized approaches to problem solving and working as helpers to clients who face problems. Some consultants are strong believers in the power of behavioural sciences and process consulting, while others favour a rigorous and systematic approach to problem diagnosis, using highly structured procedures, techniques or models.

The consultant must make every effort to become aware of his or her personal values and biases, as well as of forces and interests within the consulting firm and the client's environment, which may affect impartiality and objectivity. An open discussion with the client on these issues may be necessary and helpful. In many cases, objectivity can be increased by reviewing the approach and the solutions envisaged with other members of the consulting firm, who have faced similar problems with other clients. In an extreme case, a real professional would decline an assignment where he or she cannot be objective.

Internal consultants should be particularly aware of their dependence on their own organization and of the factors which might make them less impartial than an external adviser. They should not be given assignments where they clearly cannot think and behave impartially.

Confidentiality

Confidentiality is another universal principle of work done by independent professionals for their clients. Management consultants engage themselves neither to disclose any confidential information about clients, nor to make any use of this information to obtain benefits or advantages personally for their firms or other clients. The clients must be convinced that they can trust consultants. Here too, the consultant has to exercise self-control. The client may forget to specify what information must be treated as confidential and may be unaware of the various risks in working with information.

In internal consulting, the situation with regard to confidentiality can be complicated. In certain cases consultants have had an obligation to (or there is a possibility that they might) disclose information on the client to a common superior (minister, director-general or other official). Under such circumstances, managers regard internal consultants as central management's spies and are reluctant to use them. To counter this, many business corporations have declared confidentiality as a principle that will be scrupulously respected in using internal consultants as well as external ones. A similar approach tends to be increasingly taken within the public sector.

Confidentiality can also be violated unintentionally — by carelessness in handling documentation, naïvety in discussing work-related issues in social contexts, or lack of precautions in quoting confidential information in public speeches or articles.

Commissions

All commissions are not equal to bribery. Yet certain commissions are bribery, or can be perceived as such, if not disclosed to the client. In any event, commissions are a delicate issue. Codes of ethics do not ignore them, but most codes fail to provide sufficient guidance.

It is of course impossible to give universal guidelines on the acceptability of commissions from the viewpoint of professional ethics. Local business practices and cultures are difficult to ignore. In some countries, commissions and discounts constitute an inevitable means of obtaining and doing any business, including professional services. In other countries any unreported and untaxed commission is illegal. As a general rule, the client should be informed of commissions or similar favours received, paid or promised by the consultant in connection with the assignment.

Within a professional firm, the issue of commissions may constitute an ethical dilemma. Some consulting firms have lost important contracts only to see that a less competent winner was chosen thanks to greater "flexibility" in offering a commission to the right decision maker.

In consultants' circles, the prevailing position on commissions is the following:

— a commission paid by the consultant to the client or his staff in order to obtain an assignment, or to get the consultant's proposals accepted, is unethical;

— a commission accepted by the consultant in order to make certain recommendations, which may concern an issue within the client organization, the selection of a supplier or another issue where the choice proposed by the consultant is likely to affect the client's decision, is also contrary to the code of ethics;

— a commission paid by the consultant to a person or organization that introduced him to the client, or acted as an intermediary in a similar way, is acceptable in most cases; such commissions are normal practice in many countries; however, the client should be aware of such a possibility and find it acceptable.

Value for money

The fees charged to clients (see Chapter 26) raise several ethical questions. Professionals are concerned about the relationship between the benefits drawn by the client and the cost of the assignment. If they feel that the outcome does not justify the price, or that the benefit will be none or too small, they warn the client before the job starts. Generally speaking, professional ethics require that consultants charge "normal" and "reasonable" fees, judged by the profession's current standards and prevailing practice.

Charging excessive fees to uninformed clients is clearly unprofessional. Undercutting fees and working at a loss in the hope that this will eliminate competition is unprofessional too, in particular if the consultant does this with a new client, knowing that he will soon have to readjust the fee to the normal level. Furthermore, certain fee formulas may be regarded as less appropriate or even unethical.

Wider social concerns and the client's ethics

Consulting assignments often involve issues where the client's interest may be in real or potential conflict with wider social interests. Or the consultant may uncover practices that, according to prevailing social norms or in his personal opinion, are socially harmful and undesirable, if not illegal. The consultant may face a real ethical dilemma. He may have an opportunity to seek advice from senior colleagues and friends, but eventually he must himself resolve such a dilemma, which may be a difficult thing to do.

Codes of consulting ethics provide some guidance on the consultant's behaviour, e.g. on avoiding conflict of interest in working for a client; but they leave it entirely to the consultant to distinguish between ethical and unethical behaviour of the client.

Unfortunately, despite years of research and the proliferation of publications, the concept of managerial and business ethics has remained vague and controversial.[2] True enough, there are extreme situations of clients involved in illegal or fraudulent dealings. A professional consulting firm would withdraw from an assignment where such client behaviour has been discovered or suspected. The vast majority of situations are less clear, and recommending a course of action that meets both commercial and ethical criteria may involve difficult choices. As a minimum, the consultant would draw the client's attention to the possibility of conflict between these criteria. As an optimum, the consultant and the client should work towards decisions where business and ethics are in no conflict.

Defining what can be judged as ethical in a given context is in itself a difficult choice. Ethical norms are social, culture-bound norms, and different social groups may hold different views. Consultants would be of little help to clients if they took a moralistic stance. They can be more helpful by suggesting how to minimize potentially harmful consequences of business decisions, or how to optimize these decisions in terms of financial and social benefits to the various stakeholders who will be affected.

6.3 Professional associations and codes of conduct

Professional associations

In a number of countries management consultants have established voluntary professional associations to represent their common interests (for names and addresses see Appendix 2). These associations have played a leading role in promoting professional standards of consulting and helping this young profession to gain the confidence of management circles and a good reputation in society.

By and large, associations of management consultants contribute to the strengthening of the profession by:

- developing a common body of knowledge;
- determining minimum qualification criteria for new entrants to the profession (education, type and length of experience, references, examinations);
- certifying (accrediting) management consultants;
- defining and applying a code of professional conduct and practice for their members;
- investigating complaints of violations of the code of conduct and taking disciplinary action;
- examining various aspects of management consulting, organizing an exchange of experience and making recommendations to members on improvements in consulting methods, management of firms, training of consultants and other questions important to the development of the profession;
- organizing training events for consultants;
- providing information on services available from members and helping to identify suitable consultants at potential clients' request;
- defending their members' common interests in dealing with governments, organizations representing clients and other stakeholders interested in the development of consulting and the use of consulting services.

Membership of a professional association is voluntary, but is governed by several conditions defining the member's profile and commitment to a collectively endorsed moral obligation. Not all consultants are members. There have been cases of important consulting firms which do not subscribe to all conditions of membership, or whose management has taken an elitist approach, feeling that a well-established and strong professional firm can define its own standards and does not need any guidance or supervision by a professional association. There are individual consultants, too, who are not members because they do not meet some admission criterion, or do not see what benefits they could draw from membership.

In some countries, there are two types of consultants' organization: associations of firms, and institutes or associations of individual consultants. This reflects the different perceptions of what consulting firms need as distinct from individual persons employed in these firms or working as sole practitioners. Associations of firms tend to focus on the development of firms and questions in which the whole consulting industry is interested, while the institutes are mainly interested in the qualifications and development of individual consultants. This dichotomy is quite common in the Anglo-Saxon world, although several attempts have been made to convert the "friendly cohabitation" of these voluntary bodies into direct collaboration and even integration.

Where the two types of membership organization exist, dual and overlapping membership is quite common: a consulting firm is a member of an association, while some or all of the consultants it employs are members of an institute where membership is individual.

On average, about 50 per cent of consultants, practising individually or employed by consulting firms, are organized in voluntary professional associations of management consultants in various countries. This figure includes both consultants who are members as individual persons, and consultants who are not members as individuals, but work for firms that are members of a consulting association. It is a low figure bearing in mind the rapidly changing shape of consulting and the need to strengthen professionalism. There are consultants who would join the association if it were stronger and if it provided more services to members. They do not realize that, to be more relevant and influential, a voluntary association needs active members, and that associations can be improved from inside, not by passive observation and criticism from outside.

The international scene

At the international level, the management consulting profession lacks a world federation that would organize collaboration among national associations and harmonize national and regional efforts to develop the profession. The leading organizations covering the three principal markets for consulting services are ACME (United States), FEACO (Europe) and ZEN-NOH-REN (Japan).

ACME (Association of Management Consulting Firms) is the oldest association of firms, established in 1926. Its profile is increasingly international since ACME's leading members are large United States based multinational consultancies, and non-American firms can also become members.

FEACO (European Federation of Management Consulting Associations) is a regional federation of national associations of management consulting firms (one per country). Most large United States based firms have branch offices or affiliated companies in several European countries and participate in FEACO's work through the national associations. FEACO also works directly with large multinational consultancies through a special committee.

ZEN-NOH-REN is a national association with a wider membership base, including other professional organizations in management and productivity in addition to consulting organizations.

Thus the profiles of these three partners are different. Yet they have started to cooperate on matters of common interest, e.g. by jointly organizing major management consultants' conferences and comparing regional experiences.

Collaboration among national management consulting institutes (with individual membership) has been organized by the ICMCI (International Council of Management Consulting Institutes), established in 1987. The Council has chosen to focus on professional development and quality by promoting consultant certification by individual member institutes (members must be committed to the idea of certification), and its international recognition by the profession and the users' community.

Codes of conduct

Professional associations of management consultants attach great importance to the codes of professional conduct (ethics, deontology, professional practice), which they use as basic instruments to establish the profession and protect its integrity, and to inform clients about behavioural rules observed by the consultants. They regard the codes as statements that signify voluntary assumption by members of the obligation of self-discipline which can reach above and beyond the requirements of the law.

Appendix 3 reproduces the full text of two codes: (a) the Code of Professional Practice of the FEACO, to which all national associations grouped in FEACO must subscribe, and (b) the Code of Professional Conduct of the Institute of Management Consultants in the United Kingdom. Both codes are supplemented by explanatory notes.

It is, of course, not the code of conduct itself, but its rigorous and intelligent application by all members of the association which determines the real professional value and integrity of consulting services. Many codes have a clause by which the consultants engage themselves to do nothing likely to lower the status of management consulting as a profession. This leaves much to the discretion of the consultants themselves.

This is quite understandable. A code cannot be excessively detailed and specific, since it would not be applicable to all members and all situations in which they intervene. Furthermore, a code cannot anticipate new problems and future situations in which consultants may have to weigh what is professional and what is not. As pointed out by Gordon Lippitt, "the process of continually evaluating one's code of ethics and the application of those ethics must continue throughout one's professional life, with the use of trusted colleagues as testers and clarifiers. The acquisition of ethical competence reduces anxiety and increases effectiveness in the situational decision making that is a constant in the consulting process".[3]

Assisting professional development

Consultants' associations can help their members to raise the standards of professional service in many ways. These can include training courses for new consultants, refresher training and workshops for experienced practitioners, conferences aimed at broad information and experience exchange, research into new consulting approaches and methods, information on useful literature and on what goes on in other professions, examining new trends in management and business and their implications for consulting, and so on.

As the consulting profession is a young one, all these activities should have a strong educational dimension, by which we mean that in addition to strengthening technical skills they should emphasize professional ethics and behaviour as defined by the association's code.

6.4 Certification and licensing

Whether and how to apply certification (accreditation) or licensing to management consultants is a notoriously controversial subject, debated not only in consulting firms and associations but also in users' circles. This debate is indicative of both the professional aspirations and the growing sense of social responsibility of consultants, and of the various factors that slow down professionalization.

Certification, it is felt in some quarters, would be a step towards a wide recognition of management consulting as a true profession. Business, governments and the public at large want to have a guarantee that management consultants associated with important decisions in the private and public sectors are proven professionals. Certification should enhance the international position of management consulting and help it to compete with other professions, where certification has been a long-established practice. It should put more order into the consulting business and help to separate the wheat from the chaff. Finally, certification should be applied to individuals, not to firms: "No true profession can be based on the qualifying of firms", wrote in 1962 James Sandford Smith, Founding President of the United Kingdom Institute of Management Consultants.

On the other hand, various objections are raised: that certification cannot really guarantee anything more than the application of general and rather elementary criteria of admission to the profession; that it cannot show whether a consultant is actually suitable for a given job; and that, after all, consulting to business is itself a business and a consultant who passes the market test by finding enough clients does not need any paper certifying his or her competence.

Opponents to certification also evoke the difficulties involved in defining the scope of management consulting, the lack of a generally accepted body of knowledge, and the overlapping between consulting and other professional sectors. Some larger firms contest the consulting institutes' legitimacy to certify their employees. At best they would agree to the certification of individuals who operate on their own.

Developments towards certification

Facts show that certification has been making modest progress. In several countries the national management consulting institutes have introduced a voluntary certification procedure; candidates who meet the criteria become "certified management consultants" (CMC). Or the consultant must meet certain criteria to become a full member of the institute; full membership is thus equal to certification.

For example, full membership of the Institute of Management Consultants (IMC) in the United Kingdom is available to consultants on the following conditions:

— full-time engagement in management consultancy;

— a degree or equivalent professional qualification;
— a minimum of five years of full-time management consulting experience (reduced to three years if the applicant is an associate member and has been employed by a consulting firm with IMC-recognized training arrangements);
— recommendation by two fellows or members of the Institute;
— an interview with a Membership Review Board.

Other institutes may have chosen different conditions, including written examinations, participation in a special consultant development programme, or membership reserved to external consultants.

To promote and standardize certification worldwide, the ICMCI has developed an international model (box 6.4) as a set of minimum requirements to be met by national certification procedures. The model aims to achieve international reciprocity among member institutes, whereby the certification awarded by one member institute would also be recognized by other institutes participating in the scheme.

Box 6.4   International model for consultant certification

Requirements

Experience	Three years in management consulting
Education	Recognized degree or professional qualification or additional five years in management consulting in lieu of a degree
Age	No minimum age requirement specified
Time spent	1,200 hours per annum in active management consulting during the three qualifying years over the preceding five years and currently active in management consulting
Independence	Owner or employee of a firm in independent practice or internal consultant where currently eligible for admission to the institute

Qualification process

Examination	Written examination or structured interview to test knowledge of the code of professional conduct and common body of knowledge
Sponsors	Two sponsors who are full Members or Fellows (CMC, FCMC, MIMC, FIMC or equivalent)
References	Written descriptions of five assignments or five client references verified through interview

Designations

Designation	Professional designation exists
Retention	Member may retain designation even after leaving management consulting as long as he or she remains a member in good standing

Source: ICMCI.

However, the advancement of certification has been slow and the controversial questions have yet to be answered. Few clients are aware of the existence of certification, which is therefore seldom used as a qualification requirement in selecting consultants. The number of certified consultants has remained small: some 3,600 in the United Kingdom (15-30 per cent of the consultant population, depending on the definition used), but not more than 1,700 in the United States (some 2 per cent), which is less than in neighbouring Canada (2,200).

Licensing

Certification and similar procedures are voluntary, and fully in the hands of a private membership organization. Licensing or official registration can be made compulsory. This means that, to be authorized to practise, a professional (firm or individual person) must request and obtain an official licence, which is granted if the professional meets certain criteria. Certification does not have to be a criterion. The licence can be withdrawn in instances of malpractice. Licensing can be directly by a government authority, or delegated to a semi-official agency or a membership association, which carries it out under government guidance and surveillance. Box 6.5 gives some examples of licensing.

By and large, management consultants have little experience of licensing; their views on this practice reflect mainly their general attitudes to free competition and to government intervention. Some consultants are strongly opposed to the idea of licensing, which they regard as an unnecessary infringement of their freedom. Others tend to recognize that progression towards professionalism may require some form of flexible and non-bureaucratic licensing, with a key role being played by professional membership organizations enjoying a high reputation and the full confidence, not only of the consultants, but also of clients, government authorities and the general public.

6.5 Legal liability and professional responsibility of management consultants

Management consultants, as any other professional advisers, are not immune from being held legally responsible in certain cases where their advice or recommendations are deemed to cause pecuniary damage or loss to their clients or, perhaps, others in a relationship with their clients. While the possibility and size of such legal liability might be greater in the case of engineering or computer consultants, it is not at all insignificant in the "pure" management consulting area. It is the purpose of this section to look briefly into the standards used in various legal systems in determining liability and in assessing the amount of recoveries awarded, as well as the question of insurance available to consultants to cover such possible liability, and other means by which consultants may protect themselves from liability.

Box 6.5   Examples of licensing

Licensing is common in several professions, although national practices vary considerably. In France, for example, the public accounting practice is regulated by legal texts in considerable detail. The *experts comptables* [accounting experts] have to be registered members of the national *Ordre des experts comptables et des comptables agrées* [Order of accounting experts and certified accountants], which administers and supervises the profession within a framework stipulated by law. The government can overrule the decisions of the superior council of the Order, and the national disciplinary commission of the profession includes three government representatives and two elected members.

An interesting initiative has been taken in Canada through the efforts of the Institute of Management Consultants of Ontario. In 1984, the Ontario provincial legislature recognized management consulting as a self-regulating profession. The designation CMC is recognized by law as certifying the competence and professionalism of a management consultant, and the Institute is authorized to determine conditions of membership and enforce the code of ethics. However, compulsory licensing was not introduced, so consultants can practise in Ontario even if they are not recognized as CMC.

In contrast, in Austria, to be authorized to practise, management consultants have to become members of the *Bundeswirtschaftskammer* [Federal Chamber of Economy] and obtain a licence, which is granted if the candidate meets certain requirements concerning education and experience, and succeeds in a written and oral examination. However, Austrian consultants have doubts about the actual impact of the procedure on the enhancement of professional standards in consulting.

First, however, it should be pointed out that in those countries where the courts have too easily found liability stemming from professional advice given by consultants, and where clients/plaintiffs are awarded unduly large amounts of damages, one undesirable effect has sometimes been to induce a certain reticence on the part of consultants to recommend bold, novel and imaginative solutions to their clients' problems. In other words, fear of possible legal action can lead to over-cautiousness and risk avoidance on the part of consultants in advising their clients. Even where insurance may be available (usually at considerable expense) to mitigate the consultant's actual loss, the mere fact of being deemed responsible for negligence or for contractual breaches, and the repercussions on the consultant's reputation, may be sufficient to dampen his or her enthusiasm and innovativeness in advising clients.

Liability: Why and when?

This being said, legal liability will normally, and in principle, flow only from a clear showing of malpractice in the form of non-professionalism bordering on or carrying over into the realm of gross negligence or fraud. Although not always respected in practice, the rule should be that an honest error of professional judgement in and of itself should not entail legal liability as regards the consultant. As a minimum there should be a demonstration of non-compliance with an accepted standard of care for the profession and/or deviation from the requirements of the consulting contract.

While this is not often easy to establish, in certain legal systems (many cite the very litigious American practice) lawsuits are more frequently brought and won (and judgements or settlements are larger) than in others. Where this is the case, a contributing factor may be the nature of the defendant/consultant, i.e. where a big firm is involved which, in the eyes of a court or jury, can easily pay large judgements. The same effect may be felt where it is known that the defendant consultant is covered by insurance, and the insurance company itself is seen as having "deep pockets". In both cases the finder of facts, jury or judge, may pay less heed to a thorough search for real fault on the part of the defendant. In fact, in some societies there may be an outlook that reflects the idea that where there has been loss, there must be a legal remedy. In any case a trend towards finding liability more easily, and compensating (sometimes problematical) harm more handsomely, is in evidence and warrants consideration and possible defensive action on the part of the professional management consultant.[4]

It should be noted that it is normally no defence for the consultant to assert that he or she was merely giving advice or recommendations. The client has the "right" to rely on the expertise proffered by the consultant. The fact that the client was under absolutely no obligation to follow such advice or accept such recommendations counts for little, juridically speaking, where it can be demonstrated that what the consultant has done was patently unprofessional and did not meet the standards of the profession. Of course, in order for a plaintiff to prevail, damages or loss directly consequential to following the advice and recommendations of the consultant must in principle be shown as well. In other words, the loss or "injury" must be directly traceable to the negligence (or contractual non-performance) of the consultant.

Another significant aspect of this whole question is the financial situation of the management consultant and, in particular, the single practitioner or the very small firm. If the consultancy is organized as a limited liability company, or even in the case of those without a corporate structure, its assets may not be such as to offer the allegedly injured client the possibility of a financial recovery consonant with the loss or damages suffered, or even sufficient to make a lawsuit economically worthwhile. Nevertheless, as suggested earlier, it is far from pleasant to be accused of unprofessional conduct in the exercise of a consultancy.

Minimizing liability

One way of minimizing possible legal liability is for consultants to ensure that the terms of reference and specifications of the consultancy are clearly and unambiguously spelled out in the consultancy contract. It is not infrequent that ambiguities in this regard lead to expectations on the part of the client which are not intended by the consultant. Such misunderstandings can in turn lead to allegations of failure by the consultant to perform the contract, and to claims and lawsuits. Such a situation should be avoidable if due care is taken in drafting the contract.

Another means of attenuating, if not eliminating, possible liability for the consultant is for him or her to negotiate a clause in the consultancy agreement in which such liability is limited to a specified amount. It would appear that it is not uncommon to find clauses which specify that the consultant's maximum liability for professional acts of misfeasance or nonfeasance (or breach of the consultancy contract) is to be limited to a specified amount or to the total amount of the fee. Obviously such a clause must be negotiated and mutually agreed, and agreement will depend on the relative bargaining strength of the consultant and the client.

In view of the tendency towards litigation shown in certain countries, there is a practice in some of these for consultants to include an arbitration clause in the consultancy contract. Such clauses normally provide that in case of disagreement as to the fulfilment of the obligations of the contract, or in case of disputes otherwise arising under the contract, recourse is to be had to agreed arbitration (a single arbitrator or board of arbitrators) rather than to the courts. In this alternative form of dispute resolution the idea is that arbitration of claims by clients before an arbitrator or arbitration board which is knowledgeable and impartial will guarantee that the consultant is not an innocent victim of the tendency of certain parties to sue at the drop of a hat and for judgements to be out of line with reality. Of course any such clause must be agreed to by the client who, at times, may take the initiative to include an arbitration clause in the consulting contract to better protect his or her interests.

Professional liability insurance

Insurance against professional fault and liability becomes a serious consideration for management consultants who wish to protect themselves from possible economic disaster resulting from the practice of their profession. In some situations the client may insist that the consultant carry appropriate insurance in order that the client is protected in case of damage or loss owing to the activities of the consultant. It may also be mentioned that consultants may insure themselves either generally over a period of time or in respect of a single project. Indeed, the contracting of insurance is current practice for many of the bigger consultancy firms, and particularly those whose practice can give rise to the possibility of costly claims by clients. However, insurance coverage can be quite expensive, with rather high "deductibles" (the insured's contribution in meeting losses) and is not everywhere available. Where it is, premia can amount to a significant percentage of gross billings (as much as 5 per cent or more for consultants who are considered to present higher risks).

Such insurance coverage is not very standardized, even in the United States and Great Britain where it is probably more common than elsewhere. Thus the policies, both in terms of the risks covered, "deductible" amount, premia and other aspects, are frequently to be negotiated between the consultant and the insurer. Obviously, in these negotiations, the particular nature of typical or specific consultancies performed by the consultant will figure prominently in assessing the risk component. There appears to be some movement in certain countries towards professional associations either arranging for or sponsoring individual or group liability insurance for their members.

Finally, consultants would wish to consider whether their insurance coverage should include personal injury claims of third parties (e.g. employees or clients of the client) who may have claims allegedly resulting from the activities and recommendations of the consultant.

Liability awareness and diverse jurisdictions

In any case, consultants should be aware, at least in a general way, of the possible liability they may be exposed to in undertaking consultancies. This is obviously of even greater importance (and more difficult) where consultants operate internationally and hence are subject to differing legislation and jurisprudence depending on the country in which the consultancy takes place. There may, in this regard, be a possibility for the consulting contract to specify the governing (applicable) law, in the event of legal claims arising out of the agreement, by reference to a particular country that is related in one way or another to the contractual relationship (e.g. place of conclusion of the contract, domicile of one or the other of the parties, place where the contract is to be performed, etc.).

For this and other reasons connected with the consultancy, consultants may wish to seek competent legal advice, particularly where the assignment may involve more than minimal risks of possible liability. In availing themselves of recourse to legal advice, consultants, in particular cases, may seek out those lawyers who have specialized in legal liability of professionals, a group of lawyers which is growing in a number of countries.

Professional responsibility

It may be appropriate to conclude this chapter by some thoughts on the relationship between legal liability and professional responsibility in consulting.

Generally speaking, it is a relationship between law and ethics. Legal liability of professionals is a legal construct. It is imposed on professionals by law and is applicable if there are appropriate rules or laws, and an institutional framework able to enforce them. In contrast, professional responsibility can be defined as a set of voluntarily adopted and self-imposed values, norms and constraints, reflecting the professionals' conception of their role in the economy and in society, and their responsibility towards the clients. It is an ethical and cultural concept. Differences in the application of legal liability in various countries are due to different legal systems. Differences in professional responsibility reflect different social and professional cultures.

As discussed in the previous sections of this chapter, professional responsibility covers a wide range of issues in which a consultant can and must choose among alternative modes of behaviour. The quality of the consulting service is the best example. In most assignments, the quality of the services provided will depend entirely or predominantly on the consultant's own judgement, which in turn will be guided by his or her sense of responsibility towards the client. Legal liability will be applicable only to a very small number of extreme cases, where service quality has dropped to the level of malpractice that has caused damage to the client.

A strong sense of professional responsibility, and not a cautiously formulated consulting contract, is therefore the best safeguard in helping the consultant to avoid legal liability. Most instances where the consultants' or other professional advisers' legal liability is called into question are not due to bad intentions but can be traced to obvious breaches of professional responsibility such as inadequate research and fact finding, appointment of incompetent staff, hasty and superficial judgement, or the failure to make the client aware of the risks involved and issues that could not be taken into consideration.

As explained in this chapter, it is the policy of professional consulting associations to define ethical and behavioural norms which express their members' professional responsibility above and beyond the requirements of law. In this way the professional associations guide and educate their members and protect the profession. This protection also includes disciplinary procedures and measures in cases of violation of the codes of conduct. However, in management consulting these disciplinary measures tend to be rather exceptional and their impact has remained limited. Professional associations can deal with cases of conduct that are contrary to the adopted codes if such cases are brought to their attention. They have no mandate and no resources for acting, on a continuing basis, as inspectors of their members' professional behaviour.

Therefore, in the end it is the consulting firm which must define for itself its perception of professional responsibility and integrity. This includes instilling a high sense of professional responsibility in every consultant employed by the firm.

---

[1] See Institute of Management Consultants: *The ascendancy of professionalism* (London, 1993), p. 15.

[2] For a recent discussion of the topic see A. Stark: "What's the matter with business ethics?", in *Harvard Business Review*, May-June 1993, pp. 38-48.

[3] G. Lippitt and R. Lippitt: *The consulting process in action* (La Jolla, California, University Associates, 1978), p. 74.

[4] In some countries a counter-trend may be apparent in very recent years. This legislative and practical development is probably a reaction by law-makers and the judiciary to the excesses of past years.

PART II

THE CONSULTING PROCESS

ENTRY

7

Entry is the initial phase in any consulting process and assignment. During entry, the consultant and the client get together, try to learn as much as possible about each other, discuss and define the reason for which the consultant has been brought in, and on this basis agree on the scope of the assignment and the approach to be taken. The results of these first contacts, discussions, examinations and planning exercises are then reflected in the consulting contract, the signature of which can be regarded as the conclusion of this initial phase.

Entry is very much a matching exercise. The client wants to be sure that he is dealing with the right consultant, and the consultant needs to be convinced that he is the right person, or that his firm is the right consulting organization, to address the problems of this particular client. Such a matching exercise can be difficult technically, but there may be other even more difficult psychological problems. True, it is the client who has invited the consultant, or agreed to consider his offer, and when doing so the client certainly has had some purpose in mind. It may be that he has turned to the consultant with great hopes, or regards him as a last-resort solution in a crisis. Nevertheless, the consultant is a stranger to the client organization. There may be mistrust, uncertainty, anxiety. The consultant has probably been in similar situations before. He knows, however, that his past successes with other clients are by no means a guarantee of repeated success. Furthermore, the client may have decided to talk to several consultants before choosing one for the assignment.

Thus the contacts and activities that constitute the initial phase of the consulting process have to achieve considerably more than the definition of terms of reference and the signature of a contract. Experience shows that the foundations of successful assignments are laid down at this very early stage by establishing mutual trust and empathy, fully agreeing on the "rules of the game", and starting the assignment with shared optimism and a vision of what can be achieved.

The full range of initial contact activities described in this chapter concerns *new* assignments with *new* clients. If a consultant returns to a familiar client organization in repeat business, entry will be simplified. But even in such cases it must not be forgotten that a new assignment with a previous client may involve making new relationships between people.

7.1 Initial contacts

The consultant makes the contact

Contacting potential clients without being solicited by them is one of the ways of marketing consulting services (this will be discussed in detail in Chapter 25). A cold call can arouse the interest of the client, who may decide to keep the consultant's name in mind for the future. Only rarely would a cold contact lead immediately to an assignment.

If the consultant contacts a client about whom he has enough information, and can show that he knows about that client's problems and intentions and has something very relevant to offer, the chances that such an initiative will produce an assignment are better. This can also happen if the consultant is introduced by another client for whom he has worked in the past.

A special case is when public authorities or other organizations publicly announce their intention to carry out a consulting project, and invite consultants to manifest their interest or submit proposals. In such a situation, the consultant will almost certainly not be the only one who offers his services.

The client makes the contact

In most cases it will be the client who makes the first contact. This implies that he or she senses some performance and management problems and some need for independent advice in his or her organization, and for some reason decides to bring in a management consultant. In addition, the client must have a reason for turning to a particular consultant:

- he or she has heard about the consultant's professional reputation;
- a business friend was satisfied by the consultant's services and recommends him or her (very frequent);
- the client found the consultant in a register or directory (less frequent);
- the consultant's publications or interventions at management conferences have impressed the client;
- the client may remember having been contacted by the consultant previously;
- the client likes to return to a consultant who satisfied him or her fully in the past (as we know, repeat business can be very important).

In any event, the consultant will want to find out why the client selected him or her. This will not be difficult.

First meetings

The importance of the consultant's behaviour and performance during the first meetings with the client cannot be overemphasized. While meeting a client to negotiate a specific assignment the consultant is marketing his or her services and it is not certain whether a contract will be concluded. The first meeting should therefore be regarded as a short opportunity to gain the client's confidence and make a favourable impression.

The consultant wants to make sure that he or she will meet the decision maker — the person who is not only technically interested in the assignment but also able to authorize a preliminary diagnostic survey, and who will make sure that resources required by an assignment will be available. If a top executive (managing director, senior administrator) of an important organization agrees to meet the consultant, the consulting firm should send a representative who is at an equally high level.

The question of who should go to the first meeting with the client may present a problem if a consulting organization uses one group of consultants (partners or other seniors) for negotiating assignments, and another group (including both senior and junior staff) for executing them. Some clients know about this pattern of organizing professional services and do not object to it. Many clients do not like it. They emphasize, rightly, that a productive consultant-client relationship starts with the first meetings and preliminary surveys and that it is at this moment that they decide whether they like to work, not only with a consulting organization, but with particular persons in it. Also, they resent an approach whereby the best people represent the consulting firm at the beginning in order to impress clients, but execution is in the hands of lower-calibre staff.

Preparing for initial meetings

Initial meetings require thorough preparation by the consultant. Without going into much detail, he or she collects essential orientation facts about the client, the environment, and the characteristic problems of the sector of activity concerned. The client does not want the consultant to come with ready-made solutions, but expects someone who is very familiar with the kinds of problems that may be found in his or her company. The consultant should find some subtle way of demonstrating this.

In collecting orientation facts, the consultant starts by finding out which products or services the client provides. This information is easily obtained during the very first contact with the client, or by asking for sales literature to be supplied. The nature of the products or services will place the client within a specific sector or trade, and the consultant will want to know its main characteristics and practices. Usually he or she will gather information on:

— terminology commonly used;

— nature and location of markets;

— names and location of main producers;

- types and sources of raw materials;
- weights and measures used in the industry;
- processes and equipment;
- business methods and practices peculiar to the industry;
- laws, rules and customs governing the industry;
- history and growth;
- present economic climate, and main problems and development prospects of the industry.

Trade journals and government publications will provide much of the information, especially on industry sector trends. As regards technology, it is important to find out if the client expects the consultant to know it well or merely show some familiarity with its main characteristics and trends.

Turning to the position of the client's business, the consultant needs some selected information before he meets the client. He may be able to learn the client's financial position, recent operating results and immediate expectations and problems from published annual reports or returns filed in a public registry or credit service. He can also scan brief biographies of the top managers in a publication of the *Who's Who* type (if one exists in the client's country).

Agenda for the meeting

The meeting is a form of investigational interview in which each party seeks to learn about the other. The consultant should encourage the client to do most of the talking: he or she wants the client to speak about his or her firm, the difficulties, hopes and expectations. It is as well for the discussion to develop from the general situation to the particular and to focus eventually on the real issue.

When listening and when putting his or her own questions, the consultant assesses the client's needs in terms of sound management and business practice, personal concerns, perception of consulting, and readiness to work with consultants assuming different types of role. The consultant decides how best to describe the nature and method of consulting as it applies to the client's context. He or she must be sure that the client understands what his or her own role and responsibility will be (see also Chapter 3).

The consultant's key objective at the meeting will be to convince the client that he or she is making the right choice. "Unless their skills are truly unique, professionals never get hired because of their technical capabilities. Excellent capabilities are essential to get you into the final set to be considered, but it is other things that get you hired"[1] (box 7.1).

The individual who invited the consultant into the organization may be the "contact client" and not the "main or primary client" as described in section 3.3, i.e. the person who "owns the problem" and will play the main role in solving it. All too often the consultant is invited in by top management to act as an adviser to somebody lower in the hierarchy of the organization. This "client" may not

> **Box 7.1   What a buyer looks for**
>
> ● In selecting a professional, I am not just buying a service, I am entering into a relationship. Your selling task is to earn my trust and confidence — with an emphasis on the word "earn".
>
> ● How you behave during the interview (or proposal process) will be taken as proxy for how you will deal with me after I retain you.
>
> ● The first thing that will catch my attention is your preparation. There is little so off-putting as someone who begins by asking me some basic facts about my company or situation that they could have found out in advance. Preparation is your opportunity to demonstrate initiative.
>
> ● Professionals who are over-eager to impress come across as insensitive to me. I do not want to hear about you and your firm, I want to talk about me and my situation. Show a sympathetic understanding of my role in my company.
>
> ● You've got to give a favour to get a favour. There is no better way to win my trust than to be helpful to me right from the beginning.
>
> ● Give me an education. Tell me something I did not know. Demonstrate your creativity.
>
> ● To avoid coming across as arrogant, patronizing and pompous turn your assertions into questions. By doing so, you convert possible signs of assertiveness into evidence that you'll respect my opinions and involve me in the thinking process.
>
> ● Don't start telling me how you can solve my problems until I have acknowledged that there's a problem or an opportunity here. Convince me that the issue is big enough to bother with.
>
> ● If I interrupt you, deal with my question. I want to see how you handle yourself if I ask a question, not how practised you are at your standard spiel.
>
> ● Don't try any "closing techniques" on me. If you try to rush me, I'll take it as a sign that you are more interested in making a sale than in helping me.
>
> ● The key is empathy — the ability to enter my world and see it through my eyes.
>
> Source: Excerpts from D. Maister: "How clients choose", in *Managing the professional service firm* (New York, The Free Press, 1993).

feel the need, or may even resent being forced into a consulting assignment by a superior. The consultant may have to spend some time clarifying these relations. Clearly, the client who will work with the consultant should be specifically identified and a rapport should be established between them.

The client may wish to discuss the proposed work with other clients of the consultant, former or current, and may ask for references. This may happen at any moment during the entry phase. In giving names, the consultant must remember confidentiality and cite only those clients who have agreed to provide references.

As regards fees, the client may know how consultants charge for their interventions and be aware of the rates applied. If not, the consultant will have to consider at what stage of the entry phase this information should be given to the client. Some clients prefer to ask about standard fees and other costs right at the outset; others wait with these questions until the consultant has formulated a proposal and made an offer to the client (on consulting fees see Chapter 26).

The client may be eager to proceed without any preliminary diagnosis and planning or, on the contrary, may be hesitant in making up his mind, even though he obviously has problems with which the consultant can help. The consultant should use care and patience in explaining and persuading, and keep mainly to the potential benefits to the client. Pressing for an immediate decision is not a good tactic; it can spoil everything. It is no good, either, if the client gets the impression that the consultant badly needs the assignment because he does not have enough work.

The consultant should not be insistent if he or she is clearly not on the same wave-length as the client. If the client has firm ideas on how the consultant must proceed, and the consultant does not subscribe to them, it is better to drop the assignment. This could be suggested either by the consultant or the client.

Agreement on how to proceed

If the consultant and the client conclude that they are interested in principle in working together, several further questions must be answered. With the exception of straightforward cases, which are often an extension of past work, it would not be reasonable to start an assignment immediately without some preliminary problem analysis and work planning. The terms of business must be discussed and agreed. These are the activities that follow the first meeting.

If the client is ready to agree to a preliminary problem diagnosis,[2] the discussion can move on to the arrangements for it, and cover:

● scope and purpose of a preliminary diagnosis;
● records and information to be made available;
● who should be seen and when;
● how to introduce the consultant;
● attitudes of staff to the matters to be surveyed;
● when to conclude the preliminary diagnosis and how to present proposals to the client;
● payment for the diagnosis.

In addition, the consultant wants to be informed about the selection procedure. The client may have contacted several consultants in order to be able to choose from alternative proposals. He should, in principle, tell the consultant about it. In some cases a formal selection procedure is applied: the consultant's proposals have to be presented in a predetermined format by a given date. The client will then allow a period of time (say 30-45 days) for comparing the proposals received and making a choice.

As regards charging for a preliminary diagnosis or survey, the prevailing practice is that a very short diagnosis (say one or two days), which the consultant needs to do in order to prepare a proposal for the client, is not charged for.

However, if the contract is awarded, the consultant may bill the client for the time spent on this preliminary diagnosis. In contrast, if the preliminary diagnosis is needed to prepare for a complex assignment, and requires a longer time, the opinion prevailing in consultancy circles is that the client should pay for it. This helps to avoid two practices that are considered as undesirable:

— some consultants' practice of using free diagnostic surveys as a marketing tool (since the consultant cannot really work for nothing, another client will then pay for this "free" survey); and

— some clients' practice of collecting a large amount of information and ideas from several consultants (who were all invited to make the same survey), without paying anything for this service.

The practice of free diagnostic surveys used to be quite common in some countries in the past, but recently has tended to disappear.

7.2 Preliminary problem diagnosis

To be able to start an assignment, the consultant must know exactly what the client expects from him. That is why, during the initial meetings, the consultant encourages the client to say as much as he can about his personal perception of the problem that needs to be resolved and the work to be actually done by the consultant. Many organizations insist on doing a thorough internal examination of the problem before deciding to contact a consultant. The client may even have drafted terms of reference (see section 7.3) outlining what he wants the consultant to do.

Yet there is no guarantee that the client's perception and description of the problem is correct and that the consultant receives complete and unbiased information. Before starting to plan the assignment and proposing a specific job to the client, the consultant should undertake an independent problem diagnosis. In fact, an experienced consultant starts such a diagnosis right from the very first moment he is in touch with the client. Everything interests him: who contacted him and how; how he is received at the first meeting; what sort of questions the client asks; if there are any undertones in those questions; what the client says about his business and his competitors; if he is relaxed or tense, and so on. There comes a moment, however, when the consultant has to sort out this information, get some hard data, and complete the picture by looking at the problem from new angles — for example, by talking to people other than those who were involved in the first meetings.

Scope of the diagnosis

The purpose of the preliminary problem diagnosis is not to propose measures for solving the problem, but to define and plan a consulting assignment or project which will have this effect. The preliminary diagnosis limits its scope to a quick gathering and analysis of essential information which, according to

147

the consultant's experience and judgement, is needed to understand the problem correctly, to see it in the wider context of the client organization's activities, achievements, goals and other existing or potential business and management problems, and realistically to assess opportunities for helping the client.

The scale of this preliminary diagnosis depends very much on the nature of the problem. Very specific and rather technical issues do not normally require a comprehensive survey of the whole client organization. On the other hand, an experienced consultant knows that he or she must avoid the trap of accepting a client's narrow definition of a technical problem without personally looking into constraints and tendencies that may make the solution of that problem an impossible task, or may show that the problem is much more or much less serious than the client assumes. Therefore even if the problem lies in one functional area only, or concerns the application of some specific techniques, a truly professional consultant will always be interested in the more general and global characteristics of the client organization.

If the consultant is brought in to deal with a general problem, such as deteriorating financial results, or inability to maintain the same pace of innovation as competitors, a general and comprehensive diagnosis or management survey of the client organization is essential.

The time allocated to preliminary problem diagnosis is relatively short. As a rule, one to four days would be required. In the case of more complex assignments concerning several aspects of the client's business, five to ten days may be needed. If an extensive diagnostic survey is required (e.g. in preparing company turnarounds, major reorganizations, buy-outs or mergers, or for any other reason), this is no longer a preliminary diagnosis, but an in-depth diagnostic survey, which will be described in Chapter 12.

An outline of a management survey, including checklists of topics to be examined in various areas of management, is reproduced in Appendix 4.

Some methodological guidelines

Preliminary problem diagnosis follows the same basic rules and procedures and uses the same analytical techniques as any problem diagnosis. These will be reviewed in detail in Chapter 8. Many consulting firms have developed their own approaches and guidelines for a quick assessment of clients' businesses.

The diagnosis includes the gathering and analysis of information on the client's activities, performance and perspectives. It also includes discussions with selected managers and other key people, and in certain cases also with people outside the client organization. Basically, the consultant is not interested in details, but is looking for principal trends, relationships and proportions. An experienced consultant keeps his eyes open and can sense potential problems or opportunities behind apparent details that may escape another observer: the way people talk to each other and speak about each other, the respect for hierarchical relations, the cleanliness of workshops and offices, the handling of confidential information, the courtesy of the receptionist, and so on.

It is essential to take *a dynamic and comprehensive view* of the organization, its environment, resources, goals, activities, achievements and perspectives.

Dynamism in this context means examining key achievements and events in the life of the organization and probable future trends as reflected in existing plans and assessed by the consultant personally. The client's strengths and weaknesses ought to be viewed in a time perspective — a present strength may be merely short term, while a new weakness, hidden at the present time, may become a threat to the client's organization in the long term. The consultant is particularly interested in future opportunities — indeed, the detailed diagnosis and further work to be proposed to the client should be oriented towards these opportunities above all.

This approach is summarized in figure 7.1.

Figure 7.1   The consultant's approach to a management survey

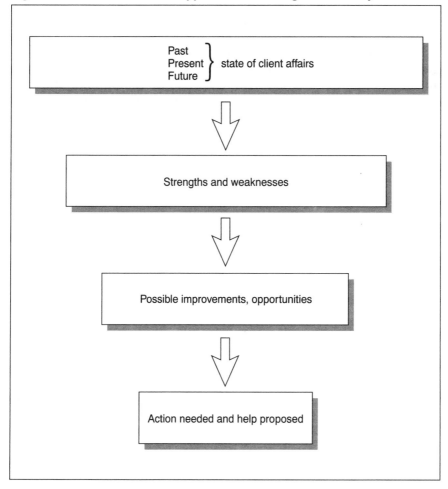

As already mentioned, even if the problem is, or is likely to be, in a single functional area, the consultant will take a comprehensive view of the organization. How far and how comprehensive is a matter of experience and judgement, and no universal recipe can be given. As the purpose is to determine what to achieve in the course of a consulting assignment of a certain size and duration, most management consultants emphasize the need for some wider appraisal of the organization before confirming the existence even of a fairly limited problem, and the feasibility of handling it within certain terms of reference.

It is recommended that the consultant should proceed *from the general to the particular*: from overall objectives and global performance indicators to the reasons for substandard performance or missed opportunities (or to interesting future opportunities), and then to an examination in some detail of selected areas of the organization's activities. An approach which starts the other way round, by examining each management function (production, purchasing, marketing, etc.) in turn and hoping for a balanced synthesis at the end, will entail much unnecessary work and might well prove misdirected. The movement from the general to the particular helps the consultant to limit the preliminary diagnostic survey to matters of critical concern to the client organization, or conversely may persuade him that, to stand the best chance of achieving the results expected, the inquiry must take into account every aspect of the enterprise's operation.

Such an approach implies that the consultant's analysis will focus on basic relationships and proportions in the client organization, such as the following:

- relationships and proportions between major processes, functions and activity areas (e.g. allocation of human and financial resources to marketing, research and development, production, administration);

- relationships between main inputs and outputs (e.g. sales related to materials consumed, the wage bill and the total workforce);

- relationships between the principal indicators of performance, effectiveness and efficiency (e.g. productivity, profitability, resource utilization, growth);

- relationships between global performance indicators and main factors affecting their magnitude in a positive or negative way (e.g. influence of the volume of work in progress on working capital and profitability);

- the contribution of the main divisions and product (service) lines to the results (profitability, image, etc.) achieved by the organization as a whole.

The comprehensive, overall approach is combined with a functional approach as necessary. For example, the precarious financial situation of a company may be caused by problems in any functional area: by badly organized production, by costly or ineffective marketing, by excessive spending on unproductive research, by the shortage or high cost of capital, or something else. As already mentioned, if an assignment is likely to be exclusively or mainly in one technical area, this area will need to be examined in greater depth than other areas, and the examination of the organization as a whole will be limited to what is necessary.

In summary, this approach will tell the consultant if the work envisaged can make a meaningful contribution to the principal objectives of the client organization and what critical relationships and linkages are likely to affect the course of the assignment.

Using comparison

The consultant is fully aware that every client organization is unique and will have to be treated as such. However, he or she needs reference points which could guide him or her in a preliminary quick assessment of strengths, weaknesses, development prospects and desirable improvements. The consultant will find them by making comparisons with:

— past achievements (if the organization's performance has deteriorated and the problem is essentially corrective);

— the client's own objectives, plans and standards (if real performance does not measure up to them);

— other comparable organizations (to assess what has been achieved elsewhere and whether the same thing would be possible in the client organization);

— sectoral standards available in the consulting firm or another source of data for inter-firm comparison.

A comparison of well-selected data with sectoral standards or with data from specific similar organizations is a powerful diagnostic tool. It helps not only in quick orientation, but also in making the client aware of the real situation, which may often be quite different from what he or she believes.

The consultant would make comparisons not only when working with figures, but also in assessing qualitative information (e.g. the organizational structure, the corporate culture, the computer applications, or the market-research techniques used). In other words, the consultant's work is greatly facilitated if he can ask himself what levels of performance and what sorts of problems he would normally expect to find in that type of organization to which the client enterprise belongs.

Such a question is meaningful if the consultant has some method of classifying and comparing organizations (e.g. by sector, product type, size, ownership, market served and the like). For each class there would be a list of various attributes that are characteristic of it. Well-established consulting firms try to provide their consultants with such data and guide them by means of manuals and check-lists for management surveys and company appraisals. It is in the interest of the younger firms in the profession to acquire or develop such documentation.[3]

Notwithstanding certain general rules, senior consultants undertaking diagnostic surveys tend to have their personal priorities and specific approaches. Many of them start by looking at principal financial data, since these reflect the level and results of the activities of the enterprise in a way which best lends itself to synthesis. Others emphasize production: they believe that a simple factory tour is most revealing and tells an experienced observer a great deal about the quality of management. Still others prefer to examine markets, products and services before turning to a financial appraisal and further investigations. These are just different starting-points reflecting personal experience and preferences: eventually the consultant has to study all areas and questions needed for a global diagnosis in order to see the problem in the right context and perspective.

The client's involvement

It would be an error to think that while the first contact meetings involved intensive and direct interaction between the consultant and the client, the consultant then carries out the preliminary problem diagnosis single-handed, confining contacts with the client to interviewing certain people and requesting information. The dialogue with the client is pursued during problem diagnosis. This will show how the client feels about various aspects of the business: what its goals, objectives and technical and human capabilities are, what its potential is for making changes, and the style of consulting that should be applied in his case. The client, on the other hand, learns to know the consultant better and has an opportunity to appreciate his or her professional way of obtaining information, establishing contacts with people, grasping the overall situation and distilling essential facts from the vast amount of data that can be found in any organization.

Sources of information

A successful diagnostic survey is based on the rapid collection of selective information that reveals the type and extent of help that the consultant can give to the client. Diagnostic data tend to be global in nature. The consultant is interested in details only if they are indicative of some major problems and help to elucidate the problems for which he or she has been brought in. For example, some detailed insights into the work style of top management may help to diagnose overall management patterns and practices that determine the working atmosphere in the whole organization.

The main sources of information for a preliminary diagnostic survey are *published material and records* (box 7.2), observation and interviewing by the consultant, and contacts outside the client organization.

Observing activities and interviewing key people are vital to information gathering. Tours of the client's premises, seeing people in action and hearing their views, worries and suggestions, give first-hand knowledge of how the organization works in practice, how it lives, the pace it sets and the relationships between its workers. These are invaluable insights which records cannot convey, but extensive interviewing and observation of activities are beyond the possibilities of preliminary surveys.

Contacts with other organizations associated with the client may be made either by the consultant, or by the client personally. During their work, consultants make contact with many organizations apart from those of their clients. These contacts not only assist the current assignment but also establish a relationship which can be used in future work. For example, contacts may be established with trade unions, employers' and trade associations, sectoral research institutions, or management associations.

The consultant informs the client of the purpose and nature of any contact made. The client personally may contact some outside bodies (e.g. employers' associations), and should know of any consultant contact. Talking to the client's customers is an essential source of information and ideas for management consultants, but contacts with customers should not be made without the client's agreement.

Box 7.2   Information materials for preliminary surveys

Client's publications:

— annual financial and activity reports;
— financial, statistical, trade and customs returns to government, trade associations and credit organizations;
— economic surveys;
— sales promotion material such as catalogues and advertising brochures;
— press releases, interviews given by management, etc.

Information from other published sources:

— conditions and trends in the client's economic sector, including technological developments;
— information on business firms in the sector;
— industrial outlook studies;
— trade statistics and reports;
— industry norms and key business ratios;
— regulations which the client must observe;
— corporation income tax returns (if published);
— labour-management relations.

Client's internal records and reports:

— information on resources, objectives, plans and performance;
— information on plant, technologies and equipment used;
— reports on financial results and costs of activities, services and products;
— minutes of board and management committee meetings;
— tax returns;
— sales statistics;
— movement of material;
— staff appraisal, etc.

Documentation files of the consulting firm:

— information on the client if not a new one;
— information on the sector and similar organizations.

Alternative approaches

The approach described in the previous paragraphs is the classical consultant's approach: it is the consultant who performs the diagnosis as an expert, using data collection and analytical techniques of his or her choice, with some participation on the part of the client. Moving closer to the process function along the continuum of consulting roles, the client and his staff become more active and the consultant focuses on providing effective diagnostic methods instead of personally carrying out the diagnosis.

For example, some consultants have used *problem-identification workshops* which can be run as part of a problem- and action-oriented management development programme, or used directly as a technique for identifying problems on which the organization will have to act. In this workshop or group approach, the members of the group develop their own lists of problems requiring action, compare and discuss their lists, and agree on a joint list and on priorities. They then work separately on a more detailed definition and analysis of the principal problem(s) from each list, paying attention to relations between various problems. This is followed by other meetings, where individual analyses are compared, a collectively agreed analysis is made and action proposals are developed.

This exercise can be organized in *one group*, or as *a system of groups*. The initial groups can be heterogeneous (from various levels and functions of management), thus enabling one organizational process or problem to be examined from several angles. Alternatively, technically homogeneous, functional or departmental groups can first look at one problem from their specific technical angles (financial, organizational, production, staffing, etc.), followed by workshops involving representatives of the groups, who meet to compare and harmonize the different viewpoints and develop a problem definition that is endorsed by all groups. Often it is more effective if groups look at organizational processes rather than at fragmented tasks and units.

Management can decide to involve an external or internal consultant in these group exercises. The consultant's approach may be low-key, reminding the group of the appropriate procedure, of criteria that may have been overlooked, and of methodological errors that might lead to false conclusions.

The use of the group approach is often preceded by a thorough explanation of diagnostic, problem-solving and performance-improvement methods. If appropriate, the consultant also provides technical information on the problem under discussion (e.g. data from similar organizations for comparison), or helps to collect input data on which the groups can start to work.

Self-diagnosis by individual business owners or managers is another approach which has been used in assisting smaller firms in various countries. The consultant meets with a group of owners or managers of small firms, provides them with a self-diagnostic instrument adapted to their needs, and explains the method to be used. He or she is then available to review the results of the diagnosis and proposals for action with each individual. Alternatively, the business people may agree to meet again and compare the ratios and other indicators characteristic of their firms, and exchange views on factors explaining differences in performance. They will then decide individually or as a group on the courses of action to follow in each firm. The consultant may be engaged to help them in further group work, or work separately with individual members of the group (see also Chapter 18).

Self-diagnosis can be an individual exercise undertaken by one client firm from the outset. The consultant may supply check-lists and methodological tools for the client's use. Or the client applies his or her own diagnostic approach based on industry experience and practices, and the consultant's role is to check the client's self-diagnosis for completeness and accuracy. The consultant would also help the client to view the business from a wider perspective.

Further approaches are described in section 4.6.

7.3 Terms of reference

Terms of reference (see box 7.3) are the initial statement of the work to be undertaken by a consultant. As mentioned in the previous section, when the consultant first meets the client, he or she may find that the client has already prepared terms of reference for the assignment. This is the approach taken by one category of clients, who prefer to do their own problem identification and diagnosis before talking to any consultant.

There is a second category of clients, whose practice is to draft the terms of reference after preliminary problem diagnosis done by a consultant. They may use one consultant specifically for preliminary diagnosis and drafting terms of reference. These terms are then used for initiating a formal selection procedure to designate a consultant who will execute the assignment. The consultant used to produce the terms of reference may even be excluded from this procedure.

Box 7.3   Terms of reference — Check-list

1. Description of the problem(s) to be solved
2. Objectives and expected results of the assignment (what is to be achieved, final product)
3. Background and supporting information (on client organization, other related projects and consultancies, past efforts to solve problems, etc.)
4. Budget estimate or resource limit
5. Timetable (starting and completion dates, key stages and control dates)
6. Interim and final reporting (dates, form, to whom, etc.)
7. Inputs to be provided by the client (further information and documentation, staff time, secretarial support, transport, etc.)
8. Exclusions from the assignment (what will not be its object)
9. Constraints and other factors likely to affect the project
10. Profile and competences of eligible consultants
11. Contact persons and addresses

A third category of clients does not use any formal terms of reference in preparing an assignment and choosing a consultant. Such clients leave the definition of the work to be done to the consulting contract.

The main reasons for these different practices are explained below.

(1) If terms of reference are used:

— the client's policy is to do as much analytical and planning work before considering to use a consultant; often this will be the case of assignments dealing with relatively narrow and well-defined technical issues;

— the client (usually in the public sector) is obliged by existing regulations to draft formal terms of reference, and obtain their approval, as an initial step in a formal consultant selection procedure.

(2) If terms of reference are not used:

— the client (usually in the private sector) prefers to select a consultant thoroughly, do preliminary problem diagnosis and define the scope of the assignment jointly with him or her. The client then confirms the choice on the basis of a proposal (offer) received from the consultant, without using the intermediate stage of drafting terms of reference.

Most management consultants are able to adapt their approach to these various client preferences. Yet when presented with terms of reference drafted by the client or another consultant, the consultant must be cautious in deciding whether to accept these terms at face value. If these terms describe an assignment that is not feasible, the consultant might be caught in a trap.

7.4   Assignment strategy and plan

During his or her initial contacts with the client and the subsequent preliminary problem diagnosis, the consultant should have collected and evaluated enough information to be able to plan the assignment. This is what the client expects at this stage: he or she will want to receive not only the consultant's findings on the problem to be tackled, but also a proposal describing what the consultant suggests doing and under what terms help is offered.

In fact, right from the first contact with the client the consultant has been thinking of the approach to take, but has suspended judgement until after he or she has become better acquainted with the situation. For example, the co-operation of the client's staff during preliminary problem diagnosis shows what consulting mode may be most appropriate (see Chapter 3), and the quality of the data found during this activity suggests how much time will be needed for detailed fact finding and analysis.

A fundamental aspect of designing and planning a consulting assignment is the choice of *assignment strategy*. By this we mean the respective roles to be played by the consultant and the client, the consulting mode chosen, the pace of operations and the way (and the time sequence) in which they will apply and harmonize their interventions, and the resources allocated to the assignment.

The *assignment plan*, including the strategy that will be followed, is formally presented to the client as a proposal, as described in section 7.5 below. Assignment planning and drafting of a proposal are not normally finalized at the client's premises. Unless it has been otherwise agreed, the consultant returns to the office with the data collected during preliminary problem diagnosis and works on the proposal, often in collaboration with other senior members of the consulting firm. The consultant should never take more time than the client expects. Momentum can be lost and relations can cool down if the client feels that the matter is not receiving enough attention.

The main elements of assignment planning are given below.

Summary of problem identification

The conclusions from preliminary problem diagnosis are summarized and the consultant presents a description of the problem. This may include a comparison with the original problem definition made by the client: the consultant may suggest widening or narrowing down this definition, or refer to other problems discovered and to possible developments (e.g. the effects of recession, or tensions in labour relations) that may take place during the assignment. As appropriate, the problem will be set in the wider context of the client's objectives, trends and resources.

Objectives to achieve and action to take

The assignment plan then outlines the objectives to be achieved and the kind of technical activities which the assignment will consist of (redesigning an information system, reorganizing distribution networks, introducing a new staff training programme, and the like).

Whenever possible, the objectives should be presented as performance measures *in quantified terms*, describing benefits that will accrue to the client if the assignment is successfully completed. Global financial benefits are commented on to ensure that the client understands the implications. For example, savings from a reduced inventory of finished goods would only be achieved when stocks had been run down, and this might require production to be cut back for some time. Benefits in other terms are stated as appropriate, e.g. output would increase from one level to a new level (in this case the client would be warned of the need for orders to keep the factory occupied).

Social and qualitative benefits may be difficult to express in figures. They are described as precisely and clearly as possible and carefully explained. Vague notions that lend themselves to many different interpretations should be avoided.

However, at this early planning stage, before a detailed investigation has been carried out and some work on alternative proposals done, it may be impossible to indicate all benefits with absolute precision. If this is the case, it is preferable to indicate the order of magnitude of the benefits to be achieved (e.g. sales increased by 20 to 30 per cent). Also, if the consultant regards certain objectives as feasible on condition that the client takes certain measures (which may include difficult restructuring, organizational or personnel decisions), these conditions should be specified as clearly as possible.

Phases of the assignment and timetable

The steps in which the assignment will be undertaken have to be programmed in some detail. Basically, the consultant will follow the logic of the consulting process as briefly outlined in section 1.4 and described in detail in Chapters 7-11, but will adjust it to the nature of the assignment and to the client's conditions and preferences. This is essential, not only for work scheduling but for several other reasons.

The nature of the consultant's and the client's activities will be changing from phase to phase. Both parties must know exactly what the other party expects at each phase. In particular, the client will want to know whether the assignment is making headway towards its final objectives. To make control possible, the assignment plan will describe the outcome of each phase and define what reports to the client will be submitted at what points during the assignment. A major phase may require an end-of-phase report, but in long and complex assignments short interim reports may be required at the end of each subphase or periodically (monthly, quarterly), for monitoring progress and allowing regular payments to be made to the consultant.

The time dimension of the assignment plan is a key element of strategy. What pace of work should be adopted? The urgency of the client's needs is the main determinant. But there are other considerations, such as:

- the client's and the consultant's technical, manpower and financial capacities;

- the feasible and optimum pace of change (as discussed in Chapters 4 and 5);

- the desirability of a phased approach to implementation (starting in a unit that is best prepared for change and willing to cooperate, introducing the new scheme on an experimental basis first, etc.).

Role definition

This is another strategic dimension of assignment planning. The consultant will suggest the style or mode of consulting that he or she considers most appropriate with regard to the nature of the problem and the motivation and capabilities of the client's staff. A general definition of the mode to be used is not enough. Precise arrangements have to be proposed. They should specify:

— what activities will be carried out by the client or by the consultant;

— what data and documents will be prepared by whom;

— what meetings, working parties, project groups and other forms of group work will be used and who will be involved;

— what special training and information activities will be undertaken.

It may be both possible and desirable to foresee a shift in roles during the assignment. For example, intensive training of the client's staff in the subject area covered and in problem-solving and change methodologies, carried out at the beginning, may enable the consultant to suggest reducing his presence and changing his role during subsequent phases.

Lack of precision in defining role expectations for each phase of the assignment causes much misunderstanding. As already mentioned, this happens frequently in connection with implementation. Is the consultant's objective to design a new scheme and submit it in a report, or to help the client to implement the scheme? Who is responsible for what? Where does the consultant's responsibility end? What does the client actually want? Does he want another report, or is he really keen to complete a change? In designing an effective assignment these questions must not remain unanswered.

Following a detailed role definition, the consultant can determine the resources required by the assignment in each phase. These include resources to be made available:

- by the consultant (consultant time, material, clerical support, special computing, research, legal advice, and other services), including their cost;
- by the client (management and staff time, liaison arrangements, administrative support, office facilities, resources for testing, experimental work, computing, and so on).

Obviously, the client will want to know what resources provided by the consultant will be used and paid for. But more than that: the client will participate, too, and the inputs required from his or her organization may be high. The failure to figure them out as precisely as possible may cause considerable difficulties once work has started and the client learns, to his great astonishment, that he is supposed to do something which he has not counted on doing at all.

It may be difficult to tell the client at this stage how much implementation will cost: it is the action planning phase (Chapter 9) that will generate precise figures. None the less, a preliminary assessment ought to be made in all assignments that are likely to propose costly changes (e.g. new investment or compensation to staff whose employment will be terminated). The client should have the opportunity to look into these probable financial implications before deciding whether to embark on such an assignment.

The costing and pricing of an assignment is discussed in detail in section 26.7.

7.5 Proposal to the client[4]

As a rule, the assignment proposed will be described in a document presented to the client for approval and decision. It may be given different names: survey report, technical proposal, project document, project plan, contract proposal, and the like. Some clients require the consultant to present the proposals in a predetermined format. This facilitates study by the client and his evaluation of alternative proposals received from several consultants. Furthermore, the format of the proposal may correspond to the format of the consulting contract to be signed.

A proposal submitted to the client is an important selling document. It is not enough for the consultant to have a clear vision of how to execute the assignment to make it a total success: he or she must be able to describe this vision on paper in a way that will make it clear to other people. This may include individuals who did not meet the consultant on the first visit to the client organization, and will be formulating their opinions of him or her solely on the basis of the written proposal.

The client should be impressed by the technical quality of the proposal and pleased by its business-like presentation. Writing "winning" proposals is an art that no consultant can afford to ignore.

Sections of the proposal

In most cases the following four sections are included in the proposal to the client:

— technical section;

— staffing section;

— consultant background section;

— financial and other terms section.

The technical section describes the consultant's preliminary assessment of the problem, the purpose to be pursued, the approach to be taken, and the work programme to be followed. These topics were reviewed in sections 7.2 to 7.4 above.

One caveat has to be made: the consultant and the client may have a different conception of how detailed and specific this technical section should be. If it is too global, the client may feel that the consultant is not really explaining what he or she proposes to do. In contrast, if it is too detailed and specific, the consultant may have gone beyond assignment planning, and may already have embarked on executing the assignment without having obtained the client's agreement. This may present no problem if a cooperative relationship has already been established and the consultant is sure to get the assignment. If it is not clear who will be chosen (e.g. if several consultants were invited to submit proposals), this may prove to be a reckless approach: giving away free expertise before the assignment has been approved.

The staffing section gives the names and profiles of the consultant's staff who will be executing the assignment. This also includes the senior consultants (partners, project managers) who will be responsible for guiding and supervising the team working at the client's organization. As a rule, the proposal guarantees the availability of particular persons for a limited period of time, say six to eight weeks. If the client delays the response, or decides to postpone the assignment, he knows that he will have to accept other consultants of a comparable profile, or renegotiate the assignment.

The consultant background section describes the experience and competence of the consulting organization as it relates to the needs of the particular client. There may be a general subsection with standard information given to all clients (including a section on ethical standards and professional practice adhered to by the consultant) and a specific subsection referring to similar work done and providing evidence that the consultant will be the right partner to choose. References concerning former clients will be used only with these clients' prior agreement.

The financial and other terms section indicates the cost of the services, provisions for cost increases and contingencies, and the schedule and other indications for paying fees and reimbursing expenses, and settling all commitments. If the client applies a selection procedure, the financial section may have to be submitted separately.

The consultant may have a standard description of his or her terms of contract or business and attach it to the proposal. Conversely, some clients insist on using their own terms and the consultant may have to comply with these if he or she does not want to lose the contract.

Presenting the proposal

Many consultants prefer not just to mail the proposal, but to hand it over to the client in a meeting which starts with a short oral (and visual) introduction of the report's summary. The consultant is ready to answer questions about the start of the proposed assignment. If the client is keen and ready to begin, there are obvious advantages in doing so while the enthusiasm is there and the contacts established are fresh in people's minds. But an early date may not be easy to meet because of existing commitments.

Although the consultant would obviously like to have a decision before the end of the meeting, the client may have good reasons for not wanting to give one. He or she should not be pressed. A professional consultant knows whether his or her performance was good enough and can only exercise patience over the outcome.

If the client wants to read the proposal prior to the oral presentation, or wants no oral presentation, the consultant will hand the report over without insisting on a meeting.

The client's reaction

A public-sector client is usually bound by rules which specify a minimum number of tenders and an internal evaluation procedure before awarding a contract. But private-sector clients may also use a selection procedure based on the evaluation of alternative proposals, in particular for large and complex assignments. In such cases it may take several weeks or months before the client will be in a position to decide.

The consultant wants to know by what criteria he or she will be judged. As a rule, the client will inform the consultant about these criteria in the original invitation to submitting proposals. In most cases, the client will also give the names of the competitors. The consultant should be aware of the relative weight that will be assigned to the various aspects of the proposal in the selection procedure. For example, the World Bank recommends its borrowers to give a weight of 10-20 per cent to the consulting firm's general experience, 25-40 per cent to the work plan, and 40-60 per cent to key personnel proposed for the assignment.[5] Thus, even a highly competent consulting firm stands little chance in a selection procedure if it does not propose consultants of the right calibre.

Negotiating the proposal

The client may be keen to use the consultant's services, but may not be happy with some aspects of the proposal. For example, the client feels that he or she can play a more active role than foreseen by the consultant and personally undertake various tasks not requiring costly external expertise, or he or she wishes to suggest a different timetable. It is normal to review these and similar technical aspects of the proposal and to make changes if the consultant is able to modify his or her approach.

As regards fees, many consultants emphasize that their rates represent a fair charge for a high-quality professional service and hence are not negotiable. A minor provision for the negotiation of fee rates is sometimes made in countries where this is the customary way of doing business (see Chapter 26).

What is not included in the proposal

In parallel with drafting his proposal to the client, the consultant is preparing internal (confidential) notes on the client organization and ideas for the approach to take (box 7.4). These notes (sometimes called "survey notes")

Box 7.4   Confidential information on the client organization

1.   Names of managers met and information collected on them

2.   Comments on organizational relationships, management style, and cultural values and norms

3.   Attitudes of various people in the client organization to consultants and likely reactions to the assignment

4.   Best sources of internal information. Sources that cannot be trusted

5.   Additional comments and data on the problem for which the assignment is proposed

6.   Other problems identified, potential problems, or areas of further work not tackled in the proposed assignment and not discussed with the client

7.   Useful background information collected and not used in the proposal to the client

8.   Any other suggestions to the operating team that will execute the assignment

---

are particularly important in a larger consulting firm if different professionals are used for planning and for executing assignments, and if several units of the same consulting or multi-service professional firm may be in touch with the same client organization on various matters.

7.6   The consulting contract

The entry phase of the consulting process can be regarded as successfully completed if the consultant and the client conclude a contract whereby they agree to work together on an assignment or project.[6] What is the usual form of such a contract? What can we recommend to our readers?

Contracting practices regarded as normal and advisable depend very much on each country's legal system and customary ways of doing business. New consultants have to seek legal advice on the form of contracting authorized by local legislation and preferred by business and government organizations. In addition, they can get advice from the local consultants' association and from professional colleagues. Where alternative forms of contract are admitted, choosing one or more will be a matter of the consulting firm's policy and judgement on what is most appropriate in dealing with particular clients. The form chosen must ensure that mutual commitments will be understood and respected, and misunderstanding avoided on either side.

In some countries the contracting practices in professional services are well defined and enough literature is available. In other countries this is not yet the case. Thus a consultant doing work abroad may have to compromise between what is customary in the home country and what the law and practice in the client's country demand.

The three main forms of contracting are verbal agreement, letter of agreement and written contract. The aspects of consulting assignments that are normally dealt with in contracting are listed in box 7.5 (overleaf). These aspects do not represent sections of a standard contract since various arrangements are possible (for detailed comments see Appendix 5).

Verbal agreement

A verbal agreement is one given by the client orally either after having reviewed the consultant's written proposal, or even without having reviewed a proposal if the client feels that the consultant is the right one and will have the required professional approach. Verbal agreement was used extensively in the first decades of management consulting, but now the tendency is to use written contracts. Nevertheless, those who believe strongly in the power of the written word and legal texts would be surprised to find out that even nowadays a lot of consulting is undertaken on the basis of verbal agreements.

Verbal agreement may suffice if the following conditions exist:

— the consultant and the client are well versed in professional practice;

Box 7.5 What to cover in contracting — Check-list

1. Contracting parties (the consultant and the client)
2. Scope of the assignment (as discussed in sections 7.4 and 7.5: objectives, description of work, starting date, timetable, volume of work)
3. Work products and reports (documentation and reports to be handed over to the client)
4. Consultant and client inputs (expert and staff time and other inputs)
5. Fees and expenses (fees to be billed, expenses reimbursed to the consultant)
6. Billing and payment procedure
7. Professional responsibilities (handling confidential information, avoiding conflict of interest, and other aspects as appropriate — see section 6.2)
8. Copyright (covering the products of the consultant's work during the assignment)
9. Liability (the consultant's liability for damages caused to the client, limitation of liability — see section 6.5)
10. Use of subcontractors (by the consultant)
11. Termination or revision (when and how to be suggested by either party)
12. Arbitration (jurisdiction, procedure for handling disputes)
13. Signatures and dates

— they trust each other totally;
— they are familiar with each other's terms of business (the client knows the terms applied by the consultant and the consultant knows what to expect from the client, e.g. if the client is able to make any advance payment, or can accept monthly billing, how long it takes to approve a payment, etc.);
— the assignment is not too big and complex (if this is the case, it may be difficult to manage the relationship from both sides without any formal document).

Verbal agreement would be used more frequently in repeat business than with new clients. If a verbal agreement is used, the consultant may produce a detailed record of what was agreed, for his or her own benefit and to make sure that other colleagues in the firm are fully and correctly informed. Sending an information copy to the client may be useful.

Letter of agreement

A letter of agreement (other terms used: letter of engagement, of appointment, of confirmation, of intent) is the prevailing way of contracting professional services in many countries. Having received the consultant's proposal (proposal letter), the client sends him or her a letter of agreement confirming that he or she accepts the proposal and the suggested terms of reference. The letter may set out new conditions which modify or supplement the consultant's proposal. In this case it is the consultant who in turn replies as to whether or not he or she accepts these new conditions. Or all this can be negotiated orally and then reduced to a written agreement.

Alternatively, it is the client who drafts the letter describing the work required and the proposed terms of reference, and the consultant who gives the written agreement.

Written contract

The use of a written consulting contract duly signed by the parties involved may be required for various reasons. It may be imposed by law or by the client's own regulations on the use of external services (this is the case in nearly all public organizations and international agencies, and many private businesses). It is often the best form to choose if the consultant and the client come from different business and legal environments and might easily misinterpret each other's intentions and attitudes. It is advisable, albeit not absolutely necessary, in the case of large and complex assignments involving many different people on both the client's and the consultant's side.

It may be the client's practice to use a standard form of contract. Most management consultants are quite flexible and accept various forms of contract. However, they should not underestimate the need for consulting their lawyer if a new and unusual form of contract is proposed to them by a client.

As a rule, the consultant will know in advance that he or she will have to sign a formal contract. He or she should obtain the standard form from the client, show it to a lawyer, and keep it in mind in preparing proposals for the assignment. Thus the consultant will be able to formulate the proposals so that they could be directly included in the body of the contract, or attached to it without making any substantial modifications.

A consulting firm should also have its own standard form of contract. It will be used with clients who do not have a standard form of their own and expect the consultant to propose one.

Built-in flexibility

The purpose of contracting is to provide a clear orientation for joint work and to protect the interests of both parties. This implies a certain degree of imagination and flexibility.

At any stage of the assignment, the nature and the magnitude of the problem may change and other priorities may become more urgent. The consultant's and the client's capabilities and perceptions of what approach will be effective are also evolving. Obviously, a professional consultant will not insist on continuing with a job (as stipulated in a contract) if that job is no longer required and causes unnecessary expense to the client.

Whatever form of contract is used, it should be agreed under what conditions and in what way either the consultant or the client can withdraw from the contract, or can suggest a revision. In some cases it may be better to contract only for one phase of the assignment (e.g. fact finding and detailed diagnosis) and delay a decision on the work to follow until enough information has been collected and examined.

Psychological contract

In an era in which more and more features of our lives are regulated and constrained by legislation, and formal contracts tend to become more and more common in professional sectors, it is useful to underline that the formal legal side of contracting is *not* the main one. We have explained why a well-drafted formal contract may be required. However, the reader should keep in mind that excellent consulting assignments are those where another type of "contract" exists, which is not codified in any document and is not easy to describe: a psychological contract, under which the consultant and the client cooperate in an atmosphere of trust and respect, believing that the approach taken by the other party is the best one to bring the assignment to a successful completion. Such a "contract" cannot be replaced by even the finest legal document.

---

[1] D. Maister: "How clients choose", in *Managing the professional service firm* (New York, The Free Press, 1993), p. 112.

[2] Various terms are used: preliminary problem diagnosis, diagnostic study, management survey, diagnostic survey, consulting survey, diagnostic evaluation, business review, business diagnosis, pilot study, management audit, company appraisal, etc.

[3] Similar classifications, with empirical or recommended performance data, can be obtained from engineering consultants, sectoral research and information centres, suppliers of equipment, centres of inter-firm comparison and other sources.

[4] A more detailed discussion of consultant selection, including various procedures, criteria and forms of contract used, can be found in M. Kubr: *How to select and use consultants: A client's guide*, Management Development Series No. 31 (Geneva, ILO, 1993).

[5] World Bank: *Guidelines for the use of consultants by World Bank borrowers and by the World Bank as executing agency* (Washington, DC, 1981), p. 14.

[6] See also Kubr, op. cit., Chs. 4 and 6; H. L. Shenson: *The contract and fee-setting guide for consultants and professionals* (New York, Wiley, 1990); and N. Pyeatt: *The consultant's legal guide* (Washington, DC, Bermont Books, 1980).

DIAGNOSIS

8

8.1 Conceptual framework of diagnosis

What is diagnosis?

Diagnosis, the second phase of the consulting process, is the first fully operational phase. The purpose of diagnosis is to examine the problem faced and the purposes pursued by the client in detail and in depth, identify the factors and forces that are causing and influencing the problem, and prepare all information needed for deciding how to orient work on the solution to the problem. An equally important aim is to examine the relationships between the problem in question and the global objectives and results achieved by the client organization, and to ascertain the client's potential to make changes and resolve the problem effectively.

The diagnostic work should start with a clear conceptual framework in mind. To embark on extensive and costly investigations without such a framework could be a hazardous undertaking. In any organization the consultant encounters a host of problems varying in importance and nature: technical and human, apparent and hidden, substantial and trivial, real and potential. He or she will hear many critical opinions as to what the main problems are and what should have been done about them. In diagnosing the problem, the consultant will be constantly exposed to the risk of taking a wrong direction, becoming unduly influenced by the views expressed by others, and collecting interesting but unnecessary facts while omitting essential facts and ignoring some important dimensions of a complex problem, or interesting new opportunities.

Diagnosis is sometimes viewed as equal to collecting, dissecting and analysing vast amounts of data, including a great deal of data that may have no relevance to the purpose of the assignment. This is a misconception, however. While there is no diagnosis without data and facts, it is equally true that (a) diagnosis embraces considerably more than data collection and analysis, and (b) effective diagnosis is confined to selected data and is consistently focused on the purposes of the project.

In principle, problem diagnosis does not include work on problem solutions. This will be done in the next, action-planning phase. Diagnosis may even lead to the conclusion that the problem cannot be resolved, or that the purpose pursued cannot be achieved and the problem is not worth the effort of resolution.

Yet in practice it is often difficult or inappropriate to make a strict distinction and draw a line between the diagnostic and the action-planning — and even the implementation — phases of the consulting process. It is not only that diagnosis lays down the bases for the work to follow. Frequently diagnostic work will already identify and explore possible solutions. In interviewing people it may be impracticable and undesirable to confine the discussion to problems and their causes, carefully avoiding touching upon a wider context and possible solutions. Thus, operations that are separated in our text for methodological reasons will have to be combined by the practitioner in a pragmatic way, likely to lead to results in the client's particular case.

Restating the problem and the purpose

The assignment plan prepared during the entry phase and confirmed by the consulting contract (see sections 7.2 to 7.5) has provided guidelines and a basic time-schedule for diagnosis. It may, however, require revision and adjustment before diagnostic work is actually started. There may be a time-lag of several months between the end of the entry phase and the start of the diagnostic phase, and the client's situation and thinking may have evolved.

Furthermore, many consulting contracts are signed on the basis of general and vague problem and purpose definitions. When the work is actually starting, the consultant may find out that the client wants something else or has a different interpretation of the general and inaccurate terms used in the contract text. Often the reason is that the people who start working together on the project are different (on both the client's and the consultant's side) from those who negotiated and signed the contract. Explaining what was intended is not enough since there may be a genuine disagreement over the original problem and purpose definition.

Thus, it is always useful to review and restate the problem and the purpose of the consultancy when starting diagnosis. A special meeting with the client may be arranged to this effect. Experience shows that in the vast majority of assignments some adjustments in the objectives and the time-table are inevitable when the work actually starts.

The people side of diagnosis

There is another significant phenomenon. As we know, the very fact that a management consultant is present in the organization and starts asking questions puts the change process into motion. There may be an immediate impact on the organization. Many of us do not have to be told what to do; it may be enough if someone asks us a question which implies that there might be an alternative way of doing the job. Sometimes an employee is heard to say, "I didn't know they wanted me to do the job that way. Had they spoken to me about it, I would have done it!"

This can have very positive effects. By gradually developing a complete picture of the situation, diagnosis increases awareness of the need to change and indicates more specifically the sorts of change that will be required. If well managed, data collection and analysis can involve the client's staff more and more in the assignment, thus enhancing their sense of "ownership of the problem". As a result, at the end of the diagnosis people in the client organization will be better prepared to cope with the necessary changes than at its beginning.

There can be a useful learning effect, too. The client and his or her staff should not only feel that they are themselves discovering the full truth about their organization or unit and suggesting what to improve, but also gain a conviction that the consultant is sharing his diagnostic method with them. The client's problem-solving potential can be considerably enhanced during diagnosis. If this opportunity is missed, it may be too late to start soliciting people's involvement in developing and implementing action proposals.

Certain negative effects may also occur. Some clients try to maintain secrecy within the organization about using a consultant. It is doubtful whether such a secret can be kept but, even more important, an attempt to do so can cast doubt upon the consultant and on the entire process. The informal communication network in an organization (all organizations have their "grapevines"!) will quickly disseminate the information. In the absence of a formal communication from the client to the system, the informal communication system will tend to generate negative data. This will seriously inhibit the ability of the consultant to perform effectively.

Unless the client system is prepared to accept the consultant, the entire relationship can be doomed to failure from the outset. Therefore, if possible, the client should prepare the organization for the introduction of the consultant. As clients are not always aware of this need, it may become necessary for the consultant to plan a course of action during the entry phase. Obviously, such preparation is in itself an intervention in the organization. It must be handled with extreme care, with all the competence required of the consultant from the outset (see also section 27.2).

The consultant must use a variety of approaches to dispel any fear or misinformation. One way to do this is by being readily available to all those in the organization who would like to meet him or her. Particularly when consulting on human resources and organizational development, the consultant should be generally visible and very accessible.

Diagnosis can be a painful exercise in an organization in difficulties. But in any organization diagnosis may uncover situations and relationships of which the client is not proud, which he or she is unable to handle, and which he or she would have preferred to hide from anybody coming from outside, and even from other colleagues within the company. The consultant, however, may badly need this sort of insight to be able to do anything useful for the client. Diagnosing delicate situations requires a great deal of tact. An aggressive diagnostic attitude (e.g. if people can deduce from the consultant's questions that he or she is looking for errors in their work and is going to criticize them) will invariably generate resistance.

Another type of potentially negative effect is spontaneous change of work methods before a new method has been properly developed, tested and adopted for general use. Often such changes are not real improvements even if they are well intentioned. Energy may be wasted if there is a misunderstanding about the purpose of the project and likely direction of the change effort and about the sequence of steps in which the consultancy is being carried out. Some people may be disoriented — they change their method of work in good faith, but this is not appreciated by the consultant and by the managers.

These and similar misunderstandings can be prevented by giving *frequent feedback* from diagnostic work. The client and his or her staff need to know how the assignment has progressed, what facts have been established, what solutions are shaping up and what findings are preliminary — requiring further fact finding and verification — or final, capable of serving as a basis for action. There should be no ambiguity and no suspicion about the type of action that diagnosis is likely to recommend and about the moment at which action can start.

On the other hand, getting the client's reaction to the feedback given to him or her is feedback to the consultant. The consultant should seek this feedback as much as possible during the whole diagnostic phase.

8.2 Diagnosing purposes and problems

Purposes

In *Breakthrough Thinking*, Gerald Nadler and Shozo Hibino explain why focusing on purposes is fundamental to successful problem solving.[1] They emphasize that defining the purposes of working on a problem ensures that you will apply your efforts in areas where you can have the greatest impact. Instead of starting diagnosis by asking "What's wrong here? What's the matter?", the consultant should ask first "What are we trying to accomplish here? What are we trying to do?" This will help to avoid (a) the conventional urge to start by collecting data and analysing the situation, and (b) working on or being sold a solution to a wrong problem ("moving faster in the wrong direction").

An array of purposes to be achieved by the project should be constructed. In this way the consultant will acknowledge the fact that there is a wide range of motivations and results possible in applying change to an existing condition. The problem will be seen in the right perspective if the array of purposes listed is broad enough, including small and immediate purposes as well as very broad and far-reaching purposes that are beyond any possibility of actually implementing a solution.

It will then be important to identify *the focus purpose*. It will be one that can meet all or most of the criteria discussed and chosen by the consultant and the client (such as management's desires, potential financial benefits, cost and capital factors, time limitations, constraints imposed by legislation, future development potential, employment potential, learning opportunities, etc.). Small, limited and trivial purposes that cannot meet these criteria will be eliminated. Excessively broad, distant, risky, costly and unrealistic purposes, as well as purposes that the stakeholders are not prepared to support, will also be eliminated.

Box 8.1   The focus purpose

For example, in one company the problem presented to a consultant was described as a deteriorating quality of several important products, and a growing number and frequency of customer complaints about quality. The discussion of possible purposes of a consulting project defined an array of purposes:

● restoring quality to previous level and preventing its deterioration;

● preventing customer complaints;

● improving quality management (including better motivation for achieving and maintaining quality);

● increasing customer satisfaction;

● achieving an image of a high-quality producer;

● becoming a sector leader internationally in terms of quality.

The focus purpose chosen was "increasing customer satisfaction". This embraced narrower purposes such as improving product quality and assuring quality management, but eliminated wider and probably too ambitious purposes, such as international sector leadership in quality. Furthermore, it was agreed that improvements would need to be pursued in after-sales and maintenance services, customer information, behaviour of the sales technicians, product modernization practices, etc. This permitted a diagnosis and the subsequent activities of the consultant and the client to be focused on a clear and realistic purpose.

Problems

It may be useful to recollect what was said about business and management problems in section 1.2. There is a problem if (a) there is a difference between two situations: one real (past or present) and one potential or desired (past, present or future), and (b) someone is concerned about this difference and wants to change it. This difference defines the problem with which the consultant is supposed to deal.

Thus, to establish this difference or discrepancy we will be comparing two situations. It is not so difficult to find out what was or is actually happening, i.e. *the actual situation*. In this chapter we will describe a number of fact-finding and analytical techniques whose mastery helps the consultant to identify and understand the actual situation. To determine what should be happening in the future, i.e. *the ideal or desired situation*, is infinitely more complex, but it is an essential part of problem diagnosis. For it is only in this way that the problem can be described and analysed, and the consultant's work focused on purposes, future opportunities and improvements.

Box 8.2   Minor changes or radical improvements?

Let us take an example of growing production costs. The costs of a particular product have increased from 10 to say, 10.80, i.e. by 8 per cent, over the last year. But the market price has not increased and the distribution agents cannot reduce their margin. There is a suspicion (or it has been established) that some competitors offering the same product have maintained the same level of production costs, and others have even been able to reduce them. Technologies making production considerably cheaper are known and some radically different technologies are being developed, but these, as usual, can be efficient only under certain conditions.

What then is the problem? The actual level of production costs is known, but how can the desired level be determined? What will be the purpose of the assignment? Bring the costs back to the original level? Change the product radically? Drop the product from the production line? Absorb the cost increase by making savings elsewhere? These may be difficult choices. Without clarifying the purpose, the client has no criterion for making these choices and directing the consultant. The consultant could spend months on examining and developing alternatives only to find out that most of them would be unacceptable.

The consultant and the client may have to face a very important choice: going for minor improvements to bring the costs under control (knowing pretty well that this will be a provisional and not fully satisfactory solution), or aiming at radical changes in product design, technology and organization (which, however, will involve different investment costs, risks, and requirements on management and employees). The client's purpose may even be so defined that the product in question could be dropped and another product line launched. Would the client be ready for such a change? Would this be a long-term solution? How will customers react? Do facts speak in favour of a radical approach or against it? Is now the right time to take such an approach?

The client's problem will be identified by the following five principal dimensions or characteristics:

(1) **Substance or identity**. The substance or identity of the problem has to be described (low performance; shortage of competent staff; lack of ideas on how to invest idle capital; desire to improve after-sales services). It has to be established what basis of comparison is used and how it is justified. Why do we say that performance is low? Low by what standard? The various symptoms of the problem have to be described as well.

(2) **Organizational and physical location**. In what organizational units (divisions, departments, subsidiaries) and physical units (plants, buildings, stores, offices) has the problem been observed? What other units are or might be affected? How widespread is the problem? Does it affect external relationships (e.g. with customers or suppliers)?

(3) **Problem "ownership"**. Which people — managers, staff specialists, workers — are affected by the existence of the problem and primarily interested in resolving it? Who is likely to make difficulties?

(4) **Absolute and relative magnitude**. How important is the problem in absolute terms (e.g. amount of working time or money lost, volume of

underutilized productive capacity, potential future gains)? How important is it in relative terms (e.g. in comparison with other problems, or the total turnover)? How does it affect the unit where it has been observed, and the people who "own the problem"? How important is it to the organization as a whole? What will the organization actually gain if the problem is resolved?

(5) **Time perspective**. Since when has the problem existed? Has it been observed once, or several times, or is it recurrent? How frequently does it appear? What is its tendency: has the problem been stabilized, or is it increasing or decreasing? What forecasts can be made about the future evolution of the problem? Are we anticipating a future problem?

Furthermore, diagnosis will aim to establish:

— the causes of the problem;
— other significant relationships;
— the client's potential to solve the problem;
— possible directions of further action.

The causes of the problem

A key task in diagnosis is to identify the forces and factors which are causing the problem. The purpose is to understand the issue, not to point the finger to one or more culprits. The exercise will start with some preliminary knowledge or assumptions about what these causes might be. This will help to establish hypotheses on possible causes. It is useful to form as many hypotheses as possible, without, however, embarking on superficial speculation. Data gathering and analysis will then focus mainly on the hypothetical causes, eliminating hypotheses that cannot be justified by facts, and adding new hypotheses which will emerge from interviews with the client or from other sources. A rigorous scientific approach should be applied. The fact that it is difficult to find data in support of a hypothesis does not mean that the hypothesis should be dropped. Eventually the consultant should be able to identify the real cause or causes amongst the many factors which are in some way related to the problem (see section 8.4).

Other significant relationships

Any business and management problem is interwoven with other problems; and there are other relationships in addition to that which can be established between a problem and its cause or causes. There may be factors which aggravate or alleviate the problem without being its direct cause. They can make the solution of the problem more or less difficult. In solving one problem, new problems may be discovered or created. Quite often a new bottleneck is created by removing an existing one. These relationships and potential problems and risks have to be investigated and identified.

The client's potential to solve the problem

The client's potential has several dimensions. It is necessary to find out whether he or she possesses the material and financial resources and the technical expertise required for solving the problem. If not, the consultancy will have to provide for developing this potential and extending help to the client as necessary. The time perspective is important. What has been the client's experience in solving other problems and making organizational changes of varying nature and magnitude? What is the client organization's culture as regards change? How quickly is the client able to act? What will be the likely future development of the client's resources in relation to the problem to be solved? Can he or she mobilize other resources? What attempts have been made to solve the given problem? Have past attempts failed? Why have they failed?

Considerable attention will be paid to *the client's attitudes to the given problem*. How do people (at various levels and in various categories) perceive the problem? Are they aware of it and keen to make a change? Are they motivated to make a special effort? Are they prepared to take risks? Have they experienced the problem for so long that they have accommodated themselves to living with it?

Possible directions of further action

The purpose of diagnosis is preparation for action. Throughout the investigation, information and ideas on how the problem could be resolved and how this would contribute to meeting the client's purposes and improving his or her business will be collected, recorded and analysed with the same care and determination as data on the nature and the causes of the problem. This will provide a link to the next, action-planning phase. Action proposals should emerge logically from diagnosis. However, the consultant will keep in mind the pitfalls of premature changes started before the facts have been established and conclusions drawn from diagnosis.

Main steps in diagnosis

The general framework provided above can be used by the consultant when making a detailed plan for diagnostic work, bearing in mind that the scope and methodology of the exercise will have to be adapted to the nature and complexity of the problem, and to the profile and the attitude of the client. Diagnosis consists in seeking answers to the questions in the areas reviewed above: the purposes pursued; the nature and characteristics of the problem itself; the causes of the problem; other significant relationships; the client's potential to solve the problem; and possible directions of further action. The exercise starts with some information obtained through preliminary problem diagnosis during the entry phase, and with assumptions and hypotheses which the consultant will be able to make at the beginning in collaboration with the client. Hypotheses and tentative answers will be replaced by definite answers, and missing data will be collected and evaluated.

Box 8.3   Issues in problem identification

It is useful to recall briefly some common mistakes made not only by clients in defining their problems, but also by some consultants. The way we define problems limits our ability to solve them!

- **Mistaking symptoms for problems.** This is the most common error. Some very obvious issues which worry management (e.g. falling sales, shortage of innovative ideas in the R&D department, absenteeism) are looked upon as problems, although they may be only symptoms of more profound difficulties.

- **Preconceived ideas about the causes of problems.** Some managers and consultants feel that, thanks to their experience, they know pretty well what the causes "must" be and that analysing facts cannot really reveal anything new.

- **Looking at problems from one technical viewpoint only.** This happens frequently if the diagnosis is made by a manager or a consultant with a strong background and bias in one technical area (e.g. engineering, accounting, behavioural science) and if the interdisciplinary nature of management problems is disregarded.

- **Ignoring how the problem is perceived in various parts of the organization.** For example, the consultant may accept the definition made by top management, without finding out how the problem is seen by the lower management echelons.

- **Unfinished problem diagnosis.** Owing to time and cost constraint or other reasons, the consultant may be tempted to conclude diagnostic work prematurely. He or she will not find out about further problems and opportunities that may be directly related to the original issue presented by the client.

- **Failure to clarify the focus purpose.** The purpose is vaguely defined and the consultant wastes time and energy by looking into many issues that will eventually be ignored. He or she works on a wrong problem or on totally unrealistic proposals.

In planning the diagnostic phase it is essential to determine the degree and form of the client's involvement in each activity. If the process-consulting mode is chosen, the client and his team will accept the main responsibility for collecting and analysing data, and the consultant will act mainly as a catalyst, making the client aware of the approach taken and drawing his attention to questions and to facts that should not escape his attention. In other instances, however, the consultant will carry out the bulk of the diagnostic work. As a general rule, it is useful to plan for gradually increasing the involvement of the client and his or her staff in the course of the diagnostic phase.

The same approach and sequence of steps may not fit every situation and every consultant's personality. Every client organization is unique and so is every consultant-client relationship. This general rule also applies to the planning of diagnostic work. For example, Jerome Fuchs described his experience in the following terms:

> My personal approach involves techniques which I find most useful. I do not attempt to analyse or compartmentalize data into fact finding, analysis and

synthesis, but let it flow as it begins to come in. I let it overlap to a certain extent in each of these stages until a pattern begins to develop. Only then do I begin to weave raw factual material into the analytical phase. When my facts are complete I want them to be so clear that they mirror what the ultimate conclusion of the study will be.[2]

8.3   Defining necessary facts

Facts are the building-blocks of any consulting work. Consultants need a considerable number of facts to get a clear picture of the situation, arrive at a precise definition of the problem and relate their proposals to reality. Facts are also needed if the assignment is trying to develop something very new and using a great deal of imagination and creative thinking. Collecting facts may be the most tiring and painful phase of the consultant's work, but there is no alternative.

When diagnosis starts, a certain amount of data will be handed over to the operating consultants by their colleagues who did the preliminary problem diagnosis during the entry phase. The diagnostic phase will go much further, and will define issues and collect facts in considerably greater detail.

The kinds of facts collected will depend on the area in which the assignment takes place, and on the definition of the problem and the assignment objectives. Facts should enable the examination of processes, relations, performances, causes and mutual influences, with special regard to underutilized opportunities and possible improvements. The conceptual framework reviewed in section 8.1 indicates the main areas in which facts are normally collected.

Plan for collecting data

Fact collecting has to be prepared for by thoroughly defining what facts are wanted. Experienced consultants will continue to apply the principle of selectivity, although they know that at this stage they need more detailed and precise facts than their colleagues who did the preliminary diagnosis and negotiated the assignment. They appreciate that virtually unlimited amounts of factual information are available in any organization, but that an excessive amount of such information easily becomes unmanageable and cannot be fully utilized in any assignment.

The cost of fact gathering cannot be ignored, especially if some data are not readily available and special schemes (observations, special record keeping, numerous interviews) have to be established to obtain them. But the definition of facts and their sources must not be too restrictive. If it is, this might exclude facts from which significant information might be drawn, and these facts are often found in unexpected places. At the beginning of the assignment, the consultant may well cast his or her net fairly widely, rejecting some data after preliminary examination, but adding other data, and so on.

In defining the scope of data the management consultant keeps in mind that the purpose is neither research nor establishing responsibility for past flaws.

"The purpose of diagnosis is to mobilize action on a problem. Action that will improve the organization's functioning."[3]

The facts to be collected and investigated have to be defined in closest collaboration with the client, especially with those members of the client organization who know what records are kept, how reliable they are, and what data will have to be sought from other sources. This includes the definition of the content of data, degree of their detail, time period, extent of coverage, and classification and tabulation criteria, as described below.

Data gathering may be a lengthy process and in a complex case some logic should be followed, e.g. by making sure that each step (finding data on marketing and sales) provides information for the next step (data on production) and so on. This should be reflected in a work plan to be agreed on with the client.

Planning for data gathering also includes deciding what aspects of the problem and what relationships do not require detailed data. This concerns cases when the consultant, thanks to experience, can arrive at reliable conclusions on the basis of global data and through comparison with similar situations in other organizations.

The client may not understand why the consultant insists on finding certain sorts of information. This often happens if, in the client's opinion, the assignment should be kept within a limited technical area and the consultant should not become involved in other areas. The consultant has to explain why he or she wants to obtain certain data on events, situations and problems that may be somehow related to the problem at hand. This may make the client aware of relations to which he or she was paying no attention, and provide further evidence of the consultant's methodical approach.

Content of data

Every experienced consultant knows only too well that apparently identical types of data may have a different meaning or content in different organizations. For example "work in progress" may be defined in a number of different ways: it may or may not include certain items, and its financial value may be determined by various methods. The definition of categories of employees (managers, technicians, supervisors, administrative personnel, production and other workers, etc.) is also subject to many variations. In old firms with established traditions definition is complicated by the existence of their own jargon, which may differ from terminology prevailing in the industry to which they belong. The uniformity of data used in the management of various organizations will be higher in countries where accounting and reporting have to observe government regulations. But even in these cases many differences will be found, especially in the production area.

For quantities, the consultant specifies the units of measure, e.g. the number of products, or their weight or volume, and sets the limits of accuracy, e.g. to the nearest 100 or to the last unit. Accuracy depends upon the purpose for which the data are to be used. Work study to set standard operating times may require accuracy to the nearest second, with an error allowance of 5 per cent. By contrast, a forecast of total volume of production per year may approximate to the nearest thousand, with an error allowance of 10 per cent. If the consultant fails to set the limits of accuracy before data are collected, he or she may not obtain what is required and the recording process will have to be repeated, e.g. if operating times are recorded in minutes or tenths or hundredths of minutes, when seconds are required.

Degree of detail

The degree of detail required for facts will generally be higher than that needed for data used in preliminary diagnostic surveys. While general diagnosis stems from aggregate figures (e.g. total time spent by machines on productive work), change rests upon more detailed data (e.g. machining time for each operation, or time spent on productive work by certain types of machines, or in certain shops). Information on individual persons and their attitudes to the problem concerned may be needed.

The more detailed the facts, the more time they will take to collect. At the start of an assignment the consultant may have difficulty in evaluating the advantages which detailed facts will yield. Before collecting the data he or she cannot know what weaknesses or opportunities for improvement they will reveal. He or she will probably point out problems that deserve close examination. Otherwise the consultant may first collect data in broad categories (e.g. total number of days of sick leave taken by all workers). Analysis of these data will suggest more detail for certain categories (e.g. number of days of sick leave taken by each age group during the winter months). Data may thus be gathered in several stages before the consultant has a sufficiently detailed picture of the present situation to suggest ways of improving it.

Period of time

Defining the period of time is equally important. For example, to design an inventory management system for finished products, the consultant must know the number of products sold. For how many years must he or she calculate the sales and at what intervals? The answer might be for each month over the last three years. The period of time should be long enough to set a firm pattern of activity, indicate rates of growth or decline, and reveal fluctuations in activity due to seasonal variations or economic cycles. A longer period will be chosen in enterprises producing large capital goods, with a lead time of several years in product design, manufacturing and installation, than in enterprises producing current consumer goods.

Periods of time need to be comparable: months or weeks have to include the same number of working days and so on. Periods when exceptional events occurred should be excluded, but recognized and accommodated in the new situation. Periods preceding major changes in operations (e.g. introduction of new products and dropping of old ones) have to be examined separately from periods of normal operation.

The choice of a period close to the start of the assignment recognizes that the mere presence of the consultant may affect the results. In a particular instance, material wastage dropped substantially from the moment the consultant began to ask questions about it and before he actually did anything.

Obviously the choice of the period of time takes account of the availability of past records, and of changes that the client may have introduced in recording procedures.

Coverage

When it comes to coverage, the consultant must decide whether to collect total information (on all products, all employees, whole units and processes), or a selection only. As a rule, information will be collected for the vital few items that account for the bulk of activity in the current period, and for such items as are likely to become vital in the future (prospective new products, etc.). If the productive capacity is clearly limited by one group of machines which have become a bottleneck, the solution of the problems of this group may be a key to the solution of most other problems of the given department. In other cases, data will be collected for representative samples.

Organization and tabulation of data

Finally, the preparatory work for fact collecting includes decisions on organization and tabulation of data, which are made in the light of the ultimate use of the data. Typical groupings are:

- for *events* — time, frequency, rate, trends, cause, effect (e.g. number of accidents resulting from specified causes that occurred each day of the week during the past year);
- for *people* — age, sex, nationality, family status, qualifications, occupation, length of service, earnings (e.g. average annual earnings of female employees with selected educational qualifications during each of the last five years);
- for *products and materials* — size, value, technical characteristics, source (e.g. value of materials by type and size in the inventory at the end of the last 12 calendar quarters);
- for *resources, inputs, outputs, processes and procedures* — rates of activity (sale, consumption, production), location, control centre, geographical distribution, use of equipment (e.g. numbers of specified parts produced by selected processes during each of the last 24 months).

To arrange facts in digestible form the consultant plans how to tabulate them. Descriptions and narratives may be noted under selected headings on a separate sheet of paper or card for each heading (e.g. responsibilities of each manager). Answers to a questionnaire can be tabulated on a "summary questionnaire", i.e. using the same form of questionnaire that will be distributed to the respondents. Processes and procedures may be represented by a chain of symbols, such as the activity symbols used by systems analysts or in work study. Shapes are best shown on drawings. Figures are usually set out in tables.[4]

It may be useful to anticipate data processing by a computer. This will involve the selection of a suitable model and programme, or the elaboration of a new one if none is available for the particular analytical purpose and the coding of data for computer processing.

The consultant's preliminary notes will tend to be wordy and speculative while he or she is feeling the way and getting the situation into focus. As the course of the investigation becomes clearer, recording of the facts becomes more systematic. General note-taking may give way to charting and other analytical methods. The original decisions on tabulating and classifying data are verified and amended.

The orderly way the operating consultant keeps his papers, and how he files them for retrieval of information, will help him to keep on course and allow for easy reference by the supervisor. The meaning of notes should be as clear months after the event as when they were written. No figure should be recorded without being precisely qualified by its terms.

8.4   Sources and ways of obtaining facts

Sources of facts

By and large, facts are available to consultants in three forms:

— records;

— events and conditions;

— memories.

Any of these sources may be internal (within the given organization), or external (publications, statistical reports, data on customers and competitors, opinions of people outside the organization).

Records are facts stored in forms that are readable or can be transcribed. They include documents (files, reports, publications), computer files, films, microfilms, tapes, drawings, pictures, charts, and so on. Facts from records are obtained by retrieval and study.

Events and conditions are actions, and the circumstances surrounding them, which can be observed. Hence facts of this kind are obtained by observing, and recording the results of observations.

Memories are all the information stored in the minds of people who work in the client's organization, are associated with it, or simply are able to provide information of use to the consultant (e.g. for comparison). This encyclopaedia of knowledge embraces hard proven facts, experiences, opinions, beliefs, impressions, prejudices and insights. The mind stores all this data in the form of words, numbers and pictures which the consultant cannot see, but can obtain from people by means of interviews, questionnaires, special reports, and so on.

A skilful consultant will avoid having recourse to indirect and time-consuming ways of collecting information if the same information can be obtained directly and simply. In many cases this means — go and ask people. People at all levels in industrial firms and other organizations possess an unbelievable amount of knowledge about their organization, and nearly everybody has some ideas on needed and possible improvements. But they do not divulge this information if they are not asked.

Retrieval of recorded data

Records are a prolific source of information, and some records will be examined and studied in any management consulting assignment. Clearly, consultants will give preference to the use of information which is already available in records before looking to other ways of data collecting. There are, however, certain pitfalls to be avoided in retrieving recorded data:

- Many records are not reliable and give a distorted picture of reality. This is common in such cases as records on machine breakdowns and stoppages, or waste. Materials may be charged to products for which they were not used. Factory plans and layouts may be claimed to be up to date but seldom are. Organizational and operational manuals may include detailed descriptions of procedures which were abandoned long ago. Even fairly sophisticated computer systems may provide misleading data if inputs are incomplete and unreliable. If the consultant or the client personally has doubts, the validity of existing records should be verified before they are used.

- It is common in organizations, both business and government, to find that various departments have different records on the same activities, inputs or outputs. The departments may be more or less careful and disciplined in record keeping. The records may differ both in the criteria used and in the magnitude of the recorded data.

- Criteria and values used in recording are modified from time to time and the consultant must find out about all such modifications.

Special recording

Special recording can be arranged if information is not readily available in existing records, or cannot be relied upon. It may be established for a limited period, say a month or two, according to criteria proposed by the consultant. As a rule, the client's employees working in a given area will be asked to record data and pass them to the consultant. For economy reasons such recording should be kept simple and last no longer than necessary for reliability. Everyone should know at the start how long the period will be, and why special recording has to be introduced.

Observing

Observing is the method the consultant uses to obtain information which is not readily recorded. He or she is present while an event occurs (e.g. while a manager instructs his subordinates, or while a worker performs a task), and uses the faculties of sight and hearing to note how the event occurs, so that he or she will be able to suggest an improved practice at a later date.

In process consulting, the consultant can observe management and staff meetings during which it is possible to identify group processes and behaviours that are related to the problem. Usually, the observation will be of groups, rather than individuals. If, however, the purpose of the consultation is to help an individual improve performance, then the observation can focus essentially on that individual. This would be the case where a high-level employee in the organization has been experiencing interpersonal problems. This client may seek an external consultant who could observe him or her in action in a variety of situations, and provide help (e.g. by personal counselling) in improving the interpersonal aspect of his or her management performance.

Alternatively, the consultant can observe socializing patterns. Where do people gather to talk and exchange information? Who has frequent working or informal contacts with whom? Who is avoiding whom? What pattern emerges from these contacts?

Information which the consultant usually obtains by observation includes:

- layout of factory, warehouses and offices;
- flow of operations, materials and people;
- work methods, work pace and discipline;
- working conditions (noise, light, temperature, ventilation, orderliness and cleanliness);
- attitudes and behaviour of higher and middle managers, supervisors, staff specialists and workers;
- interpersonal and intergroup relations.

Because most people feel uncomfortable under scrutiny, the consultant must take special care to put them at their ease before starting to observe their activities. First the consultant should tell them what he or she is going to do. He or she should never start watching workers or other employees without warning. The consultant should explain the purpose of the survey and make it clear that it is in no way critical of particular persons but simply aimed at obtaining reliable information on how the activity is performed. An exchange of views with those under observation, allowing them an opportunity to point out all the factors influencing the activity or the work relationships and inviting their suggestions for improvement, will probably enlist their cooperation. As far as possible they should behave normally under observation and make no attempt to give a better or faster, or worse or slower, performance than usual. If there is any unusual occurrence, the observation should be disregarded and repeated when conditions return to normal.

If procedures, operations and processes are observed, the consultant would choose one of the many methods that have been developed for that purpose and whose description is available in the literature.[5]

Where the assignment deals primarily with human problems and relations between individuals and groups, the consultant may have to explore the attitudes and behaviour of the client's staff in depth. In other assignments he or she probes less deeply into these aspects. Nevertheless, the consultant observes the inclinations, preferences and prejudices of people to the extent necessary to understand how these affect the problems he or she is concerned with, and to enlist cooperation. Such observation continues throughout the assignment. It starts during the introductory meetings when the consultant gains first impressions. These will be verified during later encounters. To a considerable extent the consultant gathers information on attitudes and behaviour as a by-product of interviews to question memories, exchange ideas or develop improvements. However, during interviews not directly concerned with personal traits, the consultant would distract both himself and the client by writing down his impressions. He should therefore make mental notes and only afterwards put them into writing and classify them.

In doing this, the consultant will be interested in information such as:

— experience;
— beliefs;
— degree of self-confidence;
— ambitions;
— likes and dislikes;
— special interests or motives;
— people the interviewee respects and those he or she doesn't;
— sociability;
— willingness to cooperate;
— management style (autocratic, consultative, permissive);
— extent of original thinking and innovation;
— receptivity to new ideas;
— motivation for change.

By taking such personal traits and attitudes into account, the consultant will increase the chances of understanding factors that affect change in the client organization.

Special reports

Individuals or teams in the client organization may be requested to help in the assignment by giving thought to particular aspects of the problem and putting suggestions on paper in the form of a special report. This would include any supporting information that the author might be able to supply. This method is selective — in cooperation with the client, the consultant would choose those employees who are likely to have specific views on the problem in question, who are aware of various pitfalls, and who are a source of good ideas. If, however, anybody in the client organization offers to prepare a special report on his or her own initiative, this should be welcomed, although treated with some caution.

Questionnaires

In management consulting a questionnaire is useful for obtaining a limited number of straightforward facts from a large number of people (e.g. in a market survey), or from people widely separated from each other (e.g. reasons for equipment failure from users throughout a whole region). They are generally unsatisfactory for gathering all but simple facts.

The questionnaire may be distributed to correspondents with an explanatory note asking them to complete and return it, or canvassers may question people and note their answers on the questionnaire. Either case calls for a full explanation, telling the respondent:

- why he or she is being asked the questions;
- who is asking them;
- what the questioner will do with the replies;
- who else is being asked.

Before drawing up the questionnaire the consultant decides exactly what information is wanted, how it will be used, and how the answers will be summarized and classified. Then precise, simple questions free from ambiguity are framed. As far as possible, "yes" or "no" or numerical answers should be invited. Where longer answers are required, it may be useful to provide a list of possible answers and ask for the right one to be marked. Questions should be arranged in logical order so that each answer leads to the next.

If there are some doubts about the respondents' ability to understand the questions and give clear answers, the questionnaire should be subjected to preliminary tests.

Interviewing

In management consulting, interviewing is certainly the most widely used technique of data gathering, together with the retrieval of recorded data.

One advantage that questioning during an interview has over the use of questionnaires is that every answer can be tested and elaborated. Questions supplement and support each other, confirming, correcting or contradicting previous replies. They also lead to related facts, often revealing unexpected relationships, influences and constraints. The interview is flexible and adaptable. If one line of questioning fails to produce required data, another can be tried. This may be suggested by the interviewee's answers.

The consultant learns not only from the direct replies received but also from the inferences, comments, asides, opinions, anecdotes, attitudes and gestures that accompany them — provided that he or she is alert and attentive. As we know, non-verbal messages can be very significant!

In interviewing people the consultant is guided by general rules of effective interviewing, which have been described in various texts.[6] Some more specific experiences and suggestions concerning the use of interviews in management consulting are given below.

In planning the interviews, the consultant determines what facts he or she wants to obtain, from whom, when, where and how.

What facts. In setting down the facts needed the consultant takes account of the knowledge he or she can expect the interviewee to have — for example, a production manager is unlikely to know precisely what terms of credit are extended to customers, while a district sales manager is probably not informed about the planned maintenance of machines. For background information, a general discussion may suffice. On the other hand, information that will help to solve problems or develop improvements needs to be thoroughly examined, probed and understood (e.g. workers' attitudes to simplifying working procedure in order to raise output).

Who should be interviewed. Obviously interviewees should be those dealing with the activities under study — for example, for billing procedures, the invoice clerk should be the best source of information. To obtain full co-operation and avoid slighting anyone, however, the consultant should first approach the manager responsible and allow him or her to designate informants. Later the consultant may refer to others to complement or confirm information. During initial interviews he or she can ask who will have supporting information.

When to interview. Information gathered from interviews makes more sense if it comes in logical order — for example, if products are known it is easier to follow the operations for manufacturing them. Interviews should therefore follow a sequence so that each builds on information derived from those preceding it. They should be preceded by a careful study of records, so that time-consuming interviews are not used to collect data available in another form. The amount of time an interviewee can make available for the interview and his state of mind cannot be ignored.

Where to meet. Selection of a meeting place takes into account the following:

— proximity to the activity under study;
— the convenience of the interviewee;
— avoidance of noise and interruption.

Generally, people are more relaxed and communicative in their own surroundings. They also have all information to hand there. Only if the interviewee's workplace has serious drawbacks, such as noise, cramped space or frequent interruptions, should the consultant invite him or her to meet elsewhere (perhaps in the consultant's office at the client's premises).

How to proceed. Although the conduct of an interview varies according to the characters of the interviewee and the consultant, their relationship, and the circumstances under which they meet, the guidelines summarized in box 8.4 usually apply.

In interviewing, the consultant may encounter unexpected resistance. This can be expressed in many different forms: questions are not answered, answers are evasive or too general, doubts are expressed about the usefulness of the exercise and the consultant's approach, and similar (see also section 4.4). If this happens, the consultant should quickly consider whether he or she is not provoking resistance by aggressive or tactless questioning, or by asking questions that the informant considers banal or poorly prepared. It may be good tactics to ask the informant directly about his or her feelings concerning the interview: this may unblock the situation. There is, however, not much point in pursuing an interview in which the informant clearly refuses to cooperate.

Data-gathering meetings

Another possibility in diagnosis is for the consultant to arrange a special meeting, a sort of collective interviewing, the purpose of which is to generate data related to the problem under consideration. Caution must be exercised, for it is also possible for the meeting to move into discussing possible solutions in general and in detail before sufficient data have been gathered.

Data gathering should involve all those who are related to the problem in any way. Sometimes the consultant may suggest including others who are not directly related, but whose presence could be helpful for data gathering. However, a data-gathering meeting should not be too large; this can inhibit some of those present and prevent the sharing of needed information. It may be preferable to schedule several small meetings in order to offer the more intimate climate essential for data gathering, and to hold separate meetings with people who would not give their views openly in the presence of their superiors or other colleagues (e.g. supervisors may speak more openly in a meeting where the production manager and the personnel manager are not present).

Employee attitude surveys

Attitudes of people in the client organization play some role in most consulting assignments. The consultant is alert to attitudes in observing operations and processes, in interviewing people, and in any other contacts with the client and the staff. There are, then, assignments where a special employee attitude survey may be required. This may be necessary in assignments involving changes in employment and working conditions if the consultant needs to establish how people feel about present conditions and how they could react to the change likely to be proposed. As a rule, a survey is more likely to be needed in a larger organization than in a small one if it is suspected that different opinions and attitudes exist, but the number of people concerned makes it difficult to judge

---

Box 8.4   Principles of effective interviewing

(1) Before the interview

- Prepare questions likely to reveal the required facts (the list will merely serve as a guide and a check that the interview covers all the necessary ground, and will not prevent the exploration of related topics).
- Inform yourself about the interviewee's job and personality.
- Inform the interviewee of the purpose of discussion.

(2) During the interview

- Give further detailed explanations to the interviewee at the beginning and request help in solving the problem.
- Start the interview in a relaxed and pleasant atmosphere, making sure that you break the ice at the opening.
- Ask questions likely to lead towards required information, allowing the informant to follow his or her own line of thought so long as it does not stray too far from the subject under review or become too trivial.
- Encourage a spontaneous flow of information by asking further questions, making judicious comments supplementing the interviewee's statements, and showing interest by smiling, nodding, mentioning that information is really interesting and new to you, etc.
- Except for such encouraging interjections, don't interrupt. Don't appear critical of the way things are done now since this may antagonize the informant. Don't argue and don't jump in with suggestions for improvements.
- When the questions are answered vaguely, pursue them in a non-aggressive and pleasant way until they are fully clarified.
- Be alert to non-verbal messages, feelings and impressions.
- Note facts and opinions during the interview (with the respondent's agreement), note impressions and feelings after the interview.
- Before leaving, confirm what you have noted. Thank the informant for help, thus leaving the way open for further interviews if necessary.

(3) After the interview

- Read over the notes of the interview, list points to be checked and transcribe reliable information in the assignment's classified data record.
- If appropriate send the interviewee a typed summary for verification.
- Use information from one interview to prepare questions (e.g. cross-checking or tentative) for other interviews.

---

the relative importance of different attitudes without surveying them in a systematic manner.

The organization and the techniques of attitude surveys are described in specialized publications.[7] If he or she is competent in this area, a management consultant may undertake such a survey. Alternatively, the consultant can turn to a specialist in social and behavioural research. The main techniques used would be those described above, including observation, interviews and questionnaires. There are, too, special techniques, used for instance in socio-metric studies or motivational research. Their effective use requires special training, but they would not be needed in most management consulting assignments.

Estimates

An estimate is makeshift and never fully replaces established data. Only when proven facts are not available, or for some reason are difficult to obtain, should the consultant consider estimates.

Estimates are best made by people performing the activity concerned, who have first-hand knowledge and who, in addition, will more readily accept proposals based on data they themselves have supplied. But wherever possible estimates should be obtained from more than one source and checked. If there are significant differences, the informants themselves should try to resolve them. If they cannot do so, a test may be applied, observations taken, or special re-cording installed.

The consultant may accept the client's estimates:

- in respect of facts familiar to the client (e.g. frequent machine operations, or regular patterns of work);
- on aspects of the present situation that need not be precise (e.g. percentage of total costs represented by administrative overheads, in order to decide whether to control these costs closely);
- to indicate whether further observation would be rewarding (e.g. incidence of machine breakdowns, or stock-outs of finished products);
- to ascertain whether benefits from improvements are worth more accurate measurement (e.g. savings from substitute materials or change of product design);
- where the estimate can be tested (e.g. if estimates of operating times to be used for production planning and control would result in a product cost permitting the client to sell at a fair profit).

The last example illustrates a sound use for estimates. For both control of production and control of costs it is necessary to know for each product the quantity of each material used in production, and each manufacturing operation and the time taken to perform it. Obtaining all this information by observation and measurement is a lengthy and painstaking task which would cause long delay in installing controls. Supervisors, technicians and workers, however, can provide close estimates because they are familiar with the materials and oper-ations. From their estimates a product cost can be calculated. If this permits the client to sell the product at a fair profit, estimates can be used to start production control and cost control systems. Later, precise measurements can replace the estimates and improve controls.

Before using estimates the consultant checks their validity against proven experience. An effective way of doing this is to use a known total volume, quantity, or cost for a recent period or a known capacity. This is compared with the measurement or capacity that results from multiplying an estimate for a single item by the total number of items. For example, the estimated quantity of material required to manufacture a product is multiplied by actual numbers produced during a recent period. This is compared with the quantity of material actually issued from store to production.

Another means of checking estimates is to compare them with data recorded elsewhere. Such a comparison must be made with care and will only be valid if the data being compared relate to identical circumstances. Data for comparison may be found in trade publications, in the files of the consulting organization or from organizations that have agreed to collaborate in benchmarking projects.

In addition to checking the validity of estimates the consultant needs to consider the *degree of error* they entail and decide whether this is tolerable. Where there is a strong probability that the error will remain within the limits of tolerance, the estimate will be used. For example, procedures can be installed to trigger remedial action by management when the limit is reached. In an opposite case the consultant has to devise ways of obtaining more precise and reliable data instead of using an estimate.

Estimates often concern data on developments and trends that are independent of the enterprise concerned (e.g. market prices, energy prices, transportation tariffs, exchange rates, interest rates, inflation). Many of these estimates can be obtained from competent specialized sources, such as government agencies, banks, business research institutes, or financial and market analysts. The consultant should choose an external source of estimates with extreme caution, bearing in mind that not all sources are equally reliable. It is good to know how the estimate was made — is it a "best guess", a common opinion shared by many experts on the topic, or was a forecasting model used? On what concepts was that model built? In particular, the consultant should never blindly accept, and provide to the client, estimates on the basis of which the client will have to make important investment and financial decisions. This does not mean that all risks can be eliminated, but the use of false information must be avoided.

Cultural issues in data gathering

Sensitivity to cultural factors, a general characteristic of excellence in consulting (see Chapter 5), is very important in data-gathering activities, in which the consultant interacts with many different individuals and groups in the client organization. In this respect the consultant must keep in mind both the country's and the organization's culture (box 8.5, overleaf). Even the particular micro-culture in different parts of an organization can be expected to influence how an interview is conducted or whether the group can be observed during work. It may be difficult and time-consuming for the consultant to determine the cultural norms of different groups, but it is essential.

Box 8.5   Cultural factors in data gathering

- In many countries, the interview cannot possibly start until the host (respondent or consultant) has first offered a beverage to the visitor.

- There may be cultural biases that hamper the use of a data-gathering technique. In a country where English was not the first language, a consultant went through the usual steps in preparing a questionnaire to be administered to a large group of people. When the data were reviewed, the unanimity of responses was surprising. As the consultant pursued this with some members of the client system, he discovered that it was the custom in that country for those answering a questionnaire to provide the information that they thought was wanted by those administering the questionnaire. It would have been impolite to do otherwise! The respondents had all shrewdly determined the kind of answer the consultant would want and had provided it.

- In a Muslim country, a consultant was on an assignment that required gathering data from workers, some of whom were female. When the interview was held, the consultant was surprised to find that the respondent brought along another woman, even though the consultant was herself a woman. Obviously, having another person present during the interview raised a question as to the validity of the data. After several interviews had been conducted, the consultant discussed this with the client. Only then did she learn that in that Muslim country (and there are differences among Muslim groups) a woman was not permitted to converse with a stranger, even another female, without an older female from her own household being present.

8.5   Fact analysis

Data cannot be used without *analysis*, whose purpose goes beyond research and appraisal. The ultimate aim of the consulting process is to initiate and implement change, and fact analysis should bring us closer to achieving this.

A correct description of reality, i.e. of conditions and events and their causes, is therefore only one aspect of analysis. The other, more important aspect is to establish what can be done, whether the client has the potential to do it, and what future benefits should be obtained from the envisaged changes.

There are, therefore, no clear-cut limits between analysis and *synthesis*. Synthesis, in the sense of building a whole from parts, drawing conclusions from fact analysis and developing action proposals, starts somewhere during fact analysis. Thus, fact analysis evolves gradually to synthesis. Indeed, to an experienced consultant analysis and synthesis are two sides of one coin, and he or she applies them simultaneously. The consultant does not have to discover new wholes by combining parts each time he or she undertakes an assignment — theoretical knowledge and practical experience help in synthesizing while he or she is analysing.

If the consultant knows a general rule and can establish that the problem observed falls under that rule, he or she will apply the deductive method. Instead of collecting and analysing a vast number of facts in order to establish what rule applies in a given case, he or she will proceed in the opposite direction, assuming that the relationships described by the rule also exist in the case being dealt with. But the consultant has to avoid the traps that data and past experience may set for him or her, such as the temptation to draw hasty conclusions from superficially analysed facts and allow ideas to become fixed before examining facts in depth ("This is exactly the same case I have seen many times before!"). Put in other terms, it is not possible to use *deduction* where *induction* applies, and vice versa. In practical consulting work, the two methods are combined and complement each other as analysis and synthesis do.

Box 8.6   A minicase of fact analysis

In a manufacturing enterprise, production records and observations have indicated that an important share of productive capacity is wasted owing to machine breakdown and stoppages. Waiting for the arrival of qualified repair workers has been given as a cause of the length of stoppages — in fact, the maintenance service is physically centralized in one place and organized in one unit reporting to the production manager, although the enterprise has a number of workshops located in various parts of a vast urban area. The consultant is tempted to suggest a decentralized organization of maintenance (e.g. a repair worker in every shop, or several maintenance centres each located close to a group of shops). In this connection, the consultant gives consideration, among other things, to repair workers' waiting time, since decentralization would increase their number and full use of their time could not be guaranteed. The next step reveals that the production manager is opposed to decentralization of technical support services and generally prefers their centralization. For a while the consultant is tempted to see this attitude as a major obstacle to solving the problem. But he hits on the idea of re-examining the technical causes of machine stoppages and the attitude of workers to machine breakdown. He collects more data and discovers that the wages of machine operators are not related to the effective working time of the machines. He also finds that most stoppages are caused by minor faults, and that the operators could easily be trained to remove certain defects themselves. In his proposals, the consultant finally concentrates on changes in the wage system in order to motivate workers to keep machine stoppages to a minimum, on training operatives in minor maintenance and repairs, and on some adjustments in the functions of the central maintenance service.

Editing the data

Before being subjected to the analytical operations described below, data need to be edited and screened. This includes checking their completeness, verifying clarity of recording and presentation, eliminating or correcting errors, and making sure that uniform criteria were applied in data gathering.

The most obvious case is that of recording a production operation: if 19 recordings show a duration of between four and five minutes, one recording indicating 12 minutes cannot be used for calculating an average figure. But this happens in quite different contexts — for example in accounting, where overhead costs may be inaccurately distributed among various products, or where one account may include items which should be put in a different account.

Cross-checking helps in some instances: for example, in the case of information obtained in an interview, which can be verified by subsequent interviews. In other cases there is no possibility of cross-checking and it is the consultant's experience and judgement, together with advice sought from the client's staff, that help to "clean" the data prior to using them for analytical operations.

Classification

The classification of data was started before the beginning of fact finding by establishing criteria for the organization and tabulation of data (section 8.2). Further classification, and adjustments in classification criteria, are made during fact finding (e.g. the consultant decides to use a more detailed breakdown of data than originally planned) and after it. If facts are recorded in a way which enables multiple classification (e.g. in a computer), the consultant can try several possible classifications before deciding which one is most relevant to the purpose of the assignment.

Both quantified and other information needs to be classified. For example, if complaints about the shortage of training opportunities come only from certain departments, or from people in certain age groups, the classification must reveal this.

The main classification criteria used by consultants are:

- time;
- place (unit);
- responsibility;
- structure;
- influencing factors.

Classification of data under *time* indicates trends, rates of change, random and periodic fluctuations.

Classification by *place or organizational unit* helps in examining problems of various parts of the organization and devising solutions related to specific conditions of each unit.

Classification by *responsibility for facts and events* is a different question — in many cases responsibility is not identical with the place (unit) where a fact has been identified. The consultant may need to identify responsible organizational units and/or particular persons in these units.

Classification according to the *structure of entities and processes* is an essential one and uses a number of criteria. Employees, materials, products, plant and equipment, customers, and so on, can be classified from many different points of view. An important objective in this case is to define how changes in components affect the magnitude of the whole entity, and to direct action towards those components which have major influence on total results. For example, the total lead time of a steam turbine may be determined by the machining and assembly time of one component — the rotor. Classification of customer complaints by products or production units indicates where to focus quality improvement efforts.

Operations in a production process can be classified according to their sequence in time and presented in a table or diagram, or on the plan of the workshop (which makes it possible to indicate the directions and distances of material movements in reduced proportions). Organizational relations and informal relationships in organizations can be classified by means of charts, diagrams, matrix tables, and so on.

Classification by *influencing factors* is a preparatory step in functional and causal analysis. For example, machine stoppages may be classified by factors that cause them: lack of raw material, break in energy supply, absence of worker, delay in scheduling, lack of spare parts, and so on.

In many cases simple classification (by one criterion) does not suffice: *cross-classification* is used, which combines two or more variables (e.g. employees classified by age group, sex, and length of employment with the organization).

Analysing organized data

Data that have been prepared and organized by classification are analysed in order to identify relationships, proportions and trends. Depending on the nature of the problem and the purpose of the consulting assignment, a variety of techniques can be used in data analysis. The use of statistical techniques is common (averages, dispersion, frequency distribution, correlation and regression), and various other techniques, including the use of mathematical modelling or graphical techniques, are often used. The reader is referred to specialized literature for detailed discussion of these.

Statistical and other quantitative analysis is meaningful only where qualitative relations can be identified. For example, association between two variables can be measured by correlation, but correlation does not explain the nature and the causes of the relationship.

The main objective is to establish whether a specific relationship exists between various factors and events described by data and, if so, to examine its nature. If possible, the relationship is quantified and defined as *a function* (in the mathematical sense of the term), where one or more dependent variables are in a specific relationship to one or more independent variables. The purpose is to discover and define relationships which are substantive and not just accidental. For example, the consultant may find out from data gathered in various firms that the cost of a major overhaul of machine tools is in some relationship to their purchase price. If such a relationship is defined as a function, the consultant can forecast the cost of overhaul and its influence on production costs in other firms using similar equipment.

Using ratios

A common way of expressing and measuring relationships is ratios. They may test whether inputs to an activity generate commensurate outputs, examine whether resources and commitments are properly balanced, or express the internal structure of a particular factor or resource.

In detailed analytical work the ratios of global aggregate data may be broken down into analytical ratios. For example, a series of ratios is often used to measure labour productivity:

$$\frac{V}{E} = \frac{V}{DH} \times \frac{DH}{PW} \times \frac{PW}{W} \times \frac{W}{E}$$

where V = value of production,

E = total number of employees,

DH = total direct labour hours,

PW = total number of production workers,

W = total number of workers.

There are no limits to the construction of detailed analytical ratios in any business and any functional area of management. Here again, working with a quantitative ratio makes sense if there is some qualitative relationship, and if using a ratio makes the analysis more meaningful by measuring this relationship and comparing it to a standard or another known case.

Causal analysis

Causal analysis (see also box 8.7) aims to discover causal relationships between conditions and events. It provides a key to planning change and improvements. If causes that have brought about certain situations, results or problems are known, these causes can be examined in greater depth and action can focus on them.

But how do you discover that there is a causal relationship? Remember that in most cases you would start the investigation with one or more hypotheses as to what the cause(s) of a problem may be. As a consultant, you are approaching causal analysis with a certain amount of knowledge and experience. Therefore you may have an idea about possible main causes — and to confirm this you need to have a comprehensive, synthetic view of the total process or system you are examining, and of the whole organizational context.

Only rarely would a consultant face situations in which unusual causal relationships would be discovered. But this happens as well; for example, a consultant from an industrialized country working in a developing economy may discover causal relationships between certain cultural factors and the economic performance of an organization which are unknown to him from his previous studies and work (such as different causes of absenteeism, or ethnic factors affecting the distribution of roles within a factory).

Box 8.7   Difficulties and pitfalls of causal analysis

- **Cause and effect**. Frequently conditions are observed that influence each other and there is a risk of mistaking an effect for its cause. A typical example is the relationship between poor staff morale and low performance of the organization. Is poor staff morale a cause of low business results, or do low results depress the staff and lower morale? If a static view is taken, these conditions influence each other, and there may be a vicious circle; but which condition is the cause of the other?

- **Basic or primary cause**. Suppose that the consultant establishes that falling sales and profits are the cause of low staff morale. What then is the cause of poor business results? The consultant finds out that it is the loss of an important foreign market. But why was that market lost? It was lost owing to a serious mistake in pricing policy. Why was that mistake made? And the exercise goes on . . .

  In diagnosing business and management problems, consultants face *chains of causes and effects*. The issue is how deep and how far to go in looking for basic (or primary) causes. Here again, it helps to keep the purpose in mind. The consultant will have to consider one cause as basic. It will be "relatively" basic. As a rule, it will be one upon which the client will be able to act. The consultant will thus be able to propose solutions that will address fundamental causes, without suggesting the impossible.

- **Multiple causes of one effect**. A problem frequently has two or more causes, although one of the causes may be more important than the others. This is often observed in personnel problems (a manager's behaviour and performance are affected simultaneously by problems encountered in the office or at home), or in organizational problems caused by parallel but independent events (e.g. changed foreign-exchange rate *and* death of an outstanding marketing manager).

- **Multiple effects of one cause**. The opposite also happens frequently: one condition is found to be the cause of a number of effects. For example, the existence of a political or ethnic clique in an organization can be the cause of numerous personnel, managerial and performance problems.

- **Cause or culprit?** The temptation to designate a person responsible for the existence of a problem may be strong. While this may be inevitable in instances of flagrant mismanagement or personal irresponsibility, in most situations the identification of a real cause will thus become more difficult and resistance to change will increase.

It is always necessary to proceed very methodically, examining in detail, on the basis of the information collected, whether a hypothetical cause could really have created the effect actually observed. A theoretically ideal situation is one in which the removal of one hypothetical cause does not result in the disappearance of the effect, indicating that we have not found the main cause. For example, in a workshop with bad working conditions workers get tired quickly and every day the output drops considerably after three or four hours of work. If these conditions (e.g. ventilation or lighting) are changed and output does not increase, or only very slightly, we have to look for a different cause. It may be malnutrition. Bad working conditions may aggravate the situation, but are not its main cause.

Unfortunately, to experiment by removing one or more hypothetical causes is not possible, or would be too lengthy and costly, in dealing with management and business problems. In most cases it is the quality of diagnostic work that has to eliminate some hypothetical causes and establish the real one.

Force-field analysis

A possible way of looking at relationships and factors affecting change is force-field analysis, developed by Kurt Lewin (figure 8.1). In this concept, the present state of affairs in an organization is thought of as an equilibrium maintained by two sums of forces working in opposite directions: driving (impelling, helping) forces move towards change, while restraining (impeding, hindering) forces hamper change.

Figure 8.1 Force-field analysis

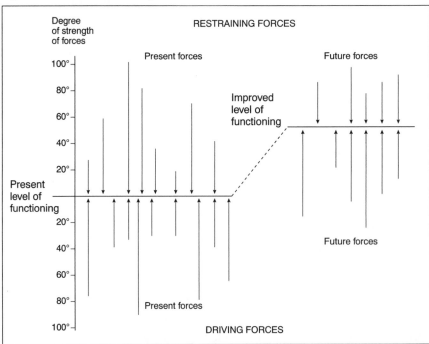

In analytical work, these two sorts of forces have to be identified and the relative strength of each force assessed. Change occurs when imbalance is created between the two groups of forces (e.g. by adding one or more new forces, or increasing or decreasing the strength of an already existing force). When a new state of affairs is attained, a new balance between driving and restraining forces is established. And the process continues.

Comparison

Comparison is an essential analytical tool, closely interlinked with the methodological tools discussed above. The principal alternatives for comparison which are commonly used in preliminary diagnostic surveys were mentioned in section 7.2. In detailed diagnostic work the same alternatives apply, but in addition to global appraisal, comparison is used to examine operating details and develop solutions. The various bases for comparisons made *within* the client organization are represented in figure 8.2. The consultant can compare C with A, C with B, C with D, E with C and so on.

Figure 8.2   Various bases for comparison

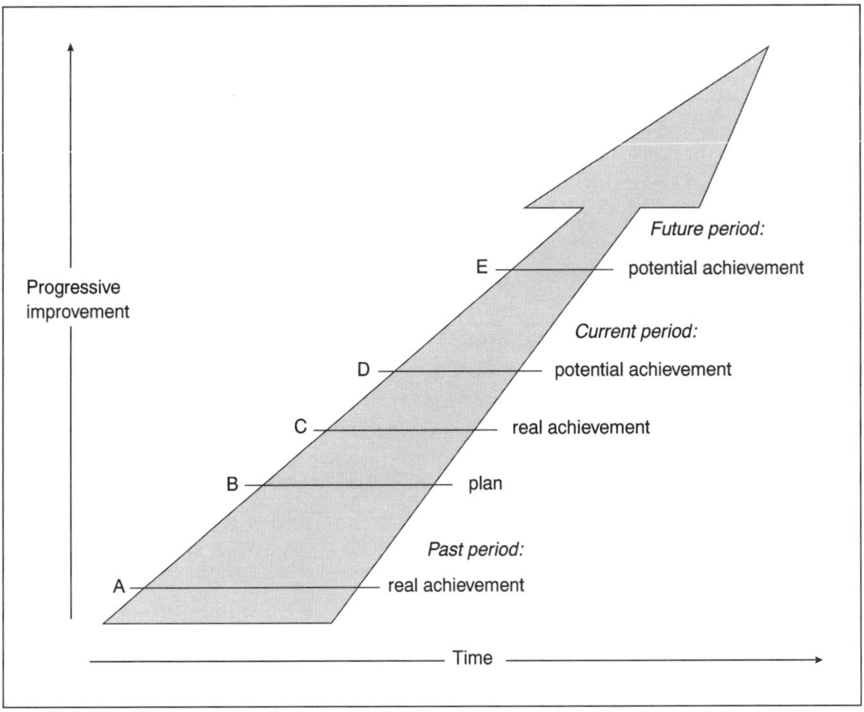

Of special interest is comparison which helps to establish future standards (of potential achievement) and thus provides guidance for the development of future-oriented proposals. It is particularly in this connection that comparison turns to examples, models and standards from outside the organization and even outside the sector and country. The consultant considers whether the diversity of conditions permits such comparison, especially if this is to be used for more than general judgement — namely for specific suggestions to the client as to what he or she should do.

Interfirm comparison is often used to assess global performance indicators against comparable data from other firms, or against sector standards. *Bench-*

marking is a more analytical technique owing to its focus on specific processes, operations and functions within organizations. It has been used by many firms to identify standards achieved by other organizations collaborating in the same benchmarking project or scheme, compare experiences and conditions, and develop specific proposals for improvements (see also section 4.6).

Analysing the future

Owing to its focus on action and results, all consulting work must be essentially future oriented. Whether the consultant works for a client struggling for survival or for a highly profitable company looking for new business opportunities, the key questions will always be: What will be our future opportunities? What shall we do in the future to achieve our purposes? Shall we focus on correcting past errors or shall we take a completely new path?

This future orientation gives a particular slant to fact analysis. For consultants have to collect or establish data on a situation that does not yet exist, in addition to collecting data on existing realities. They have to assess these data and recommend desirable courses of action that the client should take.

This statement is not exactly correct, since the future is related to the past and to the present. Many future events and relationships can be predicted. It is therefore essential to analyse trends in data describing the environment and the organization concerned. All consultants are interested in trends, whether the assignment deals with business strategy or with a narrower technical problem such as simplifying production records.

Unfortunately, the most common approach to future-trend analysis is *simple extrapolation*. We tend to think of the future as a mere extension of past trends, because we are unable or unwilling to consider whether these trends will really continue and what new developments may alter them radically. In periods of rapid technological, social and other changes — and we are living in one such period — it is normal for past trends not to continue into the future without substantial alterations.

Data on future trends collected from various external sources of information have to be examined cautiously and their reliability needs to be assessed. For example, a consultant working for a client enterprise with highly energy-intensive production processes obtains information on new power-generating capacities in construction, on their planned completion dates and on foreseen changes in the price of electricity. He should know that new power plants can be years behind schedule, that their actual cost tends to be higher than the original projected cost and that the price of energy will depend on many variables, including the government's tax policy. How will this affect the future development structure of costs in a client organization which is a major consumer of electricity? It may be necessary to develop alternative plans and estimate with what probability they are likely to become a reality.

Careful analysis is required when thinking of future developments within the client organization. These developments will be affected by environmental changes. For example, in analysing the time dimension of a product-life cycle it is necessary to consider whether the curve which is usual in a given sector applies, or whether progress in technology imposes the use of a different curve, as has been amply documented by the pace of developments in the computer industry.

The same applies to ratio analysis. Some ratios may become less important or even meaningless. In retail selling the ratio of sales per employee retained its meaning with the transition from small shops to department stores, super-markets and self-service. However, it is losing its meaning with the advent of automatically controlled sales surfaces if even the cashiers are replaced by electronic control and billing equipment. Ratios such as sales per square metre of selling surface, or sales per $1,000 of invested capital, become more sig-nificant. In general, ratios permitting the assessment of total factor productivity are becoming more important than labour productivity ratios, and so on.

Synthesis

To a management consultant the analytic method and the synthetic method are two sides of one coin. As fact analysis is progressing, the consultant's approach will increasingly involve synthesis — he or she will be identifying basic relationships, trends and causes, differentiating between fundamental and secondary events and factors, and defining factors and conditions that have to be changed if a whole process or organization is to change. In particular, the consultant operates as a synthesist when looking ahead and helping the client to define an action programme for preparing the future of the organization.

In management and consulting practice, synthesis is considerably more difficult than purely analytical work. Many bulky analytical reports are difficult to use, although they are based on vast numbers of facts and define long lists of problems. But they lack synthesis and key measures are not identified. As all the measures proposed cannot be introduced at the same time or with the same vigour, action starts in a haphazard way or is soon abandoned.

The spirit to synthesize and skill in synthesis are not given to everybody. Using synthesis is probably one of the main things that a new management consultant has to learn. Of course, consultants are not the only people who may have problems with synthetic thinking and using the synthetic method effec-tively. As Alvin Toffler has pointed out:

> Our civilization placed an extremely heavy emphasis on our ability to dis-mantle problems into their components: it rewarded us less often for the ability to put the pieces back together again. Most people are culturally more skilled as analysts than synthesists. This is one reason why our images of the future (and of ourselves in that future) are so fragmentary, haphazard and wrong . . . Today we stand on the edge of a new age of synthesis.[8]

Synthesis is the aspect of diagnostic work that provides a link with the next phase of the consulting process — the action-planning phase, which will be discussed in Chapter 9.

8.6   Feedback to the client

Throughout this chapter we have been referring to the desirability of actively involving the client in data gathering and other diagnostic operations. The objective is to build a truly collaborative consultant-client relationship at an early stage of the assignment, and to prevent various negative attitudes and reactions on the part of the client. These are difficult to avoid if he or she is poorly informed about what is actually going on, and if the consultant's findings and conclusions come as a surprise. We have mentioned, too, the need to give feedback to the client during the diagnostic phase.

What is giving feedback?

Giving feedback provides the client with information that can:

● tell the client something new and meaningful about his or her organization;

● make the client aware of the approach taken by the consultant and the progress made in the investigation;

● increase the client's active contribution to the assignment;

● help the consultant to stay on the right track, or reorient the investigation if necessary.

The notion of feedback implies that it concerns not just any useful information, but information collected, analysed and selected by the consultant while working with the client.

Feedback used during diagnosis is itself a diagnostic method. The assumption is that properly selected and presented information will provoke some reaction on the part of the client, and so you should keep firmly in mind what reaction you want to generate:

— Do you need more information on the topic?

— Do you seek information on a new topic, about which the client was reluctant to speak?

— Should the client criticize your data?

— Do you want to shake up a lethargic client by showing alarming data?

Giving feedback to the client is simultaneously an intervention technique used to stir up change:

● Is this what is wanted?

● Do you have enough reliable information to feed back to the client with the intention of stimulating change?

● Is there is a risk of generating premature changes?

● Should the client be warned against this risk?

When to give feedback

Feedback is more than reporting on the work performed. Therefore it should be given at moments when it can serve a specific purpose. An example is when feedback shows the client that the data collected so far indicate the existence of some new problem or opportunity, not foreseen in the negotiation and planning of the original assignment, or when the consultant feels that he or she has enough information to eliminate certain hypotheses formed at the beginning, but prefers to discuss this with the client. A consultant who pursues the strategy of " many small steps" may give feedback each time he or she has enough information to decide on the next step to take.

To whom to give feedback

In principle, feedback should be given to those from whom the consultant expects further help, more information, or some action related to the problem concerned. It is often emphasized that if feedback is too restrictive (reserved to selected individuals or small groups of senior managers), it is unrealistic to expect that other people will be interested in helping the consultant. Some authors regard this as a question of consulting ethics: if people readily provide information and demonstrate their interest in the assignment, they have the right to receive feedback on what has been done with their information. In theory, all people interviewed should thus receive some feedback fairly soon after the interview.

In practice there are limits to this. Some information will clearly be confidential and cannot be divulged to a large number of employees. Deciding who should be informed on the consultant's findings, and at what stage, is also a question of consulting tactics. For example, individuals who originally refused to give information to the consultant may change their attitude if they see that the consultant is sharing information with them.

What feedback to give and how

The consultant wants to show that he or she has not been wasting time and has important information to share. But the purpose is not to impress people. The consultant should be selective, sharing information that is meaningful, about which the client is likely to be really concerned, to which he probably will react, and which will activate him.

Giving feedback is not telling the client what he or she knows. This is a general rule, to be consistently observed in reporting and communicating with the client. But when the information collected contains factors that are genuinely news to the client, or shows unsuspected links between effect and cause or hidden strengths and weaknesses, it is wise to give feedback on these issues.

Giving feedback is not evaluating the client. Therefore, the consultant avoids value judgements; it is the client who should be able to draw such conclusions from information chosen and presented to him in an impartial manner. The purpose should always be kept in mind. For example, it is not good tactics to speak only about problems and difficulties, and more problems and more difficulties, encountered by the consultant. Feedback should also point to the client's problem-solving potential, and suggest strong points that might be developed.

Form of feedback

The need for careful preparation of the data and of the form of feedback to be used cannot be overemphasized.

Individualized oral feedback to important members of the client organization is very common. Another form is written information (e.g. interim reports or memos). Many consultants like to use feedback meetings with various groups in the client organization. These meetings can provide valuable additional information and help the consultant to focus the investigation on key issues. They invariably reveal attitudes to the problem at hand and to the approach taken by the consultant.

Closing the diagnostic phase

The end of the diagnostic phase provides an important opportunity for feedback. Before submitting a diagnostic report, consultants may find it useful to suggest one or more feedback meetings to review the main findings; this may help them to identify the last gaps in the analysis, and also prepare clients for the conclusions that will be formally presented to them.

Even if the assignment is to continue (i.e. if it is clear that there will be a smooth transition from the diagnostic work to action planning and then to implementation), there may be a good case for submitting a progress report at what is ostensibly the end of a predominantly diagnostic stage in an assignment. The period of obtaining and examining facts may have been lengthy, and costly to the client. Many managers may not have been involved very deeply, although they are interested in what the assignment will produce. A good progress report will certainly be welcomed. It should tell the client clearly how the work was focused, whether diagnosis has confirmed the choices made or discovered new problems and opportunities, and how the work on action proposals should be oriented.

There are, then, assignments that will have no further phase, such as management audits and comprehensive diagnostic studies of organizations, in which the consultant is required to establish and analyse facts, but for some reason the client does not want him to go beyond this point. In such cases the diagnostic report will also serve as an end-of-assignment report (see Chapter 11).

If the assignment is to continue, obtaining the client's agreement before embarking on action planning (e.g. on designing a new information system or workshop layout and planning its application) is essential. Consulting contracts often specify in detail what exactly will happen at the end of the diagnostic phase, before deciding if and how to pursue the assignment.

---

[1] This section is inspired, with the acknowledgement of the origin, by the discussion of the "purpose principle" in G. Nadler and S. Hibino: *Breakthrough Thinking: The seven principles of creative problem solving* (Rocklin, California, Prima Publishing, 1994).

[2] Jerome H. Fuchs addressing the Society of Professional Management Consultants in New York.

[3] P. Block: *Flawless consulting: A guide to getting your expertise used* (Austin, Texas, Learning Concepts, 1981), p. 141.

[4] Many books on business research methods are available on the market. For various methods of representing work processes see G. Kanawaty (ed.): *Introduction to work study* (Geneva, ILO, 4th (revised) ed., 1992). See also S. Nagashima: *100 management charts* (Tokyo, Asian Productivity Organization, 1987).

[5] See, e.g., Kanawaty, op. cit.

[6] See M. Kubr and J. Prokopenko: *Diagnosing management training and development needs: Concepts and techniques*, Management Development Series No. 27 (Geneva, ILO, 1989), or J._Quay: *Diagnostic interviewing for consultants and auditors* (Columbus, Ohio, Quay Associates, 1986).

[7] See, e.g. T. K. Reeves and D. Harper: *Surveys at work: A practitioner's guide* (London, McGraw-Hill, 1981).

[8] A. Toffler: *The third wave* (London, Pan Books, 1981), p. 141.

ACTION PLANNING

9

With action planning the consulting process enters its third phase. This phase includes developing solutions to the problem diagnosed, choosing among alternative solutions, presenting proposals to the client, and preparing for the implementation of the solution chosen by the client.

The continuity between diagnosis and action planning cannot be over-emphasized. The foundations of effective action planning are laid in excellent diagnostic work, i.e. by defining and analysing problems and purposes as well as the factors and forces that stimulate or hamper the change process in the client organization. Diagnosis provides basic orientation for action-planning efforts.

However, despite this emphasis on continuity and on the need to base action planning on diagnosis, there are significant differences in approach and methodology. The emphasis is no longer on analytical work, but on innovation and creativity. The objective is not to find more data and further explanations for the existence of one problem or another, but to come up with something new. Obviously, not all solutions to clients' problems will involve totally fresh approaches. Often there will be no need to develop a new solution from scratch because a suitable one already exists somewhere else. Yet, even transfer and adaptation require imagination and creativity. Ignoring the uniqueness of the client's condition and mechanically transplanting solutions that have worked in other organizations is one of the worst (though not one of the rarest) consulting mistakes.

It is highly desirable that in action planning the client's involvement should become even more active than in the diagnostic phase. There are several reasons for this:

— extensive conceptual, design and planning work on one or a small number of alternative solutions should not be undertaken if it is not certain that the client is fully familiar and in complete agreement with the approach taken, and will be able to go along with the alternatives that are being pursued; this agreement can best be established by working jointly with people who are in a position to ascertain what the client organization will accept and be able to implement;

— action planning requires mobilizing the best talents and examining all good
ideas; it is ineffective if the client organization's talents do not contribute
to this effort;

— as with diagnosis, the client's personnel can do a great deal of design and
planning work with backstopping from the consultant, thus reducing the
cost of the project;

— participation in action planning generates commitment that will be necessary, and put to a test, at the implementation stage;

— lastly, action planning provides a new range of learning opportunities for
the client; these opportunities are even more interesting that those offered
by diagnosis, but will definitely be lost if the consultant is left to proceed
alone.

Once more, the reader should refer to section 4.6 describing various intervention techniques for assisting change. Some of these techniques can be used
for working on action proposals in a team with the client and his or her staff.

Time may have become a constraint. In many assignments too much time
is spent on collecting and examining facts, and when it comes to the development
of proposals there is a general desire to finish the project as soon as possible.
The consultant is left with little time to prepare alternatives and rapidly develops
only one solution. But even work on one proposal may have to be concluded
somewhere short of perfection. This can be avoided by properly scheduling the
assignment and making sure that enough time is left for creative search for the
most appropriate solution.

9.1 Searching for ideas on possible solutions

The client expects that the consultant will find and recommend the best
solution to the problem, or suggest the best way of taking a new opportunity.
However, it is seldom possible immediately to point to an obvious best solution
(although this can happen). Most business and management problems have more
than one solution and in some cases the number of alternative solutions is high,
especially if the purposes pursued are complex. The consultant may be aware
of some possible solutions, but unaware of other alternatives. Often the complexity and the originality of the situation are such that no clear-cut solution
comes to anybody's mind immediately. New situations cannot be dealt with by
old approaches, and management consultants operate in a field which is
changing extremely rapidly.

The action-planning phase starts therefore by searching for ideas and
information on possible solutions to the problem. The objective is to identify all
interesting and feasible alternatives and subject them to preliminary evaluation
before starting detailed design and planning work on one proposal. Thus the
consultant will be sure to offer the client the best possible solution. The client,
on the other hand, will feel confident that he or she is not being forced into
accepting one solution without being informed about other possibilities.

Orienting the search for solutions

The main factor to be considered is the nature of the problem, especially its technical characteristics (functional area; techniques or methods to be changed), complexity (technical, financial, human and other aspects of management involved; importance to the client organization; need to respect sectoral technical standards), and degree of newness (whether the consultant and the client are familiar with the problem involved; whether a completely new solution has to be developed, or an established solution can be applied with or without adaptation).

The consultant, in collaboration with the client, will have to decide whether to direct the search towards solutions that may be available (e.g. purchasing a standard software package from a computer firm), or towards a new original solution (developing new software using the client's own resources, or commissioning such work from a specialist in software design). It is necessary to decide how far this search should go. Should it be limited to the client organization? Could possible solutions be found in other organizations, sectors, or countries? Is it necessary to screen technical literature? Should we turn to research establishments? Box 9.1 (overleaf) provides a check-list of some questions to consider in deciding how to focus the search for feasible solutions to the problem.

Using experience

In devising ways of improving the client's situation, the consultant often draws on experience. He or she considers methods successfully used elsewhere, on the basis of knowledge derived from a variety of sources:

- previous assignments and clients;
- the consulting organization's files and documentation;
- colleagues in the consulting organization who have worked in similar conditions;
- professional literature (books, periodicals, research reports, etc.);
- producers of equipment and systems software, who may have developed improvements or have been working on them;
- staff in other departments of the client organization, who may have knowledge of the particular process;
- organizations which are prepared to communicate their experience.

An obvious purpose is to avoid reinventing the wheel. An even more important purpose is to make sure that all available experience will be identified and considered, so that the client gets advice that could be qualified as "state of the art", or a solution reflecting the best experience that could be found.

This is an acid test for the consultant, who must not cede to the obvious temptation to choose the most comfortable way — suggesting what he or she has done in similar situations with previous clients, or choosing the first solution

---

Box 9.1   Check-list of preliminary considerations

(1)   What should the new solution achieve?

- what basic purpose?
- what other purposes?
- what level of performance?
- what quality of output?
- what new product, service or activity?
- what behaviour?

(2)   How will the new situation differ from the present?

- different products, services or activities?
- different method?
- different system(s)?
- different equipment?
- different location?
- different way of managing?

(3)   Are the effects likely to last?

- are the client's business and market changing rapidly?
- is competition likely to come with better solutions?
- is there a possibility that people will revert to present practices?
- should further developments be foreseen?

(4)   Where could solutions or ideas be found?

- in the same unit?
- in the same enterprise?
- from business partners or friends?
- in literature?
- in a research institution?
- in the consulting firm?
- from other consultants?
- in different sectors?
- anywhere else?

(5)   What difficulties may arise?

- technical problems?
- managers' and staff resistance?
- work hazards?
- quality problems?
- over-production?
- shortage of materials?
- customers' reactions?
- shortage of finance?

---

(6) Who will be affected?

- are employees receptive?
- is management receptive?
- what should be done to prepare them?
- how should they be involved?
- do matching changes have to be made elsewhere?

(7) When is the best time to change?

- at the end of a season?
- during holiday time?
- at the close of a financial period?
- at the beginning of a new calendar year?
- any time?
- as soon as possible?
- in several stages?

that will come to mind. For example, a solo practitioner may have completed a thorough diagnosis of the client's problem, but when it comes to proposing a better system there clearly is a need for expertise that he does not possess. What will he suggest? Will he go for the second-best solution or admit that another professional should be brought in? The same problem exists in larger consultancies, where the partners and other managers do not always appreciate the need to back up the operating consultants with all the collective expertise and information sources of the firm when looking for the best solution of a particular client's problem.

Creative thinking

In current consulting, there are more and more situations where experience cannot offer any satisfying solution and where both the consulting team and the client organization will have to come up with a totally new approach. In this connection, it may be useful to review some principles and methods of creative thinking.

Creative thinking has been defined as *the relating of things or ideas which were previously unrelated*. It combines a rigorous analytical approach with intuition and imagination. The purpose is, of course, to discover or develop something new. Nothing is taken for granted. The history of science and business is full of examples of discovery based on creative thinking, and there is no reason why the consultant could not approach many practical industrial and management problems by the same method. Creativity can be learned, and is worth learning.

There are five stages in the creative thinking process, and all need to be practised consciously to get the best results:

(1) PREPARATION: Obtaining all the known facts; applying analytical thinking as far as possible; getting the problem defined in different ways, i.e. restating the problem and the purposes pursued.

(2) EFFORT: Divergent thinking, which will generate multiple ideas, concepts and approaches. It will lead either to possible solutions or to frustration. Frustration is an important feature in the effort stage and in the full creative thinking process. It is usually followed by the production of really good ideas.

(3) INCUBATION: Leaving the problem in one's subconscious mind while one gets on with other things. This also gives time for inhibitions and emotional blocks to new ideas to weaken, and gives opportunities to pick up additional ideas from what one sees or hears in the meantime.

(4) INSIGHT: The flash of illumination that gives an answer and leads to possible solutions of the problem.

(5) EVALUATION: Analysing all the ideas obtained in the last three stages so as to find possible solutions.

Two of the stages — preparation and evaluation — require analytical thinking. The three central stages — effort, incubation and insight — require suspended judgement and free-wheeling. Wild ideas are deliberately fostered, the aim being quantity, not quality. Large numbers of ideas are obtained, new ideas being sparked off by earlier ideas. The key to successful creative thinking is the conscious and deliberate separation of idea-production and idea-evaluation.

Techniques of creative thinking include, among others:[1]

Brainstorming. This is a means of obtaining a large number of ideas from a group of people in a short time. Typically a group of eight to 12 people take a problem and produce ideas in a free-wheeling atmosphere. Judgement is suspended and all ideas, particularly wild ones, are encouraged. In fact the wildest ideas can often be stepping-stones to new and very practical ones. Ideas are displayed on sheets of newsprint and are produced very quickly; a session may produce over 200 ideas in about an hour. Brainstorming is the best known and most widely used of the techniques. Its main disadvantage lies in the fact that all ideas are to be evaluated. Many of them are foolish or totally irrelevant and have to be discarded to arrive at a few really good ideas. Also, the term "brainstorming" is often misused, to describe any discussion about an existing problem.

Synectics. In this technique, which is similar to brainstorming, a group of about nine people take a problem. The "client", whose problem it is, explains it, and participants put forward a suggestion for solving it. After a few minutes the client analyses the suggestion, saying what he or she likes about it before touching on the drawbacks. Then new suggestions are put forward and analysed until possible solutions are found.

Attribute listing. This technique lists the main attributes of the idea or object, and examines each one to see how it can be changed. It is normally used on tangible rather than intangible things. For example, a screwdriver has the following attributes: round steel shank; wooden handle; flat wedge end; manual operation; torque by twist. Each attribute is questioned and changes are suggested. Some modern screwdrivers, i.e. with ratchets or a cruciform head instead of the wedge end, are examples of improvement.

Forced relationships. This technique takes objects or ideas and asks the question, "In how many ways can these be combined to give a new object or idea?" For example, a manufacturer of furniture could take the items he makes and see if two or more could be combined to give a new piece of furniture.

Morphological analysis. This technique sets down all the variables in a matrix and tries to combine them in new ways. For example, if a new form of transport is required, the variables could be as shown in box 9.2. Although the matrix does not give all possible alternatives, the various combinations of the variables listed give an impressive number of forms of transport, many of which exist. Many alternatives will be discarded, but some are worth considering and may suggest new, practical, useful and feasible solutions.

Box 9.2   Variables for developing new forms of transport

Travelling in	air, water, space, land surface, underground
Travelling on	wheels, rollers, air cushion, magnetic cushion, skids, moving belt, aerial ropeway
Travel path	reserved, shared with other vehicles
Control	under operator's control, externally controlled
Energy provided by	electricity, petrol, gas, special fuel, atomic power, wind, water
Energy transmitted by	pulling, pushing, ejecting, own engine
Energy transmission	internal: to wheels, propeller (air), propeller (water), caterpillar tracks, ejection
	external: magnetic, hydraulic, pneumatic, mechanical, via cable, via moving belt, via screw transmission
Position of traveller	sitting, lying, standing, hanging

Lateral thinking and PO. If a problem is tackled analytically, it is necessary to go into greater and greater depth and detail — this is vertical thinking. Creative thinking involves the examination of all options, including those that appear to be outside the given problem area — that is to say, lateral thinking. Edward de Bono has recommended deferring judgement by prefacing an idea with the letters "PO", which stands for "give the idea a chance, don't kill it too quickly, it may lead to useful ideas".[2]

Check-lists. These may be used as pointers to ideas. Lists may be particular to an area (e.g. marketing, design) or general. Osborn's generalized check-list[3] is well known; the main headings are: Put to other uses? Adapt? Modify? Minify? Substitute? Rearrange? Reverse? Combine? Check-lists need to be used with care, as they can inhibit creativity by limiting the areas of inquiry.

The Six Thinking Hats. This approach, developed by Edward de Bono, suggests the use of different thought processes for different purposes. Each hat has a different colour and is used as a symbol for a particular way of thinking (*white* — for assessing available and required information; *red* — for feelings and emotions about the issue; *yellow* — for looking at gains and advantages; *black* — for constraints, criticism and risks; *green* — for creativity, new ideas and possibilities; and *blue* — for pulling the whole thinking process together and managing it). Participants in creative thinking sessions are asked to actually wear these hats during the session when they are applying a particular way of thinking.[4]

Breakthrough Thinking. This approach, developed by Gerald Nadler and Shozo Hibino and mentioned in section 1.4 (box 1.5) and other parts of our book, provides "seven principles of creative problem solving". It does not follow a constant pattern of inquiry, but proposes a general flow of reasoning. An opportunity for a breakthrough must be continually sought in order to increase the probability of one of the three distinct types of breakthrough: (1) the brilliantly creative idea; (2) the solution that produces significantly better results; or (3) bringing to fruition the "good idea", in order to make it real and implement an outstanding system or solution.[5]

The search for new creativity techniques continues. For example, *daydreaming* has been suggested if long intensive work on a problem does not generate any innovative solution; in such a situation complete relaxation and virtual dreaming may bring about creative insight. The *"group-genius"* technique gathers in one group several individuals who normally use different ways of creative thinking, thus forming a team able to combine these techniques.[6]

In summary, no matter which technique is used, the following four guidelines apply:

● SUSPEND JUDGEMENT — Rule out premature criticism of any idea.

● FREE-WHEEL — The wilder the ideas the better the results.

● QUANTITY — The more ideas the better.

● CROSS-FERTILIZE — Combine and improve on the ideas of others.

Barriers to creative thinking

In business and management practice, there is a need to struggle against barriers to creative thinking. Most people are educated and trained to think analytically, but only a few are trained to use their creative ability. Creative thinking is also restricted by:

— self-imposed barriers;

— belief that there is always one right answer;

— conformity or giving the expected answer;

— lack of effort and courage in challenging the obvious;

— evaluating too quickly;

— fear of looking a fool.

Awareness of the barriers to creative thinking, and a conscious effort to break them down in a creative situation, open a vast area of new ideas, or ways of tackling problems. Suspending judgement is a particularly pertinent example of how a better understanding of the creative thinking process can help towards a fuller use of creative abilities in seeking solutions to difficult management problems.

Respect for authority is a major barrier which is difficult to overcome. Even if a person perceived as an authority (a manager, a chief designer, a consultant, a writer, an older person) does not explicitly require conformity and uniformity, and encourages colleagues to look for new ideas, challenging his or her views may be difficult if not impossible in many organizational and national cultures. This is one more reason why managers in both consulting firms and in client organizations should refrain from expressing preference for one solution if the search for the best solution is to continue!

Success can be a serious barrier to creativity. In a successful company, management can easily become locked into methods and practices that have been its strong points, and may be unwilling to recognize that there can be an even better approach, or that owing to its success the company has stopped working on further improvements.

Excessive individualism and the failure to use teamwork is another serious barrier. If people work in a team examining a complex problem from various angles, information on a new idea put forward by one team member usually helps other members to widen or correct their outlook, and to come up with other new ideas. Members of a team can not only help but also emulate each other.

The solution-after-next principle

This principle of Breakthrough Thinking,[7] referred to earlier, suggests developing alternative solutions that take into consideration future needs. The principle states that the change or system you install now should be based on what the solution might be when you work on the problem the next time.

This implies anticipating future changes: in the environment, in demand for the client's services or products, in competition and within the client organization itself. An obvious requirement is that by adopting a new solution we must not block the way to further solutions that may become necessary in the future (e.g. by building a production capacity or a data base that cannot be expanded). Viewing the problem and the solution from a future perspective helps to arrive at the best possible current solution. It may be useful to visualize an ideal future system. Even if such a system cannot be implemented immediately, certain elements will be usable and the vision of the future will improve the quality of the solution that will be adopted. Box 9.3 gives three check-lists as pointers when searching for an ideal solution.

9.2   Developing and evaluating alternatives

Preselecting ideas to be pursued

As mentioned in the previous section, in the search for innovative ideas judgement has to be deferred to avoid blocking the process of creative thinking.

There comes a moment, however, when new ideas have to be sorted out, reviewed, discussed and assessed (e.g. very interesting; interesting; trivial; useless; not clear). Since it would be impossible to pursue a large number of ideas, a preselection is made. For example, only "very interesting" ideas will be followed up.

How many ideas should stay on a short-list and what criteria to use in classifying certain ideas as "very interesting" is a matter for judgement. The selection should be made in close collaboration with the client. If the client feels that several ideas may lead to acceptable solutions, he or she should also realize that, while parallel work on several solutions may increase the chance of arriving at an ideal solution, the length and the cost of the assignment will probably have to be increased, too.

Box 9.3   Searching for an ideal solution — Three check-lists

A. To inspire group creativity, you might:

(1)   Prohibit any criticism when ideas are being generated, allowing a later time for judgement and assessment.

(2)   Encourage free-wheeling, however wild the ideas that may emerge.

(3)   Involve someone who is not a stakeholder in the project.

(4)   Record all ideas so that each receives due consideration.

(5)   Pose questions that stimulate or motivate creativity:

    (a)   What system or value-added services and outcomes would make us an acknowledged world leader?

    (b)   What would the solution be if we faced no constraints?

    (c)   What would the ideal system look like if we could achieve all the purposes larger than the one we selected?

    (d)   What would the solution look like if we started all over again (clean slate, green field, blank piece of paper)?

(6)   Focus discussions on how to make suggested solutions work, rather than on why they won't work. Play the believing game.

(7)   In using all of these tools, have fun with humorous activities that stimulate imagination. In generating ideas, humour is a serious matter.

B. Here are some "red flags" to watch out for
on your solution-finding journey:

●   "We can't go beyond our scope."

●   "Stay on your own turf."

●   "Don't exceed the local budget."

●   "If it looks like it will work, we'll make it work."

- "Let's get on to the next problem."
- "There's only one correct solution for this problem."
- "That's totally unrealistic."
- "Let's get real here."
- "In our department (group, organization) that's not possible."
- "That's just not done in our industry (profession)."
- "It won't work. Ten per cent of our customers want rhubarb pie."
- "We can't go back to zero."

C. Always ask yourself these specific questions:

— Have I generated many solutions-after-next or ideal systems?

— How should we achieve these purposes if we had to start all over again?

— How do I see this purpose and each bigger purpose being accomplished ten years from now?

— What regular occurrences can help us develop the best ideal solution? (Remember to avoid the trap of 15 per cent irregularity. Focus on the 85 per cent that a solution will work.)

— What today is impossible to do but, if we could, would fundamentally change the business?

— Am I seeing the right targets toward which our recommendations should lead?

— Have I looked for a second right answer? A third? A fourth?

Source: Excerpts from Ch. 6 ("The solution-after-next principle"), in G. Nadler and S. Hibino: *Breakthrough Thinking: The seven principles of creative problem solving* (Rocklin, California, Prima Publishing, 1994).

Working on alternatives

If the preliminary screening of ideas has retained more than one alternative, the detailed design, systems development and planning work should in theory be started on all alternatives that were short-listed. In practice a pragmatic attitude is needed since the client and the consultant may be short of resources for working on a number of possibilities simultaneously, and detailed design and planning of several alternatives may be inefficient if only one is to be retained.

A phased approach may help. For example, work may be started on two or three alternatives, but carried only to a pre-project or sketch-plan level. This will make it possible to collect more factual data, including tentative figures on potential costs and benefits. An evaluation of alternative pre-projects can result in the conclusion that from that moment only one will be pursued or, on the contrary, that the client wishes the design of two or more alternatives to be completed.

Another possibility is to start by developing the alternative that received the highest preliminary rating as an idea. This alternative may be pursued as long as facts show that it would provide a satisfying solution. It would be dropped, and work on a second alternative started, only if assessment revealed that the course of action taken was incorrect, or that cost-benefit analysis was not showing satisfactory results.

It could be objected that these (and similar) approaches do not give a 100 per cent guarantee that the ideal solution will be found and applied. This is true, but the solutions are being developed in real life, within given time, financial, human and other constraints. The ideal solution may be within the consultant's and the client's reach — but the time or cost required could be prohibitive.

Evaluating alternatives

It can be seen that the evaluation of alternatives is not a one-off action to be undertaken solely at a defined point in time in the assignment. When data are collected and analysed, this is being done with due regard to the forthcoming evaluation exercises. At the beginning of the assignment, the consultant pays attention to the definition of the reference period during which data will be collected and used for comparing new solutions with the existing ones. When action planning has started, preliminary evaluation may be made in several steps to eliminate ideas and to reduce the number of alternatives on which the consultant and the client will start doing detailed work. A comprehensive evaluation is required when the client finally opts for one particular alternative.

Some comments on *the evaluation criteria* may be useful. There are some comparatively easy cases, such as the choice between two or three machine tools (of different technical level, productivity, service and maintenance requirements, and price) for the same production operation. The number of criteria is limited and can be quantified, especially if production records are reasonably good. In contrast, there are complex cases, such as a major reorganization in a manufacturing company, an acquisition of another company or a new marketing strategy, which are very much "open-ended". There may be several alternatives. Personnel and training measures will be involved, and so on. In these cases some criteria lend themselves to fairly exact calculation of costs and benefits (e.g. the cost of training needed). Others do not (e.g. the greater effectiveness of decision making obtained following decentralization of authority and responsibility in marketing and product-policy matters, or the improved image of the company following a merger with a well-chosen partner).

In consulting on management and business issues, the following situations prevail:

— alternatives which are ideal by all criteria used are rare, and in most cases there is a need to compare positive and negative consequences of several alternatives;

— the number of criteria is high: certain basic criteria are met by all alternatives and further criteria have to be examined;

— some important criteria (especially environmental, social, cultural and political criteria) are difficult, if not impossible, to quantify;

— the evaluation involves some assessment of criteria which are not directly comparable (e.g. financial and political criteria);

— this introduces a strong subjective element into evaluation: in the absence of hard data somebody has to decide how important various criteria are in the given case, and make the evaluation using these "soft" criteria in addition to hard data.

To overcome this last difficulty, and to increase the element of objectivity in subjective evaluations, various attempts have been made to associate numerical values with adjectival scales. The principle is to use a group of experts (from the client organization, the consulting firm or other) to assign point values to particular criteria. The values thus obtained are then used in an evaluation model, e.g. in decision analysis. The scale may be as follows:

Major improvement	=	10
Considerable improvement	=	7
Some improvement	=	4
No change	=	1
Some deterioration	=	–2
Considerable deterioration	=	–5

The evaluation technique used will be selected with regard to the nature and complexity of the particular case. It may be a simple break-even analysis, cost-benefit analysis, return on investment analysis, linear programming technique, decision analysis, or some other technique. Broader social and environmental consequences of managerial decisions will, as mentioned, be difficult to quantify and compare with economic and financial costs and benefits. Notwithstanding, the number of techniques which attempt to account for these aspects in evaluation models and schemes is growing.

9.3 Presenting action proposals to the client

When work on action proposals and the evaluation of alternatives has reached an advanced stage, the consultant has to consider the time and form for the presentation to the client. This will depend mainly on the type of project undertaken and the working relationships between the consultant and the client's managerial and specialist staff.

In long and complex assignments, involving strategic issues and costly investment or other measures, the client's staff is usually very much involved and keeps the senior management informed about progress. The consultant submits progress reports and seeks further guidance from the client at several points during the assignment, so the presentation of final proposals does not bring up anything completely new. Essentially, information that the client has had from previous reports and other contacts with the consultant is summarized, confirmed and put up for approval.

In other cases, the reporting which has preceded the presentation of proposals may have been limited. The scope of the assignment may not require reporting and discussions at each step; or, in assignments that will affect some vested interests (e.g. reorganizations), the client does not want to hold many meetings and have information circulated before the solutions have been defined and thoroughly examined by a restricted managerial group. Hence the need for a well-prepared presentation which, in the latter case, may convey completely new information to a number of people.

The presentation

Most consultants prefer to be able to make an oral presentation with the backing of all written evidence and any audiovisual aids needed to support the case. A combination of written and oral presentation is often required. The consultant can make an oral presentation, introducing documentation that will be left with the client, to be followed by another meeting once the client has examined the proposal in more detail. Alternatively, the client may prefer to receive the proposal in writing first and arrange a presentation meeting after having read the proposal.

The objective of the presentation is, of course, to obtain the client's acceptance of the recommendations. The degree of persuasion will depend on many factors and must be anticipated, prepared for and built into the presentation. The presentation meeting is held between the consulting team (including the supervisor), the client and those members of the staff chosen to attend. The client's liaison officer and other staff specialists may have an important role to play. Having taken part in the investigation they may be informed about many details and should be completely in favour of the recommendations.

The consultant's presentation works through a logical series of steps, building up the case for the recommendations in so effective a manner that the client should have little or no hesitation in accepting them. At least, that is the idea. No presentation should be made unless the consultant believes that the probability of acceptance is high.

The presentation must never flood decision makers in the client organization with analytical details, or try to impress them by techniques that are normally the specialist's domain. However, the techniques used in evaluation should be described. A clear picture of all solutions that have been envisaged is given and the choice proposed by the consultant is justified. The consultant must be absolutely honest with the client, especially when he or she is explaining:

- *the risks involved* (the solution has never been used before; some employees will probably be against it; the real investment and /or operating costs may be higher than foreseen);
- *the conditions that the client must create and maintain* (a high discipline in recording primary data is needed; maintenance has to be improved; some members of senior management must be transferred);
- *the tasks that could not be completed* (the search for potential partners could not cover all countries; some evaluation criteria had to be ignored due to lack of data or time);

- *the future perspectives* (the solution proposed does or does not anticipate future developments such as capacity expansion, automation, transfer to affiliated companies, more stringent environmental protection norms).

There may be circumstances known to both parties owing to which acceptance at this point may be in principle only. There may be an agreed intention, but a final decision may be contingent on a detailed study of written proposals by the client, on consultations with important shareholders or on the recommendations being explained to and accepted by employees' representatives.

Where there have to be further presentations to representatives of trade unions, staff associations or other stakeholder groups, the role of persuader and negotiator shifts to the client. Under no circumstances should the consultant take this on alone. He or she is, of course, ready to back up the client and help to organize whatever explanatory campaign is necessary — and he or she should strongly advise against trying to get everything over at one mass meeting.

Plans for implementation

One section is often missing from action proposals presented to clients: a realistic and feasible plan for the implementation of the proposals. The client receives a static picture, describing the new project or scheme as it should look when implemented. Yet there may be a long way to go to achieve this desired condition, and several different paths may be available. Moreover, the planning of stages and activities to put the new scheme into effect can reveal further problems and needs, allowing the proposal to be further improved before the final version is submitted to the client.

Thus an effective action proposal shows not only *what* to implement but also *how* to do it. A plan for implementation should be included in the proposal in any case. The client and the consultant can agree that this plan will be a global one, leaving the details to a later stage, immediately preceding each step towards implementation.

The decision

It is the client and not the consultant who decides what solution will be chosen and applied. On no account should the client feel that the consultant has made his own choice which the client must follow in order not to upset the whole scheme. A client who feels that a solution was imposed on him will not be very active during the implementation phase, and will take the first opportunity to put the blame on the consultant if matters do not work out as suggested.

The client's decision on the consultant's proposal is subject to the same influences as any other management decision. The number of important decisions that are determined by emotional rather than rational criteria is surprisingly high. Furthermore, the client's conception of rationality may differ from the consultant's conception because their cultural background is not the same.

It is essential that the consultant is aware of *the client's personal preferences*, and of *cultural and other factors* affecting decision making in the client organization. This awareness helps him or her to avoid proposals which will not be accepted, and to recognize again that consulting is much more than presenting technically perfect solutions: it also involves patient persuasion and explanation to the client and the staff so that they will accept rational measures as their favourite personal choices.

The decision taken on the consultant's proposals may be the final point of an assignment if proposals are accepted for immediate or later implementation, and the client wants to undertake the work personally. It will act as an introduction to the next step in an assignment if the client prefers to involve the consultant in implementation.

------

[1] See, e.g., J. G. Rawlinson: *Creative thinking and brainstorming* (Farnborough, Hampshire, Gower, 1981), and various publications by Edward de Bono.

[2] E. de Bono: *Lateral thinking: A textbook of creativity* (Harmondsworth, Middlesex, Penguin, 1977).

[3] A. F. Osborn: *Applied imagination* (New York, Charles Scribner's Sons, 1957).

[4] E. de Bono: *Six Thinking Hats: An essential approach to business management from the creator of lateral thinking* (New York, Bowker, Ingram, 1987).

[5] See G. Nadler and S. Hibino: *Breakthrough Thinking: The seven principles of creative problem solving* (Rocklin, California, Prima Publishing, 1994).

[6] See R. L. Bencin: "How to keep creative juices flowing", in *International Management* (Sutton, Surrey), July 1983.

[7] See Nadler and Hibino, op. cit., Ch. 6.

IMPLEMENTATION

10

Implementation, the fourth phase of the consulting process, is the culmination of the consultant's and the client's joint effort. To implement changes that are *real improvements* from the client's point of view is the basic purpose of any consulting assignment. The consultant, too, wants to see his or her proposals not only well received in meetings with the client, but put into effect with good results.

If there is no implementation, the consulting process cannot be regarded as completed. This is the position if the client does not accept the consultant's proposals presented at the end of the action-planning phase. It demonstrates that the assignment has been poorly managed by both parties. If the consultant and the client collaborate closely during the diagnostic and action-planning phases, the client cannot really reject proposals that are the product of joint work. If there is any doubt about the focus of the consultant's work during action planning, and about the feasibility of the proposals that will be forthcoming, corrective measures should be taken immediately, without waiting until the proposals have been finalized.

It may happen, too, that the consultant does not find any solution to the client's problem. Maybe the problem as formulated does not have a solution (e.g. the goal set was too ambitious and unrealistic). Such a situation should also be discovered and the work on proposals redirected at an earlier stage, so that action planning comes up with realistic proposals on how to deal with a redefined problem.

In planning an assignment and negotiating a contract, the client and the consultant should not forget *to define what they mean by "implementation" and "results"*. If the consultant is developing and helping to introduce a customized information system, what operations have to be completed and what parameters have to be achieved so that the system can be regarded as fully implemented? What do we mean by implementation in an action-learning programme — increased competencies of the participants, an approval of the proposals developed in action-learning teams or the actual completion of all the change measures proposed? To agree when a very complex project, such as a business restructuring or turnaround, should be regarded as completed may be difficult indeed. However, the failure to clarify these questions early enough is a frequent cause of misunderstanding between consultants and their clients.

10.1 The consultant's role in implementation

Why the consultant should be involved

In Chapter 1 we gave some arguments justifying the consultant's involvement in the implementation phase of an assignment. The issue is important enough to be reviewed once more.

As we know, the ultimate responsibility for implementation is with the client. It is the client, not the consultant, who makes all the management decisions and sees to it that they are put into effect. This, of course, is more easily said than done. The more complex the assignment, the higher the probability that implementation will be an equally or more difficult matter than diagnosis and action planning. The plan or project presented by the consultant is a model of future conditions and relationships, assuming certain behaviours on the part of the client, as well as particular environmental and other conditions affecting the client organization. The consultant can make mistakes in developing such a model. In addition, many of the conditions can change after the proposal has been presented and accepted. The consultant's co-responsibility for implementation helps to overcome these difficulties.

The issue of the consultant's participation in implementation should never be underestimated, but always thoroughly examined and discussed when designing a consulting project. Both the consultant and the client should give their arguments for and against this participation and consider various alternatives.

The consultant does not have to be involved in implementation:

- if the problem is relatively straightforward and no technical or other difficulties with implementation are anticipated;
- if joint work during the diagnostic and action-planning phases shows that the client has developed a very good understanding of the problem and a capability to implement the solutions proposed without further assistance.

The client's reluctance to involve the consultant may be motivated by financial reasons. By the end of the action-planning phase the cost of the assignment may already be high and the budget may be exhausted. Or the manager who has to approve the contract may feel that involving the consultant in implementation implies expenditures that can be avoided. Here again a frank discussion helps. The consultant can suggest a more economical design for the assignment in order to free resources that will allow him or her to be involved in implementation.

Finding a suitable arrangement

The failure to involve the consultant in implementation often reflects a lack of imagination and flexibility on either the consultant's or the client's part. Of course the client worries about the cost of the assignment, and the more time the project takes, the stronger may be the feeling that the consultants are staying for too long. The following arrangements can keep the consultant involved in implementation without imposing high charges on the client:

— the size of the consulting team present at the client's premises will be gradually reduced during the implementation phase;

— only one consultant will stay during the whole implementation phase, providing advice and bringing in additional expertise from the consulting unit if appropriate;

— the consultant will deal only with the more difficult tasks in implementation, leaving all other work to the client;

— the consultant will visit the client periodically, or at agreed points during implementation, to check progress and provide guidance;

— the consultant will be available to intervene only at the client's special request.

Clearly, every consulting unit will not be able to offer all these options. Larger firms can be more flexible. A sole practitioner will be working with a new client when a former client calls for help in implementation. It may be necessary to warn the new client that the consultant has not fully completed a previous assignment, though he is phasing himself out of it.

The alternative arrangements described above ought to be given consideration irrespective of the fee formula used (section 26.4). If a lump-sum or contingency fee is applied, the consultant will make a provision for involvement in implementation when calculating the total fee. The client should be aware of this. In addition to defining the end result of the project, the assignment plan and contract should be as precise as possible in defining the roles played by both the consultant and the client in the implementation phase.

10.2 Planning and monitoring implementation

A set of proposals for implementation should be part of the action plan presented to the client, for reasons explained in section 9.3. Before implementation starts, a detailed work programme will be prepared.

Steps to take

Planning a campaign to introduce a new method or system is another instance of the usefulness of network planning or bar-charting techniques. The day chosen as "implementation day" will be more definite if planned for in this way. The time needed to obtain equipment and to design detailed procedures may be relatively easy to estimate. When there is a major physical move, as required by, say, a new factory or general office layout, a scheduled sequence of individual moves is necessary. When there has to be "business as usual" during the move, the schedule recognizes the need for the minimum of upset. Sometimes a short, sharp campaign can take place during an annual shutdown. When it does, all employees are briefed on what they will find when they return so as to avoid some days of chaos.

Defining responsibilities and controls

Implementation will create new tasks and relationships, while abolishing old ones. People's commitment and participation cannot be solicited without specifying their contributions. Such a specification will be particularly helpful in drawing up a training programme and in establishing controls for monitoring implementation.

Furthermore, the programme of implementation should define controllable and, if possible, measurable results of individual tasks, operations and steps. This is essential for monitoring.

Pace and lead-time of implementation

Obviously, various technical and resource factors will have a bearing on the pace and lead-time of implementation. As a matter of principle, the consultant will aim to schedule implementation in the client's best interest (e.g. to make new production capacity operational as early as possible, or to avoid situations in which the client has to deal with several difficult projects or use old and new information systems simultaneously).

The feasible and desirable pace of change (see Chapter 4) is a most important criterion. It may be necessary to gain the commitment and support of a number of individuals, who will constitute a kind of critical mass. Considerable time and persuasion may be needed to create this critical mass, but once attained its existence will accelerate the whole process. These are important aspects of the strategy of planned change.

Built-in flexibility and contingency

The more complex and innovative the assignment, the greater the chance that the work programme will need to be adjusted several times during the implementation phase. Monitoring will show this need. However, adjustments are easier if some flexibility is built in. Completion of the assignment should not be scheduled for the very last moment (i.e. the time when the new scheme or plant must be in operation); some time should be kept in reserve for final adjustments. The same may apply to the allocation of resources and to provision for further help by the consultant during implementation.

Detailing procedures

When a good deal of new methodology is involved, it is usual to prepare a manual for guidance in the procedures to be followed. Virtually all forms of reorganization, irrespective of their functional or interfunctional aspects, and all new systems, require instructions on how to operate them. New stationery has usually to be designed. The consultant may do this personally or may adopt part or all of some proprietary system.[1]

Monitoring implementation

When implementation is about to start, the consultant checks that all conditions have been fulfilled and all prerequisites are on hand.

At the commencement of the running of the new system and for a time after, the consultant is available to answer any queries and to help the client's staff to deal at once with any problem that may arise. This is as much a question of tactics as of techniques, since little deficiencies and misunderstandings at the moment when a new system is starting up have a tendency to grow and become major difficulties if not dealt with immediately. In this the consultant may have more experience than the client.

It is not uncommon for decision makers, including the consultant, to experience uncomfortable afterthoughts once a decision has finally been reached and implementation commences. This phenomenon is known as *cognitive dissonance*. Prior to reaching a decision, the decision makers usually spend an inordinate amount of time focusing on the benefits of the new scheme and the disadvantages of the present, or alternative, scheme. However, once a firm decision has been reached, the implementation process commences and the first problems inevitably appear, it seems that a good deal of time is now spent on reviewing the advantages of the previous, or displaced, scheme, while comments are voiced on the drawbacks of the new scheme currently being implemented.

It is readily conceded that it takes considerable talent to examine an existing scheme and, on the basis of investigations and results obtained, devise a new, more effective one, but it also takes considerable courage to proceed with the implementation of the new scheme when problems are met with in the early stages of the implementation phase (as is usually the case). When this happens the consultant would do well to take note of the maxim: "Take time to plan your work, then take time to work your plan."

Jointly with the client, the consultant makes a regular and frequent assessment of the progress of implementation. Attention is paid to the pace of implementation and its broader consequences (e.g. whether the changes in plant layout and organization of the production department are proceeding according to schedule and the delivery of any new product will start as promised). Adjustments in the time schedule, the approach taken, or even the original design of the new scheme are made as appropriate, but in an organized manner, avoiding ad hoc, blind panic decisions.

The consultant's poised behaviour during this phase of the work affects the attitudes of the client and his or her staff towards implementation. The consultant must be seen as an enthusiastic senior colleague who feels fully involved and co-responsible, who has a vision of what should be achieved, and who is able to explain the roles and responsibilities of others engaged in the project.

10.3 Training and developing client staff

In Chapters 1 and 2 we have shown that the link between consulting and training is logical and natural. Both have the same ultimate objective — to improve organizational performance and results — and they support each other. In most operating assignments some training and development of client staff is foreseen in the work programme. It may take a variety of forms and its volume will differ from case to case.

Developing the cooperating team

Perhaps the most interesting and efficient, although the least formalized, method is the development of client personnel through direct cooperation with the consultant during the assignment. In a smaller enterprise this may concern the owner-manager personally. In other organizations it will concern some managers, the liaison officer and other members of the team who are responsible for the project jointly with the consultant. A good consultant uses every opportunity not only to pass on routine jobs (such as data collection) to client staff, but increasingly to involve them in the more sophisticated operations demanding skills and experience, and stimulating self-education. As this is an excellent learning opportunity, it is useful to assign to this job talented people with good development potential, and not just those who can be spared from their normal duties for the period of the assignment.

Managers in senior positions will also learn from the assignment if the consultant knows how to communicate with them and if they are keen to find out what the consultant's work methods are. That is why it is more interesting for a senior manager who finds a really good consultant to interact with him or her frequently instead of just meeting formally at the beginning and then reading the report at the end of the assignment.

Training for new methods and techniques

A common element in assignments is the training of client staff in specific techniques. This concerns those staff members who are involved in the introduction and use of the technique (e.g. time measurement, statistical quality control, standard costing). A number of people may have to be trained; this may necessitate a precisely defined and scheduled training programme which precedes implementation and may continue during its first stages. A number of approaches are possible, such as:

— on-the-job training by the consultant;

— training of in-company trainers by the consultant;

— training of experimental groups whose members will then train the remaining staff;

— formal in-company training courses (run by the consultant, by special trainers brought in for this purpose, or by the organization's internal trainers);

— participation of selected staff in external training courses;

— appreciation programmes for those who are not directly involved, but should be informed.

Staff development in complex assignments

As the problems tackled by the consultant become increasingly sophisticated and complex, the related training and development of staff also become more difficult to design and organize. This is the case, for example, in assignments aimed at major changes, such as extensive reorganizations and restructuring, important changes in product and market strategies, or the establishment of a new plant including the installation of a new management system. In addition to specific training in new techniques which may be needed, there is a case for a collective development effort which should bring about more substantial changes in management concepts, strategies, communication and styles.

In these situations, training in particular work techniques may have to be supplemented by programmes aimed at behavioural change. These may include seminars, working groups, discussion groups, special project teams, individual project work, exchange of roles, counselling by the consultant and by in-plant trainers, and so on. Some of these intervention techniques were described in Chapter 4.

In addition to practicality, another important feature of training provided in connection with consulting assignments is that it generates interest in further training and self-development. Sound management stimulates and nurtures this interest, which may actually be the most lasting contribution of many consulting assignments.

10.4 Some tactical guidelines for introducing changes in work methods

In this section we summarize a few practical guidelines on how to introduce new work methods and help people to master them without major difficulties. Here again, the purpose of the guidelines is to make the consultant alert to what might happen and suggest in what direction to search for a remedy, not to provide universal recipes for handling any situation. The guidelines that follow should be read in conjunction with Chapter 4, which the reader may wish to review at this point.

Tactic 1: The best method

It was mentioned in Chapter 4 that the process of change involves (i) identi-fication with the change, and (ii) internalization of the change. Whether these phases are carried out in sequence or simultaneously is not very important. The essential point is that they require commitment, involvement or partici-pation by the person doing the changing. The change must be tested by the individual as he or she moves from the general (identification) to the specific (internalization).

Therefore the people concerned in the change process should be involved as early as possible, so that these two vital elements can be comprehensively covered. However, a strong note of warning is offered as to how participation might be achieved. Apart from attending meetings or brainstorming sessions for specific purposes (such as to provide a data bank of ideas for the solution of creative problems), individuals should not start using their own new methods for performing tasks if the idea is to develop a best method for general use. Results of studies show that where individuals are encouraged to adopt their own approaches and the best method or approved solution is later imposed, those people will exhibit some conformity to the new proposal but will still diverge significantly from the approved method in following their own.

However, where persons in groups are provided with a best method or approved approach in the first instance, it is found that subsequently individuals will vary only insignificantly from the set procedures. Diagrammatically, these results can be shown as in figure 10.1.

In case 1 the end result is that individuals perform in a manner significantly different from the approved method, although not quite as widely different as during their initial trials. There is some tendency towards the norm. In case 2 there is in subsequent performance much less divergence (significant in a statistical sense) from the approved norm because individuals have not had an opportunity to rehearse in any other manner than the approved one.

Thus, where feasible, the consultant should attempt to introduce the approved method as a scheme applying to the whole group where individual differences can be kept to a minimum (often as a result of normal group pressures, coupled with the fact that no opportunity to develop individual ad hoc approaches is provided).

Tactic 2: Spaced practice

Improvement in performance occurs more quickly, in greater depth and lasts for a longer time (i.e. the decay or extinction curve is longer) if new approaches are introduced in relatively short periods, with ample provision for rest periods, than if continuous or massed practice periods are employed.

A generalized improvement in performance noted where the "quick and often" tactic is employed (compared to a continuous practice scheme) is shown in figure 10.2 (page 230).

Figure 10.1   Comparison of the effects on eventual performance when using individualized versus conformed initial approaches

Case 1: Subsequent behaviour diverges significantly from the conformed approach when individualized approaches are used prior to the introduction of the conformed approach.

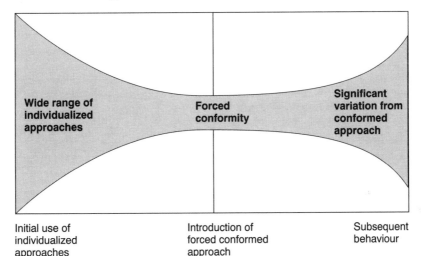

| **Wide range of individualized approaches** | **Forced conformity** | **Significant variation from conformed approach** |

| Initial use of individualized approaches | Introduction of forced conformed approach | Subsequent behaviour |

Note: Although subsequent behaviour usually differs significantly from the conformed approach, it is not as widely divergent as the initial individualized approaches.

Case 2: Subsequent behaviour diverges very little from the conformed approach if no opportunity is provided for individual experimentation prior to the introduction of the conformed approach.

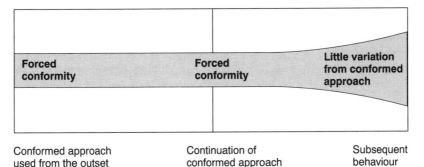

| **Forced conformity** | **Forced conformity** | **Little variation from conformed approach** |

| Conformed approach used from the outset | Continuation of conformed approach | Subsequent behaviour |

Note: Subsequent behaviour is significantly less divergent from the conformed approach in case 2 when compared to case 1.

**Figure 10.2   Comparison of spaced practice with a continuous
or massed practice approach in terms of performance**

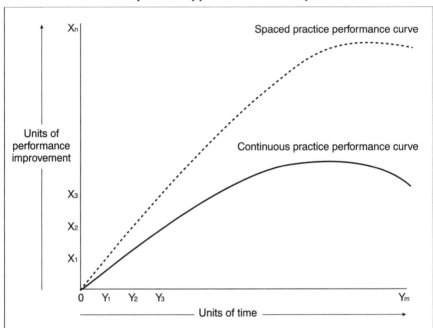

From figure 10.2 it can be seen that when a spaced practice approach is used and the results are compared with those of a continuous or massed practice approach for the same period:

● improvement using spaced practice is quicker, i.e. the performance curve is sharper;

● improvement using spaced practice is greater, i.e. the performance curve is higher;

● improvement lasts longer, i.e. the decay or extinction curve is shallower.

These performance curves will almost invariably be obtained where improvement in skill can be measured as a result of practice or rehearsal. Thus the consultant is well advised to consider introducing change gradually using relatively short practice sessions rather than relying on one great training input.

Tactic 3: Rehearsal

It is a proven fact that where skill is involved, results constantly improve with spaced practice, provided, of course, that the correct procedures are followed.

As shown in figure 10.2, performance constantly improves with continued practice until a ceiling or plateau of performance is reached. Continued practice is then required to maintain this level of performance.

Although there may be grounds for debate as to whether or not learning (i.e. the cerebral functioning involved) of a new technique takes place:

— as a sequential process, i.e. a little-by-little approach,

— as an all-or-none process (e.g. the "Eureka — I've got it!" type of phenomenon),

— or by repetitive exposures of the same input in different settings,

the learning method is not really relevant since the learning process cannot, as yet, be appropriately measured. However, there is no escaping the fact that performance, which can be measured, always improves with practice. Constant practice can eventually lead to a condition known as over-learning in which routine and procedures become virtually automatic reactions.

The consultant must therefore make provision for appropriate training and practice sessions (rehearsals) when introducing new approaches.

Tactic 4: Moving from the known to the unknown

There is considerable evidence that the knowledge of a prior skill can have either a positive or negative transfer effect on the acquisition of a new skill.

As mentioned earlier, the consultant is usually faced at the beginning with the need for an "unfreezing" phase, designed to break down old habits. Surprising as it may seem, in order to be able to facilitate new learning it is usually more effective to have the learner in an "anxious" rather than a "comfortable" state, because he or she is then more likely to actively seek information to reduce the level of anxiety. In a "comfortable" state, the learner is more likely to select information which will continue that state, to reinforce old habits rather than seek new approaches.

The consultant can use this attention-rousing device by showing that the "known" procedures are no longer suitable for present purposes. If we move directly to the introduction of new methods without first breaking down established practices, there is a grave risk of negative transfer effects taking place.

When introducing a totally new approach, however, there may be some benefit in building it on an appropriate existing procedure. In short, when introducing change, move from the known to the unknown (new approach).

Tactic 5: Setting demanding but realistic goals

According to S.W. Gellerman, "stretching" is desirable when goals are being established.[2] By this he means that targets should be set a little higher than would normally be expected. D. C. McClelland supports this notion and adds that the goals should be realistic and neither "too easy" nor "impossible", but such that a feeling of achievement can be experienced when they are reached.[3]

There is ample evidence to show that high expectations coupled with genuine confidence in a prestigious person often result in an individual undergoing change attaining higher performance and productivity. This effect can become cumulative — the improved performance encourages the individual to assume more responsibility and so creates in him or her greater opportunities for achievement, growth and development. Conversely, low expectations may lead to low performance and substandard results which, in turn, leads to a situation in which credibility is lost and distrust and scepticism become the order of the day.

When introducing change, the consultant has to ensure that all those involved readily understand what this means in terms of goals. Such goals should be expressed in terms which are:

— quantitative (able to be measured in numerical terms);

— qualitative (able to be described specifically);

— time-phased (provision of commencement dates and expected duration before final attainment).

It is important to correctly determine the time by when a new goal has to be achieved. Because attitudes and work habits take a long time to form, time must be allowed for replacing them by new ones. Unless there is a perceived dramatic need to institute a change immediately, the process may take longer than originally expected.

Tactic 6: Respecting the absorptive capacity

People differ tremendously in their capacity to absorb new information and their ability to undertake new activities. Many writers have argued that there is a maximum number of "units of information" which an individual can absorb and process at any one time. In this connection G. W. Miller refers to the "magical number seven" (plus or minus two, to allow for variations in individual capacity).[4] By confining information inputs to the lower end of the scale (namely five), the consultant can avoid overtaxing any of his audience, although he may cause some degree of impatience among the most gifted.

The information can first be presented as a single whole and can then be broken down into subunits for more detailed study, or it can be built up gradually by synthesis of the individual parts. The method chosen will depend on the nature of the problem, the composition of the audience and the consultant's personal preference.

During the introductory and concluding phases of an information session, it is as well to provide a summary of the complete presentation. There is support for the idea that the attention of an audience reaches its highest level shortly after the commencement of a session and again shortly before its conclusion. At the outset the exposition probably has a novelty value, which begins to be dissipated as physical and mental fatigue build up. Shortly before the conclusion is reached, however, the decrease in the level of attention accounted for by lack of concentration is usually removed as the audience begins to anticipate the end of this activity and the beginning of a new one. These high points in concentration are illustrated in figure 10.3.

**Figure 10.3 Generalized illustration of the high points
in attention level of a captive audience**

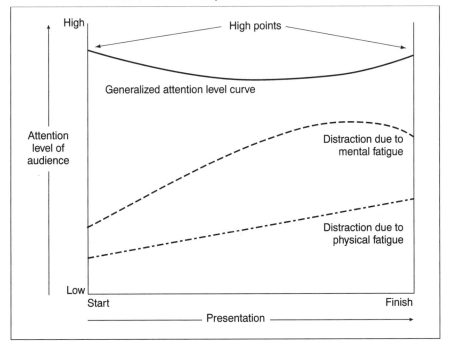

Tactic 7: Providing evidence and feedback

Verbal persuasion is inherently unstable and requires support in terms of proven facts. Action speaks louder than words. The consultant must keep records of all performance improvements as support for the change process. For example, although daily output figures may decrease immediately following a change process, it is possible that errors or accident rates may decrease even more significantly at the same time.

Successful introduction of change requires presentation of appropriate feedback information to permit the necessary adjustments on the part of those undertaking the change process. The consultant must make provision for review and reporting sessions, not merely as morale-boosting devices, but as a requisite for control and correction.

10.5 Maintenance and control of the new practice

If a new scheme is to survive and yield more in benefits than it costs, it has to be protected against a number of more or less natural hazards. Standards, systems and procedures are as prone to deterioration through wear and tear and neglect as are machines. Like machines, their performance may be eventually reduced to zero.

Maintenance and control should start while the consultant is still with the client organization, but must continue after his or her departure.

Backsliding

A maintenance and control system has to guard against simple backsliding, which is liable to occur as long as people remember what they used to do before the change. Backsliding is not always reactionary. If a new method breaks down through trouble with a computer system, equipment, supplies, and so on, work can only continue by doing something else. The most natural thing is to revert to the old practice if that is still possible. While the consultant is well advised never to stop anyone working to the old method until it can be completely replaced, he or she should also make sure that after the new method has been proved it is impossible to revert to the old one.

The way this is done will depend, as always, on the function of the assignment and the nature of its problem. A few examples are given below.

Paperwork. When a new documentation procedure is installed, the stock of old forms is destroyed. Some official is made responsible for maintaining stocks of new forms and signing orders for reprints. The purchasing clerk does not pass on orders for printing signed by any other person.

Operating standards. The maintenance of factory work standards requires similar vigilance. Working to standards must be made easier than working to non-standards. Any work outside the specification of the product or method should not be feasible using the standard forms and documentation. This is not to say that departures from standard are never allowed, but when they are they are made self-evident.

Drawings. In an engineering drawing office it must not be easier to make a new drawing for a part than to find whether an existing part may be used. When a drawing is permanently changed, all old prints are tracked down and removed. An adequate control system would prevent unauthorized prints being in circulation at any time.

All such measures are, of course, preventive. In their absence, the alternative is often not a cure but a temporary expedient with a strong likelihood of a recurrence of the problem.

Control procedures

A system of control does not necessarily stop at maintenance in the narrow sense of keeping a scheme in the same state. After a time, any piece of reorganization will begin to suffer from old age, if nothing else. Other changing influences may render it less and less appropriate; the objective for which it was designed may no longer be there. Without a means of control, opportunities to modify and develop in line with changing circumstances may be lost.

It is, however, as easy to overdo control for its own sake as it is to become fascinated by any other technique. The consultant needs only to identify the key points at which significant departures will show up and choose the times at which they are to be checked. It is unnecessary to check everything every day: the criterion is usually how long it would take for anything serious to happen if it were not checked. More frequent checks are needed immediately after a change than later on, when stability at a new level has been reached.

In financial areas, checks are part of budgetary control and made as often as the sensitivity of the situation demands. Labour performance checks may be built into weekly payroll/production analyses. Inventory controls may be in accordance with the main categories of stores.

Business companies accept the annual audit of their books as a matter of course, but may forget that a periodic internal audit of their organization and administrative methods is equally necessary. Apart from those detailed safeguards already mentioned, a periodic audit may be the only way of checking the whole system. Only an audit may reveal whether the total objectives are still being met, or are even still the same. Failure to make such a check allows the passage of time to erode insidiously the good work and its benefits.

Staff turnover is a common source of danger. If new staff members are not adequately briefed, they have little option but to act as they think fit. They may pursue surprisingly different objectives. The number of shortcomings that the consultant has met in the client organization may be an indicator of habitual neglect. If he or she does not change the client's basic attitudes to controls, his or her own work may get no better treatment.

Further improvements

Conversely, it would be unrealistic and totally wrong to assume that the implementation of the consultant's proposals will make the client's business perfect and that for a long time no further changes will be required. Improvements may be suggested by the managers, specialists and workers involved in a new scheme, by customers, by the consultant personally or by other professionals working for the same client. Improvements may become possible and necessary due to developments in information technology and other changes that could not be fully considered in the course of the current assignment. Any such improvements may be suggested and become necessary surprisingly soon, much sooner than the consultant imagined when submitting the new scheme to the client.

There will be improvements that can be easily accepted and introduced during the implementation phase. Other improvements will not fit the scheme that has been chosen, but it will be useful to record them and keep them in mind for the future. Remember the "solution-after-next" principle discussed in Chapter 9. There is no point in aiming to propose and implement definitive and closed solutions to clients' problems if we know only too well that change is the only constant of our times and that better solutions will become both feasible and necessary in the future.

---

[1] In the latter event it has to be remembered that suppliers of such systems have a vested interest in selling stationery and that standard packages may not fit the given situation very well.

[2] D. C. McClelland and D. G. Winter: *Motivating economic achievement* (New York, The Free Press, 1969).

[3] S. W. Gellerman: *Management by motivation* (New York, American Management Association, 1969).

[4] G. W. Miller: "The magic number seven, plus or minus two" in *Psychological Review*, Vol. 63, No. 2, Mar. 1956.

TERMINATION

11

Termination is the fifth and final phase of the consulting process. Every assignment or project has to be brought to an end once its purpose has been achieved and the consultant's help is no longer needed.

It is not enough to execute the assignment in a professional manner. The disengagement also has to be fully professional: its timing and form have to be properly chosen and all commitments ought to be settled to the mutual satisfaction of the client and the consultant.

It is the consultant who has primary responsibility for suggesting at what point and in what way he or she would withdraw from the client organization. He or she bears in mind that the client may feel uncertain about the right moment for terminating the project, in particular if the consultant's presence has clearly contributed to important improvements in management and the client has become used to seeking advice on important items. The client may feel more secure if the consultant continues to be available to help with any new problems that may arise. This, however, could make the client excessively dependent on the consultant, who would, to use an analogy, function as a crutch needed by a permanently handicapped patient instead of an orthopaedist who helps the patient to recover all physical capabilities.

Termination concerns two equally important aspects of the consulting process: the job for which the consultant was brought in, and the consultant-client relationship.

First, the consultant's withdrawal means that the job in which he or she has participated:

- has been completed;
- will be discontinued;
- will be pursued, but without further help from the consultant.

In deciding to terminate the assignment, the consultant and the client should make it clear which of these three applies in their particular case. There should be no ambiguity about this. It is of no benefit to anybody if the consultant is convinced of having done a good job while the client waits only for the consultant's departure in order to stop the project. Thus the consultant and the client should jointly establish whether the assignment can be qualified as a success, a failure, or something between these two extremes.

Second, the consultant's withdrawal terminates the consultant-client relationship. The atmosphere and the way in which this relationship is discontinued will influence the client's motivation to pursue the project, and his attitude to possible future use of the same consulting organization. Here, too, the assignment should not be terminated with uncertain and mixed feelings. Ideally, there should be satisfaction on both sides about the relations that existed during the assignment. The client should be convinced that he has had a good consultant, to whom he would gladly turn again. The consultant should feel that he has been trusted and respected, and that working again for the same client would be another stimulating experience. The relationship has a financial dimension, too: both parties should feel that a proper price was paid for the professional service provided.

Professional consultants attach great importance to the way in which they terminate assignments. The last impressions are very significant, and an excellent performance at the end of assignments leaves the door open for future work. We know how important repeat business is to management consultants. Repeat business, however, is available only to those whose performance remains flawless until the very end of every assignment.

11.1 Time for withdrawal

To choose the right moment for withdrawal is often difficult, but if a wrong decision is made a good relationship can be spoiled and the success of the project jeopardized.

Planning for withdrawal

Some assignments are terminated too early. This is the case if:

- the consultant's work on the project could not be completed;
- the client overestimated his or her capability to finish the project without having been sufficiently trained for it;
- the client's budget does not permit the job to be finished;
- the consultant is in a hurry to start another assignment.

Instances of assignments that finish later than necessary are also frequent. This happens if:

— the consultant embarks on a technically difficult project without making sure that the client is properly trained to take over from him or her;

— the job is vaguely defined, and new problems are discovered in the course of the assignment;

— the consultant tries to stay longer than necessary.

To avoid these situations, the question of timely withdrawal should be discussed right at the beginning of the consulting process, when the consultant presents the whole assignment cycle to the client. The consulting contract should define when and under what circumstances the assignment will end. As already mentioned, the choices are numerous. The assignment can end after the diagnostic phase, after action planning, at some stage during implementation, or when implementation is completed and agreed results achieved.

It may be difficult to determine the right moment for withdrawal when signing the contract. At such an early stage it is often impossible to foresee how implementation will progress, how deeply the client's staff will be involved, and what new relations and problems will emerge or be discovered during the assignment.

That is why it is recommended that the assignment plan is reviewed at critical points during the assignment; at each review it should be asked how much longer the consultant should stay, and what remains to be done before the assignment could be terminated.

Gradual withdrawal

Gradual withdrawal has already been mentioned in section 10.1. In many situations this can be the best arrangement from both the client's and the consultant's point of view.

Watching withdrawal signals

Withdrawal signals, as some consultants call them,[1] show the consultant that the client would like to terminate the assignment. They can be very overt, or indirect and hidden. The client may start being less frequently available to meet the consultant, or may indicate in some other way that enough time has been spent on the project. It is essential to be alert to these signals. This does not necessarily mean that the consultant should immediately pack up and leave if he or she has valid professional reasons for pursuing the work, but the point should be frankly discussed with the client.

Never stay longer than necessary!

If the client is convinced that he can proceed alone, the consultant should never insist on staying longer even if he does not share his client's opinion. After all, he who pays the piper calls the tune. It is the client who is paying the consultant, not vice versa.

Staying longer than necessary is unprofessional and damaging to the consultant's image. Unfortunately, as one practitioner has put it, "some consulting outfits are like a fungus that gets inside the client and keeps finding new areas not in the original agreement and stays on and on, sucking the blood out until someone pulls the plug and says 'enough'. Their advice is superb, but it just gets to be too much".[2]

11.2 Evaluation

Evaluation is a most important part of the termination phase in any consulting process. Without evaluation, it is impossible to assess whether the assignment has met its objectives and whether the results obtained justify the resources used. Neither the client nor the consultant can draw lessons from the assignment if there is no evaluation.

Yet many assignments are never evaluated, or their evaluation is superficial and of marginal interest. This is due to certain difficulties inherent in the evaluation of change in organizations and human systems. The number of factors affecting such systems is considerable and to isolate factors changed following a discernible consulting intervention may be difficult. For example, if the purpose of the assignment was to increase output, evaluation cannot take for granted that any higher output achieved by the end of the assignment is due only to the intervention of the consultant. It may be that the increase is due to other factors and the assignment actually made no contribution. Some changes are difficult to identify, measure, describe and assess.

In addition, evaluation can be the most delicate part of the consultant-client relationship and it may be more comfortable to avoid it, in particular if the client is not very happy with the consultant's performance and if there is a feeling that they would not collaborate again. Financial reasons also play their role: even the simplest evaluation exercise will cost some time and money and the client may feel that this money can be saved, because it is not used for developing anything new.

Who should evaluate

As with the whole consulting process, effective evaluation requires collaboration. Both the client and the consultant need to know whether the assignment has achieved its objectives and can be qualified as a success story.

The client has, of course, certain specific interests and viewpoints. He is evaluating not only the assignment but also the consultant and his performance. If the client is keen to perform better next time, he also makes a self-evaluation, assessing his own technical and managerial performance in cooperating with the consultant, monitoring the progress of the assignment and making use of the advice received. In the same way, the consultant will evaluate his own and the client's performance.

How much of this will be a joint exercise and what information will be shared is a matter of confidence and judgement. In an assignment that has been a true collaborative effort, evaluation is usually open and constructive. Yet no one can force the client and the consultant to share all conclusions from their evaluations.

Evaluation will focus on two basic aspects of the assignment: the benefits to the client and the consulting process.

Evaluating the benefits to the client

The reasons for evaluating the benefits of the assignment are self-evident. The benefits define the change achieved, a change that must be seen as an improvement, as a new value added to the client's business. Remember our discussion of consulting purposes and objectives in Chapters 1 and 7. Basically, the benefits are evaluated by comparing two situations, one before and one after the assignment. This is possible if the evaluation was foreseen in designing the assignment, i.e. in defining results to be achieved and criteria whereby the results actually achieved will be measured and assessed.

Evaluation will seek answers to the following questions:

— Has the assignment achieved its purpose?

— What specific results and benefits to the client have been achieved?

— What expected results could not be achieved?

— Has the assignment achieved some unexpected and supplementary results?

In typical management consulting assignments there are six kinds of benefit or result:

● new capabilities;

● new systems;

● new relationships;

● new opportunities;

● new behaviour;

● new performance.

New capabilities. These are the new skills acquired by the client: diagnostic and other problem-solving skills, communication skills and change-management skills, as well as special technical or managerial skills in the particular areas affected by the assignment (e.g. new ways of raising finance for the business). New client capabilities in serving customers are particularly important (e.g. ability to deliver new products and services or to meet quality standards in new countries). New capabilities also include qualities such as the client's increased ability to take action, creativity, entrepreneurial spirit, ability to innovate, sensitivity to environmental issues and similar. In a nutshell, the client should have become a more competent and more independent decision maker.

New systems. Many assignments help to introduce specific systems changes, such as new information systems, marketing systems, production and quality management systems, personnel recruitment and appraisal systems, preventive maintenance, and so on. These systems can be considered as assignment outcomes if they are, or are likely to become, operational.

New relationships. The assignment may have helped to establish new business and other relationships essential to the future of the client's business, such as new strategic alliances, subcontracting arrangements, consortia for implementing complex construction projects or agreements on benchmarking.

New opportunities. These may concern various parts and aspects of the client's business. The consultancy may have identified new potential markets, cheaper sources of raw materials, new technologies to be explored, land and buildings to be acquired and so on.

New behaviour. Changed behaviour means doing things in a different way. This term is mainly applied to interpersonal relations (e.g. between managers and their subordinates, or between cooperating teams from two different departments). However, it also embraces individual behaviour in work situations (e.g. whether or not a worker uses a safety device preventing accidents, how sales personnel treat customers or whether a general manager has actually stopped postponing unpleasant decisions).

New performance. New performance is achieved if changes in the five areas mentioned above produce improvements in economic, financial, social or other indicators used to measure performance. These changes can be observed at individual (workstation), unit (workshop, team, group, plant, department), or organizational (enterprise, agency, ministry) level.

Higher performance is an overriding goal and should be used for evaluating outcome and showing benefits whenever possible. Consulting which would improve capabilities without aiming at improved performance could be an academic exercise, and a luxury from the financial point of view. It does happen, however, that changed performance cannot be used to assess results (e.g. new capabilities have been developed and opportunities identified, but the client has to postpone the application of measures that will bring about superior performance). Also, the client's improved business and managerial capabilities can under certain circumstances be regarded as more important benefits, and of longer duration, than immediate measurable improvements in economic and financial performance.

Short-term and long-term benefits

In some assignments it may be necessary to distinguish and compare the short-term and long-term benefits. Impressive short-term results may ignore the future prospects and needs of the business and may be achieved to the detriment of the client's longer-term interests. Conversely, modest or no short-term results may be justified if the assignment has focused on longer-term benefits. The future prospects of the client's business, and long-term results, should be always kept in mind, even if the assignment has pursued short-term benefits above all.

Evaluating the consulting process

The evaluation of the consulting process is based on the assumption that the effectiveness of the process strongly influences the results of the assignments.

This concerns assignments aimed at behavioural changes above all: if new sorts of behaviour and processes are to become established in the client organization (result), the consultant must choose and propose to the client a consulting style and intervention method (process) that can produce the desired outcome. For example, it is unlikely that a real change in the client's problem-solving capabilities will be achieved by giving a lecture or distributing a technical note on problem solving and decision making.

The consultant-client relationships and the intervention method develop during the assignment. Different methods can be used, and the process can become more or less collaborative and participative, and more or less effective. The evaluation should reveal this. The principal dimensions of the consulting process to be evaluated are as follows.

The design of the assignment (the contract). It is useful to start by examining the start of the relationship. The questions to be raised include these:

- How and by whom was the need for the consultancy established?
- How was the consultant chosen? What criteria and procedures were used?
- Was the purpose of the consultancy clear? Was it not unduly narrow or vague?
- Was the design of the assignment clear, realistic and appropriate with regard to the client's needs and particular conditions?
- Did the original definition of purposes, objectives and inputs provide a good framework and guidance for the assignment plan? Were the objectives sufficiently demanding but not impossibly so?
- Was the consulting style properly defined, discussed and understood? Were people briefed about their roles and responsibilities right at the outset?

The quantity and quality of inputs. In addition to assessing the original definition of required inputs made in the assignment plan, evaluation includes the examination of inputs that were provided by the consultant and the client. The main questions are:

- Did the consultant provide a team of the required size, structure and competence?
- Did the client provide the resources (human and other) needed for the assignment?

The consulting mode (style) used. In this section, the consultant and the client assess in retrospect the events that took place and the relationship that existed during the assignment. They ask in particular:

- What was the nature of the consultant-client relationship? Was there an atmosphere of mutual trust, understanding, respect and support?

- Was the right consulting mode (style) used? Was it adapted to the client's capabilities and preferences, and adjusted to the task at hand?
- Was every opportunity taken to increase the client's involvement in the assignment?
- Was proper attention paid to the learning dimension of the assignment? What was done to transfer knowledge and know-how to the client?
- Did the consultant scrupulously observe all ethical and behavioural norms of the profession?

The management of the assignment by the consultant and the client. Gaps and errors in the original assignment plan can be corrected and modifications required by changed conditions can be made if the assignment is aptly managed by both partners. An evaluation addresses the following questions:

- Was the necessary flexibility built into the original design of the assignment?
- How did the consulting firm manage and support the assignment?
- How did the client control and monitor the assignment?
- Did the consultant and the client respect the timetable?
- Was there an interim reporting and evaluation at key points in the assignment? What action was taken on the basis of it?

Evaluation tools

Priority is given to collecting and examining hard data permitting measurement and quantitative assessment. In addition, identifying and examining opinions is important, particularly for evaluating the consultant-client relationship and the consulting style. Classical techniques are used, including interviews, observations, questionnaires and discussions at meetings (see Chapter 8).

A frank discussion between the client and the consultant is essential. Step by step, the discussion should try to review what happened in the client's and in the consultant's opinion, as well as the causes underlying particular attitudes and behaviours, achievements and errors.

Evaluation should be summarized in a short report, which can become a part of the final assignment report, or be presented separately (e.g. if the evaluation of results takes place several months after the completion of the assignment).

When to evaluate

There is a case for evaluation when the assignment is coming to an end. Some benefits to the client may already be identifiable and it is possible to evaluate the consulting process in retrospect. The end-of-assignment evaluation is certainly the most important one. But it should not be the only one. Delaying evaluation until the end of implementation can mean that it is too late to suggest any improvements in the assignment strategy, methodology and management. Such suggestions are of interest only for future assignments. That is why interim evaluations should be foreseen at the end of the diagnostic and the action-planning phases. They should be treated as a normal part of the joint control and monitoring of the assignment by the consultant and the client. If necessary (e.g. in long and complex assignments), even within diagnosis, action planning and implementation, there may be a need for several evaluation exercises to review progress and interim results and, possibly, to adjust the assignment plan and the work methods used.

On the other hand, it is often impossible to complete evaluation right away at the end of the assignment. If measurable results cannot be identified immediately, or if the projected performance cannot be achieved until some time later, there is a case for follow-up evaluation.

Independent evaluation by the consultant

Clients have their own policies and practices for evaluating the use of consulting and other professional services. A client may even choose not to evaluate a completed assignment at all. To a consultant, assignment evaluation is one of the basic tools for managing quality, controlling and developing staff, and building excellent relations with existing clients. As a matter of principle, a consultant should evaluate every assignment for his or her own benefit, even if the client has decided to skip the evaluation.

The questions to be asked are not different from those mentioned above, although their focus may be slightly modified. The consultant will stress self-evaluation, looking specifically at issues where the consulting firm has experienced problems and is keen to make improvements.

It is difficult to be objective and unbiased in practising self-evaluation. Excellent consulting firms therefore seek feedback from clients, using various data-gathering and evaluation instruments.

Questionnaires submitted to clients are the preferred instrument. The questions asked should invite the client to be outspoken about every aspect of the relationship and the work performed, including the competence and attitude of the consulting staff, their flexibility, behaviour, creativity, availability, help-fulness and other qualities that make the difference between mediocre and excellent assignments.[3] If the client takes the trouble to answer, the consultant should in turn provide feedback to thank the client and tell him what action will be taken on his answers and suggestions.

Other frequently used instruments include interviews, discussions with senior personnel in client firms, follow-up visits, study of the client's internal evaluation reports (if made available to the consultant) and similar.

It should be noted that in quality certification according to ISO 9001 standards, assignment evaluation using feedback from clients is a compulsory procedure (see Chapter 28).

11.3 Follow-up

The client and the consultant often agree to terminate a particular assignment without completely discontinuing their working relationship. If further work done by the consultant is still related to the current assignment in some way, we call it follow-up. The desirability of some follow-up is often identified in evaluating the assignment. If the consultant is convinced that follow-up is in the client's interest and that he or she has something more to offer to the client, this may be suggested in the final report and meeting with the client.

The advantages to the consulting organization are obvious. A follow-up service is an invaluable source of information on the real impact of operating assignments and on new problems which may have arisen in the client organization. New assignments may develop from these visits, which may not cost the consulting organization anything if the follow-up is provided on a paying basis.

Many client organizations may also find that follow-up services are a useful form of assistance through which new problems and opportunities can be discovered and addressed before they become a headache. However, no client should be forced to accept a follow-up arrangement if he or she is not interested in it.

Follow-up of implementation

There are many options for the consultant's involvement in implementation. In addition, new technical developments will take place in the area covered by the assignment and there may be other reasons why the client wishes the consultant to take a fresh look at the situation created by the implementation of the proposals.

Therefore the client may be interested in a follow-up arrangement. For example, the consultant will pay him or her a short visit every three months over a two-year period. The purpose will be to review progress on implementation, to help to take any necessary corrective measures, and to find out whether or not new problems have arisen. If a new intervention is required that exceeds the scope of these periodic visits, the client will receive a separate proposal for this, but will be absolutely free to accept or decline it.

Retainer arrangements

Follow-up visits related to specific assignments are normally programmed for a limited period of time. The client may be interested in maintaining a more permanent working relationship with a consultant who gave satisfaction. This can lead to a retainer arrangement (see section 1.4).

Many retainer arrangements are the result of successfully implemented consulting projects. This is quite logical. Why should a client enter a long-term collaborative relationship with a consultant without having seen him or her at work?

11.4 Final reporting

Before and during the assignment the client has received several reports:

— the report in which the assignment was proposed, based on a quick (preliminary) diagnostic survey;

— progress reports, whose number and scope varies, and in which modifications in problem definition and assignment plans may have been proposed;

— reports and documentation linked with the submission of proposals for the client's decision prior to implementation.

Whatever the pattern of interim reporting, there is normally a final assignment report issued at the time the consultant withdraws from the client organization. Furthermore, the consulting firm requires reports which will be of help, above all, to its members who may be called upon to undertake similar assignments.

Report to the client

For a relatively short assignment, this may be the only report and so has to be comprehensive. For longer assignments, the final report may make passing reference to previous reports and go into detail only on the events since the last report was written. In every case, as a closing report, it tidies up all the loose ends and covers the essential end-of-assignment facts and confirmations. It should be known before it is written whether the consultant is to provide a follow-up service. If so, the report may not be quite as "final" as it otherwise would be.

In addition to a short comprehensive review of work performed, the final report points out the real benefits obtained from implementation and makes frank suggestions to the client on what should be undertaken, or avoided, in the future.

Some consultants, especially in the OD sector, regard final reports as redundant if the client has worked closely with the consultant throughout the assignment and there is obvious satisfaction with the approach taken and the results. Final reports are not compulsory. However, the fact that one has to be produced (it can be a very short one) encourages discipline and rigour and stimulates thinking on what was really achieved and what could have been done in a better way.

Evaluation of benefits

An evaluation of benefits is included in the final report if this is practical, i.e. if the consultant is leaving the client after a period of implementation which lends itself to evaluation. In other cases, it may be submitted later as already discussed.

Through the evaluation of real benefits the consultant proves the correctness and accuracy of both the preliminary assessment (given when proposing the assignment to the client) and the evaluation of alternative solutions (presented to the client for decision prior to implementation).

Clearly, implementation must have progressed far enough, and the conditions of operating the new technique or system must have become normal and stabilized, if an evaluation of benefits is to give objective information. The consultant emphasizes direct benefits obtained as a result of the assignment and leaves the consideration of indirect benefits (e.g. no increase in fixed costs) to the client.

In presenting the benefits the reports should focus on measurable economic, financial and social benefits that have been or will be drawn from superior performance. However, the report should also describe the new capabilities and new systems, opportunities and behaviours created by the assignment and show their impact on superior performance, as discussed in section 11.2.

Most management consulting firms prefer not to point out the savings/fee ratio. Such analysis is left entirely to the client, who appreciates that all benefits cannot be costed and that this ratio may be high in many simple, low-risk assignments, whose impact on overall and long-term business results is limited.

Evaluation of the consulting process

Whether to include the evaluation of the consulting process in the final report is a matter of judgement. There may be a strong case for doing so if the client can learn from it for the future, and if the client's behaviour during the assignment was the reason for some superior or substandard results achieved. The consultant and the client should agree on how detailed and open this section would be, and what matters would be discussed, but not included in the final report.

Suggestions to the client

Although the job is completed, the consultant shows that he or she sees the client organization in perspective by pointing out possible further improvements, opportunities, bottlenecks, risks, action that should not be delayed, and so on. In any case the consultation has to make suggestions on how the new system introduced with his or her help should be maintained, controlled and developed after his or her departure. An agreement reached on a follow-up service would also be confirmed in the final report.

A good consulting report should be capable of commanding the respect of the client, who will consider it a source of further learning and guidance. He or she will also be pleased to show it to business friends and associates as the record of a worthwhile achievement.

Further suggestions on writing and presenting consulting reports can be found in Appendix 10.

Assignment reference report

In addition to the final report to the client, consultants compile an assignment reference and evaluation report for their own organization (see also section 27.5).

The client's internal report

Some organizations using consultants prepare internal reports on completed assignments. In addition to summary information the report includes the client's assessment of the job done and of the consultant's approach and performance. Although this is a most useful practice, it is not very common. This report is not intended for the consultant. Nevertheless, some clients are happy to share it with the consultant, who in turn should not miss an opportunity to obtain a copy.

---

[1] See, e.g., D. Casey: "Some processes at the consultant/client interface in OD work", in *Leadership and Organization Development Journal* (Bradford, West Yorkshire), No. 1, 1982.

[2] *Consultants News* (Fitzwilliam, New Hampshire), July/Aug. 1991, p. 6.

[3] See, for example, the client feedback questionnaire suggested by David Maister in *Managing the professional service firm* (New York, The Free Press, 1993), pp. 85-86, and also reproduced in M. Kubr: *How to select and use consultants: A client's guide*, Management Development Series, No. 31 (Geneva, ILO, 1993), p. 176.

PART III

CONSULTING IN VARIOUS AREAS
OF MANAGEMENT

CONSULTING IN GENERAL AND STRATEGIC MANAGEMENT

12

This chapter is the first of a series of 11, each dealing with consulting in a specific area of management. The authors' intention is not to provide an exhaustive analysis of management techniques, practices and problems in each area covered, but, in keeping with the spirit of the book, to show how management consultants can help clients and how they normally operate in these areas. This opening chapter, and the following ten chapters, can serve, therefore, as an introduction to a more detailed study of consulting in various areas of management. Appendix 11 provides selected reading lists for all chapters in Part III.

12.1 Nature and scope of consulting in corporate strategy and general management

A considerable amount of management consulting concerns the very existence, the basic goals or "mission", the business policy and strategy, and the overall planning, structuring and control, of an organization. These problems were at one time defined as *general management*, but are now more commonly referred to as *corporate strategy* or *strategic management*. Consultants who concern themselves with these issues are strategy or general management consultants — as distinct from specialists who intervene in one functional area (finance), or deal with a particular technique such as computerized production control or employee incentive schemes.

But how do we find out if an enterprise requires the assistance of an all-round management consulting generalist? In some cases this is quite obvious from the state of the business: its deteriorating overall performance, the growing dissatisfaction of the staff, the generally bleak prospects of the industrial sector, and so on. The business may be in crisis, or very close to it, and it is not clear how to restore prosperity. In other cases, a problem that seems at the outset to be a special or functional one (inadequate marketing methods, say) has ramifications in other areas of management and eventually is found to be only a symptom of a much deeper general management problem affecting the whole organization.

In such organizations it is common to find that top management lacks any clear idea of where the company is going or what it is trying to achieve. In short, there is a lack of strategic direction. In others, top management has some sense of strategic objectives but has failed to communicate its vision to middle and lower management and to the workforce — and, in consequence, the strategies are never implemented. These problems are addressed in later sections of this chapter.

Multifunctional and interdisciplinary problems

The most prominent characteristic of problems handled in general management consulting is that they are:

— *multifunctional:* the consultant deals with several functions of the business (production, technology, organization, marketing, etc.) and focuses on the interaction between these functions and on problems involving more than one function;

— *interdisciplinary:* the consultant must be able to view business problems from several angles; typically, a business strategy problem may have technological, economic, financial, legal, psycho-sociological, motivational, political and other dimensions.

General managers, too, have been chosen for their ability (real or expected) to deal with multifunctional and interdisciplinary problems. Experience shows that many of them find this difficult. There are cases of general managers, previously excellent plant managers, who continue to be plant managers in their new position! This is an area where a management consultant can be of great help to the client — the general manager who has to change his habits, learn how to deal with new functions, look at the problems of the business from new angles, and above all free himself from day-to-day operating concerns sufficiently to be able to think about longer-term strategy.

In fact, a general management consultant is also a kind of specialist: his or her speciality lies in combining other specialities into a balanced and coherent multifunctional and interdisciplinary approach. Like the general manager, however, the general management consultant turns to other specialists when appropriate. He or she must know how to use the specialist's skill and advice, and help the client to do the same, to prevent situations where specialists (e.g. market researchers or financial analysts) would dominate the business.

Paths to organizational excellence

In Chapter 1, achieving the organization's basic goals and organizational excellence was shown to be a common "super-ordinate" goal of management consulting. Consultants help to nudge organizations towards excellence. They therefore require a validated vision of excellence in order to raise the expectations and ambitions of managers to the effort necessary to change organizations for the better. They need, furthermore, a conceptual framework for devising action objectives and programmes that lead to excellence, or at least bring organizations closer to it.

Interest in organizational excellence waxes and wanes; it is now higher than it has been for decades.[1] Research on excellent organizations shows that they mutate: excellent organizations today are not exactly like those of yesterday. They tend to share certain common features: for example, many of them exploit technological frontiers — the railways of the 1860s, the motor companies of the first half of our century, and the electronics companies of the 1980s. Another common feature is that they are well adapted to the needs and aspirations of their workforces, and, paradoxically, this is where they can differ very considerably from one another, because of the differences in both workforces and cultures. Invariably, excellent organizations are more sensitive than other organizations to their environments, and to the needs, wishes and satisfaction of the clients in particular. This sensitivity to the needs of customers has engendered a growing emphasis on quality, and the "total quality management" (TQM) philosophy is currently recognized as a hallmark of excellence.

Thus there is no one single, simple path to excellence. The management of today's organization requires a holistic and integrated approach in devising and implementing programmes for achieving excellence. The consultant should beware of simplistic solutions and explain to the client that there is no panacea, no "quick fix" for achieving high performance, productivity, effectiveness or excellence (see also Chapter 22).

Unfortunately, management theory does not provide the general management consultant with a research-based and generally accepted conceptual approach to designing and evaluating action programmes leading to excellence. What is available, and certainly of interest to the consultant-practitioner, is a range of pragmatic and experiential models describing organizations and analysing the causes of their successes or failures. Some of these models assist in the determination of corporate strategies, through a better understanding of the industry structure and competitive forces. Some models of this type will be examined in the following section. Others are more concerned with the ways in which strategy is implemented.

For example, the so-called "seven-S" framework developed by the McKinsey organization in the 1980s examined high-performance organizations under the following main headings: strategy, structure, systems, style, shared values, staff (people) and skills, emphasizing that these variables constitute an interdependent reinforcing network. Implementation is facilitated by identifying the blocks and obstacles likely to be encountered in each of these areas, and considering how they can be avoided.[2] Another framework suggests the following five tracks: (1) culture; (2) management skills; (3) team-building; (4) strategy structure; and (5) the reward system.[3] Research into factors affecting organizational excellence is likely to continue, and will no doubt pay increased attention to factors that are specific to various socioeconomic and cultural settings, especially those which differ from the environments of the United

States and Japan where most current research into organizational excellence has been based.

Diagnosing organizations

As explained in detail in Chapter 7, many consultants prefer to carry out a quick preliminary survey of the organization before proposing a specific problem-solving assignment. Thus the first technical contact between the client and the consultant is often at the general management level, before the consultant moves into specific areas identified by the survey.

There are situations where a very thorough diagnostic survey (diagnosis, audit, etc.) of the whole organization is required in preparation for important decisions on the future of the business. A comprehensive diagnostic survey may precede a major restructuring or reorganization, an acquisition, a merger, a privatization or a decision to close down a business. The consultant's mandate is to help the client to diagnose the organization concerned; he or she may even be asked, as an independent expert, to examine the organization in order to provide an objective and neutral report on the status, strengths, weaknesses and development prospects of the business. The assessment of the management systems used and of senior managerial personnel may be included. The assignment may end with the consultant submitting a report on the diagnosis. Diagnostic surveys of this type may be fairly extensive and difficult assignments. While a quick survey is a matter of a few days, comprehensive and in-depth surveys may take several months, depending, of course, on the size and complexity of the organization and on the nature of its problems.

Some comprehensive diagnostic surveys intervene too late, when the company concerned is no longer susceptible of rescue, or when rescue would require resources that are not available. In certain cases such a crisis could have been prevented by undertaking a thorough diagnosis at an earlier date, and arranging for a periodic business diagnosis, or self-diagnosis, as a preventive measure. The consultant may have an opportunity to help a client to design and install a self-diagnostic scheme on a regular basis. This opportunity should not be missed!

Organizational level of interventions

In many cases the general management consultant intervenes at the highest level in the organization: with the chief executive in person, or the top management team. Even leaders keen to introduce change often do not realize what will be involved, or do not see that they ought to start by changing themselves. They frequently have a particular self-image, though the consultant may find that this image is not shared by other people in the organization. The consultant's problem then lies in persuading management of the need to change thinking and behaviour at the very top.

The possibility of working directly with the chief executive and the management team provides an excellent introduction to the organization, rapid access to key data, a true picture of the operating style of top management, and usually strong support from the top for the consultant's work. Yet it is often risky to confine intervention to top management level. The general management consultant needs to find out how top management is perceived throughout the organization, and how management policies influence the work style, performance and job satisfaction of employees. Furthermore, general management is also practised at intermediate and lower levels in the management hierarchy, and eventually affects every single worker. For example, supervisory management is often underestimated and constitutes one of the weakest links in the management hierarchy.

Consulting style

In general and strategic management more than in any other area, the consultant cannot avoid dealing with issues affecting management's personal interests, self-image and authority. Advice on crucial issues of a company's direction, strategy and leadership can easily be perceived as criticism aimed at particular persons. Yet the objective is to strengthen and improve management, not to undermine it. Also, the consultant does not want to see his or her proposals rejected by senior management. Experienced consultants therefore attach great importance to choosing the right consulting style.

Many entrepreneurs and senior managers are very lonely and isolated people when it comes to discussing their basic goals and values and their style. The general management consultant may well be the first person able and willing to talk to them about these issues. Personal counselling (see section 3.7) may be needed, and the consultant should not hesitate to offer it tactfully to the client.

A frequently debated issue is the choice between participative and process consulting approaches, and those where the consultant acts primarily as an expert in the subject. If the client is not able or willing to participate, the consultant may decide to give the best expert advice possible, which the client may decide to use or to ignore. However, in strategy and general management consulting, the risk of rejection is extremely high as witnessed by countless consulting reports, plans and proposals that have been ignored by the client. Furthermore, core issues concerning the very existence, mission, strategic direction or organizational structure of a client company can hardly be fully understood and properly resolved if handled by outsiders only. All the reasons that speak in favour of participative consulting in any area of management are doubly valid when dealing with strategy, organization, corporate culture and similar general management issues.

12.2 Corporate strategy

The concept of corporate strategy has made a significant contribution to the advancement of management practice and theory over the last 30 years. Consulting in corporate strategy (business strategy, strategic analysis, strategic planning, etc.) has become a rapidly growing area of management consulting. Some consultants have made corporate strategy their main or exclusive field of intervention. Consulting in corporate strategy has been strongly influenced by changing fads and fashions. During the 1970s there was a growing use of quantitative techniques and models, and strategic studies began to be dominated by young econometricians and operational researchers, with excellent education but often without business experience, and with no knowledge of people, or of social and other problems that determine strategy in reality. The following decade saw a welcome swing back to pragmatism.

A further development of the 1960s and 1970s was that many business firms created strategic planning units, and planning was seen as a distinct staff department function. The 1980s saw a strong swing away from such departments, which in any case rarely commanded the attention or respect of top management. It is now increasingly recognized that strategic planning is far too important to be left to planning staff, and that participation in the formulation of strategies is an intrinsic part of the work of senior management.

Even though the role of the planning department has diminished, however, the need for the external consultant has increased. Senior operating executives must always have some difficulty in stepping back from their immediate priorities and thinking about the longer term. Their workloads make it difficult for them to track all those developments in the company's environment that need to be taken into account in the formulation of strategic plans, and it is notoriously difficult for them to make an honest evaluation of their organization's weaknesses relative to competition. The consultant brings an open mind to these issues. Many boards of directors develop long-term relationships with consultants who advise them on strategy development, and clearly find such advice invaluable.

Strategic vision

Corporate strategy is usually defined as the organization's response to environmental opportunities, challenges and threats, consistent with its resources and its competences relative to its competitors. This latter point is so important that some writers define strategy entirely in terms of the search for competitive advantage. It is important to remember, however, that strategy is not an aim in itself but a set of paths and choices for achieving the organization's goals in the future. This is where a consultant can start helping the client. Many organizations practising strategic planning actually lack a vision of the future. Some do not even have a clear understanding of the present; they have not asked the strategist's fundamental question: "What business are we in?". Yet an understanding of this must be the starting-point of any sound strategic analysis.

A strategic vision should be as rational as possible and not a result of wishful thinking. However, total rationality is not achievable for one simple reason — the future is unknown and is being shaped by a myriad of independent actions all over the globe; the client's own actions will form only a tiny fragment of this future, however important his business is. Nor is it possible to evaluate every possible course of action. The personal values and judgement of the key decision-makers therefore play a vital role in positioning the organization for the future. Harold Leavitt has described this role as "pathfinding".[4] Other writers describe it as a "sense of mission".

It is for this reason that current thinking on corporate excellence and strategy puts so much emphasis on *organizational leadership*. A leader is an individual (or team) with a vision of the future position of the organization. Furthermore, a leader is able to express this vision in goals understandable to people in the organization, and influence and motivate people to achieve these goals. There is a unity of vision, and a unity of actions guided by this vision.

Industry and competitor analysis: Determining competitive advantage

A competitive advantage is a key dimension of survival and success in environments where organizations must compete with each other. This advantage is not a trick that can last a few months (e.g. a smart advertising campaign), but an inherent capacity to sustain superior performance on a long-term basis. The search for such advantage must therefore start with a systematic analysis of the industry and sector in which the enterprise operates, and of the competitive forces at play.

Much of the most important development in strategic thinking in the past decade has been in concepts and models that facilitate this kind of analysis. The "five forces" model proposed by Michael Porter identifies five key areas that management needs to understand: (1) the competitive structure within the industry/segment itself; (2) the threat of new entrants; (3) the threat of substitute products or technologies; (4) the power of suppliers; and (5) the power of customers.[5] Kenichi Ohmae suggests "key success factors" on the basis of which the business unit should compare itself with its competitors.[6] Another of Michael Porter's concepts, the "value chain", assists in determining where in the enterprise's operating cycle these key factors are to be found. Products and market positions can be brought into better perspective by using product/market life-cycle models. None of these models claim to describe reality for any one particular company: rather, they are an aid to thinking about reality. They are certainly tools which any consultant working in this area needs to have in his or her tool-kit.

Equipped with such tools, the consultant can be most helpful in examining whether the client business does indeed enjoy any competitive advantage, or in developing a strategy for achieving one. He or she can draw the client's attention to the ways in which organizations regarded as excellent achieved and maintained their competitive advantage. He or she can point out certain factors that tend to be characteristic of all firms that possess such an advantage (for example, priority attention paid to the clients' needs and satisfaction, and to the quality of products and services). But above all, the consultant can help the client to think honestly about the industry's characteristics, the keys to success, and just how the client's enterprise matches up to the competition in these key areas.

After the analysis comes the moment of truth: specifying the strategy to be followed. The consultant can help the client organization in choosing from alternatives that are available to it, and which reflect the real possibilities of the technical and production staff, production facilities, marketing networks, business experience and the like. Once again, recent thinking on the subject of corporate strategy has provided insights that can clarify the decisions that have to be made. Michael Porter has highlighted the distinction between two fundamental approaches or, as he terms them, "generic strategies". One of these is to concentrate upon becoming competitive through "cost leadership", i.e. by having the lowest costs in the industry (though this does not, of course, necessarily mean having the lowest selling prices). The other is to concentrate upon "differentiation", which means offering the customer superior quality and a unique package of features. Clearly, no enterprise can afford to ignore either costs or quality completely. Porter believes, however, that no company can hope to dominate its field in both cost and differentiation, and that any attempt to do so will lead to being "stuck in the middle" with neither the most competitive costs nor superior product features.

Practical examples of the strategic choices to be made are:

— offering state-of-the-art technologically advanced products not available from other firms or available from very few (differentiation), and regularly abandoning these products and moving on when the technology becomes common and prices start dropping;

— providing service to clients with speed and reliability superior to that offered by competitors (a further form of differentiation);

— selling high-quality and particularly reliable products for relatively high prices, and/or producing "tailored" products to the particular needs of clients who find standard products unsatisfactory (differentiation again);

— selling standard products of acceptable but not particularly high quality at very competitive prices (cost leadership).

In defining a competitive advantage, emphasis is put on the adjective "sustainable". This stresses the fact that the client will have to evaluate, and enhance as appropriate, his or her ability to adapt to changed conditions, and to innovate. For example, only organizations that are closely linked to technological research and where the flow of technological innovation has become a permanent internal process can choose the provision of state-of-the-art technology as their business strategy and hope to sustain differentiation on this basis.

Technology in corporate strategy

The role of technology in developing differentiation and implementing "winning" corporate strategy is another area where management consultants can be extremely useful to their business clients. There are several reasons for this:

A company that integrates technology into its strategy significantly improves its chances of reaping benefits from technological changes. Whether it decides to be a technological leader or not, the results of integrating technology into strategy can improve a company's determination of priorities among technology options, identify the technical resources needed to achieve business goals and speed up the movement of ideas into production.[7]

However, technological developments occur simultaneously in so many areas, and so rapidly, that even large companies with well-staffed R & D departments and information services find it increasingly difficult to keep abreast of developments, and think of possibilities offered by technologies and materials created in other sectors and countries.

Increased emphasis on technology strategy and its impact on manufacturing, marketing and other strategies is a new challenge to many management consultants, who often used to handle strategy simply as a factor affecting marketing and finance decisions. Some consultants have already responded by establishing R & D departments which can both participate in consulting assignments in corporate strategy and undertake specific R & D tasks for their clients. Evaluating the potential of new technologies and providing technological information analysed from the viewpoint of its potential business applications has become a rapidly growing service. Several important consulting firms already offer such a service to their clients. Consultants advising on business development opportunities and projects in developing countries are increasingly involved in questions of technology transfer, helping to choose both the appropriate technology to be used and the terms under which such a transfer can be effectively implemented.

This trend is likely to continue, and management consultants who devise new services in response to clients' pressing needs will themselves gain a distinct competitive advantage.

The environment of business

The whole environment in which organizations operate is becoming so complex, variable and even confused that managers find it more and more difficult to identify significant information and monitor changes that should be reflected in corporate strategy. Writers in the field of strategy increasingly refer to the need for systematic "PEST " analysis — a convenient shorthand for the areas that such an analysis needs to examine:

- the political environment;
- the economic environment;
- the sociological environment;
- the technological environment.

Here again, management consultants can be of great help. Some clients may need guidance in order to become more aware of the environment and so realize that ongoing or forecasted environmental changes can have far-reaching consequences for their businesses. Other clients may be aware of the scope and depth of environmental changes, but are short of the skills and resources needed to collect necessary information and draw the right conclusions from its analysis. They find it difficult to consider what information is relevant, or may be relevant in the future.

As a result, many consulting firms provide services to clients in matters of corporate strategy which focus increasingly on environmental information and analysis. In addition, these firms help clients to devise systems and procedures in which environmental analysis is not undertaken as a special study, but is internalized to become a standard part of the strategic management system in the client organization. In some cases (e.g. in small and medium firms in rapidly changing industrial and service sectors), the clients may require long-term support from a competent information agency, which would screen and monitor the environment, or some aspects of it, on their behalf. Some consultants have already decided to build up a new client service for this purpose.

Environmental analysis tends to embrace new issues in addition to classic marketing, economic, demographic and financial information. For example, new regulations concerning product quality, safety, or the protection of the natural and living environment, can determine the life or death of firms whose products or technologies are affected. Some of these regulations have a long gestation period, while others become adopted very quickly. Political and social interests, as well as organizations, are involved in the promotion of new regulations. Seen from another angle, new regulations also offer new opportunities to firms which adapt their products faster than their competitors, or which come up with new products that specifically serve the purpose of increased safety or reduced pollution.

As regards the legal environment of business in general, many companies find it impossible to keep track of all strategically significant changes in their home country, let alone changes having an impact on foreign operations. Management consultants can respond (in collaboration with law firms if appropriate) by helping the clients with this task.

Implementing strategy

Strategy that remains on paper is of little use. It is essential to help the client to develop operating systems, procedures and technical capabilities for putting the strategy into effect. This raises, among other questions, that of communications. While certain strategic choices may have to be kept strictly confidential for obvious reasons, the failure to communicate important choices to staff will mean that no one in the organization (with the exception of the planners and top managers) will adhere to the strategy chosen. Activities such as production planning and control, inventory management, quality improvement and staff development, as well as leadership and management style, become critical to the successful implementation of strategy.

The consultant can help the client, too, in developing competence for *adapting strategy* to new opportunities and constraints. No strategy is valid forever, and the rapid pace of change in the business world and its environment means that strategy formulation and review must be an ongoing process. There is a clear need for a monitoring, or "early warning", system for detecting trends, events and ideas that may lead to a change in corporate strategy. Once again, internal management may have neither the time nor the detachment to undertake this task properly. The company's management system, including procedures for auditing and redefining strategy, should be flexible enough to make adaptation possible. This means, in particular, encouraging people in marketing, production, R & D and other departments to "keep their eyes and ears constantly open" for signals and ideas that may have a bearing on strategy and should lead to its modification sooner or later. It is in pulling all of this information together and determining its implications that the consultant's role is invaluable.

Consistency with internal capabilities

Emphasis on implementation and adaptability to new conditions underlines the principle whereby consistency with the internal capabilities of a company is as important in consulting on strategy as the alignment of the firm with the business environment. Every pattern of corporate strategy has its own requirements as regards the technical profile and capabilities of the staff, as well as managerial and work style and employee motivation. Clearly, an ambitious differentiation strategy intended to maintain the company at the cutting edge of technological innovation, without much concern for costs and prices, requires a different style and working climate to a strategy which is not too demanding as regards latest technology but seeks to achieve cost leadership through rigorous cost control of standardized, high-volume work operations.

Ideally, not only management but also other staff members should be associated with strategy formulation. The *process* of defining strategy is even more important than the *content* for achieving staff commitment and a shared belief that the strategy chosen is a way to success.

Some special strategic patterns

Management consultants are often called in when the development pattern of a company deviates substantially from the normal pattern. These tend to be difficult assignments, uncertain as to the chances of success, often carried out under severe time pressure if the client organization is in financial difficulties, or, on the contrary, feels that it would miss an exceptional opportunity if the consultant takes too much time over the analysis.

How to cope with an excessively high rate of growth has been a problem faced by companies wanting to take the maximum opportunities offered by a favourable business climate. In such cases the consultant can point out the possible negative impact of rapid growth on liquidity and on the capability to sustain operations if growth suddenly slows down. In trying to maximize sales, a company is often tempted to expand production capacity and increase inventories beyond reasonable limits, instead of looking for better utilization, modernization and maintenance of existing capacity, or product and service quality. In the expansion new staff are recruited, but training is inadequate. All this can be a serious threat to long-term survival, and adaptation to new conditions may be very painful.

Mergers and acquisitions

The systematic analysis described above may well point to the fact that the enterprise can best fulfil its objectives through a programme of growth through acquisitions. Advising clients on mergers and acquisitions has become an "elitist" area of consulting. This is not totally unjustified as wide business experience and sound judgement are required in these cases. The financial side of the scheme has to be examined carefully (see Chapter 13). However, the consultant should not by any means confine himself to the financial aspects of the acquisition proposal; a good "strategic fit" must come first. A scheme which is perfectly feasible and looks very attractive from the financial point of view may involve unrealistic strategic choices as regards marketing, production capacity, staff capabilities or compatibility of organizational cultures, and in such a case the elusive "synergy" will not be realized.

Company turnarounds

A general management consultant may be asked to assist with a turnaround of a company that is in trouble. A turnaround strategy often involves total restructuring and reorganization, and usually affects all functions and activities of a company. This is a particularly difficult kind of strategic assignment. Probably the consultant will be brought in at a very late stage, when the threat of bankruptcy is imminent. He may be regarded as a potential saviour — or the last hope. The management of the company is often paralysed and starts panicking under extreme pressure from creditors, banks, trade unions, tax collectors and others.

The consultant should consider whether his experience is adequate for an assignment involving so much risk and responsibility — and what the cost of failure will be. If he accepts the assignment, he should make sure that his and the management's roles are clearly defined and understood, since there will be no time for lengthy discussions and negotiations and some measures will need to be approved and executed immediately. If the consultant feels that senior management itself is the cause of trouble, or one of the major causes, he should make it clear that personnel changes may be necessary before committing himself to the assignment.

A quick preliminary diagnosis will help the consultant to evaluate the overall situation. In particular, he has to assess whether the company can still be rescued, and if so, how much this is likely to cost and whether the task is beyond the management's capabilities or not. If it is too late, or the cost of a turnaround operation would be prohibitive, there may be no other solution than to sell or liquidate the company.

Following this preliminary assessment, it is not advisable, and often not possible, to start a turnaround by lengthy in-depth diagnostic studies. There is a crisis situation; some creditors have to be paid today, others tomorrow, and the most competent people may be thinking of leaving the sinking ship. Emergency measures have to be given priority: for example, a dialogue with the creditors is essential, and resources ought to be concentrated in order to make those payments that cannot be postponed in any way.

The emergency measures needed will involve decisions that produce immediate savings, or that stop a further deterioration in the company's financial condition (e.g. recruitment freeze, restrictions on foreign travel, termination of temporary help, increased emphasis on timekeeping and work discipline, cuts in entertainment costs). Though spectacular, some of these measures do not produce major savings, but rather help to create a new atmosphere in which people start realizing how serious the situation is. At this point the consultant should make sure that employees are invited to contribute to the turnaround in every possible way. This may involve the establishment of various means of making such participation possible, without, however, divulging information that has to be kept confidential.

Stock should be taken as quickly as possible of existing resources and financial and other commitments since the company will have to avoid further crises, pay interest and settle certain liabilities, while progressing with the turnaround. Step by step, the consultant will be able to complete the picture of the client company's condition. It is essential to identify the real causes of trouble. They may be external (depression in the whole sector, prices of raw materials too high, important markets lost for political reasons), or internal (incompetent management, antagonistic conflict between management and trade unions). In many cases, external and internal causes are combined (external factors cause serious trouble because management did not spot them early enough, or management gradually became depressed and paralysed under the influence of adverse external conditions). Financial and other controls have to be tightened in all departments.

The external partners in the game, in particular the creditors, must see that a serious turnaround exercise has been started and is producing results. In some countries (e.g. in the United States under Chapter 11 of the Bankruptcy Code) a company can obtain temporary protection from creditors' claims while it is restructuring its finances and reorganizing operations in order to become solvent again.

Following the inevitable emergency measures, the turnaround programme should turn to strategic measures needed to recover financial health and viability in the long term. Time continues to be short, therefore every change planned has to be carefully programmed and the timetable controlled. Also, responsibilities of all managers and departments must be clearly defined, and their contribution to the total programme specified to permit evaluation and rewards corresponding to real results.

It sometimes happens that, when helping with a turnaround, the management consultant, with the client's formal or tacit agreement, steps out of his strictly advisory position to tell the client what to do, or even to give direct instructions to the client's employees. No general rule can tell how far such behaviour can go, in particular if it helps avoid a crisis. Then, there have been cases of consultants recruited to assist in a major turnaround who have accepted managerial positions with the client company in order to bring the whole programme to successful completion.

12.3 Processes, systems and structures

The structuring of an organization concerns the division of tasks and responsibilities among people, the grouping of tasks and people in units, the definition of vertical and horizontal information flows and collaborative relations, and arrangements for coordination. The purpose of structuring is to provide a more or less fixed and stable framework for an effective functioning of organizational processes and the total organization, i.e. of all its members, resources and units, in achieving common goals. The products of structuring are various systems and subsystems — organization systems, management information systems, decision-making systems, control and evaluation systems, systems for handling emergencies and crises, and so on. Any complex organization is operated through and with the help of these systems. However, experience shows that structures and systems can easily become a strait-jacket, for example, if they try to standardize and prescribe behaviour for situations that are very specific and where standardization does more harm than good. The design and maintenance of systems is a costly affair; some kind of cost-benefit analysis is therefore required in starting a project to design or revise a system. Many organizations need help to prevent proliferation and overlapping of systems, as well as to avoid lack of coordination and conflicting requirements of various systems for supplying and interpreting information.

Current thinking emphasizes core organizational processes as the principal criteria for developing systems and structures. Traditional fragmentation of activities and tasks tends to give way to integration enabled by modern technologies, by information technology in particular. In describing the business process re-engineering approach, Michael Hammer and James Champy stress "focus on redesigning a fundamental business process, not on departments and other organizational units". As they put it, "the fragmented processes and specialized structures are unresponsive to large changes in the external environment — the market, . . . and display appalling diseconomies of scale, quite opposite of what Adam Smith envisioned".[8]

Decision-making systems and practices

In many organizations it may be the method and organization of decision-making (for both key and routine matters) which cause trouble. Excessive centralization of operational decisions may deprive the organization of the flexibility needed to react to new market opportunities. Fragmentation of processes and responsibilities makes quick decisions extremely difficult. In another case, an autocratic owner may be taking decisions without conferring with professional experts on his or her own staff, who could easily prove that many of his decisions were based on wishful thinking rather than rational analysis.

The need to examine and reform the decision-making system may be the very reason why the consultant has been brought in; it may concern:

— the classification of decisions in groups by their nature, urgency, financial implications, degree of complexity, etc.;

— the ways in which typical decisions are taken (this may be quite difficult to find out);

— the respective decision-making roles played by staff specialists and line managers;

— the role of collective bodies in preparing and adopting decisions;

— the participation of employee representatives in decision-making;

— the decision-making and advisory roles of individuals in informal positions of influence;

— the responsibility for decisions, their implementation, and control of implementation;

— the use of decision-making techniques, models or formalized procedures.

The possibilities of improvement in this area are tremendous and general management consultants are well advised to pay close attention to them.

Management information systems

Most managers do not ignore the fact that information has become a strategic asset of business and that the whole world is undergoing a real "information revolution". However, it is a long way from recognizing this new role of information to actually developing and implementing effective management information systems.

Many general management consultants focus on this area and offer services such as analysing the existing information system; defining information required for strategic management and operational control; harmonizing and integrating systems used in various departments; and choosing and introducing appropriate information processing technology. This work concerns both external information (on the environment, including the enterprise's relations to this environment) and internal information (on resources, processes and results achieved). The purpose is to make sure that the client does not ignore information essential to strategic and operational decisions, but at the same time avoids collecting and developing information that is of no direct use to him. To decide where the limits are is difficult, and it may be advisable to cast the "information net" more widely rather than to save money at the risk of missing some essential information.

In today's consulting, management information systems are often handled as a problem of information technology, including the choice, installation and effective use of appropriate hardware and software. Yet this is only one side of the problem. Information technology is a key factor determining what sort of information and how much of it a company will be able to collect, process and analyse. Choosing information that is needed for preparing and making decisions is not a computer specialist's problem but an information user's (and his or her management consultant's) problem. Close collaboration between the two has to be established and maintained in developing effective information systems (see also Chapter 17).

Organization structure

To examine and redesign the organizational structure used to be the "classical" intervention of many general management consultants. When the basic structure was agreed, the consultant continued his work by producing detailed diagrams and charts, as well as job descriptions for each unit and position within the client organization. The end-product was often a set of organizational charts and instructions but, in fact, the principal benefit to the client was the effort and analysis that went into this job. Forgotten and "orphan" activities were rediscovered, activities for which nobody seemed to be responsible were defined, and overlapping activities were reassigned or done away with.

Today's management consulting has overcome the rather narrow approach taken by the "reorganization experts" in the past. As mentioned above, structure is treated as one of the factors of excellence, which is linked in many ways with strategy, organizational culture, the competence and motivation of employees, new technology and other factors. Competent and committed staff working in a loosely organized framework will produce better results than incompetent people inserted in a "perfect" formal structure! In any event, every consultant must realize that formal organization reflects only a small part of the very complex network of relations existing in an organization.

Reorganizations destroy existing work relations, collaboration patterns and socialization habits. Unjustified and frequent reorganizations paralyse enterprises and institutions, and generate lethargy instead of enhancing innovation and efficiency. A decision to reorganize often reflects management's failure to identify and tackle the real issue. Therefore consultants are more and more cautious, and tend to prescribe reorganization only if there are very valid reasons for it (e.g. a new division must be established because the existing structure is clearly not willing and able to maximize efforts and resources to put a new product on the market in the shortest possible time).

12.4 Corporate culture and management style

Finally we have to turn to the "soft" and "intangible" side of organizations. The meaning of culture was explained in Chapter 5. We emphasized that, when entering a new organization, the consultant has to find out as much as possible about its specific culture. This is done in order to develop a full understanding of values and motives underlying managerial and employee behaviour, and so assess the organization's potential for making improvements. Organizational culture may be found to be one of the causes, or even the main cause, of the difficulties experienced (e.g. due to the conservatism of senior management and the impossibility of submitting new ideas). In such a case, culture may even become the central theme on which the assignment would focus.

Consulting in corporate culture became extremely popular at the beginning of the 1980s, in the United States in particular. Some consultants have not escaped the danger of regarding and prescribing cultural change as a panacea: "Corporate culture is the magic phrase that management consultants are breathing into the ears of American executives", wrote *The New York Times* in 1983.[9] Nevertheless, in warning against the corporate culture fad we must not throw out the baby with the bath-water. Interest in corporate culture and in the impact of culture on long-term organizational performance is basically a positive phenomenon, needed to reinstate a balanced approach to organizational problems. If organizational culture is ignored, a sophisticated planning or management information system is unlikely to lead to any improvements in performance.

A change in corporate culture will rarely be an explicitly stated task in a consulting assignment.[10] Yet in some situations corporate culture requires the consultant's special attention:

- when a company is in difficulties. A strong traditional and intransigent culture may prevent the company from assessing its condition realistically and proceeding with changes that have become inevitable;
- when a company has grown very rapidly. There may be various problems. The original culture of a small family company may have become a strait-jacket. There are many new managers and workers, coming from different cultures. Growth by acquisitions may lead to serious cultural clashes;
- when major technological and structural change is planned. Revolutionary changes in products, technologies, markets, and so on have strong cultural implications;
- when there seems to be a conflict between the company's culture and values that prevail in the environment — for example, if the public increasingly requires a company to behave in ways that are contrary to its culture;
- when the company's operations are internationalized and the problem is how to adapt to foreign cultures.

Corporate culture: What to recommend

The consultant will try to "separate wheat from chaff", and ascertain what in corporate culture stimulates and what inhibits further growth and performance improvement. He or she will point to values and norms that need to be discarded or changed, and to those that should be preserved and even reinforced. If the consultant has had enough experience with corporate culture issues, he or she may be able to be more specific in suggesting what to do (e.g. in defining corporate mission and objectives; explicitly affirming the value system; enhancing consultation and participation; modifying symbols used to obtain cultural cohesion; changing established role models; reorienting the rewards system; or providing training and information needed to support new cultural values and norms), and similar. The consultant who finds out that the client organization's culture is hardly noticeable may be able to suggest how to create a stronger culture, congruent with the goals, resources and external environment of the organization.

Leadership and management style

Leadership and management style are closely related to corporate culture, and certain aspects of style can become part of the organization's culture. Managers in organizations tend to behave in coherence with the culture, in ways in which the owners, other managers and employees expect them to behave. At the same time, the style of an individual manager is co-determined by his or her personality, which may be in harmony or in conflict with existing corporate culture. If there is a conflict, it is usually resolved in one of two ways: either the style of a strong personality at the top will affect corporate culture, and be accepted as a feature of a new culture, or the existing strong culture will reject the person's style and he or she will have to alter it, or leave the organization.

Here again the consultant may face a wide range of rather delicate situations in which, even if he or she has no explicit mandate to make proposals in respect of leadership and management style, it may be necessary to find a tactful way of making the client aware of the problems, and help to resolve them by coming up with a feasible solution.

The following situations and problems are quite common in organizations:

(1) People would like to support the manager, but they do not really know what he or she wants and they do not understand his or her priorities; there is a problem of formulating ideas and goals clearly enough, and of communicating them to people.

(2) The manager uses an authoritarian style rather than consulting people, discussing problems and priorities with them, and explaining decisions.

(3) People are puzzled by the way in which the manager allocates his or her time: he or she speaks about priorities, but spends time in dealing with trivial issues.

(4) Innovation is encouraged on paper, but the manager neither gives it any overt support in planning and distributing work, nor shows personal interest in innovative projects, nor rewards innovators for their achievements.

(5) Although the situations with which the manager deals are different, he or she consistently treats them in the same way; this rigidity means that the style used is adequate in one situation and inadequate in another.

(6) Because a strong personality at the top exhibits a strong style (which can have either positive or negative characteristics), and favours people who use a similar style, managers throughout the organization try to copy this style even if it does not fit their own personality.

The consultant can achieve a great deal by making a manager aware, through personal counselling, of the strong and the weak sides of his or her style. Awareness of one's style is a first step towards its improvement! Even if you do not wish or are not able to change your style radically, it is useful to be aware of your weaknesses, to mitigate them and to compensate for them.

12.5 Innovation

Whether a consulting assignment deals with strategy, structure, systems, culture, staff development, motivation or any other aspect of managing a company (including aspects and functions that will be discussed in the following chapters), there is usually an overriding theme: the client wants his or her organization to become more innovative and more flexible, and hopes that the consultant can help. Typically this is a problem of established companies which have performed well for years, but eventually find out, at a moment when new, aggressive competitors enter the market, that their ability to innovate and change is no longer what it used to be. When faced with this problem the consultant tries to find out whether the client lacks technical know-how, or whether the existing policies and systems or corporate culture inhibit innovation.

If lack of technical expertise is the reason, solutions may be costly but quite straightforward. Either the client company will be able to strengthen R & D and accelerate the transfer of new ideas from research into production, or it will have to look for know-how outside (e.g. by purchasing a patent or licence, or establishing a joint venture with another company).

The task is more difficult if innovation is inhibited owing to archaic procedures and cultural barriers. A thorough diagnosis will be required, and the consultant will try to learn as much as possible from managers who head units with direct responsibilities for innovation (technological information, new product design, testing, production engineering, quality control, technical marketing).

The main sources of information will be the "doers" — professional researchers, design engineers and salespersons as well as shop-floor supervisors and experienced workers. Essential information can be obtained directly from the customers. The consultant will probably come to the conclusion that the company could recover its innovative capability if it removed red tape, reduced centralization of decisions and controls, encouraged experiments, appointed managers who understood what innovation meant, used financial and other rewards to show how innovation was valued by the company, and fostered a climate favourable to innovation.

The 1980s saw the advent of new formulas and incentives that encourage entrepreneurship within large business corporations. The term "intrapreneurship" has been used by some authors. The object is to tap valuable innovative talent existing within the company and create conditions under which enterprising and dynamic people will not only stay with the company but be able to act with considerable freedom, as if they were running their own "business within a business". Under these formulas, the "intrapreneurs" (individuals or teams) have broad authority to gather and organize resources and decide what to do to achieve the object of their venture. This includes responsibility for profits and losses, and the possibility to do business directly with other partners outside their mother company.

The search for new approaches and methods that stimulate creativity and innovation in business and other organizations is likely to continue. The management consultant will be well advised to be at the forefront of these efforts.

---

[1] See, for example, T. Peters and R. H. Waterman: *In search of excellence: Lessons from America's best-run companies* (New York, Harper and Row, 1982); or T. Peters: *Liberation management: Necessary disorganization for the nanosecond nineties* (London, Macmillan, 1992).

[2] ibid.

[3] R. H. Kilmann: *Beyond the quick fix: Managing five tracks to organizational success* (San Francisco, California, Jossey-Bass, 1984).

[4] H. J. Leavitt: *Corporate pathfinders* (Chicago, Illinois, Irwin, 1986).

[5] See M. Porter: *Competitive strategy* (New York, The Free Press, 1980), and idem: *Competitive advantage* (New York, The Free Press, 1985).

[6] K. Ohmae: *The mind of the strategist* (New York, McGraw-Hill, 1982).

[7] A. L. Frohman: "Putting technology into strategic planning", in *California Management Review* (Berkeley, California), Vol. XXVII, No. 2, Winter 1985, p. 48.

[8] M. Hammer and J. Champy: *Re-engineering the corporation* (New York, Harper Business, 1993), pp. 40 and 29.

[9] S. Salmans: "New vogue: Corporate culture", in *New York Times*, 7 Jan. 1983.

[10] For a more detailed discussion of corporate culture, see T. E. Deal and A. A. Kennedy: *Corporate cultures: The rites and rituals of corporate life* (Reading, Massachusetts, Addison-Wesley, 1982); and E. H. Schein: *Organizational culture and leadership* (San Francisco, California, Jossey-Bass, 1985).

CONSULTING IN FINANCIAL MANAGEMENT

13

All consulting projects and assignments involve the use of financial and accounting data, and all management consultants, whatever their particular field of specialization, inevitably find themselves concerned with financial issues and practices. There are two reasons for this. The first is quite simply that finance and accounting provide the working language of business, and it is virtually impossible to analyse the operations or results of any complex organization except in financial terms. The second reason is that there are close and complex linkages between the finance function and all other functional areas. Decisions made in any area of line operations (such as an increase in the social benefits provided to workers) will have an impact on the organization's overall financial position, and may call for a revision in existing financial plans and budgets. Equally, a decision which appears to be entirely financial in nature, such as a reduction in short-term bank borrowing, may lead to a shortage of working capital that imposes a real constraint on other operating areas, particularly marketing and production. Virtually all consulting assignments uncover such linkages.

The purpose of the present chapter is to focus upon the special problems of consulting in decision areas that are specifically financial in nature, such as the financial structure of the company and the analysis of capital investment projects, rather than the use of financial information in general. Even here, however, the impact of financial decisions and policies on other areas of activity cannot be overlooked, and such issues will be examined as they arise in the course of the chapter.

It remains to ask whether the management consultant is the person best qualified to assist clients in this complex area. After all, there are other professionals who work in the financial area: bankers and accountants. Are they not the obvious source of such advice? Both groups are specialists, however, whose competence covers only a part of the financial area.

Managers who need advice on financial matters will frequently turn first to a firm of independent accountants, and in many cases this will be the firm which has also been charged with the responsibility of auditing the company's financial statements. Most accounting firms regularly provide such assistance, and are a valuable source of advice on the design of budgeting and reporting systems, and on taxation. The accounting company which has an ongoing relationship with the client has the advantage of a close working knowledge of many aspects of operations, and will have a shorter "learning curve" than another consultant brought in from outside.

There are, however, some serious limitations in the use of accountants as general management consultants. There is a fundamental difference between advising (where the client is the management of the company) and auditing (where the accountant's responsibility is to the shareholders, creditors and the general public). The potential conflict of interest is clear. An accountant who has advised the company in key financial decisions should not be placed in the position of having to produce a critical evaluation of the results of those decisions in the audit report. Some countries, indeed, legislate to keep audit and advisory work separate, although the combination continues to be accepted in Anglo-Saxon countries.

Apart from the question of probity, there is also an issue of competence. A distinction must be made here between the major public accounting firms and the smaller firms and sole practitioners. The larger companies have developed "management services" divisions, organizationally separate from the audit function and equipped with a wide range of consulting skills. The smaller firms and independent accountants, however, are often far from being "full range" financial specialists, and the specialist training of a conventional accountant may make it difficult for him or her to recognize the limitations in established accrual accounting and to think in cash-flow terms, to plan on the basis of probabilities and alternative scenarios, or to accept some of the more recent developments in costing and budgeting.

The company's commercial bank is an alternative source of financial advice. In the field of liquidity management and credit control, the advice of the local bank manager may be very useful, particularly as it will be supported by specialized knowledge about the financial situation and general credit rating of actual and potential customers. But again, it must be recognized that the training and experience of commercial bankers are biased; they may be highly skilled in credit assessment, but are likely to know little about company valuation or the workings of the securities markets.

The merchant banker (investment banker in United States terminology, or *banque d'affaires* in France) is much more actively involved in consulting. The traditional role of merchant banks has been to act as agents and intermediaries in the issue of securities, advising as to the terms of the issue and providing underwriting services. In recent years, however, their role has expanded to include a wider range of advisory services. Yet their role remains a specialized one; they are actively involved in merger and acquisition activities, and are increasingly in competition with the commercial banks in risk management and other treasury operations, but they are not much involved in day-to-day corporate financial operations such as credit and liquidity management.

The constraints and specializations of these various types of organization provide an opportunity to the general consultant who can take a wider viewpoint spanning the full range of financial decisions. Preparation for such a role involves a major investment of time, but the consultant willing to make such an investment will be in a position to offer a unique service to the client.

13.1 Financial appraisal

It will be difficult for the consultant to assist his client in the finance area unless the client is himself "financially literate": that is, possesses some basic understanding of accounting and financial terms and procedures, and is able to use them in a simple financial analysis. Bringing the client "up to speed" in financial appraisal is therefore a prerequisite for further consulting work in finance.

This book is not the place to set forth the basic principles of accounting or of financial analysis. We assume that a professional consultant has already mastered some basic financial skills. It may still be in order, however, to offer some advice as to how he or she should go about educating those clients who do not yet possess such skills. A wealth of instructional material on financial analysis and appraisal is now available. So much material is offered, in fact, that the consultant can play a useful role by reviewing as much as possible of it and selecting an appropriate combination for the client's needs.

Whatever medium is selected to provide instruction for the client, however, there are certain essential elements that need to be covered, and which therefore form the basic criteria that the consultant will bear in mind in putting together a training package.

Bookkeeping

The conventional approach to the teaching of accounting invariably started with bookkeeping. We believe that for managers this is time-consuming and unnecessary. The concepts of "credits" and "debits" can also be dispensed with. The emphasis should not be upon how financial information is collected, but upon how it is used in managerial decisions.

Accounting principles

There are some basic accounting principles which clients must understand because financial statements will otherwise be meaningless. The essential items here are:

— the accrual concept, and the resulting differences between " accounting" and "cash-flow" figures;

— conservatism, and the "lower of cost or market" rule;

— the concept of non-cash charges (depreciation and amortization);

— the distinction between the company (corporation) as a "legal entity" and its owners.

Financial statements

Clearly, the client must be familiar with the basic components of a financial report. Understanding the balance sheet is important. Some trainers and consultants, however, give undue emphasis to the balance sheet and largely ignore the income statement. The consultant should seek out material which not only gives "equal time" to the analysis of the income statement, but then brings together information from both documents to produce a "sources and uses of funds" analysis.

Ratio analysis

Virtually all financial analysis involves the calculation and use of ratios. Here the problem is that there are so many ratios, and so many variations on them, that the client is likely to become thoroughly confused. Fortunately, nobody needs to be familiar with scores of different ratios. It is much better to select a dozen or so, and then become completely proficient in their use. But although a very few ratios will suffice, the short-list must include representatives of four quite different areas. They are:

- Ratios concerning *liquidity*, or the ability of the company to pay its bills as they become due. The "quick ratio", or "acid test", is clearly the most important ratio in this respect. For companies making significant use of debt financing, the "times interest earned" or "interest coverage" ratio is equally important.

- Ratios concerning *managerial efficiency*, as expressed in turnover figures. The most important ratios here are accounts receivable expressed in average daily sales, and inventories expressed in average daily cost-of-goods sold.

- Ratios concerning *capital structure*: the relative proportions of debt and equity funds. The actual ratio used may be long-term debt to equity, total debt to equity, total debt to total capital, or one of many other possible formulations. It is important to choose one of these ratios and to use it *consistently*.

- Lastly, but most important of all, ratios which measure *profitability*. These include return on total assets, return on equity funds, and many possible variations on these. While all of these are acceptable, it is important to supplement them with the one ratio which removes the influence of existing financial structure on profitability: "earnings before interest and taxes as a percentage return on total assets".

Equipped with these basic tools and concepts, the client will now be better able to explain his requirements and to understand the consultant's analysis and recommendations. There are, of course, instances in which the client will prefer the consultant to do the financial appraisal, or comment on the financial appraisal done by the client himself. Here again, the consultant should use these opportunities for developing the client's competence in basic financial analysis.

13.2 Working capital and liquidity management

It should be asked at this point what financial management seeks to achieve. Most current financial theory is based upon the assumption that the underlying objective of all financial decisions should be the maximization of long-term stockholder (shareholder) wealth — a viewpoint that has led to the pre-occupation with the formulation of models to determine the value of financial securities under " efficient market" conditions that now dominate financial literature. Some commentators reject this view, and argue that the organization's responsibilities are to all its "stakeholders", creditors, employees, and society in general as well as to the stockholder group. It is certain, however, that the organization cannot benefit anybody unless it continues to exist, and that in order to survive it must be able to meet all its commitments as they fall due. In everyday language, it must be able to pay its bills on time.

Working capital definitions

Accountants define working capital in accounting terms as the difference between current assets and current liabilities. This is a static approach, and not a very useful one. Liquidity — the ability to meet commitments and to pay bills — comes from the availability of cash. A company could have considerable working capital in the accounting sense (because of very large inventories) but no cash at all, and thus be on the point of insolvency. The approach taken here will be based upon *cash flows* rather than upon accounting concepts, and one of the most useful services that the consultant can perform is to educate the client to think, and to plan, in cash-flow terms.

Working capital and the operating cycle

Every manufacturing business has an intrinsic "operating cycle", in which materials are purchased, stocked, converted into finished products and finally sold. Even service industries have such a cycle, though its duration is shorter. Cash flows out of the organization when purchases are made, and returns when accounts receivable are collected. The task of the consultant is to help the client to understand his or her organization's own unique operating cycle, and then to find ways of increasing operating efficiency so that the cycle is shortened and cash is conserved. Experience has shown that in most organizations improvements of 25 to 40 per cent in cash utilization may often be made simply by careful analysis and the use of common sense.

One of the factors that the consultant should remember here (and one of the advantages he or she has over the banker or the accountant in this area) is that the changes leading to these improvements in cash utilization are as likely to be in production or other operating areas as in purely "financial" ones. Improvements in inventory control leading to a reduction in average stock levels, and improvements in quality control that produce a fall in wastage and scrap, will reduce the cash tied up in the operating cycle just as effectively as an improvement in collection of accounts receivable, or an acceleration in the transfer of funds from remote locations to a central concentration account. The very fact that most managers working in these non-financial areas do *not* fully understand the cash-flow consequences of their activities makes this a field in which the consultant has a particularly valuable contribution to offer.

Managing cash

Even though the entire operating cycle has cash-flow implications, the management of cash itself should not be overlooked. Here, the banks are indeed the experts, and most major banks have actively developed and marketed cash management systems in recent years. The consultant can play a useful role even here, however, by assisting the client in evaluating the bewildering array of different "packages" in which the banks offer combinations of concentration banking, lock-box collection systems, remote disbursement, zero-balance accounts, intra-group payments netting and so forth, and in finding a solution appropriate to the client's needs.

13.3 Capital structure and the financial markets

Every business organization needs an adequate capital base to support its operations. It has been repeatedly demonstrated that operating a business with inadequate capital — which in British financial circles is called "overtrading" — is one of the most widespread causes of business failure. In addition to having adequate capital, the business must have an appropriate capital structure: the right mix of equity funds and debt. All of this is easily said, but difficult to achieve in practice.

Determining an effective capital structure

A major portion of current financial theory is concerned with the capital structure of companies and with the effect of long-term financing decisions on the organization's cost of capital. Most of the theory is based upon assumptions that do not reflect reality, however. In addition, such theory is usually expressed in a highly quantitative form. Once again, a consultant who is conversant with the current financial literature can play an invaluable role in helping clients to identify the usable and useful concepts which are now beginning to emerge from this mass of theory.

The management of an organization's capital structure actually involves a two-stage decision process. The first task, when any new financing operation is proposed, is to review the organization's current capital structure in the light of management's policies, accepted debt/equity ratios, market conditions and, most important of all, expected cash generation and use over a period of some years. On the basis of this analysis a decision can be made whether to seek new equity funds or additional debt. Once this is complete, the second stage involves the determination of the exact type of security to be issued, the selection of under-writers, the pricing and timing of the issue, and so forth. These second-stage decision areas are the distinct professional field of the investment banker (merchant banker in British terminology), and the general consultant should ensure that the client seeks such specialist services at the appropriate time. But in the first stage of the process — reviewing the overall financial position to decide what kind of funds should be sought — the consultant's help can be invaluable.

Using debt funds

The advantages of using debt funds are very great: judicious amounts of debt increase the earnings per common (ordinary) share through the leverage effect, and the fact that interest charges are tax-deductible makes the net cost of borrowed funds relatively low. In general, debt financing will be the first choice if the company can safely add the proposed new borrowing to its existing debt. The key task in capital structure management, then, is to determine the company's *debt capacity*. There are many possible approaches to this question, but few of them are satisfactory. Policies which allow some external standard or institution to determine the decision (for example, keeping a debt/equity ratio more or less equal to the average for the industry, or limiting borrowing to what can be done without lowering the "rating" of the company's debt securities by the rating agencies) are unlikely to produce optimal results.

In most cases, the consultant will face a difficult task in this area. He will have to "re-educate" clients away from rules of thumb, and convince them that nothing can replace a systematic analysis. The ability of a company to use debt depends upon its ability to *service* that debt: to meet all interest charges and repayments of principal as they fall due. This in turn depends upon cash flows.

The importance of debt management has recently been brought into sharper focus by the experiences of many companies during the recession of the early 1990s. The period of rapid growth in the countries of the Organization of Economic Co-operation and Development (OECD) during the period from 1985 to 1989 was characterized by an unprecedented increase in both corporate and consumer debt, particularly in the United States, Japan and the United Kingdom. The reasons for this were complex. Although strong growth in output (over 4 per cent in 1988) gave rise to an upsurge in capital investment, conditions in the capital markets made many companies reluctant to issue equity. A particular factor in the United Kingdom was that the large privatization issues, all of them somewhat underpriced, tended to squeeze corporate issuers out of the equity market. In consequence, the average "gearing" or leverage of the British corporate sector doubled between 1987 and 1989. The economic slowdown after

1990 therefore caught many United Kingdom companies with unprecedented levels of debt. Interest rates were kept high by the Government's Exchange Rate Mechanism (ERM) policy. Companies quickly found that cash flow fell below their debt servicing commitments, and a high rate of corporate failures and liquidations was the result.

Could such problems have been foreseen and avoided? Yes: but in times of high growth the attention of line management is understandably concentrated on expanding output to meet demand rather than thinking about the next downward cycle. Yet we know that a GDP growth rate of 4 per cent is not sustainable for long in mature economies, and by 1989 there were clear warning signals from the commodities markets as well as from the financial world. Both consultants and outside directors should have been looking ahead and advising caution.

The consultant's task, then, is to persuade the client company to undertake a long-term projection of the cash likely to be generated by its operations, not only under "normal" economic conditions, but also during periods of economic uncertainty and recession. This is likely to require the use of simulation techniques, and the development of a computer-based model of the company's financial dynamics.

Few companies can undertake such projects without outside assistance. Effective consulting work in this area depends upon the availability of a consulting team which combines financial expertise with electronic data processing (EDP) systems analysis and programming skills. Consulting organizations that are willing to develop such teams can expect growing needs for their services as more and more companies realize the fundamental importance of such an analytical approach to financial decisions.

13.4 Mergers and acquisitions

Mergers between companies or the acquisition of one company by another provide many opportunities for consulting work. Most of these opportunities come in the post-merger phase, when work begins on the rationalization of the production and marketing activities, and the task of reconciling the different budgeting systems, personnel policies and a host of other procedures. There is, however, one key financial task that must be undertaken before the merger, and in which consultants are very often needed: the determination of the *fair value* of one or both of the companies involved. The consultant may also be called upon to advise as to the method of payment to be used. He or she will normally have either the acquiring company or the one to be acquired as a client, but in some cases of "friendly merger" may be advising both organizations.

Valuation of a company

There are essentially four approaches to the valuation of a going-concern company. Value can be based upon:

- the current market price of the company's common stock (if the stock is listed and actively traded);
- the market value of the assets;
- capitalized future earnings; and
- "replacement" or "duplication" value which involves an attempt to estimate the cost of building up a similar organization from scratch instead of making the acquisition.

The first of these, the current market approach, is widely used. It does not in fact give the fair value of the company, but provides a "floor price" below which negotiations cannot go: if the common shares have recently been changing hands at, say, $50, then any offer price that values the total company at less than $50 per share is unlikely to be acceptable. The other three approaches do try to establish a real fair value. The consultant may be called upon both to advise upon the method to be used and to assist in its implementation.

In recommending a *basis for valuation*, the consultant will obviously pay close attention to the client's particular situation and needs. If the client is the company which is receiving the offer, then the appropriate method will be whichever yields the highest value: the consultant will not suggest a price based upon current earnings if he estimates that the realizable value of the physical and financial assets of the company might be higher. But when the client is the acquiring company (that is, the company making the offer) the situation is more complicated. The appropriate valuation method now depends upon the company's motives for making the acquisition, and these motives in turn are vested in its corporate strategy and long-term plans. If the acquisition is being made simply as part of a diversification strategy and the company that is being purchased will be allowed to continue its operations largely independently, then a figure based upon capitalized earnings will be appropriate. In this case the main task of the consultant will be to scrutinize the current and forecast earnings of the company being taken over to ensure that they are credible and based upon sound accounting practices, and that no special "window dressing" has taken place to increase reported earnings at the expense of long-term financial health.

The consultant is likely to be most deeply involved in those cases in which the client organization is making an acquisition for operating reasons rather than pure diversification: in order to gain additional production capacity, for example, or to acquire new products that will complement its own existing product range. In such a situation it will be necessary both to establish asset values and to adopt the "replacement" approach. Some consultants have developed particular expertise in asset valuation and have become known specialists in this area.

Method of payment

The selection of the method of payment to be used in making the acquisition is a highly complex question which requires both expert knowledge of the financial markets and special skills in determining the tax consequences of the method used. The choice of possible methods includes a simple cash payment for the shares of the other company, a cash payment for assets, a "stock for stock" exchange, and the use of bonds or notes, preferred stock, convertible bonds, convertible preferred stock, or any combination of these. The transaction may be at a fixed price, or may use a sliding-scale payment contingent upon future performance. The complexity of the matter is such that the consultant is urged to recommend to the client the use of an appropriate team of specialists, which will include investment bankers, tax specialists and legal advisers.

Methods of control

Where the client organization has been systematically growing through acquisitions and now has many subsidiaries and affiliates, an important question now arises as to how these activities should be controlled. The optimal pattern of relationships between corporate headquarters and the operating entities will in fact depend upon the nature of the underlying growth or diversification strategy and the extent of the diversification.

In those organizations in which acquisitions have been made only in areas and activities closely related to the original business, an approach often called the "core strategy" (and also known more colloquially as "sticking to the knitting"), the relationship is typically one of continuing determination of all key policies by the corporate headquarters. This approach is described as "strategic control". In such an organization the line executives in operating units will make major decisions on current operations only after discussion with the corporate level or within clear policy guidelines, and heads of staff activities in the subsidiaries will be similarly subject to supervision and control by their corporate counterparts.

An alternative philosophy exists, however. The completely unlimited approach to diversification, buying whatever appears to be a bargain without consideration of its strategic fit, was the hallmark of the "conglomerates" of the 1960s and 1970s and is now in disrepute. Organizations created in this way proved eventually to be unmanageable. But a number of large organizations — with the Hanson Group in the United Kingdom and United States markets being the best-known example — have been very successful through a policy of expansion into "manageable" activities: any product or service that can be allowed to operate largely independently with a minimum of head office involvement. For Hanson, this means activities which are concerned with "commodity" type products and services, requiring little capital investment and no sophisticated research and development.

The significance of this philosophy is that in such an organization the corporate headquarters directs through a system of essentially financial control. The management teams appointed to run the subsidiary activities are given performance objectives set in financial terms, particularly return on investment. Superior performance is rewarded, and under-performers are replaced. In such an organization the setting and monitoring of financial objectives are clearly amongst the most vital of all activities.

13.5 Finance and operations: Capital investment analysis

Most business organizations tend to generate more investment proposals than they can immediately finance. They therefore require a systematic method of calculating the economic attractions of such investment proposals, and of ranking them in order of preference so that the limited funds available go to the most productive investments. In a majority of companies the analysis of capital investment proposals is still done partly or wholly on the basis of "rules of thumb" or personal preference, so yet again the consultant has a useful task to perform.

Choosing among analytical methods

The consultant's first task in this area is to persuade the client that outdated and simplistic methods of investment appraisal, such as a simple rate-of-return analysis or the "years to payback" principle, are unsatisfactory and yield misleading results. He should instead encourage the use of one of the techniques based upon the time value of money. The general term used for this approach is *discounted cash flow* (DCF) analysis. There are, however, two different methods of implementing this approach. Most textbooks advocate the calculation of *net present value* (NPV) and the use of net present value per dollar invested as the decision criteria. The consultant should note, however, that this method requires the company to calculate its overall average cost of capital, which is then used as the discounting rate, and that this figure is difficult to develop and often unstable. The alternative approach, the *internal rate of return* (IRR), has some theoretical disadvantages but also enjoys the practical advantage of not requiring a cost-of-capital calculation. It is much more widely used than the NPV approach and should be the consultant's first choice.

The selection of an analytical method and a decision criterion, however, by no means solves all the problems in this area. The various investment proposals facing a company are likely to be very different in nature. In particular, some of them, such as proposals to replace old machinery which is giving rise to high maintenance costs with new but similar equipment, involve neither risk nor uncertainty. Other projects, such as the replacement of a known but outdated technology with an advanced but unfamiliar one, clearly involve both uncertainty and risk. It becomes very difficult to rank one project against the other unless some adjustment is made for the differing degrees of risk.

Sensitivity analysis

In order to arrive at a ranking for proposed projects, many companies will need outside assistance. The most satisfactory solution is to adopt a "sensitivity analysis" approach. Those projects that are seen as important but also as involving a high degree of uncertainty should be modelled (simulated), so that the model can be run many times with different values for key variables. A project to build a plant for the production of a radically new product, for example, may involve considerable uncertainty both about the time needed to bring the new product into production and about its market acceptance. The model would therefore require numerous reruns ("iterations") with different assumptions about the time needed to bring the plant on stream and about the likely sales volumes, and a probability distribution of expected net cash flows will be developed from the results.

It will be obvious from the above paragraph that this is yet another area in which the consulting organization will best be able to help its clients if it can offer the services of specialist teams in which financial consultants work closely with computer experts.

Follow-up of project effectiveness

There is yet another valuable service that the consultant can provide in this area. Many companies, even those that have adopted relatively sophisticated procedures for the evaluation of project proposals, overlook the need for systematic follow-up and monitoring of subsequent project performance. A project is adopted because it appears to promise a very high discount-adjusted rate of return. If it fails to perform as well as the project proposal promised, it is important to find out *why*. Was there an unexpected downturn in the economic environment? Did the project encounter technical problems that were not foreseen? Was the marketing staff unduly optimistic in predicting sales? Or were the forecasts of sales and earnings consciously inflated for political purposes by an "empire-building" divisional head? The development and installation of a follow-up system to answer such questions will rapidly pay off in improvements in project selection, and is one of the most useful tools that the consultant can provide.

13.6 Accounting systems and budgetary control

Financial consultants may be invited to assist their clients in the development of accounting systems by means of which various transactions are recorded, collected and classified, entered into the various ledgers and books of account, and finally used to prepare the organization's formal financial statements. This, however, is properly the work of qualified accountants, and consultants who are not themselves also accountants will recommend their clients to obtain proper professional assistance in this area.

Budgetary versus accounting systems

Consultants participating in general "management services" activities are very likely to find themselves called upon to assist in the design of budgetary systems rather than formal accounting systems. The emphasis here will be upon "management accounting": methods of collecting and analysing data to support internal decision-making rather than formal financial reporting. Both the objectives and the methods of management accounting are different from those of financial accounting, and the difference is essentially one of timeliness versus accuracy. Financial accounting emphasizes accuracy and detail, but produces reports that are historic. If decisions are not made until formal financial accounts are available, it is likely to be too late for those decisions to be effective. The consultant realizes that clients need information quickly to support their decision-making, and that information which is approximate but timely is of far more value than that which is accurate but three or more months late.

The budgetary and control system should be developed for an individual organization rather than bought "off the shelf", and will therefore differ from company to company. For most manufacturing companies, the component parts will include:

— a profit plan;

— the capital investment budget;

— wage and salary budgets;

— purchasing budgets and inventory control procedures;

— manufacturing direct cost budgets;

— general overhead budgets;

— sales, marketing and promotion budgets;

— recruitment and training budgets;

— the overall cash budget.

Most of these budgets will be further broken down by division and by department, reflecting the structure of the company.

Budgetary control

The consultant needs to keep in mind the multiple objectives that underlie any system of budgetary control. They are:

● that expenditures of funds and commitments of resources resulting from decisions in the various operating areas do not reach an overall aggregate that places an unacceptable strain on the company's financial structure and resources;

● that all revenue and cost items be planned and coordinated in order to ensure a positive stream of earnings and cash flows, and to guarantee the organization's liquidity;

● that all actual revenue, cost and expense items can be monitored and compared with budgeted levels, and the variances understood and corrected.

One consequence of the recent recession and the resulting strain on corporate cash flows has been a growing temptation to depart from carefully prepared list prices and to accept any order which appears to cover direct costs and to make at least a contribution to overheads. This places a renewed emphasis upon the distinction between "full" and "marginal" costs as a basis for pricing and output decisions.

The issue is clearly not well understood by many managers. Enthusiasts of marginal costing point to situations in which the company will clearly maximize its cash flow by taking decisions on a contribution basis. Others point out that in the long run an organization can stay viable only by ensuring that all of its costs are safely covered by its revenues. Both are of course correct. Marginal costing should not be the basis of pricing strategy, but it may still be valid to use it in tactical decisions. The key is to understand the importance of lead times and of opportunity costs. Although it has been said that in the long run no costs are fixed, on a shorter time scale most of them *are* in fact fixed, and any additional contribution to covering them is welcome. The consultant can be of great help in identifying appropriate time scales for the various categories of decision.

The contribution concept is not only used in making pricing decisions and in deciding whether or not to accept a particular order. It is also widely used in making product mix decisions. These decisions lie on the borderline between finance/accounting and production/operations, and like many other borderline decisions are often made on the basis of imperfect knowledge and mis-conceptions. Most managers will readily accept the logic of trying to maximize the production of those product lines on which the contribution appears to be greatest. Developments in the operations area, however, increasingly raise questions about the validity of this approach in some important cases. Where scarce capacity in some particular process acts as a "bottleneck", it is the contribution per product per unit of scarce resource time that should be the basis for decision-making. Consultants will find that this is yet another area in which they may have to educate clients — and should note that there are some excellent and enjoyable personal computer (PC) based simulation games to assist them.

The consultant must be acutely aware of the fact that designing a budgetary control and management information system involves much more than itemizing what budgets are needed and how often they should be prepared. Attention will have to be given to the company's organizational structure and existing pro-cedures. In a large company it may be necessary to create a number of "profit centres" or "investment centres", or even to designate some divisions as near-autonomous "strategic business units". In smaller organizations, a simple "cost centre" approach is likely to be used.

Once the organizational structure is agreed, it will be necessary to design procedures for the collection and submission of data for the development and review of budgets by higher authorities and for the determination of corrective action. Paper forms and/or EDP programmes and documentation must be selected. In this, as in most other areas, the development of the new procedures will involve a partnership between the consultants and key company people from the finance, organization development, EDP and personnel departments, while line management must be consulted at all stages to ensure that the completed system meets all its needs. Finally, the consultants will be actively involved in training company staff to operate the new procedures and will probably remain on call until the system has successfully been implemented.

13.7 Financial management under inflation

In the mid-1990s, inflation was not an immediate problem in any of the major industrialized countries. In the countries of Western Europe, North America and Japan the rate of increase in both producer and consumer price levels was below 5 per cent per annum, and in such conditions inflation can be overlooked in business decision-making without disastrous consequences.

Companies which operate in other parts of the world, however, need to take inflation more seriously, particularly if they anticipate making capital investments in such areas. In many parts of Latin America (and in the former USSR) the rate of price escalation approaches hyperinflation. Few managers fully understand how to take anticipated inflation into account in their planning and budgeting.

Inflation accounting

The aspect of inflation that has been most widely discussed in business circles is its impact on reported earnings. Conventional accounting permits only the original purchase value of capital goods and of inventory items to be used in calculating operating earnings. The resultant profits figure is therefore seriously overstated because the calculation of profit has not made proper provision for the replenishment of inventory or for the replacement of capital assets as they wear out. There has been very widespread debate concerning the introduction of new accounting rules that would provide for "inflation adjustment" and thus generate a lower but more realistic earnings figure.

Much of the "inflation accounting" debate has hinged upon the method of adjustment to be used. All the proposed systems seek to establish the use of more realistic current values of assets rather than using the historic (original) ones, but differ in their methods.

One approach, the "replacement cost" or "current cost" method, necessitates finding the current price in the market of equipment similar to that being used, and using this current market price as the basis for depreciation.

The alternative method — "index adjustment" or "current purchasing power" — retains the historic purchase price as its basis but multiplies this historic price each year by a factor obtained from an inflation index to give a new depreciation base.

The first method is clearly more accurate but administratively tedious and costly; the second method is more approximate but much easier to apply.

Up to the present time, the "inflation accounting" debate has been sterile for three reasons:

(1) accountants have been unable to agree as to which adjustment method should be used;

(2) some accountants do not accept any form of inflation adjustment, believing that any such system would turn accounting into a highly arbitrary and inexact process;

(3) most serious of all, very few tax authorities will accept inflation-adjustment accounts for the determination of corporate tax liabilities, and until such accounts are acceptable for tax reporting purposes it is unlikely that many companies will be willing to adopt them as the primary reporting vehicle.

Financial operations under inflation

Successful management under high inflation is not simply a matter of changing accounting procedures. There are practical operating steps to be taken. The consultancy can provide services to its clients in many areas, primarily the following:

- the development of inflation rate forecasts, either by primary analysis on the basis of monetary aggregates or by combining the forecasts readily available from official bodies and financial institutions;

- the incorporation of inflation expectations in the company's strategic planning procedures;

- the modification of capital investment analysis procedures to take explicit and systematic account of inflation expectations, particularly inflation differentials where wage costs, for example, are expected to rise more quickly than selling prices;

- the review of working capital management procedures, in recognition of the increased need to speed up the conversion of financial assets and to minimize unproductive cash balances under inflationary conditions;

- the recognition of the close relationship between inflation rates and interest rates, and the anticipation of likely interest rate changes in planning the company's capital structure;

- continuing emphasis upon the close relationship between inflation rates and changes in the value of currencies in the foreign exchange markets, leading to an increase in the importance of foreign currency exposure management.

Although at the time of writing inflation rates have fallen below their peaks in most OECD countries, this area is likely to be one of uncertainty and concern for many years to come. Yet many executives still find it difficult to think logically about inflation or its effects, and attempt to ignore it — with grave results. The educational requirement in this area is one of the greatest challenges facing the financial consultant at this time.

13.8 Cross-border operations and the use of external financial markets

Where the client company is engaged in any form of cross-border operation, either selling its products and services in foreign countries or purchasing some of its own materials from foreign suppliers, a number of important additional complications arise. Many of the issues involved are unfamiliar to corporate executives. The field of international finance is, then, a fruitful one for the consultant who develops the requisite expertise.

The most important issues arising in this area can be grouped under three subheadings, as follows:

— determining foreign exchange exposure;

— hedging techniques and decisions;

— using external money and capital markets.

Determining foreign exchange exposure

Very few companies engaged in cross-border trading are able to invoice their products and purchase their imported supplies entirely in their own domestic currency. As soon as sales are invoiced in a foreign currency, or the company contracts to purchase items priced in a foreign currency, a foreign exchange exposure exists. Many companies are unable to identify the exact extent of their exposure, and the consultant may be of considerable assistance here. The confusion which exists in many companies arises from the fact that there are three distinct kinds of foreign exchange exposure. The consultant needs to understand them all and to be able to assist the client in recognizing them, determining their relative importance and deciding what to do about them.

Many multinational companies, especially those whose headquarters are located in the United States, are much concerned with *translation exposure*: the risk of gain or loss when the assets, liabilities and earnings of a subsidiary are "translated" from the foreign currency in which the subsidiary's books are kept into the parent currency (US dollars). Such losses are "real" in so far as they influence the parent's overall reported profit and loss, and taxes on income. In another sense, however, they are "unreal" in that they arise from a particular accounting convention, and that a change to a different accounting basis may change a translation "loss" into a translation "gain". The consultant must be familiar with the current rulings of the client's national taxation authorities and the degree of freedom permitted under those rulings. Where there is no freedom of manoeuvre under the regulations, it may be necessary to advise the client to change the currency denomination of his or her liabilities to minimize the translation exposure.

Transaction exposure is simpler to understand and affects all companies which engage in international trade. Whenever a company commits itself to a transaction — whether a sale or a purchase denominated in a foreign currency, there exists the risk of gain or loss if the value of that foreign currency changes in relation to the company's own domestic currency. If a Swiss company supplies pharmaceutical drugs to a British buyer, giving 90 days credit and invoicing in pounds sterling, then that Swiss exporter will make a loss if the value of the pound falls relative to the Swiss franc during 90 days: the seller will receive only the agreed number of pounds, and those pounds will now buy fewer francs. The exporter's home currency cash flow is reduced, and the loss in this case is very clearly a real one. The consultant will probably not need to become much involved in the determination of exposures of this type: most companies are aware of their transaction exposures. They may still, however, be very unsure what to do about them.

The third type of exposure, which is now increasingly referred to as *economic exposure*, is more complex. It deals with the impact of an exchange rate change upon the organization's overall long-term profitability, rather than simply its effect upon currently outstanding transactions. Assume, for example, that a Swiss exporter sells watches to a distributor in the United States, and that the value of the dollar now falls abruptly against the Swiss franc. The immediate effect may be a transaction loss if a recent shipment of watches, invoiced in dollars, has not yet been paid for. The longer-term effect is much more serious: the Swiss manufacturer must choose between keeping the same dollar price, which will now yield fewer francs for every watch sold or, alternatively, holding the price in Swiss francs constant, which means increasing the dollar selling price, probably losing sales and market share, and handing customers over to competitors from Japan and other lower-cost countries. The need for professional advice in this area is clear.

It is surprising to recall that when earlier editions of this book were being prepared the size of the currency market was unknown. Best estimates suggested that total transactions in the foreign exchange markets probably amounted to something like US$200 billion per working day, a very large amount of money. The first systematic measurement of the market (by the Bank of International Settlement) was not undertaken until 1989, and published in early 1990. It revealed that transaction volume had reached US$650 billion per day. By early 1993 the market was believed to have grown further, and to have approached 1 trillion dollars. These astonishing figures mean that total currency transactions in a year are now more than ten times as large as total world trade in goods and services. It now becomes questionable whether the central banks of the world — even when acting together — can hope to control these markets effectively.

The importance of understanding and managing currency exposure was even more clearly underlined by the events of September 1992. During the previous 18 months there had been increasing reason to believe that, at least in Western Europe, exchange rate volatility could be discounted: the Portuguese escudo and the pound had joined the ERM of the European Monetary System, and both the Swedish krona and the Finnish markkaa had been linked to the ECU. It appeared that both the actual and the prospective members of the then European Community were moving rapidly towards currency unification. The need for currency management was expected to diminish accordingly.

The wave of speculation that was triggered by the Danish referendum dramatically changed the nature of the currency markets. Within a very few days the lira and the pound had left the ERM, the Spanish peseta had been devalued within the mechanism, the Swedish krona and the markkaa had been cut loose from their ties to the ECU, and the French franc was under heavy downward pressure. Volatility, which had been unusually low for more than a year, rose to its highest level since the collapse of the dollar in 1985. The lesson is clear. The currency market is unpredictable, and its size makes it unmanageable. Companies cannot afford to ignore or be complacent about their exchange exposures.

Hedging techniques and decisions

Once the foreign exchange exposures have been determined, the next step is to decide whether they should be "hedged" or "covered", and if so, how? Many companies turn to their commercial banks for advice. The local bank manager, however, probably has no experience of, or special training in, foreign exchange management. Consequently, his advice is likely to be highly conservative. Many bankers tell their clients: "You are in the business of making and selling products, not speculating in the foreign exchange markets. You should therefore cover all outstanding exposures by buying or selling the foreign currency in the forward market."

Any consultant working in this area should realise that this advice is an oversimplified answer to a very complex problem. A policy of 100 per cent cover by using the forward market does at least lock in a known rate of exchange, but not necessarily an advantageous one. Using the forward market can in fact be considered just as much a speculation as holding an open (uncovered) foreign exchange position: both policies will ultimately provide either a gain or a loss, depending upon the relation between the forward price when the transaction was generated and the spot price on the day the transaction matures. Beware of textbooks offering nonsensical formulae which claim to calculate the "cost" of hedging at the time the transaction is undertaken: the cost can only be calculated retrospectively when the final spot price is known.

The most important service that the consultant can provide in this area is to show the client that there are no simple golden rules or magic formulae available, and that foreign exchange operations require a systematic step-by-step analysis and decision process. The required steps are as follows:

(1) Determine overall foreign exchange exposures and distinguish between the different types of exposure as described above.

(2) Evaluate these exposure positions in the light of the best available forecasts and expectations concerning foreign exchange price movements, and decide if there are serious exposures that may produce foreign exchange losses. If so, hedging will have to be considered. For most companies, it will only be practical to cover transaction exposures on a continuing basis.

(3) Consider the possibility of hedging the exposures by operational means, rather than purely financial ones. A company which is regularly exporting goods to Italy and invoicing those sales in lire, for example, may be able

to offset this exposure by purchasing some of its own raw materials and supplies from Italian companies. Another method, particularly useful for large transnational companies with a high level of intra-group transactions, is "leading and lagging": a deliberate acceleration of some payments and delay of others in order to take advantage of expected exchange-rate movements.

(4) If operational hedging is not possible and some form of financial operation is to be used, the next question is whether the risk is so serious as to require 100 per cent cover, or whether partial hedging is acceptable. The specialized services which supply foreign exchange forecasts will usually also advise upon this point.

(5) The next step is to obtain from the banks the best available quotation for a "forward" transaction, and to compare this with management's expectations about what might happen to the spot rate. A British company has, for example, an exposure in French francs, and the exposed position is expected to continue for 90 days. The spot rate is, say, £1 = 7.80 French francs, but the banks quote a 90-day forward outright bid rate as £1 = 8.20 French francs, a significant "forward discount" on the franc. The question now is not whether the French franc will fall, but whether the spot price in 90 days' time will fall below 8.20. If it is expected to fall to a price below this, then the transaction should be covered. If it is expected to fall, but only to, say, 8.10, then it will be cheaper *not* to cover the transaction.

(6) The consultant will find that many client companies, including some that have been making regular use of the forward markets for hedging purposes and consider themselves quite sophisticated in this area, do not realize that it is possible to achieve the same result by using the money markets. For example, a company which is based in Switzerland, but sells regularly to the United Kingdom and invoices in sterling, will have regular "long" sterling exposure. Rather than hedge such exposures by selling the pounds forward, the company could borrow pounds in the London money market, use those pounds to buy Swiss francs, and use the francs for working capital purposes. The pound borrowing creates a sterling liability which offsets the long sterling position arising from the exports. The consultant should be able to show the client how to compare the cost of such an operation with conventional hedging, and to explain that when the local currency generated (Swiss francs in this example) can be used to repay an existing overdraft or credit line, the interest saving may be enough to make this the least-cost form of covering.

(7) The period since 1982 has seen the development of another and quite different approach to foreign exchange hedging in the form of the currency option. Active trading in such options started in the Philadelphia stock exchange, but is now spreading rapidly. Other exchanges (Chicago, London) are offering similar facilities and, even more significantly, major banks are selling such options on a "custom-tailored" basis. The option is essentially different from any other form of hedging in that its use is indeed "optional": the right to buy or sell currency at a stated price if the option-

holder chooses. There is no obligation to exercise the option if it is not advantageous to do so. This approach therefore offers a degree of downside protection if the currency movement is adverse, coupled with the possibility of still making a profit if the movement is in a favourable direction. The pricing of options is very complex, and the markets have unique procedures and jargon.

(8) The option form itself is still not well understood by many treasurers, some of whom consider it to be an exotic instrument that can only be used by "rocket scientists" with advanced degrees in mathematics. This is particularly unfortunate in that the basic option is now being supplemented by more specialized derivatives such as the "double option", the "average rate" option, the "knockout" or "exploding" option and the "compound" option. These are very important developments, and can be used to solve some kinds of exposure in uniquely effective ways.

Space limitations preclude the examination of all of these recent developments, but one in particular will be described to illustrate the kinds of unique feature they offer. Many companies are engaged in exporting their products to foreign buyers on a regular basis. A British company, for instance, exports monthly consignments to a buyer in Germany, and invoices the sales in Deutsche marks (DM). The exchange rate of the pound to DM fluctuates. In those months in which the DM is strong the company makes additional sterling profits, while in those months in which sterling has strengthened against the DM the company loses out. However, the company's overall profit at the end of the year will not depend upon the exchange rate at any particular point in time but on the average pound/DM exchange rate over the year. The development of a form of currency option based upon the average rate enables the company to hedge its real exposure position — and compared with the alternative of hedging with options on each individual shipment the cost saving will be about 40 per cent.

Here again there is an opportunity for the consultant to perform a valuable service. The client needs to be assured that options and other recent derivative financial instruments are both relevant (even for the smaller company) and readily available. But even once the client has accepted the usefulness of such techniques, the pace of development is such that he will have great difficulty in keeping his understanding up to date. There is a need for continuing assistance here.

Using external money and capital markets

Smaller companies in most countries automatically and quite logically look to commercial banks in their own country as the normal source of external funds. As companies grow in size and sophistication, however, the possibility of using external financial markets presents itself. Corporate management will initially have little knowledge about such markets, and probably believe them to be very exotic, perhaps dangerous or open only to the multinational giants. This is a further area, therefore, in which the management consultant's role is primarily an educational one.

The consultant will point out to the client that a number of international financial markets exist: the Eurocurrency market (sometimes called the Eurodollar market, although the dollar segment is only a part of it), the Eurobond market, and several "foreign bond markets" existing in various centres, particularly New York, London, the Swiss and German financial centres, and Tokyo. The various international bond markets cater primarily to the "high quality" borrower and a relatively small company may find access difficult. The Eurocurrency markets, however, despite their ability to accommodate single transactions of US$5 billion or more on a "syndicated" basis, are readily accessible to the medium-sized company, both as a source of loan funds and as a temporary investment medium for corporate cash that will later be needed for working capital purposes.

Corporate management will probably be surprised that banks operating in the "Euro" market can often pay a slightly higher interest rate on funds deposited than can the domestic banks, but at the same time can charge a slightly lower rate on the loans they make. The consultant will point out that this is a perfectly logical outcome of the fact that the Eurobanks have cost structures that are significantly different from those of domestic banks, the most important difference being the absence of any reserve requirements against their deposits. The lower operating costs allow them to work on a smaller "spread" between their borrowing and lending costs than can domestic banks, and their customers benefit accordingly.

Nevertheless, the area is a complex one, and the consultant will have to guide the client through a mass of new terms and procedures. In Eurocurrency lending virtually all loans are "floating rate", and are priced not at a stated percentage of interest rate but at a "spread" or "mark-up" over a base rate such as LIBOR (the London interbank offered rate), this latter being the wholesale cost of money in the interbank market. The procedures for determining "value dates" for repayment are complex, and these in turn can affect the overall interest cost. Lastly, although most financial institutions active in these markets are of undoubted superiority and creditworthiness, a few are of distinctly lower quality. There is much for the consultant to learn here. It can be a rapidly developing field for his professional services once the consultant has become familiar with these fascinating markets.

CONSULTING IN MARKETING AND DISTRIBUTION MANAGEMENT

14

Consulting work involving the client's marketing activities differs in several ways from that dealing with other functions. It is in its marketing that the firm finds itself in contact with external entities (competitors and customers) having an independent existence. The firm's very survival depends upon how well it manages to adapt to the market conditions influenced by the activities of these entities.

One of the paradoxes of the marketing function is that when it is looked at closely it tends to disappear, like a stream going underground. It is first found at the very highest level of the firm, in its overall strategy formulation. It then resurfaces in the organization and management of the various market-related activities: sales, advertising, product development, market research, and so on. This leaves a definite gap in the organization chart. Matters concerning the firm's overall strategy, of which marketing strategy is an important part, can only be decided at the topmost level of the organization, while running the various activities is predominantly a middle management function. As compared with his or her counterparts in the other management functions (production, finance, and so on), this leaves the senior marketing manager in a somewhat ambiguous position, and the same necessarily applies to a management consultant working with this manager.

Thus a consulting assignment that embraces the marketing function will usually develop into two quite separate tasks, one at the *strategy formulation level* and the other at the *activities or implementation level*. These two tasks are treated separately below. It is convenient here, however, to note briefly a third type of consulting activity.

The third type is *market research*, the study of the prospects and performance of a firm's products in the market. Market research consultants do not necessarily carry out marketing consultancy, but their findings can notably affect strategic direction. However, marketing management consulting assignments may involve some market research to verify (or invalidate) the client's assumptions about the corporate image, the nature of customers, and so on. Since this work is often very specialized and may require the availability of substantial numbers of trained interviewers, the consultant, unless he belongs to an organization with its own market research division, may find it more efficient and less time-consuming to subcontract the research to a specialist rather than to undertake it internally. The consultant should therefore keep informed of market research organizations, the areas in which they specialize and the quality of their work. The consultant should also keep up to date on trends and changes in the market research field.

Information technology (IT), based on computers linked together by the telephone network or other means, is now firmly established in many areas of marketing and distribution. Its growth is likely to be explosive. Applications, for the next few years at least, will be limited more by the ingenuity of the users than by the capabilities of the technology. Its effects have been profound, and the marketing consultancy which does not keep in touch with developments in this field will rapidly become obsolete. Some newer developments that are of interest to consultants will be reviewed in Chapter 17.

14.1 The marketing strategy level

Strategic decisions in marketing have far-reaching implications for the enterprise as a whole and for the management of particular functions, such as production, product development or financial control. It is no wonder, therefore, that even minor proposals may meet with strong objections from senior management of other departments. Major changes, such as dropping or adding product lines, committing substantial funds to advertising or product promotion, or changing overall pricing policies, are clearly general management decisions to be taken at top levels.

A useful starting-point is to classify the client's orientation towards the market. Three classifications are recognized: *product-oriented, production-oriented*, and *market-oriented*. In a product-oriented firm the emphasis is on the product itself, while in the production-oriented firm the dominant considerations in product design or modifications are those of ease, cost-efficiency or capacity of production. In either case market considerations are ignored or suppressed. In a market-oriented firm the decisions are based upon the analysis of market needs and demands. The object is to capitalize on the opportunities the market offers. This approach can produce any of the good effects of the other two orientations, and avoids their drawbacks. More importantly, it can identify new opportunities. Figuratively speaking, the management of the firm asks the following questions:

- What are the problems of our customers that our products (or services) can solve more efficiently or better than products of other suppliers?
- Who, in addition to our current customers, has these same needs?
- What are the particular circumstances of our customers, actual or potential, which would suggest modifications in our products, conditions of delivery, service after the sale, etc.?

●   Can we offer an effective and affordable solution to the problem and still produce an acceptable profit?

The idea of thinking in terms of providing solutions to problems is a very useful one in marketing. It helps considerably in identifying new markets, finding new products for existing customers, finding new customers for existing products and, most importantly, discovering potential and possibly unsuspecting competition.

As a very simple case, consider a manufacturer of nuts and bolts. This enterprise probably thinks of itself in the metalworking business, and looks for new business on this basis. But what about its customers? Their problem is joining things together. So the firm could meet competition from firms making welding equipment, rivets, cotter pins, or glues. This threat is also an opportunity, since the firm's sales force and distributors are already in touch with people who form a potential market for these items, which suggests that they could profitably be added to the firm's product line if they could be manufactured with existing facilities. The costs of marketing are high, so that anything that can add to the effectiveness of the various marketing functions (i.e. reduce the unit costs of marketing activities) can be surprisingly profitable. Such help can come from selling more items per sales visit, sending out shipments with more items, and turning small, unprofitable accounts into at least medium-sized ones. Creatively developing unique products is a key to success.

Another theme emerging is that of the "global market". The thesis here is based on the observation that a very wide range of branded goods, from jet aircraft to cars, compact disc players and jeans to hamburgers, are being sold worldwide with little or no adaptation to local conditions. Production for a global market gives substantial economies of scale compared with production for a national market, and even compared with multinational firms which adapt their production to what they believe are local national preferences. Thus national and multinational firms are vulnerable in the face of firms which adopt a global strategy.

Stated in this way, this thesis appears to advocate a product orientation rather that a market orientation, and it is ironic that the chief proponent of the global market strategy is Theodore Levitt, whose 1960 article was such a devastating attack on those firms obsessed with their products.[1] It can also, however, be interpreted as an assault on the marketing excesses of the boom years when marketers became hypnotized with their own jargon, marketing departments were swollen beyond all reason, markets were segmented for segmentation's sake, and so forth.

The global market concept is still a controversial subject, but it appears to be widely accepted that the firms which most successfully weathered the recent hard years were those which had adopted and understood the marketing concept, and applied it in pursuit of clear objectives. Marketing has emerged leaner and fitter.

Marketing strategy analysis

Since the firm's products are the hub of its whole marketing strategy, the first step in a marketing assignment should be to analyse the client's whole product line in the way described above, checking whether the products (1) provide answers to consumers' problems, (2) are mutually supportive, and (3) can be modified to solve consumer or market problems. Ideally, all the products in the line should be of interest to every customer, and should fit in well with the production facilities. This ideal is unlikely to arise in practice, of course, and a certain amount of departure from it must be tolerated. Consultants should pay attention, however, to the "odd" product, which is in line because it fits the production facilities but requires a different set of customers and thus requires undue sales effort in proportion to its potential sales. Such spare production capacity might be better used in producing for other firms under contract or subcontract. Also, a check needs to be made for gaps in the product line which could be filled by buying-in, in order to make full use of the available sales efforts. Since each product maintained in inventory requires space and cash, seeking opportunities to eliminate slow-selling items (line consolidation) can be equally beneficial as a cost-cutting/profit improvement issue.

Such an analysis should provide a sound basis for the consultant's recommendations for product additions or deletions. Sometimes it will indicate areas that need further investigation. For example, the marketing manager might insist that some sizes in a product line, although very small sellers, are necessary because the firm's distributors demand a "full" line from their suppliers. This should be investigated (sometimes "demand" means simply a mild preference), as should the possibility of "buying-in" the more extreme sizes. The analysis is also, of course, a prerequisite for a review of the client's new product development programme.

One of the interesting points noted by various studies during recent recessionary periods (and recessions are widely believed, probably correctly, to bring managers back in touch with business basics that are too easily forgotten in boom times) was that quality of goods and reliability of delivery (supply) were generally perceived as more important than price, especially by industrial purchasers. The implications of this marketing strategy are clear.

In many enterprises pricing is regarded as a special province of accountants, who determine at what prices the marketing staff must sell. Yet this is an area in which both marketing considerations and cost criteria apply. If a marketing consultant finds that prices are set by unilateral decisions of accountants, the consultant will be interested in reviewing how this affects marketing and the volume of sales. This may lead to a revision of pricing policy, including the establishment of new procedures for price setting in the client organization. The ultimate objective would be to make better use of prices as a marketing tool, but without running the risk that an increased volume of sales of underpriced products would cause a financial loss.[2] It should be noted that absorption costing and other cost accounting methods can give rise to misleading ideas about the profitability of different items in the product line.

Another problem area for consideration by top management is the firm's public image — the opinion that customers, actual and, more importantly, potential, have of the firm. This should be broadly consistent with the image the firm has of itself, and which its product line, advertising, public relations and salespersons are expected to create (box 14.1).

The consultant who suspects that such a clash between the client's internal and external images exists should investigate this possibility thoroughly. How to approach it is a question of consulting strategy. To change the firm's image is a difficult decision to take; the case for change must therefore be very strong. For example, the marketing consultant may call for the help of an independent market research consultant of good reputation, familiar with attitude research techniques. In any case, the relevant evidence should be collected and presented by a disinterested party, so that the client is assured of the objectivity of the recommendations.

Box 14.1 Various images of the firm

Different perceptions of a firm's image can be illustrated by the results of research into the public image of three department stores in a North American city, carried out by a local business school. When the students interviewed the store managers, one manager said that his store's image was built on quality, the second said his was built on prices, and the third said his store's strength lay in service. The research on consumer attitudes revealed that the same three images, of price, quality, and service, indeed existed, but that each of the three managers was wrong about the image attributed to his own store. Thus each manager was, and for some years had been (1) wasting most of the advertising expenditure; (2) wasting most of the effort expended in training salespersons: and (3) failing to give customers the type of treatment they expected from his store. It was extremely fortunate for each of these managers that the other two had misread the market as badly as he had himself. In the meantime the smaller stores in town were profiting from the way the big three were failing to cash in on their advantages.

Concentration in retailing

The trend towards concentration, apparent for many years in food retailing, is, if anything, intensifying and extending into other goods. For example, hardware is being sold increasingly through do-it-yourself outlets, themselves often subsidiaries of other retailers. This trend will have increasingly profound effects on the marketing of such goods:

(1) The major firms will obviously use their purchasing power leverage to get the greatest possible discounts; this drive will be strengthened as the chains fight for market share. In order to maximize purchasing power many chains have moved to centralized purchasing, which means that all buying, for many regional divisions, is being consolidated into one central buying office.

(2) The major retailers will try to influence and to participate in the manufacturer's advertising. In recent years, the "power" has shifted from

the manufacturer to the retailer; retailers now aggressively sell advertising and merchandising support without which a manufacturer's products cannot survive.

(3) Selling techniques have changed. A large part of the role of the salesperson dealing with independent firms and small chains is to function as "order takers", and the actual selling function is relatively limited. With re-ordering being increasingly automated through the use of sophisticated computer programs and electric point-of-sale ordering, the order-taking function is being reduced, and centralized purchasing means that the sales-person now deals with buyers who are sophisticated negotiators with abundant data at their disposal. This will entail corresponding training for sales representatives if they are to hold their own in these negotiations.

(4) The spread of "house brands" and "generics" means that in many lines of goods major retailers are in effect competing directly with manufacturers on ground of their own choosing. Some brands such as Sears Craftsman or Kenmore have built brand identity and brand loyalty.

(5) New retail formats, which reflect the further specialization in merchan-dising, are proliferating: in the United States, for example, club stores (Sam's, Pace, Price Club) and specialty retailers such as Circuit City (appliances), Toys 'Я' Us (toys), Kids 'Я' Us (children's clothing), Home Depot (home improvements and hardware), Office Depot (office supplies), CompUSA (computers), PetSmart (pet supplies), etc.

At the other end of the scale, many small food retailers are being forced to find a niche for survival by becoming convenience stores. The different mix of goods sold by such stores is reflected in changed stocking and purchasing patterns by their wholesalers; this may work back in due course to different assemblages of manufacturing facilities.

These trends are affecting, and will continue to affect, the overall and marketing strategies of all the firms involved, and the marketing consultant must become aware of them and of the effect they will have if he or she is to provide sound advice to clients.

What the advice is will depend on various factors, such as the strength of the client's brand name, the technology behind the products (a new product which can be copied in a matter of months has no market strength), the negotiating skills of salespersons, and so on. One practice that must be looked at with concern is that of recouping the discounts exacted by large customers by charging high prices to small customers. This hastens their demise and makes the manufacturer even more dependent on a few large customers, any one of whom could de-list his products and bankrupt him in a matter of months.

There would seem to be very good prospects for the consultant who knows how to show groups of (non-competing) manufacturers how to provide low-cost support to corresponding groups of wholesalers and retailers. It must surely be safer for a manufacturer to have a hundred healthy customers than four or five overgrown ones. Whether the client has the vision to perceive this is a matter for question.

14.2 Marketing operations

Different firms have different ideas about which operations are part of the marketing function and which are not. Selling, advertising, promotion, dealing with distributors, packaging, package design, new product concept development and market research are considered by almost all enterprises to be the responsibility of the marketing manager, but the responsibility for transportation and storage of finished goods (physical distribution) is usually less clear.

For example, the case has been reported of a Canadian firm that for over two years deferred action on a consultant's report which recommended building an intermediate storage and distribution warehouse, with expected savings to the firm of about Can$2 million a year. The simple reason was that no one could decide which department was to operate the proposed warehouse. While this degree of organizational futility is rare, the case nevertheless shows that top managements may have difficulty in making positive decisions concerning the administration of activities that cross departmental boundaries.

Such situations should be detected at the diagnostic stage and the assignment formulated to include the appropriate recommendations. The operating marketing consultant who detects such a case would be well advised to consult his or her supervisor, because organizational fuzziness in these areas could slow the progress of the assignment very substantially.

Sales management

The consulting activities in this field are straightforward. Proper training and motivation of salespersons are key items to be checked, as is the way that sales staff share their effective selling time between existing and potential customers, and among large, medium and small accounts. Another point to check is whether the client's advertising is being used to increase the salesperson's effectiveness by generating curiosity and interest in the minds of customers. Such interest makes it easier to obtain appointments and helps interviews to get off to a good start. This aspect of advertising is particularly important in marketing industrial goods.

Motivation of sales staff is a complex matter, given the conditions under which they work. A wide variety of incentive programmes are in use. The primary motivator, of course, is the payments system which usually includes a base salary (or draw), a commission and a bonus component. The consultant should check that the incentive system is at the same time fair to the salesperson and is designed to obtain the results desired by the enterprise (to encourage the selling of profitable items in preference to less profitable ones.)

Application of information technology can do a great deal to increase sales effectiveness. It can save much time spent in producing reports, preparing orders, and so on, and leave more time for active selling, and it can promote more effective selling by making up-to-the-minute information on stock position and other relevant matters available during the sales call.

As the marketplace becomes more diverse and complex, so must the sales management process. The vice-president of sales must manage field sales managers, sales channel specialists (i.e. club stores, convenience stores, military commissaries, etc.), sales promotion or sales merchandizing specialists, private label specialists, and so on. Many of these field sales managers must also be trained to motivate brokers and/or distributors through whom they sell.

Advertising and promotion

Usually the consultant's client can obtain good advice on these activities from an advertising agency, but occasionally a situation can arise in which those responsible for advertising and promotion are rather uninspired, both at the client's end and at the agency's. The consultant should check that the role of advertising and promotion in the client's marketing mix has been fully thought out, and is consistent with the type of product being sold: for example, "push-pull" advertising for fast-moving consumer products, producing leads for salespersons of industrial goods, or image-building for prestige goods; next, the consultant should ensure that this role has been properly communicated in the instructions given to the advertising agency; finally, the consultant should ensure that the agency has correctly interpreted the instructions in terms of the advertising message and the choice of media.

A common but undesirable practice is that of setting advertising expenditures purely as an arbitrary percentage of sales, either past sales or forecast sales. It is much sounder to plan advertising campaigns in terms of objectives and to calculate the money needed to attain these objectives. This amount may be quite out of line with the resources available, in which case the objectives should be redefined on a more modest scale. This method has the advantage of giving the client some idea of what might be expected from the advertising expenditure.

Recent advances in information technology, allowing the use of large demographic data bases, are leading to changes in advertising practices and the way campaigns are planned and managed.

In working with a client's advertising agency, or with issues which may be considered "the agency's responsibility", the consultant must continually be aware of the political sensitivity of the client/agency relationship and should avoid becoming an adversary of the advertising agency; such a situation is unproductive and could lead to the consultant's dismissal from that phase of the project.

Distribution channels

The trend towards concentration in the retailing of consumer goods is bringing with it corresponding changes in the channel structures for these goods, the manufacturer being increasingly replaced by the retailer as the "channel captain". The reduction in numbers of independent retailers, and their share of trade, is also reducing the importance of the wholesaler, and this trend is being reinforced by the increasing sophistication of the physical distribution process, which reduces the need for the intermediate storage function performed by wholesalers. Interest charges increase the costs of holding stock and also contribute to the weakening of the wholesaler. This reduction in available options will mean that the marketing consultant will be less involved than previously in assignments involving channel policies. These will be replaced to some extent by assignments concerning physical distribution.

In developing countries this increase in retail concentration is also present, although so far it is not as advanced as in the developed countries. In developing countries the wholesaler is still an important factor in the distribution channel. However, the consultant should be aware that many manufacturers, particularly the larger ones, have a tendency to maintain large sales forces who visit retailers directly, bypassing the wholesalers. This may be due to a desire by marketing managers to keep tighter control, but unless the manufacturer has a wide product range it is likely to be excessively costly. The consultant should be able to evaluate the costs of these alternatives.

Franchising is a form of distribution channel which has been widespread in the United States for many years, and is now increasingly being found elsewhere. Marketing consultants have seldom had much work with franchises, but this will probably change as an ever wider variety of goods and services are marketed through this type of structure.

New product development

This is very much an interdepartmental process, involving overall strategy, marketing, R & D, engineering, production, finance, sales, and so on. Information about the size of the potential market, competing products, competitors' possible reactions, prices, the way customers will use the product, even the levels of skill that the distributors' staff will be able to devote to servicing and repairing, should be analysed and evaluated at the inception of the product, if the design work is to start off in the right direction. The marketing department's involvement should, if anything, increase as the development progresses.

The consultant's role in this function is twofold. In the first place, the consultant should verify that the marketing department can supply reliable information of the type described and, if not, advise on how to develop that capability. Secondly, he or she must ensure that accurate and usable data are provided to all functional groups involved in the process.

New product development is a vital function, because the firm's future lies in these products or services. Yet the process of new product development is very often a hit-and-miss affair, which attracts little top-management attention (unless a top manager has suddenly had a "brilliant idea", usually with disastrous consequences).

Packaging

Package design, both structural and graphic, is an intrinsic part of new product design (and is often the major component in refurbishing existing products) and its importance, particularly in the case of fast-moving consumer goods, is often underrated. The package can be used, as in the case of window-cleaners in spray containers, to enhance convenience of use (or even in after-use, as when honey manufacturers package their products in coffee mugs or beer mugs), and thus give otherwise indistinguishable products a distinct competitive edge.

Packaging design is an indispensable way of attracting customers' attention on crowded supermarket shelves, particularly in health and beauty aids, which also offers the talented designer the opportunity of creating a coherent brand image by developing a "matched set" of containers for a range of products. At the same time the package must satisfy retailers' requirements for stackability (there was a case of an otherwise excellent product which flopped because it was in a wedge-shaped package which could not be stacked on the shelf), and protection against pilferage and damage in transit and storage, or tampering at the retail stage. At the wholesaler and bulk transport level the package has to adapt to the dimensional requirements of palletization and containerization, without excessive waste of space.

In the industrial goods field as well, packaging must primarily take into account the requirements of palletization and containerization. But even here the "value added in packaging" concept can be used constructively. For example, diesel-generator sets could be shipped in standardized containers which could be reassembled on site to form sheds for the equipment.

Modern materials and techniques are making packaging a rapidly developing area. The consultant who expects to undertake marketing assignments should keep abreast of these developments. Subscriptions to one or two of the relevant trade journals and visits to exhibitions could be good professional investments.

14.3 Consulting in commercial enterprises

In this sector stock turnover is one of the key issues. In a well-run firm this forms the focal point of all activities; purchasing and stock level planning are based on target stock rotation objectives. The consultant's first task in such enterprises is to check the *stock-control procedures*. Often these will be found to be unsatisfactory and suitable procedures will have to be established. Different types of goods need different stock-control systems.

The establishment of stock (inventory) control procedures comes first, because further work will need the data such procedures will produce. Indeed, very often the assignment aims to achieve no more than installing good stock-control procedures and training management in using stock-control data in planning and administration.

In recent years the concept of just-in-time (JIT) inventory management has become very popular. It allows a business to keep inventory levels at a minimum while reducing the risks of out-of-stock situations.

Some assignments, however, will also have various general management aspects (e.g. setting up management-by-objectives — MBO — programmes in multidepartment firms), and sometimes training in specialized techniques will have to be arranged.

The above account for the bulk of what might be called corrective or remedial consulting activities in commercial enterprises. But there are firms that get themselves into more serious trouble through unsound policies. In these cases the remedies are usually obvious, if drastic, and the consultant's main function is to provide management with the support needed to make disagreeable or unpalatable decisions.

For example, a retailer of luxury goods (watches, sports goods, and so on) might have been enticed into giving extended credit terms because it is so much easier to sell such goods in this way, only to find accounts receivable equal to six months' sales or more, which are largely uncollectable.

Quite often retailers will pick store locations unsuitable for the goods they handle, for example, trying to sell large household items in a convenience store site or vice versa. A variation of this situation is the case of the real-estate developer, innocent of all knowledge of retailing or consumer behaviour, who builds a shopping centre and then leases space to retailers who are inappropriate for that location. Problems of this kind appear and consultants are called to deal with them, soon after the shopping centre "boom" starts in any area. They are quite common in many developing countries and areas.

14.4 International marketing

There was a time when international trade meant that developing countries exported raw materials to, and imported manufactured goods from, developed countries. This simple dichotomy is no longer valid. A rapidly growing variation of this theme (which will probably become dominant in the not-too-distant future) is that developed countries export manufacturing technologies to developing countries, with manufactured goods flowing in the other direction. This leads to corresponding changes in marketing consulting, with developed-country consultants being asked to evaluate prospective host country markets in connection with proposed technology-transfer activities through joint ventures or other arrangements, and developing-country consultants having to evaluate developed-country markets for manufactured goods and set up suitable marketing channels. Consultants in both developed and developing countries will have to polish up their knowledge of export credit guarantee systems, preferential tariff systems, "most favoured nation" and GATT agreements, and other arrangements that influence international trading. They will also, of course, have to find out how much of their marketing experience is culture specific, and so not transferable to other countries.

In the future, international trade alliances such as the North American Free Trade Agreement (NAFTA) between the United States, Canada and Mexico, or the Maastricht Treaty in Europe could substantially alter or change the way products are produced and marketed in these areas.

In addition to these new trends in international marketing, the consultant may be asked to advise on the more traditional form of export marketing. This differs from international marketing in degree rather than in kind, the principal differences being the complications of the required paperwork (shipping firms will usually take the responsibility for executing this) and the additional difficulties of working with distributors in a remote country (language, distance, product training and support, etc.). Bankers, with their international contacts, can be helpful in checking references and credit ratings, and the exporter and his consultant can call upon the services of the commercial attaché of the national embassy in the destination country.[3]

The main point to keep in mind about going into exporting is that it is not a quick fix for getting rid of surplus goods or finding an outlet for spare production capacity. Developing an effective international distribution network requires time and effort, and must be taken very seriously if any success is to be obtained. There must be a definite commitment of financial and human resources to a planned programme with a specific objective.

14.5 Physical distribution

At long last physical distribution is coming to be regarded as a distinct (and serious) activity, accounting for a substantial part of the total costs of an enterprise. Consultants will find themselves increasingly being asked for advice in this area.

Complications arising in such assignments will have three sources. First, there is the problem of arriving at a clear definition of the authority and responsibilities of the distribution manager, as the physical distribution function is affected by decisions made in all departments, from purchasing through to sales, and procedures that minimize costs within each department will not necessarily result in the lowest overall cost. This can result in difficulties in reconciling conflicting objectives. Secondly, very few firms have cost-accounting systems geared to reporting physical distribution costs, so the assignment will usually have to be extended to include changes in cost accounting. Thirdly, although a substantial amount of operations research work has been done in this area and some useful results obtained on some topics (for example, vehicle scheduling), there are still no algorithms which can conveniently be used in physical distribution planning, for calculating how to arrive at overall lowest costs. Trial and error methods are too time-consuming to be practicable in a system of any complexity. Computer-based simulation programmes ease this problem, and the advent of decentralized computer availability can make such programmes part of the regular tool-kit of physical distribution management.

14.6 Public relations

This is an area which is both a part of marketing, in that it is a component of the marketing mix, and at the same time transcends marketing in that it addresses a much wider audience than simply the firm's customers. This audience includes the general public, government regulating agencies, shareholders, and the firm's employees themselves. However, it is in the nature of public relations (PR) that the corporate image which PR seeks to create in the minds of these various sub-audiences will inevitably feed back into and affect the image held by the firm's customers — a presentation given to stock market analysts and reported in the financial pages of the newspapers cannot be kept secret from customers — so it is important for the marketing department to be involved in the design of PR campaigns; if not, conflicting images could be created.

Expenditure on PR has increased dramatically in recent years, as companies have started to use it proactively rather than simply reactively. Press conferences are tending to replace (at much greater expense) press releases. PR consultants are being brought in, some to train executives how to handle media interviews, and others to advise on corporate image creation.

As far as the consultant is concerned, this tendency means that he or she should check that the images which the client's advertising and PR efforts seek to create are consistent with each other, and that the client's internal organization is such that there is close liaison between the marketing and the PR functions. The consultant may also recommend training in dealing with media interviews for a selection of the client's senior managers. Statements made by named officers of the firm carry much more conviction than those made by an anonymous spokesperson, but this is a two-edged weapon, and a poorly handled interview can generate undesirable publicity even if the underlying situation is favourable to the firm.

---

[1] T. Levitt: "Marketing myopia", in *Harvard Business Review*, July-Aug. 1960. See also idem: *The marketing imagination* (New York, The Free Press, 1983).

[2] See R. A. Garda: "The successful marketing managers gain the decisive pricing edge", in *Management Review* (New York), Nov. 1983, pp. 19-22.

[3] Very useful publications on export marketing, market studies, trade fairs, packaging and other topics are available from the International Trade Centre (ITC) in Geneva.

CONSULTING IN PRODUCTION MANAGEMENT

15

Production is essentially a process of transforming certain inputs into some required outputs in the form of goods or services. As such, a production function does not apply exclusively to manufacturing operations but also to other activities, such as construction and transport operations, health or even office services.

This process of transformation requires decision-making on the part of the production manager with a view to getting an output of the desired quantity and quality delivered by the required date and at a minimum cost. The consultant's task is to advise management, whenever necessary, on the best means of achieving such an objective. In most cases, production management consultants are able, in the performance of their functions, to measure and assess the fruits of their work quite tangibly.

Production forms part of the *value chain* which comprises marketing, inbound logistics, production, outbound logistics, sales and after-sales service. Production consultants will therefore consider the effect of their propositions on the overall value chain. There are many examples where improved production efficiency leads to a reduced performance of the overall value chain.

15.1 Basic choices in the production area

How can production consultants contribute to improving the performance of production systems having in mind an optimization of the whole value chain? Problems submitted to the consultant may have very different degrees of importance to the client organization.

At one end of the scale there are problems which belong to the group of "basic choices". A production consultant may have an important say in a team which is examining the client's business strategy.

At the opposite end of the scale there are myriad problems whose common denominator is the need to meet certain criteria with regard to productivity, cost, or job satisfaction in the performance of specific production tasks. Such problems tend to be operational in nature. But the consultant will be well advised not to lose sight of the broader needs of the client organization, as it is not unusual for assignments in very specific production fields to disclose problems that are much more profound and lie outside the scope of the production area itself.

Therefore, in defining an improvement programme or project, consultants should, together with their clients:

— establish competitive performance criteria and levels;

— develop a clear understanding of available production choices (best practice);

— select the consulting approach.

Performance criteria and levels

Speed, quality, productivity and customer focus, as well as their continuous improvement, characterize the worldwide production objectives of the 1990s:[1]

● The *speed imperative* is translated into criteria such as time to market for new products or services, response time to orders of internal or external customers, and manufacturing lead time for production.

● *Quality and productivity* are increasingly defined in terms of the customers' desire and translated into product specifications by using tools such as quality function deployment.[2] In product development, productivity and quality mean achieving high leverage from critical resources, as well as an increased number of successful projects developed in a truly cross-functional development process. With tools such as total quality management (TQM), efforts are made to improve quality and productivity in operations by increasingly concentrating on processes and not only on products.

● *Customer focus*, the third competitive imperative, aims at meeting increasing expectations of ever more segmented customers who are offered, for most products, a wide variety of choice. Here, the efficient translation of these demands into products and services with distinction and integrity has to be tackled.

Consultants are used to implement all three performance criteria or competitive imperatives, as shown in box 15.1. In the present drive to restructure production, consultants should, however, be careful not to generate too many projects which cannot be "digested" and sustained by existing production facilities and staff.

To define performance criteria and set performance standards, a client company assisted by a consultant is well advised to search for those best practices of superior companies, competitors and non-competitors, which are relevant to achieving superior performance.

Benchmarking (see description in section 4.6) has been used by many consultants in helping clients to establish performance levels in production and operations by comparing the client's current practices with those of sectoral leaders, competitors or other companies able to offer, and willing to share, useful practical experiences. In the approach developed by the Xerox Corporation, the interfirm comparison methodology, traditionally used with financial data, has been applied to product design, manufacturing and customer services by seeking to identify, evaluate and use the best approaches developed by successful competitors.[3]

Box 15.1   Performance criteria of production

Performance criterion	Driving force	Consultants contribute to
Speed	– Intense competition	– Shorter development cycles
	– Fast-changing customer expectations	– Better targeted products
	– Accelerated technological change	– Accelerated capital rotation
	– Shrinking product life cycle	– Reorganization of processes emphasizing speed
	– Reduced contribution margins	– Instigate continuous improvement
Quality and productivity	– Exploding product variety	– Promote creativity combined with total product quality
	– Sophisticated, discerning customers	– Emphasize quality of manufacturing processes
	– Increasing complexity of process technology	– Tap and develop knowledge of all staff
	– Environmental concerns	– Develop cross-functional problem solutions
		– Focus on "value added"
Customer focus	– Customer expects to be treated as individual	– Define quality in terms of customer
	– Intense competition	– Streamline supply chains inside/outside the company
	– Crowded/saturated markets	

Source: Adapted from: S. G. Wheelwright and K. B. Clark: *Revolutionizing product development* (New York, The Free Press, 1992).

Making production choices

In implementing performance improvement programmes according to the above criteria, the most complex task is perhaps the wide variety of choices a consultant faces, a summary of which is given in box 15.2 (overleaf). Often these choices are sold as a complex package such as "lean production".[4] *Lean production* advocates a reduced vertical integration, where the original equipment manufacturer (OEM) produces only about 20-30 per cent of the product value. Parts and components are bought from a reduced number of suppliers with whom close collaboration is developed. Suppliers take up product development tasks and synchronize their production (just-in-time) with the OEM. Consultants are often called in either by the OEM or by suppliers (vendors) to develop lean production practices which make such an enterprise network operate efficiently.

Another package of choices concerns the implementation of information technology in operations aiming at computer-integrated manufacturing. In several cases, this introduction has been made or is being sought to "keep up with the others", and without the necessary preparatory work being thoroughly done. Computer applications have found their way into production through computer aided design (CAD) and computer aided manufacturing (CAM). There have been several developments in CAM, as well as the introduction of flexible manufacturing systems (FMS). Production consultants would do well to remind their client organization that if the layout is poor, the product design old, production planning and control not the best, and standards loose, transferring these ills to a computerized manufacturing system is not going to help much.

Furthermore, it is the rule rather than the exception that new technology is introduced side by side with traditional technology. This may be a permanent feature or a transition phase, and the consultant must be able to diagnose the problems and improve the efficiency, particularly of traditional technology, either for increasing productivity and cutting costs or as a prelude to the introduction of new technology.

Box 15.2 Major types of manufacturing choice

Capacity	Amount, timing, type
Facilities	Size, location, specialization
Equipment and process technologies	Scale, flexibility, interconnectedness
Vertical integration	Direction, extent, balance
Vendors	Number, structure, relationship
New products	Hand-off, start-up, modification
Human resources	Selection and training, compensation, security
Quality	Definition, role, responsibility
Systems	Organization, schedules, control

Source: S. G. Wheelwright and R. A. Hayes: "Competing through manufacturing", in *Harvard Business Review*, Jan.-Feb. 1985, p. 101.

Selecting the consulting approach

There is not only a wide variety of production choices, but also a variety of consulting approaches that are applicable to production and operations.

Process or product focus. In order to improve the performance of production systems, consultants have to decide together with their clients whether to focus on certain products or certain processes, or concentrate on cutting overhead costs independently of products and processes. For a company wishing to improve delivery speed, for example, it would be useful to look into order processing, which generally would be similar for a whole range of products. If the task is to increase the contribution margin of A-products (products which have a high share of sales), then the consultant would be well advised to analyse the production sequence for this product. An overhead reduction approach would be appropriate if there is a high percentage of overhead costs and if there are too many products and processes to achieve short-term performance improvements.

Technical expertise or change management skills. While production consultants have traditionally acted very much as industrial engineering or technology experts, they have had to learn how to lead and assist in complex organizational and technological change processes. And it is still a major challenge for an engineer to acquire process consulting skills and be sensitive to people's concerns in proposing changes in established production practices. The failure of consulting projects can often be attributed to an imbalance between technical expertise and the skills required to lead change processes.

Radical re-engineering or incremental improvements. If a client decides to call in a consultant in production management, it is increasingly due to a need to modernize operations and to achieve "quantum leaps" in speed and efficiency. For such cases, consultants have devised the business process re-engineering (BPR) approach, described in section 4.6. BPR aims to identify and radically improve processes that are essential for creating value and meeting customers' demands; other processes are not restructured, but are discontinued and dismantled. State-of-the-art production and information technologies are essential factors for achieving process integration and reorganization, which is the opposite to traditional process fragmentation into thousands of small tasks.

Re-engineering ignores what *is* and concentrates on what *should be*; thus it is more like business reinvention than restructuring. The traditional question of a consultant is, for example: How can we perform customer credit checks more efficiently? In a re-engineering approach the consultant would ask: Does customer credit need to be checked at all?

In contrast, continuous and incremental improvement following the principles of *Kaizen* (in Japanese, "gradual unending improvement") builds on existing systems with the objective of using every opportunity and involving everyone — top and middle management, supervisors, specialist staff and workers — to make small improvements. To achieve incremental improvements, a consultant may be given the task of "installing" continuous improvement processes: a total quality approach, for example. Such an evolution of production systems instead of the re-engineering revolution is appropriate if a company is already a leader in quality, productivity and speed, and wants to sustain this leadership on a long-term basis. For example, "if a company falls 10 per cent short of where it should be, if its costs come in 10 per cent too high, if its quality is 10 per cent too low, this company does not need re-engineering but incremental improvement".[5]

Radical re-engineering should be followed by an incremental improvement approach to sustain overall high performance levels, as there is a well-known tendency of production systems for performance levels to erode with time. Furthermore, even if the latest production and information technologies have been applied, there is always scope for smaller improvements suggested by the customers, the company's own staff, the suppliers of the technology or the consultants.

Notwithstanding the approach taken, the consultant in most cases will have to deal with three major components of production systems:

— the products;
— the methods and organization of work;
— the people involved.

The consultant can concentrate on any of these areas in line with the agreement reached with the client. In many cases, however, this classification is somewhat artificial — problems to do with product quality, for example, may be due to poor methods of work, or poor training of workers, and so on. Nevertheless, for the purpose of structuring his or her thoughts the consultant will find this approach helpful.

Within each area, the consultant has at his or her disposal a variety of production and management techniques ranging from the simple to the more

---

Box 15.3 Current issues of Japanese production systems

Since the 1960s, production systems and methods that have their origin in the Japanese manufacturing sector have revolutionized production organization and management worldwide. Their impact on productivity and quality has been dramatic. The best-known examples include:

● TQM (total quality management): A programme to provide an environment in which the employees are involved in the process of management and make constant efforts for improvement on a daily basis.

● JIT (just-in-time): A system to integrate the sales, development, production and physical distribution in which only what is really needed in the market is provided.

● Techniques and tools for improvement and individual systems to promote the above: 5 Ss (which in Japanese stand for organization, neatness, cleanliness, standardization and discipline); visual control; suggestion schemes; quality circle (QC) activities; productive maintenance (PM) activities; *Kanban* system (just-in-time inventory management).

However, the recession of the early 1990s, and recent economic and social changes in Japan, demonstrate that no production and management system can provide a long-term guarantee of high competitive advantage and performance. Various elements of Japanese production methods have been effectively utilized in the United States in developments such as lean production systems or business process re-engineering. In Japan, lifelong employment has started to be challenged, the need to base remuneration and careers on merit is becoming pressing, and organizational structures and information systems require modernization.

In response to these challenges many manufacturing businesses are currently addressing the following issues:

(1) to organize the flow of the logistics of product distribution — manufacturing — procurement in order to shorten lead time and to obtain faster speed and response to market;

(2) to shorten the lead time of product development and production preparation;

(3) to simplify and clarify the rules, control items and evaluation criteria, and to open the information to all employees;

(4) to make the organization flat, self-disciplined and self-controlled;

(5) to reorganize systems so that the overseas production bases can act on their own;

(6) to improve the productivity of management, support and functional departments;

(7) to place emphasis on the merit system in personnel evaluation and to develop specialists;

(8) to improve the information system, which is critical in order to achieve the above goals. Positive investment will be seen in this area from now on. Theoretical development has not been seen for the past 20 years in terms of production control information systems, but there are signs of development with new concepts in this area;

(9) to develop education programmes that will activate an entrepreneurial spirit.

Furthermore, the role of government regulation and protective policies will need to be revised. While Japanese industry has benefited from them in numerous ways, they have now turned into barriers with the result that market principles can no longer work.

Many (but not all) Japanese companies have already started reforming their production and management systems. Other businesses will follow. Once more, major innovations can be expected. Management consultants will have excellent opportunities to contribute to these changes, while simultaneously widening their perspective and practical knowledge of modern and highly competitive production systems.

Author: Takeyuki Furuhashi.

complex. In the production planning area, for example, techniques used in solving planning problems can range from simple bar charts to network planning to more advanced operation research tools such as waiting line models. The choice invariably depends on the situation faced and the degree of sophistication of the industry concerned. No attempt will be made in this chapter to describe

315

these techniques. They can be referred to in various publications dealing with production management and operations research. Instead, we will concentrate on the systematic approach to identifying and prescribing methods for improving productivity, reducing production costs, and improving quality, speed and customer focus, so that the consultant develops an approach which is process and problem oriented rather than single technique oriented.

15.2 The product

The product range

A product starts as a single substance or a multitude of raw materials, processed so as to give quality characteristics that match a predetermined standard. It is rare, however, to find enterprises that produce only one product. What we usually have is a "product line", or a composite of many products, which are sometimes produced to order or produced for stock, or both. In the majority of cases, only a few products will either form the bulk of items produced or represent the most expensive (and presumably yield the highest rate of return). The consultant would then be well advised to start the assignment by analysing these product lines to identify the one or more products representing the bulk of production, or the highest value, and to focus attention on certain major areas in respect of this particular product or products. At the same time, this analysis may help to bring another question to the fore: Is there a need for all these product variations, or can some products be eliminated or standardized?

In recent years, outsourcing (make or buy) has become a major strategy not only to concentrate on the core competences of a company but also to offer a wide range of complex products.

Increasingly, environmental considerations play a part in decisions about the continuation, modification or discontinuation of products. The selection of reusable or biodegradable materials, product modifications to enable cleaner production processes, and a "cradle to grave" approach in defining product specifications open a whole range of new consultancy tasks in production.[6]

Consequently, "pruning" the product range would be the first task in systematically restructuring production systems before looking closer into the remaining products and their production.

> Why do some companies move quickly and efficiently to bring to market outstanding new products, while others expend tremendous resources to develop products that are late and poorly designed? How do designers, engineers, marketers, manufacturers, and senior executives in these companies combine their skills to build competitive advantage around product and process development? ... What can managers do to bring about significant improvement in the performance at their development process? [7]

These are questions that clients increasingly ask their consultants with a view to restructuring product development processes.

To render product development efficient, consultants will have to look into the following four areas.

Product development strategy

In assisting a client to define a product development strategy, a number of common problems arise (see also box 15.4, overleaf):[8]

- *The moving target*: The basic product or process concept misses a shifting technology or market.

- *Mismatches between functions*: What one part of the organization expects or imagines that another part can deliver may prove to be unrealistic or even impossible, e.g. engineering may design a product that the production department cannot produce, or only with difficulty.

- *Lack of product distinctiveness*: New product development terminates in disappointment because the new product is not as unique or justifiable as the organization anticipated.

- *Unexpected technical problems*: Delays and cost overruns can be traced to overestimates of the company's technical capabilities or to its lack of resources.

- *Unresolved policy issues*: If major policies have not been articulated clearly and shared, short-term decisions will have to be made during the "heat of the battle", often with negative implications for the whole organization.

Translation of customer demands into products

Here the consultant has to focus on *cross-functional information flows*, particularly between marketing and research and product development, and on the structural processes of translating this information into *product specifications* via techniques such as quality function deployment, for example. The tendency of engineers to "over-engineer" products should be limited by introducing *target costing techniques*. A cost target is set for the whole product and subsequently broken down into cost targets for components, to avoid cost and price overruns which are quite common for new products. Target costing also allows better negotiation with suppliers based on a fixed cost target.

Design for manufacturing (DFM)[9]

In many cases, a traditional or a successful product will continue to be produced for years without enough thought being given to its design features. In other cases, product design is considered to fall solely within the domain of the marketing staff, and it is left to them to make all decisions in this area. Development work leading to a design involves more than just producing an appealing product. It should be based on the full cooperation of several enterprise functions, particularly marketing, production and costing.

Box 15.4 Central themes in ineffective and effective development projects

Problematic projects		Outstanding projects
Characteristics	Consequences	Selected themes
Multiple, ambiguous objectives; different functional agendas	Long planning stage; project becomes vehicle for achieving consensus; late conflicts	Clear objectives and shared understanding of project's intent throughout organization; early conflict resolution at low levels
Focus on current customers and confusion about future target customers	Moving targets, surprises and disappointments in market tests; late redesigns; mismatch between design and market	Actively anticipating future customers' needs; providing continuity in offerings
Narrow engineering focus on intrinsic elegance of solutions; little concern with time	Slipping schedules; schedule compression in final phases	Maintaining strong focus on time-to-market while solving problems creatively; system view of project concept
Reliance on engineering changes and manufacturing ramp-up to catch and solve problems; "we'll put a change order on it when we get to manufacturing"	Poor, unrepresentative prototypes; many late changes; poor manufacturability; scramble in ramp-up; lower than planned yields	Testing and validating product and process designs before hard tooling or commercial production; "design it right the first time"
Narrow specialists in functional "chimneys"	Engineering "ping-pong"; miscommunication and misdirected effort; use of time to substitute for integration	Broad expertise in critical functions, team responsibility, and integrated problem solving across functions
Unclear direction; no one in charge; accountability limited	Lack of a coherent, shared vision of project concept; buck passing; many false starts and dead ends	Strong leadership and widespread accountability

Source: S. G. Wheelwright, I. Clark and R. A. Hayes: *Dynamic manufacturing* (New York, The Free Press, 1988), p. 14.

On the production side, the consultant is concerned with the fact that a design will normally predetermine the process and method of work, the type of raw materials, jigs or fixtures, or materials-handling equipment that will be used. This is true of the product as well as of its constituent parts. The most frequent questions that the consultant needs to ask are:

— How many parts is the product composed of? Can some parts be eliminated through better design, and have any unnecessary features been removed?

— Can certain component parts be standardized to match parts of other products and so enable the use of the same machines, tools, jigs and fixtures?

— Can some components be replaced by cheaper ones which would perform the same function?

— Does the design lend itself to easy handling?

— Can a change in the design eliminate one or more processes? (For example, a process of stamping a metal production may eliminate one or more processes of assembly, though it could also alter the appearance of the product.)

— Can some component parts be standardized, and yet by using them in different combinations can variety in the product line still be obtained?

The consultant knows that products have to be matched with the equipment on which they are manufactured (e.g. with its dimensions, precision, productivity and cost), and vice versa. In a number of cases, he or she may have to examine this relationship and make recommendations to the client concerning either the product, or the equipment used, or both. As mentioned earlier, any proposed modifications in product design should be checked with the marketing specialists for their marketing penetration potential.

Organization of the product development process

By reorganizing the product development process, it is not unusual that development time and costs are reduced to one-third compared with traditional systems.[10] To reach such results, consultants should look into the following:

● cross-functional problem solving (including at least marketing, R & D, manufacturing, purchasing, logistics, financial controlling);

● development team structure;

● project management techniques.

These elements should ensure that products are designed for marketing and manufacturing in a simultaneous (concurrent) engineering process, entailing a substantial reduction in costs and time to market.

15.3 Methods and organization of production

Under this major heading, attention will be given to the following areas:

— characteristics of high-performance work systems;

— flow of work and layout;

— materials management;

— production planning;
— setting and improving performance standards (at workplace level);
— maintenance;
— cleaner production and energy saving;
— quality control.

Characteristics of high-performance work systems

Companies worldwide are trying to overcome autocratic, highly hierarchical and Taylorist organization concepts which cannot cope with the competitive imperatives of customization, speed, productivity and quality. Consultants play a major part in facilitating the transition process to high-performance work systems exhibiting the characteristics shown in box 15.5.

From this list it becomes clear that a consultant in production management will have to be qualified to deal with the human and technical aspects of production in an integrated manner. Furthermore, the consultant has to help the client to choose among all these practices and techniques, and to effectively combine and apply those that are appropriate in a particular client context.

It is sometimes difficult for consultants to convince their clients that the traditional approach of fine-tuning subsystems without reviewing the overall organizational structure will not yield the desired success. Therefore, optimization of the aspects of production systems described below should always be carried out with a view on the overall concept of production organization.[11]

Flow of work and layout

The organization's production operations normally fall under three major descriptions. The first is *production by fixed position*, in which case the product is stationary and the workers and equipment move, as in building aeroplanes, heavy generators, or ships. Improvement in layout can sometimes be brought about by attempting to shorten the distances travelled by workers, materials and equipment. However, the margin of manoeuvrability is rather limited.

The second is *in-line production*, where the equipment and machinery are arranged according to the sequence of operations, as in bottling plants, car assembly and food canning operations. In these cases, the layout is more or less inherent in the sequence of operations which determines how the machinery is placed. Nevertheless, two sorts of issue can be examined by the consultant: the original balance of operations; and the problems which result from the fact that, in many cases, as the enterprise develops and the product line expands, or demand for the product changes, additional lines may be added which do not often work in harmony with the original line. The operations can therefore become unbalanced with certain stages producing at a faster rate than subsequent or preceding stages. A schematic diagram showing the sequence of operations and the time it takes to perform each one can be quite helpful. Depending on the type of problem faced and the complexity of the situation, correcting for balance

---

Box 15.5 Key characteristics of high-performance work systems

1. Clearly expressed and communicated "management philosophy"
2. Emphasis on training, career planning and personal development
3. Flat management hierarchy
4. Efficient continuous improvement systems
5. Salaried status with common fringe benefits package
6. Skill-based payment system with gain sharing
7. Allocation of meaningful "whole pieces of work" to teams
8. Self-managed teams with elected leaders
9. Team responsibility for goal setting and task allocation
10. Team control over quality and absenteeism
11. Teams select new members
12. "Multiskilling" and skill sharing
13. Team review of skills and salaries
14. Process layout supports continuous flow teamwork and communications
15. Some support functions carried out in teams
16. Fewer support personnel in engineering, scheduling and quality control
17. "Zero defect" quality policy
18. Just-in-time production philosophy and systems
19. Flexible manufacturing equipment or specialization via "plant in the plant" concept
20. Provision of team meeting-rooms with personal facilities
21. Common entrance and car parking
22. Common plant eating and recreation areas

Source: Adapted from E. E. Lawler: *High involvement management: Participative strategies for improving organizational performance* (San Francisco, California, Jossey-Bass, 1986).

---

can range from simple proposals, e.g. increasing workstations on parts of the line, additional machines or improvement in the method of work, to more sophisticated heuristic methods.

The third type of organization is that of *functional arrangement*, where all identical machinery is grouped together and the products move between these machines, depending on the sequence required for each. This is the case in many woodworking workshops and in the textile industry. This type of arrangement allows the consultant to do more to improve productivity through a better layout and organization of operations. The key is to identify whether among the many finished products there is one or more constituting a sufficiently high percentage in terms of volume. The machinery needed to produce such items is then detached from a functional layout and arranged along a line layout flow. The gains in productivity in this case can be substantial.

The consultant could arrive at improvements, both for a functional and a line type of layout, by looking for the following:

- bulky or heavy material that is moved further than smaller or lighter material;
- a workplace that is either too congested (making access to machinery or equipment difficult) or too large for requirements;
- backtracking of work in progress or cross-flow with other products;
- unused space overhead, particularly in stores;
- aisles that are not free or marked, materials lying about, and untidy working conditions.

Once the need for tackling a layout assignment becomes apparent, a consultant must collect information on the space requirements for machinery, storage, work in progress, and auxiliary services (canteens, washrooms, telephone installations, etc.), calculate the space required, determine and plot the flow of work, and then integrate the space needs with the plotted flow. An important consideration is that of making cost estimates of the proposed layout by comparing savings in space, equipment and labour costs with the cost of additional space, handling or storage equipment.

Materials management

With reduced contribution margins per unit of product sold, the increase of capital rotation has become an important strategy to maintain profitability of a company at acceptable levels. In this respect, computerized materials requirement planning (MRP) packages and inventory reduction programmes have become quite popular, with consultants offering a wide range of services to reduce materials costs and improve turnover of assets. In the following, we mention only briefly what can be done in this area.

Inventory control

The consultant needs to keep in mind three types of inventory: *raw materials*, *work-in-progress* and *finished products*. One general principle should govern all these: the need to keep them at a minimum but safe level. For raw materials and finished products, a safe level is one that allows for uncertainty of delivery or avoids opportunity costs resulting from lost sales. This "safety stock", usually known as "buffer stock", is not a justification for having a high stock level, nor is it to be used indiscriminately to take advantage of quantity discounts or special modes of delivery.

For finished products, the desired level of stock needs to be determined in close consultation with the marketing and finance specialists in an effort to balance opportunity costs (the probability of lost sales if one runs out of stock) against carrying charges (the cost of carrying the inventory).

Great savings in carrying charges can be made if the work-in-progress inventory is kept to a minimum. To achieve this, however, the consultant may have to look at the balance of operations, remove or reduce bottlenecks, and propagate the virtues of a system whereby no or very little inventory is allowed to accumulate beside each machine.

In most industries, stock levels were reduced dramatically in recent years owing to the implementation of just-in-time (JIT) concepts for all three types of inventory. JIT requires close cooperation between suppliers, the producer and clients, a stable production process, and a "zero defect" quality policy. The JIT concept is also a powerful tool to stabilize production processes incrementally by reducing stock levels step by step and solving the emerging problems as inventory levels go down. Thus imbalances in production lines, planning errors, bottlenecks and so on can be reduced in a systematic manner.

Conversely, JIT is sometimes difficult to implement for reasons such as more frequent transport from suppliers to producers, congested transport networks, especially in big cities, and the tough requirements on the suppliers.

Most consultants approach the problem of the raw materials inventory by analysing the values of the various items to distinguish the "A" items (which are few in number but very costly) from "B" and "C" items (the latter being the great multitude of relatively cheap items that are carried in stock).

An ordering strategy is then developed for the "A" items resting on the use of inventory models to determine the economic order quantity by balancing ordering costs against carrying charges. Quantity discounts can also be evaluated against incremental carrying charges, and a decision can then be reached as to when a quantity discount offer can be attractive. The problem, however, lies in the determination of the buffer stock level. Under normal circumstances, this is calculated by balancing opportunity costs against carrying charges. For the "B" items, ordering is carried out through regular review of stock, or whenever a minimum level is reached. For "C" items, mass orders may be placed at certain points in time.

Materials handling

Before looking deeper into the ways of improving materials handling, a consultant should bear in mind that materials handling in production operations is a non-value-adding task and should be avoided or reduced as much as possible.

For the remaining handling tasks, attention should be given to:

- the means of intermediate storage such as containers, pallets, etc.;
- the means of transport such as conveyors, cranes, trucks, robots, etc.;
- computer-assisted materials handling and retrieval equipment.

The consultant should consider three important issues. First, economy in handling can be achieved as the size of the unit and speed of transportation are increased. Secondly, versatile equipment and methods which can be used for several products are to be preferred to those that are mainly designed for a single product. Thirdly, gravity should be used as much as possible.

Utilization of materials

While the focus of attention here is on the raw materials which go towards shaping the final product, the assignment can be extended to cover other materials used in the production process, such as packaging material, fuel, and even paints and lubricants. This is an area where substantial savings can be achieved without too much effort, particularly in certain industries such as garment making, furniture, metallic products and the like. It stands to reason that the higher the percentage of material cost, the more there is a need for a proper investigation of this area. There are three approaches to reducing waste material:

— design changes, with a view to reducing waste of raw material;

— if the design cannot be changed, then efforts may be undertaken to improve the yield, by changing the method that is used in cutting garments, metal or wood so as to reduce waste to a minimum, or by changing the original size of the raw material used;

— inevitably some waste will result during the various sequences of production. Two questions should come to mind: can this waste be reworked to yield another by-product or component, or can it be sold?

These questions have gained a particular relevance because of a number of environmental regulations forcing producers to recycle materials, operate closed systems or take responsibility for the reuse of wastes. Recycling and waste management have become a special area for consultants.

Production planning

The choice of the planning method to be used depends on the nature of the operation. In normal functional (also known as process) or line production operations, as mentioned earlier, various methods of planning can be applied, ranging from simple and traditional scheduling and charting to the sophisticated use of mathematical models for queuing, or waiting line models. However, special projects, such as the construction of a plant or building of a ship, necessitate the use of network planning methods such as the critical path method (CPM) or the programme evaluation and review technique (PERT), which allow a more rational allocation of resources.

In the case of production that is geared for distribution (as distinct from made-to-order or special projects), the starting point for a planning process is the forecast of demand which is worked out with the marketing specialists. A consultant should check the reliability of such a forecast before going into production planning itself. A discrepancy between sales forecasting and production planning can result in either lost orders or carrying excess inventory, and is often a subject of contention between the marketing and production departments. In addition to the forecast, which is translated into an aggregate of operations for various products in the product mix, the consultant has to calculate the machine hours required for each product component, determine the total working time, and introduce a certain flexibility in the planning system to allow for emergency situations.

The difficulty lies in the fact that invariably there are *bottleneck operations*, but instead of concentrating on them, many consultants gear their planning and scheduling to all operations. An effective analytical and planning exercise should indicate shortages of machines or operators' hours in certain work centres and present to management proposals to relieve these difficulties.

Production planning, particularly with a large product mix, or where hundreds of components are involved, becomes far more manageable if a computer is used. This is also true of network planning involving more than 200 activities. Finally, a control system must also be established with a feedback mechanism to check progress and adjust plans accordingly.

Setting and improving performance standards

This is probably one of the most intricate problems that faces a production consultant. Performance standards are needed for a variety of reasons, including the determination of labour costs, and hence the ability to decide on matters of pricing and bidding, in "make or buy" decisions, in machine replacement problems, and so on. Such standards are essential for production planning, wages and incentive schemes. Invariably a certain standard exists for every piece of work performed, either a formal recorded standard, or a perceived informal standard which a foreman or a worker estimates for a given job. The consultant is called upon either to review a formal standard or to establish one. A crucial point is the need to perform the assignment with the knowledge and approval of the persons whose performance is to be assessed, and of the workers' representatives.

Before setting standards, a consultant working in this field examines the way a certain operation is being performed and attempts to develop an easier and more effective method. He or she utilizes a number of well-known charts such as the operation chart, the flow chart and activity charts. The consultant should also understand ergonomics and essential elements of job design.

While numerous jobs lend themselves to methods improvement, the consultant should give priority to those that are critical, because they either constitute a bottleneck or are repeated by a number of operators.

A consultant will find it most useful to invite suggestions from workers, foremen or supervisors, and managers, to involve them in the working out of a new method. In many cases, production workers and technicians will be able to point to improvements that can well escape the consultant.

To determine performance standards for the improved systems, generally speaking, one of three methods can be used: works sampling, a stop-watch time study, or predetermined time standards. Alternatively, the consultant may opt for a combination of two or all of these methods at a given working place. For example, work sampling may be used to determine the allowances to be included in a "standard time" based on stop-watch observations.

Work sampling is probably the easiest method of assessing the percentage of time worked, and the distribution and causes of idle time. Since it is based on random observations, its reliability depends on sampling and sample size that can give a certain degree of confidence.

Stop-watch time study is probably the most widely used method of measuring performance. Through sampling and timing, a consultant arrives at a certain "observed time for a given job". This has to be converted into "normal time" by a process of performance rating in which a certain pace of performance is rated as "standard".

The transformation of a "normal time" into a "standard time" requires the addition of allowances for delays normal to the job, allowances for personal needs, and fatigue allowances. The latter two, sometimes grouped together under the title of relaxation allowances, again raise controversy. In most cases, there is no scientific basis to what the fatigue allowance should be for a given job content and working conditions.

Predetermined time standards (PTS) offer certain advantages. They permit a quantitative means of comparing alternative methods of work without disturbing the existing methods, and can be used even before an operation has been established. They also avoid the rating problem and hence help to develop more consistent standards. They do, however, suffer from several weaknesses. They are generally designed for mass production and can become expensive for individual jobs; they also have limitations in machine-controlled operations, and the basic principle on which they are based, that motions can be added and subtracted, has been challenged.

Another issue is that over 200 different systems of PTS exist at present and are known by trade names, such as Methods-Time Management (MTM), Work Factor (WF), Dimensional Motion Times (DMT), and so on. A consultant has to decide which one is most appropriate for his or her purposes.

It may be useful to summarize the approach that should be taken to determine the standards of performance, and to ensure as much consistency as possible. The main steps can be as follows:

(1) identify the jobs or the activities for which standards are desirable, taking into consideration the cost and practicality of developing and applying such standards;

(2) on that basis determine the degree of coverage needed (standards to be established for all or certain jobs, departments and/or products);

(3) break the jobs into elements and attempt to have as many common elements as possible;

(4) decide whether to use macroscopic systems (e.g. stop-watch time study) or microscopic systems (predetermined time standards), or a combination of both, in which case decide what parts of the job will be measured by what system (the nature of the job and costs being a determining factor);

(5) if stop-watch time study is used, check for consistency among common elements performed in various areas of the workplace.

Maintenance

The consultant should enquire about the methods used for maintaining and repairing equipment and machinery. In particular, he should find out:

— if a preventive maintenance scheme exists, whether it is justified and how it is implemented;

— whether a proper inspection schedule exists;

— if a cost estimate of repairs is made and kept for each machine;

— how normal greasing and lubrication are done and whose responsibility it is to do these jobs.

The consultant should also enquire about emergency repairs and consider whether increasing the size of the maintenance crew could reduce the length of time machines are down. In addition, a consultant can examine whether the life of certain individual components of equipment or machines could be prolonged through either redesign or change of lubricant. Finally, machine replacement problems should be studied in relation to maintenance costs.

If major equipment is to be overhauled, especially in process industries, the consultant can help the client to achieve considerable savings by introducing scheduling for such operations (applying network planning techniques if necessary).

Because disruption of production due to machine breakdowns can be very costly, there is a growing trend towards making production staff more maintenance-conscious. Seminars on proper identification of causes of breakdowns, and on the training of both production operators and maintenance crew (which may suggest assigning a certain responsibility to operators for simple oiling and lubrication), could be followed up with performance review seminars at a later stage. Approaches involving all personnel, not only maintenance specialists, can pay handsome dividends such as the total productive maintenance (TPM) approach.[12]

Cleaner production and energy savings

The discussions on sustainable development, along with tighter environmental regulations, have made many companies review their ways and means of production under ecological criteria.[13] Consultants are called in, for example:

● to audit production facilities and propose improvement programmes;

● to assist with environmental impact assessments of major investments;

● to perform life-cycle analyses of products;

● to implement "pollution prevention pays" initiatives, often integrated in total quality management (TQM) or in staff suggestion schemes.

With the steep rise in energy costs, in many client companies there is a need to achieve substantial savings in the use of energy. These can result from simple good housekeeping (such as checking that thermostats are functioning and properly set, steam and air leaks repaired, and so on) through minor investments in additional insulation, heat recuperators, power-factor correction and the like, up to major investment decisions about changing over to low-waste, low-energy processes. Many of these issues can be highly technical in nature and would require the intervention of specialists. Nevertheless, the production consultant's contribution lies essentially in examining whether a potential saving in energy costs can be achieved, bringing this to the attention of the client, and assisting management in deciding how to set up and implement an energy-conservation programme.

Quality control

In the area of quality control, consultants are increasingly called in to assist companies in the adoption of a quality system conforming to the international standard ISO 9000.[14] The analysis of a company's operational procedures and systems during the implementation of the ISO series of quality standards will throw a spotlight on areas of weakness, ad hoc working methods, waste of resources and avoidable quality costs, and will thus result in an improvement programme. Productivity or quality management consultants are also often used by companies that want to become suppliers to original equipment manu-facturers (OEM) and, therefore, need to prepare for the evaluation procedure used by a specific OEM.

The implementation of total quality management (TQM) may be another reason to look for an external consultant. A consultant is well advised not to underestimate the amount of work and time necessary to implement TQM. It is generally accepted that TQM means that quality activities are conducted with the total involvement of everyone throughout the company. A consultant will therefore have to assist in a long-lasting process of continuous improvement and change in attitudes. Several TQM experts have published their experiences in implementing TQM as an aid to clients and consultants coming to the topic for the first time.[15]

15.4 The human aspects of production

The quality issue is perhaps the best proof that the human element is the determining factor in any operation. It would be naive to propose, let alone implement, any recommendation without the involvement of the employees concerned and without examining its impact on people. There are two major areas in production management consultations to be considered in this respect: physical working conditions and safety improvement; and job enrichment and group work.

Physical working conditions and safety

The consultant needs to pay attention to measures at the place of work to protect the worker from adverse conditions of temperature, humidity, light and noise levels, as well as air contaminants, dust and radiation, exposure to which may cause poisoning or occupational diseases.[16]

The ideal situation exists if hazards can be either eliminated altogether, or the workers removed from direct contact with hazardous situations. If this proves not to be feasible, then either the source of hazard should be isolated or the worker provided with protective equipment and clothing.

A common misconception is to concentrate on the so-called technical aspects of accident prevention — the provision of protective gloves, boots or goggles, and guards for machinery. In most plants, however, over half of the accidents are caused more through human misjudgement and negligence than through the absence of guards or protective equipment.

The consultant can discover much revealing information by analysing, from past accident records, the causes of accidents, the department, hour of the day, and day of the week in which they most frequently occur, and even the person injured. This information can prove invaluable for a concerted plan of action to introduce a scheme of safety which should invariably include training.

Since accidents can happen despite all precautions, it is appropriate to check on the availability and adequacy of health care, first aid and emergency and sanitation facilities, as well as fire protection systems.

Job enrichment and group work

Many production consultants are productivity conscious and underestimate both the need for job satisfaction, and the impact of job satisfaction on productivity.

In a production environment, the process design, the method of work, the arrangement of work assignments and physical working conditions greatly affect the worker's satisfaction. There are several ways that job satisfaction may be increased, including the possibility of both job enlargement and job enrichment. Task time cycles can be lengthened, particularly in the case of tedious monotonous jobs; work can be made more varied by adding other tasks to the original one; or more authority may be delegated to workers who can then take their own decisions on certain work-related matters.

In the last 20 years considerable research has been done on group work under various names: new forms of work organization, socio-technical systems, industrial democracy and semi-autonomous groups. Whole factories (for example, the Volvo plant in Kalmar, Sweden) have been designed around these concepts, and many industries in Japan, Europe, North America, Australia, and some developing countries, have introduced such systems with a reasonable degree of success. These systems rest on two fundamental concepts. First, in designing and modifying work, it is necessary to consider the technical and social issues together. Thus improved methods of work have to be reconciled with the social needs of the working group in terms of factors such as the variety and the degree of challenge the job offers, the opportunities of learning and advancement and so on. Secondly, people performing a certain task should participate in redesigning their own job.[17]

In this respect, small-group activities in particular are well known. Quality circles have over the years extended their scope of activities to cost reduction and productivity improvement. The success of the quality circles idea prompted many companies in developed and developing countries alike to follow the

Japanese model, adapting several of its features, with varying degrees of success. It is clear that the participation of production workers and supervisors in issues relating to their work is gaining wider acceptance.

Involvement and participation at the shop-floor level may sound at odds with a production consultant's job perceived in a traditional way. This is not the case; all depends on the consultant's and the client's attitudes. A consultant who approaches the assignment claiming to know all the answers and wanting to impose his views will invariably fail. There are many technical and human aspects of each job that have to be taken into consideration when designing or modifying an operation, and a consultant cannot be expected to know every detail. He may be surprised to find how readily people will respond to his enquiries (and offer helpful suggestions or improvements) if they feel he is sincere, appreciates their views and has their needs and interests at heart. A consultant who develops such an attitude will soon find out that involvement and participation, far from being obstacles, are key factors in the success of any assignment in production and operations.

---

[1] See, for example, S. G. Wheelwright, I. Clark and R. A. Hayes: *Dynamic manufacturing* (New York, The Free Press, 1988); or R. Schonberger: *World class manufacturing* (New York, The Free Press, 1982).

[2] J. R. Hauser and D. Clausing: "The house of quality", in *Harvard Business Review* (Boston, Massachusetts), May-June 1988, pp. 63-73.

[3] See, for example, R. C. Camp: *Benchmarking: The search for industry best practices that lead to superior performance* (White Plains, New York, Quality Resources, 1989). The American Productivity and Quality Center (APQC) at Houston, Texas, runs an International Benchmarking Clearing House.

[4] See J. Womack, D. Jones and D. Roos: *The machine that changed the world* (New York, Rawson Associates, 1990).

[5] Cf. M. Hammer and J. Champy: *Re-engineering the corporation* (New York, Harper Business, 1993).

[6] See, for example, K. North: *Environmental business management: An introduction*, Management Development Series, No. 30 (Geneva, ILO, 1992).

[7] S. G. Wheelwright and K. B. Clark: *Revolutionizing product development* (New York, The Free Press, 1992), p. xi.

[8] ibid., pp. 29-31.

[9] For an introduction see D. E. Whitney: "Manufacturing by design", in *Harvard Business Review*, July-Aug. 1988, pp. 83-91.

[10] For an example from the automobile industry see K. Clarly and T. Fujimoto: *Product development performance* (Boston, Massachusetts, Harvard Business School Press, 1991).

[11] Many of the topics covered here are treated in more detail in G. Kanawaty (ed.): *Introduction to work study* (Geneva, ILO, 4th (revised) ed., 1993).

[12] See S. Senju (ed.): *TQC and TPM* (Tokyo, Asian Productivity Organization, 1992).

[13] See North, op. cit.

[14] See, for example, UNCTAD/GATT/ILO: *ISO 9000 quality management systems: Guidelines for enterprises in developing countries* (Geneva, 1993).

[15] See A. V. Feigenbaum: *Total quality control* (New York, McGraw-Hill, 1983); or R. Collard: *Total quality* (London, Institute of Personnel Management, 1993).

[16] Extensive literature of these topics is available from the ILO.

[17] See J. E. Thurman et al.: *On business and work* (Geneva, ILO, 1993).

CONSULTING IN HUMAN RESOURCE MANAGEMENT

16

16.1 The changing nature of the personnel function

Personnel management, one of the traditional areas of management consulting, has undergone many changes over the last 20 to 30 years.

When consultants started dealing with the "people" side of business organizations, most of them tended to confine their interventions to problems grouped under the term "personnel administration". In French-speaking countries personnel problems were included in the so-called "*gestion administrative*" (administrative management). In nearly all countries, a personnel administration specialist typically dealt mainly with personnel records, regulations and procedures, questions of job evaluation and remuneration, and "employment" issues such as recruitment, selection, induction, discipline and termination of employment, and grievance handling. Over the years this has broadened considerably. The main changes that currently affect the nature and role of the personnel function occur in the following areas.

First, the subjects of personnel management — people working in organizations — have changed in many respects. People have become better educated and prepared for their jobs, more aware of their rights, better informed and more interested in many issues of national and even international economics and politics. Their value systems have changed; their employment and life aspirations have increased. Human relations within organizations have become complex, diversified and difficult to handle. These changes in organizations reflect not only technological changes but also the significant trends of political and social change, such as the democratization of life in more and more countries (most dramatically, of course, in the former communist bloc), or the emergence of new social organizations and pressure groups (e.g. the environmentalists or the consumerists).

Second, an increased number of personnel issues, including conditions of employment, work and remuneration, are affected by legislation, or have become the subject of collective agreements between workers' and employers' organizations. When dealing with these questions the personnel consultant must be fully aware of the existing legal and labour-relations frameworks, of the role of the trade unions, and of the need to inform or consult them in conformity with local practice.

Third, it is apparent, particularly in the developed countries, that organizations are increasingly recognizing the value of their human resources, both in terms of cost and contribution. For most organizations labour is the major operating cost item. Even where it is not, as in high-technology organizations, the skills and abilities of individual employees become critical. Human resources are the only ones which can generate added value out of other resources. Thus, achieving the right balance between the cost and capacity of human resources becomes a critical factor in organizational effectiveness and success. Hence, along with the previous points, has arisen the concept of "human resource management" (HRM), as distinct from the more narrow concept of "personnel administration" or "personnel management". According to this concept, employees are viewed as the most valuable resource of an organization and a number of conclusions can be drawn from this basic premise as to ways of treating people and motivating them for higher performance, the role of leadership, the investment in training and development, or the choice of staff development systems.

This has been linked with advances in the behavioural sciences, in particular in psychology and sociology applied to the functioning of organizations and to the relations between individuals and groups within organizations. A wide range of "organizational development" theories and concepts emerged, and began to be applied to the analysis of human problems in organizations, and to methods likely to increase the effectiveness of individuals and groups in achieving organizational goals. On the other hand, a focus on the cost side of the equation would involve a series of steps to limit spending on human resources and to link people more closely to results. It could include, for example, "buying in" labour capacity from outside the organization. It would be an error to think that any "human resource manager" will by definition apply a more scientific and more comprehensive approach to managing people than his predecessor — the "personnel manager". Yet the understanding of human aspirations and motives and of interpersonal processes has increased quite considerably, and a growing number of personnel specialists, as well as general managers, make use of this knowledge in their work.

Fourth, technological changes have had a significant impact on the way people are managed. This impact has taken place throughout the environment of HRM, ranging from its effect on the global integration of business right through to the way that communication with employees is conducted. Before identifying a few key effects it is worth making the point that throughout the world there are vast numbers of employees almost untouched — at least directly — by technological change. Even within highly technical industries, international airlines for example, there are still people whose job is mainly to shift heavy materials by hand. Having made that point, however, it is also true that the impact of technological change operates at all levels. At the global level technological change has "shrunk the globe", making it easy to transfer goods and services around the world, improving the position of some nations and putting others under real pressure. At the national level technological change has led to a transfer of employment from primary industry (agriculture, forestry, fishing) to manufacturing and from manufacturing to services. In broad terms, the richest countries have the highest proportions of people in services and the lowest proportions in the primary sector. Within industrial sectors, technological change has led to the collapse of some industries or companies and the emergence of others, and to the reduction in employment in some workplaces and the expansion of others. Inside the organization, technological change has had a major impact on the structure of jobs, on the way work is done and even on the shape of the organization. In the information-technology sector, for example, it is now possible for employees to work hundreds of miles away from their employer's offices, in their own time, linked to their superiors just by the telecommunications system. At the most practical level, the new technology enables an employer to address "personal" letters to each of a large number of employees. This vast range of effects of new technology, from very significant to very local, has had an inevitable and extensive impact on HRM.

Fifth, the increasing internationalization of economies, the development of multinational trading blocs and the growth of international organizations (profit or policy based) have also had an impact on HRM. It is increasingly recognized that the management of people is more culture bound and value laden than any other area of management. Practices regarded as standard in one country or organization may be unthinkable in another environment (e.g. flexible

---

Box 16.1 Human resource management in "high-tech" companies

"High-tech companies" are not all the same, either in the way they are managed generally or in their management of human resources. However, they do have many_ aspects in common which makes them distinctly different from traditional employers as regards their HRM practices:

● Employees are often highly educated and highly skilled, and their skills are in short supply. They are often highly individualistic. They are less inclined to join trade unions.

● Employees are technologically capable, able to use the full range of technology available and to work in small units, at distance, etc.

● Workplaces are usually small; rarely do they include large numbers of individuals. They sometimes have new work practices (such as "warm desks", where workspace is shared with one employee taking over from another as and when space becomes available).

● Jobs are often flexible or project-based, with a focus on the achievement of particular tasks rather than attendance or the performance of set routines.

● Jobs are often short-term, with the employees changing to different tasks on a fairly frequent basis. The employees are also more likely than others to change firms.

This is a new, vibrant and mobile sector attracting people who take similar approaches to work.

working hours, open-plan offices, dining-rooms common to all staff irrespective of position and grade, direct access to top managers, or the use of confidential personnel files). Both personnel practitioners and management consultants have become more cautious and more selective in transferring personnel practices from one environment to another when dealing with people of different ethnic, social, cultural, religious and educational backgrounds. Sensitivity to these differences has increased with the growth of international business, the advent of modern enterprises and organizations in developing countries, the expanding employment of foreign workers and managers, and improvements in management education.

Thus, we find ourselves living in an era in which the role of personnel and human resource management is being reassessed and enhanced, new demands are formulated and new approaches developed. This creates many fresh opportunities for consultants. Both the personnel specialists and the general managers face increasingly complex human problems and find it difficult to keep informed about all conditions and factors to be considered in personnel decisions. In many cases they will appreciate help from an independent and objective human resource professional.

16.2 Policies, practices and the human resource audit

Human resource management consultancy can take many forms, from the most comprehensive (the assessment of the labour force of a company that the client may be considering purchasing, or a total evaluation of the way in which the client's employment practices contribute to overall corporate strategy) to the very limited (a single management seminar or advice on dealing with a difficult employee).

In the early stages of an assignment the consultant and the client may agree that a thorough diagnosis of the human resource management function is a desirable starting-point and should be undertaken before deciding how to focus the consultant's intervention. Often the consultant will be told that there are organizational policies for dealing with the major elements of the personnel function — for example, recruitment, staff development, promotion and transfer, salary increments, labour-management relations, and so on. The consultant may first attempt to conduct an appraisal of existing personnel policies and procedures by investigating, analysing and comparing policies with actual results obtained over a set period, by means of a systematic, in-depth audit.

Before starting to prepare a research design to uncover the necessary hard data, the consultant is likely to find that the alleged "policies" are often only pious hopes and good intentions. For a personnel policy to be worthy of the name it should fulfil several criteria:

- policy should be written, understandable, and present a comprehensive coverage of the function;

- provision should be made for ensuring dissemination and comprehension of important elements of policy to all the relevant sections of the organization;

- policy should be soundly based, and consistent with public policy and current legislation;

- policy should be internally consistent with the organization's stated general objectives and policies;

- specific personnel policies (e.g. staffing, development and administration) should be mutually supportive;

- policy should be established as a result of multi-level discussion and consultation throughout the organization, including consultations with employees' representatives as appropriate.

The major purpose of the audit is to provide information for and explanation of human resource management and development practices. To achieve this, information should be sought both vertically through the personnel department and horizontally across other departments. In other words, the audit is conducted throughout the organization.

The procedures for conducting the audit can vary considerably. Basically, they consist of obtaining information of a quantitative and qualitative nature from various records and reports, supplemented by interviews, questionnaires, surveys, informal discussions, and so on. Information may be obtained by means of a latitudinal study (e.g. a department-by-department assessment of safety records or absenteeism in which the percentage of lost time and other ratios are calculated on a comparative basis). Alternatively, a longitudinal study may be used in which a sample of individuals is examined in depth over time, in the light of the effects of the organization's policies on their performance. Hard data should be sought.

If possible, data (e.g. on turnover, absenteeism, grievances, accidents, etc.) should be compared with those available from other organizations.

A recommended method for setting out a human resource audit is to list the organization's policies in sequence, to write down the practices regularly employed by the organization and the results obtained from the study, and then to draw the appropriate conclusions and recommendations. An example is given in figure 16.1 (overleaf). A list of personnel policies for audit purposes would include references to the full range of practices influencing the cost, capability and effectiveness of employees: organization; manpower planning; recruitment; selection; induction; transfers and promotions; assessment; training and development; communications; remuneration and allowances; job evaluation; fringe benefits; social and welfare benefits; safety and health; industrial relations; discipline; motivation; and administration.

A commonly used approach to obtaining information required by the audit, or by any other interventions in human resource management and development, is the *interview*. General principles of interviewing were discussed in Chapter 8 and there is no need to repeat them here. However, for the consultant working in HRM there is an additional, very significant element — *confidentiality*.

Figure 16.1   The human resource audit (data for the last 12 months)

Stated policies	Regular practices	Findings of audit
1. Recruitment		
To promote, where possible, from within the organization	Recruitment from external sources is an ongoing and continual procedure	95% of appointments made from external sources. High staff turnover of 40% per annum
2. Training		
No stated policy	Organization sends senior members to courses conducted by professional associations at request of individuals concerned	Staff claim only limited opportunities for promotion and development, feel they have to go elsewhere to "get on"
3. etc.		

The consultant can expect to receive a good deal of information that must be held in confidence. The higher the level of trust engendered by consultants, the more they can expect to receive data that is confidential or private. Not all of the data may be related to the identified problem. New problems may surface that had not been anticipated during the entry phase. The consultant may have to go back to the client to renegotiate the problem and the focus of the consultation.

If the interviews are to be effective and are to produce the data needed, the consultant must work at a high ethical level. If the respondent requests that the material gathered during the interview be regarded as confidential, the consultant has some choices and decisions to make. He or she can establish the ground rule that all data gathered will be merged and individual sources will not be revealed. This must be approved by the client, who may have other expectations. If the client agrees, then the consultant can indicate this to the individual respondent when arranging for the interview. If a respondent is still hesitant, this could indicate a low level of trust in the organization and the consultant may have to drop that person from the list of those to be interviewed.

The results of the human resource audit should, if necessary, point out the need for definition, refinement, or rewriting of organizational policies. Similarly, a review of the organization's regular practices may suggest improvements to facilitate conversion of policies to procedures. Inadequacy or total absence of data indicates that urgent attention is required in the field of personnel administration. The principal result of an effective audit is a set of conclusions as to what needs to be improved in one or more areas of HRM to be reviewed in the following sections. The client may be satisfied by the audit and convinced that enough guidance has been received to implement the conclusions without further help from the consultant. The client may agree to the consultant's suggestions in principle, but may decide not to put them into effect because they would cause difficulties among the organization's personnel. Or the consultant may be requested to assist in planning and implementing the changes that are required.

16.3 Human resource planning

The purpose of human resource planning is to make sure that the organization has the right number of people of the right profile at the right time. Many organizations do not discover this elementary truth until they face a major problem — either the shortage of competent people becomes an obstacle to further expansion or technological change, or the organization employs more people than it can afford and has to prepare itself for staff retrenchment.

In most cases a management consultant will be called in, once the problem has manifested itself, to help identify emergency measures to be taken if there is an acute shortage of competent staff, or if important redundancies are anticipated. However, an emergency situation provides an opportunity to demonstrate the advantages of human resource planning treated as part of, and coherent with, strategic corporate planning.

The consultant will be able to help the client in combining various human resource planning techniques, either global or analytical. If enough detailed information is available on the structure of production or other processes, it may be possible to define and describe all necessary job positions. This implies that a detailed job description is worked out for every job. In contrast, if detailed lists of jobs cannot be established with accuracy, or if manpower is to be planned for units with changing functions and a need to adapt easily to new conditions, it may be preferable to define broader technical profiles of the kinds of people who will be needed, describing their educational background and experience, rather than to produce a detailed list of tasks to be done.

Here again, interfirm comparison and benchmarking techniques may be of help. But they should not be used mechanically: the consultant must be able to show the client with what numbers and profiles of staff comparable organizations achieve the similar or better results, and the reasons for this difference. This underlines the relationship between the planning of human resources and of productivity and performance improvement.

Some authors advocate the consistent use of *job descriptions* in manpower planning and recruitment processes in all types of organizations and for all employees. There are valid reasons for this in many organizations, where detailed job descriptions are used for recruitment, planning training, evaluating performance, deciding on promotions and transfers, and handling organizational conflicts. Job descriptions are particularly appropriate where the organization and the environment are stable.

In many developed economies and in high-technology or high-knowledge content jobs (e.g. research, professional services), there is less emphasis on job descriptions and more emphasis on flexibility, creativity and adaptability to change (see section 16.8).

16.4 Recruitment and selection

The consultant may be asked to provide advice on how to improve the recruitment and selection of various categories of personnel, including management personnel.

Recruitment

Recruitment is the process of attracting applicants to apply for jobs within the organization. Here the consultant can help with advice on specifying the details of the job and the person required, and can clarify the means of advertising the vacancy. This may well include the perhaps most common and cost-effective method — using word-of-mouth channels — but could also involve the use of government or private employment agencies, or advertising in the local press or radio. Attention should also be paid to the efficient processing of applications.

Executive search

Executive search ("head-hunting") is a special service offered by some larger management consulting firms, or by consultants who are fully specialized in this function. It is increasingly used by a number of business and other organizations to fill important managerial or specialist positions. The advantage of using an executive search specialist is that such a person can develop information on potential sources of recruitment and undertake a systematic search and objective selection in a way that is usually outside the normal capabilities of a line or personnel manager.

Business firms turn to executive search specialists if they do not want to advertise a job publicly, or if they seek candidates in areas where advertising does not work. Most candidates also find executive search useful: some of them are glad to learn that they could have a more challenging career with another employer, while others appreciate a confidential discussion on alternative job opportunities, since their current position does not permit them to make the first contact or show interest in another job.

The executive search function involves: the building up of files and contacts needed to identify potential candidates and recruitment sources (an international search firm may have from 5,000 to 10,000 names of potential candidates in its computerized files); assistance to clients in analysing the job to be filled and defining the ideal candidate; active and methodical search for candidates (by direct approach, search through various business contacts, in some cases advertising, etc.); contacts with candidates for the purpose of interviewing them and interesting them in the job evaluation and preliminary selection of candidates; arranging the client's interviews with preselected candidates; and follow-up contacts with the selected candidate and the client.

Executive search consultants often have their own professional associations (as in the United States) or are members of national associations of management consultants. Codes of ethics for executive search have been adopted in several countries. For example, such codes forbid charging fees to the candidates and accepting any payment from them; the cost of the search operation is charged to the client according to an agreed scheme (as a rule, 30 per cent of the annual salary of the candidate recruited). Several specialized publications on executive search are listed in Appendix 11.

Selection

Selection is the process of choosing between applicants. Both the selection procedure and the criteria applied should reflect factors such as:

- the importance of the given positions in the organizational structure (job content, authority and responsibility, the possibility of correcting errors, etc.);
- the terms of employment that are to be offered (selection for long-term or short-term employment) and the possibility of terminating employment contracts;
- the normal career path of the employees concerned (likely promotions, assignments abroad, job relations);
- the legislation to be observed.

In many instances the solutions to the problems identified are straightforward. Often the selection is not done well: an insufficient number of candidates is considered, references are not checked, and recruitment interviews are superficial and conducted by personnel officers who may know little about the job. In some organizations the problems faced are delicate. Political, ethnic or other criteria may prevail over technical competence, or trade union membership may be required as a condition of employment or maintenance in employment.

The consultant's professional responsibility requires him or her to tell the client what should be changed in the best interests of the organization. But the client will be unlikely to follow advice that is deemed unrealistic owing to political or other constraints that are not under his or her control.

In most instances, however, improvements in selection and recruitment will be feasible. The consultant may identify a more objective procedure and more precisely defined criteria, or may suggest and carry out a training programme for staff responsible for selection. Particular attention will be paid to the selection of staff who will be offered permanent employment contracts in technical and managerial positions, with a view to minimizing the risk of selection errors (which are costly and difficult to correct).

Some consultants assist clients with testing and assessing candidates for managerial or technical jobs. This is done through interviews, multiple tests, special tasks and exercises, very careful checking of references and in various other ways. For example, this kind of assistance has been found useful by enterprises recruiting managerial and marketing staff for work abroad, yet lacking experience of management patterns and living conditions in foreign countries.

16.5 Motivation and remuneration

Motivation

Every organization aims to achieve certain economic and social objectives, but has limited resources at its disposal. It tries, therefore, to motivate its personnel towards the achievement of a range of goals. These may include societal, organizational, group and individual goals.

A HRM consultant may be requested to assist in determining what motivational tools and strategies should be used. This may concern, for example:

- the improvement of the overall *organizational climate* (the psychological and motivational environment of the organization). The underlying assumption is that this climate strongly affects the motivation of people at every level in the organization to work and to achieve. It is determined primarily by the people management practices of top and senior managerial staff, by the employment and working conditions, and by the encouragement given to individual and group initiative, innovation, creativity and self-development;

- the enrichment of *job content*, where, by changing the structure of the work to be performed, the consultant endeavours to assist in creating intrinsic job interest and increasing job satisfaction, and developing a more flexible and efficient workforce. There is evidence that increased team working, increased autonomy for teams and employee involvement generally have a positive motivational effect;

- *reward systems*, where the appropriate behaviour is shaped as a result of certain rewards, particularly financial and material ones. This requires a feedback system, so that the incentive used (e.g. pay) is tied as directly as possible to actual individual or group performance. However, the role of *non-financial rewards or incentives* is important and must not be underestimated when trying to enhance staff motivation.

These methods do not operate independently, but affect separate components of the motivational process and call for different levels of intervention on the part of the organization and of the consultant. A common problem faced by consultants is complaints made by clients about the lack of motivation of the managers or their staff for achieving higher performance in organizations where people are relatively well paid. A thorough study has to be prepared to determine the weight of various factors affecting staff motivation. The study may reveal that the client assumes that a good salary is a stronger motivational factor than it really is. It may be that the salary level is taken for granted by the employees concerned, that the client and the employees differ in their views on what salary level is adequate, or that certain adverse factors in the working environment negate the effect of good salaries. For example, employees often regard interesting job content and real prospects for future careers as more important for job satisfaction than the level of their salary.

Wages and salaries

In some assignments, the consultant will be requested to assist above all in the examination and reorganization of the wage and salary system. This kind of consultancy is becoming more and more frequent as increasing competition (or spending restrictions in the public sector) focuses attention on the costs of employment — a major operating cost for all organizations. In addition, the requirements of new technology and the consequent abolition or reorganization of tasks, or demands for flexible working practices, mean that pay systems have to be adjusted to fit a new reality. The challenge to existing and well-accepted structures is obvious and the importance of establishing acceptance of any new structures is clear.

In Europe and elsewhere this problem has been compounded by moves towards the "individualization" of pay (i.e. a non-union approach) and "pay for performance" (where individuals in the same job may receive different salaries depending upon managerial judgement of their performance). This has increased pay variability.

Variable pay presents major problems, particularly in the following areas. First, there is the problem of establishing clear targets and monitoring performance against them so that managerial assessments are acknowledged to be fair and not arbitrary. Second, there is the issue of what percentage of pay is variable: too much and it threatens individuals' livelihoods, too little and it fails to motivate. Third, the issue of guaranteed limits has to be addressed: if the organization is successful or people perform well, they receive pay increases — but what happens in other circumstances? Do individuals take a pay cut? These are all issues that well-prepared consultants can bring to the organization's attention and help to resolve.

In most of the developing world, and still in much of the developed world, wage and salary fixing is more traditional and a clearly structured approach will be required. The problems will be to build or develop a salary system that works efficiently and fairly from the point of view of both the organization's management and its employees (and, where appropriate, their representatives). Logically, the consultant approaches such a problem by conducting a job analysis, followed by job evaluation and the building of a job structure so as to develop an equitable salary system and a plan which will accommodate periodic reviews, supplementary remuneration and appropriate fringe benefits. Obviously, the consultant cannot see wage and salary problems as purely technical ones and has to be well informed on legislation and industrial relations practices related to wages, especially on collective bargaining.

The problems most frequently met in this area include:

— distorted salary systems (e.g. the wage differentials do not reflect the relative difficulty and importance of particular categories of jobs);

— no relationship, or a very weak one, between salary and real performance at work;

— wage and salary differentials that do not motivate employees towards training and self-development and to seek promotion to more responsible and more rewarding jobs;

— obsolete salary and pay structures, which have not been adapted to the requirements of new technologies and to the changing structure of jobs;

— the absence of flexibility in using individual and group bonuses and special rewards for encouraging high performance, and in demonstrating that such performance is important to the organization and is therefore properly remunerated by management;

— excessive secrecy in matters of salaries and other rewards, giving rise to various suspicions about the actual pay levels of certain individuals, and reducing confidence in the objectivity and fairness of management over questions of pay.

The sensitivity of pay issues, particularly in certain cultures, means that these problems are rarely easy to handle, although from a strictly technical viewpoint the solution may be straightforward. The consultant should be cautious in establishing, and assessing with the client, the feasibility of changes, and the way in which the necessary changes are to be introduced, announced and maintained.

Social benefits

There are other issues in the field of salaries and compensation which now attract considerable amounts of consultancy work: in particular those related to financial benefits other than pay — social benefits, tax and actuarial services, pensions and insurance. Throughout much of the world there are specialized consulting firms (some are quite large) whose task is to ensure that employers and employees obtain the maximum benefits from their investment of money in these areas. That often involves advising on source and location of investment opportunities and on minimizing taxation. This type of consultancy requires a detailed knowledge of financial markets and the laws of the relevant country. It is often controlled by legislation so that only qualified individuals can become involved. As financial and legal requirements become ever more complex, this is likely to be a growth area in consultancy.

Job analysis, evaluation and classification

Job analysis includes the collection, organization and examination of information on what people do in a particular job. Job analysis is used not only to produce job descriptions for recruitment and other purposes as discussed above, but also for *job evaluation*, that is, determining job worth. Depending on the job in hand, the order of complexity of the job evaluation system employed usually moves from (1) whole job ranking schemes through (2) job classification to (3) points evaluation systems and to (4) factor comparison methods. World-wide, whole job ranking is probably the most frequently used, although larger companies often prefer the points evaluation system.

344

Job classification involves the setting of wage and salary levels by classifying jobs within the organization and comparing the levels of pay with contribution to organizational success, and to competitive firms or other firms with a comparable job structure and conditions of business. The "market value" of individual jobs is given consideration, using various sources of information such as surveys and reports published by management associations, government departments, or independent business information services.

In practice, however, many jobs are not evaluated, or, if they are, their evaluation is only one of the factors determining the pay rate:

> While many employers believe that employees' pay should be differentiated on the basis of current performance, many others (perhaps a majority) believe that seniority, age and past performance and loyalty should have equal or greater weight in individual pay determination. Managers may claim that they have merit or performance-based pay systems, but many studies indicate that they are more accurately based on current performance plus seniority, or seniority alone.[1]

Changes in the way work is done (e.g. as a result of new technologies and particularly developments in new forms of work organization) have changed the jobs people do in critical ways. Thus, while some consultants started believing that in this traditional area of personnel management no further challenging assignments could be expected, the dramatic changes in technologies, job structures and staff competence requirements are generating new demands for advice and assistance. The human resource consultant should be ready to help.

16.6 Human resource development

In the last two decades human resource development (HRD) has become the most popular and fastest growing area of consulting in personnel and human resources management. There are consultants who specialize in this area, while many other firms have established important HRD divisions and trained most of their staff members in various aspects and technologies of HRD. At the same time, quite a few charlatans have tried to take advantage of the "HRD boom" by selling quickly concocted and superficial package deals to clients hoping for spectacular improvements by putting employees through crash courses on communication, team building or personal effectiveness. Fortunately, in most countries the situation has become clearer; clients tend to be better informed about HRD, and hence more cautious and competent in selecting HRD programmes and consultants.[2]

The main purpose of HRD is to help people in organizations to face the challenges created by technological and other changes, to adapt to new requirements and develop skills, and hence achieve the levels of performance needed for survival and staying competitive. A true HRD professional does not promise spectacular changes in attitudes and competence as a result of a few workshop sessions. The HRD specialist makes the client aware of the complexity of the human side of the enterprise, and of the need to consider all factors affecting motivation, behaviour, interpersonal relations and performance of people in organizations. It is important to warn the client against inconsistencies in personnel and HRD practices, as these can devalue the impact of many well-intentioned but partial and uncoordinated staff development measures.

Ideally, HRD should be allied to significant ongoing or projected changes in the organization or its policies so that the change and the development are mutually reinforcing. The specialist needs to be informed about the availability of a wide range of techniques for human resource and organization development (OD) and for productivity and performance improvement (see section 22.3), but must also be aware of the cultural bias of certain techniques and the need to avoid a mechanistic transfer which disregards differences in local cultural values and social systems.

HRD is an area which is to a considerable extent bound by national culture. The approach to career planning, the exposure of inadequacies that require training and the informal, even humorous, training style that may work very well in the United States, for example, would be totally inappropriate in China. Consultants need to be aware of this variety. Even with these wide variations, however, some general trends are discernible. There are moves to raise the profile of HRD within organizations, to make it more flexible and tailored to individuals and to take a broader view of HRD, so that people would develop through job rotation, through careful "mentoring" by a superior and by directed self-study as much as through classroom-based courses. At the same time, and perhaps rather paradoxically, companies are increasingly likely to insist that HRD is tailored to the immediately foreseeable needs of the organization, so that the cost-benefit equation is more obviously positive.

HRD is a very broad topic and this section cannot review all the approaches and techniques used. Rather it will point to certain management concerns that may call for a consultant's intervention. The reader should also refer to Chapter 4 on consulting and change, where several HRD and OD techniques are discussed in some detail.

Staff training and development

An HRD consultant can act as an adviser on how to increase the effectiveness of staff training and development, or can be directly involved in preparing and delivering in-company training. Typically, assignments in this area aim to answer such questions as:

- How can staff training and development be related to the goals and problems of the organization and make it performance-oriented?
- How can the training needs of various categories of personnel be identified?
- What should the content, methodology and organization of staff development programmes be?

- How can the real impact of staff development on organizational performance be evaluated and the level of investment in HRD determined?

- How can the training unit be organized and the competence of the training director and in-company trainers increased?

- What benefits can be drawn from sending managers and staff specialists to external courses at business schools, management institutes, consulting firms, productivity centres, and elsewhere? What sort of relationship should be established with external units offering training programmes, and should these units be used for mounting tailor-made in-plant programmes?

- How can employees be motivated for training and self-development and for using the results of training in their work? What obstacles are to be removed if training is to have the desired impact on both individual and organizational performance?

In some countries trade unions are heavily involved in the provision of training. In others the trade unions or employee representatives can be partners in training, helping to ensure that its importance is recognized, that its content is relevant and that employees themselves are enthusiastic about undertaking it.[3]

Where the consultant is directly involved in the organization and delivery of training, it is useful to go through the same check-list of questions that are noted above in relation to training policy to ensure that the programme offers maximum benefit.

One question which consultants often have to answer concerns the cost of training individuals who, in a free labour market, may leave, taking their acquired skill to another organization. Part of the answer is that few organizations can afford not to invest in the skills of their employees whatever the risk, and part is that a clear and coherent human resources management and training policy often motivates people to stay. There are also examples of competitors working together to ensure that costs are shared and cost-effectiveness of training is increased.

Career development

Career development is a significant aspect of human resource development, although its importance may not be the same in all cultures. The consultant should be able to explain the consequences of the absence of career planning to the client. Although in many organizations a detailed plan of the career path of every individual may be impossible, or undesirable, it should be possible to establish a career development policy as guidance for staff development and for motivating individual performance. Without constituting a legal commitment to every individual concerned, such a policy provides a clear model against which employees can compare their individual expectations and gear their self-development and work improvement efforts, with obvious gains in motivation and productivity.

Performance appraisal

Performance appraisal has been one of the weakest links in HRM systems. Many small organizations do not practise any performance appraisal on a regular basis. Medium-sized and large organizations have introduced structured performance appraisal schemes in many cases, but the reality tends to be very different from declared objectives and policies. The consultant is likely to find that even where regular performance appraisals do take place and performance reports are duly produced and signed, no conclusions are drawn and no use is made of the appraisals in deciding on staff development, promotions, transfers, merit increments and so on. In some organizations annual appraisals have become formalities that must be carried out but do not reflect real performance. In other cases the appraisal reflects only the subjective views and preferences of direct supervisors.

While it is not hard to find out about the formalism and other weaknesses of performance appraisals, it is much more difficult to change a deeply rooted practice. The consultant can help the client to realize that appraisal ought to be concerned with actual performance rating, that appraisers require training in performance assessment techniques, and that sensible performance appraisal commences with well-established organizational, group and individual goals. Whatever organization and techniques of appraisal are chosen, the improved system will require the support of employees' representatives and strong management commitment.

Organizational development

Many consulting interventions in the HRD field are of the OD type. The original definitions of OD emphasized the application of behavioural sciences for assisting organizations in identifying, planning and implementing organizational changes. Interventions focused on organizational processes such as communication, sharing of information, interpersonal relations, team building, the use of meetings or the ways of resolving conflicts, rather than on providing solutions to substantive technical issues involved in the process. More recent approaches aim to combine "classical" OD with diagnosing and resolving specific (technological, organizational, financial) problems, and to implement organizational performance improvement programmes in which many other diagnostic, problem-solving, process re-engineering and change management techniques are used in addition to behavioural techniques regarded as the province of OD specialists. This requires that an OD consultant should become versed in a particular area of management and business, while consultants in various technical areas of management, as well as all-round generalists, can increase their effectiveness by mastering OD principles and some OD techniques in addition to the specific technical fields they cover (finance, business strategy, etc.).

Towards a learning organization

A powerful concept reflecting contemporary thinking about change and organizations, as well as recent experience of a number of dynamic companies, is the "learning organization". It brings a new dimension to corporate strategy and to training and development. Instead of speaking of a separate training and development function, the whole organization is viewed as a learning system where individuals learn from the organization's actions and from developments shaping its environment, and where the organization as a whole learns from actively participating individuals. Both individual and organizational learning are used as two inseparable elements of strategic management and change.

These features have been stressed in the various definitions of learning organizations. For example, according to the Training Commission in the United Kingdom, "a learning organization is one which facilitates learning and personal development of all its employees, whilst continually transforming itself".[4]

In learning organizations, *continuous learning by individuals* is regarded as a necessity for organizational survival and for achieving organizational excellence in a rapidly changing business environment. It is therefore facilitated and stimulated in accordance with the following principles:

— learning is linked both to organizational strategy and individual goals;

— emphasis is on-the-job development and action learning;

— specialist training courses are available across the knowledge/skill/value spectrum;

— training to fill existing competency gaps related to current business activities is not neglected. However, the principal focus is on learning about developments in the company's environment, science and technology, and new management and business concepts that could and should be used to improve organizational performance and competitiveness in the future;

— new and open forms of training activity are utilized, including distance learning and self-development, and individuals have the main say in choosing the forms they prefer;

— learning is regarded as a continuous process, not as a sequence of separate and mutually unrelated courses or other events;

— the career and reward systems provide strong recognition for learning.

However, encouraging individual learning is not enough to become a learning organization. Individual learning must be turned into *organizational learning*. Therefore learning organizations exhibit the following characteristics:

● learning in teams is encouraged;

● various formulas are used to share information and results of individual and team learning throughout the organization; results of individual learning must be available to any other collaborator who may need them;

● managers act as trainers and coaches and are responsible for the transfer of information, ideas and competences among individuals and teams within their units, and with other units in the organization;

- managers focus learning on the organization's goals, opportunities and future perspectives without neglecting training needed for achieving short-term objectives and making immediate improvements;
- management makes sure that learning is effectively used for planning and implementing organizational changes;
- the main responsibility for staff development is vested in line managers; but human resource and training managers have a prominent position in the company's power structure and participate in conceptual and strategic thinking and planning concerning the organization's future.

Learning organizations learn from their own *internal environment* and experience, making sure that positive experience is rapidly disseminated and replicated, while negative experience is objectively assessed and acknowledged and measures are taken to avoid repeating it (e.g. in other parts of the organization or by new staff members). Ideas and critiques are collected through suggestion schemes and at meetings, opinion and corporate climate surveys are used, open discussion and feedback are practised, innovation and experimentation are encouraged, and internal records and reports are carefully studied.

Learning from the *external environment* includes:

— learning from customers (satisfaction, complaints, changing needs and demands, changing taste, ideas on new and better services, joint work on product and service improvement);
— learning from competitors and other organizations involved in comparable activities (e.g. through benchmarking);
— learning about new developments in science and technology;
— learning about market trends and changes;
— learning about economic, social, institutional and other developments.

At a minimum level, a learning organization can be responsive and take timely action on information learned and analysed. At an optimum level, it is anticipative and proactive: it changes and improves products, services and processes without waiting for such a change to become inevitable as a result of more dynamic competitors or unhappy customers.

Both HRD and strategy consultants can render an invaluable service to their clients by helping them to understand and implement the learning organization concept. It is important to see that it is not a definitive and closed model which a company would have to adopt or reject in its totality. It is a philosophy, an approach to strategy, customers, people management and learning. It can be applied at various levels of sophistication. It is therefore fully accessible to companies that are not sector leaders, to smaller companies and even to organizations in difficulties. It can well prove to be a more effective way of getting out of difficulties than various restructuring schemes in which individual and organizational learning are underestimated.

16.7 Labour-management relations

Consultants, in whatever area of management consulting, must always bear in mind that their recommendations can have implications for the labour-management relations of the enterprise (or industry) with which they are concerned. A consultant developing and recommending new remuneration systems must be aware of possible collectively bargained obligations in the pay area that cannot be avoided without further negotiations with the trade union or other workers' representatives involved (e.g. statutory works councils with powers in this sphere). Similarly, changes in work organization suggested by a production management consultant may have to be negotiated with the trade union, because of collective agreements or, as in the case of a number of countries, according to legislation. In virtually every area of management consulting consultants must themselves, or through recourse to colleagues or clients, ascertain the labour-management relations implications of various courses of action that they are considering for recommendation to their clients.

Over and above the imperative need to take account of the relevant implications for labour-management relations, a good case can be made, in appropriate circumstances, for the desirability of utilizing the existing processes and institutions of labour-management relations, and perhaps even inviting the development of new processes and institutions, in mapping out strategies for enterprise change.

This being said, it is clear that there are circumstances in which, and subjects on which, it would be highly inappropriate, given the labour- management relations system or traditions concerned to consult — much less negotiate — with trade unions or other workers' representatives. There are still some issues that are exclusively the prerogative of management and in respect of which, for various reasons, workers' representatives have no need to know; indeed, informing them prematurely could be deleterious to the effective functioning of the enterprise. A thoroughly professional consultant will know, or find out, how to distinguish between the two situations.

The contexts of labour-management relations consultancies

It is of course presumed that the experienced personnel management/ human resource management/labour-management relations consultant will already be quite aware of various legal obligations and constraints for the country or region in which he is principally operating. However, given the globalization of business and of the consultancy profession, the consultant may well have to become acquainted with the law and practice of industrial relations when operating in countries other than his own.

In all cases, regardless of the setting, the cultural context of labour-management relations must be given its due if the consultancy is to be successful. Labour-management relations advice that would be highly appropriate in the Western countries could be questionable in an Asian setting. For example, there is some doubt whether a North American or European style grievance procedure could be effective without substantial adaptation in certain Asian countries where interpersonal confrontation on an individual level is simply not countenanced. These cultural issues and their labour-management relations implications may not always be easy for a non-native consultant to appreciate and weave into the tenor of his or her recommendations, but an effort must be made to understand them and take them into account.

The remainder of this section examines various points relevant to a labour-management relations consultancy. However, it may be noted in passing that while technical advice in this field may be provided by those who are highly specialized in labour-management relations proper, consultants in personnel and human resource management often possess or develop expertise, and are called upon to advise in this area. In any case, as already alluded to, and in addition to the caveat regarding cultural issues, it is incumbent on the consultant to have a well-informed grasp of the legal, political, social and economic circumstances within which labour-management relations operate in a given country, sector or organization.

Timing and the threshold question

The consultant may be called in because problems already exist in labour-management relations, because there are internal or external forces that are likely to lead to problems, or because advice is needed in the formulation or re-fashioning of labour-management relations policies. The reform or refashioning of such policies is particularly pertinent during a period when industries and organizations are more and more concerned with problems of restructuring. Whether brought about through exclusive managerial initiative or through consultation or negotiation with workers' representatives, measures associated with restructuring, such as retrenchments, flattening out of management, work organization changes and the like, can have enormous implications for both the climate and practice of labour-management relations in the organization.

In virtually every case in which a labour-management relations consultant is called in, a key question will be the presence or absence of workers' representatives, in particular of a trade union in or for the organization and, where a trade union or another form of workers' representation does exist, the nature and role of that representation. Once it is determined that there must, should or could be a role for workers' representation in the consultant's project, the consultant must come to understand (in the case of a trade union) the representativeness of that union, the nature of the leadership of the workers' representation body, and the internal politics and power centres within it. Only then is it possible to pursue effective and constructive contacts with that body. We shall return to this point later on.

In many countries, especially in the developed world, collective bargaining and labour relations with trade unions are coming under pressure from increasing individualization. Not only are people less likely to join trade unions, but many organizations are now actively working to develop more personal and less collective ways of dealing with their employees — varying pay within the group, individual performance appraisal, personal letters to employees, and even individual negotiation of their pay and conditions. This should not be exaggerated: the evidence from Europe is that employers are likely to be developing individualization whilst retaining a commitment to good relations with the trade unions. It should not be overlooked either. Consultants may well be asked to become involved in individualization projects either implicitly or explicitly as part of "weakening the union's influence". They should be able to help the client explore the advantages and disadvantages of both collective bargaining and individualization. A key criterion is that the organization has a well thought-through, coherent and consistent approach to these issues: a good consultant will help the client to develop such an approach.

Principal areas of labour-management relations consulting

The essential questions in labour-management relations with which the consultant may be called upon to deal could include one or more of the following:

(1) Workers' representation. Advice on dealing with workers' representatives on a day-to-day basis is often an element of a consultancy. As mentioned, these may be (a) trade union representatives from within or outside the organization (including officers or staff of union federations with a unit within the organization), or (b) workers' representatives provided for in legislation or, infrequently, through general procedural collective agreements, and who are elected by all the employees of the organization. The latter generally have no direct or organic links with a union and/or are not subject to union discipline. Both types of workers representation may coexist in the same organization (or branch, if the scope of the consultancy is wider than, for example, a single enterprise). In such cases the consultant must exercise great care, through both actions and advice, in determining which — if any — matters are appropriate for interaction with one or the other type of workers' representation. This is not always easy, as the relative competences of the two types may not be clearly delineated and there may even be jurisdictional struggles between the two. It might also be noted at this point that, adding to the complexity of the question, workers' representatives are in one way or another becoming increasingly involved in the labour problems flowing from restructuring of organizations; and, of course, such restructuring nowadays can be a very conspicuous aspect of management consulting. Finally, it may be observed that recent years have seen, in a number of countries (certainly not all), a diminution of trade union militancy, and consultants may wish to consider this aspect, in respect of the specific problems with which they are dealing, when framing their advice.

(2) Disputes and grievances. A consultant may be requested to address the mechanics of handling workers' grievances, including advice on the setting up of grievance procedures, together with advice regarding other conflict resolution procedures. In this area the consultant may have to give consideration to the scope of the procedure proposed (or proposed to be negotiated with workers' representatives). Should the grievance procedure, for example, be all-encompassing or be restricted to alleged treatment inconsistent with an existing agreement? What of the protection of certain managerial prerogatives that might be called into question by a given conflict resolution procedure? And what should be the client's position with regard to the possibility of agreed arbitration procedures for unresolved grievances or on the occasion of impasses in collective bargaining? These are but a few examples of issues that could be evoked — or that the consultant may wish to evoke — in this area.

(3) **Collective bargaining**. The significance of this question will depend to some extent on the level at which bargaining takes place — for the industry as a whole, for the industry in a particular region or locality, for a group of enterprises, or at the enterprise level. Where bargaining occurs, formally or informally, at the level at which the consultancy arises, normally the enterprise level — and in most cases where there is a form of workers' representation at the enterprise or workplace some bargaining will take place at that level — then obviously this aspect of the consultancy becomes more crucial. The consultant is often called upon to carry out one or more of three functions in this regard: to develop the skills of the managers concerned with bargaining, to participate as a member of the employer's bargaining team, and/or to actually act as management's spokesperson in negotiations.

Given the recognized trend towards a certain decentralization of industrial relations, and perforce collective bargaining, in many countries where the focus of bargaining has traditionally been at higher levels, this role and function of consultants will undoubtedly be increasingly emphasized. Newer issues such as the introduction of new technology and growing labour flexibility (particularly in terms of numbers, remuneration and functions), if dealt with through collective bargaining, normally have to be negotiated at the enterprise level. But even if, for example, collective bargaining is centred at the industry or branch level, the consultant may still have to advise management on certain matters as an input that the individual employer must or should make when his or her employers' association is formulating its bargaining positions and strategy.

(4) **Management-worker consultation and cooperation**. A consultant can be asked for advice on machinery and procedures for management-worker consultation and cooperation on matters of common interest such as productivity or welfare and recreational facilities (as opposed to issues of an adversarial nature such as grievances or bargaining demands dealt with through other bodies and procedures). Newer emphasis on this area is reflected in various individual and group employee-incentive schemes, as well as in different types of quality control (QC) group programmes. Indeed, and increasingly, legislation or higher-level collective agreements call for or encourage the development of greater consultation and cooperation machinery, and even mechanisms for workers' participation in managerial decision-making (co-determination) in certain areas. At the same time care should be exercised by the consultant to ensure that appropriate distinctions (particularly where legal strictures might exist in this area) are made so as not to subvert the collective bargaining process when developing plans for consultation and cooperation.

(5) Dismissal and redundancy. Dismissal and redundancy principles and procedures (whether within or outside the context of collective bargaining) are more and more subject to treatment by consultants. Here again the freedom of action of management (and indeed of the parties) may be restricted by legislated or higher-level agreed provisions. In most countries there are restrictions against abusive or unjustified dismissals and, perhaps less frequently, arbitrary selection of those to be let go in a redundancy situation. However, within these limitations there are normally details, procedures and criteria to be worked out and the consultant may have to make a contribution on this score.

(6) Employers' position in tripartite consultations. The position to be taken by employers' associations in tripartite (government/employers/trade unions) or bipartite (either with governments or trade unions) consultations at the national level can be defined with a consultant's help. Such consultative mechanisms, sometimes ad hoc but more frequently of a standing nature, exist in most countries and deal with broad economic and social questions. As alluded to above in the discussion of an enterprise consultant's role with respect to industry or branch collective bargaining, so with national-level consultations individual employers may require guidance in fashioning their input into their association's position and strategy in such consultations. In fact, consultants would do well to impress upon their clients the importance of such input into, and participation in, association policy-making since the decisions ultimately emanating from national-level consultations often have a direct impact, and almost always have at least an indirect impact, on the fortunes of the enterprise.

Trade unions as clients

While typically it is enterprise management that engages the consultant, a fairly recent development has been the provision of labour-management consultancy services to trade unions and, in particular, to officials who "manage" trade unions. There may be cases also where the consultant is engaged jointly by management and the trade union concerned. In any of these cases, the points made in this section would still warrant the attention of the labour-management relations consultant.

Importance of the legal framework

Turning to factors to be considered in providing advice, one could mention in the first place the relevant legal framework of labour-management relations. This framework is highly individual to particular countries and, at times, to particular industries. In certain countries, for example those in Central and Eastern Europe, legislation on matters of concern to us are in a state of flux with frequent significant amendments and modifications, if not outright repeal and new enactments. For these countries it is a time of discovery and experimentation. Similarly, many countries in the developing world, particularly Latin America and Africa, have moved towards political democracy, and this has entailed radical change in labour-management law and practice.

The legal framework might reflect rules on:

— trade union recognition and the employer's obligation to treat with a given union;

— workers' representation at the workplace, and the protection (e.g. supplementary protection against dismissal or retrenchment) and facilities (e.g. time off, office space, access to members) that may have to be afforded to trade union and other workers' representatives;

— forms of workers' participation in decision making within the enterprise (e.g. rules concerning works councils or membership of workers' representatives on company boards);

— the formation and content of individual contracts of employment, and their relationship to any collective agreements which may be in force;

— legal rules (both legislated and resulting from judicial decisions) concerning termination of employment, and so on.

It is not always obvious, but it is always necessary, that consultants take account of existing legal prescriptions in charting courses of action to be recommended to clients. Moreover, even company rules on conditions of employment promulgated by management (employee handbooks and the like) may have a certain juridical or enforceable quality. Whether they do or not, consultants will wish to take them into consideration; they may even wish to suggest changes in such rules. And where particularly complex legal problems arise, or have to be resolved in the course of the consultancy, it may be necessary to have recourse to the services of a qualified lawyer specializing in labour law if the consultant does not have such training.

Provisions of collective agreements

The labour-management relations consultant must also be fully aware of the relevant provisions of existing collective agreements which apply to the enterprise concerned (whether such agreements be for the industry, the region or the enterprise itself). He or she must be aware not only of the provisions of the agreements but also, in certain cases, of possible interpretations of those provisions which may have been subject to scrutiny by labour courts, arbitrators or other decision-making bodies. Even past interpretations of collective agreement provisions made by management (and in respect of which the trade union party has raised no challenge) would probably have to be given due credence. In passing it may be commented that if this examination should result in a consultant finding that changes in the collective agreement are warranted or should be sought (and provided that this aspect is not clearly outside the terms of reference), then his or her advice may make due reference to this.

Custom and usage

Rules resulting from law and regulations, or from collective agreements, are only two of the significant sets of norms which may have to be considered by the labour-management relations consultant. In virtually all established enterprises, organizations and industries there will be labour-management customs, usage and practices which often require the same respect and attention that is accorded to legal regulations. At times these customs, usage and practices are common to a specific region or locality. Examples are *ex gratia* payments and bonuses, time off which has been traditionally granted to attend to certain family, personal or religious matters, and so on. It is essential that the consultant be fully aware of, and if necessary actively seek to learn of, such customs, usage and practices that are relevant to the consultancy. This in no way means that there will not be occasions where certain of them may warrant being dropped or changed; and the consultant may well be in a position to influence appropriate changes in established labour-management relations practices, even those that are ingrained in the organization. Indeed, this may be a crucial aspect of the consultant's assignment. However the consultant must realize that in embarking on such course of action, or in making the pertinent recommendations, extreme care should be taken, and consideration given to the possible — and sometimes unforeseen — consequences and implications of breaking with traditional practice.

There might even be legal consequences since, as alluded to above, certain practices may be interpreted as having the status of acquired and enforceable rights.

Interaction with workers' representatives

It is also very important that the consultant become familiar with the position, outlook and concerns of the trade union or other workers' representatives who will be involved in any course of action that he or she might recommend, since possible reactions from the workers' side can very well be a determinant in such recommendations. However, before entering into personal contacts with such representatives, the consultant should, in agreement with the client, consider what contacts, and with whom, would be appropriate before and during the framing of recommendations. Dealings with workers' representatives, and particularly trade union representatives, can be very delicate, and the consultant should discuss with management just what areas encompassed by the consultancy may be touched on in such contacts, as well as the limits of his or her authority to commit management should the contacts be of a nature where even tentative commitments may be made or inferred. In passing it may be reiterated that, among other things, the delicacy of contacts between the consultant and trade union representatives lies in their implications for intra-union politics and possible leadership competition. If the consultant, and the management through the consultant, is perceived to be (even if such is not the case) taking sides or demonstrating partiality towards one group or another, both the consultancy itself and labour-management relations in the organization may be compromised.

This being said, and in recognition of certain dangers as just discussed, the consultant would nevertheless be well advised to recommend that every opportunity for constructive consultations between management and workers' representatives be seized (whether or not there may be legal requirements in this regard). This is almost always desirable, but is particularly the case when new labour-management relations policies are being considered or introduced. The cooperation or acquiescence of trade union or other workers' representatives resulting from such consultations can often be a crucial factor in the success or failure of the consultant's efforts.

16.8 New areas and issues

Termination and outplacement

One unfortunate consequence of the competitive situation in industrialized economies throughout the world has been a huge growth in recent decades in terminations of employment. Many consultants now provide specialist advice on this subject, ranging from the policy level to practical support. At the policy level consultants can help an organization determine what numbers of people should be retained and how many should go, how to ensure consistency with relevant laws and collective agreements, and how to announce the resultant policy. At the practical level consultants are now often called in to provide what are known as "outplacement" services — giving psychological, career and financial planning assistance to those who will be leaving the company. The concern for the welfare of the individuals who are made redundant can ease the process considerably, and a skilful and caring consultant can do a lot to make a difficult situation more bearable.

International human resource management

One issue in human resource management (HRM) that is attracting increasing attention — and is a rapidly growing area of consultancy work — concerns international HRM.[5] The growing internationalization of the world, of business and of HRM has already been noted. This involves increasing numbers of people living and working outside their home country (expatriates). Traditionally this has involved government representatives (civil and armed services), religious groups and charities, and a number of major multinational corporations (MNCs) sending people from the developed world to the developing countries. This is now changing, as the larger MNCs tend to reduce the number of international transferees, while smaller companies move into the area. This process has been facilitated by the growth of international trade blocs such as the Association of South-East Asian Nations (ASEAN), the North American Free Trade Agreement (NAFTA) and the European Union (EU). Within the EU in particular, there are now Union-wide legislation and policies aimed at easing the movement of people seeking employment across national boundaries.

This is a field that has tended to be dominated by consultants from two areas. Accounting firms and financial consultancies will advise on pay, taxation and pension issues. Recruitment consultancies have gradually moved into international assignments as their clients have become more international. There are now a number of organizations specializing in international recruitment, particularly for the three main groups of internationally mobile employees: senior management positions, technical specialists and, somewhat paradoxically, almost entirely unskilled people such as hotel workers, construction industry labourers and household servants. One criticism that may be levelled here is that, for the managerial jobs in particular, too much attention is paid to previous experience and not enough to intercultural adaptability. In other words, it is assumed that being a successful manager in one country will mean that a manager will be successful in another country. However, there is now considerable research evidence to show that the process of managing varies from country to country. Expatriate managers are expensive and crucial people in their organization, under pressure to establish themselves and their families in the new country and having to adapt to different cultural requirements. Often they fail to make the transition successfully — at great personal and organizational cost.

There is a growing number of organizations specializing in the full range of expatriate HRM consultancy: recruitment, training, briefing, transfer, adaptation, pay and benefits, evaluation and return. Before addressing the "technical" issues of recruitment or pay and benefits, the best consultants in this area will press the client to answer key questions: "Why send expensive expatriates when there are talented and well educated locals?", "Why do you not use more (or fewer) expatriates?", "How do you know that the expatriates are adding more value than they cost?" and "What role will the expatriate undertake at the end of the assignment?".

Flexibility

Finally, it is arguable that flexibility is re-establishing itself in developed countries as a key criterion in the management of human resources. Flexible ways and times of working are traditionally more common in less developed economies. As economies advance they create "established" patterns of doing things: job descriptions, normal working hours, legal constraints on employment contracts, and so on. However, in some of the more developed economies these have again come to seem restrictive. The increasingly difficult, and often internationally competitive environment is once again leading the most sophisticated organizations to stress flexibility of human resource practices to meet the requirements of the business more exactly.

The growth in flexibility can be seen in various forms. *Numerical flexibility* — the ability to employ different numbers — is now widespread. Even the famous lifetime employment in the major Japanese companies or companies such as IBM or Daimler Benz has been overtaken by economic pressures and production requirements, and these companies have started reducing numbers. *Working-time flexibility* — working outside the "usual" morning to evening hours — is spreading as organizations find that they have to use their equipment for longer hours to cover their costs, or to be available to customers early in the

---

Box 16.2 Current issues in Japanese human resource management

In Japan, consultants have been enlisted to help managers to deal with the following human resource management issues which have become of increasing concern to industry:

- the *overall HRM system*: reprogramming to fit the diversifying human resource base;
- the *performance management system*: redesign as a key communication tool;
- the *compensation system*: reorientation from seniority to ability and performance.

The creative efforts of consultants are being used in the overall HRM system to help managers make it flexible enough to answer the needs and expectations of human resources of new, non-traditional types, especially female workers and part-time workers. Consultants and managers are working together to broaden the human resource base for successful operation in the new, highly volatile, competitive environment.

The performance management system has captured the imagination of managers and consultants as a tool to establish effective communication with the new generation of workers. Children of an affluent society, the "new workers" have arrived with a value system and work style radically different from the older generation. They are generally not as dedicated to the company and its goals, but like to stay and live within their own private world and are not responsive to the traditional informal, group-oriented communication practices of Japanese companies.

Consultants and managers are trying to build a new bridge for employee communication by designing communication-intensive, individual-oriented performance management systems. They are reinforcing personal communication elements in the system such as more frequent (even daily), formalized appraisal, a greater disclosure of appraisal procedures and criteria, and new counselling and mentoring roles for supervisors.

The traditional seniority-based compensation system has become progressively unsustainable with the gradual disappearance of supporting environmental conditions, notably the high-growth economy and regulated competition. Among consultants and managers, efforts are being made to shift the base of the system to some form of ability, starting with potential ability and edging toward demonstrated ability.

Author: Osamu Ida.

---

morning or into the evening. A wide variety of innovative working-hours arrangements in terms of part-time working, varying shift patterns, minimum/maximum hours and annual hours contracts are now common in North America and Europe. *Contractual flexibility* — appointing people to share jobs, or accept short-term jobs or a less committed relationship with the organization (of the kind consultants have!) — is now quite usual. Finally, *financial flexibility* — varying pay in accordance with the individual's performance or the organization's ability to pay — is also growing.

One important result of flexibility for workers is that it opens up new job possibilities for many people, both women and men, who may not otherwise be able to go to work. Work that offers flexible hours or that is limited to certain periods of the year may allow workers to choose jobs that suit their personal needs and preferences regarding family responsibilities (care of children or elderly relatives), educational requirements or lifestyle. Parents of school-age children, for example, could well be available for work on a part-time basis for a few hours in the middle of each day or in the evening, or for particular parts

---

Box 16.3 Current issues in European human resource management

A major HRM research programme in Europe, the Price Waterhouse Cranfield survey, now has over 16,000 responses from employers in 17 European countries. It provides hard evidence on the roles and function of human resource departments, recruitment, compensation, training, industrial relations, communication with employees and flexible working practices.

The evidence from the survey reinforces differences in HRM policies between different sizes of organization and different sectors of the economy (in particular between the public and the private sectors). The central finding of the research, however, is that while there are common trends throughout Europe there are also significant national differences.

Five key areas of common development can be identified:

(1) **Pay**. Pay determination is being increasingly decentralized from the national/ industry collective bargaining level and passed down to individual organizations or even to units within organizations. Furthermore, pay is becoming an area for increased variability, with individuals having their pay and rewards likely to increase or decrease according to managerial assessment of their performance.

(2) **Flexibility**. There has been widespread growth in "atypical" work (temporary, casual, fixed-term, part-time, etc.). This extension of different forms of employment varies by country; and countries are at different levels in their use of new employment relationships — but growth is the norm in all countries.

(3) **Equal opportunities**. Policies for providing equal opportunities for women are widespread throughout Europe, but are much less frequently translated into action. Despite recent tensions, action against discrimination on grounds of race or ethnic origin is still rare.

(4) **Training**. Training is seen as the key issue for HRM in most European countries. Spending on training and training provision continue to increase even during periods of lower economic growth. The manner in which training is assessed, organized and evaluated varies markedly between countries.

(5) **Trade unions**. Trade unions are entrenched and influential bodies throughout Europe, although membership figures vary considerably. In most, but not all countries unions have declining memberships.

Although the evidence shows common trends, there is also considerable variation across countries, and noticeably in the way these common issues are handled. The role and influence of human resource departments differ from country to country. Consultants need to be knowledgeable about the common trends in issues — but aware of the national variations in human resource departments and the way they manage these issues.

---

of the year (e.g. outside school holidays). Thus, flexible working not only attempts to match the provision of available work much more closely to the employer's work requirements, but it also opens up the labour market to a wider group of employees and hence improves the employer's ability to select the best people.

In dealing with issues of work and employment flexibility, the consultant should not overlook their wider social implications. There may be a need for improved social services, changes in public transport scheduling, and so on. The HRD consultant may be well placed to suggest to the client what new services could facilitate work flexibility, or what new arrangements should be proposed to local government or transport authorities.

---

[1] W. F. Gluck: *Personnel: A diagnostic approach* (Plano, Texas, Business Publications, 1982), p. 296.

[2] See, e.g., R. Sheldon: "Fraud in the training field", in *Education and Training* (Bradford, West Yorkshire), June 1985.

[3] This issue is examined by A. Gladstone and M. Ozaki (eds.), in *Working together: Labour-management cooperation in training and in technological and other changes* (Geneva, ILO, 1991).

[4] See M. Beck: "Learning organizations: How to create them", in *Industrial and Commercial Training*, Vol. 21, May-June 1989, pp. 21-28; Ashridge Management College: *Management for the future* (Berkhamsted, Hertfordshire, 1988) and O. Bovin: *Towards a learning organization* (Geneva, ILO, 1993; unpublished manuscript).

[5] See C. Brewster and S. Tyson (eds.): *International comparisons in human resource management* (London, Pitman, 1992); and C. Brewster and A. Hegewisch (eds.): *Policy and practice in European human resource management: The evidence and analysis* (London, Routledge, 1994).

CONSULTING IN INFORMATION TECHNOLOGY

17

Over the past 25 years, the aspect of management consulting which has grown and changed the most is that associated with information technology (IT). Whereas in the mid-sixties IT hardly existed, today it accounts for over 40 per cent of all consulting revenue even taking a fairly narrow definition of consultancy. Indications are that it will grow bigger still, although this calls into question the boundaries between management and IT consultancy.

17.1 The changed role of IT

To appreciate why consulting has become so important in this area, it is first necessary to understand the nature of the developments that have been taking place in IT and how the role that IT plays in business, and in public bodies, has changed.

Developments and their significance are always easier to understand looking backwards rather than forwards. The whole history of computer use is strewn with wrong predictions and misunderstandings. Seeing the past in perspective helps us to understand where we really stand today.

When the first commercial computers were introduced in the early 1960s, they were seen as either replacing tabulating machines or mechanizing routine clerical jobs. The perceived gain was simple efficiency, mainly in the form of a reduction in clerical labour. Moreover, most organizations saw it as a one-off change: moving from manual procedures to electronic processing. In fact, what was happening was that we were entering a new era: moving from an age in which systems virtually *never* changed to an era in which they would *always* be changing. Most of the systems which were transferred to computers had not changed in decades: stores record cards, payroll systems, accounts ledgers and the like had remained the same throughout working lifetimes.

As time progressed, computer-based systems took over more and more of the basic administrative processes of the business, eventually giving rise to total dependence on such systems for the day-to-day running of the enterprise.

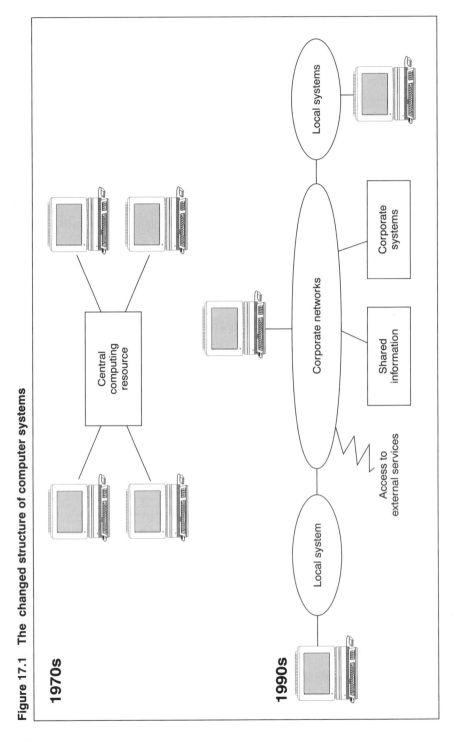

Figure 17.1 The changed structure of computer systems

However, the gains also changed from considerations of efficiency alone. Computer systems started to impact on the effectiveness of the whole business — giving the ability to market better, to control inventories more scientifically and to take management decisions based on better and more complete information. This led to a growing realization that the effectiveness of the systems used and the ability to introduce new systems quickly could give the enterprise a genuine competitive edge. The boundaries of computer systems no longer stayed within the business, but they reached out to embrace customers, suppliers and trading partners.

While this increasing use of IT was taking place, the technology itself was moving forward dramatically. It was also widening the frontiers of its application. The speed and power of computer processing were rising incredibly, matched only by a corresponding fall in cost and physical size. Computers that appeared on the desk, in the home and on the lap had the power of the biggest machines of just a decade earlier. It became clear that computer technology could be applied not only to the handling of codes and numbers, but also to voice, graphics and video. Telephone systems, which had been based on physical copper-wire linkages and simple electro-mechanical exchanges since the turn of the century, were suddenly recognized as being capable of transformation.

As the cost of technology tumbled and yesterday's "high-tech" became today's commonplace, IT found dramatic application in the office. Why should a typist retype letters or paint out mistakes when the computer could store information and make changes with ease? Three hitherto quite separate areas of technology — computing, telecommunications and office systems — converged.

Such developments moved the boundaries of IT out from the computer department and placed IT increasingly in the hands of the user. Nowadays, IT has permeated all our lives: we use it when we pick up the telephone, when we pay with credit cards and even when we drive our cars. The silicon chip has become genuinely ubiquitous.

This dramatic process of advance continues. Computer technology continues to become more powerful and to cost less in relation to performance. Our ability to store information continues to grow. Digital networks have increased local and global facilities for communication, both between people and directly between computer systems. Advances in software have enabled machines to start dealing with unstructured problems, directly learning from experience (in terms of past data and results) rather than being given fixed rules by which to arrive at a solution. From early experiments in fields such as medical diagnosis, these techniques are now finding widespread commercial application, from credit assessment to insurance premium rating and targeted product marketing.

These advances will continue for the rest of our working lives. Organizations will be required continuously to absorb new technology, new ideas and new facilities, exploiting them not only to run the enterprise more effectively and more efficiently, but also to take the business into new realms and to manage the organization in different ways. The power of IT enables us not just to replace individual systems within the business, but also to question the basic *processes* of the organization: to consider complete "business process re-engineering", as it has been termed.

17.2 The impact on management thinking

Today's managers have been largely brought up with computers. They do not share the sense of unease or the unwillingness to get involved that their predecessors had. The very term "computer" has, thankfully, lost much of its mystique and, with it, the exaggerated respect for its attendant specialists. Nevertheless, the continuous advance in technology has progressively influenced the way in which IT is perceived and used, and this will continue to happen. There is a temptation to think that we have finally come to terms with IT and what it means. The reality is that if we look back from 20 years further on, we will undoubtedly perceive that there was a great deal more to come.

A number of specific developments have taken place in the last few years that have influenced management thinking:

— *Personal computers* (PCs) have made most managers far more comfortable with IT: using the analogy of the car, PCs have taken IT out of being exclusively chauffeur-driven into the era of the ubiquitous owner-driver. Paradoxically, they have also lulled many managers into the false perception that the application and management of IT across an organization is straightforward: being able to drive a car does not qualify you to design the road infrastructure.

— *End-user computing* more broadly has empowered managers by making information more readily available and by raising the general level of information literacy. It has also equipped front-line staff to respond directly and immediately to customer queries and problems, improving customer service and contributing to the flattening of management structures.

— *Spreadsheets* and *databases* have, in their different ways, greatly changed business planning by allowing more options to be explored and trends to be better understood.

— *Desktop publishing* has raised the whole quality of office-produced — or even home-produced — documents.

— *Electronic point of sale* (EPOS) equipment has allowed much finer monitoring of sales and inventory.

— *Electronic data interchange* (EDI) and EPOS together have facilitated changed relationships between suppliers, manufacturers, wholesalers, retailers and customers.

— *Automated tellers* (ATMs) have shown that banking services need (at least in some circumstances) neither tellers nor branches.

— Developments in *telecommunications* have made international operations much easier and opened the way for new ways of doing business (such as telephone-based online banking).

— *Visual IT* has allowed engineering visualization and has transformed the design process.

— *Electronic mail* (E-Mail) has abolished distance as an operational concern in some organizations.

These developments have had an impact on a wide range of management disciplines and activities. They are changing both the shape and the operating style of organizations.

17.3 The requirements for consulting

Given the breadth and scale of the use of IT, it is hardly surprising that it has generated a whole new sector in the management consultancy profession.

Development has taken place at such a pace that, regardless of what an organization might be prepared to pay for its own specialist staff, there simply has not been, nor will there be, enough genuine expertise and experience to go round. Consultants not only play a supporting role in spreading the use of IT, but they also play a vital role. It is no exaggeration to say that the world can neither absorb nor exploit the flow of new information technologies without the services of consultants.

For the smaller organization, consultants provide expertise that the organization could not attract or justify on its own payroll. For the larger organization, consultants offer specialized skills to augment internal capability, provide additional resources to cover peak requirements and, when necessary, to implement change, and give an independent second opinion. Nowadays, virtually every major corporation in the industrialized world makes continual use of external consultants in the field of IT.

17.4 The range of services provided

The IT-related services that consultants provide cover a wide range of areas:

- reviewing and developing IT strategy;
- educating general management in a better understanding of IT, and educating IT professionals in a better understanding of the business;
- providing continuous research into developments in IT and their implications;
- evaluating the ways in which IT systems and facilities can be provided to the business;
- reviewing IT performance;
- providing specialist guidance on areas such as data structures, technical architectures, systems development techniques, telecommunications or office systems;

- recommending or providing a second opinion on the choice of hardware or software;
- reviewing projects, either at the outset or when they seem to be in trouble;
- managing projects;
- providing systems development resources ranging from supplying individual contractors to the complete provision of an "outsourced" development facility.

Let us look briefly at these areas.

Reviewing and developing IT strategy

Increasingly, it has become recognized that the day-to-day decisions on the use of IT need to take place within the framework of an overall strategy. Without such a framework, new requirements are dealt with, and corporate systems built up, on a fragmented basis. The outcome is systems that cannot be interlinked, fail to make use of common data or shared facilities, and represent a technological cul-de-sac. Such systems prevent companies from responding quickly to market changes or to competitors' moves. Witness the slow-footedness of financial services companies in responding to attacks on their market by previous trading partners (such as banks moving into insurance), foreign competitors and new market entrants such as retailers. Within many such organizations, a major asset in the form of customer information was locked away in disparate, fragmented systems, much of it duplicated, much of it inconsistent. Today, even leading international companies in areas such as consumer products, pharmaceuticals and petrochemicals are hindered in rationalizing their operations, reducing their cost base and presenting a unified front to their international clients, by incompatible systems in their various locations.

It is probably fair to say that few organizations, if they were able to start from scratch, would put in place the systems they have today. The art is in making sure this is not true of tomorrow.

A clear IT strategy is needed: a strategy which is understood and endorsed by senior management and one which fits the overall strategy for the future development of the business.

Consultants can play an invaluable role in this area: partly because of their breadth of experience in developing such strategies, and partly because of their skill in bridging the gap between commercial and technological considerations. It is probably the area in which organizations make the widest use of consultants, even to do no more than provide a second opinion. That is often a wise move; in few other aspects of the business is the penalty for being wrong so high.

Educating management and IT professionals

It is an often repeated truism that there is a gulf in understanding between general management and the IT professionals. This persists despite more than

25 years of widespread computer use. The reasons are manifold, but the most important one is that, as already explained, both the nature of the technology and the uses to which it is being put are continuously changing.

Consultants can play an effective role in improving understanding on both sides: on the one hand, educating management in how to evaluate, direct and exploit IT more effectively and, on the other, educating the IT specialists in how better to understand and communicate with the business.

Conducting research

The pace of change of IT has already been stressed. Every organization is, therefore, faced with the dilemma of identifying key trends and interpreting their implications. The problem is not so much a lack as a surfeit of information, very little of which comes from unbiased sources.

Some consultancies therefore offer research programmes which monitor developments and evaluate their likely consequences. Organizations usually subscribe to these programmes on an annual basis.

Evaluating the provision of IT facilities

Today, organizations have a range of options with regard to the development (or acquisition) and operation of information systems. The division of role between the user and the IT department is one consideration. Whether the latter should be treated as an overhead, a cost centre, a profit centre or a stand-alone business is another. Whether systems should be provided in-house or "outsourced" is yet another. The decisions are complex and often wrapped in factional issues. Consultants can provide an unbiased assessment of the options.

Increasingly, IT departments are coming under pressure to demonstrate that they are offering best value for money. As many IT activities, from systems development and maintenance, through telecommunications, to computer operations, are becoming a "commodity", alternative sources of supply start to open up.

For IT directors, used to a "captive market", the move from a cost-centre concept to a profit-centre or business concept can be a considerable culture shock. They have to face issues of becoming competing suppliers to their own firm, and of offering their services to third parties. They have to learn how to price, how to sell and how to run a successful commercial operation.

This is an area where consultants can be of great help. For example, a leading bank in the United Kingdom, having decided to set up each of its development, operations and telecommunications divisions as discrete businesses, employed consultants to help each unit establish its competitive position, determine its service costs and pricing policy, prepare a business plan, establish the management structure and acquire the skills required to become a genuine "business".

Reviewing IT performance

General management often finds it more difficult to evaluate the performance of the IT function than that of any other aspect of the business. Production, marketing and finance are all better understood. Moreover, they often lend themselves to quantified comparison. This is less the case with information technology, especially if it is already highly integrated with other areas.

It is, therefore, not surprising that consultants are often used to providing an independent assessment of whether the IT function is delivering value for money. Such an assessment may be impartial, but it has to be recognized that it is largely a subjective process. The better consultancies have a structured way of approaching such reviews and measuring productivity, but the eventual outcome must rely heavily on the breadth and depth of the experience of the individuals involved.

For the larger organization, broad-scope reviews in this area have become less common. This is largely because of much higher levels of experience and competence found in today's senior IT managers, and the confidence that the business has in them. Consequently, external reviews are more likely to concentrate on a specific aspect of IT or on policy or structural issues such as how IT should fit within the organizational framework.

Guidance on specialist issues

No organization can, on its own, stay abreast of all the issues. No one can employ all the different specialists needed to support every requirement; it would not be efficient even if there were enough experienced specialists to go round. Accordingly, great use is made nowadays of external consultants to help assess positions and evaluate options in different specialist areas. This is particularly valuable where the decisions involve technical infrastructure, a key element of an IT strategy.

Consultants will typically be engaged to evaluate the potential application of specific technology trends, for example document image processing, client server, application development rightsizing on open systems or mobile data communications. Should the business case be proven, the client might then proceed to a pilot project, with the consultant transferring the necessary skills in order to enable the client subsequently to carry out full implementation. Early investment in external expert advice can repay itself many times over in this field: ill-judged or ill-managed experiments with new technology can not only delay or prevent achievement of real business benefits, but can create a climate that is averse to innovation.

External IT consultants help the internal specialists to broaden their perspective: everyone is a product of past experience and every in-house technician has personal prejudices.

Reviewing projects

Maybe one ought to expect, after all these years of computer use, that the average systems development project would run to time and budget, and would unfailingly deliver the expected results. Regrettably, that is not the case. There have been many much-publicized examples of projects, some involving massive expenditure, getting into severe difficulties or even being abandoned. We may crack this problem one day, but we have not done so yet.

As a consequence, consultants are frequently brought in to review the status of projects thought to be in trouble. It is a classic and good use of outsiders, but what a pity that it normally occurs only after it is all too clear that the project is in real trouble. How much cheaper and more effective it would have been if a review had been carried out earlier, perhaps at the outset.

There are a number of factors relating to new projects that should trigger off the seeking of external advice: highly innovative use of new technology; a system which cuts across departmental boundaries; unproven hardware or software; an inexperienced project manager; or the sheer scale of the new development. The last point is particularly important, though often overlooked. Experience shows that for any organization there is a size of project that represents the limit beyond which the chances of serious problems, or even total failure, escalate. An empirical guide is that this limit is 50 per cent greater in scale than the largest project previously completed wholly successfully.

Managing projects

Strong and experienced IT project managers are hard to find. All too often, an individual who manages a major project successfully gets promoted and never manages another. This is very different to, say, engineering or construction, where project management is seen as a career path in its own right.

Without the necessary experience in both the project manager and the key members of the team, a new systems development project is in jeopardy from the outset. Under these circumstances it is natural that many organizations are contracting out the delivery of such systems to experienced external companies.

Provision of technical resources

Given the scarcity of good IT skills, only temporarily alleviated by recent economic recession, and the inconsistent level of demand for the different skills within any organization, it is not surprising that more and more clients are making use of contract resources. Many organizations are now only retaining in-house skills to deal with the troughs in demand, turning outside for the peaks.

17.5 The providers of consultancy

The growth in demand and diversity of requirements has given rise to a wide number of providers of IT-related consulting services. They embrace:

- strategy consultancies;
- general management consultancies;
- software and systems houses;
- computer manufacturers;
- individual consultants.

Strategy consultancies

While the international, high-level consulting groups specializing in strategic advice have in the past tended to avoid involvement in detailed, specialized areas, IT has posed them with a dilemma. Nowadays, the ability of a company to reorganize, restructure or adopt a new operating strategy is often conditioned by what can be done with its information systems. Incompatible data structures or technologies make it impossible to bring divisions or companies together quickly or to manage global businesses in a more coordinated fashion.

New technologies open up possibilities for new products, new services, new distribution channels and new ways of reaching the market. Accordingly, issues of strategy can no longer be divorced from considerations concerning the choice and use of IT.

Most of the strategy consulting firms have therefore either been equipping themselves with more IT skills or forming alliances with other types of consultancies. As a consequence, they increasingly have the ability to look at the strategic aspects of IT, how it is organized, how it is used and how it interacts with corporate strategy.

General management consultancies

Most general management and multidisciplinary consulting groups have built substantial IT practices. Sometimes these specialized practices undertake assignments related purely to IT, while at other times they provide their specialist input to multidisciplinary projects.

This work stemmed from the earlier commonplace projects, carrying out feasibility studies, selecting hardware or software, carrying out computer audits or reviewing projects which had run into trouble. While elements of this type of work remain, and indeed are still in strong demand from small and medium-sized companies, many assignments nowadays supplement or reinforce the in-house skills that most big organizations have. Indeed, the majority of the work is carried out on behalf of the CIO (chief information officer) or director of IT, rather than for the general or financial manager.

An increasing number of major projects undertaken by such consultancies are concerned with the international aspects of information systems or telecommunications networks. Clients striving to take advantage of global markets often find that their plans are inhibited by the fragmented systems which exist within the organization. Moreover, few companies have the mixture of technical competence and international systems experience to deal with the issues without outside support — not to mention the advantage of external objectivity necessary to overcome the territorial defensiveness that has often been built up within multinational groups.

The problem that all general management consultancies have had to face is how far to go in providing such services. Does the provision of project resources, systems analysts and computer programmers impede objectivity? Can a client feel comfortable with a consultant's recommendations when there is a perceived vested interest in the outcome?

Different consulting firms have taken different approaches to this dilemma. Some have simply dithered. Generally speaking, most clients appear to prefer the advantages of a consultancy that can carry through its recommendations to one that makes a great virtue of impartiality. The most successful IT consulting practice, in terms of international growth over the past decade, has gone unequivocally for the development of an implementation capability and has progressively moved into "outsourcing" or "facilities management": not simply giving advice, nor even just implementing change, but actually taking over the operation of the clients' computer systems on a continuing basis.

This has fitted in with a trend for organizations to outsource services generally, thereby reducing fixed overheads and enabling them to focus on core business.

Software companies and systems houses

The trend to extend the boundaries of consulting has brought management consultants increasingly into competition with the big software companies and systems houses: serving the same market but having come to it from different directions. The latter companies have always had problems with the more genuine "consulting" aspect of their services, partly because of the perceived lack of objectivity and partly because they have generally failed to attract the top-flight consultants who have preferred to work for companies where their own skills were more central to the main activity of the firm.

Nevertheless, the tremendous ability of software companies to implement projects, particularly when it comes to very large-scale projects, has made them an important force in the consulting services market. Many, too, have followed the path of outsourcing and facilities management. They play a key role in moving businesses forward.

Computer manufacturers

It might at first seem odd, in a book which is concerned with management consulting, to be talking about the offerings of computer manufacturers. However, they could well represent a major future source of consultancy services, particularly if one adopts a broader definition of the term "consulting" covering all the services mentioned above.

The reason that the computer manufacturers have turned in this direction is largely one of necessity. As technology has advanced, the cost of the equipment as a proportion of total systems cost has constantly dropped. Price competition has become fierce, with low-cost equipment suppliers eroding the traditional markets of the major computer companies. As a consequence, the latter have recognized that the future lies in providing "solutions" rather than "boxes".

Such a move, of course, involves a cultural shift. Above all, the supplier needs to take a broader, more client-oriented view of life. This is clearly causing some difficulties, but it would be wrong to assume that the computer suppliers will not be able to make the change: back in the 1960s most of the established consulting groups could not envisage the accounting/auditing firms ever becoming a force in management consulting!

Individual consultants

In addition to the major consulting and other organizations mentioned above, there are many individuals offering their services as independent consultants in the IT area. Their number has been swollen by the economic recession which has made many skilled individuals, including some at very senior level, redundant.

They provide a valuable source of expertise, both for the big corporation seeking a second opinion on its activities and for the smaller company wanting general guidance on its IT applications but without placing itself in the hands of the provider of the hardware or software. The risk in the latter case comes from having to put one's trust in the views of a single individual in an area where the client finds it difficult to assess the quality of the advice. In such a case, the general rule must be only ever to use an individual whom one either knows well or who comes highly recommended and has a track record of success; if there is no such assurance, it is better to rely on the systems supplier and to pin down the contracted terms for delivery and performance.

17.6 Selecting an IT consultancy

The following guidelines should help in the selection of a consultancy for an IT-related requirement:

(1) Be very clear about *what* you want, but not over-prescriptive about *how* it should be achieved.

(2) Look for genuine experience of similar assignments and take up references from the clients involved.

(3) If you have a relationship with a consultancy with whom you have worked, whom you trust and who can clearly do the job in question, why waste time with competitive quotes? What matters most is how well a consultancy delivers results, not how well it presents new assignment proposals.

(4)   Where you do go for competitive quotes, keep the short-list small, no more than three or four consultants at most. Otherwise the briefing and evaluation become too time-consuming, the best may not respond and the job may simply go to the most desperate!

(5)   Be as open as you can about the assignment budget. You want the consultants to pitch their offering to your needs, not try to guess what you might be prepared to pay nor what price their competitor might be prepared to quote. The old adage almost invariably holds good: you get what you pay for.

(6)   Make sure you know and have met the *individuals* who will be working on the project.

(7)   Decide whether independence and objectivity really matter on your particular project. If they do, make sure you know whether the consultant is allied to any hardware, software or facilities supplier. In other words, be clear on whether the consultancy has any commercial interest in the outcome of its recommendations. Independence may not be the key issue in a particular case. If you require additional services, can the consultancy provide them or will you be faced with finding and recruiting another firm and getting it up to speed? Do you want an adviser that will actively deliver what he or she recommends?

(8)   Check the breadth of skills on offer. If the project goes outside the technical considerations, can the consulting firm chosen really provide the wider expertise?

(9)   Ask how the consultant intends to transfer the necessary skills and knowledge to your own staff to avoid consultant "lock-in".

17.7 Making effective use of consultants in the IT area

The rules for making effective use of consultants in the IT area are not very different from the rules for making effective use of consultants generally. But there are a couple of special considerations. First, as far as senior management is concerned, IT is still wrapped in more mystique than the other main functions of the business, adding a higher degree of dependency on specialist expertise, whether internal or external. IT's rate of evolution makes this almost inevitable, such is the difficulty of keeping up with developments in technologies and systems, and their implications. Second, it can now be seen that getting decisions wrong on IT can have very long-term consequences for the business: the expression commonly used is "setting the business in electronic concrete".

IT is an area, therefore, where a reliable outside opinion can be invaluable even if it is a case of simply providing a second opinion for the internal specialist.

The golden rules are:

—   to recognize that if external assistance is required, then the earlier it is employed the less expensive it is likely to prove overall;

—   to recognize the different profiles and standpoints of those offering consulting services. Are they genuinely independent? Does it matter? Is the ability to implement change more important under the particular circumstances than objectivity?

Finally, one has to be aware that no use of IT specialists, whether internal staff or external consultants, can absolve management from the overall responsibility of directing and managing the use of IT within the business. One can pay for support and guidance; one cannot pay to have management responsibility removed.

CONSULTING IN SMALL-BUSINESS MANAGEMENT

18

The use of consultants by small enterprises is now an established trend in business. As activities relating to the conduct of business become more complex, the need for outside assistance usually increases. Small-scale enterprise managers who want to remain competitive need to consider using consultants as they would use other support services such as bankers, lawyers, accountants and trade associations.

Consultants can play an important role in economic development by becoming more involved in assisting people to set up small enterprises. For new entrepreneurs, the start-up phase is the most difficult; consequently, more and more consultants focus on this important aspect of enterprise development. Consultants and small-business development centres often arrange training groups of entrepreneurs who intend to initiate new enterprises.

Existing small enterprises use consultants mainly to solve specific operational problems. The duration of the consultancy will depend on the specific problem but most consultancies can be accomplished within a few months. Longer consultancies may be required if the problem concerns expanding business operations. Expansion takes time and the consultant may be involved periodically for up to one or two years.

Within economic policies pursuing structural adjustment, trade liberalization and privatization, the small enterprise sector is now identified and recognized as the key area to supply job opportunities and to provide goods and services. As a result, there has been an upsurge in consulting assignments to meet these new demands. This, in turn, has introduced a new dimension to the economic and social development field, i.e. the development of resource personnel to advise governments and non-governmental agencies in promoting small enterprise development. Essentially, these new forms of consulting service address the critical areas of policy formulation and implementation: developing strategies; designing, implementing and evaluating programmes; and managing development projects.

18.1 Characteristics of small enterprises

Definition of a small enterprise

The definition of a small enterprise tends to vary according to the nature of its activities, the purpose of the definition, and the level of development where the enterprise is located. The criteria for describing an enterprise as "small" might be the number of employees, money value of sales, capital investment, maximum energy requirements, or various combinations of these and other factors. In most discussions and writings on the subject by management consultants, it is conceded that a small enterprise is one in which the administrative and operational management are in the hands of one or two people who also make the important decisions in that enterprise. Such an operational definition has been found to include more than 85 per cent of all small enterprises no matter how defined.

The consultant should be aware of factors which usually distinguish the small from the larger enterprise. First, the small enterprise is primarily financed from personal or family savings with limited recourse to outside finance during the formative stages. Second, the manager has close personal contact with the whole workplace; and, third, the enterprise operates mainly in a limited geographical area. These "smallness" factors greatly influence the consultative process.

The small enterprise possesses distinct advantages, including the ability to fill limited demands in specialized markets; a propensity for labour intensity and low- to medium-skilled work; and flexibility to adapt rapidly to changing demands and conditions. Managerially speaking, there is an advantage in having a personal involvement in dealings which goes beyond price, product and delivery dates. Owner-managers are usually more highly motivated than salaried managers — they work longer and harder, and provide greater incentives to workers by personal example.

Simple organizational structure means more direct and less complicated lines of communication inside and outside the business. The smallness of the firm assists in identifying and developing the capabilities of workers more quickly than happens in larger firms.

The small enterprise can also experiment with or enter new markets without attracting unwanted attention from large firms. It can cater for extremes in the market — either the right- or left-hand tails of an average distribution curve — since mass marketing for the average consumer is usually taken care of by big business. Similarly, the smaller firm can more quickly exploit changing market patterns and the "floater" consumer who drifts in the market-place.

Special problems of small enterprises

Problems of small enterprises can be general or specific. Problems of a general nature involve legal aspects of business, access to credit and raw materials, and the lack of appropriate technical and managerial assistance.

Management consultants should be aware of problems at the enterprise level. These may appear more formidable to the manager of a small enterprise than problems in a large corporation might appear to its chairperson. The following list demonstrates the range of difficulties which may be encountered:

- Whereas large, well-organized enterprises can usually afford both good line-management and specialist staff, the small enterprise manager is a relatively isolated individual dealing with policy, administration and operational problems simultaneously despite personal biases and limitations.

- Small-enterprise managers often operate with inadequate or, at best, with minimum quantitative data. To save operating costs they are likely to dispense with information systems, a weakness which becomes glaringly apparent when the enterprise reaches a growth stage.

- Because the small enterprise can usually pay only minimum wages, has few fringe benefits, and offers low job security and few promotional opportunities, it is reasonable to expect difficulties in recruiting high-calibre employees.

- Professional investors are seldom attracted to the new small enterprise, and the manager is severely limited in his or her ability to raise initial capital. This problem is compounded when, as is very often the case, the enterprise runs into growth problems, or experiences operating difficulties, and the manager attempts to raise additional finance in order to cope with expansion or crisis situations.

- Because of this problem of limited reserves, coupled with low capacity to borrow, the small enterprise is particularly vulnerable to economic downturn and recession.

- Although ability to change and adapt rapidly is a natural strength of a small enterprise, this quality may be nullified when an opportunity requiring rapid change suddenly appears. The manager may be too occupied with ongoing operational problems to be able to think clearly about the future of the business.

- The hand-to-mouth financial existence of the enterprise does not encourage opportunities for staff training and development, with consequent loss in realizing the full potential of the human resources within the enterprise.

- High productivity is difficult to achieve since the small enterprise does not enjoy the low costs of the large firm which can, for example, buy at a discount, achieve economies of scale, call on its sophisticated marketing and distribution system, and engage its own research and development and systems design teams.

- The small firm is usually limited to a single or small product or service range with the result that in times of trouble it cannot diversify activities as can large-scale enterprises.

- The manager is often not able to understand and interpret government regulations, actions, concessions, and so on, to best advantage.

The small enterprise is a relatively fragile structure with limited resources to overcome its problems. Even minor problems can be life-threatening to the enterprise. In one country it was estimated that the failure rate within the first two years of operation was as high as 50 per cent for new small enterprises.

Reluctance to use consultants

Many small-enterprise managers are reluctant to use outside consultants for the following reasons:

— They believe that only large enterprises can afford the consulting fees charged.

— In many instances, consultants will not have practical experience in the type of business needing assistance.

— Identification of a competent consultant is difficult and time-consuming, because most managers have little previous contact with consultants.

— Managers are reluctant to provide outsiders with facts and figures relating to the business.

— Using a consultant may be viewed by the manager as an admission of lack of competence.

Notwithstanding these doubts and fears, many small-business managers need to talk to an attentive and helpful listener about their concerns and worries. John Harvey-Jones describes his experience in the following terms:

> I had not fully realized how lonely the life of someone running a small business can be. Of course every businessman has relationships with his customers, his suppliers, his bank manager, and so on. He also knows a number of his competitors. But remarkably few people running small businesses have any friend or confidant on whom they can test their ideas, or with whom they can talk openly about their business, its opportunities and its threats, and their feelings about the business. It seems to me that business people badly need a business equivalent of that excellent organization, The Samaritans. In many cases just talking about the way a business is running brings a feeling of support and a strengthening of conviction, which is badly needed when you feel alone and threatened by immense external forces.[1]

To overcome the preconceptions of owner-managers, consultants need to provide facts and data which will indicate the value of their services, if possible referring to specific instances of other small companies where consultants have been used. Studies have shown that most small-business owners who have used consultants have obtained the following benefits:

- an independent professional viewpoint;
- an overall, total company check-up and expert evaluation;
- ideas to cope with growth;

- manager and staff training which otherwise would not take place;
- help in developing a strategic approach.

18.2 The role and profile of the consultant

The consultant dealing with small enterprises handles the whole spectrum of management and is required to be more of a generalist than a specialist. It can be taken for granted that consultants require professional training and considerable experience in management principles as applied to small-enterprise development. Of prime importance is a knowledge of the interaction of functions of the small enterprise, since change in one function usually has immediate repercussions in others. Furthermore, it is useful for the consultant to be at least familiar with the various entrepreneurial development approaches which provide a conceptual basis for current small enterprise development practices.

As with any combination of skill and art, mastery of business fundamentals is essential for a successful career in consulting with small enterprises. When assisting the manager of a small enterprise, it is important to ensure that all managerial tasks are completed, even imperfectly, rather than having 75 per cent of the tasks completed to perfection while the remaining 25 per cent are neglected. The consultant must keep in mind the "total" picture of the business to see that functions of administration and operation are harmonized and integrated. Patience and dogged perseverance are required in encouraging the manager to complete managerial chores ranging from accounting to staff training, while preventing him or her from concentrating solely on preferred technical activities such as the actual production of goods and services.

The consultant's role becomes further complicated in that his or her main consulting duties lie in developing the manager and others contributing to managing the enterprise at the same time as being expected to provide feasible practical solutions to a wide range of specific problems — for example, finance, sales, production and purchasing. Although the subject-matter is specific, it generally exceeds the limits of a particular function or technique. The consulting technique is broad, including assistance with implementation where necessary, and informal training in many cases.

Routine consulting reports, usually submitted to larger organizations, do not apply to small enterprises. Written reports should be short, simple, limited to a minimum and often submitted only at the end of an assignment to explain what things were done and why, and what is required in the future.

The consultant should also appreciate that clients are not necessarily the best educated and skilled managers available. Moreover, there are often no training facilities readily at hand to help remedy obvious deficiencies. Thus, instead of adopting a professional air and emphasizing his expertise to influence his clients, the consultant should use a simpler style. Coaxing, praising and reprimanding are likely to be more effective in obtaining the results desired!

The client-manager of the small enterprise may suffer a severe sense of failure if forced to use a consultant. The consultant should, therefore, be alert to the possible need to restore a client's self-esteem in addition to providing technical assistance.

Unquestionably, lack of data is a major handicap in undertaking a consulting assignment with a small enterprise. Usually the sole source of information is the manager, who is often "too busy" to be interviewed. The consultant must use ingenuity, persistence and tenacity to extract the required information.

During the last 30 years, many governments, employers' organizations, trade associations, chambers of commerce and similar bodies have established special services and facilities for small enterprises, including:

— supply of credit (loans and guarantees);

— reduced tax rates (to enable accumulation of capital necessary for survival and growth);

— reserved and preferential markets for goods and services (special government set-asides, offsets and subcontracts);

— industrial estates, parks or incubators;

— product design and quality control services;

— advisory services on export possibilities;

— market and feasibility studies;

— reduced-cost bulk purchase of raw materials, etc.

Although he or she is probably able to obtain advice directly from technicians in charge of particular services, a manager or owner of a small enterprise may find it difficult to decide when and how to use such services. The management consultant has to advise on the whole range of services, and recommend priorities and acceptable costs of such services to the manager. This also includes advice on where to find relevant information. In developing countries, management consultants are increasingly involved in advising local, small and medium-sized enterprises on technology transfer, joint ventures with enterprises from industrialized countries, subcontracting, or franchising.

Good health, persistence and stamina are the consultant's chief assets. Small-enterprise managers have little respect for conventional working hours and, once preliminary fears are overcome, quickly learn to ask for help whenever and however they see fit. The consultant is very similar to the family doctor in being always on call — and some clients will, fortunately or unfortunately, take this for granted. Clients are often astonished to learn that consultants take time off for meals, and may wish to be with their families on some weekends and evenings.

Responsibility is also disproportionate. In most conventional consulting assignments for large organizations, there is some tolerance for error as reports are checked by supervisors and very important reports are examined by a manager of the consulting unit. However, when dealing with small enterprises, mistakes by the consultant can be fatal to the organization requesting assistance. Since such assistance tends to be direct and immediate, the consultant has limited time to check ideas and proposals with colleagues. Paraphrasing Reinhold

Niebuhr's famous prayer, the Asian Productivity Organization has set out the role of the small-enterprise consultant in the form of a "Consultant's Prayer":

God grant me
COURAGE to change what I can,
PATIENCE to accept what can't be changed, and
WISDOM to know the difference.

Timing may be critical. The consultant usually works under extreme pressure since assistance is often not sought until after a crisis develops and the manager is personally unable to resolve the problem. By employing a judicious blend of "resource" and "process" forms of consulting, the consultant is expected to do whatever is necessary to assist the manager. In the final analysis, it must be remembered that the consultant's job is to consult and *not* to manage. In times when consultancy advice may not be accepted or followed by management, the consultant should be guided by the saying that "you can lead a horse to water, but you can't make it drink". Similarly, the consultant should not be held responsible for the failure of a small firm, nor should the consultant claim responsibility for its success. The consultant should concentrate on the success of the assignment.

18.3 Consulting assignments in the life-cycle of an enterprise

The review in previous chapters of management situations and problems dealt with by consultants includes a number of concepts and experiences relevant to consulting in a small enterprise. However, certain situations are specific to small enterprise consulting.

Small-enterprise consultants need to change as business activity changes. They must become more aware of information and how to gain access to it. It is essential for consultants to understand the uses of software packages and computers in relation to small enterprise operations, especially how to convert computer printouts into useful information for the small-enterprise manager. An emerging area of concern for small enterprises appears to lie in the field of industrial relations in those countries where organized labour is making its claims heard and felt.

Communication skills are becoming increasingly important and may eventually overshadow even the technical knowledge and other skills of the consultant. The essential task is for consultants to use their communication skills to "pull out" problems and to "plug in" solutions. The consultant must have a good network of highly skilled technicians who can assist with specific problems. Once a solution is determined, it is the communication skills of the consultant that will convince the manager that he or she should implement the solution.

The small-enterprise owner is faced with a host of problems and the consultant should be prepared to meet these various needs. The consultant may be considered a "one-stop shop" where entrepreneurs can receive the necessary assistance. The following stages serve to illustrate the range of problems faced by consultants when dealing with an enterprise passing through a typical life-cycle.

Stage 1: At the very beginning

Biographical evidence suggests that successful small-enterprise managers, sometimes referred to as entrepreneurs (a definition which has wider implications than for small enterprises only), commonly possess distinctive qualities. They are often the first-born of a family and have had to assume a more than average amount of responsibility at an early stage in life. In many cases they are the offspring of self-employed persons, but not necessarily in the same occupational grouping, trade or service. Such people have had a sound but not necessarily extended education and, as a rule, more than five years' experience of working in real-life conditions.

From a personality point of view they are inclined to be optimistic, moderate risk-takers as opposed to gamblers or non-risk-takers, and have a feeling that control over their own destiny rather than just making money is a key motivating factor in their life. Such people are usually married, with minimum distractions caused by family life — there is usually an understanding spouse who may not, in fact, care for the kind of life-style which results, but comprehends and appreciates the demands made on the marriage partner.

A key characteristic is that successful entrepreneurs are mentally and physically very active. They are usually very well organized and manage time efficiently. Success may result not so much from quality, but from the quantity of schemes prepared and developed. In short, the greater the effort, the greater the chances of success seem to be.

When dealing with a beginner, the consultant should take stock of the client's background and interests to ascertain whether he or she is dealing with a probable or a possible entrepreneur, and develop the assignment accordingly. The project in question should be closely examined, taking into account the strengths and weaknesses commonly found in small enterprises. A check-list of items to be reviewed should be worked out.

Stage 2: Starting up

Assuming that the client wishes to launch a new enterprise, the consultant should, after reviewing and discussing the proposal, prepare for at least three possibilities and develop appropriate contingency plans:
(1)   What is the best that might happen (the "blue skies" approach)?
(2)   What is likely to happen (the basis for the "business plan")?
(3)   What is the worst that can happen (realistically assess the "downside risk")?

The consultant should talk freely with the client about the first two possibilities, which are usually "creative" problems, whereas the third alternative, which is a "corrective" problem, should be reserved for the consultant's own counsel because (a) the client is unlikely to listen to or agree with the "worst possible" alternative, and (b) encouragement rather than discouragement should help attain the full potential of the proposal. The consultant must, however, draw up detailed contingency plans for all three alternatives if for no other reason than to make allowances for "Murphy's Law" ("If anything can possibly go wrong — it will!").

A good small-enterprise manager can usually generate many ideas very rapidly. The consultant should encourage this and assist the client to obtain and record relevant quantitative data about these ideas for two reasons: first, to assist in making a logical choice between alternatives; and second, to use as supporting evidence should the manager experience uncomfortable afterthoughts about a scheme once started.

Mistakes will happen, particularly in the early stages — it is part of the general learning process. The consultant's task is to minimize errors made by the manager in these stages. It is, however, better to ensure that an ineffective scheme never takes off than to attempt to salvage an impossible project at a later date, which gives rise to the consulting maxim: "Giving birth is a lot easier than resurrection." If necessary, allow the proposal to lapse and encourage the client to try afresh when more evidence and support are available. If it is decided to go ahead with the enterprise, full commitment should be encouraged. Effective decision-making and prompt action are vital; there is little room for compromise or error in a new enterprise.

From a functional point of view the consultant should encourage clients to use the services of some specialists from the outset if they can possibly be afforded because, if the enterprise grows, the specialists will be familiar with its history, practice and results, and thus able to assist in a meaningful way. The specialists include:

— *a legal firm* (of good repute and the best which can be afforded);
— *an accountant* (possessing the same qualities as those required in the legal firm);
— *a banker* (a person, not an institution, so that rapport and trust are established at a personal level);
— *an insurance agent* (similar qualities as required in the banker);
— *a marketing representative* (this clearly depends on the type of enterprise; where the enterprise is not intrinsically marketing oriented, it is often sound practice to make links with experts or agents during the formative stages).

Small-enterprise consultants require a wide range of functional expertise, with, perhaps most importantly, emphasis on financial matters. The finance field presents problems both in attracting formation capital and in controlling expenses and income; small-enterprise management consultants not well versed in these fields are a danger to clients and cannot claim professional competence in the true sense of the word.

It is often only by thorough expert financial appraisal that the consultant is able to undertake the necessary though unpleasant task of recommending discontinuation of an enterprise rather than encouraging a holding operation which will eventually lead to insuperable problems for all involved.

This fear of tragedy deserves greater emphasis in the start-up stages of the enterprise than may seem warranted. Often family and friends' savings are used to finance the capital requirements of the new enterprise simply because "no one else will lend the money". This finding alone suggests that the scheme is probably not particularly sound. If no finance agency considers a proposal worthwhile (and they take into account an allowance for failure), why should a consultant recommend that family savings be jeopardized in a risky undertaking? There should always be proprietor equity in a venture, but not simply because no one else is prepared to support it. When preparing the third (worst-of-all) contingency plan, if project failure is likely to cause undue hardships the consultant is professionally obliged to dissuade the client from undertaking such a venture.

During the start-up phase the consultant might reflect on the following checkout routine which has been based on a considerable number of studies designed to pinpoint potential problem areas in small enterprises. In order of importance for diagnosing trouble areas the consultant is likely to find deficiencies classified as the seven "M"s:

● *managerial* (lack of experience);
● *monetary* (lack of capital, poor cost control);
● *material* (poor location, too much stock);
● *machines* (excessive purchase of fixed assets);
● *marketing* (inappropriate granting of credit);
● *mental* (lack of planning for expansion);
● *motivation* (wrong attitudes to work and responsibility).

Stage 3: Getting bigger

Having weathered stages 1 and 2, the consultant may occasionally be rewarded with a brand new set of events which emerge as the enterprise matures and the consulting assignment takes on a progressive look. This is the right time to examine thoroughly the weaknesses to be overcome, opportunities to develop further, and alternative resource allocations to help the enterprise benefit from the most favourable opportunities. When assisting the manager to allocate resources, the consultant may care to refer to the "four to one principle" which can be set up as a rule of thumb:

— 20 per cent of the customers account for 80 per cent of the sales;
— 20 per cent of the stocks result in 80 per cent of movements;

— 20 per cent of staff causes 80 per cent of the problems;

— 20 per cent of salespeople create 80 per cent of the sales, and so on.

The consultant should encourage the manager to "play percentages" and concentrate on critical areas. During this maturation phase the manager, submerged in day-to-day operational problems, is usually not able to pay attention to the long- or medium-term planning essential for continued growth and survival. Consultants can assist by encouraging the manager to look to the future. For example, they can prepare current organization charts and job descriptions and compare these with how they should look five to ten years hence, showing likely changes. New developments usually require a little inspiration, considerable incubation, and a great deal of perspiration. Therefore, the consultant should make sure that the manager plans appropriate resources and allocates the time required for future growth and development.

A noticeable feature of successful managers is that they are exceptionally well organized. This practice should be encouraged as part of the management development process by introducing systems, encouraging managers to read on management subjects, and insisting on forecasts, budgets and controls. Probably during this maturation phase an accountant (financial controller) post should be established.

The consultant will also have to draw on his or her knowledge of comparable enterprises to judge the productivity of the client under review. Knowledge of a range of interfirm comparisons, in the form of input/output and productivity ratios, is an invaluable asset, especially if corrective measures become necessary. The consultant must know where such information can be obtained.

Stage 4: Exit from the enterprise

Eventually the manager finds that the enterprise may have grown to a stage where it can no longer be considered small, and issues pertaining to growth, finance, corporate structure, delegation and the like will arise. The small enterprise consultant should then judiciously refer the manager to specialists capable of assisting in the new situation.

Alternatively, the manager may decide to forego the routine running of an enterprise and prefer to start something new, revert to becoming an employee, or retire. At that point, disposal of the enterprise becomes the problem of the moment.

Assessing the monetary value of an enterprise is usually done in any of three ways:

(1) *liquidation or forced sale value,* where the enterprise is virtually put up for auction and sold to the highest bidder (if any);

(2) *book value,* where items are assessed at cost less depreciation and sold piecemeal to selected markets;

(3) *market value,* where the entity is sold as a going concern and items such as goodwill are included in the price.

Varying conditions (such as the death of the owner) may determine which of these assessment methods will be used. Generally speaking, the market value method provides the best return to the seller.

The consultant is obliged to assist the client to obtain the best possible deal. Nevertheless, the consultant should keep in mind that the best sales are those involving a willing seller and a willing buyer. To arrive at this happy situation the consultant should encourage the seller to "leave something in it" for the new owner. By doing so the chances of a sale are enhanced, time is often saved and opportunities for recrimination are reduced. Trying to obtain the greatest possible amount of money from the potential new owner may well carry the sale beyond the borders of diminishing return.

Another end-of-the-road situation occurs when the manager is succeeded by a family member or someone else. With small enterprises, apart from areas of obvious equality and responsibility such as a partnership of doctors or lawyers, shared management seldom succeeds. For purposes of direction, control and responsibility it is usually better to have one identified manager than to split the authority between, say, two siblings. If it can be arranged, family succession in an enterprise should follow only after the offspring have been exposed to working in outside situations, otherwise managerial inbreeding is likely to occur.

18.4 Areas of special concern

Counselling the start-up entrepreneur

We examined earlier (section 3.7) the relationships between counselling and consulting in the context of working with larger organizations. The counsellor works mainly with and for individual clients, rather than for the organization. The relationship is, and should be, a personal and intense one, likely to involve areas far beyond the particular management issues leading to the assignment.

The decision to start a new business can be one of the most important steps that anyone ever takes, and involves far more than straightforward business and management issues. It is extremely important that the client alone makes the final decision. Counselling is about empowering people to take fundamental decisions of this sort for themselves rather than simply advising them what to do.

Several studies show that many people launching their own business for the first time do so because they have been jolted out of their normal career path by a shock such as redundancy, or by a personal "determining event" such as bereavement, divorce or a forced move to an unfamiliar country. Such an experience can marginalize people, and may encourage them to look beyond the ordinary and expected courses of action to new and unfamiliar fields, such as starting a new business. People in this position are often unsure and need support but, because they are marginalized, they may not have access to friends and family who might normally help on such occasions. The professional counsellor can thus fill an important gap.

Counselling usually goes beyond business issues. An entrepreneur starting a new business has necessarily to involve the whole family, since lifestyles and financial security are almost certainly going to change and the family may also have to work in the business. Some marriages break up, while others may be strengthened and enriched by the experience of starting a business. A counsellor has to ensure that would-be entrepreneurs think through all such implications.

The counsellor neither encourages nor discourages clients but only helps them to look at the situation from every angle and to make their own decisions. Some people may be over-confident or even blind themselves to possible difficulties, while others may lack the confidence to think clearly about the options facing them. The counsellor must judge whether the client needs a "wet blanket" of realism, or a "firecracker" of enthusiasm. The client should not be pushed in any particular direction but should be helped to be in the proper frame of mind to make the right decision.

Potential entrepreneurs often expect counsellors not only to be sympathetic listeners but also to provide them with useful contacts, particularly to bankers and sources of finance, or to potential customers. Successful entrepreneurs are, above all, good networkers and the counsellor should be happy to play this role. However, there should be no offer to recommend a particular contact or collaborator to the client. Names can be provided and introductions made, but the counsellor should not play the role of a "marriage broker", which could seriously prejudice his or her effectiveness as a counsellor if the two roles are confused. This is even more important when the counsellor is not being paid by the client but by a third party, such as a business support agency or even a bank. The counsellor must be scrupulously neutral in every respect.

Entrepreneurs often have to produce business plans, either as part of a course or to submit an application for funding to a bank. While preparing these plans can be a somewhat barren and automatic exercise, an effective counsellor can help clients to produce plans which not only satisfy external requirements but also provide a valuable contribution in deciding whether or not to start at all. The various components of the business plan can be used as assignments to structure the counselling process.

Counselling people starting new businesses can be an extremely demanding task, because the whole future of the client and family may be involved. It can also be most rewarding. The contribution of the genuinely effective counsellor may well be forgotten or even denied by the client, particularly if the business becomes successful, but the counsellor can take satisfaction in assisting someone through a critical stage of life.

Consulting for family enterprises

The use of consultants by small family enterprises is not common. Even after initial contact, few formal consulting assignments are ever achieved. Because of the intimate relationships between family members, they are extremely reluctant to discuss business conflicts and problems. Personal and business problems become highly intertwined and in many cases they are extremely difficult for the consultant to identify, let alone resolve.

Before attempting to solve the business problems, the consultant should meet separately with each family member in order to understand the family dynamics as they relate to the operation of the business. The consultant should attempt to gain the support and trust of each family member *before* meeting them as a group to discuss their business problems.

When family ties are strong, family pride can be a major factor in resolving the conflict. In situations where family ties are weak, it may be better to propose that some members leave the business and pursue other career and life opportunities.

A special feature in counselling the family enterprise touches on the question of succession. For the reasons mentioned earlier, there are likely to be emotional as well as managerial and business issues to consider. The consultant needs to maintain a professional role and bring up the topics of wills, death duties (if any), taxation and other items which family members may wish to avoid. The consultant might start by evaluating the enterprise's strengths and weaknesses, and recommend an orderly succession process including shareholders' and directors' interests. Once these items are in place, the consultant might introduce the subject of the profile of a likely successor. It is recommended that fees be charged on a time basis rather than on the basis of capital participation to quieten possible anxieties amongst other family members. Contingency plans should also be prepared to deal with such action such as the premature death of the senior member.

Extension services

Private consultants are not widely used by small enterprises in most developing countries. However, consulting is often provided through government-sponsored extension services to small enterprises. Extension service agents take the initiative, visit small enterprises, and provide entrepreneurs with services and advice on the spot. Such assistance may include the following activities:

- advising on all aspects of management, work organization and product design, development and adaptation; emphasis may be on price calculations, bookkeeping and financial planning;
- domestic and export marketing, including subcontracting and inventory control;
- materials procurement;
- choosing technology and solving technical problems including skill, space, public utility and equipment requirements, and procurement methods;
- advice on potential sources of finance and help in gaining access to finance, for example by preparing loan requests;

- identifying training requirements for workers and owners/managers, and potential training sources;
- explaining government regulations and dealing with related paperwork, including taxes and legal questions such as incorporation of enterprises, registration, licensing, grants, etc.; and
- quality control and standardization, particularly where subcontracting and export promotion are important.

Only rarely is it necessary or possible for the extension service to be involved in all of these functions at the same time. Specific functions will depend on the nature of the target group, both in terms of its technical qualifications and the subsector to which the target entrepreneurs belong, namely manufacturing, construction, tourism, commerce, and so on. There is general agreement, however, that an integrated approach has to be taken to assess and meet the needs of small enterprises. Such an approach would combine, for example, training, technological assistance, credit and, in some cases, physical infrastructure.

The extension service agent may be viewed as a "trouble-shooter" who identifies problem areas and refers the entrepreneur to specialized assistance such as chambers of commerce, professional associations, trade and artisan groups, private consultants, training institutions, or larger enterprises. To be of benefit to entrepreneurs, the value of the extension service must be judged by its ability to perceive their needs, to diagnose correctly problems that occur, and to provide timely and useful advice and support.

18.5 Consulting in policy development

Much has been said and written about the need for an enabling or supportive policy environment made up of legislation, rules and regulations to encourage enterprise development. In some cases, management and business consultants are requested to assist in preparing, implementing and evaluating policies designed to contribute to the development process. In such a case the client can be an economic ministry, or an employers' or small business association intending to put up proposals to government, or preparing itself for negotiations with government representatives.

One useful basis for developing a national strategy for small enterprise development is to analyse existing policies and, where appropriate, suggest ways and means of removing the obstacles and punitive measures affecting development and growth by introducing a conducive or at least a neutral and non-discriminatory policy environment.

In broad terms, policies — defined as rules based on sound analysis, proclaiming commitment to action and ensuring adequate and established resource allocations — are a product of politics. In turn, politics emanate from organized representation, and the small enterprise sector is notoriously renowned for being ill-organized, having only a limited capacity to influence policies which are usually shaped by large-scale business and well-organized political groupings. The "level playing-field", which is generally called for when dealing with the small enterprise sector, is warranted because most policies are felt to favour large-scale enterprises which have better access to and more influence over policy-makers and those who implement them. It can easily be argued that an ideal policy should treat all enterprises, regardless of size, in the same manner. Where this is not possible then we should, at least, seek to offer a fair deal to all concerned, in order to promote genuine competitiveness.

Policies that stimulate business development

It should be self-evident to all concerned that there are readily seen advantages for entrepreneurs when setting up small enterprises. These can take the form of publicly pronounced incentives set out as policies which cover areas determining profitability such as demand for output, prices of outputs and inputs, taxes and concessions. The following require consideration:

— *Macroeconomic policies* to stimulate demand are often forgotten in preparing strategic approaches to assist small enterprises, and this consequently nullifies attempts to provide supply-side assistance.

— *Trade policies* which promote trade liberalization are likely to enhance the flexibility of small enterprises to find market niches to their liking by changing product lines, provided that they can find the finance to do so.

— *Investment and taxation policies* are often biased against small enterprises through such measures as high indirect taxes, fixed levies not related to profit, and the inability to obtain exemptions, rebates and concessions which are often available to large-scale enterprises. Such disparity might be reduced by dropping all exemptions, or altering tax concessions so that they apply across the board and are not reserved solely for those who know how to apply for them.

— The need for *equality in price and distribution controls* becomes evident in cases where small enterprises lack access to state-controlled marketing and transportation channels.

— *Structural adjustment policies* generally impose restraints on demand, thus hitting the lower-income population which supports small enterprises. Appropriate compensatory measures like food security programmes can help reverse the downward spiral of declining demand and income.

An enabling environment

Entrepreneurs will logically respond more rapidly to profitable opportunities where society's attitude is positive towards a private business sector, and where there is political support for such an environment, than when there is a negative response to such issues. In economies in transition from a centrally planned to a market economy system, there is a need to convince investors that these changes will be lasting and that entrepreneurs will be protected by the legal system. It is thus essential for a conscious and visible effort to be made to provide a sound attitudinal base to business development.

Political stability in terms of government policies towards private enterprise and investment is important. Likewise, a stable economy is required, since high inflation encourages entrepreneurs to focus only on short-run, quick-return investments in preference to fixed investments and longer-term profit gains.

Regulations applying to business range from the necessary — such as protection of health and the environment — to the ridiculous — such as those that benefit only selected, usually politically acute, enterprises.

In general, it is more effective to correct the underlying problems affecting regulations than to try and compensate by introducing special exemptions. The need to simplify procedures for registering and operating businesses should speak for itself. Administering regulations can be a source of irritation for small enterprises since even when regulations are reasonable some administrators may not be. Harassment and corruption by underpaid bureaucrats may do more permanent damage to small enterprises than natural disasters. Small enterprises should pay taxes, not bribes.

There is a need for simple entry and exit procedures when running a small enterprise. Correct information should be easily obtained, and not harboured and controlled by bureaucrats. The policy issue at stake is to create a positive attitude and environment to assist rather than control and harass enterprises.

Availability of resources

Raw materials. Import and marketing policies directly affect access to raw materials by small enterprises. This is particularly noticeable when goods are distributed through state monopolies. Constraints introduced by import licensing often mean that small enterprises have to meet inflated prices by buying on the black market. One solution is to help develop strong small-business associations capable of bulk-buying for distribution to members.

Labour. Policies which encourage small enterprises can provide the advantage of absorbing labour at a lower cost than large-scale enterprises. Generally speaking, policies that subsidize capital do not encourage employment growth.

Equipment and supplies. Small enterprises need policies that provide reasonable access to improved technology if they are to be competitive and improve productivity. Policy measures which can assist include permitting the import of used equipment and facilitating the setting up of leasing companies to meet the problems of access to finance and credit. Some countries trying to develop a capacity to produce domestic equipment resort to protection measures, but these can foster inefficient and more costly local production. Large-scale firms may circumvent this by passing on costs to consumers through monopoly pricing. Small enterprises are unable to do so.

Finance. Small enterprises require a responsive financial system if they are to survive and grow. It is generally recognized that the smaller the business, the less likely it is to obtain credit from formal financial institutions. If subsidized credit policies are in vogue, the chances are that bank profitability will be affected which, in turn, will reduce the inclination to lend to small enterprises. Clearly, policy reforms would be in order in such instances.

The formal financial system is usually reluctant to lend to small enterprises because of their perceived high risk of failure at start-up. However, there are programmes which show that small loans can achieve high repayment and low default rates even with low-income clients. These are often community-based schemes employing mutual guarantees with low initial loans supplemented by subsequent loans linked to repayment performance. To introduce policies to support such approaches there is a need to propose a direct link between credit and savings schemes, and to provide them with a legal status to permit them to interact with formal financial institutions.

Infrastructure. Government efforts to support the private sector are generally through providing infrastructure. Public efforts to improve health, education, transport and access to energy not only promote small enterprises but also enhance the general competitiveness necessary for a growing and vibrant economy.

The consultant should assess to what extent existing policies negatively affect the small enterprise sector, and then suggest remedial action. In designing a strategy for small enterprise development, the consultant must consider the likely result of proposed reforms both in absolute terms and relative to their effects on large-scale enterprises, as well as constraints on the ability of small enterprises to respond.

The key questions revolve around opportunities for entrepreneurs, the supply of entrepreneurs, and the entrepreneurs' access to resources. Special concern must be paid to the interaction and complementarity of these key areas. The relative importance of these issues can be established by interviewing individual entrepreneurs and officers of their associations, suppliers of finance and credit, and agencies and institutions, both governmental and private, which assist and deal with the small enterprise sector. Policies should be closely looked at in terms of their internal content and how they are likely to be implemented.

Introducing policy reforms is not without risk. Any change must directly affect productivity until those involved learn to understand and benefit from the change. Time needs to be taken to sensitize, advise and assist entrepreneurs when new policies are introduced.

Subsidized small business consulting schemes

In some countries the policies for promoting small business development include subsidized consulting schemes. Variants of such schemes exist in countries as different as the Czech Republic, Germany, Singapore, the United

Kingdom or the United States. These schemes tend to exhibit certain common characteristics:

— the consultant's assistance is in certain priority areas such as business policy and planning, export development, job creation or quality improvement;

— the small-business client chooses (in some schemes) from a roster of consultants who have provided extensive information on their qualifications and experience, and have been approved by the agency responsible for the scheme;

— the client co-finances the project (say 40-60 per cent of the cost), and the total cost and/or the fee rate charged is within approved limits;

— the sponsoring agency has the right to review the work performed before authorizing payment.

Another form of subsidizing advisory, training and other professional services to small businesses is direct budgetary subsidies provided by governments and various development agencies to small business development institutions, such as the extension services mentioned above. These institutions are thus able to apply reduced fee rates and provide certain services (e.g. a first half-day for a quick assessment of the business and defining the need for a consultancy) free of charge.

18.6 Innovations in small business consulting

Subsidized professional services to small-business clients may be helpful in certain conditions and in less developed countries or regions. However, they provide no panacea. The small clients' needs for information and advice are tremendous and continue to grow because of the increasingly complex institutional setting and difficult business environment of most countries. Small-firm owners are unable to allocate sufficient time and resources to keep abreast of developments and take a detached critical look at their business from time to time. Conversely, many consultants and other advisers exhibit clear preference for larger business clients who have more money, can afford larger assignments and higher fees, and offer technically more interesting work opportunities (and references) to the consultants. Some consultants do not mind working for small clients, but they fail to appreciate the differences and treat them in the same way as large-business clients.

This justifies the need for innovative approaches to small-business clients. While all the principles discussed in the previous sections remain valid, consultants need to intensify their efforts to devise and apply formulas that will make their services fully understandable, easily accessible and attractive to large numbers of smaller clients. In short, small-business consulting must become more user-friendly and client centred. Let us mention some examples.

One-stop shop and integrated assistance

The so-called "one-stop" shops or counters enable small-business clients to obtain advice on various aspects of the business during one visit to an advisory or information service. This can include a wide variety of topics, information materials, help with filling in forms, preparatory work for credit requests, and so on.

In other cases, generalist business consultants can see to it that their clients receive comprehensive and complete advice from one firm rather than being directed to a number of different professionals. Thus, a consultancy can include a number of relatively small and inexpensive inputs concerning various aspects of the business, under the coordination of an all-round generalist. The client does not have to make separate searches for different specialists, sign several contracts, provide the same basic information many times and coordinate the work done. In turn, the consultant must ensure excellent selection of specialist inputs and a fair coverage of the issues at hand. It can be a good service to busy small-business clients if their consultant-generalist monitors various developments (taxation, export regulations, changes in social charges, new public markets and similar) likely to affect the business and takes the initiative to call and inform the client about such new developments, suggesting how his or her firm could help the client to react to these new opportunities or constraints.

Standard instruments and check-lists

Cheaper and more user-friendly consultancy services can be provided by combining the use of various standard self-diagnostic, business-planning and other instruments and check-lists with personalized advice introducing and supplementing the use of these instruments. If the procedure is simple enough and clearly described, a number of clients can, following a short briefing or even written instructions provided with the instruments, prepare the same data and undertake the same diagnostic or planning exercise. The consultant's personal intervention can then be limited to reviewing the results with the client and suggesting appropriate action to take. Standard instruments enable the use of junior and less costly consultants (and even business students), who would ask a more senior colleague for advice, or suggest that the client ask for such advice, only if this is warranted by the client's specific situation and needs.

"Hot-line" service

Either a private consulting firm or a public small-business development or extension service can establish a "hot-line" telephone service for entrepreneurs needing urgent information and advice. This can be a paying service on a subscription or ad hoc basis. It can also be a free (and toll-free) public service providing "emergency" help and suggesting how and where to ask for further assistance.

Working with groups of entrepreneurs

In group approaches to providing advice, more clients are served simultaneously and the cost per client is lower. In addition, the participants can learn from each other and develop useful contacts for the future. Various formulas of group approaches have therefore been used by trade and employers' associations, extension services, small-business development centres and individual private consultancies, in particular (but not only) in developing countries.

A group approach is applicable if the clients share some common problems and interests and if they are prepared to work together, which may require sharing some business information. If small firms from the same sector get together, they are likely to be competitors, although they clearly will have many common interests. If the clients are not from the same sector they still may have experience to share, e.g. on common business issues or processes and activities that exist in every business. And, as action learning, benchmarking and other approaches have demonstrated, a great deal can be learned also from entrepreneurs and managers working in seemingly completely different sectors.

Benchmarking (see also section 4.6). This technique is based on comparison of detailed and specific information on selected processes, services, and so on. This is followed by an analysis of the differences between firms and a deeper study of approaches that have helped the other participants to achieve better results. A consultant facilitating such an exercise can help to provide data for comparison, ask the right questions, make the participants aware of common issues, stimulate the discussion, help to identify best practice and introduce improvements.

Action-learning workshops (see also section 4.6 and appendix 8). Participants in these workshops get together in order to work collectively, and gain from other participants' experience, in solving problems faced by their organizations. As a rule, in the first phase the workshop focuses on problem identification and on designating those problems which are of interest to most participants and should be examined collectively. The problems selected are then analysed in greater depth by the whole group or its subgroups. Then the group comes up with one or more possible solutions. The groups could meet once a week and continue for some eight to 12 weeks. If the group's knowledge and experience are not enough, the group defines information and training requirements that are met by the consultant acting as facilitator or another expert invited for a special purpose.

Business clinics. This is an arrangement whereby a group of small-scale enterprise owners/managers meets to get advice and exchange experience on how to deal with the same or similar problems faced by all of them. It can be a one-off exercise (e.g. a one-day session) or a set of four to eight meetings similar to those run in action learning. A business clinic can be combined with interfirm comparison when the members of the group decide to compare their results and exchange experience. In other cases, a business clinic can be organized to deal collectively with problems previously identified by extension officers or other small-business advisers, or chosen by small-business owners themselves.

Self-help and solidarity groups. In several developing countries, such groups have been established by small-scale entrepreneurs with the support of technical assistance agencies, including voluntary non-governmental organizations. The groups are concerned with training, sharing experience and, in some cases, obtaining small-scale credit. A great deal of this work has been in the micro-enterprise sector — a topic to which the next chapter is devoted.

---

[1] J. Harvey-Jones: *Troubleshooter 2* (London, Penguin, 1992), p. 2.

CONSULTING FOR THE INFORMAL SECTOR

19

The previous chapter dealt with small business enterprises; but there is yet another group of businesses, which many people would not call businesses at all, but which are nevertheless in most countries a far more important source of employment and incomes, for far more people, than large or small formal businesses. These are the enterprises belonging to what is sometimes known loosely as the "informal sector", or "micro-enterprises"; that is, the vast numbers of very small-scale income-generating activities through which millions of people attempt to survive, particularly in the developing countries.

Nobody is unaware of these micro-enterprises, although we may not think of them as potential clients for management consulting. They are crowded along the pavements and in the slums of big cities, as well as in the official and the unofficial market-places. They provide a major source of income in rural areas, where many people own no land at all and for most people who do own land there is little to be gained by spending more labour hours on the tiny holdings that they call their own. They are vendors, tailors, snack-food processors, roadside cycle and car mechanics, blacksmiths, cobblers and almost everything else. Although they are often a nuisance to those of us who can afford to purchase what we need from more formal and more sophisticated sources, these micro-entrepreneurs provide essential goods and services at a place, time and price which are convenient for other poor people like themselves.

19.1 What is different about micro-enterprises?

The importance of informal sector entrepreneurs as employers and suppliers does not in itself necessarily mean that management consultants can help them in any way. It is important to recognize that they are a very different client group — if indeed they can be clients at all — from large or even small formal businesses, such as were dealt with in Chapter 18.

Heterogeneity of this target group

To provide guidance that is of any practical use, we have to acknowledge the heterogeneity of micro-enterprises and their needs for assistance. It is useful to see the difference between two major categories.

First of all, there are the very small home-based and informal enterprises, typically with one to three employees including the owner, using very basic skills and technology, with small assets, supplying a limited local market, and often having a limited life expectancy. In 99 per cent of cases they will never be in a position to consider using the routine services of private consulting firms, and paying a full charge for these services. They are businesses, however, and have to be managed. They can benefit from technical advice as can any other enterprises. Sound advice can help them to survive, adjust to changes in their environment, improve quality, product diversity and earnings, and even lay down foundations for growth.

The text that follows will focus on the specific needs of this category of the smallest and least sophisticated micro-enterprises (see box 19.1). As pointed out in the opening chapter of our book (section 1.1), management consulting is not only a separate professional service that can be purchased from independent firms on commercial terms, but also a method of providing advice and assistance aimed at improvements in management and business. This chapter will discuss mainly this second side of consulting. It will show that the consulting method can be applied by a wide range of organizations interested in assisting the informal sector, either separately, or in conjunction with other business transactions or social services (the term "embodied" consulting services has also been used). Consultants and other persons keen to render a socially useful and productive service to these entrepreneurs will have to combine technical know-how and aptitude with considerable social skills. In many cases they will have to engage in personal counselling (see sections 3.7 and 18.4) rather than strictly technical advice.

The second large category of micro-enterprises includes those that have already reached a higher level of sophistication and size than the previous group. Typically they would employ up to nine workers, use some motorized equipment within permanent premises, take part in subcontracting arrangements, and so on. The owners, especially the younger ones, may probably have acquired basic education in a local language and some formal technical training. They may still operate as informal-sector units, with all the advantages and constraints involved. This second group is in fact in several respects on the limits between the traditional informal sector and the "modern" small enterprise to which Chapter 18 was devoted. Many of them are about to "graduate" from the informal sector. Others feel that they should remain in this sector for various reasons. Consulting services for this category will exhibit some characteristics of assistance to the informal sector, but most methods and approaches to small-business consulting described in Chapter 18 will also be applicable. Depending on the assessment of the particular situational variables you will have to choose your genuine approach.

Box 19.1 A minicase of consulting in the informal sector

Laxmi is one of a large number of women in a village in northern India who earn their living embroidering the uppers of traditional slippers which are then sewn to the soles of the shoes, and sold both in the neighbouring community and in Delhi and elsewhere.

Laxmi buys the ready-cut uppers and the thread from a supplier in the village; if she has enough cash, she can choose from a number of different suppliers and then resell the embroidered part to one of several local businesses which assemble the complete slippers; if, as is more often the case, she has to buy on credit, she is restricted to one supplier and she must also sell the embroidered upper back to him; in this case, her earnings per day are about half the amount she can earn when she is free to pick her own suppliers and customers.

Laxmi's two younger sisters, and her invalid mother, provide some help in piercing the holes and other simple tasks; she does not pay them, or herself, any regular wage. Her brother drives a rickshaw in New Delhi and occasionally brings money home, and other members of the family sometimes earn a few rupees from casual work on neighbouring farms, while Laxmi makes up the necessary sums to feed and clothe the family as and when this is necessary.

A field worker from a local non-government organization which was trying to assist the leather workers in this community called on Laxmi one day. Laxmi had heard about this organization, and after some brief introductions she was therefore quite happy to tell the field worker all about her business. The field worker took careful notes on a simple pro forma which she had been trained to use by her employers, and she also looked carefully round the hut where Laxmi and her family lived, and asked a few questions about what she saw, including a fairly large pile of dusty but apparently completed embroidered uppers which were half hidden under a blanket in one corner.

After about one hour's discussion, the field worker felt able to advise Laxmi on what was clearly her main problem, namely her lack of working capital. She did not tell Laxmi what she should do, but led her through discussion herself to suggest that she should try to accumulate her own working capital by restricting her own drawings to a fixed limited amount every month. Laxmi saw that she could raise a small lump sum by disposing of the stock of finished components which she had unfortunately embroidered in a slightly outdated pattern; she agreed that it would not be difficult to find a shoemaker who would be willing to buy them, and that it would be better to to accept a lower price rather than to keep her money tied up in this way.

The field worker also told Laxmi about the savings and credit groups which her organization was helping the local people to establish; this would enable her to save more regularly, and perhaps eventually to borrow from the accumulated fund if the group so desired.

Laxmi was very happy with the discussion; when the field worker returned a month later she had disposed of the surplus stocks and had joined a savings group; she was not sure whether she could restrict and control her monthly drawings as they had agreed at their earlier meeting, but she was already making regular weekly savings of a small sum with the savings group.

Author: Malcolm Harper.

Some specific sectoral characteristics

We have seen that small businesses are usually managed by only one or two people, who have to deal with all the different functions that are entrusted to specialists in larger firms. In micro-enterprises there is no separate management function as such; the owner, who is usually the sole worker as well, is primarily a cobbler, a tailor or a vendor. She or he (and in most countries it is more likely to be "she") makes the same sort of decisions about prices, products, finance, and so on, as any other manager, but management is not conceived as a separate activity and decisions are made on an ad hoc basis as they become necessary.

The owners of formal small businesses are often criticized for not separating their business finances from their personal affairs, and consultants often have to help them to set up systems to enable them to do this. Because most micro-enterprises are a means of economic survival for the owners and their families, it is often impossible and it may be wrong to try to make the separation; the time and resources devoted to the enterprise, and the earnings from it, have to be related to the economics of the whole household. It may even be appropriate for the enterprise to operate only on a seasonal basis, since there are more profitable opportunities at some times of year. This is clearly very different from the situation of formal businesses.

Small businesses generally have little written data with which a consultant can undertake an analysis, but most micro-enterprises in the informal sector have no written records at all, except perhaps some note of amounts owed to them by customers who have bought on credit. Women in particular, who dominate the smallest end of the informal sector, are often illiterate; not only do they have no records of activities, and commercial and financial transactions, but they lack the basic knowledge to keep them or use them.

The people who own and work in these micro-enterprises also differ in other ways from the "entrepreneurs" who have established more formal businesses, in that very few of them are likely to have started their enterprises by choice. Most of them would prefer to have even a very modest job in a formal enterprise, or perhaps to work on the land; they are "micro-entrepreneurs" not by choice, but because there was no alternative. They are often people from the economic and possibly also the social margins of society, such as unemployed youth, refugees, migrants, widows or the disabled, for whom jobs in the formal business sector are not available, and this obviously has important implications for the ways in which they view the future of their enterprises.

Many of the skills needed for survival in the informal sector are very different from those required in larger enterprises, and they are certainly not the type of skills in which most management consultants are themselves experts. Successful micro-entrepreneurs are above all "street-wise": they have the right contacts, they know when and where the hand of the law is likely to fall and how it should be avoided, and they are masters — or mistresses — of improvisation. Those of us who are used to operating in a more structured and sheltered environment can probably learn a great deal from these people.

19.2 Management problems of informal sector entrepreneurs

Sub-optimal use of scarce resources

In spite of the many differences which have been outlined above, the owners of micro-enterprises do make many of the same mistakes as formal business managers, and they need similar advice. Shortage of finance is often their main constraint, and they may have to pay exorbitant rates of interest for loans, since banks and other formal financial institutions are not usually willing to lend money to people with no fixed business address, little or no formal education, and no tangible assets beyond a temporary stall, a push-cart or a few hand tools. It is therefore vital that they should deploy their funds in the optimal way, but they often fail to do this, and invest disproportionately in credit, in stocks or in other assets.

Similarly, raw materials are often an important constraint, yet many carpenters, tailors and others fail to calculate the profitability of each product. As a result, they use their scarce materials sub-optimally and produce a product mix which is less profitable than it could be. It is particularly important for an outsider to find out exactly why the business owners are behaving in this way, since there may be socio-cultural reasons which mean that apparently mistaken policies are in fact correct. Some petty traders, for instance, invest all their earnings in what appear to be excessive stocks, rather than saving money for new capital items which they admit they need; their reason, however, may be that they are all too aware that the members of their extended family will lay claim to any cash resources for personal expenses such as school fees, hospital charges or even food and clothing, but it is easier to retain money which is tied up in stocks.

Poor record-keeping

It is important not to assume that somebody who is not keeping records in the normally accepted way is not keeping them at all. Even illiterate business people usually have some system for recording sales on credit, and most people who work with money have some idea of what figures mean even if they cannot read or write words. Illiterate people are often able to remember far more information than those of us who are fortunate enough to have been taught to read and write, and some illiterate business owners have ingenious systems for controlling stocks and cash. Formal education is certainly not a necessary condition for business success at any scale; after all, there are quite a few illiterate millionaires in Europe and the United States, and even more in countries where illiteracy is more common.

The owners of informal enterprises can often benefit from keeping and using better recording systems. However, they have not had many years of formal education and usually find it very difficult to apply what they are taught in a classroom training course to the particular situation of their own business: new recording systems, and any other changes, must be designed to take account of the particular circumstances of each business and also the ability of the owner. This means that on-site individual consultancy, although it is more expensive per client than classroom training, is also more suitable for the owners of micro-enterprises.

19.3 The special skills of micro-enterprise consultants

Consultants who are used to working from written records, however inadequate, find it difficult to work with illiterate clients, and the lack of any documents that even resemble formal accounts may compound the social difficulties which consultants may have in dealing with people who have no offices and even no fixed premises. The consultant may have to meet the client in his or her shanty home in a slum, in a noisy temporary workshop or even squatting on the ground in a public market-place, where discussions are constantly interrupted by customers, the client's children or a crowd of curious onlookers whose presence severely inhibits the client's willingness to share personal financial information.

Eliciting information

It is quite possible to elicit usable financial information, even from completely illiterate business owners. But it is not easy, and the consultant must be able to avoid any form of accounting jargon and to put together a financial picture of the enterprise from information which may be obtained in a quite different sequence from that to which he or she is accustomed. It is usually necessary to cross-check information such as daily or monthly sales figures by asking for the same information in different ways. A village baker may have only a very approximate idea of the total figure of his monthly sales, but he is more likely to know how many bags of flour he uses each month, and how many loaves of bread he makes from each bag, or how many loaves he sells each day, and at what price.

A successful micro-enterprise consultant must be able to elicit, collate and analyse information on the spot, and then assemble the information into a form which shows where the money in the business came from and how it is being used, as well as giving a rough idea of the income and the costs over a period, which may be a day, a week, a month or a season, depending on the nature of the business and on the way its owner runs it. This is of course an approximate balance sheet and profit and loss account. Yet this form of analysis is as useful for a micro-enterprise as it is for a larger business, and the consultant may find that the owner's skill in managing his or her very small capital compares favourably with the management of resources in larger and more generously funded businesses.

The consultant must also use his other senses. A roadside carpenter may state that he has no stock of partly finished goods, but a dusty pile of pieces of chairs under a work-bench will show that this is not the case, or a trader who says that she never gives credit may be observed to sell a bag of flour to a customer without any cash changing hands. Micro-business people do not usually deliberately deceive people who are trying to help them, but mistakes of this sort occur because of failure to communicate. The consultant must also use his sense of touch and even his sense of smell; a finger will show up the coating of dust which reveals redundant inventory, and a smell can show up a fruit vendor's poor stock rotation methods. Simple cleanliness and good order can often make all the difference to the sales levels of a micro-enterprise, and the most immediate advice might be to sweep the floor and tidy up the stocks; these are humble suggestions, but are often relevant in far larger businesses as well.

Respect for existing business practices

Micro-enterprise consultants have to develop a special sense of respect and understanding for their clients. When a consultant observes what appears to be unintelligent business behaviour, he must ask himself what he would do in the same circumstances, with the same pressures and constraints; he may conclude that the business owner is actually coping well with very difficult circumstances. Some market traders, for instance, turn their stock over once or even twice a day, and vendors such as the people who sell newspapers and other items to car drivers waiting at traffic lights display remarkable marketing skills in their choice of potential customers and their decisions when to cut off a potential sale because the traffic is about to move and there will be no time to collect the money. Sales representatives who work in a more formal environment can learn a great deal from this form of marketing "in the raw".

Providing information

The owners of micro-enterprises are often unaware of their rights and obligations under the law, and this can be particularly important when the regulatory environment is being rapidly liberalized. Local officials may not know, or may not want to know, about old rules that have been relaxed or new rights that have been extended, and consultants can provide a vital window on the world.

Technology is also changing rapidly, and this can bring new opportunities, such as new materials to be recycled, new intermediary or maintenance services to be provided and new markets to be addressed.

Governments, at the local and national level, have traditionally been hostile to informal sector business, but this too is changing, and new sources of finance, new training opportunities, new more secure locations and new market opportunities are being made available. People working in the informal sector frequently lack the time, the facilities and the skills to obtain information about favourable changes of this sort, and it is often more difficult to disseminate information about changes in regulations than it is to make the changes themselves. Outside advisers can act as valuable intermediaries in communication of this sort.

19.4 Outreach to micro-enterprises in the informal sector

There are, therefore, many ways in which consultants with appropriate attitudes and skills can be of very significant value to micro-businesses. It is by no means easy to acquire these attitudes and skills, and the consultant may have to "unlearn" a great deal of what he or she knows before being able to work effectively with micro-enterprises. The major problem, however, is the tiny scale of each individual enterprise and the vast numbers involved. How can a consultant possibly reach out to more than a minute fraction of the people who could benefit from his or her services, and how can the costs be brought to a level which is commensurate with the likely benefits?

Approaches described in the previous chapter (section 18.6) are of interest, but here are some more ideas.

Picking winners

One approach is to concentrate only on the rather small number of micro-business people who are real "micro-entrepreneurs", with the apparent potential to "graduate" soon from the informal level and to develop their businesses into prosperous formal enterprises. It is far from easy to identify these potential winners. Furthermore, the transition to formality may not always be in the interests either of the owner or of the employees, since it involves costs such as registration fees and taxation which may not be covered by the benefits arising from improved access to formal resources. Nevertheless, many of the world's large business corporations started in an informal way, and some of today's micro-enterprises will be tomorrow's big businesses: management consultancy may help a few more of them to achieve this.

There are numerous tests for measuring entrepreneurial potential, but their effectiveness is limited with people of little education; therefore the best way to select high-potential individuals is to force them to select themselves. Many agencies offer advisory services free of charge to micro-enterprises, on the assumption that they cannot afford to pay. They may indeed be unable to cover the full cost, but the best way of ensuring that clients are serious, and that they believe that they can benefit from consultancy, is to make a charge which is significant for them. If they are not willing to make a sacrifice in order to obtain a service, the error lies not with them but with the marketing or the quality of the service; this applies as much to management consultancy as to any other product.

Lower-cost consultants

Another approach to overcoming the problem of the cost of consultancy in relation to the scale of the individual enterprises is to employ less qualified and thus less expensive consultants. Although micro-enterprise consultancy is not easy, it is possible to train people with no specialist qualifications, and no more than three or four years of secondary education, to provide an effective and useful micro-enterprise advisory service. They need regular close support and supervision, and the organization and management of such a service is more akin to an extension service than to normal management consultancy, but such services can be cost-effective.

Micro-enterprise consulting can also provide a very useful form of training for the consultants themselves. People who are learning how to provide management advice to larger formal businesses can benefit enormously from being exposed to the informal sector and trying to advise the owners of micro-enterprises. They will probably benefit far more than their clients. Indeed, as long as they are closely supervised in order to avoid making errors and giving wrong advice, management and business administration students from colleges, universities and business schools can be effective micro-enterprise consultants. Anyone who is running management courses should seriously consider introducing such consultancy as a component of the course.

Working through groups

Yet another approach is working with groups, as already discussed in Chapter 18. Not only can this reduce the costs but, more importantly, many serious problems faced by people working in the informal sector can only be solved if they get together. Consultants can help them to see the benefits of sharing experience and undertaking joint action, and advise their elected leaders on the effective management of their joint activities. For example, municipal authorities are often reluctant to allocate space for micro-enterprises, and the police and other government services may harass micro-business people unnecessarily in order to extort bribes; an individual can do little to prevent this, but if business owners come together and present a common front they can often achieve a great deal. Consultants can help with appropriate contacts and advise on strategies and techniques.

In other cases, micro-enterprises can benefit enormously from coming together not only to assert their rights but also to perform functions such as selling their products, purchasing raw materials or arranging for specialized processing, which require special skills or are not economical for a single unit to perform on its own. Micro-entrepreneurs find it difficult to initiate and organize such common activities, whether or not they are officially registered as cooperatives, because such activities are so much larger and more complex than micro-enterprises themselves. Management consultants can provide valuable technical assistance in this area. They can also help to dissipate prejudices concerning cooperative organizations, which in many countries have gained a bad reputation due to their misuse for political purposes and incompetent management.

Consulting for group activities of this sort is difficult. It is often tempting for the consultant to cease to be an adviser and to become effectively the manager of an enterprise or a grouping. The owners of the group themselves may allow or even encourage an outside adviser to do this, because their main interest is in the operation of their own micro-enterprises. The result may be that the consultant finds himself in the position of a full-time manager rather than an adviser, and the group becomes wholly dependent on the continued presence of their adviser. While this is a danger in any consulting relationship, it is particularly great in the case of group enterprises, where none of the members really "owns" the undertaking in a personal way. Such enterprises are like the proverbial village donkey: everybody feels that it is somebody else's responsibility to take care of it, and as a result nobody does.

Groups of small entrepreneurs can be informal and ad hoc, and may exist as long as the group members perceive the need to get together to discuss and resolve a common issue, or to obtain a service that no one could afford individually. More formal groupings include associations of various types and degrees of formality, as well as cooperatives.

Management consultants working with groups of entrepreneurs or co-operatives must be sensitive to the variety of interests involved, in addition to avoiding the creation of dependence. It is also tempting for an outsider to advise, persuade or even compel the owners of micro-enterprises to form groups because it appears to be in their interests. Many group enterprises have a short existence because they have come together not on the members' own initiative but because somebody else (whose livelihood did not depend on the group's success) thought that this would be the right approach.

An effective management consultancy for a cooperative or other group of micro-enterprises will indirectly help the individual members by improving their access to credit, their marketing, their raw material supply or whatever other function the group organization performs on their behalf. This does not in itself improve the management of the individual micro-enterprises. It is possible, however, to reach the individual members through their group: training workshops can be organized for such members as wish to attend, and the group's managers can require members to maintain a certain standard of quality control or other improvements as a condition of doing business with them.

This must obviously be done very carefully, since the group's managers are ultimately responsible to the members who employ them, but group pressure can be a very effective way of motivating micro-entrepreneurs to do what is in their own interest. The more successful members of a group are often very willing to act as informal management consultants to their fellow-members, in order to improve the standards and thus the earnings of the group as a whole. An effective management consultant must be able to mobilize this multiplier effect, by simplifying techniques for making diagnoses and recommendations and teaching them to the opinion leaders; the messages may seem elementary to an experienced consultant, but the communication task must be very subtly managed.

Alternative channels

Full-time management consultancy for individual micro-enterprises is not usually an economic proposition (see box 19.2, overleaf), but there are other routes through which they can be reached. Many organizations are in regular contact with micro-enterprises: manufacturers and distributors of fast-moving consumer goods such as cigarettes, sweets, contraceptives and razor blades often depend on informal vendors for a large proportion of their sales, while other manufacturers sell large quantities of supplies such as welding gas, vehicle spare parts or food ingredients to micro-enterprises. Such firms will sell more of their products if their informal outlets are better managed. Sales representatives who are in contact with micro-enterprises can help both their own employers and their customers if they are able to provide simple business and management advice in addition to selling their products.

Some banks too have started to realize that micro-enterprises can be valuable customers for financial services, both as depositors and borrowers. These banks may employ field agents to collect savings and loan repayments, who can also improve their customers' ability to save more and repay more reliably, by providing basic management and business advice along with financial services. Municipal inspectors have traditionally harassed micro-enterprises, but local authorities tend to appreciate more and more that informal-sector business activities provide both employment and important local services to the public. It is easier for inspectors to enforce health, safety or location regulations if they are able to offer management advice while carrying out their primary responsibilities.

Voluntary organizations working with the poor used primarily to provide welfare services such as elementary education and basic health care, but many of them are now starting to help people to increase their incomes through self-help and entrepreneurship. Community development staff and social workers are turning into bankers and consultants to micro-enterprises; they too offer an indirect route through which a specialist consultant can reach the owners of micro-enterprises.

"Indirect" management and business consulting through organizations such as the above is clearly very different from direct selling of business advice. A management consultant may be asked to advise and assist such organizations in their work with micro-enterprises, and to train their field workers in consulting and counselling skills. In other cases, it may be appropriate to suggest involvement of this kind to a larger client company as a way of increasing the effectiveness of field representatives, or possibly as part of the client's efforts to contribute to social development and enhance its image in the community. In these cases, the management consultant will have to assess the weaknesses and needs of the micro-enterprises with which his or her client is involved, and then suggest and demonstrate simple techniques for providing on-site management advice which can easily be taught to non-specialists.

In conclusion, it should be clear from the above that management consulting for micro-enterprises is very different from consulting for larger and even

---

Box 19.2 Private consulting services for micro-enterprises

A Philippine consulting group, established a number of years ago by ten professionals with various sorts of expertise, has chosen to work for the micro-enterprise sector in addition to serving formally established and registered businesses, government agencies and social organizations. Each member of the group works individually as a consultant on his or her own projects, but they also work together whenever required by the size and complexity of the assignment. Thus, direct consulting to micro-enterprises represents only a part of the group's activities.

The group carries out consulting for enterprises employing three to nine workers, which in the Philippines are micro-enterprises according to the official government definition. These enterprises are involved in a wide range of activities, including leather products (shoe production and repair, bags), wooden furniture, food processing (e.g. fruit preservation), processing of by-products from animal hides and skins, metal-working, etc. The micro-entrepreneurs serviced by the group often include members of the local community and personal friends.

The micro-entrepreneurs are visited by members of the group and also come to the consultants' offices when they need help. The types of services provided include: management and technical training; assistance in bookkeeping; preparation of loan applications for banks; feasibility studies; assistance in establishing market linkages and in organizing participation in marketing events (e.g. exhibits, fairs); advice on types of products and quality control; advice on policies and regulations; and referral to other sources of information and assistance. These services are provided to micro-entrepreneurs either directly, or indirectly through subcontracts to government agencies and non-governmental organizations (NGOs).

Services are provided on a short-term basis or over longer periods of time, but written contracts between the consultants and the entrepreneurs are seldom used. Rather, services are based on verbal agreements between people who trust each other.

The micro-entrepreneurs pay fees for these services either in cash or in kind (e.g. goods produced by the micro-enterprise). Advance payments are sometimes made, but more generally the members of the consulting group are paid after the services have been rendered. In many cases, payments are made on the basis of results achieved rather than on the actual cost of services.

The fees applied are a function of the services rendered, actual costs incurred (e.g. travel costs, time devoted to the assignment), and the size of the enterprise. Fees range from as little as a few hundred pesos (less than US$10) to a few thousand pesos (US$100 or more). This level of fees represents a fraction of the revenues of the group, which must seek larger consultancy contracts from government agencies, NGOs and multi-bilateral donors.

Author: Moïse Allal.

---

smaller businesses in the formal sector, both in the nature of the work itself and in the channels through which it may be necessary to reach the clients. A consultant must never fall into the trap of believing that such work is so simple that it is easy to do or beneath his or her attention, or not worth doing at all. Even though the management techniques that are needed may be very simple, the tasks of diagnosis and communication are difficult. The task is even more complex when the consultant has to attempt to reach micro-entrepreneurs indirectly, through field agents such as sales representatives or social workers who may have little or no management knowledge and perhaps misgivings about business in general.

The task is, however, well worth attempting. The number of people working in micro-enterprises is vast and their problems are often so serious as to affect the very survival of themselves and their families. For people as poor as most micro-enterprise operators, even a modest increase in income can significantly improve their whole livelihood: there are few areas where management and business consulting can have such a significant impact on the welfare of so many people.

CONSULTING FOR THE PUBLIC SECTOR

20

In this chapter, we use the term "public sector" in its broadest sense to include all levels of government: federal, provincial or state, regional and local; state-owned enterprises; public utilities; and institutions, such as hospitals and universities, supported by public funds.

The market for management consulting services in the public sector is large and challenging. In the United Kingdom, public sector consulting amounts to some 30 per cent of the domestic consulting market. The respective figures are 30-40 per cent for Canada, 40 per cent for the Netherlands and 70 per cent for Turkey. These figures may surprise many readers. Yet, on account of the current changes and new challenges, in many countries the demand for public sector consulting is likely to remain stable or even increase in the future.

Earlier, when management consulting was first introduced to public sector management, assignments tended to be general in nature. In recent years a number of factors have changed this pattern of demand. Government programmes are becoming more complex. There is a need to improve the productivity of government services in the face of shrinking budgets and the steadily increasing demand for public services. At the same time, advancements in information technology are facilitating the re-design and re-engineering of government programmes and administration. As a result, the nature of management consulting services required by this market is changing and becoming more specialized and more complex.

By and large, public sector purchases of management consulting services can be broadly classified into the following categories:

— strategy and policy advice;
— assistance in designing, developing and managing programmes/operations, and/or increasing their efficiency;
— assistance in designing and developing organizational structures and systems;
— training, development and individual counselling;
— opinion surveys.

The "strategy and policy advice" type of management consulting work is generally related to the identification of societal or administrative problems facing the public sector. These services are generally bought by the top echelon of public sector managers and politicians, looking to clarify options and to determine an optimum direction in a highly complex environment. This market is small, and is generally limited to consultants with publicly recognized experience in this area.

Far more frequent are requests for management consulting assistance in designing, developing and managing programmes and operations. These requests may be made by public managers, in reaction to an evaluation or audit, or may be triggered by consultant marketing.

The machinery of public sector organizations requires adjustment from time to time. These adjustments usually focus on organizational structures, processes, and supporting systems such as finance, procurement and human resource management. Concerns to increase productivity and use new information technology to the full have greatly intensified the pressures for public sector managers to restructure in this way.

Public sector managers often seek assistance in facilitating change processes in their organizations. Whether the change is to the structure of organization, and how it does things, or to supporting systems, the professional management of the change process itself is critical to the success of the organization. Consulting support in establishing continuous learning, total quality and performance management processes can provide the framework for the change process. With the reduction of in-house services, public sector organizations are increasingly retaining consultants to provide training and counselling services to their staff. Training will frequently be in the management and communication skills for new organizational processes, as well as in standard management and technical areas.

Increasingly, opinion surveys are used to gauge reactions from stakeholders to proposed government initiatives.

Some management consultants are aware of the special characteristics and requirements of work for public administration, services and enterprises. However, many new entrants are either overawed by the significant differences between public and private sector consultancy, or underestimate these differences to their detriment.

In this chapter, we explore the changing nature of the public sector market, the particular characteristics of the public environment, the more common types of service provided by consultants and the process of serving this market. We also briefly reflect on future perspectives.

20.1 Current trends and challenges

The role of government in modern society is pervasive. Not only do governments provide a vast array of services and regulate the services we consume, but they also provide the legislative framework for governance.

Government can achieve its objectives in many ways: produce and deliver a service itself; make direct payments to individuals and businesses; set up a government-owned commercial enterprise; provide direct grants or low-interest financing loan guarantees; offer tax incentives to individuals and businesses; and regulate the activities of individuals and organizations, both commercial and non-commercial.

In most countries government provides some or all the following services: health care; social services (social security and social welfare programmes); education; national security (police, defence); environmental protection; communication and postal services; agricultural support; tax collection; international development; capital expenditures for infrastructure; promotion of tourism; statistical services; libraries and archives; foreign affairs; immigration, employment and training services; housing and banking services, and many more. In addition, government must provide many internal services such as accounting, payroll, purchasing, personnel administration, training, auditing, inspection, and so on.

The total outlays of government attain 30-50 per cent of gross domestic product (GDP) in most Western industrialized countries, while in some developing countries the public sector can represent an even higher proportion of GDP. Governments also provide a relatively high percentage of total national employment.

The provision of consulting services to the public sector must inevitably respond to the sector's challenges and problems. In turn, these challenges and problems derive from the national, social and economic context and, in large measure, the policies of the government of the day. It is important to realize that governments turn to consultants because the challenges they face are new and complex, and the right responses are very difficult to find in the absence of precedents, accumulated experience, and resources for adequate analytical and conceptual work . In addition, governments are constantly exposed to criticism, which may or may not be justified. Comparisons with the private sector are frequently made, hence the growing interest in evaluating and using private sector experience to enhance effectiveness and efficiency in the public sector.

An exhaustive list of challenges facing the public sector in most countries would be very long indeed. An illustrative list given in box 20.1 (overleaf) shows the great variety of economic, social and administrative issues in which governments may need the help of management and other consultants. Below we discuss four selected issues that have had quite a considerable impact on the use of consulting services: rising government deficits, information and communication technologies, the issue of unemployment and growing democratization of social life.

Rising budget deficits

In most Western economies in recent years, government revenues have been lower than government expenditures, resulting in budget deficits. This has

415

Box 20.1 Challenges facing public sector decision-makers

Any of the 41 issues and trends listed in this box (and their various combinations) may be the reason for turning to a consultant. And the reader can certainly think of others.

Rising budget deficits; domestic and foreign debt
Exploding costs of health services
Inadequate social services
Problems of housing and the homeless
Growing poverty
Growing unemployment (especially long-term unemployment)
Deteriorating quality of education
Ageing physical infrastructure
Congested transport networks
Deteriorating physical environment, pollution
Depletion of natural resources (deforestation, etc.)
Toxic and nuclear waste
Population explosion
Insufficient consumer protection
Criminality (including organized crime)
Growing use of narcotics
Brain drain
Inefficiencies in public services
Red tape
Low pay and lack of motivation
Corruption
Need to reform and/or modernize the civil service
Problems of minorities and migrant workers
Political and economic refugees
Revival of nationalism
Need to decentralize
Need to balance regional development
Development of international legislation
Transfer of decision authority to supranational groupings
Market and price liberalization
Need to attract and protect investors
Privatization
Structural adjustment
Need to improve public enterprise performance
Growing power of multinational firms
Demilitarization and conversion of military industries
Rapidly changing information and communication technologies
Need to show results and satisfy voters
Criticism by general public
Criticism by political opposition
Need to match public administration with advancing democracy

---

increased government debt, internal and external, and interest charges for servicing this debt. This increasing cumulative debt situation has caused concern among economists, politicians and business leaders.

The efforts to reduce budget deficits can focus on either the expenditure or the income side. Increasingly, governments in all parts of the world are looking for services and activities that can be cut without undermining national security and provoking heavy criticism by political opposition and the general public. Often governments cut services that are politically vulnerable, which "is similar to someone cutting off a few fingers and toes instead of going on a diet to lose weight".[1] Instead of merely cutting budgets, governments have to look for ways of increasing public service productivity and efficiency, which may include major service restructuring and re-engineering. Increasing government income by raising taxes and tariffs is difficult owing to undesirable economic and social effects. Therefore governments have to look for new profitable service areas and new sources of income.

Information and communication technologies

Information technologies strongly influence both production and service processes and the organization of work. Distance is becoming irrelevant as far as information flows are concerned: thus different partners and team members can work synchronously at different places. Time can be controlled and shifted to a more convenient point: thus people working at different times can use store-and-forward and common databases as memories and as a way to shift time. Finally, all those in an organization or a network can contribute to organizational memory and to providing information in a form which is available to everyone.

The combined impact of these advances on government services and processes is profound: it concerns specific processes, information bases and flows, linkages among services and organizations, and organizational structures. The opportunities for practical application of new, faster, more reliable and ever cheaper information technologies in public services and administration are at least as significant as in business organizations (see Chapter 17).

The unemployment problem

Whatever its causes, unemployment has become a most serious national problem in many countries. No government by itself can be held responsible for the current level of unemployment and all measures needed to alleviate unemployment. However, governments are the main force that can lead and coordinate national efforts, both private and public, in combating unemployment. This calls for a vast array of measures and programmes to assist and retrain the unemployed, to generate and promote employment, and to increase public sector productivity in ways that do not aggravate the unemployment problem.

Governments are faced with a dilemma — either managing the increasing unemployment that is the corollary of competitive productivity, or governing an uncompetitive economy.

Increasing democratization

Even in traditionally democratic countries there is scope for further demo-cratization, for example by decentralizing decision-making powers and responsibilities, and bringing the management of public affairs closer to the people concerned. In formerly centrally planned and totalitarian countries, the current trend towards democracy and a market economy results in considerably more than large-scale restructuring of government services and machinery: the very nature of government is changing, with all the implications concerning policies, roles, attitudes, behaviour, competencies and motivations.

20.2 Programme responses

In this public sector context a number of innovative management responses are emerging. Three of them will be briefly reviewed below: privatization, the re-engineering of processes, and organizational restructuring.

Privatization

Worldwide, privatization emerged in the 1980s as a radical programme response aimed at reversing trends that had literally run out of control, such as the branching out of governments into many new areas previously in the private domain, and the continuation and proliferation of state-owned enterprises irrespective of failing efforts to make them more performance-oriented in the highly politicized public context. The underlying rationale of privatization efforts has been (1) that the private sector should do what it can do better, and more effectively, in the interest of the whole nation, and (2) that governments do not become stronger and more useful by running an endless number of different services and activities, but by focusing on policies, regulations, controls and services that only a government can develop and maintain on behalf of the community.

The transfer of public enterprise assets from governments to private owners has been the main form of privatization. Indeed, many people view it as synonymous with privatization. Yet there are other ways and areas of privatization. It has to be stressed, too, that privatization of ownership in the legal sense is not enough: it is much more important to create an environment which is competitive and where the market forces can play their role (see Chapter 21 for privatization approaches and techniques).

Process re-engineering

In service tasks it is important to ask the question: Why are we performing a task and what results can be expected of it? A lot of unproductive work is done when we concentrate on tasks without looking at the entire process of which the task is a component. A good example is the task of accounts payable, which is part of the process of procurement of goods. By concentrating on the task of accounts payable, we have made the task cumbersome and created several labour-intensive operations (like matching procurement orders to the receipt of goods in inventory), which must be coordinated to achieve results. Recent advances in information technology enable organizations to develop new ways of doing things which are far more efficient and less labour-intensive, and which reduce the time needed to achieve results. Using information technology to re-engineer administration and other processes has become an important strategy to improve the productivity of public sector organizations.[2]

Organizational restructuring

In the recent past, governments in Canada, Sweden and the United Kingdom, and other countries, have restructured their public sector organizations with the following objectives, among others:

- to clarify the accountability of ministers and departments by giving them more authority in functional areas;

- to separate policy-making from programme delivery activities;

- to promote innovations and risk-taking by relaxing some public service constraints on managers;

- to make organizations more efficient by improving human resource management;

- to undertake projects to pilot new work options such as teleworking.

These initiatives have resulted in some major restructuring of public sector organizations, an example of which is the creation of special operating agencies for the delivery of certain government programmes.

These agencies are given a stable policy environment, and full responsibility for the delivery of an operational programme. Special operating agencies are given a clearly defined mission, mandate and budget, and are required to operate in an efficient manner using many private sector practices. They are separate from the policy development functions of the parent department but operate within a clearly defined objective through a "memorandum of understanding". They are given wide exemptions from the constraints of the public service in matters of budgets, retaining operational surpluses from year to year, and in personnel and other policies.

Other structural changes involve decreasing the number of management levels by eliminating middle management positions, and making adjustments to budgetary processes by eliminating distinctions between salary and operating budgets. There are also numerous initiatives to improve people management by introducing modern management thinking related to quality and customer service, empowerment, training and learning, working in task force environments, and so on.

Reinventing government

David Osborne and Ted Gaebler have expressed concisely what many other scholars and practitioners have believed — government needs to be reinvented.[3] There can be no prosperous and democratic society without a strong and effective government. The issue is not private sector and private management against the public sector and government, but synergy between both sectors, each one playing those roles it can play better in the interest of the whole community and providing those services it can provide more effectively. Criticizing governments has become fashionable but sterile. What is needed are constructive and workable proposals — the government ought to be reinvented. Osborne and Gaebler suggest ten broad principles, or directions, that underscore how public organizations can structure themselves and move from centralization to decentralization, from monopolies to competition, from bureaucratic mechanisms to market mechanisms, and from funding inputs to funding outcomes or results (box 20.2).

Box 20.2 Reinventing government

The ten principles:

1. Catalytic government: Steering rather than rowing
2. Community-owned government: Empowering rather than serving
3. Competitive government: Injecting competition into service delivery
4. Mission-driven government: Transforming rule-driven organizations
5. Results-oriented government: Funding outcomes, not inputs
6. Customer-driven government: Meeting the needs of the customer, not the bureaucracy
7. Enterprising government: Earning rather than spending
8. Anticipatory government: Prevention rather than cure
9. Decentralized government: From hierarchy to participation and teamwork
10. Market-oriented government: Leveraging change through the market

Source: D. Osborne and T. Gaebler: *Reinventing government: How the entrepreneurial spirit is transforming the public sector* (New York, Plume, 1993).

20.3 The public sector environment

Most of the consulting work in the public sector is in special fields and requires specialized knowledge and know-how. At the same time, the work and the consulting needs of all governmental and public agencies share certain common characteristics, reflecting their public nature. Some of the characteristics will be reviewed in this section.

Public sector decision-making

Public sector decision-making is the process which produces a response by a government or government agency to a societal or an administrative issue.

Societal issues are those social or economic problems or opportunities which require collective action by society, generally through a government programme or agency. Government programmes — be they services produced or arranged by the government, regulatory programmes or economic grants to individuals or businesses — all require careful planning and organization.

Administrative issues are problems or opportunities related to the machinery of government. A government is a large administrative system, organized to provide different types of service or to deliver regulatory programmes. As with any large administrative system, it must develop organizational structure, policies and procedures. It must also operate a multitude of administrative services. These administrative services may or may not affect the public at large, but their quality and productivity strongly influence the efficiency and image of the whole public sector.

Figure 20.1 (overleaf) illustrates the (simplified) process by which government responds to societal and administrative issues and adopts a particular programme. The process is initiated when issues arise in society or in the machinery of government. Public sector decision-making usually comprises four major steps, in each of which there can be a demand for management consulting assistance.

To understand the nature of the issue, data gathering is required (step 1). The nature of many public issues means that the issue is frequently complex and data collection is extensive. Data collection may be from secondary sources or may require the gathering of primary data by survey or other means. It is particularly important to understand the scope of the issue being examined and the decision elements that the data collected will have to illuminate. These factors condition the extent, depth and nature of the data gathering, providing parameters that are essential to the effectiveness of this activity.

Collected data are then analysed (step 2) to develop different strategies for a programme. Once again this analysis may be relatively simple or of great complexity depending on the nature of the issue.

Consultation with stakeholders (step 3) is not unique to public decision-making, but it is of unusual importance in the government sector. Invariably societal issues and some administrative issues affect a great many people in different ways. Clearly identifying and consulting stakeholders, both internal to government and in society, can be essential to the weighing of alternatives and the eventual success of a programme. Because of the politicized nature of the decision-making process, this input may be a prerequisite to the selection of an alternative.

Figure 20.1 The public sector decision-making process

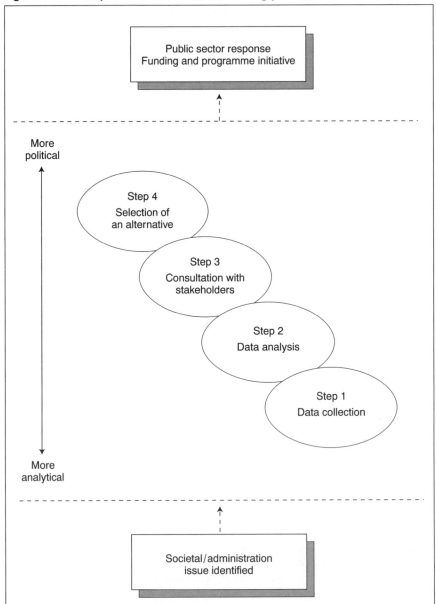

Once the three preceding steps have been completed, an alternative is selected (step 4) from which to develop a programme. This selection process is heavily influenced by the opinions of all stakeholders, not least of which may be the government of the day, the public at large, special interest groups, and the body of public servants. While good data collection, analysis and consultation can greatly facilitate decision-making, decisions themselves are strongly value based and, unlike most private sector decisions, must respond to many conflicting interests and criteria.

Once a decision has been made, it must be translated into a carefully designed programme, implemented and subsequently evaluated. This evaluation may lead to adjustments to the programme through redesign. A specific initiative may not involve all the steps of the process as described, but generally a significant initiative must go through the entire process. As shown in figure 20.1, the process becomes more political as we advance through the stages of decision-making.

The role of politics

Key decision-making processes in the public sector are political processes even if the issues concerned are highly technical. Minor administrative decisions, seemingly without any political implication and significance, may also involve political criteria and can become politicized under certain circumstances. Top and senior administrators may well emphasize their independence and non-political approach to decisions; but politics are omnipresent and the power of political parties and their coalitions shapes public sector decision-making through senior personnel appointments, reorganizations, budget increases and cuts, changes in legislation, decisions taken by the council of ministers, and more or less direct personal interventions by politicians.

Two opposite tendencies can be observed in the decision-making practices of various governments.

On the one hand, in searching for efficiency and improved performance, many governments are stressing the relative independence of their agencies responsible for particular economic services and activities. Such an approach has been increasingly applied in public utilities and enterprises.

On the other hand, there has been a tendency to politicize the civil service and increase the number of public sector appointments made on political criteria first of all (or in addition to technical criteria). Thus, an agency's independence and responsibility for cost recovery may be enhanced, but top management has been selected, and will be judged, by criteria established by the leading political party or coalition.

Social objectives

A key requirement of political decision-making is the balancing of economic and social objectives in developing and implementing public programmes, and using consultants in their support. Social objectives may include the development of specific regions, the promotion of small business firms, job creation and services for minority groups, equitable distribution of contracts and purchases, and so on.

Box 20.3 The consultant-client relationship in support of decision-making

Issue		Private sector	Public sector
1.	Identification of client	Clear or nearly clear	Difficult
2.	Nature of client	Single person or small group	Many persons or groups
3.	Client objectives	Relatively clear boundaries and targets	Multidimensional and complex; irregular boundaries
4.	Methodology	Important, but often less so than results	Very important, especially consultation and facilitation
5.	Constraints	Relatively few, known	Many, difficult to define
6.	Accountability for decision	Personal, small group	Collective, large group
7.	Decision-making	Based on objective commercial criteria	Political, value based
8.	Documentation/ report	Not always important	Very important; a public document
9.	Results	Generally measurable	Often not measurable
10.	Evaluation	Informal	Formal and complex
11.	Implementation	Almost immediate	Uncertain; depends on political will, resource allocation, etc.

Consulting support

These factors give a different dimension to the consultant-client relationship, some elements of which are summarized in box 20.3.

The complex public sector issues and client-consultant relationships give rise to fairly complex consulting projects. By way of example, a consultant intervention in the area of rail safety regulations is described in box 20.4.

Box 20.4 Minicase: Rail safety regulations in Canada

In Canada, there are several railway companies in both the private and public sectors. These companies are under the regulatory jurisdiction of a government body. The Canadian Government undertook an examination of its transport safety programmes. The primary issue was: Are the existing regulations and programmes adequate to ensure public safety? There was public concern about the level of safety on the Canadian railway system arising out of a series of derailments.

The consultants had to address many social, economic and administrative issues. These included:

1. What is an acceptable level of safety? How do you define it and measure it?
2. What are the economic implications of government regulatory programmes? What are the costs and benefits? Who should pay for these programmes?
3. What should be contained in a National Rail Safety Programme?
4. Are government programmes properly designed, well organized and adequately staffed?
5. What should be the proper allocation of funds among different regulatory programmes such as inspection and accident investigation?
6. What is the public perception of the regulatory safety programmes?

The consultant's work involved: a statistical analysis of accident data to measure trends; studying each of the many safety programmes, with evaluation and re-design where necessary; consulting with the railways on their preventive maintenance and other safety programmes; consulting with interest groups (e.g. unions and special-interest groups) to understand their concerns; conceptualizing methodological approaches to the regulation of the safety practices of commercial corporations: defining the role of government in managing safety on Canada's railways; developing a National Rail Safety Programme; designing safety programmes for the regulatory authority; developing an organizational structure, staffing levels, classification of employees, budgets for different programmes, etc.

Thirteen different reports were issued by the consultants. All were made public. The National Rail Safety Programme was reviewed by the railways, interest groups, the appropriate subcommittee of Parliament and others, and approved by the Minister of Transport. It was very difficult to define the boundaries of the project, and issues such as "What is an acceptable level of safety?" were intractable and difficult to study methodologically. Within the regulatory authority, accountability was diffused.

In summary, this project demonstrates the typical characteristics of a public sector consulting project.

Public procurement processes

The selection and procurement of consultants, as indeed of other goods and services, falls under the area of public procurement, and has to comply with criteria and rules applied to public procurement at large. A general description of consultant selection is given in Chapter 7 and Appendix 1. What, then, is typical of the public sector?

Invariably, the use of formal, precisely defined procedures prevails. There is likely to be an official document, issued by a government agency, which describes the procedure and criteria of consultant selection and provides additional information and guidelines, contract forms and the like.

The reasons for the use of formal procedures in the public sector can be summarized as follows:

- to give all eligible candidates the same chance;
- to increase the probability of identification and choice of the most suitable consultant;
- to make selection "transparent" and less prone to criticism, and to reduce the risks of favouritism, nepotism and corruption;
- to harmonize the approaches used and transfer good experience among various government departments and public agencies;
- to improve the overall quality of consultant selection and appointment in a complex public sector environment.[4]

Data banks. Many public sector organizations maintain a data bank in which consultants can register. These data banks are huge and may have thousands of consultants and consulting firms on file, registered by skill areas. In some cases, registration with the relevant data bank is a prerequisite to receiving requests for proposal or being eligible to supply services.

Competitive bids. Depending on the size of a proposed consulting assignment, competitive bids are requested from consulting firms or individual consultants. Bid documents must generally conform to detailed specifications: failure to respect these specifications leads to the disqualification of the bidder. The evaluation procedures of these bids are also generally adjusted to the size of the proposed assignment: the criteria, and often the results, are generally available to the bidder.

Budgetary constraints. There may be a strict budgetary constraint limiting the size of the assignment, or predetermining its time schedule.

Managerial discretion. Despite the predominance of formal procedures, public sector procurement of consulting is not totally inflexible. As a rule, small assignments may be arranged by direct selection. In certain cases, the appointment of consultants who have done a satisfactory job may be authorized for further services related to the previous job. Otherwise, preselection and short-listing are applied, which ensures that all eligible candidates possess the necessary qualifications.

Internal consulting groups

In marketing services to the public sector, management consultants must also be aware of the frequent presence of internal consulting groups within public sector organizations (see also section 2.5). While the number of these groups has been decreasing, they exist in many countries. Some of them provide consulting services to government clients without fee, while others charge fees (as a rule subsidized) for their services. The range of service provided varies significantly: some groups provide only limited services such as personnel and audit, while others provide a very wide range of services.

The procedures for public sector managers purchasing the services of internal consulting groups are different and generally simpler than those that apply to private sector purchases. Most internal consulting groups complement their own resources by hiring consultants on subcontract from the private sector, and can therefore be valuable clients for private sector consultants. Some internal consulting groups also manage other consultants on behalf of an agency and provide information to government on competitive consulting rates. On the rare occasion that an internal consulting group is on a full revenue dependency regime (i.e. self-financing), it can provide a yardstick for reasonable per diem rates for consultant hiring by government.

20.4 Success factors for consulting to the public sector

The worst error a consultant can make in entering the public sector is to believe that solid private sector experience provides all the answers. Indeed, drawing from private sector management know-how is one of the principal current ways of improving public management. However, experienced observers of the public sector environment are well aware of the differences in complexity, driving and impeding forces, time horizons, resource constraints, hierarchical relations, individual motivations and other factors that make public sector processes and organizations significantly different from private ones.

Developing a niche

Very few consulting firms are capable of providing the full range of services the public sector consumes. Consultants therefore need to choose their niche and position themselves as experts in their area. There are several ways to define a niche:

— by territorial criteria;

— by level of government (federal, provincial or state, local, government agencies);

— by sector (health, education);

— by functional specialization (IT, statistics, finance);

— by methodological specialization (issue identification, facilitation of meetings, change management, surveys); or

— by various combinations of these criteria.

To compete within the chosen niche, consultants should develop a competitive strategy based on a product-based differentiation from other firms. A clearly communicable focus for the firm is essential to public sector consulting success.

Understanding the public sector environment

One of the most critical and time-consuming factors in building a successful public sector consulting practice is to gain a thorough grasp of the target public sector environment. This requires a deep understanding of internal and external issues facing public sector organizations, in other words all those factors discussed in this chapter. It is the interplay of these issues, coupled with government policies, that defines the risk and reward framework for public sector managers and dictates the consulting needs of the day.

Most, if not all, public sector problems are embedded in larger social, economic, political or administrative issues. It is very important to understand thoroughly the nature of the problem and its full complexity. The problem presented is often deceptively simple, and it is sometimes necessary to build problem definition (with the various stakeholders) into the consulting process. Inadequate problem definition and an insensitive approach to environmental issues can lead to an unmanageable assignment, especially in its later stages.

Empathy for the client

It is important to develop a relationship of trust and an understanding of the client as a person. Many public managers are competent and dedicated people trapped in systems that do not encourage high performance, make changes difficult, and require special skills and approaches to get anything improved. The consultant must not only understand why certain things are possible and others not, but must sympathize with the client and develop a true partnership in working on solutions that the client can accept as his own and defend with his superiors. A negative and unduly critical attitude to public sector managers is counterproductive and inhibits effective problem solutions.

Marketing efficiently

Most marketing to the public sector (development of leads and identification of consulting projects) is through networking and personal contacts. A good network can only be developed over the course of time and requires constant effort to maintain. It will ensure direct selection (in a limited number of cases) or the consultant's preselection and short-listing (more frequently). Most large assignments in the public sector are awarded on the basis of competitive bids; the success ratio of firms bidding competitively varies but is not very high, while preparing these proposals is both expensive and time-consuming. Consultants are therefore well advised to develop an efficient process to bid competitively and maximize their chances for repeat business, which is altogether less expensive to obtain than is new business. It is useful to develop a proportion of business in sole-source, directly awarded contracts: these mandates are generally small, but they are relatively inexpensive to obtain and permit consultants to build up and maintain good client contacts.

Emphasizing consultation: Seeking pragmatic solutions

Many experienced consultants will remark that in the public sector, "people" and "process" problems prevail over "technical" problems. It is important to adopt a process approach which includes full consultation and communication with all stakeholders. Consultants can be excessively idealistic or tempted to recommend theoretically the best solutions. While there is academic satisfaction in finding a "best" solution, what matters most is finding solutions that are practical, acceptable and stand a good chance of being implemented. A recommendation that leads to real change is worth any number of elegant reports that will languish on the shelf and gather dust.

Full consultation will ensure that conclusions and recommendations do not surprise stakeholders, although it is in the nature of societal problems that all stakeholders can seldom be equally satisfied with a recommendation.

Applying the right mix of resources

A public sector problem is generally multidimensional. The consulting team, therefore, should include the right mix of resources. Frequently, three types of resources are necessary:

- "technical" (to provide methodological support);
- "process" (to guide consultation and communication); and
- "experience" (those who know the sector well, can think like the managers in it and can substitute for the abysmal corporate memories of most public sector organizations).

Consulting team leadership can be chosen based on the primary needs of the project.

Managing assignments

As with all consulting, public sector assignments must be managed for quality, scheduling and budget. Perhaps the greatest risk with public sector work lies in under-budgeting, inadequately forecasting the amount of time necessary for working with stakeholders and for the decision process in general. There are no short cuts to the process of consultation with stakeholders, and neglecting this process can have painful consequences. Another characteristic of most public sector assignments is the need to produce well-edited reports: these documents are, or can usually be, made public and are therefore worthy of care and time in their production.

Pricing the services

The pricing of services is important in marketing consulting to public sector organizations. Requests for proposals generally ask for very detailed information on pricing, including the per diem rates of individual consultants on projects and the allocation of time by individual consultants to tasks. Often maximum or set per diem rates are established by regulations, and frequently these are below market rates in the private sector (see Chapter 26).

Building an image

It takes effort to build a successful practice in public sector management consulting. A good firm develops a team which is capable of providing quality services on demand and builds a track record of providing excellent customer service and durable solutions to problems. Through successful assignments a firm develops a reputation and builds its image in the minds of its clientele. A firm cannot service clients well unless it allocates at least a small part of its revenues to research. This research should produce key information on public sector issues, and the new products and ideas which are essential for the continuous development of a consulting firm. Research also ensures the involvement of staff with current issues facing target public sector organizations, keeping their learning current in the process. Publishing the results of research can provide an excellent marketing vehicle for the consulting firm, as well as reinforcing its image. A firm should also aim to communicate its successful project experience through articles and public speaking engagements.

Box 20.5 "Shoulds" and "should nots" in consulting to government

"Shoulds" that work

1. Show knowledge of the agency's methods, procedures and processes.
2. Demonstrate genuine interest in the public sector work environment and the difficulties faced by public servants.
3. Learn the specialized jargon.
4. Understand how the agency is measured.
5. Treat each government employee as an individual, separate from governmental stereotypes.
6. Match your own staff qualifications closely to the agency's requirements.
7. Recognize that decisions often take longer than in business.
8. Respect the fiscal year constraint.
9. Identify and meet the client's perception of a good job.

"Should nots" that don't work

1. Refrain from hard-sell approach.
2. Avoid designing projects requiring a great deal of interdepartmental co-operation.
3. Don't just finish a project but "ease into the completion", suggesting review steps and follow-up activities.
4. Don't forget to keep the client fully informed and closely involved, even if the client tries to avoid responsibility.
5. Don't underestimate the role of the written agreement, especially with deliverables.

Source: W.P. Cordeiro and S.A. Bartik: "How to consult to government", in *Journal of Management Consulting* (Milwaukee, Wisconsin), Fall 1993, pp. 20-24.

20.5 Special areas of consulting

Local government

Many consulting firms confine their marketing activities to higher levels of government (federal, provincial or state), thereby missing a large-volume market at the local level. Local government can generally provide consultants with an opportunity to address problems related to urban planning, criminal justice, social services, infrastructure planning and development, and local business development. In the 1990s every level of government is finding difficulty in funding its programmes, but nowhere is the result more evident to the private citizen than in the field of municipal government. It is this lower level of government, beset by a multitude of difficulties, that provides opportunities for experimentation of new ideas.

Public enterprises and utilities

In the public enterprise sector of the 1990s, most opportunities for consulting are created by the governments' decisions to privatize, as discussed in section 20.1 and Chapter 21. However, management consultants should not overlook enterprises and utilities that will stay in the public sector, or whose privatization has been postponed for strategic, social, political, national security or any other reasons.

In this area, private-sector experience is more applicable and useful than anywhere else in the public sector. However, the governments must be prepared to start managing public enterprises and utilities as real enterprises, not as any other segments of the government and public services. This may require considerable restructuring, performance improvement and management development programmes, effective business linkages with the private sector, and performance-related motivation and remuneration. Demonopolization, deregulation and the phasing out of direct subsidies are essential — it has been pointed out that demonopolization and the creation of a competitive environment have a greater impact on performance and efficiency than privatization.

The public sector in developing countries

Considerable opportunities exist for management consultants of all nations to provide services to the public sectors of developing countries. Some of the specific opportunities in these countries include:

- **Improving the performance of public enterprises.** Public enterprises were once revered in these countries, but are now often denigrated as having failed to live up to expectations, to be adequately productive and to deliver the required economic performance. Some argue that the root cause of this poor economic performance lies in state ownership. In many cases this is true and privatization is a viable strategy, although massive privatization cannot be achieved overnight. There are obvious consulting opportunities in the privatization process, as already discussed. There is also strong demand to improve the management of the remaining enterprises and utilities which are generally large and centralized, and possess poorly defined accountabilities, with large overheads and excessive controls.

- **Improving the performance of governments.** Developing countries habitually have poorly organized machinery of government. There is a general lack of decentralization from federal, to state, to local governments. Planning is centralized and not enough diversity is permitted even where obviously required. Public services, such as health, education and criminal justice, are not efficiently delivered. There is a multiplicity of institutions, but innovation is systematically discouraged and the institutions are not properly managed. Entrepreneurship and individual initiative are stifled by strict adherence to obsolete policies and procedures.

- **Developing the volunteer and not-for-profit sector.** This sector is decaying in the face of religious and regional conflicts, lack of resources and general neglect. Yet it can play a major role in economic and social development if its organization and management can be improved.

- **Building internal consulting groups.** Several countries are making energetic and extensive efforts to improve their public sectors (very large, important organizations for energy generation, health, education, regional public transport, etc.) and have selected the route of providing internal management consulting groups to a growing number of public services.

To supply services successfully to the public sector of developing countries, management consultants must obviously develop strategies that are likely to work. Such strategies might include:

- adopting a long-term, and not a short-term, focus. There are no short cuts to acceptance in developing countries;

- being adaptive, not prescriptive. Only at a high level of generalization are management techniques universal. They must be carefully adapted to local cultures and management situations;

- being a coach and trainer — not a referee or judge;

- adopting an action-learning approach to training, coupled with the solving of specific practical problems faced by the public agencies;

- visibly developing a deep understanding of local culture and a respect for the people.

While there is an abundance of educated and knowledgeable people in developing countries, most have had no opportunity to apply their knowledge to the solution of practical management problems. Organizations have tended to stifle innovation by discouraging experimentation and change. Training offers only a partial solution, since knowledge of methods and techniques is not lacking. Very often, solutions to these problems lie in creating a favourable atmosphere and commitment to change, and illustrating how different, more flexible ways of managing can yield dividends: a bona fide consulting role.

Public management in Central and Eastern Europe

On their path to a market economy and political democracy, Central and Eastern European countries cannot avoid a radical turn-round of their public administration and service systems. The extent and depth of the changes required are unprecedented. The issue is not only government restructuring and reshuffling to cater for new functions and responsibilities, but a totally different conception of fundamental government functions in the development of modern society. There is a need for a radical departure from the command economy philosophy, procedures and work habits, to facilitating and regulating roles and to the public service concepts proper to a market economy and a democratic society. Structural and procedural changes will be important. Changes in skills, attitudes and behaviour will be critical.

The role of both foreign and local consultants in this process can be tremendous. Foreign consultants can assist in transferring public management experience of democratic countries using various forms of government. They can also help to promote collaborative and participatory approaches to problem-solving and structural changes, and to reform the education and training of public servants. However, only consultants with excellent knowledge of public management in their own and other democratic countries should be involved. Local consultants should help to adjust foreign experience to local traditions, as well as assisting in identifying attitudes and habits that were inherited from the totalitarian State and will have to be unlearned. In addition, active involvement in the transformation of public management provides exceptional learning opportunities for local management consultants, both external and internal.

20.6 Future perspectives

The current privatization movement and the demands for leaner government will free the public sector from activities and services for which the private sector is better suited, or which can be discontinued without any harm to the community. Conversely, there will be greater demand and stronger pressure for services that only governments can perform effectively. The increasingly complex interface of economic and social life, and the growing number of issues in which the community is vitally interested, will call for new governmental functions and services, and for continuous improvements in service quality and productivity.

Hence, while the public sector has already become a major user of management consulting services, it is not unrealistic to predict that it will be a growth market for consultants in the years to come. Although entry can sometimes be difficult, and the requirements for consultant competence and service quality are likely to grow, there is great potential for new business, and for a considerable amount of repeat business. The quality of work, reliability, level of service to the client and good relationships with the client will be particularly important. Clients will seek consultants whose profiles match special process and/or sector criteria and who can exhibit a record of proven performance in serving the public sector. Public decision-makers will be keen to obtain "value for money" as much as their peers in the private sector are.

The market will continue to be complex and difficult, but challenging and rewarding. Working for public sector clients should not be regarded as an occasional opportunity to gain additional income, but as a strategic option to be reflected in the consulting firm's competency, relations and image building.

---

[1] D. Osborne: "Reinventing government", in *Public Productivity and Management Review* (San Francisco), Vol. XVI, No. 4, Summer 1993, p. 350.

[2] See M. Hammer and J. Champy: *Re-engineering the corporation* (New York, Harper Business, 1993), and Chs. 4 and 22 in this book.

[3] D. Osborne and T. Gaebler: *Reinventing government: How the entrepreneurial spirit is transforming the public sector* (New York, Plume, 1993).

[4] M. Kubr: *How to select and use consultants: A client's guide*, Management Development Series No. 31 (Geneva, ILO, 1993), pp. 99-100.

CONSULTING IN PRIVATIZATION

21

The demand for technical, financial and legal advice on privatization — a systematic transfer of state-owned companies and assets and state-run activities to the private sector — constitutes an important consulting market. It started in the United Kingdom and rapidly spread to more than 50 countries, which now have active privatization programmes.

In their transition to a market-driven economy, Central and Eastern European countries use massive privatization as their main strategy. In the developing world, many governments that formerly paid lip service to the importance of the private sector have been adopting wholesale privatization. Among the developed countries in the West, too, countries such as France, Italy or Sweden are turning to privatization for reasons such as budgetary constraints and increasing public opposition to heavy government subsidies. The biggest privatization effort in one country so far has been achieved in Germany, where in the four years following reunification the *Treuhandanstalt* (the privatization agency) sold more than 13,000 state-owned enterprises in eastern Germany to the private sector.

The purpose of this chapter is to focus on the special problems of consulting in the area of privatization, such as the market for privatization advice, management consultants' interaction with other professional services, and their special tasks in privatization projects.

21.1 The principal clients

The main clients are the governments as owners of companies and property to be privatized. To achieve privatization, most ministries and other governmental institutions rely to a considerable extent on external expertise. This offers widespread opportunities for professional advisers to seek and obtain contracts for servicing governments on accounting and legal affairs, privatization procedures, enterprise restructuring, sectoral and feasibility studies, management and staff training, and the creation of an effective market-economy infrastructure.

The aims of a government, once it has opted for privatization, include:

- increasing the size and dynamism of the private sector;
- attracting and facilitating private-sector investment from both national and foreign sources;
- generating revenues for the State;
- freeing public resources for urgently required investment in infrastructure and social programmes;
- reducing the government's administrative burden; and
- achieving a radical transformation from a state-controlled and centrally planned economy to a market-driven economy (the former communist bloc countries).

The ministry most interested in privatization is generally the ministry of finance since it has to provide the funds for supporting the enterprises and will also manage the distribution of the revenues of the privatization. The relevant sector or branch ministry might also be interested in divesting itself of a whole sector or a number of companies. On the other hand, a sector ministry might sometimes try to hamper the privatization of companies since, after a completed privatization process, the ministry's importance as a "holding ministry" diminishes, officials may be made redundant and the ministry might even be abolished. To avoid this bottleneck, in some countries governments have preferred to dismantle certain sector ministries before launching privatization programmes.

In a number of countries, the key customers for consulting advice are the ministry for privatization, the privatization agency or the state property agency, which are responsible by law for implementing privatization, even though they are not always the direct owners of the enterprises. This might lead to conflicts with the sector ministry formally owning and technically supervising the enterprises if it has other or different priorities and views concerning the approach to privatization.

In many cases, the consultant is retained by the management of a public enterprise that is preparing itself for privatization. There can be various situations and scenarios. The enterprise may seek help in developing a technical, legal and financial restructuring programme to be presented to the privatization ministry in a privatization project. Enterprise management may want to tap a consultant's expertise to be sure that all important alternatives were given due consideration and the proposed privatization project will not be rejected because of poor preparation and quality. Furthermore, there may be a need for an independent expert opinion, to attest that the privatization proposals are correct and fair. The consultant's task may be to give such an opinion to the agency that will be responsible for approving the privatization project.

Privatization can in some cases lead to the closure of non-viable companies previously kept alive by government subsidies and protection. The management of the company, and in most of these cases also the unions representing the workers, may want to demonstrate that privatization is misguided. Being aware of the difficulties, the management of the enterprise will try to avoid or postpone any move by the government towards privatization. The consultant in these cases should assist the government in explaining to the public that a closure of a loss-making firm can free assets for a more productive use and reduce a financial burden on the economy and the taxpayers.

To convince management and employees that their enterprise has no future may be more difficult, especially if they are not aware of the real situation on international markets and have an unrealistically high opinion of their firm's potential for technical and efficiency improvements. The consultant may have to undertake this delicate and often painful task even if he or she has been recruited by the enterprise itself, not by a sector or privatization ministry.

Many consultants are recruited by potential buyers looking for interesting acquisitions of former public companies or their parts. A consultant in this case will help the client to maximize the benefits from a takeover through effective preparation and advice on the purchase from the government.

21.2 Profiles of privatization advisers

Many governments, international institutions and enterprises tend to choose management consultants as principal advisers for privatization. However, a lot of work in the area of privatization has been done by accountants, investment bankers or lawyers (see also section 2.6), although their competence covers only certain aspects of privatization.

Accounting firms have been very active in developing business in the privatization field because they can fulfil the first need of governments or enterprises — a good set of accounts and an independent financial audit of an enterprise to be privatized. However, the standard accounting schemes and procedures limit them to thinking in financial and accounting terms. Therefore the large international accounting firms, including those of the "Big Six" group and others, handle privatization projects through multidisciplinary teams, drawn from both their accounting/auditing and their management and business consulting services divisions.

Investment bankers also offer services in privatization and have been involved in many important privatization projects. They are limited by definition to giving advice and providing services in the areas of financial engineering, sources of finance, banking services and short- or long-term lending. If a company is to be privatized by an initial public offering on a stock exchange or via a private placement, the assistance of one or more investment bankers may be essential on account of their experience in capital markets and their capability to trade the stock of the privatized company on a stock exchange in order to smooth the fluctuations of the stock price. Conversely, an investment bank may be short of information and expertise needed for company valuation, and may lack the necessary industry-sector knowledge and understanding. In particular, investment banks specializing in mergers and acquisitions tend to concentrate on the financial transaction side of privatization deals.

A number of *law firms* have also entered the market as privatization advisers, but tend to concentrate their work on the regulatory environment, corporate governance, laws and rules affecting the company or its privatization, and the legal aspects of various contracts and agreements involved. Since law firms generally do not employ professionals with a financial and business management and strategy background, they tend to concentrate on advising governments on legislation, and the sellers and buyers on legal documentation.

The management consultant has none of the above specialized roles since he or she takes a comprehensive and multidisciplinary view of the sector and the company, which covers the whole spectrum of issues involved in a privatization. This sector-specific approach means assessing the company from an industrial investor's point of view rather than an accounting or legal perspective. Management consultants engaging in privatization projects should have a solid sectoral background and a track record showing that they are able to solve practical diagnostic, structural and strategic problems of companies.

The industry-sector approach reaches beyond the company's technical assessment and its survival chances. It also includes a pragmatic valuation of the enterprise which will — beyond the financial statements and cash flow analysis — assess other items such as technology, product quality, attractiveness to investors, technical, business and marketing know-how, the skill level of the workforce and so on. In addition, positive multiplier effects of a privatization project on the economy ought to be taken into consideration, i.e. the number of jobs and investments created directly and indirectly in the country. This industrial approach is common to the leading management consulting firms most active in privatization. It permits the assessment of a company's privatization chances and attractiveness to investors, and the development of an individualized strategy to be followed in its privatization.

As mentioned earlier (section 2.6), the borders between various professional firms tend to be increasingly blurred, and therefore the description given above may not apply to every single firm. Nevertheless, management consulting firms with a good background in sector studies, business diagnosis, corporate strategy and restructuring are well placed to take the lead in advising clients on important privatization projects. They can help clients to identify and involve on effective terms specialized advisers able to handle legal, financial, environmental and other aspects of particular projects.

21.3 Selection of consultants and contracts

In choosing consultants for privatization projects, both government and enterprise clients tend to apply rigorously the complete selection procedure described in Chapter 7.[1] There are several reasons for this:

- companies to be privatized are public property;
- the clients want to be sure that they cannot be accused of corruption, nepotism or incompetence;

- political parties, the parliament, the media and the public at large watch the privatization process in the country very closely;
- there is a desire to obtain consulting advice for a fair price;
- many assignments are financed by technical assistance from donor agencies, which insist on a precisely defined selection procedure, and control its application.

Rosters and registration

In several countries ministries responsible for privatization have established their own consultant rosters, based on information provided by interested consulting firms and individual consultants. The quality of these rosters has improved recently as both the ministries and the consultants have acquired more practical experience with privatization projects. It has become possible to start giving consideration to the consulting firms' privatization experience in general, and in particular countries and sectors, their ability to staff complex assignments and implement them rapidly, and their ethical behaviour, especially as regards loyalty to clients and avoidance of any conflict of interest. Some privatization agencies have gone beyond simple recording of eligible and interested candidates and require consultant registration. Candidates who submit prescribed documentation for registration are screened and in some cases interviewed by a committee, which then decides whether the consultant can be registered as expert in privatization.

Selection by client

In privatization projects, the consultants have to be aware of the differences between the various sorts of client described in Chapter 3. The privatization agency may be the contract client, while the main client's role may be split between this agency and the management of the enterprise to be privatized. This relationship may change in the course of the project, depending on the client's real participation in project work. If a technical assistance agency sponsors the project, which is often the case in Central and Eastern Europe and in the developing countries, it would normally act as a sponsoring client and retain the authority to approve the procedure, the conditions of the contract and possibly even the consultant who will be selected. The selection procedure may involve complex and lengthy negotiations among the various interested parties involved.

Administration

In handling projects for governments and international institutions, consultants are generally required to prepare and maintain documents and records pertaining to the procurement process and the administration of contracts following their award. The administration of the financing and/or awarding institution will monitor the project and reports. If the financing agency finds that the procurement or administration of a contract has not been carried out by the consultant in accordance with the agreed contract, it may refuse to finance the contract or its part.

21.4 The consultant's tasks in a typical privatization process

Pre-privatization studies

In preparing for privatization, some governments and large public corporations have commissioned in-depth sectoral studies. The purpose is to give a true picture of a whole sector (such as textiles, home electronics or steel), its strengths and weaknesses, position and chances in international competition, attraction to foreign investors, environmental considerations, investment requirements and future development prospects after privatization. Such studies have been found useful in orienting and planning privatization, and providing governments with basic information that was unavailable, incomplete or distorted under central planning. These studies require consultants with a broad industry-sector background, capable of finding and analysing data on technology and sectoral trends, consumption, international and national markets, impact on the environment, major customers and suppliers, government policies, regional economic groupings and similar.

Privatization policies and plans

Some governments, as a rule sponsored by technical assistance projects and grants, use consultants to assist privatization ministries in designing and planning the whole privatization process in a country and choosing among alternative privatization approaches (box 21.1, pages 442-443). This is a case for high-level policy advice, for which very few management consultancies have the right background and experience. As a rule, there is a need to establish mixed teams grouping advisers from various firms and professions, including management and business consultants, bankers, accountants, lawyers, economists and others. Since the privatization ministries suffer from acute shortages of competent staff and recruiting new staff locally is often difficult owing to low government salaries and for other reasons, there may be a tendency to use the privatization advisers (both local and foreign) for normal government work. The consultant will be well advised to be most cautious in accepting various operational responsibilities, which may be outside the original contract terms.

However, most consulting assignments in privatization concern individual privatization projects, involving one or several state enterprises that have been earmarked for privatization. In a typical assignment, the consultant would successively undertake the following tasks.

Technical and strategic assessment

After a kick-off meeting with the concerned ministry or state agency (i.e. the seller), where the engaged consultant and the seller will agree on schedules, exchange of information and task distribution, the consultant will visit the company to be privatized, discuss with management the situation, prospects and problems of the company and make a quick survey of the business premises. The consultant will then make a detailed inspection of the company and collect, together with a technology specialist, all necessary data for a technical assessment. These data would cover:

- products and services;
- licences and technical know-how (marketability, competitive situation);
- technical layout and condition of business premises (buildings, machines, technologies, processes, logistics);
- productivity, management and human resources:
  - existing organization and management structure;
  - qualification, skills, experience and know-how of management and workforce, including statistical data on the workforce (age structure, turnover, etc.);
  - productivity of the company's various units in the value-adding chain;
  - necessary improvements and investments;
  - attitudes to privatization and expectations of management and workforce.

Parallel to the technical assessment, an evaluation of the strategic and financial situation of the company will take place. It will cover especially issues such as:

- the strengths and weaknesses of the company in its present operating environment (markets, customer base, competitive situation, market share);
- the threats and opportunities for the future privatized enterprise and the company's ability to cope with these influences (market forces, competition);
- actions which may be required to secure the company's position in the local and/or international market (establishment of long-term contracts, restructuring necessities, foreign marketing networks, etc.);
- the financial performance (cash flow, profitability, current financial structure, working capital, liquidity, quality of receivables and other assets, the company's ability to finance itself with its own resources).

Owing to the generally extensive vertical and horizontal integration of many public-sector companies, especially in Central and Eastern Europe, companies often have to be split up to become manageable and attractive to investors. This has the advantage of:

- higher specialization of the smaller units to be privatized;
- a larger number of investors from different sectors for the various segments of the split-up company;
- higher purchase prices for the various units compared to the sale of the company as a whole.

Box 21.1 Taxonomy of privatization strategies

Many different terms are used to describe privatization, much like the blind men describing an elephant based on each one touching different parts of the animal. Semantic confusion is evident. Privatization is a broad concept which goes beyond the selling of state-owned enterprises and other assets held by government to individual private investors. Government activities or state-owned enterprises can be privatized by three broad strategies: divestment, delegation or displacement. The first two are more active processes, while the last is more passive. In current privatization practice these strategies come in various combinations.

I. DIVESTMENT

A. Sale
1. Private sale
2. Sale of shares to the public
3. Sale to management
4. Sale to employees
5. Sale to users or customers

B. Free transfer
1. To employees
2. To users or customers
3. To the public
4. To prior owner (restitution)

C. Liquidation

II. DELEGATION

A. Contract

B. Franchise

— concession
— lease

C. Grant

D. Voucher

E. Mandate

III. DISPLACEMENT

A. Default

B. Withdrawal

C. Deregulation

I. DIVESTMENT

I.A Divestment by sale

1. The enterprise or its part can be sold to one or several buyers (local or foreign). The sale can be negotiated, or the enterprise or its part can be auctioned.
2. Shares can be issued and offered to the public.
3. Managers can buy the enterprise or its part.
4. Employees (and pensioners) can buy the enterprise or its part.
5. Local users (organized in a users' cooperative) can buy the enterprise or its part.

I.B Divestment by free transfer

1. The enterprise can be given away to employees free of charge.
2. The enterprise or public service can be given away to users or customers organized in a cooperative or an association.
3. Free transfer to the public is an important transfer method in Central and Eastern Europe, where it is usually carried on by issuing free vouchers, or

vouchers sold for a nominal price, far below the expected value of the assets for which they can be exchanged.

4. Restitution to former owners or their heirs can concern assets that were nationalized; this may be combined with selling (at an advantageous price) assets that were added to the enterprise after nationalization.

I.C Divestment by liquidation

The enterprise is closed down and the remaining assets (buildings, equipment, raw materials, etc.) are sold in one of the ways indicated under I.A.

II. DELEGATION

II.A Delegation by contract

A government activity is restructured by contracting with a private organization, paid to perform the work. Contracting only a portion of the work can foster competition.

II.B Delegation by franchise

Under a franchise (also called a concession), government awards a private organization the right (which may be exclusive) to sell a service or product to the public. One form of franchise concerns the use of the public domain (airwaves, streets, underground space, etc.). The second form is a lease of government-owned property to a commercial enterprise.

II.C Delegation by grant

A private entity receives government subsidies for performing its task(s).

II.D Delegation by voucher

Instead of subsidizing producers of goods and services, the government issues vouchers to eligible recipients of formerly state-run services (for food, housing, health, child care, etc.).

II.E Delegation by mandate

A government mandate obliges private organizations to provide certain services at their expense (e.g. social security).

III. DISPLACEMENT

III.A Displacement by default

The private sector steps in to offer a better service than the government (e.g. private education, postal service, local transport).

III.B Displacement by withdrawal

The government deliberately discontinues a service or shuts down an enterprise.

III.C Displacement by deregulation

A government monopoly or restrictive regulations are abolished, thus opening the market to private initiatives.

Source: E. S. Savas: *Structural adjustment and public service productivity* (Geneva, ILO, 1992; mimeographed).

The consultant with his or her industrial know-how will analyse the company and as a first step suggest a horizontal separation which includes the recommendation of the sale of non-essentials via various asset deals to different investors. As a second step the company may be separated into core business units, and after this vertical separation individual parts of the value-adding chain of a company's units can be privatized separately in different asset deals. However, this splitting up in most cases will make valuation more complicated and can be time-consuming.

For any consultant, the most important focus of strategic and technical assessment must be the viability, future competitive advantage and development prospects of the company after privatization. Therefore splitting up industrial concerns into smaller and more easily manageable units must not be regarded as a panacea. There have been instances of public enterprises that have been split into several smaller units in a way that has weakened their marketing, research and business development potential for future years.

Valuation

Valuation plays a basic and vital role in the privatization process. Governments, their agencies, prospective buyers, future joint venture partners, management interested in buying out a company and also previous owners seeking restitution of business property — all have an interest in assessing the value of an enterprise to set a market price.

A consultant encounters a broad range of problems in conducting a valuation (see also section 13.4). In Central and Eastern Europe and in developing countries the valuation theories and methods must be essentially the same as those used to value a Western enterprise operating in a normally structured market economy. However, creativity in their application is often a requirement.

Assumptions about future domestic and international economic trends (i.e. interest rates, exchange rates, inflation) and a rapidly changing market, as well as the legal and financial environment, must be dealt with. Social assets and recreational facilities owned by companies must be properly accounted for in the valuation. In some companies historical financial records do not exist or are limited only to one or two previous years. In order to facilitate the valuation, the financial statements in most cases must be converted to a Western accounting standard.

The valuation of land and property tends to be particularly difficult. The level of market information available is low and rental levels might be volatile, making valuations at best problematic. Other problems include dealing with technologically obsolete equipment in the realization that past operations under government ownership will most probably not resemble future operations. In certain countries, too, existing valuation laws impose on the consultant a ceiling on the level of the discount rate that can be used in a discounted cash flow analysis. The discount factor is important if cash-flow models are used since it is the main indicator of the country and the sector risk.

For privatization purposes, consultants generally use two different valuation methods to give indications about a company's value:

● the valuation of future cash flows (capitalized future earnings); and

● substance valuation.

Valuation from the current market price of a company's traded common stock is not possible owing to government ownership, since the stock has not been quoted on a stock exchange.

In the first method, the company's value (i.e. the maximum price a purchaser might be willing to pay) is theoretically the sum of the present value of the expected future company earnings. A problem that arises in this context is the necessity to forecast future company earnings for a long period of time (actually until infinity). While problems already exist in making precise projections for Western companies operating in a relatively structured and stabilized economic environment, almost insurmountable problems arise in making this sort of estimate in former socialist and centrally controlled economies. In addition, past earnings provide minimal assistance because of the above-mentioned historical, economic, legal and financial changes which have taken place in an unstable environment, and those that can be expected for the future.

The second valuation method, the substance valuation (the difference between a company's assets and liabilities) might be used to determine a minimum transaction price, but it does not try to establish a fair value for the company. The substance valuation must also approximate what an investor or purchaser of the company would expect to pay for the reconstruction of the company, as no reliable way to estimate "free market costs" for construction exists and the depreciation methods for the enterprise might differ from those in the investor's country.

To ensure that an investor would become and remain interested, the valuation of the company would have to be tested for fairness and reasonableness and the consultant may be called both to advise upon the method to be used and to assist in its application. In most emerging markets the substance value of a company becomes the most important factor in the valuation process if the present value of future earnings is negative, cannot be determined or is lower than the substance value.

Governments have realized that (with certain exceptions) privatization is not a seller's but a buyer's market, and that overvaluation of a company and its assets can endanger privatization. Nevertheless, many governments still try to increase the value of state companies by writing up companies' assets, thus endangering privatization. In these cases the consultant should correct the excessively high valuation and advise the seller on a realistic approach.

If the seller's goal were to maximize the "social benefits" created by a privatization, the government would choose a potential investor on more criteria than just the purchase price. It would use a combination of the company's likelihood to be successful in the future, the amount of investments which the buyer guarantees to make, the number of jobs created and, only finally, the purchase price offered. This price may indeed appear to be fairly low. In privatization, it is not always the highest sales price but the continuation of a company's business on a going-concern basis which is the major interest of the selling government. Hence, that applicant who has the most appropriate conception about the future business activities and development prospects of a company chosen for privatization is the one who will most probably be selected as purchaser.

Strategy for privatizing a company

After the collection of all data and the valuation of the company, the consultant will advise the seller on the privatization strategy (see also box 21.1, above). These strategies may involve:

- privatizing the entire company as a whole (share deal) via:
  — public offering of shares;
  — sale of shares by auction;
  — sale of shares by auction limited to preselected bidders;
  — sale of shares through direct negotiation or private placement;
  — sale of shares by exchange for vouchers (if a country has opted for a voucher privatization scheme);
- splitting up the company in an economically balanced way into different smaller units;
- various combinations of these approaches.

At this stage, based on the appropriate privatization strategy, the foregoing assessment and valuation, an information memorandum will be compiled. This will contain all important data, including financial information as well as information on the product programme, staff and management, market(s), customers, locations and equipment, together with the most relevant elements of a strategy as well as a restructuring plan and requirements, as identified by the consultant or with his or her help.

In order to move quickly towards privatization, the enterprise's current management and probably its employees' collective, trade union or works council, as well as its supervisory board, should be fully involved in developing and discussing this strategy in order not to block privatization or discourage potential investors during their visits to the company.

Searching for investors and marketing

Following the agreement with the seller (the concerned ministry) and the enterprise management, the consultant will start marketing the company to the widest possible range of potential investors of quality. In this marketing effort the consultant will approach private investors (domestic or foreign), investment bankers and funds, and selected enterprises in the sector of the company to be privatized.

Normally the consultant would first approach as potential buyers those investors and companies with whom he or she has, over the years, developed good working relationships. However, no interesting potential buyers should be left out even if these are organizations with which the consultant has had no contact in the past.

The company memorandum will serve as the basic marketing tool. The consultant will also be responsible for follow-up of enquiries, responses and expressions of interest in the most appropriate manner to ensure the widest number of potential investors. The seller will be kept fully informed about any reactions to these marketing efforts.

Negotiations and documentation

The seller will expect any investor to make a written offer for the target company. Besides the offered price the seller will expect the investor also to present a detailed plan for the continuation of the company, including activities, investment, finance and employment, and any likely implications for the company's suppliers and customers. This plan should be carefully drafted because it usually forms the basis of the seller's sale decision. In many cases a consultant might be engaged to assist in the formulation of this business plan, since in this area the client may be particularly short of experience.

Once the seller has received this written offer, the consultant will assist in evaluating the offer and negotiating the purchase of the enterprise with the potential investor. The negotiation of the details of the contract will usually take place between the investor, his lawyer and his consultant(s), on one side, and the responsible representative of the seller assisted by the consultant who has helped to prepare the deal and by a lawyer, on the other side.

The seller's position on some contractual cornerstones can be summarized as follows:

Warranties. The seller in most cases is reluctant to give any warranties in relation to the company being sold. The reason is that, especially in Central and Eastern Europe and in developing countries, the seller does not know any more about the target business than the investor himself, who has had full access to all required information and performed his legal and financial due diligence on the company.

Business plan. The seller will require certain guarantees or assurances of the amount of investment and the number of employees stated in the purchaser's business plan. Guarantee clauses might stipulate that the investor has to pay a substantial penalty to the seller if the agreed objectives are not met. Therefore, any investor and the consultant who assists him or her are well advised to provide realistic investment and employment figures in the business plan.

Purchase price and terms of payment. The purchase price and the terms of payment to finalize the privatization deal are questions which require knowledge of both the financial market and the tax law environment. While the seller generally would prefer to be paid at once after the contract has been notarized, for financial, tax and legal reasons the purchaser might choose to pay in instalments or at a later stage. In these cases it is expected that the purchaser provide the seller with a bank guarantee to the amount of the purchase price. In reviewing the purchaser's options and eventually making a recommendation to the purchaser (with the assistance of tax advisers), the consultant's help can be invaluable.

Know-how transfer. In order to make the privatization project a success, the buyer is in most cases expected to provide missing technical and management know-how. Therefore the seller must ensure that know-how transfer into the company is guaranteed by the investor either through ensuring access to new technology and/or through direct managerial interventions, or through seconding management staff to contribute to the further modernization of the enterprise and to strengthening its economic power. For both the seller and the purchaser, a consultant can provide valuable assistance by advising on realistic methods of transferring technical and managerial know-how.

Closing and publicity. If desired by the seller, the consultant will also assist with the drafting of public announcements or advertisements and the distribution of information to the media (e.g. through press releases or briefings), to inform the public in the country concerned and abroad about the privatization of a specific company.

Final evaluation. Once a privatization project is completed, the consultant, as the seller's adviser, will provide the latter with a general assessment of the operation, the issues addressed, the lessons learnt and the results achieved.

21.5 Issues and risks

Privatization affects individual and group interests at various levels. It influences the future of organizations and will have a strong bearing on the future of whole nations. Therefore it is highly politically sensitive. In the relatively unstable and politically difficult context of many reforming economies, it may be impossible to reach full agreement on the best and only possible privatization strategy. Consultants need to develop political sensitivity to make sure that their proposals are politically acceptable and technically beyond any reproach, in order to survive even if governments change or the responsibilities of various agencies are redefined.

Currently most funds for consulting assignments in privatization are provided by international and national technical assistance agencies. Often in one country there is more than one source of funding, which may lead to demarcation disputes, professional jealousy between the various funding sources and overlapping of projects, as supranational and national institutions tend to pursue their own goals which can easily hamper constructive cooperation. Any consultant incurs the danger of getting caught up in the battlefield between the different agencies. The same applies to various ministries and other institutions in the country where the company is located. Much advice has been wasted because political backing for particular projects or steps within a privatization programme has been lacking.

Another problem might be consultant loyalty, especially if it is not the real client, but a donor or project sponsoring agency, that pays the consultant's fee. In various cases the consultant works in a predetermined framework or according to terms of reference set by the donor, whereas the real client might expect different tasks to be fulfilled and objectives met. Under these circumstances the consultant has to develop a sensitive way of being loyal to both sides and compromising between the interests of the donor and the main client. This may be very difficult. Also, remuneration rates for consultants in privatization are often lower than in other areas of management consulting. Furthermore, because of political pressures there may be a tendency not to select consultants on merit but to distribute the contracts to be awarded among consultants who have personal access to the contracting authority or sponsoring agency. This can happen even if a formal selection procedure is used, which in theory should ensure full objectivity.

A consultant engaged in privatization can also be subject to direct political pressure from various angles: donors, trade unions, political parties, federal, state and local government bodies, and other national as well as international pressure groups all of which — sometimes even through illegal methods — may try to influence the consultant's advice in their favour. In other cases, the client may be unable to control the consultant properly and assess his or her work for lack of information, experience and time. In the long run, only those consultants will be successful who act and advise independently and in best faith for the benefit of the client and the company. Once a consultant has given way to political pressure or even corruption, the market will soon learn about this and the consultant will be well on the way to being excluded from future projects.

The same applies to confidential information given to the consultant by the client, the company or another party, as the case may be. Frequently such information has competitive value and any consultant should be committed not to disclose it without prior consent of the client, and to treat it confidentially. It is of course understood that the consulting firm and its employees will become liable for all direct and indirect damage resulting from any breach of confidentiality. However, it may be very difficult to define such damage and prove that confidential information has been leaked intentionally or by negligence.

Finally, the concept of "consultancy tourism" sticks in the throats of many sellers, government officials and managers in state enterprises to be privatized. Often these "tourists" are consulting companies charging relatively lower fees, but lacking the necessary professional competence. This also means that they have no back-up when something goes wrong or extra work is needed at a certain stage of the project, as invariably happens in reforming economies. Companies and governments have been left with long reports but no means and assistance for implementing them.

In summary, consulting in privatization is a special market, different from classical consulting projects contracted by individual business companies or government departments. In the absence of simple rules and benchmarks to which a consultant could refer each time a delicate issue occurs, a privatization

---

Box 21.2 Václav Klaus on the Czech privatization experience

Perestroika-style economic thinking suggests that the shift from soft to hard budget constraints can be achieved, and that economic behaviour can be modified, by changing formal rules and introducing rational macroeconomic policies. Those measures, however, represent necessary but insufficient conditions for the transformation. It is privatization that moves an economy past perestroika to a real systemic change.

In some industrial and developing countries where privatization has taken place — the best known of which is the Thatcherian privatization of Great Britain in the late 1970s and early 1980s — privatization represented a partial change in an already existing, properly defined property rights structure, that is a shift of property rights between two (or more) well-defined economic agents. This kind of privatization has almost nothing in common with the task we are facing.

Privatization in Central and Eastern Europe means the establishment of a previously non-existent property rights structure. Privatization in the West may be viewed as a "reform" process. In the East, however, privatization is the road to the most fundamental objectives of a systemic transformation. It is the process within which the non-owner or quasi-owner (the government) transfers non-assets to their first (initial) proprietor, and in doing so "creates" the assets. In organizing the privatization programme of a transforming economy it is always important to understand the peculiarities of that economy. The special characteristics of transforming economies in Central and Eastern Europe call for special, non-standard privatization methods:

Revenues. The government's objective should be to accomplish economic transformation rather than to maximize the proceeds coming from the sale of government's assets. To understand that paradox is absolutely crucial.

Speed. Meagre proceeds are usually believed to be the price paid for speedy privatization. We have found, however, that in the Czech Republic and elsewhere the correlation between proceeds and time, if any, is the reverse of what has been hypothesized for standard privatization. In other words, the slower the privatization, the smaller the proceeds. For one thing, the true value of the privatized enterprise rapidly decreases due to its unavoidable pre-privatization agony and to the absence of a real owner during such a process.

We looked for privatization techniques that were faster than the standard ones. Our non-standard voucher privatization scheme proved to be rapid and efficient. It is based on selling vouchers (quasi-money applicable only in the privatization process) to every adult citizen at a symbolic price. The vouchers are redeemable for shares of privatized firms. Voucher privatization turned more than 75 per cent of Czech adults into shareholders, with shares either in the 1,500 privatized companies or in the investment privatization funds. The voucher scheme has also facilitated application of standard privatization techniques in the rest of the economy and, indirectly, speeded their implementation. The overall privatization programme also includes transfers of state property to municipalities, restitutions to original owners, transformation of "Soviet-type" cooperatives into cooperatives of real owners, privatization of small-scale business through public auctions, and privatization of medium- and large-scale enterprises through direct sales, joint ventures, tenders, and so on.

Organization. The effectiveness and speed of privatization depends greatly on the organization and administration of the process. It makes sense to concentrate

---

privatization initiatives at the micro level, not at the government level. Planning, organizing, restructuring, dividing and demonopolizing functions for the enterprises should not be imposed from above (this approach is thus entirely opposite to what has been done by the *Treuhandanstalt* in the former GDR).

Foreign involvement. The presence of foreign investors in the Czech Republic has always been considered beneficial and, therefore, most welcome. We are quite content with the continuous inflow of foreign capital and do not want to accelerate it artificially. It is one of our fundamental theses that foreign capital will enter the country on a massive scale after privatizations have been carried out since the decisions that will promote the inflow will arise from the private initiative of real owners rather than the irresponsible decision-making of government bureaucrats (irresponsible in the sense of a failure of logic). In keeping with this philosophy, we resisted strong temptations to introduce a special foreign investment law that would have accorded better treatment to foreign investors than to domestic ones.

Restructuring. Privatization is usually initiated with the goal of bringing efficiency and prosperity to individual privatized enterprises. It is a common myth, shared by many, that privatization in a post-communist country could, and should, have the same objective. But what really matters in our case is the effect of privatization on the economy as a whole. The question is not "Is the enterprise restructured?" but "Is the economy restructured?"

Individual restructuring must follow privatization. We have no doubt that it will be the new owner, not the government, who is motivated to find the ideas, time and resources for the necessary restructuring. The Czech Government has never listened to the advice that state ministries and agencies should attempt to increase the efficiency of state-owned enterprises before they are privatized. Furthermore, we consider it unnecessary to design legislation and techniques and develop perfect owners. Such an objective is beyond the capacity of post-communist governments. Besides, the first (initial) owners of privatized firms may not be the final ones.

In the early weeks and months of 1990 the Czech approach (to privatization) provoked harsh criticism from all imaginable sources. By now, however, even the most prominent international financial organizations have realized that government of a transforming country is the worst imaginable agent to take care of restructuring tasks. Moreover, it has been recognized that internationally renowned consulting firms, which are very expensive, lack the necessary country-specific and system-specific knowledge.

It has been observed — at least in the Czech Republic — that the meaning of privatization may differ substantially in different socio-political environments. I am convinced that our approach is correct — the results speak for themselves. Margaret Thatcher privatized three or four firms a year; we have been privatizing twice that many each day.

Source: *Transition: The Newsletter of Reforming Economies* (Washington, DC, The World Bank), Vol. 5, No. 1, pp. 11-12.

consultant's best guide is individual judgement, political sensitivity and personal and professional ethical standards. Furthermore, consultants should be fully aware of evolving privatization policies and of the assessment of recent privatization experience in various countries (see, for example, box 21.2, above).

The purpose of the consultant's involvement and participation in any stage of the privatization process is not only to guarantee continuity, but also to transfer know-how to the client. A consultant who approaches any privatization assignment believing that he or she knows the solutions and wanting to impose personal views and models in a standardized way will invariably fail. Each case of privatization is unique and individual, and projects demand a broad background of consulting experience, ranging from industrial, technical, strategic and financial expertise, through know-how on mergers and acquisitions to legal, accounting and valuation knowledge. Intuition, communication and negotiation skills are also most important. This combination of opportunities and abilities makes privatization one of the most challenging sectors of management consulting.

21.6 Post-privatization consulting

In a privatized enterprise, the transfer of ownership rights, and the related legal and organizational restructuring, are not an end but only the beginning of its total transformation. The ultimate objective is to develop an independent business that can survive and prosper in competition, without state subsidies, based on its own vision of the future, entrepreneurial drive, and fully competent management. Privatization changes the rules of the game and creates new opportunities. It provides no guarantee whatsoever that every privatized enterprise will be successful. On the contrary, many new owners and managers (who are often the same persons who were in charge before privatization) quickly discover that unlearning command-economy concepts and practices, and learning how to think and operate in a market-economy environment, is not an easy matter. This creates tremendous and unprecedented opportunities for management consultants in all post-communist societies, as well as in other countries that have privatized a significant part of their public sector.

Post-privatization consulting could be regarded as any other management and business consulting to private enterprises and other clients in market economies. This, however, would be a misunderstanding. There are some important differences between emerging and developed market economies. For example:

— In many privatization projects, the transfer of property rights is the culmination of the effort and the crucial point of privatization strategy; when they are finally in charge, many new owners and their managers face a host of problems and alternatives in choosing where and how to start in order to modernize the business and make it competitive.

— The organizational culture of many privatized enterprises is strongly influenced by their past experience; old habits die hard, and both managers and staff find it difficult to start thinking and acting differently.

— The management of many privatized enterprises is controlled or strongly influenced by investment funds established during the privatization process; often these funds are short of entrepreneurial and business management competence, and do not really know how to exercise ownership rights and influence enterprises in their portfolios in the best interest of all stakeholders.

— In post-communist societies, the newly privatized enterprises start operating within an imperfect and incomplete business infrastructure; ideal models that have demonstrated their effectiveness in modern market economies are not immediately applicable and enterprise management has to cope with gaps and problems in the areas of distribution, credit, bank services, bank and other guarantees, cash flow, insurance, quality certification, foreign-exchange regulations, licensing, taxation and many others.

— An insufficiently developed business infrastructure and culture and the lack of business ethics provide a fertile ground for fraudulent dealings, economic crime, unfair competition, misrepresentation and speculative deals; many managers experience considerable difficulties in making the right choices and avoiding errors that can have serious consequences for the enterprise.

Conversely, in emerging market economies many entrepreneurs and managers exhibit a great deal of dynamism and openness. They are keen to innovate and learn in order to gain a competitive edge and rapidly overcome the teething pains of their recently privatized enterprises.

Management consultants need to be aware of these and other differences, and look for solutions that are applicable to recently privatized enterprises. There will be great demand for consultants who will be able to help in "privatizing" managerial values, standards, behaviour, practices, systems and performances, following the transfer of property rights to the new owners.

---

[1] See also Ch. 4 in M. Kubr: *How to select and use consultants: A client's guide*, Management Development Series, No. 13 (Geneva, ILO, 1993).

CONSULTING FOR PRODUCTIVITY AND PERFORMANCE IMPROVEMENT

22

The role of productivity as a major factor in improving company competitiveness and increasing national welfare is universally recognized. Generally, productivity is expressed as a ratio of output against input of resources. It shows how much and how well we produce from the resources used, both human and physical. In dealing with productivity issues it is necessary to consider all the major factors which affect productivity either positively or negatively. These factors include national economic and social policies and strategies, business cycles and international competition, the natural environment, the legal, institutional and regulatory setting, demographic and structural changes, and so on. Yet the principal place where productivity growth is created is the enterprise, as it is here that the whole range of available resources come together in order to produce goods and services. The effectiveness of the combined functioning of these resources in a given macroeconomic, institutional and natural environment is reflected in productivity.

This chapter begins with a short review of the evolution of productivity consulting and of its current characteristics. It then focuses on two issues that form the core of consulting for practical productivity and performance improvement: productivity measurement and analysis; and the planning and organization of programmes for improving company productivity and performance.

22.1 A short history of productivity consulting

Helping clients to understand and increase productivity has always been one of the fundamental objectives of management consulting. However, conceptual approaches to productivity, performance assessment and improvement techniques, and the organization of productivity services have undergone many changes.

The "scientific management" and "rationalization" movement initiated by F. W. Taylor in the late nineteenth century, with its concentration on the workplace and on the simplification and better organization of production tasks, was in fact the start of productivity consulting. It created numerous work, productivity and efficiency improvement techniques of which most have remained in use until the present time. It also predetermined, for several decades, the image of productivity improvement consulting, which to many people became synonymous with improving worker and/or employee productivity by performing fragmented work operations more effectively both in production shops and in offices.

During the Marshall Plan period (1947-59), American technical assistance had a strong productivity dimension. American experts came to Europe and Japan to provide advice on productivity and quality questions in connection with post-war reconstruction. At the same time, the famous "productivity teams" (altogether some 25,000 people) travelled to the United States to see and study productivity practices developed during and after the Second World War. Their task was to act as advisers back at home in their companies, by transmitting and disseminating their findings and conclusions.[1]

Every recipient nation of Marshall Aid had the obligation to create a national productivity centre. An important network of productivity agencies was thus established in Europe and Japan. Until 1960, the European network was supported and to some extent coordinated by the European Productivity Agency. In Asia, the establishment of the Japan Productivity Centre was followed after a few years by the creation of the Asian Productivity Organization in order to promote and support productivity improvement in other Asian countries. Gradually, most of these countries have also established their own national productivity boards and/or centres. In a number of countries in Asia and in other regions, the ILO provided technical expertise and other assistance to national productivity bodies, often with financial support of the United Nations Development Programme (UNDP).

Because of the broad and integrative nature of the productivity concept, the national productivity centres tended to develop a wide range of functions and services, including information, training, advice and consulting on various aspects of enterprise productivity, efficiency and performance. In the first years their services were heavily subsidized by governmental and technical assistance funds in order to make productivity advice accessible and attractive to enterprises undergoing reconstruction, and to newly established smaller businesses.

During this period, productivity services of private consulting firms were developing alongside the various national and international productivity services. Some consultancies, both large and small, continued to work as efficiency and cost-cutting experts. Others preferred a more comprehensive approach, looking at the interface of various management functions and at the composite productivity effect of a better combination of all productive factors. Gradually, various new approaches to productivity started appearing on the market for consulting services and capturing the attention of clients in industry and other sectors.

A major impetus to productivity consulting came in the 1980s with increasingly tough international competition, market globalization, energy crises and a generally more difficult business climate. To more and more companies, vigorous action to achieve substantial improvements in productivity was no longer an option to choose or not to choose — it became a necessity, a condition of sheer survival.

In the current period, productivity improvement has without any doubt become a key element of most management and business consulting work, although often the term "productivity" is not used and productivity is described in terms of business efficiency, performance, total quality, competitive edge or in other ways. Also, productivity improvement concepts and techniques are presented under different names or are integrated with global business development concepts. Thus, the productivity dimension looms large in business process re-engineering, total quality management (TQM), company performance improvement, *Kaizen*, benchmarking or corporate excellence. This is fully understandable and quite normal owing to the diversity of business contexts and objectives, and national and corporate cultures, as well as the approaches taken by different business corporations and their consultants. However, it is essential that both the clients and the consultants see the purpose and the nature of the change behind the various techniques and parameters used. For example, there is a strong productivity improvement dimension in the approaches and tools listed in figure 22.1.

Figure 22.1   Responses to the challenge of large-scale change

• Business process re-engineering	• Theory of constraints	• *Kaizen*
	• Systems thinking	• *Hoshin Kanri*
• Total quality management (TQM)	• Theory of psychology	• Benchmarking
	• Vendor partnerships	• Experimental design
• Strategic planning	• White-collar productivity	• 7 tools of quality
• Statistical thinking	• Organizational redesign	• Learning organization
• Measurement	• Business process improvement	• Theory of knowledge
• Self-managing teams		• Gainsharing
• Total employee involvement	• Statistical process control	• Customer-driven focus
	• Plan, Do, Study, Act	• Downsizing
• Taguchi methods	• Profound knowledge	• Leadership
• Just-in-time inventory management		

Source: D.S. Sink: *A grand strategy for accelerating the rate of organizational and individual improvement*, paper prepared for the Eighth Productivity Conference, Stockholm, 1993, p. 4.

Turning to Central and Eastern Europe, the current productivity scene is different from the rest of the world and has been shaped by two significant factors.

The first factor has been the predominantly bureaucratic approach to productivity introduced and used for years by the command economy system. Productivity improvement was not motivated by the need to be better and more effective than competitors, but by the obligation to comply with planned productivity targets. It was more important to improve productivity on paper than in reality. As a result, the current generation of managers is not sufficiently productivity minded and lacks many of the skills needed for productivity and company performance improvement in modern market economies.

The second factor is the current priorities of the fundamental transformation process through which the economies of this region have to pass. The top priority is creating a real and not a fictitious market economy environment through massive privatization and restructuring. In the first phase, this restructuring is essentially legal, organizational and financial. Improving the performance of privatized and restructured companies (including productivity and quality) comes next, and in most companies this second phase has not yet been entered. The need has yet to be fully perceived by management, including those in charge of the already privatized units and investment funds. Full exposure to tough competition will be the principal condition of this fundamental attitudinal change (see also Chapter 21).

Thus, Central and Eastern Europe is not yet a major market for productivity consulting. However, it is likely to become one, and offer most interesting opportunities to consultants, in the not very distant future.

22.2 Measuring and analysing productivity and performance

Although the productivity level is of critical importance to enterprise competitiveness, there are other important parameters that should also be taken into consideration when assessing company performance. They include profitability, return on investment, quality, customer needs satisfaction, social climate, environmental impact, and similar. At the end of the day, all these performance parameters result in higher or lower productivity. Nevertheless, for management decision-making, and for focusing consulting work, productivity should be distinguished from performance, without losing sight of how these highly synthetic concepts relate to each other.

Productivity measurement and analysis form the foundation of sound productivity improvement consulting. Even as a separate element, they are effective tools of diagnosis and decision-making at all economic levels. The success of productivity measurement and analysis depends largely upon a clear understanding by all parties concerned (employers, enterprise managers, workers, trade union organizations and government institutions) of the relationship between productivity measurement and the effectiveness of the organization. Productivity measurement and analysis indicate where to look for opportunities to improve and also show how well efforts at improvement are progressing.

In enterprises, productivity is measured in order to help analyse effectiveness and efficiency. Its measurement can stimulate operational improvement: the very announcement, installation and operation of a measurement system can improve labour productivity, sometimes by 5 to 10 per cent, with no other organizational change or investment.

Productivity indices also help to establish realistic targets and check-points for diagnostic activities during an organization development process, pointing to bottlenecks and barriers to performance. Furthermore, there can be no real improvement in industrial relations and proper correspondence between productivity, wage levels and gain-sharing policies without a sound measurement system.

As mentioned, productivity is measured as a ratio of output to input, or products to resources. Total productivity measures reflect the relationship between the total output and total input of an enterprise:

$$\text{Total productivity} = \frac{\text{Total output}}{\text{Labour + Capital + Materials + Energy + Others}}$$

By using total productivity measures all the parts are assessed and then combined, which means that all resources have been taken into account.

Approaches and criteria

There are many approaches to productivity measurement and analysis since different groups of people (managers, workers, investors, customers, trade unions) have different goals. Normally the method of measurement is determined by the purpose of the productivity analysis, which may be:

— comparing an enterprise with sector leaders or competitors;

— determining the relative performance of departments and workers;

— comparing relative benefits of various types of input for collective bargaining and gain-sharing.

For example, if an organization's goal at a particular time is to maximize the return on invested capital and expand its operations, the company should measure its cost and profit structures.

Selected examples of useful measurement techniques used by productivity consultants are presented below.

Kazukiyo Kurosawa's structural approach

In this approach,[2] productivity measurement focuses on the structure of the enterprise and helps to analyse past activities and plan new activities. It can be used to set up an information system for monitoring operations. For this reason it is important that productivity measurement be built according to the decision-making hierarchy. A very general system could be as shown in figure 22.2 (overleaf).

Applying this equation over time, the consultant can use the system as a sort of interlinked index system. Value-added productivity also can be used meaningfully for productivity measurement in combination with various

Figure 22.2 Fundamental framework of productivity measurement in management

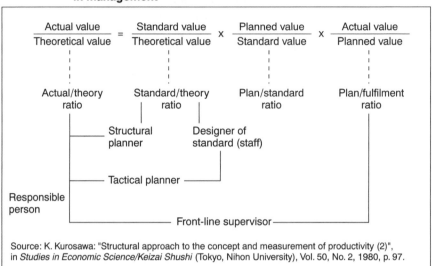

Source: K. Kurosawa: "Structural approach to the concept and measurement of productivity (2)", in *Studies in Economic Science/Keizai Shushi* (Tokyo, Nihon University), Vol. 50, No. 2, 1980, p. 97.

physical parameters as well as other related variables. As can be seen in figure 22.3, value added at the enterprise can have several forms. The selection of a suitable one depends upon management objectives. In routine business activities, value added is usually evaluated at current prices. Value added at constant prices is estimated more for analytical purposes. The essence of value-added labour productivity is in the differentiation between industries and enterprises. A commonly used method to eliminate the price effect on value added is the double deflation method.

Alan Lawlor's approach

In Alan Lawlor's approach,[3] productivity is regarded as a comprehensive measure of how organizations satisfy the following five aims: objectives, efficiency, effectiveness, comparability and progressive trends.

Objectives can be met when the total fund is adequate to meet the demands of the organization and to measure the degree to which its principal objectives are achieved. This fund is called total earnings (TE):

$$TE = Sales - Materials = S - M$$

Total earnings serve to buy services, pay wages and salaries, and invest in fixed capital, profit and taxes.

Efficiency tells us how well actually needed outputs (which could be sold) are generated from available inputs and indicates the use of available capacity. It reveals the degree of use of resources compared with the total capacity

Figure 22.3 Structure of production value and value-added variants

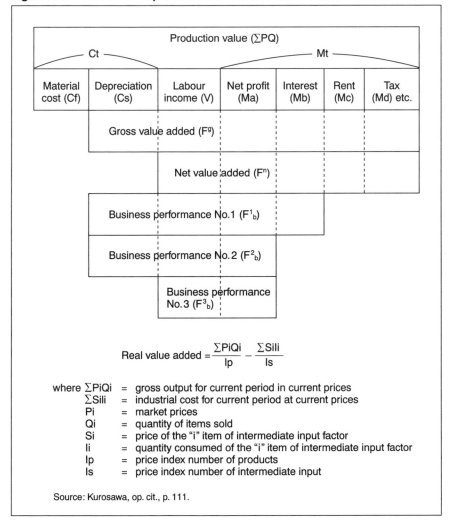

Real value added $= \dfrac{\Sigma PiQi}{Ip} - \dfrac{\Sigma Sili}{Is}$

where $\Sigma PiQi$ = gross output for current period in current prices
$\Sigma Sili$ = industrial cost for current period at current prices
Pi = market prices
Qi = quantity of items sold
Si = price of the "i" item of intermediate input factor
Ii = quantity consumed of the "i" item of intermediate input factor
Ip = price index number of products
Is = price index number of intermediate input

Source: Kurosawa, op. cit., p. 111.

(potential) and tells us where inefficiencies lie (Profit : Input is the profit-productivity ratio):

$$\frac{\text{Output}}{\text{Input}} = \frac{\text{Input} + \text{Profit}}{\text{Input}} = 1 + \frac{\text{Profit}}{\text{Input}}$$

Effectiveness compares present achievement with what could be done if resources were managed more effectively. This concept includes an output target achieving a new standard of performance (or potential new achievement):

461

$$\frac{\text{Output}}{\text{Input}} = \frac{\text{Effectiveness (what could be achieved)}}{\text{Resources consumed}}$$

Productivity improvement involves a combination of increased effectiveness and a better use of available resources. It shows four basic ratios:

- actual output divided by actual input (the status quo);
- higher output divided by current actual input;
- current actual output divided by lower input;
- maximum output divided by minimum input (the higher level of effectiveness).

Comparability is a guide to organizational performance, since productivity ratios alone tell little without some form of comparison. Generally speaking, productivity measurement means comparisons at three levels:

— comparison of present performance with a historical base performance;

— comparison of performance between units, or relative achievement;

— comparison of actual performance with a target or objectives.

Trends can be assessed by comparing current performance and a historical base in order to identify whether performance is moving up or down and how fast.

This approach calls for at least two levels of productivity measurement within the enterprise: primary and secondary. The primary level deals with total earning productivity (E) which is:

$$E = \frac{\text{Total earnings}}{\text{Conversion cost}} = \frac{T}{C}$$

where

Conversion cost (C) = Total wages and salaries (W) + Total purchased services (Ps) + Depreciation (K).

Thus, obtaining a high level of total earnings ensures a healthy organization.

Secondary productivity measurement provides the ratio of used resources to the total conversion cost of all available resources.

In summarizing his approach, Alan Lawlor provided a hierarchical structure of productivity indices (figure 22.4).

A quick way to assess productivity

Productivity measures need not be complicated. In order to monitor all aspects of productivity and the factors influencing it, a Canadian consultant, Imre Bernolak, suggests combining typical productivity and profitability ratios.[4] In most sectors, between 30 and 35 ratios are sufficient for the combined productivity/profitability analysis.

Over time, the analysis of information from the base year can be greatly assisted by showing the relative movements of the relevant ratios in a trend-chart

Figure 22.4   The framework of productivity analysis

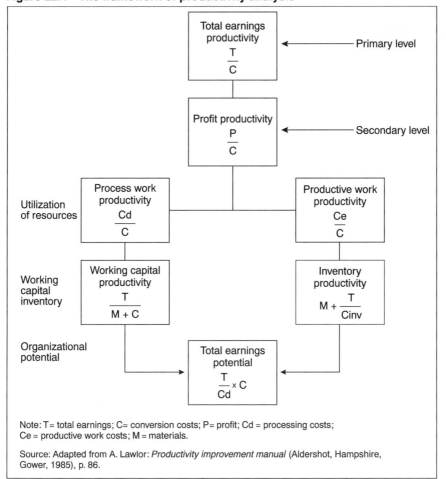

Note: T = total earnings; C = conversion costs; P = profit; Cd = processing costs;
Ce = productive work costs; M = materials.

Source: Adapted from A. Lawlor: *Productivity improvement manual* (Aldershot, Hampshire, Gower, 1985), p. 86.

form, first giving the relative movements of the main ratios, and then proceeding to analyse the components of the main elements and factors.

The integrated analysis of profitability and productivity makes the application of productivity theory very practical for enterprise managers. While profitability measures indicate the combined short-term effects of both productivity and price factors, the long-run success of enterprises is determined by proper resource utilization, i.e. the productivity factor. In the short term, the analysis of productivity measures helps to explain the causes of performance results, and forms the basis of productivity gain-sharing.

Enterprise profitability and productivity analysis starts from the finding that the most commonly used measure of the performance of an enterprise is return-on-investment (ROI). Since productivity expresses the physical relationship of output to input, all assets are therefore included in the denominator of

---

Box 22.1 Example of a "family of measures"

Customers:

- Percentage of repeat customers
- Number of complaints from customers
- Warranties, claims or returns
- Key performance characteristics of the product or service that are global in nature:
  - — percentage of deliveries on time (distributor)
  - — scores on standardized tests (school)
  - — degree of return to normal physical or mental functioning (hospital)
  - — time (to complete a service)
- Number of awards or compliments
- Number of recommendations by customers to others
- Market share

Employees:

- Education levels
- Level of experience or skills
- Personal accomplishments
- Absenteeism or turnover
- The extent to which people take pride in their work
- Percentage of employees' time allocated to education and training
- Number of suggestions submitted
- Number of grievances filed

Business and financial:

- Earnings or profits
- Costs (fixed, variable, controllable, etc.)
- Variance from budget
- Share of market
- Return on investments, return on assets or return on capital
- Amount spent on research and development
- Amount of resources allocated to the improvement of quality

Operations:

- Throughput or cycle time for the system
- Percentage yield
- Efficiency
- Volume of production or sales
- Productivity
- Backlog of orders or work
- Levels of inventory

- Amount of overtime
- Amount of scrap or rework
- Number of errors, accidents, injuries or close calls

Outside environment:

- Time allocated to industry groups or advisory groups
- Amount of community service
- Amount of discharge of pollutants
- Number of lay-offs
- Accidents or injuries related to the product or service
- Fines or violations from government agencies
- Media coverage

Source: Adapted from L. Provost and S. Leddick: "How to take multiple measures to get a complete picture of organizational performance", in *National Productivity Review* (New York), Autumn 1993, pp. 477-490.

the ratio. Consequently, the return-on-assets (ROA) ratio is used instead of the ROI as the top performance ratio of the pyramid, and the main link between productivity and management.

The ROA ratio is then broken down into the other two commonly used "primary" ratios, namely, the profit-over-sales, and the sales-over-assets ratios. If these two ratios are multiplied by each other, they are equal to the top ratio (profit-over-assets). For practical considerations, the reciprocal of the sales-over-assets ratio, i.e. assets-over-sales, is used in the profitability/productivity analysis. In industries where capital assets are relatively insignificant compared with other inputs, the profit-over-sales ratio becomes the integrating top ratio.

All cost data must be based on real cost figures rather than "standard" costs. In addition to physical productivity ratios which can be built into the pyramidal analysis system, each financial ratio can be analysed in terms of its physical productivity and price components.

Using a "family of measures" of organizational performance

Productivity improvement is the result of the combined efforts of many different stakeholders with different objectives and perceptions about organizational effectiveness. That means that the results of measurement of different parameters should be fed back to all participants to stimulate improvement.

A "family of measures" should be used since no part of an organization is so simple that it can be measured adequately by one indicator. By drawing together a set of measurements of the organization from the perspective of its various stakeholders — customers, employees, stockholders, owners, suppliers and communities — an organization can avoid the shortsightedness that often results from focusing on a single measure of success. By taking only a single measure or a few measures concentrated in one dimension, almost any group

---

Box 22.2 Problems to watch and principles to observe in productivity measurement and analysis

The problems and difficulties in productivity analysis concern both the methods used and the organization of measurement. The most common problems are:

- how to combine different types of input into one acceptable denominator;
- how to embrace all resources and business activities;
- how to deal with qualitative changes in input or output over time;
- how to separate real from fictitious improvements;
- how to keep input and output measurements independent of each other;
- how to interpret measurement results;
- how to indicate accountability and provide clear signals for managerial decisions and action;
- how to reflect significant structural changes over time, which would complicate measurement and comparisons;
- how to avoid the confusion between indirect costs and avoidable costs such as ill-designed procedures which should not be considered as input;
- how to make productivity measurement credible and easily understandable to everybody concerned in various parts of the organization.

To avoid the above-mentioned problems, observing the following principles can be helpful:

- provide simple and unambiguous signals to improve performance (productivity, profit, quality);
- break down the change in profit to reflect the contribution from each resource used in production (labour, capital, materials, energy);
- break down the contribution to change in profit from each resource into productivity terms and price recovery terms; this will isolate the effect of different elements of change in product vis-à-vis resource price;
- use price recovery terms to evaluate whether a productivity loss or gain for a given resource is appropriate;
- transform the above measures of change in profit into corresponding measures of change in profitability, in cost per unit of output, and in performance index numbers (e.g. productivity index numbers);
- provide consistent signals for profit improvement regardless of the units in which the measure is expressed;
- use a "family of measures" to reflect both "hard" and "soft" factors and changes, and to view the organization as a whole.

To choose a specific measurement approach and technique, a number of variables should be considered:

- *purpose and stakeholders:* what the measure is supposed to do and who will use it (management, investors, employees, trade union representatives, etc.);
- *commitment to measurement:* the extent to which an organization sees productivity measurement as a critical part of its effort to remain competitive;
- *awareness/understanding of management:* the extent of management understanding and awareness of productivity measurement systems;

- *centralization/decentralization:* the extent to which measurement control systems are part of the total organizational culture;
- *output variability:* the extent to which the physical characteristics of the output change over time;
- *type of technology:* ranges in technology where input and output may vary considerably over time;
- *process cycle time:* length of time for one unit of output to be produced;
- *controllability:* the extent to which management can "manage" or control input levels;
- *resources as a percentage of costs:* amount of costs associated with each of the components of resources as a proportion of total cost (In selecting a method of productivity measurement, feasibility and costs are major concerns).

can be successful in the short term by optimizing the selected measure at the expense of other important measures. The volume of production can be increased by cutting back on preventive maintenance or tests of new products, and so on. It is much more difficult to improve performance based on a family of measures than on any single measure.

Using interfirm comparison and benchmarking

These two techniques are known to the reader from Chapters 4 and 8, and some other references in the previous chapters. They are essential for assessing productivity in an organization by referring to other organizations pursuing similar objectives and activities, and drawing practical conclusions from the differences identified.

Typical *interfirm comparison* (IFC) is based on quantitative data supported by qualitative information that has been collected. The 30 to 40 ratios thus produced are then compared, either by comparing individual enterprises with each other, or by comparing an enterprise to a sectoral standard, best sectoral performance or simply average data. This provides a basic orientation for productivity assessment, which has to be pursued by going into more detail and examining factors, causes and relationships behind global ratios.

Benchmarking, a recent, more advanced, variant of IFC, provides information needed to focus and support improvements, and develop a competitive advantage. In productivity analysis, benchmarking helps to identify specific activities and practices that can and ought to be changed. Owing to its operational focus and the voluntary collaboration of several companies aiming at productivity and performance improvement, benchmarking also provides (which is not the case in traditional IFC) specific information and suggestions on what to change, and what conditions to create in order to make particular productivity improvements sustainable. Thus, benchmarking can be described as a collaborative approach whereby several organizations share experience and help each other in productivity assessment and improvement.

Resistance to productivity measurement

As is the case of any organizational change (see Chapter 4), the introduction of a productivity measurement system may encounter resistance. The specific reasons may be the following:

— **potential misunderstanding and misuse of measurement:** the fear of workers that managers who are not intimately involved with the work process will exaggerate or otherwise misinterpret the changes or trends in measurement data;

— **exposure of inadequate performance:** since many workers are not sure where they stand with their boss, a measurement system that would clarify the situation may be perceived as a threat;

— **additional time and reporting demands:** a frequently stated fear of productivity measurement is that it will increase the paperwork and take time for which management is making no additional provision;

— **reduction of autonomy:** individual staff members differ in terms of their desire for autonomy. Introduction of tighter management control as a result of productivity measurement may be seen as a constraint.

Many of the perceived threats described above are the result of problems in the organization that consultants need to understand and resolve. Implementing a productivity measurement system is an organizational change and must be managed as a change process.

22.3 Designing and implementing productivity and performance improvement programmes

General conditions of success

A sound productivity improvement strategy calls for a systems approach which recognizes the interrelationships between the elements of the system and their environment. Such strategy should, as a minimum:

— develop a clear and easily communicated definition of the productivity improvement concept;

— explain why organizational improvement is important;

— evaluate current operating situations and the reasons for the current status;

— develop models of excellence;

— develop improvement policies and plans.

The objective of productivity improvement should always be expressed in terms of "organizational" improvement. The overall objectives should be supplemented by detailed action plans. Below are some examples of questions which can indicate the state of this planning and draw attention to potential areas of productivity improvement:

- Does the enterprise have written productivity objectives and goals, and a productivity plan which covers the whole organization?
- Are the objectives set for small, identifiable groups so that their performance can be assessed?
- Does the plan include the methods by which productivity improvement objectives can be reached?
- Are target dates set for the achievement of objectives?
- Are the objectives and actions set against labour costs and other costs?[5]

Another key aspect of productivity improvement plans covering an entire company is their integration into the long-term strategy and planning of the organization as a whole. Managers should fully understand that focused efforts to improve productivity may lead to a chain of reactions among many of the operational and output variables. For example, if management intensifies efforts to control rising costs in one specific area of operations, it may hurt other cost areas badly.

The productivity improvement programme (PIP) can be successful if the following conditions are present within an organization:

— Top management is wholly committed to the programme.

— There is an effective organizational arrangement headed by someone belonging to top management.

— Full awareness and understanding of the programme objectives exist at all organizational levels.

— There should be free-flow communication between different structural elements of the organization.

— Good labour-management relations exist. Recognition of the key role played by workers is crucial and must be demonstrated through a sound productivity gain-sharing system.

— The programme is linked with measurement processes that are practical and easily understood.

— The productivity improvement techniques (technical, behavioural and managerial) chosen for the programme are fitted to the situation and needs.

— Monitoring, evaluation and feedback processes to identify results and barriers provide a basis for design improvements.

Finally, among important conditions for success the following are the most frequently cited: there is pressure for change within the organization and its external environment; the invention and development of new ideas, methods and solutions are encouraged; and top management and consultants provide leadership in programme design and implementation, as well as permission to experiment with new solutions. There are many reasons to enter into a PIP, such as red figures on the bottom line, new products and equipment, new technologies and materials, stronger competition, demand for more production flexibility, the need for shorter delivery time and better services, and many others. Both managers and consultants should be sure that there are enough positive factors to give a reasonable chance of success, that the time is right and that conditions are generally favourable.

Structuring the process

A systematic eight-step approach to designing performance improvement planning processes, suggested by Scott Sink, is shown in figure 22.5.

Figure 22.5   The performance improvement planning process

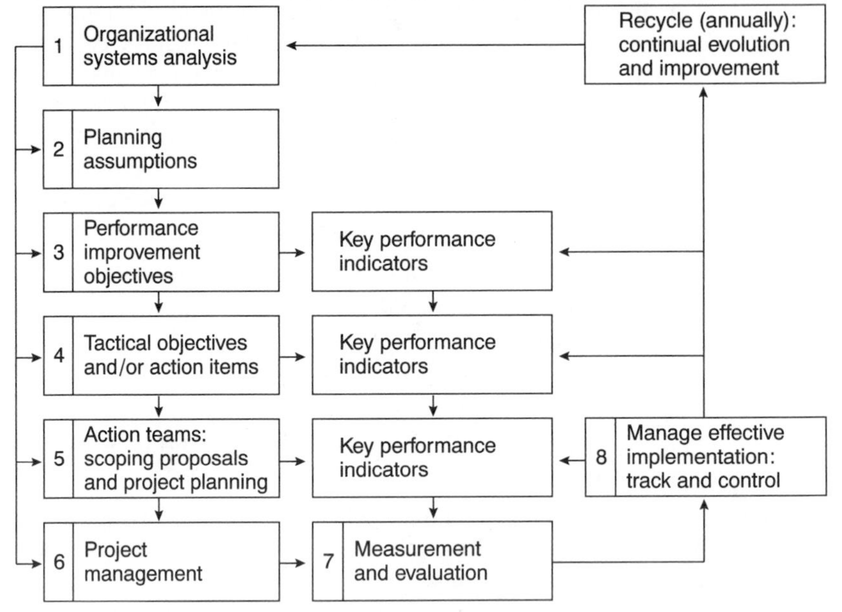

Source: S. Sink: "TQM: The next frontier or just another bandwagon to jump on", in *QPM-Quality and Productivity Management* (Blacksburg, Virginia), Vol. 7, No. 2, 1989, p. 18.

All productivity programmes operate in organizations, and to run them a programme manager must be able to suggest processes that can be used to identify problems, and to work out and implement solutions. The intra-enterprise productivity processes include, among others, suggestion schemes, quality circles, task forces, action teams, productivity committees and steering committees, which should be fully understood and used by the programme manager.

Deciding on a productivity improvement programme[6]

The decision about entering a PIP should be taken as for any other investment: the cost of the investment to be compared with benefits and risks should

Figure 22.6   Potential areas for a productivity improvement programme

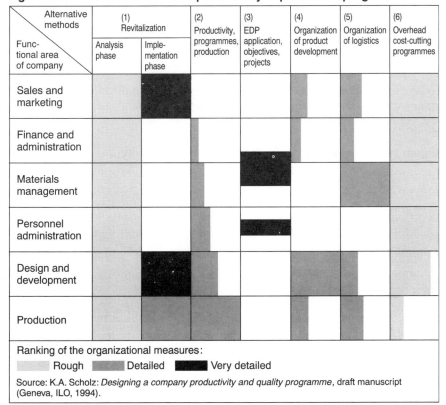

Func- tional area of company \ Alternative methods	(1) Revitalization		(2) Productivity, programmes, production	(3) EDP application, objectives, projects	(4) Organization of product development	(5) Organization of logistics	(6) Overhead cost-cutting programmes
	Analysis phase	Imple- mentation phase					
Sales and marketing							
Finance and administration							
Materials management							
Personnel administration							
Design and development							
Production							

Ranking of the organizational measures:
░░ Rough   ▓▓ Detailed   ██ Very detailed

Source: K.A. Scholz: *Designing a company productivity and quality programme*, draft manuscript (Geneva, ILO, 1994).

be taken into account. The payback period from a PIP should normally be less than one year.

To prepare the decision for investing in a PIP, the first step must be the identification and assessment of potential savings. The best way is to look at the big outputs and the large blocks of cost. Usually large potential areas are directly related to product costs: the consultant should take the "products" with highest output and look into its cost elements such as materials, value added per pro- duction area, tooling, design cost, overhead cost and distribution cost.

After having identified a good reason for a project and after knowing where the areas for big potential savings might be, one has to set the framework for the PIP. Figure 22.6 shows the main typical areas of responsibility of a company and six different approaches to a PIP. None of the approaches is confined to one functional area only. Choosing the right approach involves:

(1) Clarifying a reason to start a PIP which would make it easy to commit people to the programme.

(2) Identifying, in a quick one- to two-day preliminary analysis, where the potential savings should come from, what is the value or the percentage of

cost of the potential savings and what risks must be taken to obtain the savings.

(3) Setting the frame for the PIP by covering most of the potential savings areas, making sure that management makes the necessary decisions, and by covering those functions which can facilitate or hinder the PIP.

The following three approaches are normally used in the PIP (figure 22.7). Where a great proportion of all cost cannot be related to direct saleable output, *approach A* (value analysis) will apply. This approach mainly requires decisions, not organizational activities.

Figure 22.7 Three approaches to improving productivity

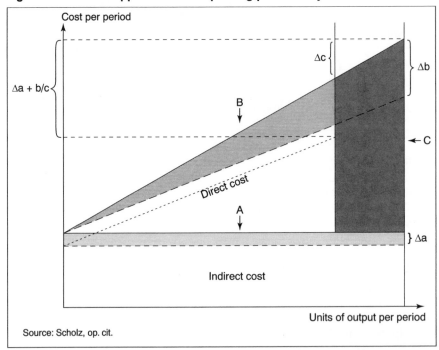

Source: Scholz, op. cit.

Approach B is the industrial engineering approach used for rationalization. It aims at cutting unit costs (expressed as Δ) by reducing waste, raw material consumption and handling per unit, combining work operations and workstations, controlling work in progress, avoiding delays and time losses, and so on.

Approach C often brings the best results. It simply consists in reducing numbers (number of tasks, number of orders, number of operations, etc.).

For example, can the quality control operation on all pieces of output (100 per cent control) be turned into an exceptional operation (statistical control)? Can the control operation on all pieces of output be turned into an automated in-process control? Can writing and mailing of order confirmations be avoided, if incoming orders are dispatched the same day, or for the next day?

In defining the aims of a PIP, the initial rules are: "Spend less!" and: "Sell more!" The project team has to know right from the beginning of the programme whether the productivity improvement aims at "spending less" only, at extra capacity which can be "sold", or a combination of both.

The "Royal Road"

The "Royal Road", used by most productivity improvement programmes, is outlined in figure 22.8 (overleaf). It consists of three phases:

Phase I — The Pre-Survey, or Preliminary-Survey Phase, to identify aims and "sell" the programme to management.

Phase II — The Survey Phase, to set and commit goals with all responsible area managers.

Phase III — The Implementation Phase, to design and develop the pro-ductivity improvement tasks in detail, implement the measures for improvement and control, and evaluate the results from increased productivity.

To run a successful PIP, it is absolutely vital to involve management in the decision-making process from the very beginning of the exercise. By incor-porating "stop/go" decision milestones into the programme after each main step, management becomes very much involved in decisions on directions, aims, expected results, necessary changes and investments to be made. In following this Royal Road there are at least two decision milestones in each PIP phase (see figures 22.9 and 22.10 on pages 475 and 476).

All reporting given by the productivity improvement project team to management is focused on decision-making. This aspect makes it easy to understand which data have to be collected and checked, and in which way measures for productivity improvement have to be presented as clear, accurate and convincing information to the decision-maker(s).

A PIP can be implemented successfully if the project team is well motivated to achieve the results aimed for. In most programmes that have been implemented, five general approaches have prevailed:

● economy of scale/the experience curve effect;

● product structuring as the basis for productivity improvement;

● "manufacturing to market" organization;

● delivery quality and service organization;

● flow-oriented manufacturing process.

At the end of the implementation phase the results should always be documented by quantitative data reflecting the improvements actually achieved.

Figure 22.8   The "Royal Road" of productivity improvement

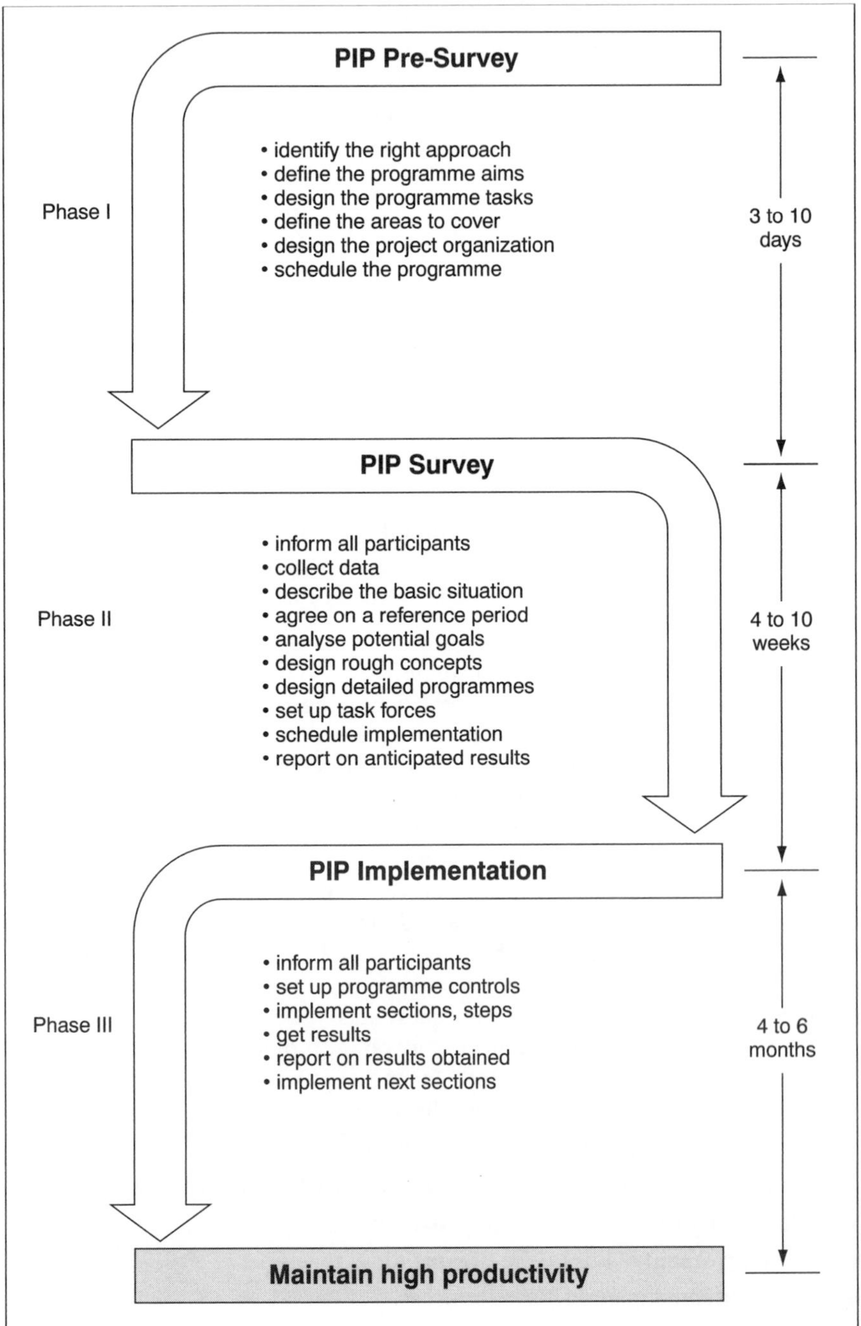

PIP Pre-Survey

Phase I

- identify the right approach
- define the programme aims
- design the programme tasks
- define the areas to cover
- design the project organization
- schedule the programme

3 to 10 days

PIP Survey

Phase II

- inform all participants
- collect data
- describe the basic situation
- agree on a reference period
- analyse potential goals
- design rough concepts
- design detailed programmes
- set up task forces
- schedule implementation
- report on anticipated results

4 to 10 weeks

PIP Implementation

Phase III

- inform all participants
- set up programme controls
- implement sections, steps
- get results
- report on results obtained
- implement next sections

4 to 6 months

Maintain high productivity

Source: Scholz, op. cit.

Figure 22.9   Phases I and II of the "Royal Road"

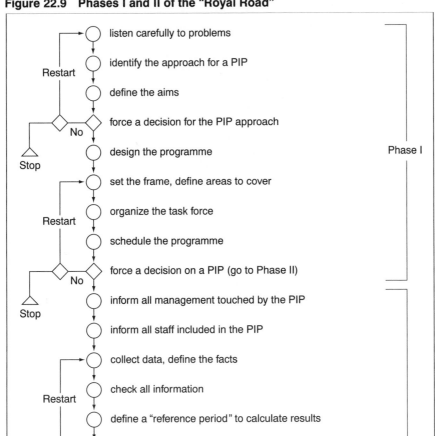

listen carefully to problems

identify the approach for a PIP

Restart

define the aims

force a decision for the PIP approach

No

Stop

design the programme

Phase I

set the frame, define areas to cover

organize the task force

Restart

schedule the programme

force a decision on a PIP (go to Phase II)

No

Stop

inform all management touched by the PIP

inform all staff included in the PIP

collect data, define the facts

check all information

Restart

define a "reference period" to calculate results

agree on data and reference period

No

Stop

analyse potential for productivity improvement

Phase II

define measures for change, following approaches A, B, C

design the concept for productivity improvement

define the goals

Restart

design the programme(s) for implementation

get decision for implementation of the PIP

No

Stop

follow the Royal Road for implementation (go to Phase III)

Source: Scholz, op. cit.

Figure 22.10 Phase III of the "Royal Road"

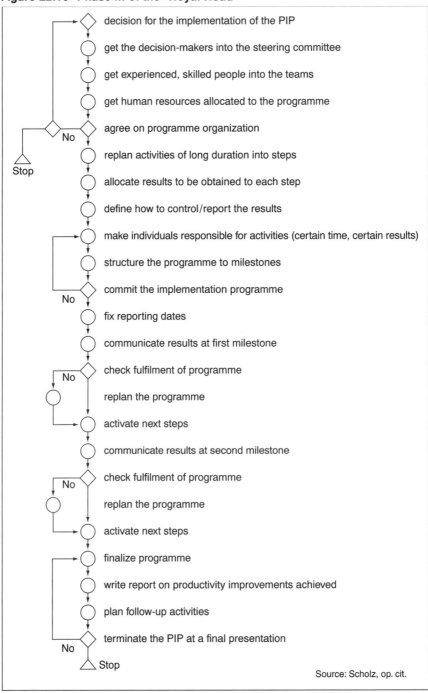

decision for the implementation of the PIP

get the decision-makers into the steering committee

get experienced, skilled people into the teams

get human resources allocated to the programme

agree on programme organization

No

Stop

replan activities of long duration into steps

allocate results to be obtained to each step

define how to control/report the results

make individuals responsible for activities (certain time, certain results)

structure the programme to milestones

commit the implementation programme

No

fix reporting dates

communicate results at first milestone

check fulfilment of programme

No

replan the programme

activate next steps

communicate results at second milestone

check fulfilment of programme

No

replan the programme

activate next steps

finalize programme

write report on productivity improvements achieved

plan follow-up activities

terminate the PIP at a final presentation

No

Stop

Source: Scholz, op. cit.

Productivity-oriented training

In many cases productivity improvement requires considerable efforts in human resources training and development. This can form part of a broader management consulting intervention in improving organizational performance, or can be designed and implemented as a special programme in support of productivity growth (see also section 16.6).

Figure 22.11 provides a general model of the links between company objectives and/or problems (present or future), the problems experienced by managers and employees, their specific training needs, and the training and development approaches that can be combined with the envisaged productivity improvement measures in a single results-oriented HRD cycle.

Figure 22.11 The results-oriented human resource development cycle

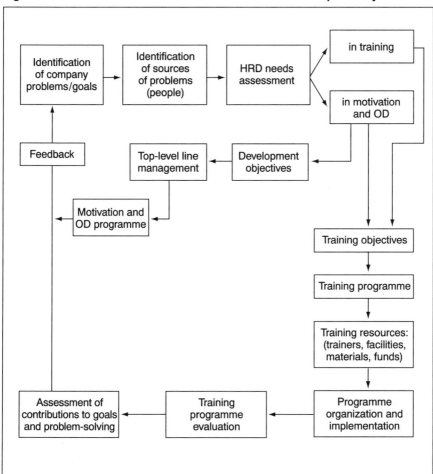

The model shows that the first phase includes identification of company goals and problems, the sources of the problems, and human resource training and development needs. The results of this first phase provide the necessary information for the next phase — identification of development and training objectives. Development objectives provide information for designing organization development programmes, while training objectives serve as a basis for designing training programmes. After both programmes have been implemented, the results are assessed and compared with the objective and with the company's needs. The cycle is closed. Ignoring the human resource development needs assessment inevitably leads to setting wrong objectives and designing (or purchasing) programmes that miss the target. From this development cycle it is easy to see that, if properly implemented, it can contribute significantly to productivity and overall organizational performance improvement. More specifically, integrating productivity or other business objectives and strategy, and training and development of human resources, help to improve organizational effectiveness by:

— making people aware of the need to change;
— assisting the development of new business strategies and solving real strategic and operational problems;
— unlocking the potential and creativity of individuals;
— converting strategy into action;
— building trust and commitment;
— preparing people for coping with new challenges and problems;
— breaking down departmental barriers.

Using business process re-engineering

Following the approach suggested by Hammer and Champy (see section 4.6), many consultants have chosen to use business process re-engineering (BPR) in helping clients to achieve radical improvements in total company productivity and performance.[7]

Hammer's classical example of a process begging to be re-engineered is the simple instance of a customer sending in an order. In most companies, this will typically pass through six to 15 different departments or units. This means that customer's needs are not being met promptly because too many people take part in processing the order, thus increasing the time taken unnecessarily. Hammer talks of the ratio between value time (VT), when work actually gets done, to elapsed time (ET), when nothing happens. "If the organization worked as we'd like it to VT/ET would equal 1. If you have VT/ET = 0.1 you should consider yourself lucky." In practice, typical ratios run from 0.03 to 0.05. Not only does this way of working take time, but it is very costly.

In most companies, overheads are one of the biggest "killers" of productivity. Overheads are "organizational glue", but with direct labour ranging from 3 to 15 per cent of total costs there is now more glue than work.

Therefore BPR programmes focus on customer needs and satisfaction to achieve high financial performance through operational excellence and process integration. Customer focus sets up an immediate opposition to the functional fragmentation of work. A recent study identified two critical factors — breadth and depth of the process. The breadth means that the process to be redesigned must be broadly defined in terms of cost or customer value in order to improve performance across the entire business. As for depth, the redesign must penetrate to the company's core.

At the same time, it should be recognized that not all company re-engineering has been a great success. There is evidence that about 50-70 per cent of those who start BPR do not achieve the results they intended. In 11 of the 20 cases that have been examined in detail performance improvement was below 5 per cent (whether evaluated in terms of change in earnings before interest and taxes, or in terms of reduction in total business-unit costs). Redesign projects often aim at processes that are too narrow and not deep enough. Even with sufficient depth, efforts may still focus on a narrow process rather than the entire business. When managers try to assess the impact of BPR, they often measure the process being redesigned rather than the business unit as a whole. Only those projects that were sufficiently broad and sufficiently deep produced widespread, and long-lasting, bottom-line results. To achieve proper breadth, managers and consultants must first identify the activities that are critical for value creation in the whole business unit for inclusion in the process being redesigned.

While the re-engineering of single functions can be important to companies with limited problems, a narrow approach to redesign cannot produce the kind of radical productivity improvement and other results that many companies are looking for. Process breadth is important for two reasons. First, if more activities are included in the process, the improvements are more likely to extend throughout the entire business unit. Second, if a process includes interrelated activities, a company may identify incremental opportunities that would not surface in single-function performance-improvement efforts. Such oppor-tunities include removing delays and errors when processes pass between functional areas, eliminating problems caused upstream of an activity, and, finally, combining steps that span business units or functions.

Many re-engineering efforts fail because of insufficient process breadth. The Hammer and Champy study mentioned above examined the re-engineering efforts of a European commercial bank. By redesigning some of its back-office processes, the bank expected to reduce process costs by as much as 23 per cent. However, the actual cost reduction, when measured in terms of total business-unit costs, was only 5 per cent and earnings before interest and taxes improved by a scant 3 per cent. The bank overlooked many back-office processes in planning the redesign; in addition, back-office costs in general represented only 40 per cent of the bank's total costs. In summary, the process was too narrowly defined to have any significant impact on business-unit performance as a whole.

Depth in successful redesign means the complete restructuring of the key drivers of behaviour through redesign, including such depth levers as roles and responsibilities, measurement and incentives, organizational structure, information technology, shared values, and skills. An effective transformation of these six depth levers requires a clean-plate approach to process redesign. Only then can companies avoid the classic re-engineering pitfall of fixing the status quo. If the redesign plans are sufficiently broad, all the old support systems will become obsolete — from employee skills to IT. Though IT is critical, the misuse of technology can produce a formidable barrier to the re-engineering programme. IT is just a component of the business system; therefore it is better to obliterate both IT and the business system rather than to automate the wrong business system.

Starting from scratch, companies can plan and build the new infrastructure required to realize the new design. This new infrastructure should include: programmes such as comprehensive training and skill-development plans that require years and not merely weeks for success; performance-measurement systems that track how well the organization is meeting its targets and how employees should be rewarded based on those objectives; communication programmes that help employees understand why and how their behaviour must change; and IT development plans that capture the benefits of new technology at a minimal investment.

To implement BPR projects successfully, the commitment of senior management is of critical importance. The involvement, even of the best consultants, without top management support and active participation, is not sufficient. Successful re-engineering initiatives start with tough chief executives. They should be able to lead organizations through a period of radical changes by combining a determination in pursuing objectives with the ability to build consensus. Strong top management commitment could also be demonstrated by placing the best people on the redesign teams and making significant investment of their own time and resources. In the most successful projects, the top executives spent between 20 and 60 per cent of their time on the project. In contrast, top managers in less successful companies refused to enlist their top people and, as a result, the team did not command respect and the project failed.

Starting from strategic goals, not from current problems

It is important to see that approaches and programmes that produce major improvements, or "quantum leaps" in productivity and performance, exhibit one common characteristic: they do not start by identifying and dissecting current problems, shortcomings and underutilized resources with the intention of devising a better method and thus increasing productivity, while having only a vague idea of what should actually be achieved, and for what purpose. Rather than that, their starting-point is the client company's vision of the future and its strong desire to translate this vision into reality: to become a sector leader, achieve a significant competitive advantage, offer a completely new sort of product or service, or cut costs not by 5 per cent, but by 30-40 per cent. Put in other terms, business re-engineering fares best if linked with corporate strategy.

Thanks to this approach, productivity and performance improvement can be directed to a future purpose, which can be very demanding but not unrealistic.

This purpose serves then as the main common target and driving force for the consultant and the client. It helps the client organization to develop a long-term perspective within which to determine and realize short-term goals, and to learn to work towards its purpose over time. The consulting approach is consistently *purposeful*.[8]

In conclusion, it is easy to see the link to consulting in corporate strategy, which was the topic of the opening chapter (Chapter 12) of this part of the book. It is the company's strategic vision, translated into specific, clearly defined and understandable goals, which is the corner-stone of effective productivity and performance improvement programmes and consulting assignments.

---

[1] J. M. Silverman: *The history of the technical assistance programs of the Marshall Plan and successor agencies, 1948-1961* (Washington, DC, World Bank, 1992).

[2] K. Kurosawa: "Structural approach to the concept and measurement of productivity (2)", in *Studies in Economic Science/Keizai Shushi* (Tokyo, Nihon University), Vol. 50, No. 2, 1980, pp. 96-135.

[3] A. Lawlor: *Productivity improvement manual* (Aldershot, Hampshire, Gower, 1985).

[4] I. Bernolak: *Effective measurement and successful elements of company productivity: The basis of competitiveness and world prosperity*, Paper prepared for the Eighth World Productivity Congress, Stockholm, 1993, pp. 4-6.

[5] J. Prokopenko: *Productivity management: A practical handbook* (Geneva, ILO, 1987), p. 66.

[6] This section is based on a training module on designing a company productivity improvement programme, written by Karl Scholz for the ILO (unpublished manuscript).

[7] M. Hammer and J. Champy: *Re-engineering the corporation* (New York, Harper Business, 1993); see also M. James: "Hammering the BPR message", in *Management Consultancy* (London), July 1993, p. 49, and "Re-engineering reviewed", in *The Economist* (London), 2 July 1994, p. 64.

[8] See also P. Stroh: "Purposeful consulting", in *Organizational Dynamics* (New York), Autumn 1987, pp. 49-67.

PART IV

MANAGING A CONSULTING FIRM

FUNDAMENTALS OF CONSULTING FIRM MANAGEMENT

23

The previous parts of this book have shown how management consultants operate in serving their clients. Part IV, which opens with this chapter, looks at the consultant's work from a different angle. It shows management consulting as a professional service that itself requires competent management if it is to provide a quality service to clients and, at the same time, achieve satisfying business results.

That management consulting itself needs to be managed may be self-evident to a large consulting firm employing hundreds of consultants and engaged in a wide range of assignments. In such a professional firm, finding work for all consultants, coordinating a number of varied assignments, recruiting and developing consultants, keeping abreast of the state of the art and achieving adequate profits all represent a formidable management task. However, a small consultancy, and even a single practitioner, also needs to manage resources, time allocation, relations with clients, administrative support, professional development and so on.

In practice this basic truth is often ignored. There are consulting firms, including some fairly large ones, which devote all their talent and energy to finding new assignments and dealing with their clients' problems. However, they neglect the management of their own operation. The inevitable consequences of this attitude are inefficiencies, internal conflicts, and flaws in the services provided to clients.

Clients are not unaware of this. We often hear, "Healer, heal thyself", or "Consultant, take your own medicine!". The message cannot be more plain. While any professional service firm requires management reflecting its nature and complexity, the case of management consultants is a particularly delicate one. Management is their daily bread and showing clients how to manage better is their main activity. If clients are to take such advice seriously, the consultant must be seen "to practise what he preaches". If this is not the case, clients become cynical about the consultant's real ability to deal with other people's problems.

This chapter provides a brief overview of key issues faced in managing consulting firms. Further chapters in Part IV will discuss these issues in detail and depth.

23.1 The management challenge of the professions

As a relatively young profession, management consulting should be able to draw some lessons from the management experience accumulated by older and better-established professions, such as law or accounting. Unfortunately, management is a new and relatively underdeveloped field in all professions. Professional firms historically have been managed in one of two ways: badly or not at all.

Management, as a distinct function and approach to running an organization, starts being practised systematically and consistently only when it becomes a recognized necessity. As long as professionals prefer to operate as individuals, independently or through loose interest groupings, sharing some physical facilities and administrative support, but each serving one's own personal clients and ignoring the clients of other colleagues, the management function looks superfluous, if not undesirable. Therefore the key factor through which the management of professions came into being was the growing size and complexity of professional firms, and of the tasks tackled.

The second factor was changes in the market and in competition. With the gradual disappearance of protective regulations and traditional practices inhibiting competition, the professional firms started being exposed to market pressures and opportunities like businesses in any other sector of the economy. Issues such as marketing, selling, product life cycle, innovation and efficiency became important, and had to be taken care of.

Conversely, certain factors have constrained the advent of modern management in the professions. First is the professionals' ambiguous attitude to management. On the one hand, they do not object to belonging to a well-established and financially strong firm. On the other hand, as individuals they cherish freedom and hate discipline. Many of them do not want to see any management, and related paperwork, anywhere near to them. This creates paradoxical if not inextricable situations. In Bruce Henderson's words, "the basic paradox is the requirement to manage the unmanageable".[1]

A second constraint has been the shortage of managers of professional service organizations. The best professionals can be the worst managers. Many excellent professionals are prepared to devote some time to management, say supervise a small team, if this does not take up more than a third or a half of their time. Few are prepared to give up all client work to become full-time managers of other professionals. Compromises have to be accepted as common practice, mostly by combining management with direct work for clients, or rotating managerial roles.

A third constraint has been the underdeveloped body of knowledge on the management of professions. Understandably, meaningful concepts and theories could not start developing as long as there was no practical ground, accumulated experience, or demand. Significant contributions are few, and these date mainly from the last decade.

In summary, the case for competent and effective management of professional service organizations seems to have been made. In addition to the competence and motivation of individual professionals, the management of professional teams and organizations is increasingly recognized as a key factor of service quality and business performance. However, many professional firms have a long way to go to become well-managed organizations.

In identifying the management requirements of consulting activities, we have found it useful to look at consulting from two different perspectives. Firstly, consulting is a professional service and some of its management requirements are determined by this characteristic. Section 23.2 will attempt to review them and to point out practical implications. Secondly, consulting practised as an independent service, for a fee, is a business activity and must be viewed and managed as a business. This will be the theme of section 23.3. The last part of the chapter will provide a synthesis of the two perspectives.

23.2 Managing a professional service

What sort of product?

It has been pointed out many times that professional services produce *intangible* outputs or products. In consulting, the product is the advice given to the client. Alternatively, if implementation is included, one could say that the final product is the change that has actually occurred and the improvements that have been achieved in the client organization thanks to the consultant's intervention.

Such a product is difficult to define, measure and evaluate. The consultant can have a certain conception of the product, while the client's view of the product and its real value can be quite different. In marketing his or her services, what the consultant is selling is essentially a promise — a promise of help that will satisfy the client's needs. Clients cannot, to use Theodore Levitt's words, "see, touch, smell, taste or test" the product before deciding to purchase it.[2] They have to look for surrogates in assessing whether the consultant is likely to deliver what has been promised.

This explains the crucial role of self-assessment, self-discipline and an ethical approach in marketing and delivering the consulting service. Often the consultant will be the only person able to judge what services he should be offering in general, and what he can promise and actually deliver to a particular client.

There are ways of reducing uncertainty by *increasing product tangibility*. The client can obtain a manual describing in detail how the business will be diagnosed, what data will be examined, comparisons made, ratios produced and suggestions developed. Or the consultant may be offering a system or a procedure, which will be delivered as such, in its standard form, or with adaptations and supplements. The role of fully or partially standardized systems and procedures has increased in consulting over the last ten to 15 years. Any larger consultancy has some "more tangible" products to offer and some small firms have been completely built around one or two proprietary systems. Yet the basic issue remains the same. Every client organization is unique and there is no certainty that even an excellent system will be effective in every client's environment.

To determine what to standardize and market as a standard product is a difficult decision. There are consultants who have spoilt their reputation by selling standard packages to clients who needed an individualized approach. On the other hand, if a standard system or methodology is applied flexibly and with imagination, it can help to increase the quality and reduce the costs both to the consultant and to the client.

Working with the clients

Building and managing a clientele is another key issue in managing professional consulting. If there is no client, there is no consulting. The consultant cannot produce for stock, getting ready for prompt delivery once a client is found. In fact, the client is a direct participant in the production of the service. As a minimum, he or she has to help the consultant in defining the scope of the advice, provide needed information, and then take the advice. In process consulting, it is the client who "produces", while the consultant, as is often emphasized, acts mainly as a catalyst.

The link between the consultant and the client is a highly individualized one. On each side of the partnership there is one person, or a small team. Whatever the size and complexity of the professional service firm, the firm sends individual professionals or small teams to clients for undertaking specific assignments. Larger consulting firms can handle more important and more complex projects, and support individual consultants with the collective know-how of the whole firm, but even a very large firm operates through a number of individualized client assignments and cannot think in terms of mass production, or of selling services to unknown customers through networks of wholesale and retail shops. Even the largest consultancy operates as a retailer.

Service quality

The intangibility and other above-mentioned characteristics of profes-sional services determine the consultants' approach to assessing and ensuring quality. Within the profession, and even within one firm, it is virtually impossible to refer to independent and fully objective benchmarks whereby quality could be measured and evaluated. Yet service quality is one of the basic characteristics inherent in a professional approach. Providing every client with a service of best possible quality is a professional goal in its own right, not merely a condition of being able to sell an assignment and to get paid for it.

Because consulting is a service aimed at satisfying specific client needs, the degree to which these needs, or requirements, have been met is normally regarded as the main criterion for evaluating service quality. Once more the consultant-client relationship comes to the forefront: service quality cannot be measured — and does not even exist — outside this relationship, but only as an intrinsic part of it.

In consulting, quality management and quality improvement are therefore built on feedback from clients and focus on increasing client satisfaction above all. When appropriate, however, quality management has to reach beyond the criterion of satisfying client requirements. This will be the case in working with uninformed clients, whose current requirements may be well below the consultant's own conception of high service quality. Also, quality means being up to date and providing a service of appropriate sophistication. Often the consultant will be better placed than a particular client, or even a whole group of clients, to judge the desirable degree of novelty and sophistication of certain services. Being proactive in consulting implies that the consultant thinks even of those needs and requirements of which a client has not been aware, and helps the client to realize all his or her possibilities and needs.

The professional workers

Professional consultants, including the beginners in the firm, are used to dealing directly with clients and spend more time with clients than with colleagues within their firm. The firm, on the other hand, must know that it can rely on the competence and integrity of its professional staff as a whole, including not only the senior partners, but also the younger colleagues.

In some established professions there is a well-defined path to the necessary level of competence and integrity, including university studies, attendance at a graduate school, and practical training and "indoctrination" over a number of years in a professional firm. Membership of professional institutions or special examinations may be required. The result of this process is a reasonably high degree of standardization of skills, permitting the definition of a range of jobs that even a relatively junior professional should normally be able to perform either without or with limited supervision. Even the attitudes of professionals tend to become fairly standardized; thus it can be predicted how professionals will normally react and behave in typical situations in which their intervention is required.

In management consulting the situation is more complex, for several reasons. It is a young profession, and consultants employed by any firm usually have different educational and practical backgrounds. It is almost necessary for them to come from various schools and business environments so that the firm can handle a variety of assignments and deal with management problems requiring a multidisciplinary approach. Contributing different insights and perspectives can be extremely valuable. Furthermore, the behavioural aspects of handling technical and human problems, and the professional's ability to work with people and help them to cope with organizational change, are probably more significant in management consulting than in other professions.

Therefore, in managing the professional staff, consulting firms face special challenges, such as:

- how to build up a homogeneous operating core with people possessing heterogeneous backgrounds and skills (e.g. finance and accounting, information science, behavioural science, statistics, economics, law or industrial engineering);
- how to develop a common philosophy of consulting and an *esprit de corps* while maintaining the diversity of personalities, attitudes and approaches needed for various assignments, which can be an important source of innovation;
- how to define the right degree of decentralization of technical decisions concerning client assignments (e.g. questions which an operating consultant on assignment can decide, and those on which a manager or partner should give an opinion or make a decision);
- how to provide consultants on assignments with technical information and support in order to make them as effective as possible to their current clients;
- how to make sure that not only the skills, but also the personalities and work styles of consultants and clients, will be matched in order to establish a productive consultant-client relationship in every single case;
- how to build, maintain and utilize a collective knowledge base of the firm;
- how to provide the sort of leadership that appeals to professional workers with a developed sense of independence.

Professional culture

Despite their high level of knowledge and skill, or perhaps because of it, consultants are difficult to manage. Many of them have become used to getting on with the job for the client and deciding what to do without waiting for any instructions from their superiors. They tend to have their own conception of management in a professional firm: managers are responsible for creating favourable conditions for professional work (which includes finding new work and securing finance), but should not intervene in individual projects and assignments. Some professionals resent any control or interference in their work with clients, while others are prepared to accept it on condition that it comes from people whom they respect.

Some consultants become strong individualists and one is tempted to ask why they actually stay with the firm. Some stay because they have chosen to work as technicians and do not want to be bothered with administrative and marketing problems. Others appreciate the advantages of teamwork and collaboration with other professional colleagues. There is a third group for whom work in a professional firm is mainly a learning experience, and who do not feel that they must stay in consulting until retirement.

The attitudes that will prevail depend very much on the organizational culture and management style of a particular firm. Indeed, consulting firms tend to exhibit various organizational cultures. The firm may be nothing more than "a collection of individualities housed under one roof", and physically not even under the same roof, since consultants spend most of their time with clients. The management of their firm may act as an employment agency, whose main objective is to find work, keep consultants occupied and provide common support services to the employees.

In contrast, while respecting individuals, many leading firms emphasize a common consulting philosophy, the service ethos, service quality, team spirit, sharing of information and know-how, the seniors' responsibility for guiding the juniors, participation in management, and pride in belonging to an excellent and respectable professional firm.

Leadership

Experience of excellent consulting firms, smaller and larger, has demonstrated the crucial role of leadership. Leadership is needed to build up a professional organization with a strong culture, whose individual members adhere to common values and work together as coherent teams in pursuing common professional and business goals. Leadership is needed to motivate individuals towards superior performance, service quality and loyalty to the firm. Without leadership, a professional firm is bound to operate below its potential, and disintegrate sooner or later.

The problem with leadership in professions is that it is a rare commodity. It requires a combination of superior professional achievement with the personal qualities of a leader: a genuine interest in people, organizational talent and an ability to set an example, maintain morale and provide encouragement. Professional workers tend to reject leaders whom they do not respect as highly competent and productive professional colleagues and as persons exhibiting genuine interest in leading and helping others.

This makes the choice for management positions difficult. If possible, managers in consulting and other professions should also be natural leaders, and should be willing to assume both leadership and administrative responsibilities.

23.3 Managing a professional business

Management consulting is a business, and has to be treated as such, in all cases where an independent service is provided to clients for a fee, and where the firm has to sell services and finance its existence and growth from its earnings. This applies to the vast majority of consultants in market economies and in countries in transition from the command-economy to the market-economy model. Internal and subsidized consulting services constitute an exception and all principles of managing professional businesses may not apply to them. Yet they can greatly benefit from being structured and managed as "quasi-businesses".

Recognizing that consulting is a business

It is not always easy to call a spade a spade. For many years, professional firms resented being regarded as "businesses", and even at the present time some professionals feel uneasy about "selling" their services or discussing fees, which they regard as unprofessional and beneath their dignity. As one practitioner has pointed out, a consultant is often "torn between being a professional and a commercial".

Yet a professional service must find a buyer (client) who is able and prepared to pay an adequate price for it. There is a more or less developed and structured market for professional services, and competition among professionals is increasingly regarded not only as normal and acceptable, but as necessary and beneficial to the clients. The marketing of professional services has undergone spectacular changes over the last two decades, and in many countries further changes are likely to occur in the years to come.

Like any other business, a professional consulting firm can and should make a profit. This profit will depend on many variables, some of which are not under the firm's control (e.g. general demand for professional services), while others are (e.g. the uniqueness and the quality of the services provided, the marketing skills, and the efficiency of operations). Profit planning, and deciding on the use of the profits, is important in every consulting firm that wants to be in a healthy financial position, compensate its people correctly and have sufficient resources for further development.

Ownership

Most consulting businesses are owned by the consultants themselves. Several legal forms of ownership are common in consulting, and these will be described in Chapter 30. However, not all consultants working with a firm are necessarily co-owners. Usually there is a group of partners who are co-owners of the firm, and a group of consultants who work for the firm as salaried employees without having any share in the ownership.

People-intensive business

A consulting business is highly people-intensive (labour-intensive) and requires relatively little capital. All a new entrant to the profession needs is a small amount of working capital to cover living and other expenses before he or she starts collecting fees on a regular basis. He or she can even borrow this money, and start working from home without renting expensive office space. Many sole practitioners have thus been able to become consultants, even if quite a few of them have had to make personal sacrifices at the beginning of their consulting career.

The labour-intensive nature of consulting affects all areas of managing consulting businesses. The professional staff constitutes the main asset, although it has no value from a strictly accounting point of view and bankers would not recognize it as a collateral. The cost of staff tends to be high in absolute terms and may exceed 60-65 per cent of the total cost of services. Staff productivity, motivation and investment in further staff development are fundamental issues of the economics of the firm.

To change products, that is to phase out old and introduce new services, is much easier in consulting than in capital-intensive businesses. Many consulting firms have been able to exploit this advantage in adapting their service portfolio to new market opportunities, and in increasing profitability by offering new and more sophisticated services.

Yet at the present time management consulting is tending to become more capital-intensive. Consultants have to invest more in information technology and related staff development. The pace of change in information technologies quickly makes this investment obsolete, thus forcing the firm into writing off these expenses within two to three years, and making further investments.

A profit model for consulting firms

The basic issues of consulting firms' economics are reflected in the profit model, developed by David Maister and applied by the Association of Management Consulting Firms (ACME) in its annual surveys of the profession's economics.[3] The profit model is a variant of the traditional Dupont formula for industrial companies, breaking down aggregate data into analytical ratios. "Return on equity" is replaced by "profit per partner" and the global formula is as follows:

$$\frac{\text{Profits}}{\text{Partners}} = \frac{\text{Profits}}{\text{Fees}} \times \frac{\text{Fees}}{\text{Consultants}} \times \frac{\text{Consultants}}{\text{Partners}}$$

$$\text{(Profitability)} \quad \text{(Margin)} \quad \text{(Productivity)} \quad \text{(Leverage)}$$

The understanding of the formula permits firm management to focus on particular factors affecting business performance, and to manage the relationships between these factors.

Leverage

Leverage ("an increased means for accomplishing some purpose", according to *Webster's Dictionary*) is one of the basic concepts underlying the structure and operation of professional firms. The general principle is simple: leverage is achieved by employing a certain number of (less experienced and lower paid) junior professionals for each (more experienced and more highly paid) senior professional. In most instances, this senior professional will be the firm's co-owner (partner), while the juniors will be the firm's salaried employees. Leverage assumes a rational and efficient division of tasks: the seniors are mainly responsible for finding and managing work, while the juniors are mainly responsible for executing client assignments under the seniors' guidance and supervision.

Box 23.1 Leverage and profitability

The relationship betwen leverage and profitability can be illustrated by many different examples.

1. In a consulting unit, one partner may have "leveraged himself" by four operating consultants. Total earnings are $600,000, i.e. $120,000 per consultant (including the partner), while their salaries are $450,000, including $130,000 for the partner and $80,000 for each operating consultant (let us ignore the overheads and other expenses). If the partner manages to use and supervise one more operating consultant, thus increasing leverage from 4:1 to 5:1, the new total will be $720,000. Earnings per consultant are unchanged, but total profit, hence profit per partner, increases from $150,000 to $190,000, i.e. by 26.6 per cent.
2. Let us assume that, to be able to guide and supervise the fifth consultant, the partner will have to alter his time allocation. Instead of doing 40 per cent billable and 60 per cent non-billable work, he will only be able to produce 30 per cent of billable and 70 per cent of non-billable work. His personal billing will thus drop from $120,000 to $90,000, i.e. by 25 per cent, and the total profit will increase only by $10,000 (from $150,000 to $160,000), i.e. by 6.6 per cent. Profit per consultant will decrease from $30,000 to $26,600, i.e. by 11 per cent, although the total volume of business increased by 15 per cent.
3. In another scenario, the unit described in (1) above will find new work that will be paid better, but will require different staff competence and structure. From five consultants (one partner, four operating) it will pass to seven by recruiting one senior (partner) and one operating consultant. The two new consultants will be able to deliver $280,000, i.e. $140,000 per consultant, while their salaries will be the same as in (1), i.e. $130,000 for the partner and $80,000 for the operating consultant. Figures for the restructured unit as a whole will show a slightly higher profit per consultant ($31,500 instead of $30,000), but a considerably lower profit per partner ($110,000 instead of $150,000, i.e. a 26.6 per cent reduction). This has happened, despite higher fees and profits per consultant, due to the change of leverage from 4 : 1 to 2.5 : 1.

The reader can certainly think of other scenarios and their impact on profits.

In practice, the principle of leverage can be applied in different ways depending on the nature of the services provided, the clients' needs and preferences, the career planning in the firm and other factors. However, the appropriate, or optimum, leverage for a consulting firm depends on the nature of the services provided. Very demanding, state-of-the-art and highly responsible work does not permit the use of the same number of juniors per senior professional as more routine, repetitive, standardized and technically simpler services.

Leverage has a strong impact on profitability measured by profits per partner (see box 23.1). Firms with lower fee levels and lower earnings per consultant, but higher leverage, can earn higher profits per partner than firms with higher earnings per consultant, but lower leverage.

Productivity

Increasing productivity means earning more fees per consultant employed. The first way to achieve this is to increase working-time utilization — an important target in all professional firms, but not an exhaustible one due to legislation, human limitations, and the simple but important truth that unreasonably long working hours result in lower quality and falling efficiency.

The second way is charging higher fees per unit of time worked for clients. This cannot be an arbitrary decision if there is a market rate and competition. Higher fees can be achieved by selling new, better and more sophisticated services thanks to innovation, programme development, training and self-education, and better utilization of know-how and experience within the firm.

Margin

The profit margin achieved by the consulting firm reflects the productivity and leverage levels above all. Higher consultant productivity and higher leverage generate higher margins. However, there are also some additional costs, such as general administration, purchase of information, and training and development costs, whose reduction can improve the margin. It is up to the firm's management to judge what is feasible and beneficial in both the short and the long term. Saving on training and administrative costs will increase the margin, but may reduce consultant time utilization (due to poor administration) and fee levels (training was neglected and the consultant's competence did not increase).

Growth

As explained above, in the consulting business improvements in earnings per partner and profitability do not always require the firm to grow. There are even growth patterns which fail to increase profitability, or which reduce it, although the total profits are higher (box 23.1).

On the other hand, the business may have to grow for other reasons (see also section 24.4):

— to strengthen its position on the market and capture new markets;

— to develop a more complete service portfolio and employ consulting staff able to undertake a wider range of complex assignments;

— to provide for new work opportunities, career development and staff motivation.

Entrepreneurship in consulting

Entrepreneurship lies at the very heart of business. In a consulting firm, the founder is the first entrepreneur. He or she is the person who has taken a life chance and linked his or her personal future to the future of the new business. Although the first investment may have been modest in financial terms, it is always important in terms of human intellect and energy.

Box 23.2 Hunters and farmers

Approaches to entrepreneurship and management in the consulting business can be demonstrated by differentiating between "hunter" and "farmer" firms.

Hunter firms attempt to maximize the entrepreneurialism of their members by creating the maximum possible degree of individual autonomy. They encourage each individual (and each small group) to respond and adapt to the local market. Marketing is a matter of individual responsibility. Firm-wide consistency (in services, in markets and in approach) is sacrificed in order to capture the benefits of local market opportunities.

To succeed, hunter firms must attract, motivate and reward the best entrepreneurs. Individuals rise and fall according to the results of their own entrepreneurial efforts. There is no central strategy — just kill meat! The focus is short term. Those who kill meat are rewarded.

Entrepreneurialism, flexibility, responsiveness, and fast adaptation to shifting market needs are powerful business virtues. Any firm that can successfully maximize these will be a formidable competitor.

Farmer firms (also called "one-firm" firms) are built on a collaborative approach to professional practice and emphasize business systems such as compensation, hiring, training, organization and choice of service lines. They build their success by investing heavily in the chosen areas. What counts is not individual performance, but contribution to aggregate success. There is no way for an individual to do well unless the organization as a whole succeeeds.

Farmer firms enter new markets (after thorough preparation) "big or not at all". Their marketing is focused. Farmers approach marketing as an organized, joint activity done as teams. Entrepreneurship is not a matter of individual drive and initiative, but a function of the whole firm's management.

Firms that attempt to capture both groups of benefits (individual entrepreneurship and collaborative strategy) must make significant compromises in management practice, which usually results in lessened performance.

Source: Excerpts from D. Maister: "Hunters and farmers", Ch. 28 of *Managing the professional service firm* (New York, The Free Press, 1993).

A consulting business needs entrepreneurial thinking and behaviour even when it becomes larger and turns into a partnership or a company employing a number of consultants. It must be prevented from turning into a bureaucracy or a research establishment. It probably needs an entrepreneurial spirit more than growing businesses in some other sectors. This is due to the rapidly changing needs of the clients, the changing shape of the profession and growing competition from other professions, and to the fact that consultants encounter new opportunities virtually every day. However, every consultant must have the will and the ability to see and take these opportunities.

It is essential to define the entrepreneurial role of consultants, in addition to their specific technical and managerial roles. Consultants will think and behave as entrepreneurs if they know that such behaviour is wanted and valued by the firm. They should know what is regarded as entrepreneurship: Is it getting new clients? More business from existing clients? Selling more assignments that will be easy to execute? Looking for innovative work methods? Demonstrating that the firm is able to come up with new ways of tackling old problems? Taking the initiative to develop new fields of consulting?

Consultants need to know, too, who in the firm is supposed to think and act as an entrepreneur. Is this a province of senior partners? Is every member of the firm, including the new recruits, encouraged to think and act as a relatively independent entrepreneur?

When consulting is not a business

Not all management consulting units are independent businesses. Internal consulting units within governments and public or private corporations (section 2.5), and most consulting units in management or productivity centres in developing countries, cannot be categorized as businesses. Some of these units provide consulting services free, or for a nominal price, instead of charging the full market rate. Their budgets may be subsidized by their parent body, or from another source.

Some of these units may be in competition with other consultants, but their independence tends to be limited in recruiting, remunerating and terminating the appointments of staff, fixing consulting fees, expanding or scaling down activities, changing the service portfolio or choosing new clients.

Not all the principles involved in managing a professional business can be applied to such a unit. However, certain principles are applicable. The effectiveness of these units can be enhanced by treating them as "quasi-businesses", providing them with relative decision-making autonomy, encouraging them to sell services and making sure that their business results have a bearing on staff remuneration and motivation, and on the future development of the unit.

Internal consulting units may compete with external consultants for work to be done within the parent organization but, at the same time, may be authorized to market and sell their services to other companies.

23.4 The management matrix

Some important conclusions concerning the nature and the scope of the management of consulting activities can be drawn from this analysis. First, each of the two sides of consulting reviewed above — consulting as a professional service and consulting as a business — has its specific management requirements and justifies certain management tasks and approaches. Secondly, management tasks in a consulting organization relate either to individual client assignments (projects) or to common and general needs of developing and operating a consulting practice as a whole. These different dimensions are shown in figure 23.1 (overleaf) in matrix form.

Figure 23.1   The management matrix in a consulting firm

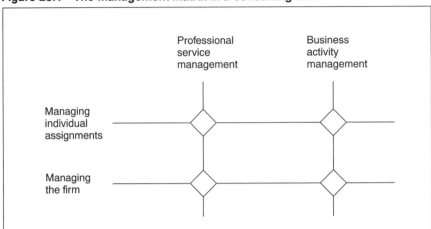

A fundamental management task in consulting is balancing, reconciling and harmonizing different needs and interests, such as:

—   professional and commercial;

—   individual and collective;

—   the clients' and the firm's;

—   the owners' (partners) and the other members' (employees) of the firm;

—   short term and long term.

Balancing professional service and business activity management

The management of a professional service and of a business activity are two sides of one coin. They can be described and examined separately as we have done in this chapter, but in real life they are not separated. Yet in every firm there may be pressures that could easily destroy the delicate equilibrium. Individuals or teams sometimes foster services in which they are personally interested, but for which there is no market, or which are no longer profitable. Some partners resent leverage because they prefer to do everything by themselves rather than relying on junior colleagues. The firm may press consultants to increase profitability by lowering quality. Operating consultants may be asked to become more productive by saving on data gathering and analysis. Juniors may be assigned to jobs which are beyond their competence, and so on.

Balancing assignment and practice management

The main task of management consultants is to work on assignments in client organizations. Every assignment has a business dimension (cost, price, efficiency of execution, contribution to the firm's income and profit) in addition to the specific technical tasks to be carried out for the client.

Assignments constitute basic building-blocks in the management system of consulting organizations. In theory, the system operates as follows. Once an assignment has been identified and a contract agreed to, the organization has to appoint a consultant or establish an assignment team and furnish them with needed resources. A self-contained management cell is thus created within the consulting firm. As assignments normally have a limited life-span, assignment teams cease to exist when the job is completed. Individual team members are regrouped to make up new assignment teams (and new management cells), while other resources (e.g. equipment, stationery, finance) have been used up or are reallocated.

It could be objected that the short life-span of an assignment does not provide for continuity in organizational relations and makes the whole management system volatile. Yet the nature of consulting services underlines the importance of assignments as basic management cells. During the assignment, the working time and the expertise of the operating consultants "belong" to the client, and the team leader must be able to mobilize and control fully the resources and guarantee the delivery of the service. Consultants whose full-time presence in assignments is not required must be able to share their time and attention among several assignments. The consulting firm supports, guides and controls the assignment teams in these efforts. The whole operation of the firm must be geared to this objective.

Assignment management is a crucial activity in any professional consulting firm. However, even the best assignment management cannot ensure the functioning and development of the firm as a whole. It can even create conflicts and imbalances by unduly favouring one assignment to the detriment of others, or of the global interests of the firm. Assignments can conflict with the firm's overall strategy. Future development can be jeopardized. Here again a balanced approach is required, putting the right emphasis on global concerns and needs of the firm in addition to managing specific client projects.

These global concerns and organizational needs include in particular:

● the firm's professional and business culture;
● strategy for achieving high professional standards and service quality;
● strategy for achieving profitability and growth;
● the development of new capabilities and products;
● market and client base development and promotion;
● management, motivation and development of the principal resource — the professional staff;
● sound financial management and control.

In summary, the art of managing a consulting practice consists of dealing with all dimensions of the management matrix in a balanced manner, making sure that both individual client assignments and the consulting firm as a whole meet their professional goals and business objectives. What this means to various management functions will be discussed in detail in the chapters that follow.

---

[1] See H. J. Hagerdorn: "The anatomy of ideas behind a successful consulting firm", in *Journal of Management Consulting* (Milwaukee, Wisconsin), Vol. 1, No. 1, 1982, pp. 49-59.

[2] T. Levitt: "Marketing intangible products and product intangibles", in *Harvard Business Review* (Boston, Massachusetts), May-June 1981, p. 96.

[3] This section is based on D. Maister: "Profitability: Health and hygiene", in *Managing the professional service firm* (New York, The Free Press, 1993), pp. 31-39; and Association of Management Consulting Firms: *ACME 1993 survey of United States key management information* (New York, 1993). See also V. E. Millar: *On the management of professional service firms: Ten myths debunked* (Fitzwilliam, New Hampshire, Kennedy Publications, 1991).

THE CONSULTING FIRM'S STRATEGY

24

In Chapter 12 strategic management was shown to be one of the principal areas in which management consultants work with business clients. Thus, many consultants are familiar with the concept of strategy and the techniques of strategic planning and management. This chapter looks at the question of how a strategic approach can also be useful to the management of consulting firms.

24.1 A strategic approach

A strategic approach is justified if there is a need for it, not because it has become fashionable. In the past, most consultants followed no particular strategy and tried to react to any opportunity and any expression of interest from a potential client. This has changed. More and more consultants realize that they cannot be all things to all clients, and that they stand a better chance of obtaining business by offering a unique service, or by serving a market segment where they will outperform other consultants. Successful consulting firms behave increasingly as strategists even if the term "strategy" is not always used.

Purpose and goals

As in other businesses and organizations, strategy in consulting consists in choosing a path that leads from one condition (the present) to a different one (the future). The starting-point is known, or can be identified by assessing the consultant's present position, resources and capabilities. This is not very difficult if there is a will to see reality as it is and not through rose-coloured spectacles.

The future is a different matter. The basic questions to answer are: What do we want to achieve, what is our basic goal and when do we want to achieve this goal? Such questions cannot be answered by doing analytical work and merely extrapolating past trends. Extrapolation can be very misleading if the environment and the markets change with high speed. What is needed is a vision of the future, which is something different from an assessment and a projection of demand and opportunities; it is the consultant's conception of what the firm should look like in the future. This is a reflection not only of ambition and imagination but also of a realistic assessment of opportunities and of the firm's strengths and weaknesses.

The two dimensions of consulting discussed in the previous chapter have to be given consideration in deciding what the consulting firm wants to be in the future. First, the consulting firm needs to define its purpose and objectives from *a professional point of view* by seeking answers to questions such as:

— What sort of professional firm do we want to be?

— What will be our culture, our consulting philosophy and our role in solving clients' problems, in helping clients to achieve high performance levels, and in developing their learning and problem-solving capabilities?

— Do we want to become leaders in technical terms, that is consultants who are always at the forefront of progress in technology and management methods, and who are the first to offer new information and new services to their clients?

— Shall we confine ourselves strictly to consulting in management, or widen the range of our service offerings? What services should we add in order to be more useful to clients?

— What new services can we afford to add to our portfolio without losing our identity and entering areas beyond our competence?

The second strategic dimension is that of *a business activity*. The key questions to ask are:

• What does our consulting firm want to achieve as a business?

• Should our strategy ensure mere survival, moderate growth or rapid expansion?

• What is the position in the market for consulting services that we want to achieve?

• What earnings and profits should be achieved?

• What should our firm's financial strength and independence be?

The unity of these two dimensions cannot be overstressed. Focusing only on commercial goals could kill the firm professionally. Ignoring the business side of strategy would undermine the firm's financial health and the proposed professional strategies could be unattainable.

Competitive edge

A strategic approach helps to achieve a competitive edge over other providers of consulting services. A fundamental question is: What is our competitive advantage, or why should a client turn to us rather than to other consultants? The reason could lie in special technical expertise, a unique product unavailable elsewhere, a wide range of multidisciplinary expertise required for complex business problems, an intimate knowledge of an industrial sector, speed and reliability of service delivery, low fees, good reputation and contacts among public sector agencies, or excellent relationships with existing clients.

It is true that every consultant cannot become a guru, and most clients do not need guru consulting in any case. Clients' needs are at various levels of sophistication, complexity and novelty, and the consulting market offers a wide range of different opportunities. However, the number of consultants competing for all these opportunities keeps growing. And clients themselves compete increasingly with their own consultants by building up internal technical, analytical and change management capabilities in areas where until recently they used to turn to consultants.

Thus, a successful consultant who is happy with his or her current achievements and current chances of getting good business is probably very close to losing a competitive advantage. Success can be the consultant's worst enemy. While you are enjoying your leading position and past successes, another consultant is probably working hard on developing something new and demonstrating that he or she can perform better than you. Privileged relationships with existing clients will not save you. Clients themselves are exposed to competition and cannot afford the luxury of retaining obsolete consultants, even if they have been getting full satisfaction from them in past assignments.

In consulting, you should be absolutely honest with yourself in examining whether you have a competitive advantage. You may feel that you are good, even very good, but are you really better than your competitors? If you conclude that you possess a distinct competitive advantage today, the next questions should be: How solid is it and for how long will it last? How can you maintain and enhance it? If you have no competitive advantage, maybe you can think of developing one. How? This will, of course, depend on many factors and there is no blueprint. But there are no limits to imagination and innovation. Not everybody will succeed, but everybody can try. After all, this is how management consulting has been developing — not by grand designs involving the whole profession, but by a myriad of individual efforts by smaller and larger firms to offer new and better services to clients.

Strategy and operations

There has been a long debate about what the concept of "strategy" means when applied to the behaviour of business organizations. Is strategic equal to long term? Is a strategic choice one that has a major impact on the nature and shape of the business? Can we talk about strategy if choice is limited and there is only one really feasible path?

In our conception, strategic decisions of consulting firms are those that will have a significant impact on the shape or profile of the firm in both professional and business terms. It is plain to see that such decisions cannot be separated from everyday operations. If a consultant who has never worked for the transport sector agrees to do a first assignment for a road transport company, this may be more than a simple operational decision. It will turn out to be a strategic decision if followed by more work from the same client and if other firms from the transport sector start coming with requests for advice. An operational decision may comprise elements of a strategic decision.

At what point can we say that an operational decision has turned into a strategic one? This is difficult to answer in general terms. However, every consulting firm must be sensitive to this issue. If not, it may find itself trapped in an important choice which has been made unconsciously and even unwillingly, just because no one has been monitoring a shifting sectoral or functional focus of operating assignments.

If a strategic choice is made by the firm's management, it is essential to turn it into marketing and operating decisions. New clients, new services, different work for existing clients, new intervention methods, significant improvements in quality, changes in the firm's public image — these are all strategic changes requiring changes in marketing and operations. There is no strategic change without change in the firm's operations.

Flexibility in the strategic approach

Only experience can show whether strategy has been chosen correctly. Another consultant, a competitor, may have chosen to offer the same new service, and has performed better in marketing and service delivery. Both your and your competitor's choices were correct when they were made, but your competitor has been more successful in implementing his or her strategy. You will have to revise your strategy, looking for one that takes the competitor's achievements into account.

However, the main reasons for flexibility in defining and redefining strategy are not management errors, or competitors' successes, but changes in the business environment. Management consulting would lose its meaning if it did not reflect alterations in technology, markets, finance, legislation, national and international politics, and any other significant changes that affect clients' businesses. Consulting strategy has to follow, or preferably anticipate, these changes. Once the financial markets have been internationalized and even smaller firms can think of borrowing on the international money market, a financial consultant's strategy cannot be restricted to the national financial market.

The need for flexibility and imagination in defining and redefining consulting strategy cannot be overemphasized. Strategy must never become a straitjacket inhibiting innovation and entrepreneurship. A consulting firm may have defined its specialization and intervention methods with great care and precision, but this should not prevent the professionals on assignments from being alert to new kinds of problem and opportunity faced by clients. Dynamic consulting firms have always encouraged their staff to think of assignment opportunities in new fields and come up with new suggestions on how to deal with old problems. The relationship between long-term strategic choices and the need for flexibility and innovation may be delicate and difficult to monitor (remember the "hunters" and "farmers" in box 23.2, page 496), but no consulting firm can afford to ignore it.

Furthermore, taking a strategic approach does not mean that the consultant must have recourse to a heavy, time-consuming, yet probably not very practical strategic assessment and planning methodology. There is no point in quantifying what cannot be quantified and making detailed projections if the future is uncertain. A "light" and flexible approach to strategic planning and management is not only more effective, but it is the only approach that has a chance of being internalized and practised systematically in a professional service firm.

24.2 Services and products

Some consultants are reluctant to be explicit and precise in describing the services that they are able to provide. They are worried that such a description could be restrictive and that they would not be considered for work that does not exactly fit the service description. Others feel confident that their analytical and problem-solving expertise is so strong that they can handle virtually any problem.

Yet service and product definition is a basic building-block of consulting strategy. It determines the firm's identity and profile, tells clients what they can ask for and expect to get, determines the expertise that the firm must build up and maintain up to date, and has considerable impact on consulting style and methodology.

In Chapter 2 the services provided by management consultants were classified under six headings:

— areas and functions of management;

— problems and challenges faced by management;

— systems development and improvement;

— approaches to organizational performance improvement and change;

— sectoral services;

— complementary services (which may be outside the management consulting sector).

Basically, management consultants choose and describe their service portfolios in line with this broad classification. Obviously, there will be some overlapping and various combinations of these services. Systems, or problems and challenges, will be in particular areas, functions and sectors. Change-management methodology may be combined with a special sectoral or problem focus, and so on.

Areas and functions of management

This alternative, common in the past and still widely applied at the present time, defines the consultant's services by functional or technical areas in which he or she can help clients. Emphasis is placed on broad background knowledge and past experience in the given area. Examples are finance, marketing, production management or general management. The definition can be kept wide, or narrowed down into sub-areas — for example, maintenance, production scheduling and control, stock control, quality control or supervisory development, instead of production management.

While it indicates the area of competence, the definition lacks focus if the consultant is not highly specialized and the subject area is broad. It does not specify what quality is peculiar to the consultant, what his strong points are, or how he differs from other consultants. It says nothing about the consultant's method of work and about the results he aims to obtain in his interventions. The consultant's identity is blurred. He has to keep up to date in a wide area of business management, which may be feasible in a large firm, but virtually impossible for a sole practitioner or small firm.

Problems and challenges faced by management

This second alternative defines the services offered by referring to typical business and management problems experienced by clients. Emphasis is put on help in problem solving and on relevant special expertise. Examples were given in Chapter 2. The underlying assumption is that the consultant will analyse the problem and provide a solution, combining specialist and generalist approaches as appropriate. Thus, a company turnaround consultant is offering to handle financial, commercial, technological, organizational, legal, personnel and other aspects of a turnaround.

The rationale behind this way of defining services is obvious: when businesses and other potential clients, including governments, have to react to new pressures and challenges, this is likely to be in areas where they are short of experience and expertise and the demand for consulting will be high. It may be a short-term demand, too.

Systems development and improvement

In this case the consultant has developed and is offering expertise needed for analysing, developing and improving management systems. These may be confined to one area or function (accounting, finance, personnel) or may integrate several functions. It may be (but not necessarily) a proprietary system, which is not available from any other consultant. It is, of course, understood that the consultant provides more than the installation of a standard system. As a rule, the service will include a preliminary diagnostic study, an adaptation of the standard system to the client's conditions, and assistance with implementation and related staff training. Further servicing and perfecting of the system may also be included, thus establishing a long-term consultant-client relationship.

A consultant who has developed competency in special systems may be recognized as a good (if not the best) source for providing systems of proven effectiveness for rationalizing and modernizing certain types of process and procedure. He or she may find it difficult to get assignments in other problem areas. Such a consultant should be careful not to acquire the reputation of someone who tries to apply the same standard package to any problem presented by a client.

Alternatively, some consultants provide systems, not as their main product, but as an accessory tool for dealing with a special aspect of the problem in hand (e.g. a production control system in a plant restructuring project).

Approaches to organizational problem solving and change

In this instance the consultant defines his or her service as a methodological approach to identifying problems in client organizations and to helping clients in planning and implementing changes. Emphasis is not put on the nature of the problem, and the content and end result of the assignment, but on effective process methodology, and on the fact that the client will personally be able to acquire a methodology for diagnosing and solving problems and managing organizational change processes in the future.

The method becomes the product offered. It may be a method whose description is specific and convincing enough for the client to understand what will be happening during an assignment, and to consider whether he or she is prepared to buy such an approach and use it in collaboration with the consultant. If the consultant's approach is not structured and cannot be easily described, then the consultant will be marketing the personality and image of a successful and trustworthy problem solver or change agent.

In an extreme case, the consulting firm may stress, as William Altier has done, "we're glad we don't know your business".[1] Clearly, this will be a very different strategy from one based on an intimate knowledge of a specific sector or functional area.

Sectoral services

By choosing sectoral specialization, the consultant has a good chance of being accepted in a given sector as "a member of the family", especially if he or she has an excellent knowledge of the sector and good relations with key personalities. Conversely, confining the firm's services to one sector could be too restrictive and risky, owing to a narrow client base, potential conflict of interest and confidentiality issues. Placing too much emphasis on a sectoral focus can lead to inbreeding.

Complementary services

The reader knows from Chapters 1 and 2 that firms in various professions may branch out of their principal area of competence to start providing additional services as part of their portfolio, for two main reasons:

- to serve clients better by offering a more complete and integrated service package;

- to develop business by capturing markets in areas previously covered by other professional firms, or in grey areas, which are usually border areas between various professions.

Services such as training and education, business information, data processing, market research, project management, executive search, interim management and many others are offered by more and more firms whose principal area has been management consulting. In these cases the synergy with consulting work should be given careful consideration:

— Do the consulting, training, information and other services support and complement one another?

— Do they constitute an integrated package of services enhancing the value of assistance provided to clients?

— Is the consulting firm more effective because it is providing other services in addition to consulting proper?

— Or is it spreading resources thinly over many different services unrelated to one another?

— Will service quality and the firm's credibility gain or lose?

Your special product

In defining the firm's service portfolio, some consultants have found it useful to develop, and offer to clients, a special product, different from services or products available from other consultants. It is easy to see that such a special product (which may be a training package, a business diagnosis methodology, an information system or other) can constitute the consultant's distinct competitive advantage if it meets a perceived client need and if the consultant is successful in marketing the product.

Such a special product, it is stressed, should be different from comparable products offered by other consultants, and superior to them. The difference must be real, not fictitious. It is not very professional to try to fool clients by using fancy brand names in marketing consulting services, especially if these services offer nothing special or different from those of other consultants.

Product innovation

Like any other product, a professional service has its life cycle; it passes through periods of design and development, testing, launching on the market, growth, maturity, saturation and decline. Some services become obsolete and have to be phased out sooner than others. As far as possible, in planning strategy the consultant should analyse the life cycle of his or her particular services in order to avoid their obsolescence and be ready to change existing services or introduce new services at an appropriate moment.

A practical approach is to classify services in groups, using criteria such as the contribution of the service to the firm's income, the rate of growth of the

Box 24.1 Could consultants live without fads?

To business journals and other observers of the consulting scene, current consulting is almost identical to faddishness. Consultants are regarded, and criticized, as the principal force behind the creation, use and abuse of management fads. "Consultants have always had a role in launching fads, . . . but they have been working overtime to roll out new fads since the 1970s" (*Business Week*, 20 Jan. 1986). And seven years later: "Fad surfing — riding the crest of the newest panacea and then paddling out just in time to ride the crest of the next one — has been big business over the past 20 years" (*Sloan Management Review*, Summer 1993). And "there is a new-look menu over at The Consultants' Café. Good old soupe of Total Quality Management and Change Management pâté are off. Perhaps you would care to try some Business Process Re-engineering instead?" (*Management Today*, Aug. 1993).

A management fad can be one consultant's special product at the beginning, and turn quickly into a popular and widely demanded technique. But what is a management fad? Is it a gimmick, an irresponsible promise and a superficial approach, or can it be a new practical and useful method whose popularity has grown beyond any expectation? It would appear that the rise and fall of management fads is due as much to the clients' attitudes to change as to some consultants' imagination and aggressive marketing. "A lot of American executives these days seem eager to latch on to almost any new concept that promises a quick fix for their problems" (*Business Week*, 20 Jan. 1986). Since American business sets the tone, managers in other countries quickly become inoculated.

If a client is looking for a fad and the consultant agrees to provide one only to avoid the real problem and please the client, it is right to talk about abuse. This is unprofessional behaviour. If a fashionable method helps to shake up lethargic management and stimulate real improvements, the fad probably fulfils a useful role. Perhaps management and business practitioners need a periodical dose (not an overdose) of fads to stimulate thinking and change. Perhaps the impact of many management fads has been more psychological than technical. What is your firm's strategy in respect of management and consulting fads?

service, expected future demand or the cost involved in developing and marketing it. Various methods of strategic analysis can be used. Analysis will reveal, for example:

- services that do not grow any more, but continue to generate a substantial part of the total income;
- services that grow rapidly, though their relative importance in the firm's total income has remained small;
- services whose volume tends to stagnate in certain markets, but which are in demand in other markets;
- services that could easily be redesigned and adapted for new markets (client groups, sectors, countries, etc.);
- services where marketing and maintenance costs are excessively high;
- routine services, which have become fairly standardized and can be staffed by junior consultants;

- services which provide opportunities for developing new competencies and entering new markets.

Research strategy

There is, then, the question of what research the consulting organization should do for its own needs, particularly for improving and keeping its services up to date, and developing new competencies and services. In many consulting firms, the senior staff is busy negotiating and preparing new assignments, while the operating staff is busy serving clients. Little is done by way of research and new product development. That is why some outstanding academics have been able to compete successfully with professional consultants: basing their advice on research, they have been able to come up with new products which have aroused the attention of the business community beyond all expectation.

Every consulting firm has to decide whether or not to carry out research for product and methodology development, and if not, how to acquire the new knowledge and expertise without which product innovation is impossible. Some larger and medium-sized consulting firms have chosen to do their own research, aimed mainly, but not exclusively, at developing new services. Another major benefit, which several consulting firms have already derived from research, is the demonstration of intimate knowledge of the business and management scene and of the firm's readiness to share knowledge and experience with a wide management public.

Sole practitioners and small firms are in a different situation; their limited resources prevent them from engaging in major research projects. Small and focused projects are within their reach. They can, furthermore, keep informed about ongoing research in universities and management institutes and make sure that they participate in workshops reviewing the methods and the results of recent research. Joint research involving several consulting firms, and research organized by consultants' associations for the benefit of their members, are under-used and deserve to be explored.

In deciding to do research, a consulting firm has to face the question of relationships between research and operations. Research projects and teams separated from current client work do not seem to be the most effective solution. Better results have been obtained from research based on work for clients, using client assignments both as a source of information and for testing and applying research results. However, adequate organizational, time and financial provision must be made if research objectives are to be pursued and met in parallel with operational objectives. Without proper arrangements, it would be unrealistic to expect that operating consultants would also find time and energy for research.

The firm's core competencies

A useful perspective in choosing products and services is that of the firm's core competencies. Core competencies are defined by activity areas (these can be subjects, intervention methods, sectors, special skills or others) in which the firm has developed excellent knowledge and know-how, employs a sufficient number of well-trained professionals, keeps abreast of developments and can without any major difficulty undertake various assignments and serve a wide range of clients. Rather than marketing a special product, the firm markets competencies for doing certain things. It would confine its service offerings to its core competency areas, without trying to branch out into areas where it does not feel strong enough. If there is a need and demand for work outside the core competencies (as a rule in complex assignments), rather than improvising or doing second-rate work the firm would turn to subcontracting, sharing the work with an alliance partner or another convenient formula. A firm recognized as highly competent for certain sorts of services would not spoil its reputation by amateurish work in other areas.

The concept of core competencies must not be static. These competencies can change with changing experience and as a result of changes in the professional staff structure. They can be enhanced by staff development, but lost owing to inertia, lack of dynamism and poor personnel policies.

24.3 The client base

Consulting services and products are always intended for a particular client base. Defining and developing this base is another key element of strategy formulation in consulting. This includes considerations on whether to serve:

— existing or new clients;

— organizations of different size (small, medium, large, very large);

— organizations in one or more sectors (e.g. energy, transport, health, banking, any other sector);

— private, public or mixed-ownership organizations;

— organizations with management systems at different levels of sophistication (e.g. firms known to be very advanced in applying new manufacturing and management technologies);

— firms in a limited geographical area, in a whole country, in other countries and regions, or multinational firms;

— a larger or smaller number of clients.

In consulting as in other professional services, having a solid clientele is probably even more important than having an excellent product to offer. Clients who know and trust the consulting firm from previous experience, and are prepared to return to it with new work, are a major asset.

Invariably, the strategists of the consulting profession put great emphasis on retaining existing clients and on marketing and other strategies aimed at these clients. This is confirmed by statistical data on repeat business, which in some firms attains 75-85 per cent of total earnings.

This, however, has to be considered in conjunction with service specialization and the firm's overall development strategy. Growth and diversification may be impossible without finding new clients, thus increasing and diversifying the client base. Conversely, the existing client base cannot be served by unchanged products. Clients stay with you, and recruit you again, only if they see that you are developing your product line in accordance with their changing needs. Otherwise they have no reason to return to the same consultant once again.

There are, too, certain other strategy considerations. It is important to decide how many clients to serve. This may be crucial to a single practitioner or a small firm. Getting large contracts from a small number of clients reduces the amount of time spent on acquisition work and ensures regular income. However, it may create an excessive dependency on one or a small number of major clients, and even on individual managers in the client organizations. It may narrow down the consultant's horizon and limit the chances to learn from new clients.

Further, the level of the clients' sophistication ought to be compared to the sophistication of the services that the consultant is able to provide. There are differences between clients (and countries and sectors) in terms of sophistication of their management systems, and competence of their managerial and specialist staff. Not every client requires, and can use, the latest innovations in management sciences and technologies. Not every consultant can claim to operate at the cutting edge of technology and a realistic assessment of one's own level of sophistication can be one of the soundest strategic moves.

24.4 Growth and expansion

In many countries and even in international markets, large consulting organizations and single practitioners operate alongside each other. Various firms have grown in their own ways and, in many cases, no particular growth strategy has been pursued. The vision and entrepreneurial spirit of the founder or managing partner, and good performance in marketing and delivering services, have been the main factors of growth, allied with a favourable business climate.

Nevertheless, the size of the firm and the rate of growth ought to be considered when defining strategy. These questions should be examined in connection with the range of services offered, the sectoral and geographical coverage, the assessment of the market, existing and newly developing competition, the consulting organization's resources, and its ability to sustain growth while maintaining or improving service quality.

Is there an ideal size of a firm?

Some consulting firms have deliberately opted for a limited size and do not try to grow beyond it. This is often justified by a combination of human and managerial factors — the desire to maintain a coherent professional team where individuals can interact with each other and a simple management structure can be used. Conversely, size has become a constraint for many smaller firms. They see consulting opportunities that are fully within their technical potential, but beyond their reach owing to the importance of the potential client, the size of the contract and the number of consultants to be assigned to the project.

Yet it is impossible to determine an optimum size of a consultancy as a theoretical concept. Instead, it is necessary to examine if there is coherence between the firm's strategic choices and plans, and its current and projected size. This analysis may reveal that there is no reason to grow, or, conversely, that the firm must grow if it wants to capture new markets, develop new service lines and satisfy the ambitions of its staff.

Growth and problems of staffing

Growth involves recruiting and developing new consulting staff. If growth is fast, it is often difficult to find new consultants, the initial training of new recruits has to be shortened, and relatively inexperienced consultants have to be assigned to jobs that may be beyond their competence. In the 1970s quite a few consulting firms which followed a fast-growth strategy had to struggle with considerable problems of staffing, training, indoctrination, coherence and integrity.

A consulting firm that does not grow, or grows too slowly, faces other problems. Its staff ages, becomes more experienced, and wants to be promoted to senior positions and obtain corresponding increases in remuneration. The firm's leverage pattern may become distorted since it will be impossible to maintain the normal ratio of juniors to partners. The cost of the firm's services also grows if the higher remuneration cannot be counterbalanced by increased staff productivity.

What is to be done? The firm may try to change its product-market scope, focusing on more sophisticated services, requiring more experienced (and better-paid) staff. In other cases, staff turnover helps. Staff members, who see no chance of promotion if the firm does not grow, may decide to leave and can be replaced by new recruits at junior level. In one sense, such problems exist in any organization. They tend to be more acute, and to have a greater effect on strategy, in professional service firms, because most of these firms are limited in size and professionals employed in them are highly competent individuals who pursue ambitious career goals. We will return to this question in Chapters 32 and 33, when discussing consulting careers and staff development in more detail.

Mergers and acquisitions

Growth and expansion can be achieved through mergers and acquisitions. In the 1980s and early 1990s, many consulting firms adopted this strategy for various reasons: to add a new service line to their portfolio (corporate strategy, information technology, marketing), to acquire access to a consulting market in another country, to become international, or just to grow and get a larger share of the market. Some larger international consultancies bought ten or more smaller firms of varying profiles. The most spectacular mergers were of course those within the Big Eight group, which reduced the group to the Big Six.

In the professions, growing through mergers and acquisitions is a courageous and risky strategy, requiring highly sensitive and open-minded management. Different corporate and national cultures have to be faced and harmonized, many structural and human problems resolved, barriers to change overcome, and clients assured that they will be getting the same and an even better service. It is not surprising that not all mergers and acquisitions have been unqualified successes.

Networks and strategic alliances

As consulting projects grow larger and more complex, and clients demand the highest quality of service, fewer and fewer consultants can rely solely on their own resources. Developing new services and capabilities with the firm's own resources takes time, and may not be the right thing to do (e.g. if demand for certain services is irregular and small).

A merger or an acquisition may prove to be the solution. However, many firms do not want to lose independence. Perhaps they have not found a suitable candidate for a merger. Or they prefer to collaborate for some time with a partner before considering a legal merger in order to ascertain if competency levels, consulting philosophies and organizational cultures are compatible.

Collaboration among independent professionals is nothing new. However, since the 1980s networking and strategic alliances have become an important feature of strategy in many consulting firms.[2] They come in various forms:

- **Informal networks**. Such a network is usually formed by a group of single practitioners or smaller firms with similar or complementary profiles and interests. The network becomes a pool from which consultants choose collaborating firms or individuals case by case for assignments that are too large for one small firm, require special technical expertise or extend to other countries.

- **Structured networks**. Some networks have become more regular and structured. For example, members are listed in a consultant's information brochure and there is a moral commitment (not a binding agreement) to treat them as preferred partners in deciding whom to invite to collaborate in an assignment.

- **Direct interfirm agreements**. Such arrangements can concern various service lines, geographic areas or forms of cooperation. For example, a general management consultancy can have a long-standing arrangement with several partner firms (or subcontractors) for work in specialized areas such as market research, organization development, valuation or information technology. Such interfirm agreements can be more or less binding and exclusive.

- **Ad hoc project consortia**. A consortium involving two or more professional firms is usually established for a particular project which exceeds the possibilities of a single firm, or where involvement of several firms is required for another reason. Technical assistance agencies often require consultants to bid for projects in a partnership with one or more consulting firms from the aid-receiving country.

Cross-border alliances are particularly important for the advancement of consulting in countries where the profession is inexperienced and not well established. Many young firms in the developing world and in Central and Eastern Europe have drawn considerable benefits from various cooperation arrangements with Western consulting firms.

If alliances fail, this is usually due to superficial selection of partners, lack of respect and trust, incompatible cultures and consulting styles, major discrepancies in competence, unrealistic expectations, poorly defined commitments or the pursuit of conflicting business objectives.

24.5 Going international

Going international is a fundamental strategic choice, with many implications for the structure, competence and operation of the firm. If the firm wants to grow, and the local market is saturated, going international may be a necessity.

By and large, consulting firms internationalize operations for the following main reasons:

— to find new markets for services;

— to respond to demands received from foreign clients;

— to satisfy multinational clients, who expect that their preferred professional advisers (consultants, lawyers, auditors and others) will provide an international service, matching the client's multinational profile;

— to tap the resources for the funding of technical cooperation, provided by a wide range of national and international agencies;

— to satisfy the consultants' intellectual curiosity and quest for challenging new work opportunities.

To many consultants, becoming international is no longer a strategic choice. They made this choice ten or 20 years ago, and their current problem is how to be more effective in managing and developing an international consultancy.

All consultants who have become international stress the need to understand the institutional, economic and cultural characteristics of every national market. Yet different internationalization strategies have been pursued, depending on factors such as the firm's general philosophy, organizational culture, resources, creativity, and also sheer luck (e.g. in finding a good local partner firm or an exceptionally talented local manager, or winning an important international contract).

Internationalization has been pursued by:

● undertaking foreign assignments from the firm's headquarters;

● establishing local practices, but providing all senior and special expertise from headquarters;

- establishing local practices by recruiting and developing local consultants, and gradually phasing out managerial and special expertise provided from headquarters;
- acquiring local firms and transforming them to fit the parent firm's professional and business culture;
- acquiring local firms but leaving them almost as they are;
- using various networking and alliance building formulas, as described in section 24.4.

A key issue is striking the balance between centralization and decentralization in developing and managing the professional service side of the firm. If a centralist approach prevails, the whole firm operates more or less in the same way, following the same guidelines and using the same type and level of expertise in different countries. Ensuring uniformity and coherence is a key task of management at all levels. In contrast, fully or largely decentralized firms operate as groupings of independent national units, which may be quite different from each other in terms of technical services and consulting style. Professional guidance from the headquarters is limited, and management focuses mainly on common business development policies and issues.

24.6 Profile and image of the firm

The strategic choices discussed in the previous sections concern the principal characteristics of a consulting firm: its philosophy, services, competencies, client base, markets, resources, growth pattern, geographic coverage, size and so on.

Taken as a whole, these characteristics determine a firm's unique identity or profile. As we have seen, many combinations are possible in choosing the firm's principal characteristics. As a result, there is an almost infinite range of different profiles among which firms can choose.

Consistency between various choices

Nevertheless, no firm is totally free in choosing its strategies. The choices must not be inconsistent. Decisions concerning the sort of services that will be offered, or the sort of clients to be served, require corresponding choices in other areas, such as staff recruitment and development, or the firm's own research programme. Furthermore, strategic choices cannot ignore the firm's past experience and record of achievement. Your future is very much predetermined by your past. Even if the firm has the determination and the resources for major reorientation of its service portfolio and profile, it is important to analyse what can actually be changed and what the cost of this change will be, and how the clients will react.

Typology of firms' profiles

To help professional firms in understanding their profile and developing coherent change strategies, several attempts have been made to develop typologies of professional firms (box 24.2).

Any such typology has both the disadvantages and advantages of simplification. Seldom would a particular firm's profile be fully identical with one of the prototypes. Most firms are hybrids, and exhibit many other characteristics. When it comes to specific client projects, they will also be influenced by personalities and cultures of individual consultants and clients. Yet such simplification is conceptually useful and helps both consultants and clients to understand what is hidden behind the professional firms' names, mission statements and general service descriptions. It also helps to develop realistic strategies for the firm's future.

Image of the firm

The firm's image is the way it is perceived by client circles and even by the general public. The image concerns various aspects of the firm's profile and, in theory, should be a faithful reflection of this profile. In practice this is often not the case, owing to factors such as the firm's exceptional achievements, recent misfortunes and its treatment by the media. Also, even if there is no discrepancy between the firm's real profile and public image, this image will usually be

---

Box 24.2 Five prototypes of consulting firms

Danielle Nees and Larry Greiner suggest five prototypes of consulting firms, based mainly on differences in their professional and organizational culture. They emphasize that consultants from these different firm prototypes bring a pre-established style to the client. Their typology includes:

- *Natural adventurers* (consultants identified with scholarly disciplines, providing leading-edge knowledge and tackling difficult issues requiring a scientific approach).

- *Strategic navigators* (consultants applying models and analytical tools to handling complex issues of the client firms' future strategies).

- *Management physicians* (consultants focusing on the anatomy and circulatory system of client firms by analysing and improving structures, procedures, culture, leadership and other factors of efficiency and effectiveness, and on implementing the proposals).

- *System architects* (consultants dealing with systems projects requiring technical solutions, often using sets of pre-established tools and procedures; this includes installing the system and training the staff).

- *Friendly co-pilots* (advisers to senior management on business strategies and policies, and other significant issues).

Source: Adapted from D. B. Nees and L. E. Greiner: "Seeing behind the look-alike management consultants", in *Organizational Dynamics*, Winter 1985.

---

reduced to a few characteristics and will provide a simplified (and possibly superficial) picture of the firm's real resources and capabilities.

The firm's image plays an important role in developing relationships with clients and marketing the firm's services. It cannot be ignored in developing strategy. In professional services, the clients' perception of what you are is as important as what you really are. You may be the best of consultants, but if the clients perceive you differently (or if you have no image), they have no reason to turn to you. Therefore every firm needs to be well aware of its image.

A self-image must not be mistaken for a real image. Professionals easily develop a self-image that is more flattering than their real image in client circles and within the profession. This can be a bad starting-point for strategic thinking.

24.7 Strategic management in practice

Strategic management is an approach, a way of thinking. Strategy is primarily synthesis, not analysis. It must not be a cumbersome procedure with a lot of paperwork and endless meetings. If it turns into bureaucracy, or if it becomes the guarded province of specialized planning units, line management and professional workers lose interest in it. Consultants advise clients to prevent such a degeneration of strategic planning. They must be able to avoid this pitfall themselves. This, however, does not preclude the use of a structured strategic assessment and planning methodology, if the consultant is versed in one and has had good experience with it. There are quite a few on the market.

Self-assessment

A thorough and honest self-assessment is a necessary starting-point irrespective of the procedure and methodology chosen. It is sometimes called "strategic audit" to emphasize the focus and purpose of the exercise. Many consultants will be able to undertake it by themselves, although it is never easy to be detached and objective in assessing one's own performance, capabilities and perspectives. A peer audit may be helpful. In some situations, however, it will be preferable to turn to an independent adviser versed in the management of professional service firms. In any event, the audit should be based on facts and figures, not on illusions.

In self-assessment, the consultant will be addressing the various issues reviewed in this and other chapters of our book. The check-list in box 24.3 gives an idea of the questions that need to be answered.

Learning from clients

The reader knows that the relationship between consultants and their clients lies at the very heart of the consulting profession. When the consulting firm is assessing and developing its strategy, clients play a special role: learning from clients is indeed a significant strategic choice. It would be arrogant, and futile,

---

Box 24.3 Strategic audit of a consulting firm: Check-list of questions

1. What kind of professional firm are we?
2. What is our consulting philosophy and ethics?
3. What is our organizational culture?
4. What is our image in client circles?
5. How solid is our client base?
6. How do we work with clients and how do we learn from them?
7. What are our core competencies?
8. How can we assess our service portfolio?
9. What is our competitive advantage?
10. What lessons can be drawn from our growth pattern and performance record?
11. What strategies have we pursued and with what results?
12. What is our financial position?
13. How can we assess the quality and development potential of our human resources?
14. What do we know about competitors and what can we learn from them?
15. What can we learn from other professional service firms?
16. What is our potential for further growth and improvement?
17. What is our vision of the future?
18. What are our strategic options for future years?
19. What strategic and other errors must be avoided?

---

to draw conclusions on the firm's capabilities and future perspectives without asking what the clients need, want and think.

First of all, the firm must know precisely what the clients think about it. Feedback from clients concerning the services provided may be available from assignment evaluation, contacts with the managers of client organizations, industry meetings and conferences, and other sources (see Chapters 11 and 25).

In assessing and developing strategy, all this information must be carefully reviewed. In addition, clients can be asked specific questions concerning their expected future needs and requirements. They can make invaluable suggestions to the consultant.

Looking at your future market

In many situations, looking at the current market and the existing client base would not be enough. This can be the case of a firm that has exhausted the possibilities of offering new services to its clients, wants to be less dependent on a small number of important clients, or feels that its products could well interest potential clients in other countries or sectors.

The identification and assessment of the potential market starts with a hypothesis as to what the market might be (bearing in mind the scope and level of the consultant's resources and capabilities). Fact-finding and market research would confirm this original hypothesis, suggest another definition of the market, confirm the original definition on condition that the consultant could improve his or her image, and so on.

A complete survey would cover:

- technico-economic characteristics and development tendencies of the sector(s) to be served: advanced or obsolete technology, growth prospects and difficulties ("smokestack" industries), position in respect to other sectors and national development strategies, inter-sectoral linkages, international competition;
- organizations in the sector: number, size, categories, leaders, monopolies, ownership pattern, traditions; more detailed information on organizations that are most likely to be a prospective market (including names and addresses of firms, and, if possible, names of owners and senior managing staff);
- the management scene: level and sophistication of management, use of management systems and technologies, prevailing attitudes and traditions, background and competence of managers;
- practices concerning the use of consultants: demand, attitudes, experience with use, special requirements.

Assessing a potential market obviously involves much more than finding addresses of firms and some global information on them. It is a thorough research effort; the consultant must know his or her potential market in considerable depth and detail. Various sources of information and research methods can be combined in order to develop a comprehensive picture of the market (business publications and reports, trade journals, official statistics, stock-market information, training events and management conferences, individual contacts and interviews, and so on). Information obtained directly from existing and potential clients is particularly useful.

The definition of a potential market is a delicate matter for a new consulting firm, which does not have any clientele and faces the risk of adopting either an excessively wide or an unduly narrow definition of its market. In the first case, the firm's marketing effort will be too costly and largely unproductive, embracing organizations where there is little or no likelihood that they will become clients. In the second case, good opportunities of finding assignments will be missed by omitting certain prospective clients.

Some consultants regard *all* organizations in the field of their specialization as a potential market, while others use a more restrictive definition and regard their market as consisting of organizations which have problems and require the consultant's help. Both approaches have their rationale. An organization that does not have a problem today may have one tomorrow, or next year, and it will be good if it is aware of the existence and reputation of *your* consulting firm! Some marketing effort may therefore be directed at creating this awareness. At the same time, every consulting firm needs assignments that will keep it occupied today, and these will be found in organizations that already experience problems. This includes not only organizations in difficulties, but also prosperous firms that are seeking new opportunities for developing and improving their business.

The concept of *market segmentation* is helpful in analysing the chances of a consulting firm successfully entering a new market. Segmenting the market involves subdividing potential clients and their business and management problems into smaller groups, by one or more criteria — by size, geographical location, technology used, ownership pattern, financial difficulties experienced (shortage of working capital, foreign exchange problems), market served (local market, exporting, re-export), or other issues. Such segmentation is meaningful if it identifies some common characteristics of the organizations involved, reflected in their common consulting needs and in the kind of services required. It will be useful to find a market segment, or niche, which (a) is likely to need a special service or product that you are able to provide, and (b) is less "occupied" by other consultants.

Box 24.4 What do we want to know about competitors?

1.   Who are they (names, founders, key executives)?
2.   How large and how well established are they?
3.   For what markets and organizations do they work?
4.   Do they enjoy a solid and stable client base?
5.   What is their technical competence and range of services?
6.   What are their consulting and marketing approaches and methods?
7.   In what areas are they ahead of us?
8.   What professional image do they enjoy?
9.   What are their terms of business?
10.   What can we learn from them and what can we do better?
11.   Are we likely to win or lose if we compete with them?

Knowing your competitors

The market analysis is pursued by assessing existing and potential competitors. As a general rule, it is essential to learn as much as possible about other consultants' profiles, strategies and achievements, addressing questions such as those listed in box 24.4.

Learning from competitors is not aping them without imagination. Less experienced consultants can easily fall into a trap by trying to do exactly what their established and experienced competitors do, although their resources are usually inadequate for this.

Whether to compete or not is a delicate but essential strategic choice. Many consultants have decided not to compete with existing firms by offering the same service, but to offer a new service or special product that is *not* currently available from other consultants. However, most consulting services cannot become legally protected intellectual property (except certain proprietary systems and software packages). Sooner or later competitors will come up with the same or a similar service. What will your strategy be then?

Understanding the business environment and climate

Your assessment of the environment has to reach beyond the market for your particular services. Various other environmental factors affect opportunities for management consulting and the approach to take in developing and marketing new services. Some of them can be found in box 24.5.

The box gives only examples of factors that may be important to your consulting firm. Whether a particular environmental factor is important or not, and should be examined in depth, reviewed briefly or ignored, is a matter for the consultant's judgement. A general management consulting firm contemplating the expansion of international operations will be interested in different environmental factors from a marketing consultant working with small businesses serving a limited local market.

Every consultant is keenly interested in the general business climate. If business is prosperous, the markets for consulting services tend to be expanding rapidly. This often stimulates consulting firms to an equally fast expansion, even if they are not always able to provide all new recruits with excellent training and maintain high professional standards.

On the other hand, economic recession and stagnation of business also affects consulting, but not necessarily all services in the same way. Services considered as essential for the clients' survival, and for achieving tangible improvements in productivity and efficiency, continue to sell well or even better. Other services tend to suffer. In many instances the recession, and falling demand, have forced management consultants to phase out training and other service packages that were fashionable and easy to sell in the period of general prosperity, but ceased to interest clients when austerity became the name of the game.

Following the developments in the profession

Although many consultants follow the developments in their profession virtually on a daily basis, a strategic audit provides an opportunity for a more

---

Box 24.5 Environmental factors affecting strategy

- the political climate;
- the current business climate and its expected changes;
- international political, economic and trade blocs and agreements;
- promotional or restrictive government policies;
- the dynamism of the business community;
- the availability and sources of finance for new development projects;
- local cultural values and traditions;
- local business practices and habits;
- labour legislation and industrial relations;
- legislation governing professional services, contracting, liability, and the like;
- technology trends likely to affect your clients in the future;
- environmental protection issues and policies;
- facilities offered to foreign investors.

---

thorough review of these trends and of their possible implications for future strategy. Important changes that affect consulting services deserve particular attention. These can be changes in consulting methods, the conception of ethics, the approach to marketing and advertising, the ways of combining management, technological and other types of consulting, the relations between consulting and training, competition with other professions and similar issues.

Choosing coherent strategies

We have already mentioned that strategic choices affecting various aspects of the consulting firm are mutually related. There is a significant relationship between the basic objectives to be pursued, the services to be offered, the market segment that will be the firm's target, the image to be built up, the marketing techniques to be used, the staff to be recruited and trained, the research and product development to be undertaken, and the resources to be allocated to these activities. The purpose is to develop coherent strategy, not a set of accidental, inconsistent or even conflicting choices.

Involving staff in strategy formulation

There are valid reasons for organizing strategy formulation as an exercise involving as many members of the consulting staff as possible. This can be done through task forces, meetings, special projects, and so on. Participation in strategic thinking and planning helps to build up an *esprit de corps*, increase the firm's cohesion, and counter the centrifugal tendencies that develop only too easily in professional firms. Both senior and junior staff members thus feel associated with the strategy that is adopted, understand the reasons for it and accept it as their own choice. They will feel like "owners" of their firm's strategy.

In discussing common strategy every professional has the opportunity to compare his or her personal strategy (if any) with that of the organization to which he or she belongs. In professional services it is not uncommon that these two strategies conflict. An individual may believe in a different mode of consulting or just prefers to do different things than the firm intends to do. He or she may decide to leave if there is no way of reconciling the two approaches.

Making strategy explicit

We have stressed that strategy should provide a framework and guiding principles for operating decisions made by all units and staff members in a consulting firm. Therefore they have to know the strategy chosen and understand the reasons behind it. Staff participation in formulating strategy has contributed to this understanding. It is useful to tell all staff about the strategy chosen by management and to keep people informed about any changes in it. Attention must be paid to strategy in the induction training of new staff. Making staff aware of strategy is particularly important in larger and decentralized consulting organizations with many relatively autonomous operating units, which are exposed to a permanent danger of losing sight of common objectives and strategic choices. Also, consultant remuneration and motivation must not operate (as they often do) against strategic choices made by the firm. For example, if the firm wants to do more work for high-technology firms and phase out routine company organization work, the firm's marketers and operating consultants must be well aware of this decision and be motivated towards getting new assignments that make this reorientation possible.

Some consulting firms have found it useful to have a strategic plan for three to five years rather than just a list of policies reflecting strategic choices. If such a plan has to be prepared, the firm is encouraged to make strategic choices explicit and express them in measurable and controllable terms. The plan is a tool for achieving coherence between the various choices discussed above, allocating needed resources and rejecting strategies that are not feasible. However, it may be unrealistic and unnecessary to set targets for three to five years if technology changes very rapidly, future business prospects are uncertain or the firm has not really gathered and analysed meaningful information. Many consultants prefer to avoid any formalized strategic planning, which they replace by a short statement of their principal strategic orientations and policies.

Strategy is an internal matter and the consulting firm may treat its strategic decisions or a statement of strategy as confidential. Yet certain aspects of strategy can be made publicly known. It may be useful to give clients, current and prospective, some information on the strategy chosen, thus helping to build up the consulting firm's image and gain clients' confidence. This is done, as a rule, through information brochures, annual reports and other publications, or in dealing with specific clients and submitting proposals to them.

Monitoring strategy implementation

At the beginning of this chapter we stressed that strategy is inseparable from operations. In theory, operating decisions and actions should be in harmony with strategy. Often they are not. Strategy is either ignored or for some reason cannot be applied.

Usually the reason is that strategy has been treated as a staff function separated from operations. Either the real state and possibilities of operations were not duly considered, or the operating consultants were kept in the dark about senior management's strategic thinking. Both cases imply that the firm has been poorly managed and its strategic planning has probably been an esoteric exercise.

Monitoring the relationships between strategy and operations is an essential management function. If deviations from strategy are frequent and important, this probably indicates that a wrong strategy was chosen, that it has become outdated or that the firm's management has been unable to translate its own strategic choices into marketing and operational practices. Alternatively, operations may have revealed new opportunities and issues important enough to justify a revision of the firm's strategy. In any event, the firm's senior management will have to act to bring strategy in line with new realities.

When and how should this be done? A major correction of strategy (e.g. to amend an error, or seize an excellent unexpected opportunity) should be done immediately when this becomes necessary, and people in the firm should be told about it without delay. Other adjustments may be made periodically within the framework of annual performance and strategy reviews.

---

[1] W. J. Altier: "We're glad we don't know your business", in *Journal of Management Consulting* (Milwaukee, Wisconsin), Vol. 3, No. 3, 1987.

[2] See also H. S. Bott: "Strategic alliances", in *Management consulting 1990: The state of the profession* (Fitzwilliam, New Hampshire, Kennedy Publications, 1990).

MARKETING OF CONSULTING SERVICES
25

A consulting firm can exist and prosper if it gets and keeps clients. This is what marketing is about: define your market, identify clients, find out what they need, sell the consulting service to them, deliver the service to the clients' full satisfaction and make sure that once you have good clients you do not lose them.

In management consulting, as in some other professions, there has been a long debate on the appropriateness of marketing and of its various techniques. Even today, some consultants feel uneasy about "selling" their services: they regard it as unprofessional and beneath their dignity. Many consultants are poor at marketing and, if they have to market, they do so with little enthusiasm and imagination.

Yet the marketing of consulting is as old as consulting itself. James McKinsey, one of the pioneers of management consulting, spent many hours having meals with prospective clients and other useful business contacts. Over the meal, he would engage in a technical discussion, aiming to gain the person's confidence and subtly explain how he could be of help. His business sense was telling him that professionals must be active in marketing their services. He was, however, cautious not to oversell.[1]

Since McKinsey's time, the leaders of the profession have always exhibited considerable dynamism in marketing their firms' services. They have systematically sought opportunities to make social contacts with potential clients, to be recommended by existing clients to new prospects, to carry out quick management surveys free of charge, or to speak at management conferences. This, in addition to the firm's reputation, used to be sufficient to attract clients to the established firms as long as the market for consulting services was small, and competition was limited.

No wonder that the firms established in the business did not favour the use of a wider range of marketing techniques, and of advertising in particular. The same attitude prevailed in consultants' associations. It was not until the late 1970s that advertising was admitted in the United States as a correct and acceptable means of marketing professional services in a competitive environment. Stress was laid on the point that competition in professional services ought to be encouraged, as it provides the client with the possibility of getting a better service for a lower price. In other countries, attitudes to the marketing of professional services have also started changing.

At the present time, it is almost universally recognized that professional services can and have to be marketed. Publications and courses on the subject proliferate. Yet many consultants have a long way to go to become fully proficient and effective in the marketing of their services.

In summary, management consultants, like other professionals, have to market their services for two main reasons:

— if they do not market in a competitive environment, they will not get the clients and the market share that they could and should get, and are thus abdicating their position in their competitors' favour;

— irrespective of competition, marketing is needed to put the right consultant in touch with the client who needs and is prepared to use him or her; the client may not know about your firm, lack an understanding of what consulting is about, or just be timid and shy, so a professional approach to marketing will surmount these obstacles and establish the required collaborative relationship.

Chapter 24 has shown that marketing considerations have a prominent place in the strategy of consulting firms. This discussion will now be pursued by reviewing the principles and methods of marketing.

25.1 The marketing approach in consulting

In consulting we often think of marketing as a distinct function, a set of activities, tools or techniques which cost us time and money and which we would prefer to avoid — if only a sufficient number of unsolicited clients came to us by themselves. According to this view, marketing is an unavoidable evil, something that we accept that we have to live with, although we do not like it.

Fortunately, more and more consultants, as indeed other professionals, regard marketing as an inherent characteristic of the service concept. Marketing does not precede a professional service; it is a professional service in its own right, needed to establish and maintain an effective consultant-client relationship. It identifies clients' needs and requirements, reveals the client's mentality, defines the best way in which a professional can be useful to the client and puts the whole consulting process in motion. According to this view, service marketing is an essential condition of a truly professional service. It does not stop when a sale is made. The consultant continues to market after the contract has been signed, when the project is being executed and after project completion.

What is to be marketed?

The marketing of consulting is strongly affected by the "intangibility" of consulting services. As we have seen (Chapter 23), clients will not be able to fully examine the product they are intending to buy and compare it to products available from other consultants. Even if product tangibility is somewhat increased when consultants supply structured systems and methodologies, it can never attain a degree of tangibility comparable to industrial products, and many other products in the service sector.

What the consultant is selling is a promise (but no guarantee) of a service that will meet the client's needs and resolve the problem. Why should a potential client buy a mere promise? Why should he or she take such a risk?

First, because the client has established, or just feels, that it might be useful to get the consultant's help.

Second, because the client has no alternative — buying any consulting service (even from someone whom you know well or whose work you have seen elsewhere) is always buying a promise. What has worked in another company may not work with you. A client who is not prepared to take this risk and buy a promise must refrain from using a consultant.

It is fully understandable that, in buying a promise, competent clients will wish to reduce risk. They will be looking for surrogates in evaluating what they are likely to get and deciding to whom to turn. In the marketing of professional services, surrogates play a prominent role. Many clients buy without having any direct knowledge of the professional firm, just because of the firm's image in business circles, or because a business friend or acquaintance has used the firm's services previously and has been satisfied.

Furthermore, the marketing of consulting services deals with both dimensions of the consulting approach described in section 1.4 — the technical dimension (the technical know-how needed to solve the client's specific management or business problems) and the human dimension (the relationship between the consultant and the client, and the consultant's ability to face human problems). Thus, the consultant has to convince the client that, from a strictly technical point of view, he has all the technical knowledge, know-how, access to information, and so on, needed to deal with the client's technical problems and produce a solution whose technical quality is indisputable. But this is not enough. Consulting is a human relationship above all, and the consultant and the client may be spending long hours in working together. Therefore the client must be convinced that he is purchasing the services of someone with whom (at worst) he is prepared to work or (at best) he will enjoy working. This concerns the consultant's ability to work with the whole "client system" as described in section 3.3.

Finally, the marketing of consulting services must not ignore the fine distinction between a consulting firm and an individual professional employed by that firm. True, in purchasing the services of an excellent professional firm clients normally expect a certain degree of quality, integrity and even uniformity, reflecting the firm's collective know-how and organizational culture. Yet consultants are human beings and absolute uniformity is not only impossible, but undesirable. Informed clients are aware of the difference between the firm's image, know-how and standards, and the capabilities, personalities and style of individual consultants. Accordingly, the consulting firm will have to market both itself and its individual members and teams.

Box 25.1 Marketing of consulting: Seven fundamental principles

Experience has shown that successful marketing of consulting services is guided by certain general principles:

1. **Regard the clients' needs and requirements as the focal point of all marketing!**

There is no point in selling to potential clients what they don't need, or don't want to buy. The client may be pleased to hear that you are a brilliant and highly successful professional, but it is infinitely more important to convince the client that you care for him or her, understand the situation, are prepared to listen patiently and can help to find and implement a solution beneficial to his or her business. This is a golden rule. Your marketing efforts must be client centred, not consultant centred. Your interest in the client must be genuine, and stronger than your self-interest.

2. **Remember that every client is unique!**

Your past experience and past achievements are an important asset. They can become a trap: you may feel that you know pretty well in advance what your new client will need — haven't you handled the same sort of situation many times before? Yet even if all other conditions appear identical (they won't be), the people involved will always be different. Acknowledge your new client's uniqueness. Show the client that you will offer an original solution, not a pale imitation of a model designed for other conditions.

3. **Don't misrepresent yourself!**

The temptation to offer and sell services in which you are not fully competent can be high. Often a client who trusts you would confide a job to you without requiring any evidence of your competence. To yield to this temptation is unethical; the client's interests can be seriously damaged. This is a matter of technical judgement, too. Competence in marketing involves your ability to realistically assess your own competence!

4. **Don't oversell!**

Marketing creates expectations and commitments. Overmarketing may create more expectations than a consulting firm is able to meet. This may be counter-productive and even unethical: some clients may need your help urgently; you promise it, but cannot deliver. Or an excessive selling effort may force you to recruit and immediately send to clients inexperienced consultants without being able to train and supervise them.

5. **Refrain from denigrating other consultants!**

Questions concerning your competitors' approaches and competencies come up often in discussions with clients. Nothing should prevent you from providing factual information, if you have it. However, it is unprofessional to provide distorted and biased information, and make disparaging comments about competitors in order to influence your client. A sophisticated client is likely to regard such comments as an expression of your weakness, not of your strength.

6. **Never forget that you are marketing a professional service!**

Management consultants have to be entrepreneurial, innovative and at times even aggressive in marketing. They can learn a great deal from marketing in other sectors. Yet you are not selling biscuits or washing powder. The professional nature

---

of the service, the clients' sensitivity and the local cultural values and norms must not be lost from sight in deciding what marketing approaches and techniques are appropriate.

7. **Aim at an equally high professional performance in marketing and in execution!**

In their efforts to find new clients some consultants have not maintained the delivery of assignments at the same quality level in staffing, controlling quality, respecting deadlines, and making every effort to satisfy the client. It is useful to view marketing as a process that does not end with the signing of the contract. The execution of assignments has a significant marketing dimension. Flawless service

25.2 A client's perspective

In client-centred marketing, the consultant does not come to the client with the desire to close another sale of a ready-made product. The approach is reversed: the assessment and understanding of the client's needs come first. The consultant is asking questions such as: Can I provide a service that will meet this particular client's needs? And if I am not the only one who can provide such a service (which is usually the case), why should a client select me and not one of my competitors? What criteria will the client use? How can I be more useful to the client than other consultants? How should I market myself to get selected?

Understanding the purchasing process

As pointed out by David Maister, "the single most important talent in selling professional services is the ability to understand the purchasing process (not the sales process) from the client's perspective. The better a professional can learn to think like a client, the easier it will be to do and say the correct things to get hired".[2] We have already pointed (Chapter 3 and section 7.1) to the role of psychological and relational factors in the selection of consultants. Since usually more than one consultant will be fully suitable from a strictly technical point of view, clients will give preference to consultants:

- with whom they are prepared to work and would like to work;
- who understand their personal worries, concerns and preferences;
- who exhibit a genuine desire to be helpful to their client;
- whom they are able and willing to trust.

Thus, it is important to keep in mind that both technical, and behavioural or psychological, criteria will be applied by clients in selecting consultants. The consultant's marketing strategy and methods used should therefore be attuned to this. Yet it is impossible to provide a blueprint for every context.

Overemphasizing good relations (e.g. never contradicting the client during first meetings even if the client is obviously wrong) may be interpreted by the prospect as a lack of technical competence, or a tactical trick. The client may even be testing the consultant by asking awkward questions. The best approach is to be honest and sincere. It is difficult to play a role which does not suit you and pretend to be something that you are not. If you do not really care about the client and are merely seeking a well-remunerated assignment, you will not be able to hide your attitude for long before your client. Some clients' concerns are reviewed below.

Reluctance to admit that a consultant is needed. Some managers do not want to admit to themselves that they need a consultant because this would hurt their self-esteem. Often the potential client is worried that a consultant's presence will be regarded by others — by subordinates, peers, superiors, shareholders, or even by competitors and customers — as an admission of incompetence and a sign of weakness.

Doubts about the consultant's competence and integrity. It is common for clients to have doubts about an external person's ability to resolve intricate problems with which management has struggled without finding any solution. Some clients feel, too, that a consultant will not really take all the trouble needed to search out a solution that is likely to work in the long term, and will simply try to place a standard package. Some organizations feel that consultants are too inquisitive and collect too much information that could somehow be misused in the future.

Fear of becoming dependent on a consultant. Sometimes the remark is heard that it is easy to recruit a consultant, but difficult to get rid of one. Consultants are said to structure and manage assignments in a way that inevitably prolongs their presence in the client organization and leads to new assignments. This can create a permanent dependence on external expertise, which could be a very dangerous thing.

Fear of excessive fees. This fear is quite widespread in smaller businesses. Owners and managers sometimes ignore how the fee is calculated and justified, and with what benefits it could be compared. They believe that most consultants try to overcharge and that using a consultant is a luxury that is beyond their means.

General feeling of uneasiness and insecurity. Asking a consultant to look into the organization's "internal cuisine" can be very disruptive. What will come out? Established practices and peaceful relations may be disturbed, but will this really be necessary? Will it be an improvement? Is it worthwhile to run such a risk? Are we not opening a Pandora's box without being forced to do so?

General criteria of consultant selection, taken from an ILO guide on the topic, are summarized in box 25.2. As all clients do not use the same criteria, it will be most useful if the consultant can find out what criteria will be applied to him or her as a firm or a person, and to the assignment proposals submitted to the client, as well as to the weight the client will assign to each criterion.

Box 25.2 Criteria of consultant selection

In selecting their consultants, most clients would apply one or more of the following criteria:

(1) **Professional integrity** (how the consultant interprets and respects a code of ethics and conduct)

(2) **Technical competence** (knowledge and experience needed for dealing with the client's technical problem and producing results of desired level and quality)

This can be refined further by:

(a) differentiating between the competence of the whole firm and the individual (team) proposed;

(b) stressing knowledge of the client's sector of industry;

(c) in international consulting, stressing intimate knowledge of specific country conditions (economic, socio-political, cultural);

(d) differentiating between hard and soft skills (the knowledge and expertise concerning technical procedures, methods and systems, on the one hand, and the ability to deal with human problems and facilitate organizational change, on the other hand);

(e) stressing creativity and innovation (which can imply that past experience will be de-emphasized).

(3) **Rapport with the consultant** (mutual understanding, trust, the client's attitude to working with the consultant as a person)

(4) **Assignment design** (demonstrating the consultant's understanding of the specific problem and context of a given client organization, and the approach to take)

(5) **Capability to deliver** (structure, size, resources, location, flexibility and other features of the consulting firm, demonstrating the ability to actually deliver what was promised, even if conditions change)

(6) **Ability to mobilize further resources** (important in assignments that may call for expertise of other firms, new business contacts, additional capital, etc.)

(7) **Cost of services** (fee level and formula; this may not be a key criterion, but excessive fee requirements may disqualify the consultant)

(8) **Certification of competency and/or quality** (formal competency certification of individual consultants and quality certification of consulting firms are taken into consideration by some clients, in support or as a surrogate of the criteria listed under (1)-(7))

(9) **Professional image of the consultant** (the principal surrogate, by using this criterion the client relies on the choices and assessment made and experience gained previously by other users of consulting services, or on the consultant's achievements outside consulting, e.g as a manager or author)

Source: M. Kubr: *How to select and use consultants: A client's guide*, Management Development Series No. 31 (Geneva, ILO, 1993), pp. 77-87.

25.3 Techniques for marketing the consulting firm

A wide range of techniques is available to management consultants for building up their professional reputation and image, or positioning their practice, in the clients' minds. The main techniques are reviewed in this section. Their purpose is not to sell individual assignments, but to get potential clients informed about and interested in the consulting firm and its products, and to create opportunities for contacts with these clients.

While certain techniques are aimed purely at public relations and image building (e.g. advertising), the reader will notice that other techniques aim to arouse the clients' interest by directly providing another useful technical service (e.g. information, or training).

Working the referrals

Word of mouth is one of the oldest and yet most efficient ways in which a professional firm becomes known to new clients. Business people and managers are used to sharing information about professionals such as lawyers, accountants, engineers and management consultants. They exchange both favourable and unfavourable information, so only a firm which has rendered a flawless service to a client can hope to have another useful referral. A manager looking for a consultant will often ask business friends for advice before turning to any other source of information.

It could appear that excellent performance in serving clients is all that is necessary to get good referrals. Experience shows that it is indeed the main thing, but not the only one. Some consultants do not leave it to chance that a happy client will recommend them to colleagues. They discuss their promotional needs and policies with their clients, asking them:

— to suggest who else in the business community may be interested in similar services;

— to authorize the use of the clients' names as a reference to prospective clients;

— possibly to give permission for describing or summarizing a successful assignment in a technical publication, in promotional material or in a management seminar;

— to speak about the consultant with other managers and business colleagues, but also with bankers, lawyers, accountants and other persons who may be asked for a good consultant's name by their own business contacts.

This requires an excellent mutual understanding between the consultant and the client. The client must not feel ashamed that he had to pay a consultant for dealing with a problem that he should have solved by himself. Rather he should be proud that cooperation with an outstanding professional has helped him to discover new opportunities and view his problems in a wider perspective. The consultant must show the client that his concern for the client goes beyond a single contract — this is best achieved by informing past clients of the latest research and the state of the art in their sector or problem area, telling them about new services the consultant can provide, having a business lunch with them from time to time to discuss new developments in the client's business and in the consulting profession, and in general maintaining frequent communication. The client will then enjoy talking about "his" or "her" preferred consultant and recommend such a person without hesitation. Happy clients become your best marketers, and do it free of charge!

Professional publications

Books for managers. Writing books that will be read by managers, or even become reference works, has become increasingly popular among consultants. Some recent publications based on experience and research in management consulting firms have become real bestsellers, and their impact on promoting new business has been quite strong.

The promotional effect depends on the nature and quality of the publication. The reader must be impressed by the author's innovative approach to topical management problems, and conclude that his or her company might also benefit from such ideas and experiences. Finding the right publisher is equally important. Publications that just repeat the same old stuff using new words may bring in a few not very sophisticated clients, but will have little effect in the long run. Writing a really good book is an extremely difficult and time-consuming exercise, and those who say that every management consultant should try it are bad advisers. Yet if you feel that you have enough to say, do not hesitate!

There is a considerable need in many developing countries and in economies in transition for original management publications reflecting the real problems and experience of local business practice. This is a real challenge and opportunity for management consultants.

Articles on management and industry topics. Writing an article presents certain advantages over publishing a book:

- the article can focus on a specific, rather narrow, topic (e.g. an interesting development in a sector served by the consultant, or an intervention technique that has helped several clients);
- the time required to write an article is short;
- the readership base will be much larger if the article is published in a widely circulated newspaper or journal;
- many busy managers do not read books, but do glance through articles on topics of concern.

To arouse interest in potential clients, articles must address important topical issues. Articles based on successfully completed assignments, and outlining the approach taken, the changes achieved and the benefits to the clients, are particularly useful.

The choice of the medium is essential. The general public or the academic community are not the primary target. We can therefore recommend:

— professional, business and trade journals, which are normally read by a wide management public (e.g. a consultant who wants to be recognized as an authority in road transport management should be known as an author to the readers of trade publications on transport in general, and on the road transport sector in particular);

— business and management pages and supplements of important daily newspapers and weeklies;

— local newspapers, in particular those read by the local business community;

— publications of trade and employers' associations.

Occasional papers and pamphlets. Both existing and potential clients appreciate it very much if a management consultant shares with them some knowledge and experience through technical and information papers, guides, reports, briefs, pamphlets, check-lists and other materials. These can deal with a relatively narrow and specialized topic, but must be of direct interest to the recipient. Therefore, you should choose a topic of concern to managers, providing suggestions and guidelines tested by experience. You do not have to divulge *all* your know-how that constitutes your competitive advantage, but you must be prepared to say something if the material distributed is not to be viewed as trivial publicity. Papers informing managers and/or specialists about the state of the art in their field, or about trends likely to affect the business, are particularly welcome.

Newsletters. A newsletter is a periodical publication whose purpose is to keep its readers abreast of developments in their field of activity on a regular basis. A management consultant can choose between a newsletter devoted entirely to news from a sector or trade, and one which also gives news from his or her consulting firm (completed projects, research done, new services started, publications, senior staff appointments, and so on). If the area to be covered is well chosen and the newsletter handled professionally, it can become a highly regarded reference service, used as essential information by many subscribers. Several special-focus newsletters launched by professional firms have achieved this standard.

All publications should include a reference to the consulting firm to which the author belongs, with some information on the firm and its services, and (if they agree to it) on client organizations from which the published experience was drawn.

Relations with public information media

Public information media such as the press, television or radio are constantly looking for the information that their audience expects to receive. Management consultants possess, or can help to gather, organize and present, some of this information — for example, on developments in business and finance, impact of technological developments on factory and office work, new energy-saving techniques, or the likely impact of trade policies on investment decisions.

Quite a few consultants have found it most beneficial to keep in touch with the media and be helpful to them. Editors and other media people have to meet imperative short deadlines, need quick help, and want to be sure that their contact is well informed, trustworthy and reliable. They want information in a format suitable for immediate use. A consultant who understands these requirements and tries to be flexible can expect to be quoted as a source or technical authority, or be invited to give an interview. This will have a much greater promotional effect than costly advertisements in the same public medium.

Being responsive to public media requirements does not mean refraining from taking any initiative. Once you understand how the media operate, and for what kind of information they are looking (and how presented), you can yourself come up with suggestions of topics, or directly offer a piece of news or a story to your contacts in the media.

News or press releases are intended for wider distribution to the media. Some consultants have had good experience with them. A news release showing that you have done something interesting in an area on which media are keen to report can be most welcome and may be used by several media, or the media may get in touch with you for further information.

Some media people have a distorted picture of management consultants and look mainly for sensational information on them (e.g. on assignments that ended up as complete failures, or on exorbitant fees charged for substandard work). Caustic articles with this kind of information appear from time to time in newspapers and business journals in various countries.

It is counter-productive to react aggressively and arrogantly. Even exposing sheer facts may be difficult because of confidentiality and for other reasons. Helping media to do their job, and demonstrating a professional approach in dealing with them, is the best way to change their attitude to management consultants.

Seminars and workshops

Management seminars, round tables, conferences, workshops, executive briefings and similar events have become very popular in the management consulting sector. Usually a consultant invites managers to attend a session on a topic of real concern to them — for example, how to handle industrial relations under new legislation, what is happening in international money markets, or how to apply new computerized information systems. The consulting firm can invite external specialists as speakers, but it is essential that its own professional staff should make a presentation to demonstrate that the firm is fully up to date and has developed interesting practical applications. If possible, work recently undertaken by the firm should be described, showing benefits derived by the clients. However, it is essential that participants perceive the seminar as a direct help to them and not merely as a selling exercise.

It is impossible to suggest one single way of organizing a seminar. You have to consider whether it is better tactics to offer it as a free service to all clients, selected clients, potential new clients or a wider public; charge a relatively high fee or charge only for the meals and printed materials provided, and similar. A seminar may be arranged by the consulting firm alone, or in collaboration with a management centre or institute, a local chamber of commerce, or a trade association. It should be brief, and the time and venue must be convenient.

If the purpose of a seminar is marketing, the participants should be potential clients. Ideally, you would use a selective mailing list and invite decision makers from organizations likely to need assistance, or to be looking for opportunities in the areas that will be discussed. You will have to assess the probability of response (which may be 5-20 per cent, depending on factors such as the topic, the reputation of your firm and the speakers, the quality of the mailing list and the managers' propensity to attend seminars). It is better if invitations look very personal.

Those who agree to attend express, by so doing, interest both in the topic and in your expertise. They may be potential clients. Their names should therefore be carefully noted. Some discussion with them will start at the seminar, e.g. in small groups built into the agenda or by individual contacts. While some of them may continue to talk further with you after the seminar, or may ask for an appointment, you will also have a focused list for future contacts (say a telephone call two or three weeks after the seminar, offering to meet to discuss their specific problems in greater depth without any immediate commitment). This may open the door for new assignments.

The reader knows that many consulting firms also run open training programmes, and that some of them have even established special training departments or institutes.

This is a direct client service whose prime purpose is skill development, not marketing. Participants do not have to come from existing or potential client companies. However, the marketing effect of these programmes is not negligible. Some participants may decide to apply what they have learned and ask for the consulting firm's help. Others leave the programme with an awareness of the firm's areas of know-how and its performance in the field of training. They are likely to remember this when choosing consultants in the future.

Generally speaking, the graduates of all training programmes should be regarded as the consultant's former clients. They know your firm and if the training programme was a useful one, your image in their minds will be favourable. Demonstrating that you care for them, providing them with useful information and contacting them selectively may create opportunities for identifying and discussing new consulting assignments.

Special information services

The promotional effect of special information services can be similar to that of seminars and newsletters. A consulting firm that becomes a recognized authority in a special area of information vital to decision makers can use its information services for promoting consulting work. A periodic information report can include a description of the firm's consulting services. Individual enquiries can be used to mention and describe other services. If the information received is highly valued by the clients, many of them will also be interested in other technical services offered by the same firm. Conversely, the value of superficial, fragmented and haphazard information will be low.

Management and business research

As mentioned in Chapters 1 and 24, the role of research in consulting is growing. This trend has significant marketing implications. In seminars, articles, news-sheets and other marketing instruments described in the previous paragraphs the consulting firm may choose to report on its own research, or on research done elsewhere but used in the firm's products and services. "We have researched and identified the critical factors determining the effectiveness of flexible production systems" is probably a more convincing marketing message than: "We have long experience with improving production systems". However, to become really interested, the potential client may prefer to learn more than that you are research-minded and use research to widen and update consulting services. You should be willing to share some significant findings of your research with the business community and other potential clients.

Advertising

The purpose of advertising is to arouse the interest of a large number of potential clients by telling them that your products or services are particularly attractive to them. Advertising is making headway in management consulting and every year we see more of it. Consultants should be aware of its advantages and its pitfalls.

Those who also consult in marketing and distribution tend to be familiar with advertising issues and may even be able to design advertisements and advertising campaigns for their own firm. A new consultant who is not versed in advertising will be well advised to turn to a professional public relations or advertising agency before embarking on a major advertising campaign and spending a lot of money on it. Quite a few mass-advertising methods and media used for promoting goods and services to the wider public are less suited to the marketing of professional services.

Press advertisements have to meet two basic criteria. First, they must be placed in journals and newspapers where potential clients are likely to see them. It is necessary to find out what managers and business people read. The longer the press run and the wider the circulation of a journal, the higher the cost of advertising space will be. A consultant who has been of help to a business or trade periodical and has developed privileged relations with the editors may be offered advertising space at a special rate.

Advertisements must meet the criteria of effective design:

● providing a small amount of essential information rather than a lot of fragmented detail;

● stressing (possibly in the heading or in another very visible way) the benefits for which the client is looking rather than promoting the firm's name and background;

- clearly suggesting where and how to contact the consultant;
- appealing to the potential clients' taste and cultural values.

Advertising on radio and television has been little used by management consultants. Yet it should not be completely overlooked. Some stations have programmes for the local industrial and business communities on topics such as creating an enterprise, soliciting credit, saving energy or increasing productivity; an advertisement may follow such a programme.

Mailing publicity materials

Mailing publicity materials is a method which probably every consultant has thought about at some point. Many consultants reject the idea, because they feel that this so-called "cold contacting" is a waste of time and money. Those who use it include both some well-established firms and newcomers to the consulting business.

It is essential to have a good mailing list. Some consultants prefer to draw up such a list themselves, using information on organizations in the sector they want to serve (e.g. on smaller firms located in a given district likely to experience maintenance or cash-flow problems). Or there may be a trade association or a special firm from which a focused mailing list can be purchased.

Only well-chosen and properly designed materials should be mailed. These include information brochures and leaflets on the consulting firm, information sheets and reports on new services, annual activity reports, reprints of articles, samples of newsletters, and similar. There is no point in flooding managers with paper; they receive too much publicity material anyhow. The materials sent should therefore be succinct and brief, and should give the potential client a piece of meaningful technical information, demonstrating the consultant's unique approach, knowledge of the business, and work recently undertaken. This should be supplemented by a short description of the consulting firm and profiles of its senior staff.

Exhibitions

Exhibitions of professional materials and services, organized in conjunction with trade fairs, exhibitions of computer, communication, teaching and office equipment, professional conventions, or management and training conferences, also provide opportunities for advertising. If a representative of the consulting firm can be present, some clients may get in touch with him or her directly at the exhibition.

The manager's professional and social activities

If you are a management consultant it is in your interest to socialize with managers and be regarded as someone who belongs to management and business circles. You expect that these activities will "make you visible" to a number of potential clients, who will prefer to deal with a person known to them from professional and social contacts rather than with a stranger. You will also get to know bankers, lawyers and other professionals who may recommend you to their own clients.

Many consultants are members of management associations and similar voluntary membership bodies, local, national or international. They readily give talks at meetings (often for free) and agree to serve on committees or working parties. They exhibit "relaxed initiative" (interest and availability), but should not overdo it by being so active that their behaviour becomes annoying and suspicious. A single practitioner has to consider in how many events he or she can afford to participate, while a larger consulting firm can be represented by various staff members in several organizations.

Private social, cultural and sporting activities provide opportunities for informal contacts which can generate new business. More than one consulting project has had its origin on a golf course!

Voluntary social work

Organizations involved in social work and community development are badly in need of members and advisers with administrative and management know-how. While their technical problems may not be the most sophisticated ones, helping them is often a most rewarding social experience.

Voluntary social and community service gives a significant social dimension to the consultant's image. This can even be expressed through formal recognition or award. It helps to establish contacts with managers and business people who also engage in these activities — in some countries quite a few of them do.

Directories

In most countries, various directories of professional services exist and many of them include sections on management consultants. In addition to the consultant's name and address, a directory would normally also indicate areas of competence, using either standard terms and definitions chosen by the publisher of the directory, or a description provided by the consultant concerned.

It is unlikely that a potential client would select a management consultant straight from a directory listing. However, a directory may be used for establishing a short-list of consultants, or for checking and completing information on them. It is therefore advisable to be listed in directories that are well known and enjoy a good reputation. This includes membership directories issued by professional consultants' associations. It is not necessary to be mentioned in every directory at all costs.

If the "yellow pages" of the area telephone directory include a section on management consultants, you should make sure that your firm is listed.

Responding to enquiries

The use of any of the marketing techniques discussed above can at some point lead to an enquiry by a prospective client. In some instances the prospects are directly invited to make an enquiry (e.g. as a follow-up to a seminar which they attended). These enquiries can cover a wide range of topics, including general questions on business and management, sources of information, profile of the consulting firm, work for other clients, or problems faced by the client who is making the enquiry.

Any such enquiry can be another effective step in preparing new business, or can spoil the emerging relationship and turn a potential client away. This risk is particularly high in large consulting firms, if the person contacted (who may be a telephone operator, but could equally well be a professional who happened to be in the office) is unable to put the client in touch with the right colleague, or to react properly to the enquiry.

It is useful to bear the following rules in mind:

— if you advertise, write articles, speak at conferences, etc., you can expect enquiries;

— resources should be made available for handling enquiries (people appointed, time reserved, answering machines installed to record enquiries in the consultant's absence);

— every enquiry should be handled with utmost courtesy and patience and at the right level (a well-informed client can be discouraged by a poor answer from a clerical assistant or an uninformed junior associate; a company manager will expect a reply from a partner or another senior consultant);

— enquiries that cannot be answered immediately should be handled in the shortest possible time;

— responding to enquiries involves marketing tactics — that is, considering how far to go: merely answering a question, showing interest in the client organization, offering a meeting, or similar;

— in certain cases the consultant will have to decide how much to reveal (it may well happen that a client could try to turn an enquiry into a free consultation);

— enquiries should be recorded in clients' files (see box 25.4, page 554), and suggestions for further follow-up should be made as appropriate.

Location and standing of office facilities

A happy medium needs to be struck between the prestigious image of a professional service and the economy of its operation. The right address is usually close to the sources of business. This tends to locate a firm in or near the financial or commercial quarter of the capital city or a major industrial centre, which in some countries is the same place. However, a "good address" is likely to be expensive and the consultant must be able to afford it.

The business-like appearance of the offices, the reception area and the meeting rooms where visitors are received, is equally important. Successful consulting firms want to show clients that they use up-to-date office equipment and elegant but sober and functional furniture, and have efficient internal administration. Exhibiting excessive luxury may impress certain clients, but will discourage most of them. Your clients will quickly conclude that you will make them pay for the beauty and comfort of your office facilities. Owners and managers of small firms definitely feel uneasy in offices too unlike their own working environment.

Name and logo

Although many consultants are unaware of it, public relations experts confirm that the firm's name and logo have their role in communicating the firm's image to the public and to potential clients.

If the firm's name is well known and has become a part of its goodwill, it should not be changed, even if it does not any longer have a real meaning. A new firm, however, can consider alternative choices.

Names of persons. Naming a firm after the founder, owner or main partners is very popular in professional services. It is useful to know who has the key role in the firm. If a consultant is successful as an author or conference speaker, potential clients can easily see his or her association with a professional practice of the same name. On the other hand, there can be some confusion. It may be difficult to maintain a clear distinction between professional and private activity undertaken under the same name.

A quick perusal of lists of important accounting and consulting firms shows that names of persons (founders or main partners) prevail in their titles. To use a person's name is not recommended if it sounds awkward in the consultant's cultural environment, or if it can evoke bizarre associations.

Activity area. To call a firm by its activity area (e.g. International Marketing Consultants, Road Transport Management Services) is another possibility. Such a name should be carefully chosen:

— it may become too restrictive if the consultant enters a new area (e.g. adds new fields of transport to road transport) — this has, in fact, happened in many consulting firms;

— it may easily lead to confusion if it is too general and if several firms in the same business community use similar names (Resource Planning Services, Resource Management Associates, Strategic Planning Services, and similar).

Acronym. It is useful to think of the firm's acronym: the original full name of many professional firms has long been forgotten and the acronym has replaced it completely.

Logo. The logo of a professional firm does not have the same importance as in mass advertising of consumer goods, but it can play a useful role in reminding the clients quickly that a message is coming from a particular firm. A logo can be used on letter headings, business cards, newsletters, reports, publicity materials, and printed and visual advertisements.

25.4 Techniques for marketing consulting assignments

Every consultant prefers clients to come to him or her. Yet many consultants, in particular newcomers to the profession, would never get enough work by merely waiting for potential clients to come. They have to find clients and market assignments to them. The main techniques are reviewed in this section.

Cold contacts

Cold contacts are visits, letters or telephone calls whereby a consultant turns to a potential client and tries to sell a service. A lot has been said and written about these contacts. The professional community regards them as the least effective marketing technique and some consultants never use them. Yet they are still used, and newly established consulting firms may be unable to avoid them.

Cold visits (unannounced) are least suitable. Managers resent being disturbed by unknown persons for unknown reasons. There are cultures, however, where this is acceptable.

Cold mailing of letters is a slightly better technique. Its purpose is not to sell an assignment, but to present the consultant to the prospective client and prepare the ground for a further contact, to follow in two to three weeks.

Cold telephone calls have the sole purpose of obtaining an appointment with the client. They also serve for answering the immediate questions that the client may ask before deciding to receive or visit the consultant.

The effectiveness of cold contacts can be increased by observing certain rules. First, the prospects have to be properly selected. They must be "target organizations", identified by researching the potential market, and the consultant must be convinced that he can do something useful for them. He should work out a list of addresses or, if he decides to buy one from an agent, he should screen it before using it.

Second, cold contacts require technical preparation. The consultant should learn as much as possible about the organization to be contacted. The worst thing that can happen is to exhibit flagrant ignorance of basic facts about the client's business in the first conversation with him or her. Letters worded in general terms, or giving a lot of detailed information of no interest to the prospective client, should be avoided. Instead, individualized letters should be written, showing the client that the consultant has something specific and relevant to offer. A telephone call also needs preparation to be effective. Some consultants have check-lists for preparing and constructing the conversation over the phone.

Third, the consultant should aim at getting in touch with the right person. In many (but not all) organizations it should be the top executive. A cold letter should be addressed to him personally. In calling by telephone the consultant should try to speak with the "target person", aiming to reach him at a time of day when he is not too occupied. Busy executives do not bother to return calls unless they have a reason to do so. Therefore, if the consultant does not reach the target person, he should not leave his name and number, hoping that the call will be returned. Rather he should call again at a moment suggested by the secretary.

A normal sequence in cold contacting would be (i) a letter, (ii) a telephone call following up on the letter and asking for an appointment, and (iii) an appointment with the client. To reach this third step does not guarantee a new assignment, but the possibility of getting one has increased.

Contacts based on referrals and leads

If a consultant "puts referrals to work" as discussed in section 25.3, there is no doubt that most contacts with new clients will take place thanks to referrals and leads. These occur in various ways:

- the prospective client asks for a meeting;
- the consultant is introduced to the prospect by a mutual business friend or acquaintance;
- the consultant gets names of potential clients from current clients.

The fact that the consultant has been recommended, or can use referrals likely to influence the prospective client's attitude, creates a favourable atmosphere for negotiating an assignment. The prospect may know a great deal from business friends and the discussion can quickly pass from generalities to specific issues. The consultant should find out how much information the client already has, to avoid repeating the obvious and forgetting to provide information that the new client needs.

If the client wants no more than information, the consultant should not force him into negotiating an assignment immediately. Experience will teach the consultant how far to go in such situations. For example, he or she may suggest another contact in which the discussion could be pursued, and prior to which he or she could look and comment — without charging a fee — at some data on the prospect's business. Or the consultant can provide some detailed descriptions of assignments carried out for clients whom the prospect knows and respects. Such a contact should be followed up by a telephone call after two to four weeks. If the prospect has lost interest, the consultant should not persist.

In a similar vein, consulting firms which organize management seminars often make follow-up contacts with participants to find out whether they would be interested in a consulting assignment. An approach in several stages (as described above) should be applied in these instances.

Responding to invitations to submit proposals

In certain cases new contacts with potential clients can be made in response to a published announcement inviting consultants to present a technical proposal for executing a project. As a rule, the client will be a public agency, or (less frequently) a private organization that for some reason has chosen to apply a formal selection procedure.

In such a situation the client has not only identified himself, but probably has a fairly precise view of what he wants to be done. His own technical services, or an external consultant, will have undertaken a preliminary investigation and developed a global description (terms of reference) of the project. This description would be made available on request.

Frequently the selection procedure is in two steps:

— in the first step (preselection), consultants who are interested are invited to contact the client and provide a *technical memorandum* on their firm's profile and relevant experience; those retained are included in a short-list;

— in the second step (selection), the short-listed consultants submit *technical proposals* (tenders, offers), which are then examined and selected as described in section 7.4.[3]

Projects thus announced are often large and financially attractive, and whet the appetite of many consultants. However, before a firm decides to tender, several factors ought to be considered and relevant information carefully examined:

● the prospect may already have a short-list, or even a specific firm in mind, when starting the formal selection procedure;

● several important consulting firms may be interested in the job and competition will be tough;

● one or more firms may already have done considerable preparatory work and a great deal of marketing;

● the preparation of a technical memorandum and of a good technical proposal is time-consuming and costly (a fairly detailed diagnostic survey, including several visits to the client organization, may be needed before drawing up a proposal); this work is done at a loss by those who are not chosen and sometimes its cost is not reimbursed even to the winning firm;

● the selection procedure may be long, the consultant may be asked to submit additional information, reconsider some of the terms, rewrite proposals and pay several visits to the client; therefore he or she should not be in pressing need of securing the job and starting it quickly.

If you decide to compete for such a project you should develop a tactical plan for winning it. For example, you may feel technically fully competent for the job, but be unknown to the client. The question is: What can be done in a short time to become known to an important new prospect? Can our former clients help? Should we organize study visits to our former clients for the prospective client's key technical staff? What else can be done without divulging confidential information?

Marketing during the entry phase

The entry phase of a consulting assignment was described in detail in Chapter 7. The reader should recall that in many instances the client will not give a final agreement to the assignment before having seen and reviewed a technical proposal based on preliminary problem diagnosis. The entry phase cannot be regarded as successfully completed before the contract has been signed, or confirmed by a verbal agreement. The implication is clear: the marketing of a new assignment does not end at the first discussion with the prospect, but continues throughout the entry phase even if some technical work on a new assignment has already started.

The marketing dimension of the whole entry phase cannot be over-emphasized. Whether there is competition or not, the consultant should think of the marketing effect of everything he or she says and does in the first meetings with the client organization, in the preliminary diagnostic survey, in formulating and presenting the proposal to the client, in giving price quotations, in for-mulating the contract and in suggesting how to staff the assignment.

25.5 Marketing to existing clients

There are two groups of existing clients — those for whom we are currently working (current clients) and those for whom we have worked in the past (former clients). In all professions, firms pursue the strategy of keeping their clients and trying to sell further services to them. In management consulting, this strategy has resulted in an impressive share of repeat business – – 64 per cent by recent ACME data,[4] a share that in some firms attains 75-80 per cent. Box 25.3 (overleaf) shows that the cost of marketing efforts is not a negligible factor.

Marketing during assignment execution

It has been stressed many times that marketing to existing clients starts during assignment execution. This includes:

- being alert to any sign of the client's unhappiness or apprehension con-cerning the approach taken, the progress made, the costs incurred, or the behaviour of the assignment team;
- keeping the client fully informed about the progress of the assignment and examining all potential problems and difficulties with the client as early as possible;
- keeping eyes open for further client needs and opportunities (beyond the scope of the current assignment) and mentioning these to the client in an appropriate way;
- fully demonstrating to the client that you care for him or her and will spare no efforts to provide a service that is most valuable according to the client's, not the consultant's, criteria;

- yet resisting any temptation to extend the assignment beyond necessary limits in order to increase your current earnings.

Box 25.3 Hard data on the cost of marketing efforts

In a medium-sized German consulting firm the average size of an assignment is about US$100,000. The records show that getting an assignment from a new client requires some seven to eight days of marketing effort (including a study of client conditions, making contacts, drafting proposals, negotiating, etc.). On average, the firm manages to win one of three such prospective new contracts. Hence, some 21-24 days have to be spent for generating US$100,000 of new work, and one new client. In contrast, to get US$100,000 of business from an existing client requires about three to five days of focused marketing effort.

The initial marketing effort needed to obtain a new client is costly. In most instances, the first assignment will be done at a loss. This can be justified (i) if you get a good client, (ii) if you are good enough at obtaining repeat business by marketing to existing clients, or (iii) if you need a new client because you are diversifying services to new sectors, countries, etc.

Winning new clients while losing existing clients is a luxury that few professional firms can afford.

Author: Karl Scholz.

Cross-selling

Cross-selling is a popular though controversial concept in current professional practice. We speak about cross-selling if established contacts and activities in one service area (audit, financial consulting) are used to sell other services (strategy consulting, engineering, legal advice) to the same client organization. As a rule, two or more units within a consulting firm or group will thus become involved.

The relationship between auditing and management consulting is often mentioned as the best example of cross-selling. Some audits point directly to deficiencies or underutilized resources, and a consulting service is then offered to remedy these. Or the approach may be more subtle. If there is a good relationship with the client in audit or another area, this can be used for establishing contacts in another sector of the firm's services, hoping that the existing relationship will ease the negotiation of assignments in a new sector. In some cases it is the client who takes the initiative to avoid a painful and time-consuming search for a new supplier of professional services.

Arguments in support of cross-selling include:

— maximizing the value of current client relationships;

— the possibility to reduce costs both to the client and the consultant since the two organizations already know each other;

— achieving synergy through better coordination of different services provided to one client.

Cross-selling has also been vigorously criticized from various perspectives:

- it constrains the client's choice, especially if, because of excellent relationships in one area, the client feels obliged to recruit from the same firm the different services proposed;

- hence the client may end up by using services of a lower quality (and possibly more expensive) than if an independent selection had been made;

- in some professional firms the various service sectors collaborate poorly and are not really motivated to do a good marketing job for another sector of the firm; if they cross-sell when working with current clients, they do so reluctantly, and only because they have been instructed by their top management.[5]

Marketing to former clients

A "former" client in our conception is not a lost client, but one for whom the consultant has done some work in the past. Satisfied former clients often return to their professional advisers:

- if they have high respect for their technical competence and their continuous efforts to be up to date;

- because they enjoyed working with a particular person and/or firm;

- because a selection process can be avoided or simplified and the work carried out promptly.

The obvious assumption is that the client has some work in the former consultant's areas of competence. Some clients do come back by themselves, without any effort on the part of the consultant. More of them come back if the consultant does not ignore them in his or her marketing efforts. There are no special techniques for marketing to former clients and the consultant may well be able to choose among those reviewed in the previous two sections (25.3 and 25.4). On the one hand, it may be unnecessary to repeatedly send basic and general information, since the firm is already known to the client. On the other hand, it is useful to send new information and ideas, demonstrating that the consulting firm is constantly developing and improving its client services, and confirming continued interest in former clients' business.

Occasional personal contacts appear to be a good form of marketing, provided that they (i) are well prepared, (ii) show to the client that the consultant follows the client's business and is aware of the client's changing needs, and (iii) are made at a proper level of managerial responsibility on both the client and the consultant sides.

The last condition does not mean that junior professionals should not be doing follow-up work with former clients. It may even be very effective to involve new people in the relationship, thus showing new faces and new competences to the client. However, junior consultants should probably talk to different people, and about different questions, than the firm's partners or principals would do.

25.6 Managing the marketing process

It is probably not an exaggeration to say that, in an increasingly competitive environment, effective marketing has become one of the key success factors in professional firms. Therefore it is not enough to state a few principles of marketing, hoping that all staff members will apply them. The marketing process has to be managed by the firm's top management. It must not be managed as a separate function, but as a process and an approach that is fully integrated with everything the firm does — staff development and promotion, partner and staff compensation, the organization and supervision of operations, quality improvement efforts, and so on. Marketing strategy is the central point of the firm's corporate strategy.

Marketing audit

An established consulting firm keen to improve its marketing should start by reviewing and assessing its current marketing practices. A marketing audit is a useful diagnostic approach for this purpose. It can be a totally self-diagnostic exercise if the firm feels capable of examining various aspects of its own marketing, including public relations, the effect of advertising, and so on. If not, specialists in the marketing of professional services or in public relations can be asked to assist. They may be useful, for example, for interviewing clients and collecting information from other external sources in order to provide unbiased information.

Generally speaking, the audit would:

— examine the past and current marketing practices (organization, information base, strategy, techniques, activities, budgets and costs) and assess their contribution to the development of the firm;

— find out how marketing is understood and practised within the firm by various units and consultant groups;

— compare the findings with the marketing approach of direct competitors and other consultants;

— consider what changes in marketing will be desirable in order to meet new requirements and exploit new opportunities of the market;

— suggest how to make marketing more effective.

The benefits of a marketing audit reach beyond marketing as such. It can identify new potential areas of business, suggest new sorts of client services, reveal gaps in the firm's technical competence and staff training, and make many other practical suggestions. It can, in fact, serve as a first step to examining overall strategy and applying strategic management systematically.

Marketing programme

A marketing programme (or plan) defines the consultant's marketing objectives and strategy and determines what measures to take in putting the strategy into effect. A written marketing programme makes clear what is to be done over a definite period of time, what resources are required and what contribution to the total marketing effort is expected from individuals or units within the firm.

Objectives of marketing

Objectives of marketing should clearly express what is to be achieved by marketing efforts over a definite period of time in both quantitative and qualitative terms:

- *quantitative objectives* may indicate the market share to be attained and the volume of new business to be generated from existing and from new clients;
- *qualitative objectives* concern, for example, the desired positioning of the consulting firm in the clients' minds, or the need to find more challenging work.

The objectives are to be achieved some time in the future — say in one, three or five years. This underlines the need to place all analytical and strategic considerations in a time perspective. For example, most of the techniques of indirect marketing used to build up a professional image take time to make any impact and have to be treated as an investment in future business.

It is not enough to define marketing objectives at the firm's level. Consulting and other professional firms often stress that every firm member should try to get new business, without, however, explaining what this requirement means in the case of each individual, and how he or she should go about it. Junior consultants in particular feel perplexed, since they have received no training in marketing and have no time to think of marketing activities in which their senior colleagues excel.

Mix of marketing techniques

The mix of marketing techniques has to be consistent with the firm's existing and desired professional profile and image and market penetration, on the one hand, and its personnel and financial resources, on the other hand. The optimum mix is influenced by so many factors in every consulting firm that it is impossible to give other than general guidelines. Experience tends to show that:

- it is usually preferable to combine several direct and indirect marketing techniques (reinforcing each other if possible);
- techniques in which you would feel uncomfortable and those for which you lack resources should not be used (if you don't perform well in front of an audience, don't try marketing through seminars, etc.);

— although regarded as least effective, cold contacts (personal, by mail or by telephone) are used by every second consulting firm (more often by smaller and young firms than by larger and well-established firms);

— newcomers to the consulting business cannot afford to wait until the market comes to them and have to use techniques that put them rapidly in direct contact with potential clients.

Suggesting that you should use those techniques that give the best results (in terms of new business compared to efforts spent) in your particular case sounds like a platitude. Yet this is the main criterion to apply, not what your competitors or the "stars" of the profession do.

Volume of marketing efforts

Reliable data on the volume of resources spent on marketing by various consulting firms are not available. As we know, the area of marketing is relatively new in professional services, and marketing practices are changing rapidly. Also, a great deal of indirect marketing can simultaneously be an income-generating activity (e.g. management seminars and information services for which the clients pay). Many single practitioners have to devote 20-30 per cent of their time to marketing. Some firms indicate that they spend between 5 and 25 per cent of their income on marketing. This figure is strongly influenced by the choice of marketing techniques — for example, an advertising campaign in major business journals will be a costly undertaking.

Planning the forward workload

The very nature of their services requires that consulting firms maintain a sufficient backlog of orders for several weeks or months ahead. For any consultant there is an optimum figure that provides a reasonable safety margin and still allows new jobs to start without undue delay. Some consulting firms consider a three-month backlog of work as ideal, while six weeks are regarded as a minimum. A backlog exceeding three months implies that the order book is lengthening and some clients will be kept waiting longer for the consultant to commence an assignment. Many consultants do not attain the six-week backlog and are happy if they have work for three to four weeks ahead. This, however, is a small safety margin.

To maintain a satisfactory safety margin, the volume of new assignments in fee-earning days (weeks or months) negotiated in every period of time (week or month) should be equal to the average volume of consulting work performed by the firm in this period, plus a provision for required volume increase. This, of course, is theory, but it provides guidance for the firm's management. If the firm is selling at a rate below this figure, its forward load is decreasing or stagnating and there may be danger ahead.

In practice, the marketing of assignments and the planning of work have to be less global. Ideally, the structure of the forward load should correspond as closely as possible to the relative numbers of consulting staff of different technical profiles. Clearly, it is easier to plan forward workloads for consultants who are relatively versatile and can undertake a wider range of different assignments.

Pacing the marketing effort

A steady monitoring of the forward workload helps to pace the firm's marketing effort in order to avoid both under-and overselling. There must always be, in the pipeline, a number of initial meetings with prospective clients, follow-up visits to former clients, management surveys for preparing proposals to clients, assignment proposals in preparation or other marketing events. If these marketing events are not generating a normal number of new assignments, it may be necessary to allocate more of the staff's time to marketing, or to examine the effectiveness of the marketing approach used. Some firms use the ratio: accepted proposals/submitted proposals. If the ratio drops, say from 1 : 3 to 1 : 5, this is a signal for examining the firm's tendering policy and work quality in drafting and submitting proposals, and negotiating them with clients.

A sole practitioner must also watch his forward workload carefully. Although he would normally allocate some 20-30 per cent of his working time to marketing, he may be tied up full time by a longer assignment, thus risking not doing enough to prepare for future work. This must be avoided. If the consultant prefers to give all his working time to a current client, he must put in more hours, and try to meet new prospects and do some marketing outside regular business hours.

The intensity of promotional activity should be heavily influenced by the duration of current assignments and the size and length of future assignments. If the average length is dropping, more time will be needed to find and negotiate the same total volume of business for the firm. For example, a firm that normally undertakes 50 assignments a year to occupy its 25 consultants finds out that it has to sell 60 assignments, i.e. 20 per cent more, to maintain the same volume of work. Its records show that it normally has to make 5 initial visits to prospective clients and 1.3 management surveys to get one contract. Can it do 300 initial visits and 78 surveys instead of 250 visits and 65 surveys? A few pointers begin to emerge from this elementary arithmetic: either the average assignment should be longer, or more consultants should be employed for marketing, or fewer operating consultants engaged.

The marketing information system

Focused and effective marketing requires a considerable amount of information. This information may be so complex and diversified that it is difficult to use unless it is systematically organized. It is useful to view and treat it as a system intended to provide both global and detailed information on existing and potential markets, and on the consulting firm's marketing activities and capabilities.

Box 25.4 Information on clients

This information is kept in client files (card index, computer files, or similar), which are normally established on all clients — past, current and prospective — and contain:

- the client's name and address; names of key owners, managers and contact persons;

- basic business information on the client (or an indication of files where this information is stored);

- summary information on past and current assignments, including the consultant's assessment of these assignments (and a reference to assignment files, reports and other documents containing detailed information);

- information on all past contacts with the client (what contact was made, by whom, with whom, and with what result);

- information on other consultants who have worked, or tried to work, with the client;

- suggestions and information needed for future contacts (e.g. who else in the client organization might be interested).

This approach involves:

— defining the kind of information to be collected, stored and analysed;

— determining in what way and how frequently this information will be updated;

— assigning responsibility for collecting, updating and analysing marketing information;

— choosing a convenient system and equipment for storing, processing and retrieving information.

Information on markets for services describes the main trends and significant developments of these markets. Focus should be on developments that create a new demand for consulting services, or change the nature of this demand. Information on competition is included. This information should interest the management of individual consulting sectors and of the whole firm.

The content of marketing information on individual clients is described in box 25.4.

Information on specific new business opportunities should be generated by systematic screening of information on markets and clients. Client files should be screened periodically for the planning of follow-up visits and new contacts with prospective clients. If the consulting firm is keen to do more work for government departments and the public sector, its information system must detect every invitation to submit proposals for consulting services published in official journals and other periodicals.

As part of their staff competency inventories, some consulting firms also record information on marketing capabilities of staff members (including special characteristics such as languages, club membership, good and bad experience with certain types of client, and similar).

---

[1] See W. Wolf: *Management and consulting: An introduction to James McKinsey* (Ithaca, New York, New York State School of Industrial and Labor Relations, Cornell University, 1978).

[2] D. Maister: *Managing the professional service firm* (New York, The Free Press, 1993), p. 111.

[3] For a detailed discussion of the procedure see M. Kubr: *How to select and use consultants: A client's guide*, Management Development Series No. 31 (Geneva, ILO, 1993), Ch. 4.

[4] Association of Management Consulting Firms (ACME): *ACME 1993 survey of United States key management information* (New York, 1993), p. 15.

[5] See also the comments made in V. E. Millar: *On the management of professional service firms: Ten myths debunked* (Fitzwilliam, New Hampshire, Kennedy Publications, 1991), pp. 5-14.

COSTS AND FEES

26

Running a consulting firm assumes healthy financial relations with the clients: both the clients and the consultant must be convinced that the cost and the price of the service and other financial terms of the contract are correct and fair. This chapter examines the main problems concerning costs and fees in selling consulting services and operating the financial side of a consulting practice.

26.1 Income-generating activities

A precise definition of services for which clients can be charged is essential to the costing and pricing of consulting services. If only chargeable services generate income, any other service and activity of the consulting firm will have to be financed out of this income.

Chargeable services

Generally speaking, a chargeable service is one performed directly for a particular client on request. It does not have to be carried out at the client's premises: the consultant can travel and negotiate on behalf of the client, search for information in a documentation centre, or work in his or her own office on a business plan. It should be clearly established, however, that these activities are part of a given assignment, and their results will be made available only to the client who commissioned them and who will be charged for them. This is quite understandable. Clients do not want to be charged for work not done directly for them.

Certain activities may or may not be treated as chargeable. *Travel time* is an example. Most consultants charge a full rate for the time spent travelling to and from the client's location and any other travel time required by the assignment. Some consultants charge at a reduced rate, while others do not charge anything (e.g. if they work for local clients and travel time is negligible).

Supervision, technical guidance and assignment control may also be charged for in various ways. Here again, some consultants prefer to give their clients precise information on the amount of supervision and similar work required by the assignment and charge a corresponding fee for it. Others consider this to be an unnecessary complication of accounting procedures, for example if a senior consultant supervises several assignments during the same period of time and the cost of his or her time would have to be apportioned to these assignments.

In summary, the prevailing practice is to charge clients directly for all services provided under a specific client contract, with the exception of services for which it is impossible or impractical to charge directly.

Services that are not directly chargeable

General management and administration of a consulting firm, and marketing and promotional activities, as well as research, product development and staff training, are activities that are not directly related to a particular client assignment. The same applies to annual leave, time lost through sickness and various other time losses, including those due to a shortage of clients or to poor management of the firm.

The cost of the time spent on activities that are not directly chargeable will be spread over all clients through overhead charges. The cost of the time lost will also be spread over all clients, or it may be necessary to treat it as a loss reducing the consultant's income.

Free client services

Strictly speaking, in a self-supporting professional practice there is no place for "free" client services: the consultant can work for free only if, for some reason, he has decided to do the work in his leisure time, if he accepts a reduction in his income, or if the service is subsidized by a governmental or other source. A service that is given free to one client will normally be paid for by other clients. Someone will be charged for every free lunch offered to a potential client!

As regards the cost of preliminary diagnostic surveys, it was mentioned in Chapter 7 that short surveys required for preparing an assignment proposal are done free of charge by some consultants and billed only if the proposal is accepted and the assignment executed. Other free services may include management seminars or information services, not charged for because they are used for marketing to existing or potential clients.

Fee-earning days

Services to clients are costed and in many cases also charged on the basis of consultant-days (or hours or weeks). It is essential to plan and attain the required number, which may be determined as shown in table 26.1 (assuming a five-day working week).

Table 26.1 Chargeable time

Item	Weeks	Days
Total time	52	260
— annual leave	4	20
— public holidays	2	10
— reserved against sickness	1	5
Time available	45	225
— reserved for training and meetings	2	10
— reserved for marketing and research	5	25
Chargeable time	38	190

The 190 chargeable days per consultant represent the expectation of a consulting firm for the planned period. This is a 73 per cent utilization of the total time, as determined by the ratio:

$$\frac{\text{Chargeable time}}{\text{Total time}} = \frac{190}{260} = 0.73$$

We have chosen a hypothetical example. It is not a standard figure; every consulting unit has to establish its own time budget based on local conditions, and the firm's experience and strategy.

An alternative way of calculating this ratio is to compare chargeable time to days available:

$$\frac{\text{Chargeable time}}{\text{Days available}} = \frac{190}{225} = 0.85$$

Consulting firms often use this second variant of the ratio and apply differential rates to various categories of consultants. A typical time utilization rate is 80-90 per cent for operating staff, 60-80 per cent for senior staff (supervisors, team leaders) and 15-50 per cent for higher management staff (partners, senior partners, officers). Operating consultants can achieve high utilization rates thanks to the marketing, planning and coordination done by their senior colleagues. Data from various countries indicate that single practitioners who take care of their own marketing and administration achieve utilization rates of 55-65 per cent. As we already know, many of them have to spend as much as 20-25 per cent of their time on marketing.

26.2 Costing chargeable services

Fee per unit of time

The time unit used by most consultants in calculating fees is one working day, but some consultants use weekly or hourly rates. The basic consideration is simple: every fee-earning day has to earn a corresponding portion of the total budgeted income. This, of course, is an average figure. The actual fee will be influenced by some other factors, as will be shown in section 26.3.

Let us use the hypothetical example of a consulting unit described in section 30.2 and assume that the time budget of the 20 operating consultants in that unit is 190 days each (table 26.1) and that the six senior consultants should achieve 130 chargeable days each. To keep things simple, the unit's director and the two trainees attached to the unit will not do any directly chargeable work. Let us assume, too, that the unit's income should attain $3,898,000, which corresponds to the operating budget (total income) shown in table 29.1 (Chapter 29). The average daily fee rate will then be:

$$\frac{\text{Total income}}{\text{Fee-earning days}} = \frac{\$3,898,000}{(20 \times 190) + (6 \times 130)} = \$851$$

Fees for various categories of consultant

Charging the same per diem rate for all consultants irrespective of their experience and seniority would be a wrong policy. Many clients would insist on having only senior consultants assigned to their projects if they could get them for the same price. In contrast, some tasks requiring less experienced consultants would be too costly. Most consulting firms therefore apply differential fee rates for various categories of consultant. In our hypothetical case the per diem rate for an operating consultant may be set at $800 and a senior consultant's fee at $1,100. This will permit the unit to achieve the same total income, assuming that the projected time utilization is attained by both categories.

The difference in fee rates charged for various categories of consultant can be quite important. For example, in 1992 the average standard hourly rates applied by consulting firms in United States were US$65 for research associates, US$93 for entry-level consultants, US$121 for operating (management) consultants, US$150 for senior consultants, US$180 for junior partners and US$225 for senior partners.[1]

Fee/salary ratio

Another ratio used by consulting organizations (the so-called "factor" or "multiple") compares the salaries paid to the fee-earning consultants with the total fees earned as follows:

$$\frac{\text{Total fees earned}}{\text{Salaries}} = \text{Factor}$$

The normal value of this ratio in consulting firms is between 2.3 and 3.5, but ratios higher than 3.5 are not uncommon in larger firms. Tables 29.1 and 29.2 (Chapter 29) show an expense structure of a hypothetical consulting firm and provide data from which the "multiple" can be calculated.

A single practitioner can often achieve a lower ratio by operating with lower overhead expenses. For example, if he or she spends 27 per cent of the 225 "days available" (i.e. 60 days) on marketing, administration and other non-chargeable activities, total annual income may be $150,000 (salary $85,000, social charges $20,000, various overhead expenses $30,000 and profit $15,000), to be earned in 165 chargeable days. The per diem fee is $910, while the "multiple" is 1.77 (i.e. 150 : 85).

26.3 Marketing-policy considerations

The actual fees are not the result of a simple arithmetical operation apportioning the total income to be earned to the projected fee-earning days. Some other factors must be taken into consideration.

Consulting fees are simultaneously an instrument of general, financial and marketing management policy. Consultants have to keep in mind not only how much the service sold costs them and what income they must earn but, at the same time, what fee is appropriate on a particular market and how much the clients will be able and willing to pay for the service provided.

Normal fee level

A "normal" fee level may be well established and generally known, and may even be recommended by a professional association (e.g. as minimum and maximum fees). Fees higher than the suggested maximum would then be acceptable only for certain special services, or might have to be justified in detail. In some countries legislation protecting free competition forbids the setting of any compulsory or recommended fee levels by professional associations or other bodies. However, statistical data may be available.

Fees charged by competitors

As in other areas, the consultant should find out how competitors calculate fees, what pricing policy they follow and what the clients think about their fees. It is equally useful to learn about the fees charged by other colleagues in the profession, who are not competitors.

Fees for different market segments

Different segments of the market served may require different fees. Typically, lower fees may be charged to small enterprises and non-profit-making social organizations than to important multinational or national business corporations. Some consultants follow this policy, while others consider it inappropriate.

Promotional fees

A promotional fee (say lower by 10-15 per cent than a normal fee) is sometimes used in launching a new type of service in order to stimulate the clients' interest. It is understood that it will be increased to a normal level at the end of the promotion period. This is acceptable if the clients are aware of it. It is unprofessional to get clients interested in a new service and then, to their great surprise, increase the fee.

Subsidized fees

Governmental consulting services may be able, or even obliged, to charge lower fees to certain or all clients. This is possible thanks to government financing, whose purpose is to promote consulting and make it available to clients who would be discouraged by high fees. In some countries even private consultants may be able to work for lower fees thanks to government subsidies under special schemes for assisting small enterprises, encouraging businesses to move to new geographical areas, helping underprivileged social groups to start new businesses, and similar. Alternatively, the consultant would charge a normal fee but the client may have the possibility to apply for reimbursement or a subsidy (see section 18.5).

Fees determined by clients

Government agencies or other clients may have established maximum fee levels and are unable to go beyond these in recruiting a consultant. Some consultants accept these imposed fee levels in working for clients from whom they are getting, or hoping to get, a fair amount of business.

Congruency of fees with the consultant's image

The level of fees charged and the fee-setting technique used are an element of the consultant's professional image. Thus, a consultant who is positioned as a high-level adviser to top managers on corporate strategy issues would consistently charge higher fees than a colleague involved in routine re-organizations of office operations.

26.4 Principal fee-setting methods

Management consultants use several methods of fee setting. This reflects the differences between the jobs they do and the various views on appropriate ways of remunerating professional services. We must remember again that both the form and the level of remuneration are part of the consultant-client relationship and contract. They have to be acceptable to both parties and be consistent with local business practices.

Fee per unit of time

The traditional and probably still preferred method is to charge a fee for the time spent working for a client. The unit of time used is one working day (eight hours) in most cases, but it can be one hour, one week, or one month (in long assignments).

As mentioned in the previous section, differential fee rates are normally used for various levels or ranks of consulting staff. The ratio between the fee charged for a senior expert and one charged for an operating consultant can be as high as 3 : 1. Research assistants and junior (entry-level) consultants are likely to be charged for at a lower rate than operating consultants (at some 30-50 per cent of their rate).

Easy and clear fee calculation and billing are major advantages of this technique. The clients are billed after agreed periods of time (e.g. monthly) for the time actually worked by the consulting team in the previous month. Many consultants consider this to be the only possible and correct method of charging for professional work.

Yet fees per unit of time raise objections. The client is billed for the time used and not for the work accomplished. He might even be billed for time totally wasted. He therefore has to trust the consultant's professional integrity and competence. Or he has to control the progress of the assignment in considerable detail to convince himself that he will pay not only for the time used, but also for the product as agreed in the contract.

Some clients object that this sort of fee encourages the consultant to take more time than necessary and to try to prolong every assignment. This does occur occasionally. However, it can be avoided by examining the consultant's proposal thoroughly, defining the maximum duration of the assignment in the contract, participating actively in the assignment together with the consultant, and monitoring the progress actually made and results achieved.

Flat (lump-sum) fee

In this instance the consultant is paid for completing a precisely defined project or job. The advantages to the client are obvious. He or she knows how much the whole job will cost, and can also have an idea of the amount of time to be spent on the project, hence the daily rates used in costing the assignment. Finally, the client may be able to withhold payment, or the last instalment of it, if the job is not completed according to the contract.

The consultant must be able to agree to these conditions. In particular, he or she must be sure that the project cannot cost more. He or she cannot accept this form of fee if the completion of the job depends more on the client's than on the consultant's staff. Thus, a flat fee may be charged for a market survey, a feasibility study, a new plant design or a training course, but not for a re-organization the completion of which depends much more on the client than on the consultant.

It does happen occasionally that a consultant who first agreed to do a job for a fixed price needs more time to complete it and prefers to do it for free rather than to ask for an additional payment not foreseen in the contract. The reason may be that the consultant did not plan and manage the job properly. Or the assignment has taken more time for unforeseen reasons; it is vital to complete it, but the client's financial position permits no overrunning of costs. This could mean that on such an assignment the consultant will make no profit, or may even fail to recover costs.

The job can also require less time than has been quoted. This can easily occur if the assignment is not precisely defined and the consultant has made a generous time allowance to avoid taking too much risk. Occasionally a smart consultant may submit an excessively high quotation knowing that an uninformed or very busy client will have little insight into the project. In such cases the client will pay too much.

These and other drawbacks of a simple flat-fee arrangement have led to the development of several alternatives:

● in preparing the contract, the client and the consultant examine, in considerable detail, the consulting time and other resources required, and the risks involved;

● to protect the client, a lump sum is set as an upper limit that must not be exceeded: within this limit, if the consultant needs less time, the actual fee is paid on a time basis;

● to protect the consultant, a contingency provision is included in the contract (to be used if unforeseen conditions or events occur);

● competitive bidding is applied and the consultants asked to justify their fees in detail; the client could then analyse several bids and review them with the consultants before choosing one of them and approving the fee.

In current consulting practice, flat fees and their variations are becoming increasingly popular. They are the preferred formula in public sector and international technical assistance contracts, where often the direct client or the agency sponsoring the project want to have a guarantee that the allocated sum of money will not be exceeded. In addition, the client may be ill-equipped for handling details and monitoring the consultant's work on a daily basis. Consultants, in turn, like these contracts because of the increased flexibility and freedom in organizing their work.

Fees contingent on results

Fees contingent on results, the so-called "contingency fees", have one or both of the following characteristics: (1) the fee is paid only when specific results are achieved; and (2) the size of the fee depends on the size of the results (savings, profit) achieved.

In theory, this could be the ideal way of remunerating and motivating consultants: the consultant is not paid for spending time at the client's offices, or for writing reports, but for achieving bottom-line results. Initiative and creativity are encouraged. The client pays only if the results are real and measurable, and if there is a healthy proportion between the payment made and the results obtained.

In practice, however, a host of problems arise:

— the consultant may be tempted to focus on easy short-term improvements, producing immediate savings, and neglect measures likely to produce benefits in the long run (such as preventive maintenance, staff development, or R & D); excellent short-term results may even be the cause of future losses;

— it is often very difficult to identify and measure real results achieved thanks to the consultant's intervention;

— the client's and the consultant's assessment of the results may be very different, and therefore friction and conflict are difficult to avoid;

— sometimes the projected results are not achieved through the fault of the client and the consultant cannot do anything about it;

— it is not easy to decide when to pay the consultant if the results can only be measured long after the end of the assignment;

— if the client company is in difficulties, the projected results may never be attained and the consultant will get no fee whatsoever.

Contingency fees have been one of the most controversial issues in the practice of management consulting. For many years they were banned by the consultants' codes of ethics. This ban has been lifted in most countries and contingency fees are no longer regarded as unethical. This, however, does not remove the technical objections to their use.

In current practice, quite a few management consultants (as well as chartered accountants) continue to reject contingency fees. Some consultants use this method of payment if they feel that they can take the risk involved, that the client will get a substantial economic benefit which will be measurable, and that contingency payment is the most correct expression of the consultant's contribution to the improvement of the client's business.

According to FEACO's guidelines (see also Appendix 3), "remuneration cannot be linked to costs reduction or profit increases". FEACO permits contingency fees —

> where this is accepted practice, such as staff selection, mergers and acquisitions and search for licenses. In circumstances where a contingent fee basis might operate in a manner which could prejudice the independence of the consultant undertaking the assignment or might prove difficult to calculate in practice or might prejudice the long-term relationship with the client, it must not be used.[2]

It is interesting to note that the use of contingency fees is more common in the United States, where it has increased over the last few years, than in other countries. Over 60 per cent of American consultants generally do contingency work at least some of the time. This is often explained by the more entrepreneurial attitudes of American consultants.

Equity participation

In searching for new and flexible fee arrangements convenient to certain sorts of client, some consultants have started accepting equity in payment for their services. For example, the formula has been used in working for very promising high-technology firms requiring substantial consulting assistance, but unable to pay the full cost of this assistance on account of a severe cash shortage.

This is a sort of contingency payment since the value of equity will reflect the results actually achieved by the client firm. The consultant is taking considerable risk and is strongly motivated to help achieve the projected results. He or she may offer to work with the client throughout the critical period, putting great emphasis on actual implementation.

Percentage fee

A percentage fee is a kind of contingency fee, tied to the value of a business transaction, such as a merger, an acquisition, a property deal, a joint venture, a bond issue, or similar. Traditionally, real-estate agents and investment bankers have been charging percentage or success fees for their services in these transactions. Percentage fees are common in architecture and civil engineering, where the consulting engineer's remuneration is often calculated as a percentage of the total project cost plus reimbursable direct cost.

A management or business consultant acting as an intermediary and a facilitator and helping a client to negotiate a merger or an acquisition may work for a percentage fee. Whichever side of the table the client sits, he is interested in negotiating an arrangement which is most favourable to him and acceptable to the other party.[3]

A typical example of a percentage fee is the Lehman formula, or the 5-4-3-2-1 formula, which continues to be the standard method of structuring the intermediary's (broker's or finder's) fee in mergers and acquisitions, although various modifications of the basic formula are in use. The classic Lehman formula is based on the acquisition price and uses a descending percentage scale as follows:

5 per cent of $1 to $1,000,000
4 per cent of $1,000,001 to $2,000,000
3 per cent of $2,000,001 to $3,000,000
2 per cent of $3,000,001 to $4,000,000
1 per cent of $4,000,001 and up.

Thus, the consultant's success fee for the sale of a $5 million company would be (0.05+0.04+0.03+0.02+0.01) $1 million = $150,000. An alternative of the formula is 5 per cent of the first 2 million, 4 per cent of the next 2 million, and so on. Another variant in use is 5 per cent of the first 5 million, 2.5 per cent of the next 10 million and 0.75 per cent of any amount in excess of 15 million. A fixed percentage fee (say 1 to 3 per cent) is also practised, as well as various bonus formulas. Such a bonus would be paid in addition to the normal fee if the selling price obtained in the transaction exceeded a certain limit. The bonus can be calculated as a percentage of the whole transaction or of the part of the price in excess of the agreed amount, which is preferable.

Some consultants prefer different fee formulas to be sure to earn something even if the deal fails. For example, a retainer or per diem fee is paid in any case, but if the deal is concluded, a percentage fee is applied and the fee already calculated and paid on a per diem basis is deducted from the amount which is due to the consultant.

It is easy to see that the fees earned by consultants, as indeed by other intermediaries, helping to identify, prepare and negotiate important business deals can be high. However, there is a risk of failure and a lot of time will be also spent on deals that never materialize. Most importantly, bringing the deal to a successful closing and obtaining a good price is a skill for which even a seasoned business person is prepared to pay a high price.

Retainer (ongoing) fee

In retainer arrangements (see section 1.4), the consultant's fee is calculated on the basis of the number of days of work in a period (say four days per month) and the consultant's normal daily fee. A retainer ensures a steady income to the consultant and saves marketing time. It is, therefore, usual to apply a reduced daily rate. The retainer fee is to be charged and paid even if the client (at his or her discretion) makes use of the consultant for less time than foreseen by the contract.

This can be a delicate issue. The client may feel that the consultant should have taken the initiative and suggest what needs to be done. This is exactly what experienced consultants do — in working under a retainer, they closely follow the client's business and do not hesitate to come up with their own suggestions on how they could be more useful to the client.

26.5 Fair play in fee-setting and billing

It is easy to see that none of the techniques discussed can guarantee absolute precision and objectivity of remuneration for the work performed and results produced. There will always be an element of uncertainty, and of subjective judgement, which may or may not be correct and fair. Despite progress in measurement techniques, fee-setting and billing for professional consulting work continues to be a matter of honesty and trust, in addition to being a matter of measurement and control. Consultants and their associations are well aware of these two sides of billing. Their concerns are expressed in the codes of conduct, which tend to pay considerable attention to billing techniques regarded as ethical, as well as to practices that are not recommended or are directly banned by the profession.

Communicating fees to clients

Clients need to be properly informed about fees and about methods used to calculate fees. They should have no reason to suspect that they are being charged an exorbitant fee and that the consultant wants to conceal an unjustifiable profit. Clients do not expect consultants to provide a high-quality service for a low price. Many clients are wary of cheap consultants. Nevertheless, consulting is costly, and clients have the right to know why it is so and what they will be paying for.

Up to a certain point, it is a matter of tactics and tact to decide when and how to communicate the fee to the client. Some clients ask a direct question in their first meeting with the consultant (see section 7.1). They should get an equally direct answer. Others make remarks which express their fears, or show ignorance about consulting fees and their justification. At a convenient moment the consultant should tell the client what the normal fee rate is and in what way he or she would charge for the work performed. If the client asks for more information, the consultant should explain the structure of the fee.

Such general information should be given at a relatively early stage in negotiating the assignment, to avoid disenchantment at a later date. Information on fees given in the written proposal to the client should not come as an unpleasant surprise. In particular, if the client believes that the consultant's standard fees are too high, this should become clear before a preliminary diagnostic survey and work on a detailed proposal is started. On the other hand, it may be better tactics to demonstrate professional competence, genuine interest and a good understanding of the client's business before starting to talk about fees.

Irrespective of the tactics chosen, there is a general rule: the client must be informed about the fees, or the basis of fees to be charged, before the work starts.

Overcharging

A universal rule concerns the adequacy of the fee to the work actually done. As regards the time taken, the consultant may be the only person who knows how much time was really needed and spent to complete an assignment. Charging for time not worked, or spent inefficiently owing to flaws within the consulting team or firm, is unprofessional, even if this is done for a wealthy client who does not have to worry about every cent. Charging an excessive fee for a simple job is equally unprofessional. As regards flat fees, we already know that their purpose is not to blur information and make sure that the client will pay more than if a per diem fee were used.

Double billing

Double billing must be avoided. A professional who will work for two or three clients during the same trip would not charge the full travel time and cost to each client separately. A consultant who, in calculating the standard fee rates, has already made a provision for various administrative and communication charges of the firm, would not charge for these expenses a second time in billing individual clients.

These are straightforward issues. More delicate questions arise in connection with research, fact finding, development and systems design work that can serve as a basis of two or more assignments, and reduce the cost of these assignments. Is it fair to charge data collection or research work performed for one client (and fully paid by that client) once more to another client at a full rate? If not, why should the second client benefit from work financed by the first client? Why should the consultant miss the opportunity to make a special profit if no one knows about this? These and similar questions require judgement based both on business policy and ethical considerations.

Price of exceptional expertise

In contrast to the situations described above, there are cases where any fee level can be justified and regarded as fair if the client is aware of it and has accepted it. This is the case of an expert who is able to help with a difficult strategic decision of far-reaching importance to the client's business, or to prevent a disaster. Usually such assignments will be short, and even an exceptionally high per diem or lump-sum fee will be only a fraction of the client's possible losses or gains.

26.6 Towards value billing

The previous sections illustrate that in a professional service it is difficult, and at times impossible, to establish a clear, understandable and undisputable relationship between the cost of a service and the results actually achieved. An ethical approach to assessing and recording time and costs, and establishing "fair" or "reasonable" fees, is essential — but it is not enough. In mature and demand-driven markets — and the consulting market in most countries tends to be one of them — clients want to pay for the value received, not for costs incurred to deliver a service. They are prepared to pay more than the costs if the value is high. Conversely, and more importantly, they resent paying a high price for a service of low value, irrespective of the real cost of that service.

It is essential to understand the difference between cost and value. Value is not a mere reflection of costs. It is, first and above all, the client's perception of what has been added to the business thanks to the consultant's intervention. This perception can be very subjective. To one client, a retainer may have a high value since he can call and rely on the consultant whenever he feels that he needs him or her. To another client, such easy availability has no value and she would not be prepared to pay for it.

Competition tends to ensure that a relationship between value and costs is maintained, and re-established when necessary. In a free and open market, professionals could not afford for long to sell a service of low value for a high price, claiming that this is justified by their costs. If the consultant believes that the price must be high because the cost is high, and the client fails to see a reasonable relationship between the value added to the business and the price paid, something is utterly wrong with the relationship.

These are the reasons behind the current efforts to apply what is now commonly called value billing, or value-added billing. In value billing, the price paid by the client should be in reasonable proportion to the value added by the consultant. This approach does not preclude the use of any form of fee setting and billing. A per diem fee may be perfectly correct and the daily rate may even be tripled if the issue at stake is important and the value to the client will be high. Yet in more and more cases other techniques of fee setting are regarded as more appropriate forms of value billing.

The time when a consultant could say, "I am a professional and this is my price" is gone. Increasingly, management and business consultants have to think of the value of the service rendered and of the degree of client satisfaction, aiming to judge them from the client's perspective, and discuss them frankly with the client. This will help to reduce misunderstandings and conflicts over the relationship between value and price.[4]

A consultant's attitude to value billing was best expressed by Gerald Weinberg in his Sixth Law of Pricing: "If they don't like your work, don't take their money".[5] This view is shared by other leading professionals. Christopher Hart's firm gives the client the following guarantee: "If the client is not completely satisfied with the services provided by the TQM Group, the TQM Group will, at the client's option, either waive professional fees, or accept a portion of those fees that reflects the client's level of satisfaction".[6] In supporting this approach, David Maister points out that "the professional firm market-place is cluttered with claims to excellence and assertions of quality, few of which are credible to the buyer ... The reality of today's market-place is that if your client is unsatisfied, you're probably going to have to adjust the fee anyway".[7]

26.7 Costing and pricing an assignment

Calculating time

The first step in costing an assignment is the calculation of the time needed to carry out the job. This calculation is based on an assignment plan (sections 7.3 and 27.1) and on estimates of time required for each work operation. Reliable time estimates can be made only if the assignment plan is precise and detailed enough. For example, we know that in planning the diagnostic phase of the assignment the consultant can choose among several alternative data-gathering techniques. The time requirements of various techniques can be very different.

Considerable experience is required for correctly assessing time for all operations and phases of a consulting assignment. Such an assessment is normally made by senior members of the consulting firm, responsible for planning and supervising assignments. Some consultants have their own tables of indicative time data to which they can refer in assignment planning (e.g. number of interviews per working day). Such data must be applied with due regard to the specific conditions of every client and assignment.

There are cases where precise time assessment is difficult, if not impossible. Two kinds of situation are quite common.

First, either the individual who assesses time may be inexperienced in consulting, or the job to be carried out may be new even to an experienced practitioner. In such a case the consultant should try to obtain information on the time required in comparable situations, say from other consultants. Or, instead of making a commitment to completing the job in a fixed number of days, he or she should only give a time estimate and suggest a more flexible arrangement to the client.

The second case concerns assignments in which the initial phases can be planned with precision, while the subsequent phases can be estimated only roughly. Typically, the consultant may be able to make an accurate time assessment for the diagnostic phase, a rough assessment for action planning, and no more than a preliminary guess for the implementation phase. This is quite understandable owing to the number of factors likely to affect implementation. In these instances, it may be preferable to use a phased approach to assessing time and costing the assignment. Only orientation data would be given for the phases where duration and volume of work required are unclear at the beginning of the assignment. Clients who understand the nature of consulting will be receptive to such an arrangement.

Costing the consulting time

As mentioned in section 26.1, the tendency is to be as precise as possible in measuring the labour costs of an assignment. The cost of the time of operating consultants would therefore be treated as a direct labour cost in any case. The cost of supervisory and control work, as well as various technical and administrative support operations, can be treated as either direct or indirect costs and the consulting firm will have to decide which is more appropriate.

If different categories of consultant are assigned to the project, it is customary to calculate and indicate the time and price for each category separately, so that the client knows how much he is to pay for the junior, intermediate, senior and very senior (top) levels of direct services to the firm. As we know, the fee differentials can be significant and the cost of an assignment could rocket if a large part of the job is done by the most expensive tier of the consulting staff.

The total time required by an assignment, and the cost of this time, should be established even if a fee-setting method other than per-unit-of-time rate is applied. In such a case, the consultant will use it as internal management information in deciding for what sort and size of fee he or she would be able to work.

Other expenses

Expenses other than direct labour costs may be either included in the fee (as overhead expenses) or charged directly to the client. It is important to make this clear to the client, who should know precisely what kinds of expenses will have to be reimbursed.

Typical "billable" or "reimbursable" expenses are travel and board and lodging expenses of consultants on assignments, special services arranged by the consultant (e.g. testing, computing, printing, purchase of special equipment, drawings), long-distance communication and document delivery. In addition to listing these items it may be necessary to indicate the values, as for example, the expenses that the consultant expects to incur in travelling to and from the client's premises, and how much the client is to pay for the consultant's board and lodging, or for local transport during the assignment.

In international consulting these "billable" expenses may be quite high, reaching 25-30 per cent of the fees. There may even be a provision for family travel and accommodation if the consultant is to work on a long assignment abroad. Expenses defined as "billable" are not a part of the consultant's fees, but a separate additional item in the total assignment budget and in bills submitted to the client.

Most consultants will ask the client to reimburse these expenses without paying any additional overhead or mark-up, but some consultants would add a 10-20 per cent mark up to cover their administrative costs.

Comparing costs and benefits

Irrespective of the fee-setting method used, the client is likely to compare the price proposed by the consultant with the value gained by the client's business. The consultant, in pricing the assignment, should make his or her own calculation of this ratio, even if the client has not explicitly asked for it and has not even thought of it.

If the value to be generated cannot justify the price in the client's eyes, the assignment design may need to be completely revised. Or the client should be encouraged to think of a different approach, for example, purchasing standard record-keeping and cost-control software rather than asking the consultant to design a customized system.

Discounts and contingencies

Under normal circumstances, if the cost of the assignment has been calculated correctly there is no reason for granting any discount on a consulting fee, and the consultant cannot actually afford to do so. Nevertheless, in certain situations a reduced fee may be justified and can be offered.

For example, a client can claim a "quantity discount" if the volume of work contracted notably exceeds the average size of assignments. Either the assignment can keep the consultant occupied for a fairly long time, or the assignment team will be larger than usual. The consultant may save on marketing time, administrative support expenses, and even on technical backstopping and supervision. A discount can also be arranged if a consulting firm already has an assignment with a client, and is offered an additional one by the same client for the same period of time.

On the other hand, in costing assignments it would be difficult to ignore changes in the cost of living and price levels. A provision for necessary cost increases can be made in various ways, depending on the client's and the consultant's convenience. For example, the contract can include an "escalation clause", whereby the fees will be adjusted upwards in accordance with the officially recognized inflation rate. Or a contingency provision (say 5-10 per cent of the total cost) is made, to be used by common agreement of the consultant and the client for justified and inevitable cost increases, and for expenses that could not be foreseen before starting the job.

Schedule of payments

Both the client and the consultant are concerned not only about the amount of the fee to be paid, but also about the payment schedule. Many clients are interested in delaying payments. Consultants, in contrast, want to be paid as soon as possible after having completed the job or a part of it, and if they can get an advance payment before starting the job, they are certainly not opposed to it.

The most common arrangement is one whereby the consultant bills the client periodically (as a rule monthly or weekly) for work carried out in the previous period. The last bill is payable within an agreed number of days after the completion of the assignment. Payments are to be made within an agreed period of time — as a rule, 30 days after billing.

There are, then, various possible arrangements:

- In some situations (e.g. international consulting), consultants prefer to receive an advance payment after the signature of the contract, but before starting the work; if the client agrees to this, he actually confirms his commitment to the assignment and his confidence in the consultant.

- If other than per-unit-of-time fees are applied, there may still be some payment of advances before the project is completed, or the consultant may propose waiting for the payment until the job is finished and the projected results achieved. For example, the payment schedule may be: 30 per cent on signature, two payments of 20 per cent each during the assignment, and 30 per cent one month after the client has received the final report and bill.

- Occasionally a schedule of payments may be so important to the client that it is necessary to redesign the assignment in order to adjust the pace of the work to the client's financial position. For example, the client may prefer to stretch the assignment over a longer period of time. Or the consultant may be able to accept a payment schedule that differs from the actual work schedule of the assignment, but makes the processing of payments easier for the client.

In fixing their fees, consultants should find out if the payment schedule matters to the client, and whether any particular constraints are to be observed. However, in the consulting business, it is not usual to encourage early and prompt payment by offering cash discounts to clients.

Negotiating the fee

Under what circumstances can a consultant agree to negotiate the fee with a client who wants to get the job done for a lower price? It is virtually impossible to think of universal rules. In the social and business cultures of some countries, professional fees are never challenged. In other countries everything is regarded as negotiable, and the local culture may require the consultant and the client to pass through a negotiation ritual before concluding a contract. It may even be customary to agree on a slightly lower price than originally demanded. The consultant should be aware of this and, if necessary, build in a "negotiation provision" in the first price quotation. Thus, the price agreed on after the negotiation will be the correct one, and regarded as such by both parties.

Irrespective of local habits, there may be technical reasons for negotiating consulting fees. The client may need more detailed information to become convinced that the fee is correctly set. A true professional is always prepared to give this information. Furthermore, in challenging the fee the client may actually be raising questions about the design of the assignment. As mentioned in section 7.5, the client may want to negotiate the consultant's proposal for various reasons. He may be thinking of a less costly approach. Often the client may be able to have some tasks performed by his own personnel instead of using consultants or their technical and administrative support services. The timetable may also have to be reconsidered for financial reasons if the client wishes to use a different schedule of payments from that proposed by the consultant.

When agreeing to negotiate the fee, the consultant should try to be well informed on the conditions under which the negotiation will take place. Will it be a formality, a ritual required by local culture? Does the client have alternative proposals (at different prices) from other consultants? Is the client happy with the design of the assignment and the competence of the staff proposed, but not with the price? Is the price proposed prohibitive to the client, or does he or she merely want to save money by pressing the consultant? Thus, the consultant should prepare for the negotiation, trying to anticipate questions and suggestions likely to be made by the client.

26.8 Billing clients and collecting fees

Professional firms bill clients and collect fees like other businesses. They may, however, face additional problems with certain clients if these do not feel sure that they are paying the right price and that the consultant has really delivered what was promised. This confirms how important it is to be clear and consistent when negotiating the assignment and informing the client about the fee rate and the billing practice.

Bills should be issued as soon as records of work performed and expenses incurred are available. This underlines the importance of reliable and smoothly operating administration.

Information to be provided in a bill

Bills should be as detailed as necessary to avoid any misunderstanding or unnecessary query from clients. Clients must know exactly what is being charged for and why. They should be able to refer to the contract (or the attached terms of business) in case of any doubt. They should find no unexpected charge in a bill, e.g. no separate charge for a service or supplies that they thought would be provided within the agreed fee. Information normally provided in a bill is indicated in box 26.1.

Box 26.1 Information provided in a bill

- Bill number
- Period covered
- Services provided (listing, dates, volume of work by each consultant)
- Fee rates and total charges
- Expenses billed separately from fees
- When payment is due
- How to make payment (currency, method of payment, account number)
- Whom to contact for queries
- Date of expedition of the bill
- Name, address, telephone and fax numbers of the consultant
- Signature and courtesy formula

Addressing and delivering the bill

Problems arise if the consultant does not know to which department and person to address the bill. This can easily happen in large businesses and in government services. The consultant should therefore find out what actually happens to the bill when it is delivered, and make sure that the right people receive copies of the bill. To deliver the bill personally may sometimes be advisable. However, there is no reason why the consultant should harass financial or other services in organizations that are known to pay their bills correctly.

Collection period

What is a normal collection period in professional services? In most countries consultants would ask for payment to be made within 30 days, and hope to receive the money not later than in 45 days. There may be local differences, and in international consulting payments may take several months.

Payments received late result in additional charges to the consultant. Rare are the consultants who can afford to extend interest-free credit to their clients! A late-paying client should first be reminded with courtesy — it may be enough to send another copy of the bill with a remark that perhaps the original was lost. If the consultant believes there is a problem, it may be wise to contact the client personally and find out the cause of non-payment. This can be done during a supervisor's visit if the assignment is still operational. A tactful reminder may be all that is necessary.

If a client still does not pay, the consulting team may be withdrawn. The client should then be told clearly what measures the consultant intends to take to collect the fees.

Uncollectable accounts

Whether to take a non-paying client to court or not is a delicate decision. The procedure risks being both lengthy and costly, and the result is uncertain. In many cases it is wiser to stay out of court and try to find a compromise settlement. In the consulting contract there may be a provision for a settlement through arbitration of disputes that cannot be settled amicably.

Some fees are uncollectable in any country. Consulting firms in sophisticated business environments report that they normally write off no more than 0.1-1.0 per cent of uncollectable fees. There are countries where this figure can be much higher. If bad debts cannot be collected, in many countries they can at least be deducted for tax purposes.

There are also countries where business clients consider it normal and ethical practice not to pay the last 5-10 per cent of the total fee for a project. If you intend to operate in such a country you must know about this!

---

[1] ACME: *ACME 1993 survey of United States key management information* (New York, 1993), p. 39.

[2] See FEACO's *Information document* (Brussels, 1994), p. 12.

[3] See W. M. McKoy and J. D. Roethle: "Consultants' fees for mergers and acquisitions", in *Journal of Management Consulting* (Milwaukee, Wisconsin), Vol. 5, No. 4, 1989, pp. 16-21.

[4] Experience of other professions facing similar problems is certainly of interest to management consultants. See, e.g., R. C. Reed (ed.): *Win-win billing strategies: Alternatives that satisfy your clients and you* (Chicago, Illinois, American Bar Association, 1992).

[5] G. M. Weinberg: *The secrets of consulting* (New York, Dorset House, 1985), p. 188.

[6] See C. Hart: *Extraordinary guarantees* (New York, AMACOM, 1993).

[7] D. Maister: "The new value billing", in *American Lawyer* (New York), May 1994.

ASSIGNMENT MANAGEMENT

27

Assignment management is important because a consulting firm performs work for clients through individual operating assignments. Whatever choices are made and principles adopted as regards the firm's strategy, quality assurance, staff development or product innovation, any such decision will need to be translated into operational arrangements and intervention methods used in individual client assignments. If not, grand designs will not leave the managing partners' offices and work with clients will continue as before. Also, individual clients will judge the consulting firm not only by the content and relevance of the service provided, but also by the organization and management of this service. Clumsy and hectic assignment management is likely to be interpreted by clients as a sign of the consultant's organizational incompetence and inefficiency. It will turn away clients.

This chapter focuses on managerial and administrative aspects of assignment execution. Therefore it supplements Chapters 7 to 11 describing the main stages of the consulting process. To avoid repetition, a number of references to these chapters will be made in the text that follows.

27.1 Structuring and scheduling an assignment

Defining an assignment and its management requirements[1]

The scope of an assignment (other terms used: engagement, project, case, etc.) is usually defined in the proposal to the client and in the contract (sections 7.4 to 7.6). The definition includes the start and the end of the assignment, the objectives, the proposed approach, the work programme, the consultants involved, the resources required, the degree and form of the client's involvement, the supervisory responsibility and the price to be paid. Checking the completeness and clarity of assignment definitions is an important precondition of effective assignment management. Even questions such as where the data will be processed and reports produced, or who will take care of the consultant's transport during the assignment, should be clarified. More important, however, are technical and human issues related to the client's problem and the approach to be taken by the consultants.

Based on this information, the consulting firm will choose how to manage each assignment. Questions on which decisions will be needed include:

- the use of a standard or special management procedure;
- the need to appoint a full-time team leader;
- the type and level of experience of senior consultants (partners) charged with supervision and backstopping;
- the desirability and frequency of detailed controls;
- the need to inform and/or involve the client firm's top management;
- the opportunity to try out or test new approaches and techniques, and the desirability of doing so;
- the importance of the assignment to future business development;
- the lessons that the firm may be able to draw for this assignment.

In making these choices, the consulting firm will be guided both by its established practices and by an assessment of the profile of the new assignment. Although there are similarities between assignments, no two assignments are exactly the same because the human context and other conditions will always be unique. If the firm has developed a typology of assignments and defined characteristic management requirements of each type, this typology needs to be used cautiously.

Assignment team leaders and supervisors

The key role in managing operating assignments is played by *team leaders* or *project managers*. As a rule, a consulting firm would have a group of senior colleagues whose experience and achievement qualify them for this critical position. The function often includes the negotiation and preparation of new assignments — the senior consultant who negotiates the assignment, does the preliminary survey of the client organization, and coordinates the drafting of the proposal submitted to the client, is then charged with managing assignment execution. Interdisciplinary general management assignments would be managed by team leaders who are all-round generalists, while functional assignments are normally managed by senior specialists in marketing, finance, production or another area.

In managing the assignment, the team leader must enjoy full authority and responsibility for operating staff time-allocation, work scheduling and organization, the method of work, and the nature of the advice given to the client. He or she is the line manager and must be regarded as such by both the consulting firm's higher management and the members of the team. This is a very important principle since the team often consists of consultants of different backgrounds and profiles. In addition, if specialist consultants have to contribute to several assignments during the same period of time, there is not only a scheduling and coordination problem, but also a problem deriving from the technical approach, intellectual involvement and commitment to one or another job.

If an assignment is small and involves only one or two operating consultants, a senior consultant is usually appointed as *supervisor* of several assignments. These supervisory responsibilities include:

— periodic visits to operating consultants on client assignments;

— control and assessment of assignment progress;

— technical guidance and support for operating consultants;

— review of important reports and proposals to be submitted to the client;

— liaison with clients on matters of assignment progress and mutual commitments.

It is always necessary to define clearly the working relations with the client, i.e. what matters should be discussed and agreed on with the operating consultants, or with the supervisors who come to control the assignment. For example, if the assignment does not progress because the client does not spend enough time with the operating consultant, the supervisor should raise the matter with the client. When conclusions drawn from diagnosis, or action proposals, are submitted to the client, the supervisor may come to meetings and support the operating consultant with his authority.

Assignment staffing and scheduling

Ideally, a consulting firm would like to see all its consultants moving directly from completed assignments to new ones, without losing a single working day. The starting dates and the schedules of assignments are negotiated with clients in order to make this possible. An ethical approach is required, however: if the client is in a difficult situation and needs help quickly, you should never try to convince him that he can wait in order to make your work-scheduling task easier!

Before establishing detailed work plans for each assignment, the consulting firm needs to make sure that the consultants selected for the assignment will be available at the necessary times and for the periods required. This may be yet another piece in the jigsaw puzzle, to be seen in the context of the total picture of operations.

First, the technical profile of the team is matched to the technical profile of the assignment. It is obvious that the choice of professional staff will vary according to the size of the consulting firm. Some larger consultancies have developed computerized inventories of staff competences (skills). Smaller firms either have to work in more limited fields, or employ highly versatile and adaptable people. In extreme cases, the problems of a sole practitioner, or a partnership of two or three consultants, are plain to see.

Second, there is the personality factor. The correct matching of client's and consultant's personalities can make the difference between good, middling and poor assignments. Guidance on the client's characteristics, in terms of likes and dislikes, habits, interests and general way of life, should have been provided (as confidential information) by the consultant who negotiated the contract (section 7.5). The consulting firm knows the personalities of its own staff.

The client and the consultant do not necessarily have to have everything in common. There are even advantages sometimes in complementing a client of one type by a consultant of another when a modifying influence appears desirable, but the consulting firm should avoid pairing two obvious incompatibles. Up to a point, it can be expected that every consultant will adapt to normal and unavoidable differences, and matching people is only a matter of avoiding clashes at the more extreme limits of human behaviour.

Third, it is equally important that the team leader and the team members get on well with each other. Consultants do not always see eye to eye in matters of individual preference any more than do other people.

Human relations and the atmosphere within an assignment team will affect work quality and efficiency as much as the technical competence of the operating consultants and the team leader. Therefore, professionally managed consulting firms tend to be open-minded and flexible in staffing assignments even if this can lead to inequalities in the workload of individual consultants. Team leaders are asked whom they prefer to have on their teams, or even encouraged to make their own proposals concerning the team composition. The operating consultants' preference for particular team leaders is not ignored either.

Even if all personal preferences and choices cannot be fully respected for obvious reasons, it is important to know about them, and draw appropriate conclusions for coaching, training and career planning. Quite often the originally proposed team structure may need to be modified. Usually this is due to a time-lag of uncertain length between the submission of the proposal, its acceptance by the client, and the actual start of the assignment.

Various circumstances may affect the scheduling of the actual start and execution of the assignment. If waiting time cannot be avoided, it is necessary to decide who will wait. The consultant may have to choose between two or more clients, deciding which one will be served first (assuming that other clients can wait and will agree to do so). Or a major assignment is scheduled to start in, say, two months, but the designated team leader is available now. Would the client agree to advance the start of the assignment? Should the team leader be assigned to another job? Should he or she be kept waiting? When is this justified and when not? What will the client do if he or she has to wait?

It frequently happens that a current assignment should have finished, but requires more time than originally scheduled, so that there is a risk of delaying a job promised to another client. As it is inconvenient to interrupt a nearly finished job, the consulting firm would probably try to negotiate a compromise with one or both clients, for example, start the new assignment gradually, as individual team members become available. These and similar situations require careful consideration and tactful negotiation with the clients concerned. Clients are not unaware of these problems, and will usually be open to a discussion of mutually convenient arrangements.

Lastly, assignment and individual work scheduling should follow a golden rule: never leave any consultant unoccupied! If time-lags between assignments cannot be avoided, the consultant should have other activities waiting for attention. The consulting firm should have a backlog of jobs for this situation (training, self-development, research, visiting former clients, etc.), and should encourage individual consultants to make their own suggestions for productive use of the time that cannot be spent with clients.

Overall assignment plan

The overall assignment plan (section 7.4) covers the whole period of the assignment. It presents the operating team's main activities against a timetable (in weeks or days). It specifies the starting and final points of these activities, the volume of work (consultant/weeks or consultant/days) in every period in the timetable, and points of time for submission of reports (interim and final) and for progress control of the assignment.

Estimates of time in the overall plan can be made:

— *top down*, when the consultant knows that he or she has a certain number of weeks and work-weeks available and tries to allocate them to a certain number of different activities;

— *bottom up*, when the consultant estimates the time needed for each particular activity and compares the total time thus obtained with the established deadlines and total estimates of work-weeks needed for the assignment.

Experience with the time taken for similar activities on previous assignments is useful in any case.

The length of assignments affects planning. A short assignment must obviously be planned in greater detail in order to complete it on time. A long assignment invites the temptation to neglect planning since there is no immediate time-pressure. If allowed to take this line, the consultants may suddenly become aware that half the time has been used, and only one-quarter of the programme accomplished. Long assignments may also tend to lose sight of ultimate objectives, particularly as the operating team becomes more accepted and part of the scene. A clear plan and its regular control avoid this.

A well-calculated overall assignment plan allows for some contingencies and should have to be altered only when major events disturb the normal progress of the assignment. The plan can be presented as a bar chart, a table giving numerical values, a network diagram (for long and complex assignments) or a combination of these.

It is useful to enter the client inputs and activities in the assignment plan in a way which permits a separate control of client and consultant inputs.

If the consultancy provides quality assurance under ISO 9001 (see sections 28.2-28.3), a quality plan may be a separate section of the assignment plan, or may be appended to this plan.

The plan is available for assignment monitoring and control both to the consulting organization and to the client.

27.2 Preparing for an assignment

Liaison officer

It is usual for the client to appoint one or more staff members to provide close and continuous liaison with the consultants. The term "counterpart" is sometimes used. These people are of great assistance to operating consultants and save their time, especially during the early investigational stages. Theirs may be full-time work. In some assignments, consultants train the liaison officers to maintain and develop the work after the end of the assignment.

Recruitment and training of client staff

The preliminary diagnostic survey may have shown that there is a shortage of competent people in the client company, with no prospect of finding suitable candidates internally. The client may personally recruit and select additional staff, or may use the consulting unit's service. Either method will take some time. Client staff, possibly including the liaison officer, may need preliminary training in certain techniques. The consulting firm may assist in finding the most suitable courses for them to attend.

Special training of operating consultants

An assignment may require certain skills in which the only available consultant is short of experience. He may receive intensive coaching in the consulting organization, or gain direct experience by joining another assignment where the team is already practising the same methods.

Office accommodation

A consulting team should not have to hunt for offices when it starts an assignment. Consultants need not have the best offices, but they will not be highly regarded by the client's staff if they have only a small table in a corner of a general area. Without suitable office space consultants cannot avoid wasting some of their expensive time. Also, operating consultants on assignments need privacy for interviews, discussions and meetings, keeping and studying documents, and writing. As a rule, meeting-rooms are not suitable for use as consultants' offices.

Consultant briefing

One person likely to know little about the assignment before the briefing is the operating consultant, who has probably been very busy winding up his or

---

Box 27.1 Check-list of points for briefing

A. Hand over

1. Report on preliminary problem diagnosis and proposal to the client
2. Internal confidential notes on the client
3. Working papers borrowed from the client
4. Published or other printed matter

B. Convey and discuss

1. Terms of reference and contract
2. Source of introduction to the client
3. Client's experience of consultants
4. Client organization's structure, personalities, general style of management, apparent centres of power and influence
5. Client's needs and desires, real and imagined
6. Probable attitudes of staff
7. Expected results; on what are they based
8. Assignment strategy and plan (including quality requirements)
9. Client's experience in the techniques the consultants intend to use
10. Key facts of the client's operation
11. Production processes, trade jargon and terms particular to the business and the locality
12. Contacts made with trade unions and other bodies
13. Previous work in the sector (for the same client, competitors, etc.)
14. Scheduled reporting and progress controls

C. Inform on

1. Commitments to the client in respect of various services of the consulting firm (training, recruitment, design, computing, etc.)
2. Arrangements for invoicing and payment of fees
3. Arrangements for starting date, time and place
4. Arrangements for office accommodation, staff liaison, secretarial and other support
5. Accommodation, travel arrangements and meeting-place of consultants before going to client organization

---

her last assignment and is in no position to give thought to a new one. If the supervisor has been involved with the entry-phase activity, that is one person who will know a great deal. Otherwise, the colleague who negotiated the assignment will brief them both. At the briefing meeting, the team takes over the accumulated documentation from the preliminary survey. All matters pertaining to the start of the assignment are then discussed. A check-list of points for the briefing (box 27.1) would guard against significant omissions.

Briefing must never be hectic and confined to administrative arrangements. Partners and other seniors must use this opportunity to discuss with the operating team what approach may be most appropriate and what techniques should be used in the given assignment. In many firms, time and clients' money are wasted by superficial and impatient briefings provided to operating consultants by their seniors who negotiated the assignment.

Client briefing

Many of the points which should be raised in a final check with the client are also covered in the list in box 27.1. The remaining precautions to be taken may depend on how much time has passed since the assignment was agreed to and what the pre-assignment activities were. Checks should be made to ensure:

- that the client's views and needs are still in accordance with the definition of the assignment and the terms of the contract as mentioned above;

- that the client has adequately explained the nature and purpose of the assignment to all managers and other employees who will be in any way affected.

Introducing the consultants

The conduct of the first days of an operating assignment is of vital importance. The client has already met senior members of the consulting firm, but may be meeting the operating team for the first time. The members of the team new to the client are introduced to the managers and other employees as appropriate. These introductions should be comprehensive and should include all staff who might resent being missed out. At the end, the consultants should ask tactfully if there are any others they should see. During introductions the consultants will sense whether the client's briefing of his staff was complete and understood. The team should be careful to remember names.

Introductions may be combined with a tour of the plant or offices (which may be limited to the area covered by the consultancy). This gives a two-way opportunity — for the consultants to begin their orientation and for the employees to get their first sight of the team. The tour could end with another tactful question: "Is there anywhere we have not been?"

During introductions the team members should talk enough to show and arouse interest, but avoid any remarks that would suggest prejudgement or over-confidence. This is the start of an exercise in patient listening.

Starting work

After introductions the team should make time to talk on their own and discuss impressions. They should re-check the overall assignment plan. If there is not already a short-term plan, they should draw one up to cover the next week or two. The date of their supervisor's next visit is arranged and a copy of his or her own programme in the meantime is left with the operating team.

With the departure of the seniors, the operating consultant is alone for the first time in the new surroundings. This can be a ticklish time, and if there is any stage fright this is when it occurs. It is essential for the operating consultant to do something immediately and establish contacts with the client's people. Making a start is more important than what precisely is done first. The longer the delay, the harder it becomes. Experience shows the consultant what initial steps would be appropriate in this new environment.

27.3 Managing assignment execution

Consulting requires considerable decentralization of operational decision-making and control. Once an assignment has started, it functions as a relatively independent project, where most matters are decided on the spot by the operating consultant or the team leader in consensus with the client. This section provides a number of thoughts and practical suggestions concerning the short-term control of assignments. The reader should consider what is applicable in the particular setting (e.g. the frequency of control visits to consultants on assignments will be influenced by distance and the cost of travel).

Operating consultants' self-discipline and self-control

The self-discipline and self-management of the operating consultants is a vital factor in assignment control. They are the full-time members of the team, and often the consulting firm's sole representatives for 90 per cent of the time of the assignment.

The consultants are constantly exposed in a situation where they are greatly outnumbered. They have to set an example for hard and high-quality work and intellectual integrity. It is primarily a matter of their own judgement to decide how the code of conduct and the unwritten rules of the profession should be applied in the conditions of the client organization, and from this viewpoint every organization has its own behavioural patterns, habits, traditions and defects. Should questions arise, the senior consultant supervising the assignment has to help the operating team with advice and guidance.

Assignment diary. At the end of the first day of the assignment, the operating consultant starts the assignment diary. This is an essential record of activity throughout the assignment. It is written up each evening with a summary of the day's significant events (or non-events) and of progress made. It is a necessary reference for the supervisor. Every paper or note written by the operating team should be recorded in the diary, and dated: sometimes the date proves to be its main value.

Time-keeping. The general rule is that the consultant on an assignment adjusts to the working hours of the client organization. But the assignment programme is usually a heavy one and the consultant may need to work long hours to complete it on time. There may be both practical and tactical advantages in starting a little ahead of the rest of the staff in the morning and leaving a little later in the evening — so long as the consultant does not appear to make a virtue of it.

The consultant's home may be far from the client's premises and he or she may occasionally need to travel on a working day. If this is foreseen, it should be discussed with the client before the start of the assignment. An agreement should be reached on how the working hours and days will be counted, and whether the consultant will be authorized to take time off for travelling home if he or she has worked overtime.

When the assignment concerns departments working two or three shifts, the operating consultant must spend enough time on each one to find out all that is needed. The consultant's reception on a night shift is often illuminating — workers and supervisors may receive him or her warmly and appreciate that somebody is interested in their problems.

Sensitivity, anticipation and reaction. The operating consultant has to be sensitive to all the points that the supervisor would normally check. This sensitivity is allied to self-control. The consultant will encounter frustrations and must endure them with patience and good humour. Anger will only arouse opposition and the consultant may end up being baited. At times people may put forward ill-considered views, or provide incorrect information. In screening and rejecting these the consultant must use tact and show tolerance, taking care to give reasoned explanations. There may be attempts to use him in internal politics, or involve him in intrigues. If he has his eyes and ears open, he may be sufficiently ahead of these games to sidestep them, and be respected the more for it. Genuine appeals must always be met with ready help: goodwill and cooperation do not come unless they are deserved.

Favours (perks) offered by clients. Sometimes clients arrange for their staff to be able to purchase goods in local shops at a discount, or they may allow the purchase of the company's products at cost rather than at market price. The consultant is not a member of the client's staff, and should not expect to participate. If he is invited to join the scheme, he should consider the privilege with care and discretion.

The same rules apply to gifts from the client. There is perhaps no danger in accepting a parting gift, made as a personal gesture at the end of a satisfactory assignment, but at any other time discretion is necessary in deciding whether and how to accept gifts.

Control by supervising consultant and client

The supervisor visits the assignment as frequently as its circumstances warrant. Visits are made more frequently when the operating consultant is new, or when the assignment is going through a difficult period. Dates of visits should be known in advance to all parties so that appointments and other preparations may be made.

The supervisor spends time with the operating consultant and client together and separately, to find out how each regards the other and the progress of the assignment. The supervisor also considers progress in relation to the wider policies and interests of both the client company and the consulting firm.

With the operating consultants, the supervisor may check some or all of the following points:

- that frequent and satisfactory contacts are being maintained with client personnel;
- that assignment progress is up to date and under control;

- that the assignment diary is in good order;
- that the operating consultants are not under stress from any form of harassment by the client;
- that in their anxiety to reach an early balance between financial benefits and fees, the members of the operating team are not tempted to go for a quick return from some potentially dangerous scheme;
- that the opportunities for reporting to the client on real progress are being used;
- that the operating consultants' morale is high, and their enthusiasm unflagging.

The supervisor is always ready to act as a sounding-board for an operating consultant's ideas and as an audience for rehearsal of presentations. He or she discusses the operating consultant's performance frankly and constructively with him or her, giving approval for work well done and guidance where improvement is necessary.

With the client, the supervisor checks:

— whether he or she is satisfied with the overall progress of the assignment, the contribution made by the operating team, and the relations that have developed between the consultants and the client's staff members;

— whether he or she has met all agreed obligations and inputs in the assignment.

To make control efficient, the client organization, on its side, must have its own procedure for examining the progress of operating assignments. The scheduled interim reports submitted by consultants should be studied, views of staff members collaborating with consultants collected, and the consultants' working methods and behaviour observed. Any problem should be raised with the supervisor.

There are periods, particularly in the early stages of an assignment, when the work shows no tangible results. The supervisor may notice signs of fretting, impatience, lessening interest, or simply "cold feet". The symptoms to be watched out for could be:

- people "too busy" to spend time with the consultants;
- defensive or reserved attitudes and a reluctance to talk;
- remarks like "Your man is taking up a lot of our time", "When are we going to see some results?", or "You people are costing us a lot of money".

The supervisor has to take these signs for what they are worth. They are not to be ignored, nor are they grounds for panic. They have to be countered by whatever overt or covert means are appropriate. It could be that in fact the client is not being sufficiently involved and does not know enough about what is going on.

From the sessions with the operating consultants, the supervisor might find that the assignment is in fact getting behind. If so, short-term measures may be agreed.

Short-term adjustments in the work plan

Sometimes, tactics of expediency in face of unpredictable occurrences might require the imposition of a short-term plan on the overall plan of the assignment, in order to break an impasse or show the way round a knotty problem.

A short-term work schedule may be used to plan a temporary increase in the number of operating consultants beyond the originally planned figures. However, the option of injecting more consultants to complete the work in a shorter calendar time is not always available. The addition of extra consultants does not reduce the time proportionally — as a rule, four consultants require more than one-quarter of the time that one would need. There are various reasons for this, one being the necessity to coordinate and sequence activities. Also, the capacity of the client to increase the pace is limited since the consultancy is an addition to his or her normal load. Additional consultants may even hinder rather than help in such a situation.

One way of gaining time is to allocate junior or trainee consultants when an assignment suits the particular stage of their personal development. They can take over parts of the plan and save time at little or no extra cost to the client. In other cases, it may be the client who can increase his or her personal involvement and thus speed up the assignment.

Supervisor's report

The supervisor keeps notes and gives reports to the management of the consulting firm in much the same way as the operating consultants keep the assignment diary. He or she may have five or more current assignments and cannot rely on the recollection of one control visit after making several others. These reports are for internal use only and can be handwritten or typed on the supervisor's PC.

Liaison with the operating consultants

Whether the location of the assignment raises difficulties of communication depends on the type and size of the consulting firm and the geographical spread of its operations. Many operating consultants may be working a long way from their headquarters for extended periods.

Though the consulting firm may have a newsletter, and may hold regional staff meetings and perhaps an annual conference for everyone, an operating consultant may feel out on a limb for much of the time. The main line of communication between him or her and the organization is through the supervisor.

The supervisor's visits are, therefore, important occasions for discussion of the consulting firm's news and achievements, and of interesting developments on other assignments, and for some informal talk on what is going on. The operating consultant is made to feel that he still belongs to an organization. The worst feeling a consultant could harbour is that so long as he is bringing in the fees nobody cares much about him. Supervisors thus have a responsibility to both their firm and their operating colleagues to keep the whole as close-knit as possible. Without it, operating consultants on a long assignment may begin to identify too much with their clients and lose their vital independence and objectivity.

Health and morale of operating consultants

A consultant's morale is unlikely to be high if he or she is not in good health. Consultants on assignments tend to go on working when client staff would go on sick leave. Furthermore, a hotel is not usually the most sympathetic place for someone who is ill. The supervisor watches the operating consultants' health carefully; delaying a visit to a doctor could mean a serious illness.

A drop in morale can occur without a loss of physical health. Isolation from one's family, frustrations of the assignment, or uninspiring surroundings all contribute. One of the tell-tale signs is that a consultant begins to hate the sight of the place he or she has to work in.

Learning by the consultants and the firm

Assignment management is the best opportunity for encouraging and assisting learning in the consulting firm. Normally the team leaders and supervisors are more experienced in the areas covered by operating assignments. While their more junior colleagues may have a better educational background, especially as regards recent economic, business management, information technology and other developments, they may be unaware of the gaps in their practical experience and broader understanding of client issues.

Experience has shown that learning must be a managed process. Team leaders and supervisors must know that they are responsible for the coaching and professional development of the junior colleagues in their teams. Time needs to be provided — a quick and superficial visit by a partner, during which an operating consultant does not dare to ask any questions, is of little help. Meetings should have a technical content, not just checking if a deadline will be met and a report properly presented. Individual discussions with operating consultants could be extremely useful and encouraging for them, and could be used to touch gently on issues for which collective discussions are less suited.

The senior consultant and the whole firm also learn from operating assignments. Most innovations in consulting are the result of creative thinking, experiments and collaboration with clients during operating assignments. Team leaders and supervisors are responsible for identifying innovations, helping operating consultants to carry them through, providing additional technical inputs to perfect the approach to be taken, and making sure that the whole firm is promptly informed and can learn from every single innovative project.

This, however, must be an organized process enjoying the strong support of higher management, not a mere declaration of noble intentions. The short-term pressure of client demands and billing targets is strong and there will always be a temptation to postpone ad infinitum activities (which are seemingly unproductive) to build up the firm's collective know-how.

Assignment progress control by higher management

Periodical (e.g. monthly) progress reviews of all assignments should be made by higher management in the consulting firm — by top management in small organizations, and by divisional or regional management or by a senior partner in large organizations. They are based on reports submitted by supervisors and/or team leaders, information received from clients (complaints, changes implemented, additional requests), and the senior managers' own intelligence gathered through personal contacts with the clients and the consulting staff.

Assignments which are on schedule and present no technical problems do not require detailed discussion, except for those which are approaching completion, and higher management should become involved in these by studying the report, planning a visit to the client for presenting the conclusions, and preparing for the transfer of the assignment team to another project. Problematic assignments should be reviewed in more detail, in particular if the supervisor concerned is not in a position to redress the situation by measures that are within his or her competence, and needs help from superiors.

Whenever necessary, assignment progress reviews by higher management should also discuss technical problems involved in assignments. This may be the case with assignments which are particularly difficult, where new consultants or new supervisors are employed, or where new and unfamiliar methodologies are applied. It is very important for the operating teams and the supervisors to know that someone higher up is interested, not only in smooth delivery and regular income, but also in the operating consultants' efforts to apply new approaches and improve the quality of the service.

All technical problems cannot (and should not) be referred to top management for advice or decision. Many consulting firms therefore use procedures whereby higher management would be consulted, or requested to approve the report to the client, on any assignment that exceeds a certain size (e.g. cost over $200,000), proposes an unusual solution (e.g. merging companies from different sectors), has major political and social implications (e.g. could provoke a strike), or would substantially deviate from routine practice in some other way.

Quality management, a key dimension of any assignment management and control in consulting, is discussed in Chapter 28.

27.4 Controlling costs and budgets

Both the client and the consultant are concerned about the financial side of assignment execution. The client is certainly pleased to see that the job is making progress, but since he or she is also paying the consultant's bills, it is normal to compare the progress achieved with the money that has been spent.

The consulting firm has a similar concern. If the contract stipulated a lump-sum payment, both the operating consultants and the supervisor involved must watch very carefully whether the progress made is really commensurate with the time and other resources spent. It does happen that through a lack of focus and discipline too much time is spent on fact finding and diagnosis, and the consultants are then completing the assignment under extreme pressure, or cannot finish it within the agreed time-limit and budget.

However, even if a per diem fee rate is applied and no fixed budget was agreed upon, the consultant's responsibility to the client requires a strict control of cumulative costs and their comparison to the progress really made in the assignment. If this relationship is ignored and the client is expected to pay the fees without complaint, this can lead to a major conflict. The assignment may be phased out in an unpleasant atmosphere, or the consultant could spoil all the chances of getting other work from this client.

The consulting firm controls assignment budgets for one more reason. It wants to know which assignments are profitable and which are not, in order to take corrective measures in respect of its service portfolio, assignment design, work organization, staff structure and personnel management, including partner and consultant compensation. Therefore many consulting firms budget and control the complete cost and the profit made for every assignment (see also section 29.2).

27.5 Assignment records and reports

In a decentralized organizational setting, where a number of assignments are executed simultaneously and many operating decisions are taken far from the headquarters, an accurate and reliable system of records and reports is indispensable for effective assignment management, for charging clients properly, and for paying consultants their salaries and reimbursing their expenses. There are many information technology applications for professional service firms that have made this relatively easy even to smaller companies (see Chapter 31).

Notification of assignment

At the beginning of every assignment the supervisor or the team leader prepares an assignment notification, which is intended to inform many sections within the consulting organization. It initiates or supplements a client file for the commercial aspects of the firm's work with that client. The form records information as indicated in figure 27.1, overleaf. When, during the course of an assignment, additional operating consultants, specialists or trainees become involved, a supplementary notification is made.

Figure 27.1   Notification of assignment

NOTIFICATION OF ASSIGNMENT	Assignment No.
Client	Industry
Address	Phone

Assigner (main contact)

Invoices to

Type of assignment
- [ ] Preliminary survey   [ ] Operating   [ ] Follow up
- [ ] Paid survey   [ ] Training   [ ] Other (specify below)

Free rate	Special invoicing instructions

Expenses rechargeable to client

Operating function

Operating consultant(s)

Survey consultant or supervisor

Other (trainees, etc.)

Starting date	Planned duration	Finishing date

Briefing and special conditions	Other comments	

Date	Issued by	Signature

Consultants' time records

Time records, or time sheets, are the source of data for invoicing clients and for much of the control information needed by firm management. If recording is manual, one standard form suffices for operating and senior consultants. It is returned to the office either weekly or monthly depending on the requirements for invoicing and control, and supplies the following information:

- consultant's name;
- dates of period covered;
- client names (for up to, say, five assignments, surveys or visits);
- fee rates for paid work;
- number of fee-earning days per client;
- number of non-fee-earning days per consultant divided into:
  — attending public and professional events
  — giving training
  — leave
  — preliminary survey
  — promotional activity
  — receiving training
  — sickness
  — supervision
  — unassigned
  — unpaid operating.

Operating consultants normally enter the name of their current client, the fee-earning days to be charged and the non-chargeable days. Other consultants (supervisors, marketers, survey consultants, etc.) enter the names of all clients dealt with personally during the period, the days spent on non-chargeable work, the days of chargeable work, fee rates, and the use made of all non-fee-earning time.

The same data can be generated and processed using a computerized time-sheeting scheme. Consultants can use their PCs, but it is important that they record the data on a daily basis to avoid omissions and misallocations of time.

Consultants' expenses

The firm may have a standard scale of expense allowances, and rules for their application which cover an assumed normal set of conditions. This is surprisingly difficult to draw up and administer: the "every situation is different" character of operating assignments often extends to the consultants' actual expenses. As a rule, consulting organizations are prepared to consider any case of higher than standard expenses at the consultant's request.

The main sources of expenses are:

- accommodation and meals while away from home;
- travelling;
- communication (faxes, telephone calls, etc.);
- use of special services (computing, printing, translation, information);
- entertainment of client and other business contacts.

Whether other out-of-pocket expenses are reimbursed by the client will depend on the terms of the contract. The expenses claim form caters for any items that are to be recharged to the client.

Receipts for various expenses

Orderly administration and bookkeeping require clear rules as regards receipts for various expenses incurred both by individual consultants and by the consulting firm.

The consultants must know that certain categories of expenses will be reimbursed to them only if they submit a receipt. The firm should keep receipts for all expenses that will be charged to clients for reimbursement. If an expense item is important, it may be good practice to provide the client with a copy of the receipt and add an explanation.

Finally, certain receipts may be required when claiming deductions for tax purposes, or should be kept available for the eventuality of tax inspection.

If an expense item cannot be documented by a receipt, it may be useful or even necessary to establish an internal check or another document to prove that the expense was really incurred and authorized, and to make sure that it will be properly recorded in the books.

Reports to the client

The reports given to the client at various points of the consulting process were discussed in Chapters 7 to 11, and general principles of effective report writing are set out in Appendix 10.

Assignment reference report

This report, called "assignment summary" by some consultants, and prepared at the end of operating assignments, is a very useful piece of information, which makes it unnecessary to read detailed client reports for single facts on past assignments. In addition, it gives comments on possibilities of further work with the client. The report provides information and comments on the points listed in box 27.2.

Box 27.2 Assignment reference report — A check-list

1. Client company name and address
2. Assigner's name and title
3. Nature and size of client organization
4. Operating function of the assignment
5. Names of members of the consulting team
6. Dates of start and finish
7. Brief summary of objectives and results
8. References to all reports and documents that give details of the assignment
9. Feedback from the client on assignment quality and results (reply to a questionnaire and any other feedback)
10. Rating of the quality of the assignment by the consulting firm
    — above standard
    — standard
    — below standard
11. Rating of the value of the assignment for future reference
    — A: excellent
    — B: average
    — C: not to be used
12. Whether the client has agreed that the consulting firm may use him or her as a reference to prospective clients (if the rating was A or B)
13. Suggested future assignment opportunities that should be pursued with the same client, and what should be kept in mind in negotiating new business with him or her

---

27.6 Closing an assignment

It is useful to establish and announce clearly that the assignment has been terminated. This will avoid confusion in longer and complex assignments involving several members of the consulting firm, a number of people in the client company, and a wide range of different activities.

The main considerations involved in closing an assignment were discussed in Chapter 11 and there is no need to repeat them. In particular, the reader should refer to the discussions of assignment evaluation and of final reporting. But there are some further points to remember:

- In the days close to the completion date, the client should not get the impression that the consulting firm is losing interest because the business is winding up and the payment will be forthcoming in any case. This may happen if a new, interesting client is already lined up and the consultant is obviously keen to start working for him or her as soon as possible.

- It is important not to leave any unfinished agenda, such as documentation that was promised but not produced, training that was started but not completed, or a new system that was supposed to be flawless but breaks down every second day. All commitments should be met by the date of termination, including seemingly unimportant ones (for example, the consultant should return all documents and equipment borrowed from the client, hand over all papers as agreed, and return the pass issued by the client organization).

● Billing will follow the established practice (section 26.8) and the specific conditions stipulated in the contract. When receiving the final bill, the client should not find an unexpected surprise or feel that there is any unfinished business. The client should have no reason to feel that the consultant is more concerned about being paid than about leaving a perfect job behind.

Before leaving, the consultant may already be able to obtain some feedback on the client's satisfaction. He or she should inform the client about the post-assignment evaluation practised by the firm (e.g. through questionnaires or personal interviews) and ask the client tactfully if he or she would be prepared to recommend the consultant to business friends.

A successful completion of a consulting project may be a good opportunity for drinks, a dinner party or another social event, which can be hosted either by the consultant or by the client.

---

[1] Little has been written and published on these questions. The reader may be interested in the Consulting Services Practice Aid 93-5 published in 1993 by the American Institute of Certified Public Accountants (AICPA) under the title *Developing a consulting services control and management program*. This publication provides a number of useful forms for assignment scheduling and work records.

QUALITY MANAGEMENT AND ASSURANCE

28

The concept and importance of service quality in management consulting were explained in Chapter 23 and many references to quality can be found in other chapters of our book. Nevertheless, the importance and the current issues of quality management warrant a separate chapter focused on quality. The purpose is to help readers in forming a comprehensive view of quality management and of current approaches to quality improvement in management consulting.

Quality and effectiveness have been concerns in manufacturing industry for a long time and management consultants have contributed significantly to the raising of standards. The debate on quality, value for money and meeting user needs has now moved very much into the service and public sectors, including the professions.

Most management consultants claim to embody the concept of quality in their objectives, placing considerable emphasis on the quality of people, on impressive experience, and on offering clients a highly responsive professional service. Yet the image of consultants among clients is patchy; while some clients respect the consultants' service as necessary and valuable, others regard them, at worst, as charlatans, or, at best, as smart alecs to be avoided.

In recent years, quality issues have been more widely debated, and management consultants have begun to address the quality management of their own firms. "Physician heal thyself" is not inappropriate given that management consultants have led in devising and implementing quality management systems in their clients' organizations. There are a number of reasons to explain this change. When the primary emphasis was on growth during the boom years of the 1980s, high utilization and the recruitment of many people new to management consulting resulted in inadequate attention to training and process disciplines. In a much tighter market-place, consulting practices often need to differentiate themselves more on quality of service than on skills and experience. Pressure on margins is also driving consultants to manage themselves more efficiently and to look more closely at service delivery.

28.1 What is quality management?

We have stressed that professional service quality is, above all, a characteristic of organizational culture, an approach to everything a professional does with and for the client. Aiming at quality is aiming at the best possible satisfaction of clients' needs and requirements. If this concept of quality is adopted, responsibility for quality is vested in every professional worker. Indeed, quality is an inherent characteristic of all work that claims to be truly professional. In many instances, there will be no other person able to judge whether the service actually provided is of high quality or needs improvement. In this sense, quality management is essentially self-assessment, self-control and self-improvement.

However, the client has a contract with the consulting firm, not with its individual employee. The firm wants to be sure, and assure its clients, that there will be no notable differences in the quality of service that can be expected from any of its members. Uncertainty and inconsistency as regards expected quality can be very damaging. Hence quality management is also a system of written and unwritten standards, policies, guidelines, controls, records, safeguards, incentives, sanctions and other measures whereby quality is assessed, maintained and improved. Quality management may involve formal declarations of policies and principles. More important will be the myriad of small steps and interventions, most of them informal, in areas such as recruitment, staff development, coaching, promotion, dealing with individual clients and listening to them, ensuring thorough problem analysis, helping poor performers to turn out work of better quality, reacting to clients' complaints, and so on.

Indeed, quality management should be omnipresent. Whatever a professional firm does (or omits to do) has a quality dimension and direct or indirect impact on the quality of services provided to clients, as well as on client satisfaction.

Furthermore, quality management must address both the strictly technical side of consulting (the knowledge base, the practical know-how, the choice of correct data and procedures, the analysis of all relevant facts, the assessment of important alternatives, etc.), and the human and behavioural side of the consultant-client relationship (caring for the clients, listening to their concerns, dispelling their worries, respecting their priorities, being helpful beyond the scope of the contract, etc.). David Maister has pointed out that while most consultants meet the quality criteria as regards the first aspect (technical quality), satisfaction levels are low, and complaints numerous, when clients are asked about the way they were dealt with by their consultants.[1]

Increasingly, clients who have themselves invested heavily in quality are expecting their service suppliers to think the same way. An example is that some of the leading commercial banks in the United Kingdom are asking consultants to provide details of their overall policy regarding commitment to quality, to indicate independent management responsibility for ensuring that quality is promoted and implemented, and to describe quality assurance procedures for project design, service quality and support. A growing number of public and private sector clients are requesting information on progress towards ISO 9001 certification (see section 28.3, below) and on the extent to which a quality management system is in place. Some larger client organizations, particularly in the public sector, who are major purchasers of consulting services, have begun to seek reassurance through imposing quality standards. For example, the Ministry of Defence in the United Kingdom requires management consultants to hold ISO 9001 certification of quality or equivalent as a precondition of tendering.

Primary stakeholders' needs

Thus, quality is above all a question of meeting clients' needs and requirements. This implies that the main focus of quality management must be on client services and satisfaction. After all, in the long run the success of the consulting firm's owners and the consultants themselves is dependent on client satisfaction. Quality management also has an essential role in helping the firm to meet ambitious targets for utilization, profitability and consultant satisfaction, thus addressing the needs of all stakeholders (box 28.1). This concept is important: a quality management programme that does not address the needs of all stake-holders is unlikely to be successful.

Box 28.1 Primary stakeholders' needs

Clients

- services and solutions that meet their requirements and expectations
- longer-term relationships
- value for money
- contractual reassurance

Owners of the consulting firm

- client satisfaction
- higher utilization
- prompt payment
- repeat business
- adequate profits
- image of the firm

Consultants

- job satisfaction
- client satisfaction
- rewards
- career prospects

Cost of quality

Quality requires an effort and has two distinct cost dimensions.

First, there is a "positive" cost of quality. This includes the costs of achieving and maintaining high quality — costs of recruitment, staff training and development, professional guidance, control of work, reliable record keeping, information and documentation files, knowledge and experience transfer among the members of the firm, contacts with client managers during and after assignments, and so on.

These costs are not normally computed and analysed from the viewpoint of quality. They are the costs of operating an excellent professional firm. We could call them hidden costs of quality. Yet a firm that cares for quality may spend more in these areas than another firm. Comparison is difficult. One firm may spend more on formal staff training, while another firm allocates more partner time to coaching young associates. Which approach represents a better investment in staff competence and quality? It is impossible to say without knowing much more about both firms . . .

Second, there is a "negative" cost of quality. This is the sum of activities and costs which are expended and fail to meet customer requirements. Rewritten reports, needlessly lost proposals, disputes with clients over fees and failure to capture repeat business are examples of the costs of quality which impact on profitability, and both client and consultant satisfaction.

The purpose of quality management is to control both the positive and the negative costs of quality: to optimize (not to maximize) the positive costs, and to minimize the negative costs.

Raising the profile of quality

It should be self-evident that a business which pays serious attention to improving quality can significantly improve its viability and performance. In practice, quality management and management consultants are not always easy bedfellows for a number of reasons:

- the recent history of many management consultancies is of high client demand and good rewards for owners and staff without any special effort to raise quality;

- consultants do not value "process" highly and are often reluctant to co-operate in introducing what may be seen as unnecessary bureaucracy;

- more is demanded of management, an already scarce resource, which may resist more calls on its time;

- initial costs can be substantial, particularly in the investment of non-chargeable time;

- quality improvement is a slow, gradual process, both in terms of application and results.

For sole practitioners who believe they are doing their best anyway, the motivation and time to address quality may be difficult to find. The benefits are that it can be done relatively simply and the rewards will flow to them as owners and practitioners. The large practice has all the problems of buying in the services of consultants who may work with a variety of skills in many sectors, and tackling difficult cultural change. On the other hand, resources can be applied usually with limited detriment to current business. Yet serious attention to improving quality is often unlikely to be forthcoming unless client pressures drive it. If the opportunity is then grasped, it can drive improvements in efficiency and profitability and the benefits can be tangible.

Responsibility for quality

In a people business, it is essential that every practitioner and support team member is clear about personal responsibility for quality. Quality service delivery is dependent on the individual. The four basic principles in assigning responsibility for quality are:

(1) *Responsibilities must be clear and clearly stated* — so everybody knows who is responsible for what.

(2) *Top management must be visibly involved* — giving credibility and clout to the importance of quality.

(3) *Continuity/succession needs to be assured* — thus dealing with the inevitable problems emanating from absences on assignments, changes in assignment staffing during project execution, etc.

(4) *Quality assurance must be applied consistently* — to all work at all times.

The main responsibilities for quality within a consulting firm are set out in box 28.2 (overleaf). In a large consulting firm, the key responsibilities for quality may be delegated to a central quality management team formed from the quality directors of practice areas or business units. This provides a vehicle for ensuring consistency across the practice, testing new initiatives and promoting quality awareness. Every individual director or partner needs to be aware of his or her responsibility for quality. In particular, the monitoring and nurturing of long-term client relationships is a major quality task for each individual director or partner. Regular assessment of client satisfaction through meetings and interviews is a valuable input to sustaining the delivery of quality work.

The associations of management consulting firms have an important and influential role in providing guidance on quality issue for their members and in giving clients a message that management consultants are concerned about and are taking the lead on quality management. In the United Kingdom, the Management Consultancies Association has published guidelines and practice notes for members seeking ISO 9001 certification, and guidance on how to achieve client satisfaction. It also provides a forum for the discussion and exchange of ideas on quality issues which have considerable relevance to the image of management consultants in the market-place.

Box 28.2 Responsibility for quality

Role	Key responsibilities for quality
Directors/partners	Set quality policy and objectives
	Allocate responsibilities
	Review activities
	Establish priorities
	Provide role models
	Demonstrate commitment
Project team leaders	Ensure that quality assurance is built into all stages of an assignment
	Allocate project responsibilities
	Publish assignment plan and deliverables
	Produce and communicate quality plan covering quality assurance procedures, technical standards and quality criteria
	Coach and support operating consultants
Individual consultants	Understand quality policy
	Follow best practice
	Document adequately
	Consult appropriately
Internal auditors	Conduct systematic third party reviews
	Provide balanced feedback
	Highlight areas for improvement

28.2 Key elements of a quality assurance programme

The definition of quality — meeting client requirements — suggests the best starting-point for any quality programme. Feedback and data from clients can provide focus and leverage to debating quality issues and introducing measures to improve performance. It is important to work to a dynamic model of quality assurance which drives a programme of continuous quality improvement. Many quality improvement initiatives have failed because they did not address real issues in a practical, sensible way so that they were an integral part of day-to-day working and relationships. Some key do's and don'ts based on experience are set out in box 28.3.

The key elements of a quality assurance (QA) programme can be considered under the following headings:

(1) Assignment management
   — assignment management procedures
   — quality plans
   — client satisfaction surveys
(2) People management
   — personnel policies and procedures
   — training and development
   — coaching on the job
(3) QA programme management
   — quality policy
   — quality organization
   — focus of the programme

Box 28.3 Introducing a quality assurance programme

Do	Start from client requirements
	Take a long-term view
	Focus on a few real quality issues
	Obtain consultant buy-in
	Empower staff to participate fully
	Simplify processes
	Feed back the benefits
Don't	Create bureaucracy
	Be over-prescriptive
	Adopt a minimalist approach (it destroys credibility)
	Re-invent the wheel
	Expect results too soon

Assignment management procedures

Client feedback is a useful lead into reviewing the necessity for, and structure of, assignment management procedures (see also Chapter 27), if only to ensure that the focus remains firmly on those matters which have the greatest influence on quality in the consultant-client relationship. It also provides a framework which consultants can more readily understand and accept.

Management consultancy is not like a factory-built standard product which can be quality tested at the end of the line. QA, together with client involvement, needs to be built into every stage of the assignment process. Remedial action at the end of an assignment may be costly and too late, and may do little to repair an already damaged client relationship. Box 28.4 (overleaf) sets out a suggested list of main assignment activities which need to be managed and monitored to assure quality work.

Box 28.4 Assuring quality during assignments

Assignment stage	Objectives	Activities
At the outset	To ensure that the right job is being undertaken	Defining terms of reference. Managing client expectations. Agreeing the assignment plan. Agreeing quality measures
During the work	To ensure that the job is being done correctly	Progress reports. Variation control. Documenting client contacts. Guiding and supervising operating consultants
At the end	To ensure that the job has been done properly and the client is satisfied	Formal review and acceptance. Internal review. Consultant appraisals
After the end	To ensure that the client is still satisfied and to review the work in the context of an ongoing relationship. To review consultants' performance	Client feedback through questionnaires and interviews. Update client records. Independent surveys. Feedback to consultant appraisals and rewards

Many consultants would claim, if challenged, that they carry out all or most of the activities listed in box 28.4. In practice, this usually involves a substantial degree of post-event rationalization and over-reliance on memory rather than documentation. The client may appear to be satisfied but a better, and more profitable, job might have been done with a more rigorous approach to quality management.

It is better for the approach to assignment management procedures to be that of the zero option rather than the comprehensive compendium which ends up as a many-volumed manual. Once published, such manuals rarely see the light of day again until consultants move offices. The mobility, responsiveness and flexibility required of consultants are not compatible with highly documented and prescribed procedures. Useful rules are:

— make full use of check-lists and "best practice" guidelines which are advisory;

— define and document mandatory (minimum) work systems and procedures;

— once communicated, monitor adherence to these procedures;

— encourage consultants to comment on procedures and to suggest improvements.

There are a couple of management tools, one used at the beginning and the other at the end of an assignment, which can give excellent leverage in establishing a QA programme. These are the quality plan and the client satisfaction survey.

The quality plan. The concept of the quality plan is open to criticism that it is bureaucratic and that it should be no different from the assignment plan, which should adequately cover quality matters. In practice the concept is valuable in helping practitioners to focus on quality assurance, particularly in large and complex assignments.

The quality plan is an extension of the assignment or project plan (see section 27.1) and can be treated as its part. Its contents will vary according to the nature and complexity of the assignment and the size of the assignment team. The following headings provide a skeleton framework:

(1) What are we trying to achieve: (a) assignment definition; and (b) assignment plan and deliverables?

(2) How are we going to ensure that we do a quality job: (a) organization and responsibilities; (b) quality assurance procedures; and (c) technical standards?

(3) How do we measure our success: quality criteria (time, cost, rework, etc.)?

The successful implementation of the quality plan lies in its scope and communication to all members of the team, including client and support staff. Particular emphasis should be given to:

● initial team briefing covering assignment plan, client expectations and QA procedures;

● progress monitoring and reporting to client;

● communications and documentation of client contacts and feedback;

● control of change implemented;

● document control;

● acceptance of final report by client.

In planning for QA, consideration may be given to allocating special responsibility for quality monitoring to an individual member of the team, or to appointing an independent quality auditor from outside the project team, who will carry out a peer review of the work.

An example of a quality plan is that prepared for a large international management information systems project. It starts with the premises that quality must be built in from the beginning of an assignment, and that the competing interests which might compromise quality are best reconciled if they are planned and managed from the outset. The relevant quality criteria are then described both for the client, (e.g. recommendations should clearly identify costs and benefits) and for the project team (e.g. no rework, clear language in presentations, meet cost targets). The next sections of the plan outline the QA principles, procedures and standards and methodologies, for example, the role of the programme manager and the content and frequency of reporting.

The client satisfaction survey. The measurement of client satisfaction through a survey is an essential component of a quality programme in every consulting firm. The survey must be handled with sensitivity and confidentiality to protect clients as well as partners/directors and staff. To be equitable and acceptable, it needs to apply to all parts of a practice, and to be subject to independent management and interpretation. It is not acceptable, for example, for an individual partner to select the clients or assignments which are polled. It is also essential to obtain the views of the project team in analysing the client's feedback.

Postal questionnaires are relatively cost-effective if a large number of clients and projects are to be covered, and if clients are not always readily accessible. Points to note are:

— the timing of sending out the questionnaire needs careful consideration;
— questionnaires should normally be returned to an "independent" director of quality to provide safeguards for both clients and consultants;
— the number and complexity of questions should be limited.

Questionnaires should cover an overall scaled assessment and specific questions on areas of satisfaction, dissatisfaction and improvement. Open-ended questions often provide powerful feedback to project teams; on the other hand, ratings are essential to providing comparative evaluations and identifying trends. The extent to which the client should be prompted in the questionnaire needs careful research and piloting to suit an individual firm's requirements.

Personal interviews with clients have the advantage that areas of concern can be thoroughly probed, and an opportunity is offered for strengthening the consultant-client relationship. The questions asked can be more thorough and extensive. However, the size of the firm and of the clientele may make extensive use of personal interviews prohibitively expensive. Also, some clients may feel safer in expressing their views in an "anonymous" postal questionnaire.

If client interviews are feasible, it is important that they are based on a standard questionnaire, so that comparisons can be made. It is also preferable that they should be conducted by a director or a partner independent of the project team.

Finally it is important to bear in mind that:

• some clients will not cooperate, but the majority will welcome their opinions being sought;
• the value of client satisfaction surveys lies in their results being fed back to all members of project teams.

Independent market surveys. Client satisfaction surveys do not provide an assessment against competitors or benchmarking on how a firm is doing in comparison with other consultants. Many firms contribute to omnibus surveys of consultancy purchasers, and use their own professional associations and networks of firms to obtain data on how they are doing competitively.

People management

Good personnel policies and procedures are essential to quality management and to ensuring that continuous quality improvement is achieved. Apart from the application of high standards, appraisal and training provide the vehicles for taking corrective action and addressing client satisfaction. Key "people" elements will be discussed in detail in Chapters 32 and 33. Let us stress at this point that quality can be enhanced by:

● the consistent application of high standards in recruiting new staff and in selecting subcontractors;

● induction and core skills training which equip consultants with the necessary competences;

● coaching and supervision on the job;

● assignment appraisals which feed into an individual's longer-term development, remuneration and promotion;

● using skills and experience databases which enable the pulling together of properly structured and highly competent teams for client assignments;

● feeding back client satisfaction survey results into consultant appraisals and training;

● defining and publishing the firm's code of ethics and encouraging voluntary membership in professional associations and institutes.

Within consulting firms, consideration may need to be given to "accrediting" consultants with specialist skills who have completed the required training and demonstrated competency. This protects both the firm and the clients by ensuring that certain specialist work, with perhaps associated high risks (e.g. financial modelling), is undertaken only by accredited experts on the topic.

QA programme management

The director or partner responsible for quality will need to agree and provide a framework which ensures that the quality programme has direction and support, and is applied consistently throughout the firm. The starting-point is the drafting and publication of a quality policy statement. This should include:

— aims of the policy, linked to client satisfaction;

— whether there is an intention to work in conformance with an externally audited quality standard (ISO 9001);

— areas in which standards will be applied (technical, client relations, cost and time quality, etc.);

— the name of the person or persons with overall responsibility.

The policy statement should be authorized by senior management, and communicated to all staff and subcontractors. It should be subject to regular review.

The quality programme needs to be supported by an appropriate quality organization (section 28.1, above) and requires a clear focus. The steps to achieving this are:

● review all activities — preferably using client feedback;

● establish priorities for quality improvement;

● determine approaches to achieving improvement (procedures, best practice, training, etc.);

● ensure that training, appraisals and performance measures support the agreed priorities.

Small consulting firms and sole practitioners

The principles of this approach to quality management can be applied equally well to small practices and sole practitioners as to larger firms. Independent review becomes more difficult for a small practice, and a sole practitioner will need to rely on self-generated review procedures. A questionnaire with a series of written observations against each question is a more powerful procedure than a check-list with uniform ticks. Customer review and sign-off of reports is a particularly valuable discipline to the smaller firm.

28.3 Quality certification

ISO 9001 quality assurance standards

In recent years there has been considerable debate among management consultants about the relevance of externally audited quality standards to their firms. Movement towards seeking certification has been at the pace dictated by the market-place, including in some cases direct pressure from public sector clients, who see certification as a necessary reassurance of attention to quality. As a result, many larger consulting firms have started preparing for, and gaining, certification for, at least, particular sectors of their business. The origins of this movement lie in several countries of the European Union, the United Kingdom and the Netherlands in particular.

The quality standard (ISO 9001 1987/EN 29001 1987/BS 5750 Part 1 1987) requires the applying organization to have a quality policy and a documented quality system and supporting procedure, and to provide evidence that the procedures are being used, conformance is being monitored and reviews are regular.

A quality audit must be undertaken by an independent certification body (such as BSI Quality Assurance, Bureau Veritas, Det Norsk Veritas). These bodies are not management consulting firms, but their function is to audit businesses and organizations in many sectors. They are accredited by government bodies, e.g. by the National Accreditation Council for Certification Bodies (NACCB) in the United Kingdom.

In theory, the quality management system (QMS) should require no more than a well-run business, which takes quality seriously, should be doing already. In practice, the disciplines of a rigorously applied QMS can necessitate substantial shifts in organizational culture and work habits.

General principles

Seeking certification should not be an end in itself; there is plenty of anecdotal evidence to support this view. A superficial approach is likely to result in rejection by the consultants involved and non-conformance being readily exposed by the external auditor. It is important that the QMS reflects the needs of actual practice and, therefore, deals with real quality issues. It is also essential to involve the staff in its preparation, so that it is not seen as a bureaucratic imposition.

The assignment model (e.g. lead/enquiry, proposal preparation, assignment plan, monitoring and controlling, and completing/closing) is well suited to the application of ISO 9001 standards. It has been shown to be applicable to all sizes of consultancy practice.

Clearly, ISO 9001 certification is not sufficient in itself as a guarantee of meeting client requirements. It provides independent certification that a quality management system is in place and that the practice is conforming with its requirements. But there is much more to do. Quality certification by itself is not a measure of client satisfaction, although the QMS should require that there are procedures for obtaining client feedback, and that these are in operation.

Cost of certification

Obtaining certification can be quite costly for both small and large consulting firms. A large firm may need to allocate the full-time resource of a consultant for six to nine months in each main business unit to obtain certification. The input from a small practice might be in the order of seven to 15 days over a six- to nine-month period. Time and expense can be much reduced by starting with a basic system and customizing it to requirements. For example, for a small British firm in 1993, the cost of assessment and registration was between £1,000 and £2,000, with ongoing assessments in the range £500 to £1,000. A large consultancy would have been faced with considerably higher costs, depending on the size and complexity of the organization. Thus, certification is not a step to be taken lightly and the costs and benefits need to be reviewed carefully. If clients insist, it is important that the QMS is used to derive benefits for the practice in improving efficiency.

Quality manual

The key documentation, and the largest cost, is the preparation of the quality manual covering the QMS. This needs to be supported by procedures and standards manuals. The QMS comprises all the elements that enable the

---

Box 28.5 Outline of a quality manual

Main headings	Subheadings
Quality policy	Standards Approval and review Client satisfaction procedures
Quality organization	Management responsibility Individual responsibility Internal audit
Quality management system	Definitions Coverage
Undertaking assignments	Problem identification Preparation of quality/project plan Agreement with client Contract review Performance delivery Completion and follow-up
Management and administration of the firm	Staff development Fee calculations External contacts Purchases
Administration of the quality system	Controlled documents Quality records Internal audit Corrective actions Consulting methodologies Client satisfaction
Use of the quality system	

---

consultancy to meet its stated quality policy. Examples can be obtained from consultants who have developed a manual for their own practice and are prepared to customize it for an appropriate fee, and from the Institute of Management Consultants in London.

Writing the quality manual is a balancing act between ensuring that it is comprehensive in its coverage and keeping it brief. Over-engineering is a common problem. While the QMS must meet the requirements of the standard, the more procedures there are, the greater the demands for conformance on individuals and the higher the risk of excessive bureaucracy. A suggested list of headings in a quality manual is set out in box 28.5.

Selecting a certification body

Fees charged by certification bodies are negotiable. As there are the on-going costs of surveillance it is worth paying particular attention to the value you will derive from the guidance of these bodies and checking out that their auditors are going to understand your business. Remember that many certification bodies are new to the auditing service and professional businesses.

Questions to be asked of certification bodies include:

- Have you been, or are you expecting to be, accredited to assess management consulting firms?
- Who recognizes your certification?
- Do you have a customer care programme?
- What are your fees?
- Can we see the curriculum vitae of your quality auditors?
- Can you provide relevant references?

The quality auditor will check the documented quality system against ISO 9001 and the applicable guidelines. He or she is likely to carry out an internal auditing and management review, and also needs to agree on the scope of the certificate, i.e. which parts of the practice (activity areas) are to be included. Three or four months' records based on the documented quality system are necessary before the conformance audit can be undertaken.

Using advisers/consultants

The time spent in preparing a quality manual and implementing a QMS can be considerable, and external assistance can provide expertise and valuable resources. It is often helpful to have an external consultant examine the system before finalizing it for assessment. Points to note are:

— before employing a quality consultancy, check its track record and take up references;

— ensure that its consultants work with your staff, so ownership is in house;

— make sure that they do not overspecify your requirements.

Scope of certification

The QMS must apply to all activities associated with service delivery. In management consulting this includes the services of any subcontractors and of support staff directly involved in service delivery. Within larger and multi-functional firms, it may be sensible to pilot ISO 9001 in a selected area of service, in order to test its impact and to reduce risks initially. This, however, brings its own problems, in that consultants from other parts of the firm may be transferred to assignments which have to be managed to ISO 9001 standards.

Problems encountered in seeking certification

It is still relatively early days to assess the real value of quality certification to management consulting firms (as indeed to other firms providing management and business services). However, there is a growing view that once the initial difficulties are overcome, there is considerable benefit in better working and higher client satisfaction.

Some of the problems which have emerged are:

● resistance by partners and staff resulting in implementation being a painful process;

● over-complication and excessive bureaucracy;

● failure to adhere to documentation requirements;

● failure to provide feedback and use information properly, e.g. on lost tenders;

● slowness of certification bodies to receive accreditation enabling them to certify management consultants.

Some small firms and sole practitioners have expressed strong views that ISO 9001 quality standards are excessively bureaucratic, and an unnecessary burden. While their voice is being heard, it is unlikely that change in certification practices will come in the short term.

Box 28.6 Eight steps to QA certification

(1) **Basic familiarization** (study the ISO 9001 standard, relevant guidance and authoritative books on quality)

(2) [Optional] **Make contact with an adviser** (if there is no internal expertise consider the assistance of an external adviser/consultant skilled in implementing quality management systems)

(3) **Decide the firm's quality policy** (this is a statement of the role of quality in meeting the firm's objectives and of the firm's intention to maintain a quality management system)

(4) **Devise a quality management system (QMS)** (document with a quality manual, preferably relatively short, supported with other reference manuals; remember that it covers all aspects of service delivery)

(5) **Make contact with a certification firm** (you may need to contact more than one to obtain a competitive quote and to test out the chemistry; obtain their view of your system)

(6) **Implement the system**

(7) **Internally audit the system** (this confirms that the system is being used)

(8) **Undergo an external assessment** (the selected certification firm carries out an independent audit of the QMS and its implementation and conformance)

28.4 Sustaining quality

In conclusion, client pressure and growing competition have moved quality higher up the management consultants' own agenda. Increasingly, service quality constitutes the consultants' competitive advantage. For long-term development and growth, both large and small consultancies will need to be proactive in working with clients on quality issues. As with any such development, clarification of objectives, standards, roles and responsibilities is an essential first step. ISO 9001 contributes by providing standards which are externally certificated. Both clients and consulting practitioners need to share the aim of achieving continuous improvement in service delivery, and to be proactive in sustaining this.

A formalistic approach to quality must be avoided. There is a real risk that some firms will be happy to have and be able to exhibit an elaborate procedure, the "bureaucracy of quality", and that some clients will be unduly impressed by the formal side of quality management. No control and certification procedure can become a substitute for the quality of people in a professional firm, for their genuine concern for the clients and for their sense of professional responsibility.

The decisions concerning quality management and assurance, and the measures taken to enhance quality, depend on the firm's attitude to quality and its determination to achieve high standards. As W. Edwards Deming said of total quality management, "You do not have to do this: survival is not compulsory".

---

[1] See Ch. 8, "A service quality programme", in D. H. Maister: *Managing the professional service firm* (New York, The Free Press, 1993).

OPERATIONAL AND FINANCIAL CONTROL

29

This chapter deals with key aspects of operational short-term management and control, emphasizing those methods and indicators that help the consulting firm to monitor operations and prevent events that could reduce efficiency or lead to crises which would be difficult to control. We assume that the reader is familiar with the basics of financial and budgetary control, and therefore the discussion focuses on specific problems of consultants and consulting organizations.

29.1 Operating work plan and budget

Operational management and control uses two basic management tools: an operating work plan and an operating financial budget. Both documents are normally prepared annually, for the next planning and budgetary year, in a monthly or quarterly breakdown. This breakdown accounts for seasonal and other variations within the 12-month period, such as a reduced workload during the holiday period, and other events, including major payments to be made or received at a foreseeable point in time.

Operating work plan

The operating work plan should reflect the firm's strategic choices and indicate how strategy will be implemented in the forthcoming year. It therefore determines:

— the volume of consulting and other services to be sold and delivered to clients;

— changes in the service portfolio (phasing out a service, introducing a new product, starting work in a new sector, new foreign operations);

— staff recruitment and training required;

— staff retirement and departures;

— the volume and orientation of promotional and marketing activities;

— the backlog of new assignments to be maintained;

— other measures needed to implement the work programme and to prepare for the future (research and development, organizational restructuring, investment, etc.);

— the ways in which consultants would be used effectively during the time not spent in working for clients.

Extrapolation of past trends is a useful technique for preparing an operating work plan. However, mechanistic extrapolation cannot be recommended. An analysis of business trends, and of the consulting firm's current opportunities and difficulties, helps to determine professional and business targets that are neither mere extrapolations nor unrealistic dreams.

Operating budget

The basic management tool for controlling the financial side of the firm's operation is the operating budget. In preparing the budget the firm has to include

---

Box 29.1 Methods of achieving efficiency and higher profits

Area of intervention	Achieved by
Efficient operations	Using staff according to competence
	Organizing and executing assignments efficiently
	Increasing staff utilization and efficiency
	Saving on overhead items
	Billing and collecting fees promptly
Fee levels	Charging more for existing services
	Charging for services provided free hitherto
Marketing efforts	Selling and delivering more work (increasing volume)
	Selling more profitable work
	Cross-selling
	Marketing more efficiently
Staff size and structure	Recruiting more consultants
	Increasing leverage
	Cutting or replacing unproductive staff
Service portfolio	Cutting unprofitable services
	Developing new and more profitable services

---

all expenses it expects to incur during the budget period, and fix the projected income at a level required for recovering expenses and ensuring an adequate profit. If budget preparation reveals that the budget cannot be balanced, it is necessary to review the work plan and the planned expenditure to keep them within realistic financial limits, and re-examine the costing, pricing and other assumptions underlying the two sides of the budget.

The budgetary planning may show that the consulting firm's costs will be too high, and therefore the fees risk being excessive, or profits too low. In this case, management can look at various methods of achieving efficiency and higher profits, listed in box 29.1. Which method to adopt will depend on the market, the opportunity to recruit new consultants and find enough work for them, the firm's ability to increase efficiency in implementing assignments, and so on. The method chosen should be consistent with the firm's strategic choices.

If growth in operations and income is planned, analysis should reveal how expenses will increase. The consulting firm will certainly keep the difference between fixed and variable expenses in mind, and subject each expense line to a more detailed scrutiny before deciding whether and how it should be allowed to grow.

A hypothetical example of an annual operating budget is shown in table 29.1. It corresponds to the (also hypothetical) consulting unit, employing

Table 29.1 Operating budget of a consulting firm

Budget item	$	%
1. Professional salaries	1 710 000	43.9
2. Social charges and benefits on professional salaries	340 000	8.7
3. Administrative and support staff salaries	250 000	6.4
4. Social charges and benefits on administrative salaries	50 000	1.3
5. Marketing and promotion expenses (other than salaries)	160 000	4.1
6. Rentals and utilities	120 000	3.1
7. Equipment, furniture, materials, stationery	110 000	2.8
8. Communications (mail, fax, telephone)	110 000	2.8
9. Taxes (other than income taxes)	70 000	1.8
10. Library, subscriptions, membership fees	80 000	2.1
11. Staff training and development	80 000	2.1
12. Other expenses (travel, entertainment, etc.)	180 000	4.6
13. Overhead expenses (3 to 12)	1 210 000	31.0
14. Total expenses (1 to 12)	3 260 000	83.6
15. Gross profit (before tax)	638 000	16.4
16. Total income (14 + 15)	3 898 000	100.0
17. Expenses billed to clients	522 000	13.4
18. Gross billing (16 + 17)	4 420 000	113.4

Note: Item 1 ("Professional salaries") includes the following: director (1 × US$100,000) 100,000; senior consultants (6 × US$75,000) 450,000; operating consultants (20 × US$55,000) 1,100,000; trainee consultants (2 × US$30,000) 60,000; total 1,710,000.

29 consultants, shown in figure 30.2 (page 636). The salary rates and other figures in the budget are therefore not intended as standards for remuneration policy, or for assessing the expense structure and efficiency of any particular firm.

Structure of expenses

Nevertheless, the expense and income structure shown is within the broad limits of normal practice in a number of management consulting firms. These limits tend to be as shown in table 29.2.

Table 29.2   Typical structure of expenses and income

Item	%
Professional staff salaries (including social charges)	35-60
Other expenses	40-60
Gross profit (before tax)	10-25
Total income	100
Billable expenses	10-30
Gross billing to client	110-130

Management consulting services are highly labour-intensive and *professional staff salaries* are therefore by far the most important single expense item in any firm. Their share in the total expense structure depends on factors such as the professional income level in a particular country and firm, and the size of the consulting firm. Single practitioners and other small firms are usually able to operate with lower overhead costs, reducing or completely eliminating certain items of expenditure without which a larger firm cannot operate. A single practitioner may even be able to operate without any secretarial and support staff, and without renting expensive office space.

Other expenses (grouped under lines 3-12 in table 29.1) include a wide range of different items linked with operating a consulting unit of a given profile, scope and level of activity. As a rule, this group includes costs that cannot be directly related to a particular client assignment; or, if they could be, it would not be practical and efficient to do so. For example, reproduction expenses can be treated as an overhead item or a direct cost item to be charged to a particular client. Routine reproduction work (e.g. reproducing consulting reports in a standard number of copies) is normally treated as an overhead cost. Reproduction of voluminous special reports, or large numbers of additional copies ordered by the client, should be charged to the client as "billable expenses". A similar choice has to be made in the case of telephone charges and for other costs.

Expenses billed to clients (billable expenses) are often not regarded by consultants as part of their business income even if these expenses pass through their accounts. Therefore, billable expenses are shown separately (line 17) in the operating budget.

Profit

Profit (before tax) is the difference between the total fees earned and total costs and expenses incurred over the budget period. It provides for:

- a profit-share or bonus to the owners, partners or other employees of the consulting firm;
- establishing security reserves;
- increasing the working capital;
- financing capital expenses;
- paying a profit (income) tax.

As shown in table 29.2, in most cases the profit margin would be between 10 and 25 per cent of the total income. The actual figure will depend upon such factors as the possibility of charging fees that provide for an adequate profit, the ability to reduce and control expenses, and the firm's need to generate resources for further expansion of its services or for other purposes mentioned above.

29.2 Performance monitoring

The monitoring of operational and financial performance is an essential, yet often underestimated, management function in consulting firms. The purpose is not to produce statistics for their own sake, but systematically to collect and evaluate key information likely to reveal negative trends (from which will spring the need for action to redress the situation) or positive trends (which may need to be reinforced so that any opportunities disclosed are not missed).

Performance monitoring aims at immediate improvements first of all, but its strategic implications should not be overlooked. It helps to reveal changes and trends that will affect the consulting firm in the long run, such as major shifts in demand for certain kinds of service, or the increasing cost of selling services to certain markets. Adjustments to the firm's strategy can thus be based on hard data instead of mere guesses and estimates.

Using comparisons

It is impossible to assess performance without making comparisons: superior or substandard performance can be identified and assessed only by referring to some other performance. Consultants use comparisons extensively when working with clients, and therefore they should not hesitate to apply them to their own operation.

Comparing results achieved with planned or projected targets can be revealing provided that the targets were based on thorough analysis and realistic goal setting, and not just on guesswork. The main documents to which this comparison refers in performance monitoring are the annual work plan and operating budget.

Comparing current and past performance helps to discover and analyse trends in performance, as well as changes in factors affecting it.

Comparing performance with other consultants can be most instructive. This can be done in various ways:

— Consultants who are business friends can exchange and compare data informally, as colleagues who want to learn from each other.

— There can be a formal interfirm comparison scheme, which can be run by a consultants' association or another agency. Under such a scheme, key data are collected, tabulated and distributed to participating consulting units on a regular basis, without revealing the identity of these units.

— Performance achieved by a specific consulting firm can be compared with data regarded as sectoral standards. Such sectoral standards would reflect "good practice", i.e. experience of consulting firms whose management is considered competent and performance adequate. Here again, such standards can be developed by an association for the benefit of its members. This book refers to a number of ratios collected from consulting firms and their associations. These operating ratios can be regarded as a form of standard.

In making comparisons, it is essential to determine the *causes* of superior or substandard performance: it can result from excellent or poor management of operations and assignment execution, but also from an unforeseen change in the business environment over which the consulting firm has little control.

Both data from other firms and any sector standards or averages have to be used cautiously. The situation and possibilities of your firm may be very different and so may be your objectives. While it is extremely useful to know how others perform, no superficial and hasty conclusions should be drawn from the data without comparing resources, conditions and the strategies pursued.

Key monthly controls

Operational controls have to be established and examined on a relatively short-term basis to permit action before it is too late. In practice, this will be on a *monthly basis* in most cases. This explains why the operating work plan and budget described above are prepared with a monthly breakdown of most data. Any deviation from the consulting unit's standards, or any undesirable trend, should be detected by management. Management will have to consider whether prompt corrective action is desirable and feasible, or whether changes in short-term indicators are signals of longer-term shifts in the market, the profession or the firm itself. The list of controls given in box 29.2 can be of help in establishing a list that suits a particular consulting firm.

Box 29.2 Monthly controls — A check-list

(1) **Forward workload (backlog)**

Most important; ideally it should be around three months and should not drop below one-and-a-half months; if it is too high, clients are kept waiting for too long.

(2) **Number of client visits (meetings, surveys) to number of assignments negotiated**

Indicative of the effectiveness of promotional work. An alternative ratio is volume of new business negotiated per client visit (meeting, survey), or number of marketing days required to get an assignment or to obtain a certain volume of new business (say $100,000). This is more precise if assignments vary greatly in extent.

(3) **Actual and budgeted utilization of total time**

Can be computed for all consulting staff or by categories, e.g. for operating consultants, supervisors, partners and officers; shows not only whether the firm has enough to do, but also whether work is properly scheduled and organized for smooth delivery.

(4) **Cumulative actual fee-earning days against planned fee-earning days**

Similar use as previous ratio.

(5) **Actual and budgeted fee rate**

Can be computed for all consulting staff or by categories of consultant; helps to assess whether the firm is in a position to apply optimum fees and gives guidance in using the staff in accordance with its technical and income-generating ability.

(6) **Fees earned against fees budgeted (monthly and cumulative)**

Synthetic indicator of actual programme delivery rate in financial terms.

(7) **Fees earned against expenses (monthly and cumulative)**

Syn thetic indicator of short-term performance in financial terms; can provide early warning of excessive expenses and cash shortages.

(8) **Expenses incurred against expenses budgeted (in total and by expense budget lines; monthly and cumulative)**

Permits detailed control by expense lines, providing suggestions for specific expense-cutting measures and for adjustments of budgets owing to price and other changes outside the consultant's control.

(9) **Monthly billing against monthly fees earned**

Shows whether the firm is properly organized to process work records and bill the clients as soon as records become available.

(10) **Number of months of outstanding fees**

Shows whether fees are collected within normal time limits (four to six weeks); an alternative ratio is outstanding fees as percentage of total (annual) income.

Annual controls

All ratios do not lend themselves to short-term monitoring and action, so not all need to be presented every month. A dropping backlog of work or falling income require immediate management attention, and therefore the data are needed monthly. The basic staff structure cannot be changed by short-term measures, and an analysis of relevant information once or twice a year may be enough.

An annual performance review, or audit, would examine the data collected on a monthly basis, plus certain additional data, such as:

- growth rate of business;
- gross and/or net profits compared to total income;
- profit per partner and per consultant employed;
- volume of work sold per consultant engaged in the marketing services;
- ratios indicating the structure of consulting staff (various categories);
- number of consulting staff compared to number of administrative and support staff;
- expense and cost structure (relative magnitude of various expense lines);
- non-collectable fees (bad debts) as part of total income.

It is often useful to analyse various other financial ratios which can be calculated from the annual financial statements. However, before choosing to do this it is necessary to consider whether they are as meaningful in consulting as in manufacturing industry and other sectors (owing to factors such as the small volume and role of fixed assets, etc.). In addition, trends may be analysed by computing and comparing data over five to seven years.

Here again, analysis should reveal causes and suggest focus for future action. Increased income can be the result of better performance, but also of price adjustments due to inflation, while real performance in non-financial terms has not changed or has deteriorated.

Organizational level of performance monitoring

The management of the consulting firm will be interested in knowing and analysing all key controls, both monthly and annual. As a rule, operating and financial performance ratios are reviewed at regular management meetings. If it is decided to take corrective action, the precise target to be achieved and the responsibility for action to be taken should be defined.

It is good practice to keep not only partners and senior members of the firm but also other consultants informed about the performance achieved by the firm, pointing out what should be improved, and in what way individual consultants can help and will be encouraged to make such improvements.

Selected performance ratios can be calculated and analysed *by units* (teams, departments, service groups, practice areas, etc.) within the firm. This opportunity should not be missed. It can show which units are the main contributors to the total results achieved, and which "problem" units have become, or may become, a financial burden. This can stimulate the management and staff of these units to be more active and entrepreneurial.

It is often useful to know performance data *for each consultant employed.* A typical example is the ratio of volume of work sold per consultant engaged in marketing the services. Rather than calculating and examining average data per consultant, some consulting firms record and analyse the marketing performance of each individual. The same can be done in assessing programme delivery by comparing the budgeted and the real income and profitability for individual consultants. If an individual's profitability is low, the reasons can be, for example:

— the fee charged is too low in comparison to the salary paid and other costs;

— chargeable time utilization is low owing to small demand for the services of the individual concerned, or for other reasons reflecting weaknesses in service marketing, scheduling and organization.

Performance by individual assignments

In a similar vein, profitability and some other performance indicators can be calculated and analysed *by assignments* (projects, products). For example, one consulting firm found that the profitability of its consulting assignments was minimal. However, most assignments generated demand for tailor-made in-plant training programmes, and also brought participants to open training seminars scheduled on a regular basis. Since these two groups of products were highly profitable, the overall result was judged as being satisfactory and the relatively low profitability of consulting assignments fully acceptable.

Information on assignment performance provides insights into questions such as the adequacy of fee formulas and fee levels for various types of assignment, assignment staffing, the use of experienced (and more expensive) consultants for the backstopping and supervision of operating assignments, the quality of assignment scheduling and administration, various expenditure (and cost) items that are not reimbursable, and so on.

The key condition is correct recording and measurement of the time spent by various categories of consultant on particular assignments. For example, it may be established that junior consultants use more time than budgeted because of poor briefing and guidance by the seniors, or that more seniors' time is used than warranted by the difficulty of the task. Furthermore, the cost of time (hour, day) of each category should be calculated (which includes a decision on whether to include and how to allocate the overhead cost).[1]

Using the profit model for performance monitoring

A general profit model for professional firms was described in section 23.3. The model can be used for a firm's periodic annual performance reviews, for example as recommended by the Association of Management Consulting Firms

Figure 29.1 Expanded profit model for consulting firms

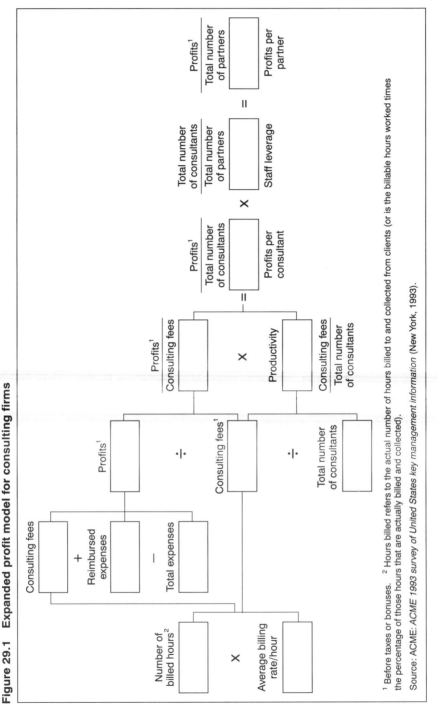

[1] Before taxes or bonuses. [2] Hours billed refers to the actual number of hours billed to and collected from clients (or is the billable hours worked times the percentage of those hours that are actually billed and collected).

Source: ACME: *ACME 1993 survey of United States key management information* (New York, 1993).

(ACME) in its annual surveys of key management information. The model provides both for a synthetic view of profitability (profit per partner) and for more analytical information on key factors that have affected the profit per partner ratio. The expanded model is reproduced in figure 29.1 and key performance indicators provided in ACME surveys are shown in box 29.3 (overleaf).

29.3 Bookkeeping and accounting

Like any business, a consulting organization needs bookkeeping and accounting to control the financial side of the operation and produce information required by law. Some comments on accounting problems faced by consultants will be made in this section, which, however, is not meant as a complete review of accounting in professional firms. Such information is available from specialized publications.[2]

Choosing your system

The purpose is to have an accounting system that is fully adapted to the nature of consulting operations and will be used as a management tool. Such a system should be as simple as possible. A single practitioner who serves a few clients and has a limited range of expenditure can use a very simple system indeed. The complexity of the system will increase with the growth of the firm and the complexity of its operations, but even a larger consulting firm should try to keep its accounting simple.

A consultant who is versed in accounting can decide personally what system to use. There are, too, proprietary bookkeeping systems and computer programmes (see Chapter 31) for smaller businesses and professional service firms available on the market; the consultant may be able to purchase such a system, including all forms and books, from a supplier of office equipment, software and stationery. In some countries, the associations of professional firms have issued accounting guidelines and recommendations for the member firms. Finally, the consultant can ask an accountant to design a tailor-made system. Often this will be the best solution, provided that the accountant does not conceive an unduly complicated system which creates an unnecessary workload.

The essential criteria to be considered include the following:

- What is the structure of the firm's income (volume, number of clients, frequency of payments, collection problems, different kinds of income)?
- What is the structure of the firm's expenses (different expense items, critical expense items, frequency of expenses)?
- What are the firm's material and financial resources (buildings, equipment, stocks of materials and spare parts, financial reserves, cash)?
- How is the firm's operation financed?

Box 29.3 ACME surveys of key management information

Every year, ACME collects data from over 100 consulting firms of various sizes and technical profiles, on a strictly confidential basis. Using the profit model for professional firms, ACME issues its annual surveys, giving key indicators for the previous year and seven-year trends in overall performance. Indicators are provided for the total population of reporting firms, and in breakdown by firm groups:

- by volume of annual fees (below US$1 million, US$1-4 million, US$4-25 million, and over US$25 million);
- by size of consulting staff (less than 15, 15-50, 50-150, over 150);
- by consulting speciality (9 specialities);
- by number of domestic offices (1, 2-5, over 5).

The following *key performance measures* are given in the survey report:

1. Profits (before taxes or bonuses) to consulting fees
2. Profits (before taxes or bonuses) per consultant
3. Profits (before taxes or bonuses) per partner
4. Profits plus partner salaries, bonuses and other cash compensations per partner
5. Consulting fees per consultant (personnel productivity)
6. Hours billed as percentage of total hours
7. Days outstanding in receivables
8. Liquidity (current assets: current liabilities)
9. Leverage (consulting staff per partner)
10. Consultants per support staff person
11. Senior partners as percentage of total consulting staff
12. Percentage of female employees per category of consultant
13. Average number of billable hours per week (per category of consultants)
14. Average standard billing rates (per category of consultant)
15. Distribution of non-billable time
16. Employee turnover
17. Percentage of employees hired from outside the firm (per category of consultant)
18. Employee compensation (per category of consultant)
19. Employee bonuses as percentage of base salary (per category of consultant)
20. Company stock ownership (per category of consultant)
21. Business development costs (as percentage of total consulting revenues)
22. Billing procedures
23. Percentage structure of the firm's income statement

The statistics included in the study provide "yardsticks" against which individual consulting firm performance can be measured.

Source: ACME: *ACME 1993 survey of United States key management information* (New York, 1993).

- What are the existing and potential problems as regards cash flow and liquidity?
- What information is critical for sound financial management and how frequently should it be provided?
- What records and reports are mandatory?

A smallish consulting firm may be satisfied with a simple single-entry system, using a cash book, though most consulting firms prefer a double-entry system. Every consultant, irrespective of the legal form of the business and the accounting system chosen, should separate his or her business accounts from private household accounts. This basic rule of financial management is generally recommended by management consultants to their small-business clients, and consultants will be well advised to follow the same principle in their own businesses.

Another possible choice may be between cash-basis accounting (only cash transactions are recorded) and accrual-basis accounting (accounts receivable and accounts payable are recorded). In the United States, for example, professional firms prefer cash-basis accounting since under this system only income for which cash has actually been collected is taxed.

What accounts to keep

In some countries there will be a suggested or even compulsory chart of accounts (called "accounting plan" in some French-speaking countries) with which both public and private business companies have to comply. In many cases, however, the consultant will be free to choose his or her own chart of accounts. In particular, he or she will be able to decide how detailed the chart should be.

The purpose has always to be kept in mind. Accounts from which statutory financial reports are produced will be needed. Accounts required for controlling important expenses (e.g. wages of administrative and support staff) should be kept separately in most cases. On the other hand, unimportant expense items do not require separate accounts, and a number of these items can usually be blocked in one account.

It is advisable to aim at coherence between budgeting and accounting to facilitate both the preparation and the control of budgets. If the firm decides to structure its operating budget as shown in table 29.1, its accounts for income and expenses should be structured accordingly. The accounting can be more detailed. For example, income may be recorded in several client accounts before being posted to the general ledger. However, inconsistencies should be avoided. Thus, if "marketing and promotion expenses other than salaries" are budgeted separately from any salaries, they should be shown in the same way in the respective accounts. Needless to say, to avoid errors and confusion, it is necessary to be precise in defining what is to be recorded in what account. For example, will all telephone charges (except those chargeable to clients) be consistently charged to the communications account, or should some of them be treated as marketing and promotion expenses if they concern marketing? Many such decisions will have to be made.

Financial statements

In most countries, consulting firms established as corporations (companies) have to produce financial statements which include:

— the balance sheet;
— the income statement (profit and loss account);
— the sources and uses of funds statement (funds flow statement);
— the statement of earned surplus;
— the auditor's certificate and notes on the financial statements.

Even if this is not required by law, any consulting firm, including the sole practitioner, should prepare financial reports at least once a year, for self-assessment and to keep control of the financial health of the firm. This can be quite a simple, though extremely useful and instructive, exercise.

The meaning and use of these statements are amply described in accounting and financial management literature.

---

[1] See also D. Maister: "Measuring engagement profitability", in *American Lawyer* (New York), July/Aug. 1994.

[2] See, e.g., M. R. Altman and R. I. Weil: *Managing your accounting and consulting practice* (Albany, New York, Matthew Bender, 1978); or M. C. Thomsett: *Fundamentals of bookkeeping and accounting for the successful consultant* (Washington, DC, Bermont Books, 1980).

STRUCTURING CONSULTING FIRMS

30

Because there is a wide variety of consulting firms, these firms use many different structural arrangements. Structure must never become a strait-jacket. Our review of structural arrangements, including the legal forms of business, will therefore refer to some typical arrangements, but without aiming to provide a blueprint for all situations. Every consulting firm is unique and its structure reflects many factors, including the nature and volume of activities, personalities, the strategy chosen, traditions, and the legal and institutional environment.

30.1 Legal forms of business

In most countries consultants can choose among several legal forms of business organization. This choice is not always completely free. Local legislation may include special regulations for organizing and operating professional services, and/or for firms with foreign ownership. Therefore an international consulting firm may have to use different legal forms in various countries. Unless the consultant is sufficiently knowledgeable in legal matters, he or she should seek a lawyer's advice. An accountant's or a tax adviser's viewpoint is equally important because the forms of business organization differ as regards registration, taxation, record keeping, reporting and liability.

Sole proprietorship

A sole proprietor (sole owner) is a person who owns and operates the whole business. This form may involve either the single practitioner, or the owner plus a variable number of associates. While normally and legally there may be no limit to the number of staff, it is usual that the "sole owner" employs only a few associates, and perhaps only for the duration of specific assignments. The firm's net income is taxed as the owner's personal income; the owner's liability for all debts incurred by the firm is unlimited.

Sole proprietorship is a simple form, suitable for those who are starting in consulting but have some previous management experience, or who prefer to remain completely independent in their consulting career. In addition to working on assignments, the sole practitioner has to take care of marketing future assignments. The risk is quite high in the case of sickness. Even if the single practitioner has health insurance, a prolonged illness may affect business contacts very adversely. The firm normally ceases to exist with the death or retirement of the owner (although his or her estate remains liable for outstanding debts).

Partnership

Partnership is a common form of business in management consulting and in other professional service sectors. It entails a contract between two or more persons who agree to set up a firm in which they combine their skills and resources, and share profits, losses and liabilities.[1] Under most legal systems, the partnership does not have to be on an equal basis — a consultant may enter a partnership with a junior colleague on a 60-40 or another basis; or one or more of the partners may wish to devote less time than the others to the partnership business and hence will accept a smaller share of both profits and losses.

The advantages of partnership include the division of labour to optimize the use of the partners' skills, the possibility of undertaking more important and complex assignments, the possibility of continuing the business in the absence of one of the partners, and a better utilization of resources such as office space, equipment or secretarial support.

The disadvantages include the unlimited liability of each partner for errors and obligations of all other partners arising from the business, the need to reach an agreement on every important decision, and the difficulties involved in harmonizing personal preferences and styles of the partners. In some legal systems it is possible to establish a *limited partnership*, which includes one or more general partners (with unlimited liability), and one or more limited partners, whose third-party liability is limited to a specific amount (which can be zero).

It is generally recommended that a clear and unambiguous partnership agreement should be drawn up, even if local legislation does not explicitly require one. Much more important, however, is the composition of the group: individuals who cannot work together, have different conceptions of professional service and ethics, and do not trust each other for any reason should avoid becoming partners.

Partnerships are usually not limited by law as to size, but in practice are often confined to a comparatively small number of people. If a unit expands beyond this number, though it may still retain something of the spirit and the title of partnership, it might be advisable to consider transforming the business into a corporation.

Corporation

Many consulting firms are established as corporations (limited liability companies). The corporation has two fundamental characteristics: (1) it is a legal entity that exists separately from the owners (i.e. does not cease to exist after an owner's death or withdrawal from business); and (2) the owners have no personal liability for the obligations and debts of the corporation (the shareholders are protected from liability incurred by the company, except in certain cases when it is established that the corporate form was abused in order to avoid personal liability).

The major advantages of incorporation include:

— considerable flexibility in doing and developing business;

— the possibility of easy changes in the number of co-owners (shareholders): there can be one sole owner, and therefore even a sole practitioner can incorporate a business;

— the possibility for individuals to be simultaneously owners and employees of the corporation;

— the possibility of retaining earnings for reinvestment in the firm;

— separate taxation of personal income (salary, bonuses and dividends) and the corporation's profits, and the possibility of deducting certain employee benefits and certain types of corporate expenses from taxable income (the level of taxation is often a major factor in deciding whether to incorporate or not).

On the other hand, a firm using the corporate form must comply with a number of requirements stipulated in the company or other law of particular countries. These include:

• compulsory registration (incorporation) prior to starting business;

• a statement of corporate purposes (objects of the company), the definition of which may be very significant as in some countries the corporation is not authorized to do business outside the scope of this statement;

• accounting and other records to be kept, with periodic reporting;

• public auditing of company reports and (in certain countries) the publication of these reports;

• the organization and definition of responsibilities of top management (shareholders' meeting, board of directors).

Moreover, corporate directors can be personally liable both civilly and criminally for certain corporate acts of malfeasance or misfeasance.

Management consultants in various countries have adopted special arrangements in using the corporate form. With few exceptions, they do not "go public", i.e. the shares are not available on the stock market, but ownership is reserved to a group of senior consultants (officers, principals, partners, etc.). Promotion to this level in the hierarchy may include not only an entitlement, but an obligation to purchase a certain number of shares and thus invest in the firm.

The maximum number of shares which can be owned by one member of the firm is often limited (in many firms the limit is between 1 and 5 per cent of the shares) and the owner must resell these shares to the company (thus recovering the money put in) when retiring or leaving for any other reason.

In some consulting firms there is one (or more) majority owner who actually controls the firm. Usually he or she would be the sole founder, or one of the partners who established the firm, who at some point decided to transform the firm into a corporation and widen the ownership base. In a small number of cases, consulting firms are owned by other business corporations (by banks, accounting firms, engineering firms, or others), or by employers' associations.

As regards the use of profits (after tax), some consulting firms use the whole profit for developing the business and creating reserves, while others distribute a part of the profit to the shareholders of the firm, or to all employees (see section 32.4).

Many consulting and other professional firms have maintained the partnership form even when they have become larger, or have continued to be managed and to behave as partnerships after having been restructured as corporations. Currently this traditional approach is being challenged. If there are hundreds of partners and consultants, the ideas on which the partnership formula has been based (undivided responsibility, direct participation and seeking full consensus in key decisions, etc.) are increasingly difficult to apply. Further difficulties are being encountered in raising capital needed for expansion and service modernization, and in facing liability issues (see section 6.5). While these issues have probably been more pressing in the accounting and legal professions, many larger management consultancies have also started looking for alternatives to the classical partnership formula.[2]

Other forms

As we know, not all management consulting units are independent businesses. Some units are established and operate as divisions in private corporations that have wider corporate purposes and offer other types of service (accounting, auditing, engineering consultancy, etc.) in addition to management consulting. In such a case, the legal entity may not be the consulting unit itself in its own right, but the organization to which the unit belongs.

There are also consulting units established as, or within, associations, foundations, public agencies and other non-profit-making organizations. However, the corporate form tends increasingly to be used for these units in order to enhance their independence, motivation, responsibility and liability. For example, a management institute can often be organized as a corporation, or a public agency can create (and own) a professional service company that sells services to clients in both the public and private sectors.

30.2 Structuring the operating core

Consultants spend most of their time working for clients on specific assignments. Normally they do most of their work at clients' premises and once an assignment is completed, they move physically to another client. In the management system of a consulting firm, individual assignments are treated as basic management cells with precisely defined terms of reference, resources and responsibilities. However, assignments are only temporary management cells and structuring by assignments would not provide for stability and continuity of internal organization. Most consulting firms therefore structure their operating core — the professional staff — in more or less permanent "home" units. Consultants are attached to these units according to some common characteristics in their background and/or areas of intervention.

Functional (subject) units

Functional or technical subject units are common. They used to be organized by the basic functions of management, such as general management, finance, marketing, production and personnel. More recently, their focus has started shifting to technical problem areas, such as strategy and policy, organization development or quality management. A consulting assignment may be fully within the function or problem area covered by the unit (e.g. in marketing), and the unit can therefore staff and supervise the assignment from its own resources. In other cases, the unit would "borrow" staff from other units for the duration of the assignment. This is particularly common in complex assignments dealing with various aspects of a business; these assignments tend to be mainly within the province of units dealing with general aspects of business strategy and policy.

Sectoral units

Sectoral units (e.g. for construction, banking, insurance, road transport, health) are often established if this is justified by the volume of business done in a sector and by the need to have teams that are recognized as sectoral experts. It is impossible to suggest a minimum size for such a unit. Even a smallish unit with all-round experts in a sector may play a useful role in developing and managing assignments, which can also make use of specialists from other units. If a certain sector generates a sizeable amount of work, a sectoral unit may become more or less self-contained and employ a wider range of specialists on a permanent basis in addition to its sector generalists.

Geographical units

Geographical (territorial) units are often established when a consulting firm decides to decentralize in order to get closer to the clients and increase efficiency (e.g. by reducing transport and communication expenses). They exist in two basic forms:

— offices whose main purpose is marketing and liaison with clients in a delimited geographical area; these units tend to be small, staffed by a few all-round generalists, and equipped by certain services for supporting operating assignments; assignments can thus be staffed both by consultants from the unit and from headquarters;

— fully staffed local (area) branches that can take care of most assignments using their own personnel; these units are effective if the volume and structure of business done in the area concerned is relatively stable, or is regularly expanding; a major advantage, appreciated by the consultants, is that they do not have to be absent from their homes for long periods of time.

Geographically decentralized units are most common in larger consulting firms. A smaller firm must weigh the advantages of getting close to the clientele against the cost of the operation and the firm's ability to keep technical and administrative control over geographically distant units. There are, in addition, various combinations. For example, a decentralized geographical unit may specialize in the sector or sectors featuring most prominently in the area covered by the unit.

Some examples

Figure 30.1 shows a general pattern of organizational structure used by a number of larger consulting companies in various countries.[3] In contrast, figure 30.2 (overleaf) shows the structure of the professional core of a consulting unit employing 29 consultants. It is a hypothetical example used to explain typical organizational considerations. A unit of this size can make up a whole consulting company, or constitute a division in a larger company or a management services department in an industrial concern.

The unit employs six senior consultants, of whom four work as team leaders and supervisors of operating assignments, and two concentrate on marketing and on management surveys. The 20 operating consultants will, as a rule, be specialists in various management functions. Among the supervisors in the unit, three may also specialize in managing assignments in functional areas, while the fourth supervisor may be an all-round general management expert, able to manage assignments covering several functional areas. The 20 operating consultants can work in assignment teams or individually on separate smaller assignments. Thus, the supervisors will either work as team leaders on larger assignments, or supervise several operating consultants working individually for different clients.

A consulting firm may never expand beyond 27 to 30 people, as the owner or manager may wish to keep personal control of all the operations and relations with clients. In this case, the manager may have a small office and staff to support the operating core.

Figure 30.1 Typical organization of consulting companies

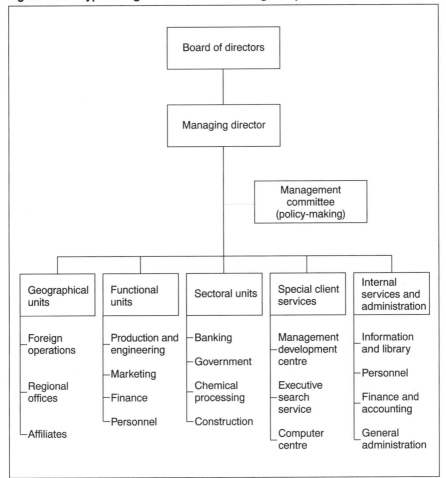

If expansion takes place, and a unit employs more than 30 consultants, it may split into two sub-units. One senior consultant may become the manager of the second unit, which is built up to full size. During this expansion more seniors will be required, and in time central support services may be set up. The additional seniors are needed to coordinate and administer these separate units, or to set up specialist units and support services.

The general criteria concerning the firm's leverage (section 23.3) will be kept in mind. Significant factors determining expansion are market demand, and the availability of operating consultants with sufficient experience and knowledge to be appointed as supervisors or team leaders. At least three to five years of experience, encompassing both a range of assignments with companies and a variety of techniques, are required. To replace the operating consultants as they

Figure 30.2 Professional core of a consulting unit

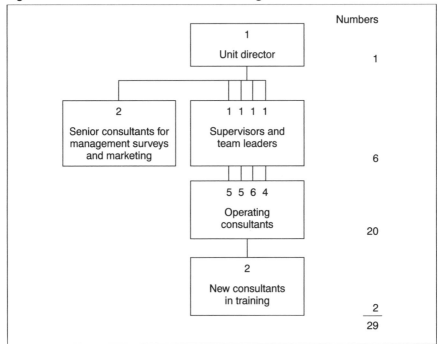

rise to higher levels or leave, new consultants must be ready trained. For this reason a stable organization includes two to three trainee consultants in every group of 25 to 30, as shown in figure 30.2.

Another factor governing expansion is the ratio of specialist to generalist consultants. Where an assignment calls for several disciplines, the supervising consultant may accept overall responsibility but call on a specialist to oversee special techniques as required. To meet the full range of client demands, the consulting firm may have to call on some highly specialized consultants, e.g. in productivity measurement, logistics, operations research or franchising. It is of course difficult to find a constant demand for these types of service within a smaller unit.

Matrix management

It results from the foregoing discussion that many consulting organizations in fact practise some sort of matrix management. Both operating consultants, and their more senior colleagues who work as team leaders or supervisors, have their "home" units — functional, sectoral or geographical. However, all assignments do not remain totally within the province of these home units.

The organizational culture of a consulting firm must provide for considerable flexibility to facilitate the rapid establishment of an effective collaborative relationship and a team spirit in starting new assignments. Any member of an assignment team must accept his or her role in the team, and the coordinating role of the team leader, as soon as the team is constituted and starts tackling the job. If this were not the case, the start would be slow and costly, to the detriment of the client.

However, the role of the "home" unit extends beyond the function of a pool of specialists from which operating consultants can be drawn. The head of a marketing consulting unit is also interested in what is actually happening in the assignments to which he or she has detached marketing consultants, even if these consultants work under the immediate supervision of a team leader from another unit.

The head of the unit is responsible for technical guidance and control of operating consultants in the special field of marketing, and carries out this responsibility in various ways: by organizing technical meetings of marketing consultants, briefing consultants before assignments, reviewing consulting reports, discussing progress of the work with the team leaders, visiting the marketing consultants on assignments, and so on. Such guidance and control have to be exercised in agreement with the team leaders and supervisors, and in a way that does not undermine the operating consultants' authority in the clients' eyes.

Flat structure

In addition to matrix management, most consulting firms prefer to use a relatively flat organizational structure. The number of rungs on the management ladder between an operating consultant and the firm's top manager is usually between none and three, depending on the firm's size, complexity and service diversification (see also Chapter 32). Such a structure encourages collaboration and interaction with peers in the operating core rather than referring matters upwards through the chain of command.

30.3 Organizing for marketing

Effective organization of the marketing function is extremely important for reasons already discussed in detail in Chapters 23 to 25. Virtually every member of the consulting staff may have some role to play in marketing, and consultants on assignments can do a lot of good marketing if they keep their eyes open and think of future business for their firm. Yet some formal organizational arrangements for the marketing function are also necessary.

Marketing manager

Whatever the size and complexity of the consulting firm, its management team will pay considerable attention to marketing. Decisions on marketing strategy will normally be discussed and taken by senior management. If possible, one member of the senior management team should be appointed marketing manager. This can be a full-time or part-time function.

The marketing manager is responsible for preparing and submitting key market analyses, strategies, programmes and budgets. He or she is concerned with the marketing function in its totality. Certain marketing activities will be his or her direct responsibility, e.g. training policy for marketing, advertising, press relations, mailing lists, and editing and distributing publicity information. He or she may have a small technical and administrative team for these functions. Other marketing functions and activities are not the direct responsibility of the marketing manager, but he or she has to monitor, evaluate and stimulate them in collaboration with other managers.

Roles in indirect marketing

Roles in indirect marketing (aimed at building up the professional image of the firm and creating opportunities for contacts with new clients) are normally shared throughout the consulting firm and assigned to those units or individuals who can use their skills to best effect. The purpose is to optimize the use of individual capabilities: not everyone can write a book or article that will promote the firm. The roles have to be precisely defined, e.g. it should be determined who will be active in what management or trade association, or who will be delegated to attend a management congress.

Roles in direct marketing

Direct marketing of specific assignments is normally the function of partners or managers, who would spend 30-100 per cent of their time in contacts with individual clients, building up new relationships, trying to sell an assignment, negotiating a preliminary diagnostic survey, or following up previous work.

In some consulting firms these senior professionals are full-time marketers. They may not be the firm's top technicians, but their social, diagnostic and selling skills make them an invaluable asset. They are the firm's "rainmakers". However, many consulting firms prefer switching the roles, e.g. by making the successful marketers also responsible for the management and supervision of assignment execution.

Direct marketing requires excellent coordination and follow-up by senior management and/or by the managers of sectors and geographical areas within the consulting firm. Uncoordinated contacting of the same client by different units of one consulting firm can damage the firm's image. Conversely, there are many opportunities to achieve synergy within consulting firms by active sharing of information on potential clients and assignments, and by keeping the interests and the possibilities of the whole firm in mind when working with particular clients.

30.4 Organizing other client services

Organizational arrangements for training, research, information, documentation, computing, product testing, quality control and other services to clients can be permanent or ad hoc. Permanent arrangements usually take the form of special divisions or centres within the consulting firms. These are justified if the volume of the service is sufficiently important and stabilized, or growing regularly. To establish a new unit for a special service may be a strategic decision if the firm intends to promote that service and wants to demonstrate to the clients that adequate resources have been allocated and a competent person made responsible for the new service. Two examples are given below, but there can be various other services as discussed in Chapters 2 and 24.

Training units

Training units are very common in consulting firms. There is a wide variety of them, ranging from smallish training sections to management development institutes. These units tend to enjoy relative autonomy within the firm and some of their programmes may be open to external participants. Training units may market their programmes quite independently of the consulting services marketed by other divisions in the firm. Training units also contribute to particular consulting assignments by providing trainers, diagnosing clients' training needs and policies, or mounting tailor-made courses in support of consulting projects. Many of them organize internal courses and seminars for the consulting firm's staff. The teachers/trainers are usually drawn from experienced consultants, many of whom return to consulting after a period spent with the unit.

Information and documentation services

Information and documentation services to clients are less common than training units. Yet some consultants have been successful in expanding their internal information units into client services. The nature of the service, including the handling of information inputs, files, processing, outputs and dissemination in a systematic matter, justifies the establishment of a separate unit structured and managed as a professional information service.

30.5 Organizing for international operations

Organizational arrangements for international operations reflect the strategy pursued by the firm (section 24.5). They also take account of factors such as the frequency, relative importance and predicted future trend of these operations, the institutional and legal setting in countries where work is to be done, the possibility of repatriating earnings, language requirements, and local practice concerning business and professional services.

Consultant missions

If work abroad is irregular and its volume small, consulting firms usually prefer to send their staff on missions from headquarters. This is how foreign operations start in most consulting firms. It can be a costly arrangement, not only because of the price of long-distance travel and living and other expenses of operating consultants, but also because of costs incurred by negotiating, preparing and supervising assignments in foreign countries.

Offices in other countries

Having gained some experience with consulting across national boundaries, a consulting firm may feel that it is more effective to have a permanent presence where the market for the services is. The establishment of a foreign (country or regional) office is often the solution. As with decentralization within the home country, this office may start as a small one, staffed mainly for marketing, liaison with local businesses and government, and as a support for operating teams coming from headquarters to work on specific projects.

Foreign subsidiaries

Fully staffed foreign subsidiaries have been founded by many large consulting firms that regularly undertake a substantial amount of foreign business. Such a subsidiary may be quite independent of the parent company in operational matters, but provision is always made for policy guidance and quality control. There is a growing tendency to staff foreign subsidiaries with local professionals, even in consulting companies which originally preferred to staff them by consultants detached from headquarters.

Association with local consultants

Some countries require foreign consultants to work in association with a local consulting firm. But even if there is no such regulation, consulting firms operating abroad often find it useful, for a number of reasons, to negotiate and execute assignments and to organize their foreign operations in association with local consulting firms. This association can have various forms, such as a shared ownership of a foreign company (on a fifty-fifty or another basis), or an arrangement whereby the precise scope of collaboration is defined separately for every assignment. In addition, there have been cases of abuse, e.g. if the association is established with the sole intention of bypassing legislation in order to get contracts and the local consultant is a "man of straw".

30.6 Administrative support services

Many single practitioners and other smallish consulting units are proud of having minimal administrative expenses because they are able to handle many jobs personally, with the help of a spouse, a part-time assistant or a bookkeeper. However, as the consulting firm grows, its administrative and support services reach a volume that justifies permanent staff and solid organization. Reliability, versatility and initiative are the key qualities required in addition to technical proficiency and discretion. Consultants busy with client matters, and often absent from their own offices for long periods, must be absolutely sure that they can trust their administrative assistants and other collaborators as regards messages, travel arrangements, contacts by clients, report processing and transmission, search for information and many other services that cannot, or should not, be directly handled by the professionals.

Office staff

Because the majority of the professional staff — the operating consultants — are able to make some use of their clients' administrative services, and more and more consultants use their own personal computers when working with clients, consulting firms usually need only a small office staff at their headquarters. The smaller the staff, the more it is necessary for its members to be able and willing to help in any part of the daily work.

In a small unit the following staff may be employed:

- administrative assistant (who may also act as the manager's secretary and/or office manager);
- accounts clerk/cashier (who would keep time and other records, invoice clients, pay salaries and expenses, purchase office supplies, etc.);
- receptionist/telephonist/typist (who would help in typing correspondence and reports);
- one or two more secretaries/typists if necessary.

It is logical that larger units will require more office staff. At some point the establishment of an administrative service unit, headed by a senior administrative assistant or office manager, will be justified.

Organizing bookkeeping and accounting

In organizing bookkeeping and accounting the consultant is faced with several alternatives. Many single practitioners do their own accounting, not only to save on administrative expenses but in order to be constantly in control of their financial position and of the efficiency of their operation. Even a consultant whose main field of intervention is production or personnel may find it useful to do his or her own accounting.

In small consulting firms, routine bookkeeping may be done by an accounts clerk or administrative assistant as mentioned above, while financial and tax reports would be prepared by one of the professionals, or by an external account-ant employed on a part-time basis. Some consultants have all bookkeeping and accounting (including tax returns) done by an external accountant, but this may be a costly arrangement.

As the firm grows, a point is reached at which it is necessary to employ a qualified accountant on a full-time basis.

30.7 Library and documentation

A dynamic and reliable information and documentation service is needed for two principal reasons:

— information on new developments in management and business relevant to the work of the consulting firm has to be collected and channelled to the consultants (who often work far from their headquarters, in localities where new books, professional reviews or other information sources are not easily available, and on projects which keep them too busy to search for new information);

— information on the methods and procedures used and the results obtained in previous assignments must be available for any new assignment.

Information services are costly, but consultants must keep up to date. Some excellent work for clients can often be traced to an idea picked up from an article or book not necessarily directly related to the particular subject.

Information service

The information service has responsibility for collecting, extracting, storing and retrieving managerial and technical information contained in important publications and other sources. It must be able to act on request (information on topics designated by the consultants in connection with particular assignments) and to systematically collect and provide information in selected areas of interest to the firm and individual professionals. A proactive service is required, able to take the initiative in identifying information and suggesting useful sources to the consultants. A highly selective approach is equally important. A consulting firm cannot afford to collect vast amounts of information for vaguely defined purposes.

Any management consulting firm should have at least a reference library of:

- standard handbooks and dictionaries;
- essential business legislation;
- a selection of the best books on management in general and on management functions and new concepts;
- references on special techniques;
- basic books on management consulting;

- literature on change management, communication and training concepts and methodologies.

Furthermore, consulting firms need to subscribe to leading management and business periodicals, selected newsletters and in some cases also to an abstracting service. While some periodicals may be for general circulation within the firm, an information service may select and photocopy articles and abstracts that are of direct interest to particular consultants. The firm may also subscribe to those newspapers that regularly cover business or industrial issues, or use an agency specializing in screening and copying published matter for its subscribers.

Whoever runs a periodicals or clippings service may also collect companies' annual reports, brochures, advertising and descriptive matter, government economic reports and statistics, and so on. In addition, or as an alternative, the information officer should know how to search major computerized databases providing business and management information.

The organization and use of the information service require inputs from both ends of the information flow. The information section should take the initiative in looking for new sources and suggesting what might interest whom, while the consultants should present specific demands clearly indicating the nature and scope of the information required for their priority tasks and keep the information service fully informed of new and changing demands of the firm. If consultants do not collaborate with their librarians and information officers, they cannot expect to get relevant and prompt information when they need it.

Internal manuals and training materials

In established consulting firms a great deal of accumulated experience and know-how is embodied in manuals, guides, check-lists and other materials concerning various aspects of the firm's practices and procedures. Some of these materials were first produced for a client, but may be of more general interest. Any such materials must be properly recorded and kept in the information centre to be easily accessible both to operating consultants and to new recruits. The same applies to the firm's own training materials, which can also interest operating consultants who are engaged in training the clients' personnel or looking for self-development materials.

Reports library

The third essential part of an information service is the reports library. Survey reports, survey notes, proposals to clients, contracts, and interim, final and follow-up reports have to be classified, indexed and filed. They grow into an invaluable reference library, a real treasury for the whole firm. Although complete solutions cannot usually be transferred unchanged from one situation to another, the methods used and results achieved provide examples, give inspiration and can sometimes be partially used in different settings. Reports are also needed for training new consultants, and for the development of internal guides and manuals.

The reports library must have an efficient means of information retrieval, and for this an indexing system has to be established and maintained. Reports may be indexed by client, consultant, sector, country, operating function, subject within a function or technique applied. Thus, an enquiry as to what work has previously been done in, say, production planning in food canning with the use of information technology (IT) could result in either the extraction of a report, or the reply that no assignment of this nature has been undertaken, or that there has been one assignment, but without any IT application.

A long-term view is needed when deciding on an indexing and filing system. It is easier to start with something that will be suitable in 20 years' time than to change reports going back 20 years from one system to another.

Clients' reports are confidential papers and the library must be run on lines of strict security. Copies lent to consultants must not be taken into other clients' premises, nor left open in public places.

30.8 Office facilities

Headquarters accommodation

In all circumstances, headquarters accommodation should be designed round the fact that consulting is predominantly a field operation and not a head-office activity. While a "good address" enhances the firm's image and has other advantages, such as the proximity of many clients, the total office space required can be relatively small.

The accommodation needed for the internal administrative and support services is self-evident. The reports library may start in a small way with a few lockable filing cabinets, but in time may need a room of its own. At the beginning it may share this room with the reference library of books and other documentation files, but with the growth of the unit more space will be needed.

As for consulting staff, the partners and other senior staff members involved in supervision and practice development need office space at headquarters. Operating consultants and associates need at least a desk each (though not individual offices). In addition, it is useful to have a meeting-room, space for training workshops, and some small rooms for receiving clients and other visitors.

The number of consultants sitting at their desks instead of working with clients is generally considered to be a signal which requires examination.

Sole practitioner's office

A sole practitioner may be able to operate from home without renting any office space. However, this is not always desirable from the client-relations viewpoint. In some countries, an office in a business area may be essential. To avoid excessive office accommodation and administrative costs, sole consultants and other professionals often choose to share an office, and a secretary or assistant, with other independently operating colleagues.

Office equipment

Good-quality office and communication equipment is a major asset in a consulting organization. Word-processing equipment and personal computers are now within easy reach of all consultants (see Chapter 31). The hardware and software chosen should be flexible and versatile enough to serve several purposes including record-keeping, filing, bookkeeping, billing, electronic mail, facsimile communication, word processing, preparing proposals for clients, editing and printing reports, and so on. Some document reproduction equipment (or easy access to such equipment) is needed in any consulting firm; high-capacity photocopying and printing equipment will probably be justified only in firms where large numbers of documents are reproduced on a regular basis.

30.9 General management organization and coordination

Collective bodies

The pattern of the consulting organization's top management depends very much upon its legal statute. In firms constituted as corporations (limited companies) there will be a board of directors. In a small firm the directors would generally be the general manager (managing director) and the senior consultants (partners). In a large firm there may also be external board members who, being non-executive, may play a useful role in the sense that they may preserve the same detachment in guiding the firm as the consultants have in advising their clients. They also tend to be chosen because of their range of business interests and contacts. In partnerships, decisions on key policy matters may be reserved for periodical meetings of all partners.

Consulting units that are not independent firms may have a governing body comprising a cross-section of managers from private and public enterprises, representatives of chambers of commerce and employers' associations, senior government officials and possibly other members in addition to one or more senior managers from the unit.

Chief executive officer and management committees

The key position in the management hierarchy is that of the chief executive officer (CEO), who may be called (in various countries and organizations) principal, general manager, president, managing director, managing partner, director-general, or simply manager or director. In a partnership, the CEO would be elected by a partners' meeting for a fixed period.

The CEO may use a management committee in the usual way for involving other managers or designated senior partners in dealing with issues requiring collective discussion or decision. Other committees may be established for dealing with issues such as strategy, quality, business promotion and marketing, IT, or staff compensation. They may be permanent or ad hoc. As in other businesses and public organizations, there may be a tendency to create a committee each time an issue cannot be immediately resolved or needs to be examined in a collective. A proliferation and overlapping of committees (and meetings of the same people under different committee denominations) are not signs of effective management.

The individual at the top will most probably be a career consultant (a senior partner) with considerable experience and managerial talent. On reaching the top, he or she may experience problems similar to those faced by managers of research and other professional services — he or she must stop thinking and operating as a technician and concentrate on managing (see also Chapter 23). Some consulting organizations have recruited top managers from outside, from among individuals who have been excellent business managers, but not necessarily practising consultants. There is no universal rule — the candidate's competence and personality will determine whether he or she will be able to cope with the challenge of the job, provide strategic leadership and strengthen the firm by subtle but persistent coordination.

---

[1] See, e.g., D. B. Norris: "To be or not to be — a partner", in *Journal of Management Consulting* (Milwaukee, Wisconsin), Vol. 7, No. 3, Spring 1993, pp. 46-51.

[2] For a recent discussion of the problem see, e.g., "Partners in pain", in *The Economist*, 9 July 1994, pp. 63-64; and V. E. Millar: *On the management of professional service firms: Ten myths debunked* (Fitzwilliam, New Hampshire, Kennedy Publications, 1991), pp. 39-44.

[3] Adapted from an organizational chart developed by a FEACO research project.

INFORMATION TECHNOLOGY IN CONSULTING FIRMS

31

Information technology (IT) has moved from being a back office function to a position where it can be exploited by consultants to enable a wider, more effective service to be provided to their clients. The techniques now available permit more effective communication within consulting firms and allow firms to obtain greater value from the information at their disposal. The key to the delivery of these benefits is recognition of the changed role of computing in professional service firms.

31.1 Current trends

Information technology has changed in scope

In the 1970s and early 1980s the hardware, software and staffing costs associated with the provision of a computing service were such that their utilization was only considered cost-effective in the larger of the professional firms. Typically, professional firms keep very tight control on their internal costs and, given the high level of initial investment required to install computer systems, investment was only made where the volume of work could justify the expenditure required, which was then a major item. As a result, the focus for computing expenditure was on administrative procedures and staff savings.

The situation has now changed dramatically (see also Chapter 17). The basic costs of hardware and software have decreased, while power has increased. A powerful personal computer (PC) that can be purchased for under US$1,500 is at least equivalent in capacity to a mainframe computer in the 1970s. Cost of power has therefore ceased to be a barrier. Additionally, the smaller hardware units do not require the space and specialized environment that are the hallmarks of mainframe systems.

System architectures have changed from central mainframes supporting dumb terminals to *networked personal computers* being used to access and manipulate data held on central shared files. This approach, often described as a "client server", is becoming the preferred method of provision for systems, and the majority of new software developments are now aimed at exploiting this infrastructure. PC software, such as spreadsheets and word processors, are now regarded as the normal method of operation. Consultants and other professionals use such techniques as part of the standard means of fulfilling their professional role, and therefore accept and appreciate the potential for IT to assist in both the "back office" and "front office".

The availability of networked systems provides the opportunity for information (data, text, image and even voice) held electronically to be shared among users. The ability to group and process such information in a varied number of ways, without incurring an additional clerical overhead, improves its value to the organization. It is often said that IT has now reached a level of sophistication at which it can begin to address the information (as opposed to data) needs of the knowledge workers.

This wider exploitation of IT is being harnessed at a time when the need for service differentiation is becoming key to the successful competition for business, as the buyers of consultancy services have become highly sophisticated and selective.

Consulting services have evolved

The last decade has seen major changes in the scope of services offered by individual consulting firms. The market-place is no longer divided into discrete sectors, and the ability to cross-sell services between multiple disciplines within a firm is an important means whereby companies are aiming to maximize revenue while containing selling costs. Swift access to comprehensive information, and the ability to exchange information electronically, have become key features of consulting and other professional firms' competitive advantage.

The information on which consultancies draw is expanding rapidly. Estimates show that the information used in business is expected to double in the next six years. Consultants have to be fully informed, and therefore require swift, accurate and comprehensive access to such information (for example new legislation, international trade and demographic statistics, and technical literature).

Speed of service has become a major differentiator between organizations. A recent survey conducted by the Boston Consulting Group showed that, worldwide, organizations that recognized speed of service as a factor of business differentiation were growing, on average, 50 per cent faster than those which did not. IT is a central component in the delivery of the improved and streamlined services. The need to recognize the importance of speed of service applies equally to consulting firms and to their client base.

Finally, more and more emphasis is being placed on the adherence to quality standards. Firms are having to institute total quality management or quality assurance programmes (see Chapter 28) as a means of guaranteeing the currently expected level of service to their clients.

Figure 31.1   Functionality is dependent on power and structure

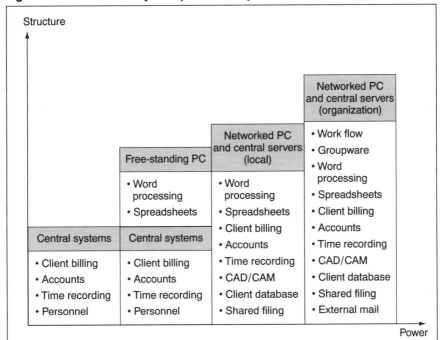

Potential use of IT

As a result of these changes in both the availability of systems and the demands on the systems provided, the use of IT is now an intrinsic part of the operation of the majority of consultancies. Computing can be viewed as being exploited in three separate ways:

— to support business administration;

— to support professional service productivity and quality;

— to improve market exploitation.

Below we discuss these three areas in more depth, and describe the types of system adopted within each area of operation. Finally, having considered the scope of computing, and the benefits to be derived, we highlight the issues that must be addressed if the full benefits that derive from investment in new technology are to be realized. The relationships between IT structures and the range and sophistication of functions being delivered to the users are illustrated in figure 31.1.

31.2 Support to business administration

It was in this arena that IT was first used within consulting firms. In common with all early commercial use of IT, the focus of the systems was the streamlining of administrative processes. The main generic areas in which consulting firms introduced systems were time recording and accounting, including client billing. Where specific sector-focused consultancies offered professional services that required access to computer processing (for example portfolio management and valuation, and engineering designs), support systems were developed to meet these needs. Initially systems were bespoke, written to meet the individual needs of each organization. The market has now matured, and "off the shelf" central system, PC and network-based packages can be purchased to handle these requirements. The packages vary in complexity, and cater for all levels of need, from those of a small organization through to major firms operating across multiple sites and providing services in a range of different disciplines. The functions described below are supported by all main package vendors.

Time recording

Computerized time-recording systems vary greatly in their sophistication and scope. The basic functions supported are:

- recording time against job numbers;
- maintaining records of work in progress;
- calculating costs (internal charges) and fee income against a job.

Additionally, systems are now often enhanced to fulfil many of the functions associated with project (assignment) management:

— application of direct expenses to a job;

— maintenance of resource estimates against individual jobs;

— forward load by job and by individual consultant;

— reporting of exceptions showing job overruns;

— cash-flow forecasting, based on the expected work plan and the client payment profile (monthly, end of phase, etc.);

— consultant availability.

Systems provide managers with a comprehensive mechanism by which to obtain the data for measuring business performance, as described in the previous chapters. The means by which the time data are collected are themselves changing, as individual consultants have access to networked PCs. Originally, time sheets were collected centrally and entered into time-recording systems by data-entry clerks. More and more the prevailing practice is for individual consultants to accept responsibility for input of their own time sheets into the system, using PCs as the data collection mechanism, and thereby removing the need for central data preparation. Systems are now being marketed that enable time data to be downloaded to the recording system from hand-held devices, such as the Psion Organizer, thereby reducing still further the effort required for data capture.

Accounting

A wide range of packages is available to support both client billing and company accounting systems. As with the time recording systems, these vary in sophistication. At the top end of the market the packages available will interface both one with another and also with an associated time-recording system.

Modern packages are, in the main, built using industry standard databases, for example, Oracle and Ingres for major systems, with products such as Foxpro, Clipper and Access being exploited for PC-based solutions. The advantage of the approach is that the database structure enables the need for ad hoc information to be addressed. This would enable users to address such questions as "What percentage of our customers is in the petrochemical industry and what has been the average job value and profit on sales to this market over the last two years?"

All major types of billing can be handled by database systems, including stage payments and retainers. Company accounting systems can cater for the accounting requirements of partnerships and both public and private companies.

The management information available not only includes the standard accounting returns, but will enable the profitability of a specific client to be measured in total. This will allow the management to view the profit on an individual job, as well as to allocate sales and market costs to the client, in order to obtain a fuller picture of the interaction with that client. Attributes can be assigned to individual clients, for example industry sector plus size of company, enabling more detailed analysis of the profile of the clients, both existing and potential.

Customer service provision

Where consulting firms offered services to clients which required intensive use of data and statistics, for example chartered surveyors offering consultancy advice on valuation and portfolio management, these systems were initially tailor-made for each consultancy. These requirements are now supported by software packages. The availability of relatively cheap software to support the complex mechanistic aspects of such requirements has enabled smaller firms to offer services where previously they could not compete owing to the level of the skills and resources required to handle the work manually and the prohibitive cost of bespoke software.

31.3 Support to professional service productivity and quality

It is in this second area that the exploitation of IT has changed dramatically over the last five years:

- access to a PC is now regarded as a standard provision for any professional worker, in the same way that all employees expect to have access to the telephone;
- the advent of the portable PC now enables consultants to gain access to computing power regardless of location;
- the availability of corporate networks allows information to be exchanged and more cooperative methods of working to be developed;
- the scope of systems that can be hosted on a PC has improved dramatically with the constantly increasing power of the PC.

Below we describe the key areas in which, by exploiting new technology, major benefits can be delivered within consulting firms.

Word processing

The opportunities afforded by word (text) processing were recognized early by consulting firms. Firms invested in word-processing systems to meet the needs of the central typing resource. Documents were handwritten and word processed by either the central typing pool or secretarial support. Corrections were marked on draft copies by the consultant and returned for correction. While such techniques reduced the time necessary for final document preparation and improved the quality of the final document, they relied heavily on the consultant being available to change the drafts.

The advent of the PC now enables a more flexible approach to be adopted and, more and more, word processing is being used cooperatively. Work submitted on paper to the typing resource is word processed and the files generated are mailed electronically to the consultants, who then make minor modifications directly using their PC.

Most consultants now use PCs to generate drafts of their reports. This is of increasing importance where consultants work away from their base and must report their findings swiftly and to a high standard of presentation.

This approach relies on compatibility between the software in use on the consultant's PC and that in use within the central word-processing function. This is not always the case: the PC systems may not be compatible with the central shared systems. While conversion between word-processing products is provided, the conversions are not always without problems and do not always support the full range of features available. Many consultancies are now having to re-appraise their approach to word processing to ensure that synergy and cooperation can be effected between professional and support staff.

Electronic mail

The advent of electronic mail (E-mail) as a supported, standard mechanism for communication and data exchange enables new ways of working to emerge. Consultants no longer have to be working in proximity to each other for working documents to be passed easily between them.

Firms can now exploit E-mail to help in the assembly and review of proposals and reports, thus reducing the time necessary to move text, spreadsheets, graphics and so on between staff. This, again, assists in helping to improve speed of service.

E-mail between organizations is now seen as a standard method of communication, and for many organizations it is becoming the preferred method. The oil company Esso has published a leaflet stating that they wish, wherever possible, to use E-mail as the means of communication both to and from their business partners. Some buyers of consultancy services only issue invitations to submit proposals to interested companies using E-mail, and the availability of E-mail for communication between buyer and supplier is, for some buyers, now one of the criteria in bid evaluation.

E-mail has been used to increase both the speed of delivery and the profitability of jobs. Law firms use E-mail to obtain expert opinions on international legal issues directly from lawyers in the country involved. This has been especially effective between Europe and Japan, where the time zone differences and language problems are such that telephone communications become problematic. Where consultancies themselves operate in the field of IT, systems designed in Europe and the United States are being built in various parts of Asia, using the locally available workforce. All communications are conducted using E-mail.

Image processing

The cost of image systems has now dropped to such a level that consultants are considering the use of image processing within their own organizations. The main area of application is in the maintenance of client files. The external client-generated paper documents are scanned into the firm's client filing system and indexed together with the electronic documents that have either been generated internally or provided via E-mail or another file-transfer mechanism. Access to the equivalent of the full "paper file" can then be made available electronically.

The advantages of such systems lie in:

— the added security they provide, as files are never missing;

— the fact that multiple access to a single file can be obtained, thereby allowing several members of the firm to work simultaneously on the same files;

— requirements of records management can be invoked automatically.

These facilities assist greatly where firms wish to gain quality accreditation such as ISO 9001 or its national equivalent. The consultancy can show that all documentation is maintained and filed in a manner that is secure and easily accessible.

Additional benefits are gained where image processing is augmented by *intelligent character recognition* (ICR). Using this technique, images of typed (and even some handwritten) documents are converted into word-processing format. Once the document is in this format it can be interrogated in the same manner as internally generated documents. This facility is now widely used by legal firms in the *"discovery"* processes and also in the field of forensic accounting.

Workflow software

While not as yet extensively used within consultancy firms, workflow software has the potential to assist in many of the administrative areas of the consulting business. Workflow software is typically used in conjunction with word processing, E-mail and image processing. The technique enables the automation of the administrative procedures that have to be undertaken in the support area. Examples of areas in which workflow is already being exploited by both public and private sector organizations, and in which benefits could be delivered to consultancies, include:

- personnel (job application management);
- contracts (checking of contract details and contract set-up);
- report production and approval;
- expenditure approval.

The technology relies on the presence of an effective office infrastructure, as it typically combines features such as word processing and forms processing, and exploits E-mail to transfer items between users. Its introduction is therefore closely linked to the provision of PC terminals and effective networking.

Voice mail

Where consultants are often away from their offices, voice mail can provide a valuable means by which to maintain contact and also to ensure that information can be disseminated quickly and effectively. Currently few voice-mail systems are integrated with PC-based IT. This, however, is changing rapidly. The systems operate as a sophisticated "answer phone", enabling (1) messages to be left, (2) replies to messages to be sent, and (3) messages to be broadcast or sent to predetermined distribution lists.

Because the systems are available over the telephone network, they can be easily accessed without recourse to sophisticated technology. Consultants can log onto the systems in the same manner from a client's site, a hotel or their own home.

External information sources

Consultants need to be able to conduct their research speedily and effectively. Services are now available from third-party information providers that enable research to be conducted without the need for the corporate librarian to carry out all research internally, or for the consultant personally to visit a library or an information centre. The scope of the systems is wide-ranging and growing. Among the topics on which information can now be provided by access to an on-line information service are, for example:

— European legislation;

— IT developments;

— company performance;

— international trade figures;

— any mention in the press of specific topics (using key word and ICR techniques).

Professional support products

In addition to the standard office products described above, systems are now being developed to address the needs of specialist consultancies.

Geographic information systems (GIS) are being exploited by environmental and market-research consultancies. The systems enable data to be linked to specific geographic locations and analysed as required. For example, by using a GIS to link demographic information with road network information consultants are able to advise on locations for facilities as diverse as retail outlets and hospitals. The systems and their associated data are comparatively expensive to obtain and maintain, their value being totally dependent on the range of geographic-based information associated with the system. The services therefore tend to be provided by specialist organizations from whom consultants buy both the required information and necessary analysis.

Sophisticated *computer-assisted design* (CAD) packages, that run on PCs, are also available. Where consultancies work in the engineering, design or logistics arena, such techniques are heavily utilized and are now regarded as the standard method of operation. The final product is delivered to the client electronically.

Market research companies are also using hand-held PCs, and bar-coding and ICR techniques to enable data to be gathered from the general public swiftly, accurately and without incurring the overheads associated with the transfer of information from paper questionnaires to computer-based analysis systems.

As mentioned above, when image systems were discussed, the use of ICR enables the images to be translated in word-processing format. The text can then be interrogated using *free text retrieval* (FTR), which enables searches to be performed on the text file(s) looking for a specified set of characters anywhere in the files. This facility has been used by consultants in many different ways:

- within accounting firms and financial consultancies the technique is used to access data relating to bankruptcies where fraud is suspected, thanks to the ability to search for any mention of specific items (names, values) or a combination of such items;

- ICR techniques are also used where consultancies are assisting in stock market flotations; the capability of the software to detect "near matches" can be used to identify multiple and fraudulent applications;

- when applied to internal documentation (reports, proposals, records of sales meetings) of the firm, ICR can be used to ensure that a full picture of all dealings with an individual client or industry is identified.

The range of products and techniques, described above, has moved IT from being solely a mechanism supporting administrative functions into an arena where its exploitation enables the work content of professional members of the firm to alter dramatically.

In organizations where office systems are now fully exploited, tangible benefits are being delivered as the professional to support staff ratios are altered. Introduction of advanced office systems, in conjunction with a revised method of working, can enable the ratio of professional staff to support staff to be improved by up to 50 per cent, dependent on the effectiveness of the initial structure and working methods. Improvement in this ratio can have a major and immediate effect on the profitability of a consulting firm.

31.4 Information for marketing of services

In the previous sections we considered how IT techniques, such as ICR and FTR, are being brought to bear to improve the operation of internal processes and procedures in consulting firms. In this section we consider use of these facilities for improving the marketing and selling abilities of consultants.

Once the systems described above are in place, a valuable information infrastructure has been provided. The administrative accounting and billing systems provide information about current clients and the sales effort in hand. At the same time, office systems used to support the professional consultants enable information to be captured effectively and disseminated throughout the firm.

To these techniques can now be added information access products which are already being exploited by large consultancies. By combining databases with such products, easy access and dissemination of both structured and unstructured information can be provided, thereby encouraging the sharing of information. Users can be given access to details of all work undertaken, proposals submitted and marketing meetings held with a specific client. As a result, meetings with the client can be conducted with full awareness of all the issues surrounding the potential sale.

By combining information relating to clients within a specific market sector, trends can be identified in terms of key products, buying patterns and similar. This can be exploited to focus the marketing effort on the key areas of client needs. Furthermore, information relating to any issues arising on a job can be swiftly shared, the experience of other consultants brought to bear and the problem potentially solved before it becomes a major issue.

Once the technical infrastructures are in place, and consultants understand the potential benefits that can accrue from sharing and exploiting information, the use of such systems within the consulting arena will escalate.

Also, more and more work has to be won through a competitive tendering process. The clients' expectations, relating to the quality of proposals and presentations, are constantly increasing. Consultants must exploit technology to deliver effective sales and marketing materials:

- Advanced word processing and desktop publishing, combining text with graphics, are used to improve proposals and reports.

- Drawing packages are used for slide presentations and reports.

- PC-based systems are replacing 35mm slides as the medium for presentations.

- Final results of a diagnostic or other type of consulting study may involve interactive video. For example, in layout planning, and in architectural and environmental consultancies, "active" models of new structures can be generated in order to assess their impact.

An additional marketing tool now available is the vast and growing use of the Internet World Wide Web (WWW). Companies can use the Internet services both to improve their own awareness of the market-place into which they are selling and also to provide information relating to the services they themselves provide. It is now possible to link WWW and Lotus services, providing, for the first time, the potential for the full exploitation of both internal and external information.

31.5 Realizing benefits

Computing is now capable of fulfilling a pivotal role in consulting firms and being a major driving force in the reduction of overheads, the improvement of lead conversion and the generation of extension business. If this role is to be realized to its full potential, and the benefits maximized, the management and development of computing must be addressed at the firm level. IT offers value, regardless of the size of the consultancy. The emphasis, however, changes. This section reviews effectiveness and management issues faced by larger firms. Section 31.6 will then focus on the areas in which small consulting firms and sole practitioners can gain value from IT.

Recognizing computing as a corporate asset

To date, in many professional service firms, the expenditure on computing has been fragmented across the separate areas of responsibility. The key benefits that can now be derived from IT stem from the ability to access and exchange information across disciplines and practice areas within the firm. However, unless central direction is given, major investment can be made with few benefits being realized, as issues arise relating to compatibility, connectivity and data integrity, interpretation, ownership and management. Corporate management mechanisms need to be in place to ensure that central directives can be implemented in order for the investment in hardware and software to deliver its full potential.

The extent to which IT is exploited will depend heavily on the size and nature of the consultancy firm. In figure 31.1 (page 649) we illustrate the types of application that we would expect to see being exploited across firms of differing size.

Providing corporate management

The management and administration of IT must be addressed as a corporate requirement:

- a *mechanism* must be put in place whereby the resources available are focused on the areas of greatest need, rather than automatically satisfying, one by one, those users who take the greatest personal interest in IT;
- the *responsibility* for the allocation of funding must be assigned, and a mechanism put in place that ensures that the rationale and justification for projects are clear, unambiguous and agreed within the organization;
- a *clear IT strategy* must be formulated in order to ensure that the organization implements systems in a coordinated manner, enabling incremental growth and the optimization of benefits;
- the firm's *training policies* and programmes must provide the required skills and stimulate all consultants' interest in using IT.

In order to achieve these goals, larger consulting firms are adopting a *steering group or committee approach* to the management of IT. An IT steering group is set up from within the senior management of the organization. It is chaired at board or management committee level and represents the key user groups together with the administrative and financial functions.

The steering group is responsible for:

— agreeing overall IT staffing and budgets;

— agreeing work priorities and overall schedules;

— acting as the project board for the developments undertaken (or to delegate project responsibility to a lower level, dependent on project size).

— ensuring that the interests of IT are represented at board level.

The head of the firm's IT unit (department) should report to this steering group. For all projects undertaken a project manager is appointed and is responsible for reporting progress to the project board. The project manager does not necessarily have to be drawn from the IT department. Depending on the nature of the project, the manager may be a senior user, a member of the IT staff or even an external consultant. All project managers report to the project board and the head of IT should also be involved in this reporting mechanism.

Providing support

Once computer systems become an essential part of the day-to-day working methods of the consultants, they must be supported, maintained and enhanced as the need arises. The need for in-house technical expertise has to be recognized. While systems were purchased as discrete packages and minimal exchange of information took place, little in-house expertise was required. However, the disciplines and knowledge necessary to provide integrated access to all administrative, office and advanced groupware systems of a firm are not known to the majority of consultants. Technical support must be available if the systems are to be usable by all staff, regardless of their location and individual levels of IT literacy.

A word of warning must be issued here. In many firms professional consultants have, for many years, had to act as their own IT "gurus", deflecting effort from their mainstream consulting activities. Such skills are often jealously guarded. Opposition may be encountered among professional staff who see little value in conforming to corporate standards and wish to continue operating in virtual isolation, using systems chosen on the basis of personal preferences.

This problem can be addressed in three ways:

- by showing the benefits to the individual consultant of the adoption of a corporate approach;
- by ensuring that adoption of the central standards offers some personal advantage to the consultant, for example, automatic securing of personal data, or technical advice and backstopping hitherto unavailable;
- by providing individualized training, flexibly meeting each consultant's particular needs and preferred ways of learning.

Ensuring confidentiality

In addition to these internal issues, an external issue must be dealt with. Computing techniques can, in theory, make information easily available across an organization. The need for data confidentiality must therefore be addressed. Consulting firms must be able to show that their systems can maintain confidentiality of information. This is essential if, for example, financial advice is being given to more than one client company. Consultants must be able to identify potential conflicts of interest and avoid them by ensuring the security, privacy and integrity of the information provided by their clients.

Where implemented with vision and used as a major corporate resource, computing now has the ability to be a critical factor of differentiation, enabling consulting firms to offer a focused, cost-effective and fully-informed service to an ever-widening client base.

31.6 Information technology in small consulting firms

Small consultancies do not need complex IT systems, but they do need sufficient IT to allow them to present themselves and operate as professionally as their larger competitors. Today, with the advent of low-cost computing, this is easily possible. Below we give some indications of what was available in 1995. As computer technology is constantly changing, the reader should obtain as much information as possible before making any decision.

Today no small consultancy can survive without information technology, but it does not need to spend a fortune. The equipment and software described here are available for some US$3,000-6,000 (1995-96 prices).

Basic hardware and software needs

Basic hardware. Initial priority should be given to a desktop computer which provides the desired power and graphics quality; later on a portable computer is likely to prove useful. A consultant doing a lot of text processing and other computer work outside his or her office may decide to start with a portable computer or to acquire both.

An independent dealer should be able to advise on the size and capacity of various machines, their operating systems, their advantages, and so on. Current hardware includes a central processing unit (CPU — a minimum capacity is 486 DX 50 if Intel is chosen), dynamic memory (a minimum of 8-16 megabytes is becoming necessary), a graphic display screen, a keyboard, a mouse and permanent disk storage space (hundreds of megabytes). The market currently offers three types of hardware — Intel-based PCs from many suppliers, the Apple Macintosh, and various computers based on the Unix operating system (which are less frequent and take some 10 per cent of the total market).

Operating systems. All computers run an operating system. The choice today for PCs is MS-DOS with MS-Windows (most common), OS/2, or one of the Unix operating systems such as SCO or Solaris. The Macintosh runs System 7; other computers run the version of Unix that corresponds to the hardware, e.g. OSF/1 for DEC machines.

Graphical user interfaces. The current standard is a graphical user interface with a mouse. It provides a user-friendly environment which is intuitive and more productive for the user than the previous character-based interfaces. One should remember that software packages from different suppliers will run on the machine, so these should be compatible with the chosen operating system and graphical user interface. An independent specialist should be approached to advise on the pros and cons of different machines, operating systems, graphical user interfaces, and so on, to suit the specific needs of the consultant. Getting advice from another management consultant may be useful, but there is a risk of bias due to personal habits and preferences, and incomplete information.

Printing. A laser printer which permits the production of quality documents is a "must", and one should not skimp on the investment.

Scanner. A scanner is not essential, but could be useful for "reading" documents direct into the computer. The early ones were not very reliable, but they are getting better all the time. If you decide to buy one, our advice would be to pay the extra and get a flat-bed scanner. The hand-held units are quite cheap, but less effective.

CD-ROM. A CD-ROM reader, double speed or better, is a very worthwhile addition to the equipment. Many extensive databases are already available cheaply on CD-ROM, and the range of uses of the CD-ROM technology is expanding very rapidly.

Compatibility issues and the consultant's choice

The choice of the computer workstation and the operating system will limit the choice of future software packages and additional hardware. Probably 100 consultants use PCs for every ten that use a Macintosh and one that uses a Unix computer; however, there may be exceptions in certain consulting domains. For example, one would expect to see Macintosh being used in the publications field and Unix systems being used in the petrochemical industry.

The consultant must select the packages that he or she wishes to use. The basic needs for small consulting firms are for word processing, a spreadsheet for data management, and graphics, primarily for overhead projector transparencies. A program for desktop publishing will be appreciated by those who want to produce their own brochures and take camera-ready copy to their printers. These programmes should be compatible, as you will wish to transfer data between them. It is also worth considering the IT standards used by your main clients, who may wish to use the materials generated by your firm, and vice versa.

With this equipment the small consultant can easily compete with larger firms in making effective use of IT technology and producing highly professional documentation without an enormous investment in time and money.

Administrative computing

The equipment already purchased and the spreadsheet package can be used for basic budgeting, bookkeeping and cash flow management. For the management of customer records the consultant will additionally need to purchase a database programme (something simple will do). This enables the consultant to keep client records and provides easy access to them.

For the larger consultancy it may be useful to purchase a small accounting package, but for the smaller business this can be more trouble than it is worth. Billing can be done using the word processing and spreadsheet or database packages for records. Cash flow can be managed using the spreadsheet. This, we find, provides sufficient controls.

Marketing

Finding clients on a continuing basis is especially difficult for small firms, whose resources are normally fully stretched in coping with current work, and the failure to properly manage new business generation inevitably leads to "gaps" in the work plan. Here the computer can be essential. For example, using the database programme the consultant develops a database of, say, 100 potential clients. He or she then uses a well-briefed and well-trained telesales person whose job is to speak to these potential clients every month and prospect for work. The database is continually updated, with new prospects being added and the poorer prospects being removed.

Communication

If one wishes to communicate with external telecommunication networks, the computer must have the required power and a modem. The modem and its software allow the computer to connect to public and private electronic services via the public telephone lines. Some modems can send and receive faxes.

For most small consultancies it is not practical to operate their own network, but many service providers such as Internet or CompuServe offer worldwide E-mail facilities "on line", and direct access to financial and other databases at affordable prices. Such systems are worth investigating as they provide cheap and rapid means of data access and data transfer over any distance.

PART V

DEVELOPING MANAGEMENT CONSULTANTS AND THE CONSULTING PROFESSION

CAREERS AND COMPENSATION IN CONSULTING

32

In the previous parts of this book, management consulting has been shown to be a special profession with its own objectives, methods, rules and organization. To individuals who join this profession, consulting is a career in which they may spend the main part of their working lives.

32.1 Personal characteristics of consultants

To become a career management consultant is to make a major life decision. Both individuals considering the career and consulting organizations should therefore think very carefully about the characteristics which make someone a suitable candidate.

Management consultants have discussed these characteristics many times and useful advice can be found in several publications.[1] As in any profession which has attempted to prepare a profile of an ideal candidate, there is no perfect model against which every entrant can be measured, but there are certain common characteristics affecting the consultant's success and personal job satisfaction. These common characteristics differentiate the consulting profession from other occupations that also require a high level of technical knowledge and skill, but have other objectives and use different methods of action (e.g. research, teaching, or management jobs with direct decision-making authority and responsibility). In management consulting, particular importance is attached to analytical and problem-solving abilities, as well as to special competence in the behavioural area, in communicating and working with people, and in helping others to understand the need for change and how to implement it.

What kind of person is able to perform the multiple roles required of a management consultant appropriately? It seems that the qualities a consultant needs fall into two broad categories: a number of distinctly *intellectual abilities*, and a number of distinctly *personal attributes*.

Dilemma analysis ability

Intellectually, the consultant needs the ability to make a "dilemma analysis", because an organization which uses a consultant is probably faced with a situation that appears insoluble. If the difficulty could easily be solved by the operating manager, a consultant would not be needed. The consultant must recognize that a dilemma, whether real or not, exists in the minds of those within the organization. The consultant's role is to discover the nature of the dilemma and to determine the real cause of it, rather than what is thought to be the cause.

To accomplish this, the consultant must have a special type of diagnostic skill, and should approach a study of the organization's dilemma by means of an existential pragmatism that takes into account the total client setting and all situational variables. It is only through skilful examination of the organization's fabric that the structural relationships between the various subsystems that comprise the total organization can be seen, together with the interdependent nature of its individuals, groups, substructures and environmental setting.

In order to make this kind of dilemma analysis, insight or perception and intuition are necessary. Insight or perception is vital because any dilemma requiring outside assistance will be part of a complex situation. The ability to penetrate this complexity and isolate the key situational variables is the toughest task. Unless the important factors can be sifted from the maze of detail, and cause separated from symptoms, accurate diagnosis is impossible.

Sense of organizational climate

Intuition or "sensing" must be coupled with perception in order to assess the nature of power and politics in the organization. Experience with bureaucratic and managerial structures, both public and private, tends to indicate that these do not function optimally. Underlying and intermingled with the functional operations the organization performs are the crucial dynamics of internal power and politics. Invariably, people are vying with other people for organizational influence, or for some internal political reason. Very often the consultant has been asked to help, not just to provide needed assistance, but also as an instrument of a strategy designed to secure an objective related to this influence.

Unless the consultant can intuitively sense the organizational climate, he or she runs the risk of being only a pawn in a game of organizational politics. The consultant who has the ability to recognize and understand the dynamics of the internal power and political relationships can use them masterfully in pursuit of whatever change objectives client and consultant conclude are appropriate.

Apart from these diagnostic abilities, the consultant needs implementation skills. Obviously, he or she must have some basic knowledge of the behavioural sciences, and the theories and methods of his or her own discipline. But more than these, the consultant needs imagination and experimental flexibility. Dilemma-resolving is essentially a creative enterprise. No real-life situation is going to fit perfectly into the mould suggested by standard techniques or textbook methods. Diversity and unique circumstances will almost always exist.

The consultant must have sufficient imagination to innovate adaptations and tailor concepts to meet real demands.

Furthermore, the consultant must be able to visualize the impact or ultimate outcome of the actions proposed or implemented. But, as happens so often, this is as much a process of experimental trial and error as it is one of *a priori* solutions. The courage to experiment and the flexibility to try as many approaches as needed to solve the problem are important ingredients in the practitioner's make-up.

Integrity is essential

The other important qualities required of the consultant are what we call personal attributes. Above all, he must be a professional in attitude and behaviour. To be successful, he must be as sincerely interested in helping the client organization as any good doctor is interested in helping a patient. The consultant must not conceive of himself as, or portray the image of, a huckster of patent medicines. After all, the consulting role in management and business is no different from that role in any other profession. If the concern of a consultant is primarily to make an impression or build an empire, and only secondarily to help the client organization, the organization's leaders will soon recognize that the individual is a phoney and deal with him accordingly. People in management are generally astute individuals. They can identify objectivity, honesty and, above all, integrity (see also Chapter 6).

When entering a client system, a strong tolerance for ambiguity is important. The consultant's first acquaintance with an organizational problem tends to be marked by a degree of bewilderment. It takes time to figure out the true situation, and during this period the consultant is going to experience a certain amount of confusion. One must expect this to occur and not be worried by it.

Coupled to this type of tolerance must be the qualities of patience and the ability to sustain a high level of frustration. Curing a client's ills is likely to be a long and trying experience. Substantive changes, full cooperation and complete success are unlikely in the short run. Inevitably, attempts to change people's relationships and behavioural patterns are going to be met with resistance, resentment and obstructionism from those who are, or who think they may be, adversely affected. It is important for the consultant to have that kind of maturity and sense of reality which recognizes that many of his or her actions and hopes for change are going to be frustrated. Such maturity is necessary to avoid experiencing the symptoms of defeat and withdrawal that commonly accompany the frustration of a person's sincere efforts to help others.

Sense of timing and interpersonal skills

Finally, the consulting practitioner should have a good sense of timing, a stable personality and well-developed interpersonal skills. Timing can be crucial. The best conceived and articulated plans for change can be destroyed if introduced at the wrong time. Timing is linked to an understanding of power and of the political realities existing in the change situation, and to the kind of patience that overrides the enthusiasm surrounding a newly conceived idea or training intervention that one is longing to try out immediately.

Obviously, consulting involves dealing with people rather than with machines or mathematical solutions. The consultant must have good interpersonal skills and must be able to communicate and deal with people in an atmosphere of tact, trust, politeness, friendliness, change and stability. This is important because the impact of the consulting practitioner's personality must be minimized to keep it from becoming another variable in the existential setting and so making a contribution to the existing complexity of the situation. Beyond this, success will depend on the persuasiveness and tact the consultant uses in confronting the interpersonal relationships on which the helping situation is based.

How to interpret these requirements

Box 32.1 attempts to summarize the key intellectual abilities and personal qualities of a management consultant in telegraphic form. It could be objected, and rightly, that only a very mature and exceptionally capable and versatile person can possess all the qualities mentioned. In recruiting a new consultant it is therefore necessary to consider what qualities the person must possess on recruitment, and what qualities he or she will be able to acquire, or improve, through training and experience.

32.2 Recruitment and selection

The foundations of successful careers in consulting are laid down at the moment of recruitment: only those candidates who meet certain criteria will have good chances of becoming fully competent consultants and advancing up the career ladder to their own and the consulting firm's satisfaction. Hence the extraordinary importance of a careful search and a thorough appraisal of candidates.

Recruitment criteria

Although consulting firms apply different requirements in recruiting new consultants, the comparison of their practices allows for some general conclusions concerning personal characteristics, education, practical experience and age.

Personal qualities were discussed in the previous section and there is no need to return to them.

Education is carefully examined in every case. University (first degree) level or a higher degree (a master's degree or doctorate) is required at the present time for nearly all management consulting positions. The relevance of the field of study to the particular field of consulting is considered, and in some cases

Box 32.1 Qualities of a consultant

(1) **Intellectual ability**
- ability to learn quickly and easily
- ability to observe, gather, select and evaluate facts
- good judgement
- inductive and deductive reasoning
- ability to synthesize and generalize
- creative imagination; original thinking

(2) **Ability to understand people and work with them**
- respect for other people; tolerance
- ability to anticipate and evaluate human reactions
- easy human contacts
- ability to gain trust and respect
- courtesy and good manners

(3) **Ability to communicate, persuade and motivate**
- ability to listen
- facility in oral and written communication
- ability to teach and train people
- ability to persuade and motivate

(4) **Intellectual and emotional maturity**
- stability of behaviour and action
- independence in drawing unbiased conclusions
- ability to withstand pressures, and live with frustrations and uncertainties
- ability to act with poise and in a calm and objective manner
- self-control in all situations
- flexibility and adaptability to changed conditions

(5) **Personal drive and initiative**
- right degree of self-confidence
- healthy ambition
- entrepreneurial spirit
- courage, initiative and perseverance in action

(6) **Ethics and integrity**
- genuine desire to help others
- extreme honesty
- ability to recognize the limitation of one's competence
- ability to admit mistakes and learn from failure

(7) **Physical and mental health**
- ability to sustain the specific working and living conditions of management consultants

candidates must have a specific educational background — for example, a doctorate in psychology, or a degree in computer science. The consulting firm is equally interested in the performance of the candidates during their university studies, in particular in project assignments during which the students have practised fact-finding, communication and other consulting skills.

Practical experience (a minimum of five to ten years) used to be required by all consulting firms, but this has changed in recent years. Some important firms have started recruiting up to 30 to 50 per cent of new consultants directly from university or business school, particularly in special fields where it is difficult to recruit people with required technical knowledge and experience from business firms. The idea is that talented and dynamic individuals will quickly acquire the necessary practical experience by working in teams with more senior consultants. Executives in business and consulting firms tend to agree that recruiting young consultants without experience is not ideal, but they see no alternative.

The *age at which candidates are recruited* reflects the required education and experience. The lower age limit is usually between 25 and 30 years. In many cases there is also an upper age limit. It may be difficult for a senior manager or specialist, who has reached an interesting position in terms of employment, to switch over to consulting unless he or she is directly offered a senior position with a consulting organization. This would happen only in special cases — for example, if senior people have to be recruited from outside to start new lines of consulting and head new divisions.

However, as a general rule, most consulting firms try to avoid recruiting new staff at senior (partner) level. Consulting emphasizes certain work methods and behavioural patterns, and some people would find it difficult to learn and internalize these after a certain age and at a higher level of seniority. Also, it is not easy to adapt to a firm's culture and style. The upper limit for recruitment therefore tends to be between 36 and 40 years. Of course, if an individual decides to open a private consulting practice, he or she can do it at any career point. There are retired business executives and government officials who start consulting at the age of 55-60. Some redundant managers have chosen to turn to consulting, at various stages of their careers, rather than to start looking for another management job in a saturated labour market.

Recruitment sources

There are two main sources: business enterprises and universities. But any other source is acceptable, provided it gives the candidate the required kinds of experience and skill. Many consulting firms advertise job opportunities in business journals and management periodicals, thus opening their doors to any candidates who meet the criteria.

A good source might be found in the client organizations, although under normal circumstances a consultant must not use this source owing to conflict of interest (see Chapter 6). But there are exceptions. A client may willingly authorize a consultant to offer a job to an employee whose personal qualities would be better utilized in consulting than in the present job.

When recruiting directly from universities and business schools,[2] consulting firms aim at getting the best students. They may interview 20 or more candidates for one job position. In some countries, consulting careers with leading firms enjoy such a reputation that it is not difficult to get the best graduates interested.

Interviewing and testing

Candidates for consultants' posts are asked to fill in the usual application forms (personnel questionnaires), supply detailed curricula vitae, and provide other evidence of professional work (articles, papers, a doctoral thesis, etc.). References given by the candidate and other references identified by the consulting firm are carefully checked for every candidate who looks interesting (by correspondence, personal visits or telephone calls).

Applicants are subjected to multiple interviews: by the personnel officer, a manager of the consulting firm, a supervising consultant to whom the candidate might be attached after recruitment, and one or two other consultants. Both structured and unstructured interviews are used; emphasis is on obtaining as complete a picture as possible of the technical knowledge and experience of the candidate and of personal characteristics which are essential to consulting.

In some consulting firms (more frequently in the United States than in Europe) tests are used as aids in selecting new consultants. These include both cognitive tests (designed mainly to measure knowledge) and psychological tests (related to personality, attitudes, interests and motivation). If personality and attitude tests are used, the evaluation of results should be made by a professional psychologist.

Tests can convey useful information about the candidate, but their importance in the choice of consultants should not be overrated. They sometimes provide distorted information because of the ambiance in which the test is administered, or because some tests that are widely used become well known and hence less effective. In general, mature candidates do not like these tests.

Medical examination

A medical examination will be required, as is usual in the case of long-term employment. This will take account of the life-style of consultants, which in most cases is more demanding on the individual's physical and mental fitness, resistance and endurance than many other jobs with a comparable technical content.

Selection

As any new entrant to the profession is to be seen as a potential career consultant who may stay with the firm for many years, the selection of those who will be offered employment requires very careful evaluation of the applicants, based on all information provided by each applicant, reference checking, multiple interviews and, possibly, tests. Managers of consulting firms should avoid making authoritative decisions on selection without consulting a number of experienced colleagues: every case of recruitment warrants a collective assessment.

32.3 Career development

The great diversity of career structures in consulting firms reflects their different history, size, technical areas covered, consulting modes used, and even personal preferences of the key decision-makers. But certain common patterns tend to emerge from this diversity.[3]

In larger firms, the consultants progress through four or five principal grades, or ranks, during their career. Smaller firms use only two or three grades. In pursuing flatter and leaner structures, some larger firms have also reduced the number of rungs in their consultants' career ladders.

Career progression implies that the consultant will take on more responsibility, which can be:

- supervisory (team leadership, project management, supervision of assignments);
- promotional (management surveys, marketing, negotiation and selling of new assignments);
- managerial (managing organizational units in the firm; functions in general and top management);
- technical (directly performing assignments that require particularly experienced and knowledgeable consultants, training of new consultants, development of methods and practice guides);
- various combinations of these four alternatives.

A summary description of a typical career structure is given in box 32.2.

Factors affecting careers

In a typical consulting career there is a significant relationship between progression in rank and role. A higher rank means a more difficult role, and more responsibility.

This relationship is not the same in all firms. Certain firms prefer a more conservative approach, whereby precisely defined functions are assigned to each rank in the consulting hierarchy. Thus, only a consultant of a higher grade would be used in negotiating with a potential client. In contrast, many firms are increasingly flexible in deciding what a consultant can and should do irrespective of rank. For example, a consulting project can be managed by an individual in any of the four principal grades (starting at the operating consultants level),

Box 32.2 Career levels in a consulting firm

First level: junior consultant (trainee, research associate, analyst, entry-level consultant)

This level exists only in some firms. These firms recruit new consultants as trainees (for 6-12 months), whose main task is to master the essential consulting skills as quickly as possible.

Second level: operating consultant (resident consultant, associate, associate consultant, management consultant, consultant)

The operating consultant is the front-line professional who does most of the consulting work at client organizations. Every operating consultant has a special field of competence, as a rule in one management function or in special techniques. Normally the consultant would undertake a number of operating assignments in varying situations, individually and as a team member, for a period of three to five years before being considered for promotion to the next level.

Third level: supervising consultant (team leader, project manager, senior associate, senior consultant, manager)

The main responsibilities of consultants promoted to this level include team leadership (e.g. in assignments requiring expertise in general management and involving several functional areas) and supervision of operating consultants (e.g. a marketing supervisor may be in charge of four to six different assignments in marketing). A consultant at this level also continues to execute assignments directly if these require a more experienced person. Further responsibilities may include training, management surveys, the marketing of new assignments and maintaining contacts with clients.

Fourth level: junior partner or equivalent (principal, manager, survey consultant)

Consultants at this level carry out a number of marketing and management functions. Typically they spend most of their time in promotional work (visiting clients, doing management surveys, planning and negotiating new assignments). Some may be personally in charge of important client assignments, while others head organizational units within the firm, or coordinate and control a number of client projects.

Fifth level: senior partner or equivalent (officer, director, partner, managing partner, vice-president, president)

Senior and top management responsibilities prevail at this superior level. These include strategy and policy direction, and senior management positions in the firm. Consultants at this level are also concerned with practice development, do promotional work with important clients, and may be personally in charge of complex and major assignments. In most firms they are the owners, but there are firms where the junior partners of principals (the fourth level) also belong to the group that owns the firm.

depending on the scope of the project and the capabilities of the individual. These firms encourage young operating consultants to assume responsibility for more difficult jobs and for managing assignments, and thus to expand their capabilities, as soon as possible after joining the firm. Even consultants whose experience is relatively short are expected to demonstrate project managers' abilities and to be in a position to present the results of their work both to their supervisors and to the clients.

Career advancement is based on achievement above all. As seniority is difficult to ignore, individuals who cannot demonstrate high achievement are encouraged to move on. If they stayed, they would see their younger colleagues advance more rapidly, which inevitably creates jealousies and leads to frustration. It is often emphasized that every young consultant should be regarded and treated as a potential partner, and that career development to partner level should not take longer than 6-12 years.

Fast career progression has a positive motivational effect on the consultants and creates a dynamic and competitive working environment. However, a firm that adopts fast career progression as a policy must be prepared to cope with certain problems:

— if the firm's growth is fast enough, the number of senior positions grows as well and promotions can be fast also, but if growth slows down or stops promotions become difficult;

— some firms have therefore introduced special promotion schemes for technically competent and experienced individuals for whom supervising and managerial jobs are not available, or who are not interested in these jobs;

— an alternative is reorienting the firm to more complex assignments and thus increasing the demand for senior consultants — this enables the firm to change the overall ratio of operating to senior consultants (for example, instead of employing two seniors for every five operating consultants, the new mix of projects would permit the firm to employ three seniors and change the ratio from 5 : 2 to 5 : 3); this, however, is a sensitive issue of the firm's economics and strategy, as the reader knows from Chapters 23 and 24.

Staff reviews

There are two reasons why systematic staff reviews (performance assessment) are probably more important in consulting and other professional firms than in other sorts of organization:

• the career patterns described above as prevailing in consulting require consultants to develop rapidly and be able to assume a widening range of responsibilities — it is difficult to find work for consultants whose growth potential is limited and who will not be able to keep pace with their more dynamic and ambitious colleagues;

• the operational environment in which a consultant works (individual role in an assignment, team leader, immediate colleagues, client staff) changes frequently, and an operating consultant may be a member of three or more different teams within one year; performance evaluation must therefore be organized for collecting and assessing all information needed for the consultants' careers and professional development in this constantly changing work environment.

Thorough evaluation of a new consultant is therefore started during his or her initial training. First, several reports are prepared (see Chapter 33).

The second element in systematic staff evaluation is formal performance reviews at the end of each assignment. These reports are prepared by the team leader or supervisor, discussed with the consultant, and filed in his or her personnel record.

The third element is periodic performance appraisals, which take place in most consulting organizations once a year. As a rule, they are more frequent in the first two to three years of the consultant's career. They are based on reports from all assignments and evaluate performance and competence in areas such as:

- the technical subjects covered;
- consulting methodology and style;
- teamwork;
- team leadership, supervision, coordination;
- marketing and client relations;
- training and self-development;
- special personal characteristics, manners, interests and talents.

Every periodic performance appraisal must aim to tell, openly and clearly, both the consulting firm and the individual where to focus improvement efforts. If an individual consultant ought to start looking for a career outside consulting, a performance appraisal should reveal this and make an unambiguous recommendation! It is unfair not to tell young consultants that their career prospects are limited, thus creating unrealistic expectations and merely delaying a painful decision.

Staff turnover

Not all consultants will stay with one firm until retirement. Staff turnover figures are quite high in consulting: an annual turnover of 10-15 per cent is considered as normal, a 5-10 per cent turnover as low. The reasons for consultants' departure include:

— different views on how to do consulting;

— different views on advancement in careers;

— entrepreneurship (quite a few consultants employed in consulting firms decide to start their own consulting practices);

— personal preference for other careers (business management, government administration, university teaching, politics, etc.);

— insufficient promotion prospects;

— personality clashes.

Large consulting firms tend to have a higher staff turnover than small firms. Many young professionals join these firms in order to gain diversified experience in a relatively short time, without intending to stay in consulting. This is less common in smaller firms. In addition, small firms try to be more adaptable to the needs and aspirations of individual staff members even if this means reorienting and restructuring the firm.

In a larger firm, most consultants who want to leave do so at the operating consultant's level, before being promoted to the partner level. Voluntary departures at the partner (junior or senior) level are more the exception than the rule. However, forced and negotiated departures of partners (before retirement age) have recently become more frequent. In searching for leaner structures and competitiveness in a more difficult business climate, quite a few consulting firms have come to the conclusion that they cannot afford to sustain large numbers of highly paid partners without undermining the firm's financial health and staff morale.

A sole practitioner's career path

What, then, is a typical career path of a consultant who has decided to work as a sole practitioner?

Most individuals who start their own consulting business do it, for reasons already known to the reader, after some 8-15 years of practical experience in functional or general management, or after having worked for several years for a consulting firm. Those who go directly into independent consulting without any previous experience usually set up in special fields where technical knowledge acquired at university is in great demand and businesses are prepared to use technical experts without practical experience.

A sole practitioner has no one who could promote him or her to a more senior position. What normally happens is that, as he or she becomes more experienced and ambitious, a sole practitioner is able to undertake more complex and difficult jobs, and also to charge higher fees. Nevertheless, many sole practitioners get into situations where important career choices have to be faced. They could progress technically and take on more responsible assignments, but this may require giving up personal independence and agreeing to work in a team. One consultant will decide to expand the firm and start employing other consultants. Another will join a larger consulting firm if a senior position is offered. A third will establish a network and cooperate with other sole practitioners. A fourth will reject all these alternatives and look for assignments requiring high-level special expertise and a great deal of experience, but small enough to be undertaken by an individual. The consulting business offers enough opportunities to satisfy a wide range of different career aspirations.

32.4 Compensation policies and practices

Compensation policies and practices of management consulting firms are based on similar principles to those in other firms in the professional service sector. Compensation reflects factors such as:

- the technical complexity and special requirements of consulting work;
- the quality of individual talent;
- the situation in the market for consulting services and professional staff;
- the financial performance of the firm;
- the actual contribution of the individual consultant to the development and financial performance of the firm.

Financial compensation is not regarded as the only way to motivate consultants. Long-term motivation is emphasized by demonstrating to the new recruits that in due course they will be promoted to the partner level and start earning considerably more. The nature and the job content of consulting, as well as exceptional learning opportunities and business contacts provided by consulting assignments, are also strong motivational factors.

Entry-level and operating consultant compensation

At entry level, consulting firms compete among themselves and with other employers for the best talents. As a result, salaries offered to new recruits tend to be relatively higher than those offered by business firms in industry and commerce. In the total remuneration package, the share of the base salary exceeds 90 per cent and may attain the full 100 per cent. Hence, the role of bonuses and profit sharing is relatively small, although some firms stress that consultants at all levels should be eligible for some bonus.

The bonus paid to junior and operating consultants may be discretionary and may depend only on the profitability of the firm as a whole. Alternatively, the consultants may be getting a bonus which is in some proportion to the fees they (or the team of which they are members) earn from their own clients, and to new business that they are able to generate for the firm.

If individual fee earning and new business generation are strongly reflected in the bonus paid, the message is clear — this is what the firm expects from you. As a result, the young consultant will become less interested in helping other colleagues, engaging in teamwork and spending time at activities for which no bonus is likely to be paid.

Experience has shown that even a small and discretionary bonus is valuable for any level of consultant. However, it should not be paid automatically, without reviewing the consultant's work performance. It should not send wrong signals on what the firm values most in the junior and operating consultant's behaviour and performance.

Box 32.3 Minicase: Consultants' careers and compensation at INTRA

INTRA is a medium-sized German consulting firm (about 50 consultants) active mainly in general and operations management. It has opted for a flat structure (teamwork rather than hierarchy), democratic decision-making (key decisions are made by the partners' assembly meeting four times a year) and individual consultant self-control and self-motivation (every consultant is treated as a profit centre). The firm's philosophy stresses professionalism, service quality, enjoyable work and entrepreneurship. New staff members are recruited at junior level (university plus two to three years of experience in business or teaching) and the firm wants them to become fully productive in the third year. A new recruit knows that he will be elected partner in five years if his performance meets the firm's standards. After the second year with the firm this is already confirmed, or the young consultant is encouraged to look for another career, and the firm helps to find an interesting one.

Consultant compensation is based on the principle of relatively low fixed salaries and a high share of profit calculated for each individual. An individual's income (from client billing or priced internal services) is divided as follows:

— 50 per cent to the individual;
— 25 per cent to the marketing and supervising consultant(s);
— 25 per cent to the firm (contribution to common expenses).

An individual's annual income and cost structure may be as follows (in DM):

Income		Costs	
50 per cent of fees	150 000	Salary	90 000
Reimbursed travel expenses	15 000	Social contributions	10 000
		Travel costs	16 000
		Car depreciation	8 000
		PC depreciation	2 000
Total	165 000	Total	126 000

The positive balance of 39,000 is the consultant's profit share. However, as new consultants enter a well-established setting, they start operating with a "debt" of 100,000 to the firm. This must be repaid before the consultant can really start collecting the profit share. Normally this is done in two to three years and the consultant starts getting his or her share of profit in the third or fourth year. However, this "dividend" is actually paid only if the whole firm is profitable. Also, the total sum of the positive balance of individual consultants computed as described above is compared to the total gross profit of the company, and only a proportion corresponding to what the company has actually earned over expenses is distributed to consultants. Thus, the company as a whole cannot really make a loss. The same system applies to every member of professional staff and to all activities. Management jobs are assigned a value in days, e.g. 80 days per year for the managing partner. Consultants can earn days for internal projects selected by the firm's management, for which they are paid fees covering their real costs.

Author: Karl Scholz.

Partner compensation

Partner compensation is a most complex and delicate issue of management in professional firms. The partners are in a dual position — they own the firm, therefore they are entitled to a part of the profit, and they carry out specific managerial, marketing or consulting jobs, for which they are paid a salary. The prevailing formula used in partner remuneration practices tends to be base salary plus profit share or bonus. For example, between 1986 and 1992 senior partners in American consulting firms received bonuses amounting on average to some 21-32 per cent of their base salaries. The corresponding data for junior partners were 14-23 per cent. In larger firms, the total senior partner remuneration is about two to three times higher than that of an operating or senior consultant.[4]

Partners and other professionals in equivalent positions manage the firm and play key roles in promoting the business. Their roles and performance ought to be correctly reflected both in the compensation formulas used and in the actual level of compensation. If partner compensation criteria disregard, or are in conflict with, the firm's goals and policies, even the best strategic plan will be nothing more than a piece of paper.

In small consulting firms with a few partners, simple income or profit division formulas are quite common. If there are three partners in a firm, each of them may be allocated one-third of the profits. The formula causes no difficulties if within this small team there is a clear division of responsibilities and an understanding of who does what for the development of the firm. Probably the three partners will be able to speak frequently and openly about these questions and change the focus by mutual agreement (eg. spend more time on coaching a new associate or start looking for a new line of business). It may be unnecessary and even contrary to the firm's well-established practices to formally reflect such agreements in changed partner compensation.

The matter gets more complex with the growth of the firm's business and the number of partners and consultants employed. There will be a need for a compensation plan for partners, reflecting and supporting the firm's strategic goals and priorities. As a rule, the plan will use a combination of a few criteria (say three to five) which may be quantitative and measurable (e.g. the partner's personal billings) or qualitative and judgemental (e.g. the partner's contribution to junior staff coaching and training, or to building up the firm's image in professional and client circles). Each criterion will be assigned a weighting. Consistency between the criteria declared and actually applied will be essential (see box 32.4, overleaf).

The practical impact of each criterion needs to be carefully considered. Furthermore, periodical performance evaluation ought to be applied even to partners in senior management positions, using a formula that stresses collective assessment and is acceptable to senior professionals. For example, a partner can be asked to prepare a self-assessment of performance using the main criteria chosen by the firm. This is then reviewed in a compensation or management committee and discussed with the partner in a committee meeting or individually.

Box 32.4 Criteria for partners' compensation

(1) Seniority

Widely used. Still an exclusive criterion in some distinguished professional firms. Encourages partners to get used to a stable income level irrespective of current personal effort and achievement.

(2) Profitability of firm

Widely used. Encourages partners to focus on helping each other, promoting teamwork and improving the whole firm's results.

(3) Profitability of activity supervised or managed

Widely used. Puts a high premium on actual results of the partner's projects (assignments) or of a unit for which the partner is directly responsible.

(4) Personal billing

Widely used. Stimulates interest and initiative in doing individual billable work. Also remunerates for a high personal billing rate (fee rate) reflecting individual competence and image (which can be a separate criterion).

(5) Personal selling

Encourages finding new clients and projects, or obtaining new work from existing clients. Possible refinement: differentiating between new work of routine (repetitive) nature, and projects providing for acquiring new competencies, entering new sectors or similar.

(6) Client satisfaction

Encourages partners to care for clients, assure high quality and manage assignments to their clients' full satisfaction.

(7) Training and development of consultants

Stresses transfer of experience and know-how, and the partner's role in coaching and developing younger consultants.

(8) Contribution to the profession

Remunerates voluntary association and other work serving the profession.

(9) Contribution to the success of others

Rewards collaboration and help to other units through sharing of information, providing advice, giving leads, helping to negotiate new assignments, etc.

(10) Contribution to technical developments in the firm

Rewards research, new method development, writing of practice guides and other work enhancing the firm's knowledge base and competence.

(11) Building up the firm's image

Encourages writing of articles and books, reporting at conferences, membership of government and mixed committees, etc.

(12) Self-development

Stimulates the learning of new technical, managerial, communication and other skills to enhance the partner's competence and contribution to the firm.

(13) General management

Remunerates for general management positions within the firm's structure.

Applying a fair compensation policy

In conclusion, it is useful to stress that a compensation policy impacts strongly on the climate in the consulting firm. Consultants at all levels should know what the policy is and how it is justified. They should have no reason to suspect that the firm's management uses a double meter in applying the policy to different firm members and different levels of the consulting hierarchy. The purpose of compensation policy is to motivate the whole staff, not to promote privileges and create tensions between groups and categories of consultants.

---

[1] The first significant attempt to define these characteristics was made by the Association of Management Consulting Firms (ACME) in the United States. See P. W. Shay: *The common body of knowledge for management consultants* (New York, ACME, 1974). In 1989 ACME published a revised edition of this first guide under the title *Professional profile of management consultants: A body of expertise, skills and attributes.* See also Ch. 10 in G. Lippitt and R. Lippitt: *The consulting process in action* (San Diego, California, University Associates, 2nd ed., 1986).

[2] To facilitate contacts between consulting firms and students, the Harvard Business School has established a Management Consulting Club. The School and the Club publish a periodical career guide. See, e.g., *Management consulting 1991-92* (Boston, Massachusetts, HBS Press, 1990).

[3] There is little published information which permits a comparison of the career patterns in various consulting firms. Information from several North American firms can be found in the consulting career guide of the Harvard Business School, op. cit.

[4] See ACME: *ACME 1993 survey of United States key management information* (New York, 1993), pp. 47-50; and idem: *ACME 1993 survey of European key management information* (New York, 1993), pp. 19-20.

TRAINING AND DEVELOPMENT OF CONSULTANTS

33

The reader knows from the previous chapter that all entrants to the consulting profession should have an excellent educational background and that a great many will also have several years of practical experience. Yet consulting has its own special training and development requirements that are additional to whatever a new consultant may have learned at university, at business school, and in former jobs.

There are four main reasons for this. First, consulting on how to do a job is different from actually doing that job. A new consultant must develop a full understanding of this difference and acquire the technical and behavioural skills that are specific to consulting.

Second, the breadth and depth of technical knowledge required for advising clients usually exceed what a new consultant has learned during his studies and previous employment. A new consultant with five to ten years of business experience may have worked in two to four jobs and experienced a relatively small number of business and management contexts. This does not provide the consultant with enough experience for giving the best possible advice to the client. In addition, a new consultant may have to update and upgrade the technical knowledge acquired during university or business school studies.

Third, most new recruits will join the firm without any prior education in consulting *per se*. University and business school courses in management consulting are rare. Those which exist are elective and attended by small numbers of students.

Fourth, the new entrant is joining a consulting firm which, it can be assumed, has chosen a particular consulting philosophy and strategy. This will concern issues such as the objectives of consulting, the methods and techniques used, the ways in which clients should participate, and ethical considerations. There is a need to "indoctrinate" the new recruits to make sure that they will learn the consulting firm's professional approach, and identify themselves with its philosophy and culture.

However, the consultant's education can never end with the completion of initial training. "Least of all can consultants afford to take the attitude that the old ways of doing things are good enough. Probably no group is more severely challenged by the information explosion than management consultants. Learning must be a life-long job for consultants", wrote Michael Shays in 1983, when he was President of the Institute of Management Consultants in the United States.[1]

How does a consultant learn? What is the most effective way of developing a competent consultant? University education can provide the future consultant with a solid fund of knowledge and some analytical tools. Excellent education is necessary. However, like managers, consultants learn from experience above all. This includes the consultant's own direct experience, on assignments in which the task is to deal with problems and situations that provide meaningful learning opportunities. In doing so the consultant also learns from the clients' experiences. Furthermore, the consultant learns from other consultants — his or her colleagues in a team, the team leader and other superiors, consultants who worked for the same client previously, and other members of the profession.

Learning on the job, by practising consulting, is therefore the main and generally recognized method of learning. This is how most consultants acquired their proficiency in the past, and even at the present time some consultants advocate that on-the-job learning is the only way of becoming competent in consultancy. However, learning on the job alone is not enough and should be supplemented (but not replaced!) by other learning opportunities, including formal training in courses and workshops. This is the approach that we have adopted in this chapter. Such an approach tends to be increasingly supported by leading firms and professional associations of consultants.

33.1 What should consultants learn?

A remarkable diversity of personalities, clients, subjects handled, intervention methods and consulting firms' philosophies is a prominent feature of the consulting profession. Because of this diversity, there are probably as many different paths to individual proficiency as there are consultants. As in other professions, some individuals will learn faster than their peers and achieve higher proficiency, owing to a happy concourse of a number of circumstances: talent, drive, educational background, complexity and novelty of assignments executed, and leadership and support provided by the consulting firm.

Training and development policies of consulting firms, and of the profession at large, tend to respect this diversity, offering an adequate range of choices that permit the harmonization of learning with individual needs and possibilities.

At the same time, the profession has aimed to achieve a necessary minimum of uniformity and standardization, reflecting the common and prevailing needs of consultants at various stages of a typical professional career. Leading consulting firms and professional associations have devoted a lot of energy to these questions. As the profession is a young and rapidly evolving one, and distilling common needs and principles from constantly changing diversity is not easy, the task is far from being completed. Nevertheless, some useful guidance and support materials, outlining the consultants' professional profiles and common knowledge base, are available.[2]

Elements of consultant competency

Generally speaking, a consultant's competency can be described in terms of personality traits and aptitudes, attitudes, knowledge and skills. These elements of competence are interlinked and influence each other.[3]

Personality traits and aptitudes were mentioned in the previous chapter in discussing recruitment criteria. Traits determine how a person will react "to any general set of events which allow the trait to be expressed".[4] Thus, traits define a typical thought pattern and resultant behaviour characteristic of a person in a variety of situations. Examples of personality traits are: propensity to take initiative, ambition, flexibility, patience, self-confidence, shyness, and the like. Examples of aptitudes are manual dexterity or linguistic ability.

Attitudes are a person's feelings for or against certain issues, and therefore they reflect values that a person holds. They concern matters of human preference and result from choices between competing interests. Examples of attitudes or values are preference for oral before written communication, tolerance of other people's religious beliefs and cultural values, or preference for having people of certain nationalities or technical backgrounds as direct collaborators.

Knowledge is retained information concerning facts, concepts, relationships and processes. It is useful to distinguish between general and specialized knowledge. In consulting, general knowledge concerns economic, social, political and cultural processes, institutions and environments that constitute a general background for consulting interventions in specific organizations or systems. There are then two sorts of specialized knowledge. The first area concerns the object of consulting, i.e. the consultant's special sector and/or technical area of intervention. Examples of sectors are manufacturing, banking or insurance, while examples of technical areas are marketing, production organization, job evaluation or corporate strategy. The second area of knowledge concerns consulting *per se* — its principles, processes, organization, methods and techniques.

Skills are the abilities to do things: to apply knowledge, aptitudes and attitudes effectively in work situations. Skills too can be broken down into several groups. Some of the consultant's skills will be generic, e.g. social and cultural skills. Other skills will be common to consultants and their clients (managers and entrepreneurs) using consultants. The difference will be in the required breadth and depth of mastery of certain skills. Probably the consultant will be more skilful in interviewing and providing advice than a typical manager, but may lag behind managers in the skills of organizing, coordinating, mobilizing people or speedy decision-making. There are, then, the skills that are particular to consultants, advisers and other helpers whose job has been described as "getting things done when you are not in charge".[5] These professionals have to be competent in assessing problems and opportunities of organizations for which they are not responsible and where they have not worked, developing and presenting proposals, providing feedback and reports to decision-makers and their collaborators, and so on.

The difference between the content and the level of competency is significant. Thus, various elements of managing consultancy projects (assignments) are listed among key consultant skills and components of their body of knowledge. However, there will be a difference in required level of this competence between an entry-level consultant and a partner supervising several major projects. This difference will have to be duly reflected in training programmes for various levels of consultants.

Box 33.1 Areas of consultant knowledge and skills

Orientation to management consulting

- Nature and objectives of consulting; consultants and clients; consulting and change
- Basic consulting styles and approaches
- Types of consulting services and organizations

Consulting and other professions

- Management consulting as a career
- Organization of the profession
- Professional ethics and conduct
- Historical development, present position and future perspectives of consulting

Overview of the consulting process

- Framework and stages of a consulting assignment (project)
- Entry
- Diagnosis
- Action planning
- Implementation
- Termination

Analytical and problem-solving skills

- Systematic approach to problem solving in management and business
- Methods for diagnosing organizations and their performance
- Data collection and recording
- Data and problem analysis
- Techniques for developing action proposals
- Creative thinking
- Evaluating and selecting alternatives
- Measuring and evaluating project results

Behavioural, communication and change management skills

- Human and behavioural aspects of the consulting process and the consultant-client relationship
- The client's psychology
- Behavioural roles of the consultant and the client
- Consulting and culture
- Techniques for diagnosing attitudes, human relations, behaviour and management styles
- Techniques for generating and assisting change in people and in organizations
- Managing conflict
- Communication and persuasion techniques
- Teamwork and the conduct of meetings
- Using training in consulting; assessing client training needs; designing training programmes
- Management and staff training concepts and techniques
- Courtesy and etiquette in consultant-client relations
- Effective report writing and presentation

Marketing and managing assignments

- Principles of marketing in professional services
- Marketing approaches and techniques
- Consultant selection criteria and procedures
- Proposals to clients (planning, preparation, presentation)
- Consulting contracts and their negotiation
- Fee setting
- Structuring, planning and staffing an assignment (project)
- Managing and controlling an assignment (project)
- Reporting to the client and to the consulting firm

Managing and developing a consulting firm

- Considerations in establishing and structuring a consulting firm; legal forms
- Economics and strategy of a consulting firm
- Governance, organizational culture and management style in professional firms
- Recruiting, developing and remunerating consultants
- Financial management
- Operational management and control; performance monitoring
- Quality assurance and management
- Professional responsibility and liability
- Information technology in professional firms
- Internal administration and office management

A body of consultant knowledge and skills

In Chapter 6 we referred to a "body of knowledge" — a listing of the areas of competence of a mature and experienced management consultant. As a rule, such a document will indicate common threshold competences, not those required for doing a particular job and achieving superior performance. In compiling their body of knowledge, several national institutes of management consultants and the International Council of Management Consulting Institutes (ICMCI) pursued certification as the main criterion in deciding what to include: the body describes competences to be mastered by consultants wishing to be certified (accredited) by one of the national institutes.

It is useful to refer to a complete text of a body of knowledge in designing a training programme for consultants. However, it is important not to forget that these documents are not intended to lay down the scientific foundations of consulting as a field of learning. The reader may well conclude that, in his or her particular context, other topics should be covered in training, or the topics listed should be grouped and presented in a different way.

Irrespective of differences in terminology and layout, the principal areas covered in a common body of consultant knowledge will normally be close to those outlined in box 33.1, above. The multidisciplinary nature of the science and the art of consulting is obvious, as the topics listed draw from sociology, psychology, statistics, economics, management and organization theory, and other disciplines. Some topics are confined to the description of good or best experience without aiming at scientific analysis and theoretical justification.

Substantive area of management and business expertise

In current consulting, training and development in the substantive areas of the consultant's expertise are becoming ever more important. There are several reasons for this. New recruits may have an excellent technical background but a rather narrow perspective and limited knowledge of the business, management and social environment. While progressing in their careers and accepting more complex assignments, many consultants need to master new areas and widen their knowledge base in addition to their original background and main area of competence.

Another reason is the extremely high speed with which management concepts and techniques emerge, gain importance and popularity, and become obsolete — to be replaced by other concepts and techniques in many cases. This race for originality and novelty forces consultants to be always fully up to date and well informed. While it is not easy to recognize the difference between essential state-of-the-art developments and passing fads, a management consultant cannot really afford to answer a client enquiring about a new technique: "Never heard of it", or "You can ignore it, it's not important to you".

Furthermore, information and telecommunications technology is omnipresent and rapidly changing in all sectors and functions of management. Training and retraining in IT and its management applications has therefore become a normal part of any consultant development programme.

Consultants who specialize sectorally need to keep abreast of sectoral developments, including sector-specific technologies, principal products, leading producers and distributors, competition, restructuring of firms, economic trends and prospects, employment and social issues, environmental considerations and the like.

Consultant development matrix

The consultant development matrix in figure 33.1 (overleaf) gives a rough idea of how training needs change in the course of a typical consulting career. To simplify, three stages in the career are shown (initial, advanced, managerial). Between these stages, there is a shift in emphasis from basic, operational and methodology issues, dominating initial training, through assignment (project) marketing and management, to firm (practice) management and development. The table also shows that owing to the rapidly changing state of the art in consulting, every area requires some updating at all levels of the hierarchy.

Impact of the firm's strategic choices

Finally, remember that in Chapter 24 we stressed the close relationship between the consulting firm's basic strategic choices, and the training and development of its professional staff. Although some common basics have to be given to all consultants, normally firms do not develop their staff to make them more competent in general terms, but to fit the firm's particular profile and to understand and implement its strategy. Strategies can be very different, and so will be training policies and programmes. For example, firms engaged mainly in the development and installation of management systems will provide a great deal of formal and structured staff training in the design and application of these systems. Firms practising action learning and process consulting as their principal intervention technologies will put more emphasis on behavioural, communication and human resource development approaches and techniques.

33.2 Training of new consultants

Objectives of training

The overall objective of an initial training programme for new consultants is:

> To ensure that the consultant has the ability and confidence to carry out assignments in his or her field of management.

As consulting is not easy, initial training must explain and demonstrate this, but at the same time provide enough guidance for new entrants to start their first assignment confident of their ability and enthusiastic in their determination.

Figure 33.1 Consultant development matrix

Areas covered	Level			
	Initial	Advanced (project manager)	Managerial (partner)	Updating (all levels)
1. Substantive expertise				
1.1 Main area	★ ★ ★	★ ★	★	★
1.2 Context, environment	★ ★ ★	★ ★	★ ★	★
1.3 Related areas	★ ★ ★	★ ★	★	★
2. Consulting approach				
2.1 Basics, general principles	★ ★ ★	★		★
2.2 Methods and techniques	★ ★ ★	★ ★		★
2.3 Managing change	★ ★ ★	★ ★ ★	★ ★	★
2.4 Ethics, professionalism	★ ★ ★	★ ★	★ ★	★
3. Managing the process				
3.1 Marketing assignments	★ ★	★ ★ ★	★ ★	★
3.2 Managing assignments	★	★ ★ ★	★ ★	★
4. Managing the firm				
4.1 Practice management		★ ★	★ ★ ★	★
4.2 Practice development		★ ★	★ ★ ★	★

The overall objective quoted above can be broken down into four sub-objectives, as follows:

> 1. To ensure that the consultant can investigate an existing situation and design improvements.

This requires the ability to gather information and analyse it critically, to identify all aspects of the problem, and then to design practical improvements using imagination and creative ability.

> 2. To ensure that the consultant can develop a collaborative relationship with the client, gain acceptance of the proposed changes, and implement change satisfactorily.

The ability to make contacts with people easily, an understanding of factors stimulating or inhibiting change, a sound knowledge of the techniques of communication and persuasion, and good interaction with people during implementation, are vital parts of a consultant's armoury. They are stressed and practised during initial training.

> 3. To ensure proficiency in the consultant's field or discipline.

This includes knowledge of the technical aspects of the field, some of which consultants may not have encountered in their previous career, and the ability to apply them to a client's problems. At the same time, consultants must be able to see the problems of their particular functional field in the broader context of an overall management strategy, and relate them to other functional areas and to the environment in which an enterprise operates.

> 4. To satisfy the management of the consulting firm that the consultant is capable of working independently and under pressure to the required standard.

It would be unrealistic to require new consultants to be able to tackle any difficult assignment immediately after training. Nevertheless, by the end of the initial training period they must have demonstrated their ability to handle a field assignment. At the same time, a systematic evaluation of the trainees' performance should give the firm enough information about the strengths and weaknesses of new colleagues for the team leader to be able to help them by proper guidance and coaching during the first assignments.

Patterns of initial training

The design of an initial training programme depends on many variables, including the specific needs of individual trainees and the resources and policies of the consulting firm. The practices of consulting firms vary. There is a broad range of initial training programmes, from precisely planned and structured programmes to totally informal training of undetermined duration. It is not the purpose of this chapter to prescribe one particular pattern for all conditions.

There are, however, certain principles which should be reflected in any programme for new consultants, and also certain patterns which have given good results in varying situations.

Individualization. New entrants have different backgrounds in terms of knowledge and experience, and different personal characteristics. There should be no uniform initial training programme, although some elements of initial training will be given to every new consultant. We will show below how the training programme can be individualized without becoming too difficult and expensive for the consulting firm to organize.

Practicality. Some aspects and methods of consulting can be explained and simulated during a course, but most of the training has to take the form of practice in carrying out the various steps of a consulting assignment and in interacting with clients, under the guidance of a senior consultant. The programme must include both the observation of experienced consultants in action and a direct execution of practical consulting tasks.

Stretching the trainees. The programme should demonstrate that consulting is demanding in time, effort and brainpower, so that trainees are under no illusion about the responsibilities and performance standards they have accepted in their newly chosen profession.

Length of programme. Although it could be argued that new consultants will need several years of experience to become fully competent and able to operate with a minimum of guidance and supervision, it would be impractical, and psychologically unsound, to maintain new consultants in the category of trainees for too long. Assuming normal conditions of recruitment, the period of initial training would not exceed 6 to 12 months.

Coaching. The new consultants' learning will be strongly influenced by the nature of the work assigned to them and by the behaviour of their supervisors and other senior colleagues. Therefore professional firms in consulting and other fields make their partners and other seniors personally responsible for the development of their younger and less experienced associates. Most of this development is done informally, at work, by discussing technical, behavioural and other relevant issues.

Basic components of the training programme

An ideal programme of initial training will have three basic components:
— training courses for new consultants;
— practical field training at client organizations;
— individual study.

A *training course for new consultants* will cover those aspects of consulting which have to be given to all trainees, and can be dealt with in a classroom situation, using a variety of training methods as discussed in section 33.3, below.

As a rule, this will be a full-time residential course and its total duration may be between 2 and 12 weeks. Large consulting firms can afford longer courses, and hold them at their own headquarters or training centres. Small firms may have to send their new members to an external course for management consultants, complementing such a course by short workshops dealing with their specific policies, work concepts and issues.

Field (on-the-job) training is intended to develop a range of practical skills, demonstrate consulting in action, and mould the trainees' attitudes towards their new profession on the basis of personal first-hand experience. It should provide opportunities and time for improving characteristics such as good judgement, analytical and problem-solving ability, interpersonal relations, and ability to communicate and persuade. The training programme will also aim at improving other qualities such as self-confidence, integrity and independence. In planning this part of the training the consulting firm enjoys great flexibility, provided that it has enough clients willing to receive newly recruited consultants, and experienced consultants who have the time, ability and motivation to train and coach new colleagues.

Whether the trainee's time spent at a client organization should be charged to the client is a delicate matter which should be frankly discussed with clients, without imposing arrangements that clients would accept reluctantly. In examining the curricula vitae of consultants proposed for an assignments, the client will easily identify new recruits with no or little consulting experience. He will wish to be informed not only about these new consultants' capabilities and usefulness, but also about financial arrangements. While it is justifiable to ask clients to pay some fee if a trainee's work produces tangible results, it is neither reasonable nor fair to expect individual clients to bear directly the cost of training new consultants. This should be a general overhead in the consulting firm's costs. A compromise solution may be found by charging a reduced fee, or a fee paid for a part of the trainee's time. The same applies to the trainer's time — if the trainer is an operating consultant, time spent on guiding and coaching trainees should not be charged to the client.

Assignments for which the client will be charged a flat fee may provide a more favourable training ground than if the fees are time based. The client who knows that the fee will remain the same irrespective of the number of consultants used and time spent will feel more comfortable about the use of inexperienced consultants in a project team.

Individual study is another component which provides for flexibility of training. A new consultant can fill some knowledge gaps by reading professional books and articles, final assignment reports, operating manuals and other documentation.

In an ideal situation these three components of the initial training may be combined and scheduled as follows:

- first (introductory) part of the course for new consultants (say between two and six weeks);
- field training (length as necessary and feasible);

- second part of formal training (say one to six weeks), including one or more specialized seminars and/or workshops on operating methods, and familiarization with technical services, people and documentation at the consulting firm's headquarters;
- field training continues as appropriate;
- no specific period is reserved for individual study — this will be done in parallel with the course and with field training (the consultant may have to make allowance for many overtime hours).

A consulting firm may, however, find it impossible to follow this schedule for various practical reasons: the number of trainees may not warrant an in-house course, or the firm can only afford a short introductory workshop for new entrants. The training task may thus become more difficult for everybody concerned and a new entrant will have to pick up much more through individual study and by observing other colleagues at work.

The trainer's role

During recruitment and selection, new consultants meet senior people in the organization only for a short time. Thus the trainer is the first member of the organization whom new consultants get to know well. He sets an example of how a consultant behaves, and how he achieves results largely without the authority to impose his ideas. The trainer therefore plays an important part in developing the characteristics that differentiate consultants from managers, executives, accountants, auditors or researchers. Apart from instilling knowledge, the trainer sets the tone for new consultants in their work with clients, and helps them to identify with the consulting firm's philosophy and culture.

The *head-office trainer* is a senior person with wide experience of consulting and training. He or she has overall responsibility for the training of new consultants, including the programming of field training. He or she is in charge of the central training course for new consultants and will personally give a number of sessions in the course.

In a training course for consultant induction, each trainee is viewed as an individual who will spend much of his or her time as the sole operating consultant on an assignment. Behaviour within the group and ability to join in the common cause are also noted. So are the trainee's reactions to the problems and ideas discussed during the course. The trainer does not take a teacher-and-pupil attitude and the atmosphere in the course room is not that of a schoolroom. This point may seem obvious, but a trainer also has to learn to do the job for the first time and may start by being something of a pedant. A trainee should find the trainer a good friend and counsellor on whom he or she can rely at any time for guidance and help.

Field trainers are operating consultants or team leaders working with clients. They are already practising in the field in which the new consultant will operate, and arrange for him or her to gradually take over a part of the assignment. They too must have training and coaching capabilities, be sympathetic to the needs of the new consultant, and be able to impart enthusiasm for working with a client. The field trainer develops a very special relationship with the new consultant. As the two of them will be spending some evenings together, a bond of friendship is usually born, and this may persist for many years after training is completed.

Evaluation of training

New consultants' progress in training is carefully watched by those in contact with them and a series of reports is issued. The purpose is to ascertain whether the training is achieving its objectives, propose corrective measures (extension of the training programme, inclusion of new subjects for individual study and the like), and gather information on the strengths and weaknesses of new members of the firm (this is invaluable to those who will supervise their first assignments). Needless to say, evaluation also helps to improve the training policies and practices of the consulting firm.

Many consulting firms use a system of confidential reports in which the trainers (both at head office and in the field) give their personal appraisal of the trainee.

At least two reports are required: one at the end of the induction training course and one at the end of field training. Additional reports may be required if the initial training is broken down into several assignments involving different team leaders, or if the length of field training warrants interim progress reports.

The reports (see an example of a report form in figure 33.2, overleaf) evaluate the new consultant under a number of headings. The assessments are usually on a numerical scale with supporting comments and examples. The scale can use a range of numbers or letters, a common system being a five- or three-point scale, as follows:

1. Excellent	A. Satisfactory
2. Very good	B. Satisfactory with reservations
3. Standard	C. Unsatisfactory
4. Poor	
5. Unsatisfactory	

The standard against which the new consultant is measured is the standard expected by the firm of operating consultants on their first assignment. The question to be answered is: "On present showing, will he or she be ready to operate at the end of the training?" Consistency of interpretation of the standard by the central trainer, field trainers and supervisors derives from their common experience and their knowledge of current operating requirements.

The trainers review with the trainees how they are progressing, informally during work and training sessions, and in formal discussions which are held when an evaluation report is prepared. New consultants must be told of their strengths, weaknesses, and any other aspects of their work.

Figure 33.2 Training report form

TRAINING REPORT (confidential)		Report number	Date
Trainee		Trainer	
Supervisor		Client	

Type of report	☐ Interim report ☐ Final report	☐ Head office training ☐ Field training

Reporting period	Starting date	Finishing date	Duration in weeks

Description of work performed

Evaluation (mark X in the appropriate column; comments are required if marked other than satisfactory)	A - satisfactory			
		B - satisfactory with reservations		
			C - unsatisfactory	
				Comments
I. Personal attributes				
Intellectual capacity				
Professional conduct				
Physical appearance and bearing				
Initiative and energy				
Person-to-person communication				
Social behaviour				
II. Technical qualities (general)				
Diagnostic skills				
Preparing suggestions				
Techniques of introducing change				
Verbal reporting				
Written reports				
III. Specific functional or sectoral skills				

Figure 33.2 *(cont.)*

Evaluation	A	B	C	Comments
IV. General observations				
Attendance and punctuality				
Course contribution (as individual)				
Course contribution (to group work)				
Contribution to field work				
Meeting set deadlines				
Speed and accuracy				

Overall assessment by the trainer

Supervisor's comments

Recommendations concerning first assignments and future training

Other comments or decisions

In addition to these discussions, senior members of the consulting organization meet with new consultants during training. Apart from giving all the participants an opportunity to talk about the work and progress, these meetings ensure that new consultants become fully integrated members of the firm. They show that management is interested in the new consultants, aware of their progress, and making plans for their assignment after completion of training.

The importance of open criticism and frankness need hardly be stressed. Both the future effectiveness and life of the consulting organization, and the long-term career prospects of new consultants, depend on the excellent professional work of each individual. Any doubts about a new consultant's ability are not hidden, but are discussed with him or her and with the supervisors. If the doubts cannot be resolved by the end of the training programme, a decision is required on whether the new consultant stays or terminates employment. On balance, termination of employment at this early moment may be the better choice, both for the new consultant and for the organization. However, an early termination can be an exception if the initial selection of candidates is carried out in a competent manner.

At the end of the initial training programme it is useful to draw conclusions on the further training needs of the new consultant and on the best ways of meeting them (by giving preference to certain types of assignments at the beginning, by further individual study, by attaching the consultant to team leaders chosen for their particular qualities, etc.).

The design and execution of the training programme also require evaluation. Trainees may be asked to comment on the course in the usual way. These can be general or specific comments on the content of individual exercises and the performance of each trainer. Care is necessary to preserve confidence — trainees may be reluctant to openly criticize their current or potential future superiors. However, the feedback to individual trainers can spur them to improve their sessions.

Comments and criticism may be obtained from senior consultants responsible for the early assignments. They may find the new consultants lacking in specific skills; these deficiencies may be due to omissions, or poor coverage of certain subjects, either in the initial head-office training course or during the field training. New consultants should also be asked, both during and after field training, whether they found the practical preparation for the first assignments adequate.

33.3 Training methods

Training course methods

The training of new consultants uses a variety of training methods, with emphasis on participative methods, and on those where the trainee can adjust the pace of learning to individual capabilities.

Box 33.2 Training in process consulting

Internal development programmes need to draw on knowledge in such fields as industrial sociology, political science, organizational behaviour, psychology, social psychology and interpersonal communication. But such programmes need to emphasize skill more than knowledge, through discussion and role-playing sessions in which the skills are acquired through practice, reflection, and experimentation. The discussion should not be about what you *should know*, nor even about what you *should do*, but about what you *are doing*, here and now, and about what you have done and will be doing, in specific interactions with members of a client organization. In other words, process-skill development sessions should primarily consist of open discussion among colleagues of specific client case situations, supplemented by role plays of actual and desired consultant-client interactions. The sessions should be led by someone expert at facilitating this kind of experiential learning, who can bring to bear, when relevant, simple but powerful behavioural concepts to assist in understanding past events and to stimulate useful experimentation with new approaches.

The three most relevant skills to develop for an effective consulting process are, in my opinion: diagnosing behaviour, listening, and behaving authentically.

Diagnostic skill is developed by examining and discussing what is taking place within client organizations. These discussions develop hypotheses that can be tested in subsequent client contacts. In such discussions and experiments with different approaches, consultants may discover, perhaps to their discomfort, that effective diagnosis of behaviour is often in part an intuitive and not just a logical process.

Listening of a very special kind is an essential consulting process skill. Good consultants learn how to listen with understanding to what is meant as well as to what is said, to feelings as well as to facts, to what is hard to admit and not just easy to say. There is no way to develop this skill except by practising it, with the benefit of feedback from a friendly audience which has heard the same words and observed the same non-verbal signals. It is easy to tell consultants how they ought to listen and have them agree that this is desirable. But to help them to learn that they do not listen as well as they think, and then to produce a worthwhile improvement in this ability, in practice, requires a series of carefully designed and effectively conducted workshop sessions. It does not happen all at once.

Behaving authentically needs to be seen as an equally necessary skill. Consultants need to be able to be themselves, to behave according to their own values, and sometimes to confront clients with unwelcome facts and opinions. Again, small group discussions and role plays of actual experiences provide the best setting in which to develop the skill of understanding oneself as well as others, and of usefully and constructively expressing one's own point of view even when the other person may not want to hear it.

Author: Arthur Turner.

Subjects which involve mainly the imparting of knowledge may require some lecturing, but this should be supplemented by discussions, practical exercises, case-studies and other techniques. In many cases, lecturing can be replaced by the reading of texts (e.g. on the origin and history of consulting, on types and specialization of consulting firms), or by using audio-visual learning packages (e.g. videotapes). Subjects involving skill improvement require techniques that permit practice. This can be done to some extent in a training course by using properly chosen learning situations and exercises. Experience with methods suitable to training in process consulting skills is summarized in box 33.2 (page 699).

Case-studies can introduce the new consultant to various consulting situations and provide good material for discussion; the consulting firm may be in a position to prepare its own case studies, or histories, from previous assignments.

Practical exercises can lead the new consultant through common consulting practices, such as:

- effective speaking and persuasion;
- interviewing;
- analysing company accounts and preparing ratios;
- discussion leading and control;
- written communication;
- methods charting and work measurement;
- designing systems and procedures.

Role-playing provides an excellent way of introducing consulting practice into learning situations. It takes place in a controlled situation, i.e. in a classroom, where mistakes are used to enhance learning and have no disastrous consequences. For example, as a large part of a consultant's work on assignment consists of presenting proposals to clients and their staff, it is useful to organize role-playing exercises in:

— interviewing staff to obtain facts about an assignment problem and find out about their expectations;

— dealing with awkward situations or complaints from staff about proposed changes;

— persuading members of the client's staff to accept a new method of operation;

— explaining to the client conclusions drawn from his financial reports;

— presenting an assignment report to the client;

— dealing with embarrassing questions from the client or members of his staff.

Role-playing exercises need to be realistic, and test the participants under conditions as near as possible to those found in everyday life. Feedback after the exercise is essential. This suggests four requirements:

- a trainee playing the part of a consultant;
- other trainees playing client or other roles;
- at least two trainees acting as observers, with a brief to watch for certain features of the players' behaviour;
- the preparation of thorough briefs for all participants.

Time is allowed for briefing the role-players and observers, and for the absorption of the material including the preparation of any figures. After the role-playing, observers comment and a general discussion leads to the identification of lessons to be learned. Aids such as tape recorders or closed-circuit television may be used.

Field-training methods

In field training, the consultant learns mainly by doing practical diagnostic, problem-solving and project work in direct collaboration and interaction with other consultants and the client. As this is carried out in a real-life situation, which may be very sensitive to errors and *faux pas*, at the beginning the trainee will be guided and controlled by the trainer in more detail than might be necessary in another situation. It may not, however, be easy to find situations in which new consultants could practise not only a few, but a wide range of the techniques that should eventually make up their consulting kit.

Here again, feedback on what the consultant did and how he or she did it is an essential dimension of training. The team leader or supervisor acting as field trainer must provide this feedback, creating an atmosphere in which any aspect of work and behaviour can be openly discussed without embarrassing the new colleague. The whole assignment team may participate in such discussions.

Role-playing can be used to rehearse activities before the "live" show later. In this form of role-playing, the new consultant and the trainer rehearse in the office or at home in the evening, and are able to anticipate and correct snags.

In certain cases a whole real, not fictitious, consulting project can be designed and used primarily as a training experience. This has been done in several courses for consultants, as well as in various types of course for managers and students of management. Such a simulation exercise can be very close to an actual situation. Yet the differences should not be lost from sight: if the client has agreed to a consulting project, but does not pay a normal fee for it, this may affect the participation and attitudes of the client staff when working with the trainee consultant.

33.4 Further training and development of consultants

We know that in management consulting lifelong education is a must. This idea is not new. Many consultancy firms have gained and maintained their excellent reputation precisely because of their continual efforts to upgrade staff competence.

Principal directions of consultants' development

Most staff development activities in consulting firms fall under one or more of the following four areas.

Upgrading functional proficiency. Keeping abreast of developments and becoming more knowledgeable and competent in his or her own field together form the basis of an operating consultant's further development. Many training and development activities in consulting firms are geared to this objective.

Mastering new fields. A consultant may learn new subjects complementary to his or her main field in order to broaden the ability to undertake assignments touching on several management functions, perhaps with a view to becoming an all-round consultant, able to lead teams of mixed functional specialists, to act as adviser on general management problems, and to undertake diagnostic surveys of business companies and other organizations. Another reason for learning new subjects may be the consulting organization's intention to become active in new technical fields. Many consulting firms prefer to transfer their more dynamic consultants, familiar with the organization's philosophy and practices, to these new activities rather than staff them with new recruits.

Upgrading behavioural and process-consulting skills. Experience has amply demonstrated that initial training of a new consultant is just a first step in developing the know-how needed to perceive, diagnose, understand and influence human behaviour in organizations. Further training of all consultants (without any exception) therefore deals with the "how" of management consulting as it relates to people, including effective client-consultant relations, the consultant's role in organizational change, and the process-consulting skills required for various situations.

Preparing for career development. This includes personal development needed for the positions of team leaders, supervisors, division heads, partners and other senior positions concerned with client relations, management and business expansion. Career advancement carries with it the need to use a broader approach and develop technical competence in several fields.

Organization and methods of further development

Certain features of consulting practice make further training and development difficult to organize. Typically, consultants working with one firm in the same discipline are geographically dispersed on individual assignments. To arrange a technical discussion among specialists may require a special organizational effort. Furthermore, the highly individualized character of many consulting assignments encourages consultants to become individualists, and this creates a constant problem in sharing work experiences with other colleagues.

Nevertheless, the profession also has many features which facilitate the consultant's development. A consultant's energy and time are much less absorbed by routine matters and established procedures than those of a manager involved in the same technical field. The consultant can approach every new assignment as a challenging exercise where innovation is both possible and desirable, and can thus refine his method almost continually. He is never short of opportunities for the practical application of ideas and suggestions found in the literature or other sources. Furthermore, a consultant learns a great deal from any client organization, but to reinforce learning he must compare, evaluate, generalize, conceptualize and try to apply a new, more effective approach to successive assignments. He has to avoid the pitfall of forgetting that every client organization and every assignment are unique, and mechanically applying past solutions to new situations.

Clearly, most of the learning from experience, including the consultants' own and their colleagues' experience, as well as the clients' experience, takes place on the job: it is learning by doing and by observing how others do. It should, however, be enhanced by other learning opportunities and approaches.

Professional guidance by senior consultants. Partners, supervising consultants and team leaders, among others, are generally responsible for the development of more junior consultants who report to them. They provide guidance when assigning work, examining work progress and discussing solutions to be proposed to clients. Such discussions can easily be broadened to inform the operating consultants of experience from other assignments, or techniques used by colleagues. A major feature of coaching by senior consultants is that it should help operating consultants to develop their personal qualities and communication skills. Informal discussions should be arranged within the assignment teams on experience gained from joint work, and used for staff development on a regular basis.

Workshops and conferences. Short workshops and conferences for professional staff are organized in many consulting firms. There may be an annual conference which deals with technical and methodological topics useful to all consultants, as well as policy and administrative matters. Workshops and seminars may be organized in functional divisions, on a regional basis, or in other ways. There are also various external seminars on management and consulting topics from which consultants might benefit. Such services are available from consultants' associations, management institutes, and in some countries also from private consultants who concentrate on training other consultants.

Information to consulting staff. While dissemination of information by itself does not guarantee training and development (e.g. information may be ignored or misunderstood), it is a basic input for learning in the consulting organization. A properly organized system of information and documentation should supply operating consultants with facts and ideas which they should know. Additional information may be forthcoming as a result of a consultant's membership of a professional association. This can be a consultants' institute or a specialized association in fields such as applied psychology, training, management development, marketing or other.

Reading. Consultants have to acquire the habit of reading the main business and professional periodicals, technical papers, important new publications and internal consulting reports relevant to their field.

Research and development assignments. Special project assignments, such as developing a new line of consulting, or preparing an operating manual, are excellent learning opportunities for senior staff members.

Training others. One of the best methods of self-development is training other people. Consultants have many opportunities to do this: for the client's personnel during assignments, at the consulting firm's training centre, as supervisors of younger consultants during operating assignments, as part-time teachers at management institutes and schools, or as speakers at professional conferences.

Training for supervisory and managerial functions. Promotion to the role of supervisor usually takes place after several years in an operating role. Some experience of the role is gained by seeing seniors in action, and by guiding new consultant trainees. Training on promotion is usually quite short and is provided by experienced seniors who are good trainers. Training is given partly in formal sessions at head office and partly with experienced seniors in action. Head-office training and briefing require about three weeks, while coaching by an experienced senior may extend over some months. During this time the promoted consultant works largely alone, with only occasional guidance and advice from a more experienced colleague.

Planning and budgeting

The diversity of individual consultants' career paths and training needs, as well as the desire to be flexible in meeting current clients' requirements, make it difficult to plan staff development and to observe what has been planned. Yet some planning is useful.

Some consulting firms use indicative standards showing the amount of formal training which, on average, a staff member would undergo in one calendar year: for example, between 40 and 60 hours of formal training. A corresponding budget can then be worked out, bearing in mind whether the training will be arranged internally or externally. As a rule, the cost of training per staff member will be higher in comparison to the cost of training per manager or staff member in many other sectors.

Individual planning is even more important. It is useful to establish training objectives which reflect career objectives and against which the consultant can measure his or her progress. In particular, such training objectives should be defined for the first years of operating, based on the evaluation made at the end of the initial training programme, and the subsequent periodical performance reviews. While some flexibility in deciding on participation in specific training events will always be required, training must not constantly be put off in order to cope with the current workload.

Motivation for consultant development

In consulting, more than in many other occupations, the individual bears the main responsibility for his or her own development. The consultant's professional development is self-development above all, and the results achieved will depend mainly on a person's ambition, initiative, determination, perseverance and intellectual capabilities. This is self-evident to the sole practitioner, who knows very well that he or she takes full responsibility for his or her own future. However, a member of a consulting firm working on jobs assigned to him or her by management can also show a great deal of initiative and interest in achieving his or her career goals and training objectives, and can find a great many opportunities for improving competence.

Most consultants understand that to stop learning is equal to becoming very vulnerable, less interesting to clients and an easy target for competitors. Invariably, personal development and learning get high marks in rating consulting firms' priority concerns. To many consultants as people, learning is a vital need, a natural part of their lifestyle. There are, however, forces and constraints that can hamper consultant development quite seriously.

A consultant's natural desire to learn tends to wane if he or she sees that the firm is more interested in, and remunerates its staff better for, achieving short-term objectives such as high personal billing and bringing in new clients. In a similar vein, if the firm is keen to get more of any business, the consultant will be discouraged from looking for assignments that provide good opportunities for learning something new, but are more difficult to negotiate and/or execute.

If promotion and pay clearly favour other criteria (e.g. seniority or higher management's personal preferences), this policy may have a negative effect on self-development. To see senior partners who for years occupy the same positions and collect the same pay cheques without any self-development and performance-improvement effort is demotivating not only to younger consultants, but also to other partners.

A poor choice of trainers can be equally damaging. This has happened in those consulting firms where the trainers' jobs were given to those seniors who were not so good at dealing with clients or managing operations.

Most importantly, all professional firms without any exception stress that training and coaching the staff members assigned to them is a crucial responsibility of all professionals, including those in the highest management functions in the firm. In practice, however, many senior professionals devote all their time and know-how to firm management, business promotion and dealing personally with important clients. This tends to be encouraged by the compensation system, which may ignore, or allocate a small weight to, the senior consultants' contribution to the development of other staff members. If this has been the prevailing practice for years, it has probably turned into a cultural value. Senior professionals who remember well that they "had to make it" without any help from their superiors often think that the next generation ought to be treated in the same way.

In summary, to be successful in consultant development, a consulting firm has to achieve coherence between policy statements, strategic objectives, resource allocation, current assignment management, organization of training and staff motivation at all levels, starting with the newly recruited trainee and ending with the firm's managing partner. Consultants must know what the policy is and must be encouraged to comply with this policy throughout their career.

33.5 Options available to sole practitioners

To survive and progress in his or her field, a sole consulting practitioner needs to continuously improve competence. However, a sole practitioner lacks the knowledge base, training resources and interaction with colleagues available in larger consultancies. Conversely, he or she enjoys more freedom and flexibility in choosing clients, moving to new fields of intervention and deciding about his or her own future.

There are forces that discourage sole practitioners from spending time and money on self-development. Paradoxically, success and high earnings from current business are the most dangerous enemies. A consultant who is in great demand will be tempted to think that he or she is the best expert and that there is no reason to worry about future earnings.

Other consultants complain that they lack time for self-development, are too tired after a heavy working week, cannot concentrate on studying in hotel rooms, or must use every free moment to look for new business. These reasons may sound quite realistic and understandable. Yet they cannot justify the lack of self-development in any profession.

If you are a sole practitioner, the following principal options are available to you.

Self-assessment

From time to time, or periodically and regularly if you find it easier (but at least once a year), you can take a short pause, sit back and think about your career path:

— Are you getting closer to your goals?

— Are clients fully satisfied with your work?

— Are you satisfied with what you have been doing for your clients?

— What have you learned and applied since the last self-assessment?

— Do you feel tired, burned out and out of date?

— Have you once more continued to do the same without any perspective?

When assessing motivation for learning and self-development, it is essential to be honest with oneself. Ambitious professional goals and a strong will to learn go hand in hand:

● Are you motivated enough to work hard for your professional future?

- Do you want to be one of the best experts in your field or are you merely looking for survival in the business?

Networking

In the absence of large-firm professional environment and resources, a single practitioner can draw a lot of benefit from networking with other professionals who have similar concerns.

Informal contacts with other consultants and managers are the simplest form of networking. Association work comes next. Associations are a useful source of contacts, information and learning opportunities. An active participant in association work can suggest and help to start new association activities and recommend priority topics as themes for meetings, committees and workshops.

Business alliances with other independent professionals can be helpful not only for finding new work and delivering projects that exceed the possibilities of one consultant, but also for learning from others.

There is no networking without reciprocity: while you want to learn from others, they are keen to learn from you! They will give if you give.

Looking for technically challenging assignments

Learning is encouraged and becomes a necessity if the consultant keeps looking for assignments that are not a mere repetition of work done many times before. This, of course, is more easily said than done if new business is scarce. Yet it is an objective that can be pursued as a matter of deliberate personal choice.

Formal training opportunities

Short seminars and workshops are a useful form where sole practitioners can update and widen their knowledge of management and business topics or consulting approaches. Careful selection is required in order to avoid losing time and money in training events that, because of their purpose and quality, are not suited for consultants.

Preparing for certification

In several countries, professional institutes practise voluntary certification of management consultants (see section 6.4). Preparing oneself for certification may be a good opportunity for studying new literature on consulting and reading about topics not usually handled in everyday work.

---

[1] E. M. Shays: "Learning must be a life-long job for consultants", in *Journal of Management Consulting* (Milwaukee, Wisconsin), Vol. 1, No. 2, 1983.

[2] In designing training programmes for consultants, it is useful to refer to materials produced by consultants' associations and institutes. In 1989, the Association of Management Consulting

Firms (ACME) in the United States published *Professional profile of management consultants: A body of expertise, skills and attributes*, and *Management consulting: A model course*. This model course is intended for university programmes in consulting, but it provides useful guidance for other consultant training courses. In 1992, the International Council of Management Consulting Institutes compiled its *Uniform body of knowledge for management consultants*, supplemented by a paper giving definitions of topics in the body of knowledge. More recently (1993), the Institute of Management Consultants in the United Kingdom produced *The practice of management consultancy: Training modules for consultants*, intended for four levels in the consultant hierarchy (analyst — consultant — engagement manager — practice manager). The suggested duration of formal training needed to cover all topics in the modules is 60 days.

[3] See R. E. Boyatzis: *The competent manager: A model for effective performance* (New York, Wiley, 1982), and M. Kubr and J. Prokopenko: *Diagnosing management training and development needs: Concepts and techniques*, Management Development Series No. 27 (Geneva, ILO, 1989).

[4] Boyatzis, op. cit., pp. 28-29.

[5] See G. M. Bellman: *Getting things done when you are not in charge* (San Francisco, California, Berrett-Koehler, 1992).

PREPARING FOR THE FUTURE   34

This is the final and concluding chapter of our guide. It is neither an attempt to summarize the preceding 33 chapters, nor an exercise in futurology. We have preferred to take a short look at the future prospects and challenges of consulting by focusing on developments and trends that are already with us, or are likely to emerge in the near future.

Two perspectives are of particular interest to those concerned about the future of management and business consulting: the future developments and opportunities concerning the environment and the markets for consulting services, and changes in the profession itself.

34.1 The changing demand

The future of consulting as a sector of professional services is assured thanks to the ever-changing nature of demand. The world of business, and its technological, social and economic environment, are changing rapidly. Business and government clients will face more and more challenges. To many potential clients, turning to a consultant will be more than a pragmatic decision on how to optimize the use of resources: it will be a necessity owing to the novelty and complexity of the issues at hand, and owing to clients' desire to avail themselves of the best expertise before taking important decisions.

At the present time, a relatively small part of all consulting work deals with state-of-the-art issues of business and management practice. This part is likely to increase, thus creating new service opportunities for consultants. Clients will be increasingly sophisticated and able to handle, with their own resources, many issues for which they used to turn to external consultants in the past. They will prefer to work closely with consultants on issues that are new, difficult and risky, and require a great amount of information, speed of analysis and action, an interdisciplinary and intersectoral perspective, an innovative approach, understanding of social and environmental implications, and availability of special expertise.

Box 34.1 Significant trends that will shape consulting

"The future of management consulting is tied not only to the future of business but to global forces and trends on a much broader scale . . . and with a mandatory interweaving of two primary thrusts:

— Technology: the 'hard' areas of computers, information, automation, communications, biotechnology, etc.
— Humanities: the 'soft' areas of informal management, self-determination, changing personal values, motivation."

James H. Kennedy

"Four issues will shape the consulting industry. Firms that can come to grips with them are likely to be among the largest and most successful: (1) technology; (2) global reach; (3) human capital; and (4) relationship management."

Ed Pringle

"Five objectives will be central to consulting's success in the 1990s: (1) building tighter, more effective links between strategy and the implementing functions; (2) creating working/workable global networks of effective practitioners; (3) driving value-based principles into operating practices; (4) managing change and cultural values; and (5) refocusing corporate organizations around core service activities."

Tom Doorley

"Which will be the strongest-growing service lines? There is little doubt that amongst them will be: (1) human resources, including management training; (2) information technology; (3) logistics; (4) sales and marketing; (5) environmental consulting; and (6) strategy consulting."

Ken Dawson

"To succeed internationally we as consultants will have to think internationally. This means staying on top of developments — economic, financial, political and social — that will affect our clients' enterprises around the globe. We need to be proactive, advising and leading clients on trends worldwide that will affect their businesses."

Jim Kielley

"Services in the general management area will have to be more tightly linked to areas of specialized knowledge and experience. Beyond this, it is going to become essential that consultants focus on emerging issues, particularly those caused by public and private sector interaction. And this means they must learn new roles: combining objective and professional management analysis with greater sensitivity to the social environment."

Tom Cody

Business Week has predicted that "in the next 10 to 15 years the leading management consulting firms could well see their influence and power increase exponentially. That's because the top consulting groups, almost all of them American, probably control the deepest reserve of knowledge on how to manage globally and build worldwide networks of information technology".[1]

In box 34.1, six observers of consulting give their views on significant trends likely to shape the profession in the years to come. In these and all other predictions concerning future demand there is a clear message. Although the body of knowledge underlying the consulting profession has not been fully and precisely defined and may remain largely undefined for a few more years, the demand will be for consultants exhibiting high-level specialist knowledge and able to demonstrate that they always keep abreast of developments in practice and theory.

To say that the time of the consultant-generalist is over would be an exaggeration, and it would contradict our statements about the need to understand and handle interdisciplinary and intersectoral issues. However, to be merely a generalist will not be enough. The general management approach will have to be based on, and coupled with, excellent knowledge and expertise in one or more special fields. Conversely, narrow specialists will be difficult to use as consultants in management. Those specialists will be in great esteem and demand who are modest and wise enough not to think that they are God's gift to the human race, but to acknowledge that, used in isolation, their special knowledge is of little use in dealing with the increasingly complex problems of business and human organizations.

34.2 The changing geographical perspective

Towards a global economy

The current trend towards internationalization and globalization of the world economy has already triggered off some significant developments in the consulting sector. In future years, consulting practices will be more and more international and global, and this trend will be reflected in developments such as:

— providing consulting services to clients in other countries;

— developing multinational consulting practices;

— strengthening collaboration and forming alliances with consultants in several countries;

— recruiting consultants of various nationalities and cultural backgrounds, and requiring the mastery of several languages;

— using international consulting teams;

— applying a multi-country perspective in dealing with business issues;

— handling problems of international and intercultural management;

— adjusting business and management approaches to various country contexts;

— transferring business and management experience among countries, communities and cultures.

In internationalizing their services, management consultants need government support, mainly by lowering and removing barriers to free trade in services, including free movement of information, money and people. Box 34.2 gives an overview of current trends and efforts in this area. It should, however, be stressed that no government and no international agreement has the power to remove deeply rooted and often self-imposed barriers that are due to language, culture, religion, local habits, social or ethnic prejudices, and fear of the unknown. Management consultants keen to think and operate as internationalists must learn themselves how to cope with these barriers.

Box 34.2 Removing barriers to trade in services

To grow as an international service sector, consultants need freedom to operate in foreign markets. Therefore they will greatly benefit from the results of the Uruguay Round of the GATT (General Agreement on Tariffs and Trade) negotiations, concluded by the 108 participating countries on 15 December 1993. The so-called GATS (General Agreement on Trade in Services) foresees further liberalization of international trade in services and urges governments to identify and reduce barriers related to market access and national treatment.

- For *market access* we are referring to issues such as maximum foreign ownership restrictions, restrictions on establishing a local representation or restrictions on choosing a legal form of business.

- With respect to *national treatment* we are essentially talking about measures or practices which restrict competitive opportunities for foreign service companies. These cover the limited use of a company's title or logo, discriminatory restrictions on the mobility and employment of foreign personnel, an exclusion of foreign companies from government contracts, an obligation to involve local consultants in projects, foreign exchange restrictions or scope of practice restrictions applied to foreign consultants.

In assessing the real impact of GATS on consulting or other professional services, the key will be found in the country schedule and the particular government's willingness to bring local legislation and practice gradually into conformity with the general principles of GATS. As of 15 December 1993, the effective close of the Uruguay Round, 103 countries had submitted schedules of specific commitments across the whole range of tradeable services, including in many cases management consulting services. Subsequent negotiating rounds between member countries will aim to eliminate or further reduce restrictions on trade in services.

Source: Information provided by Mario A. Kakabadse, World Trade Organization.

The North American market

Since the advent of consulting, the North American market has established and maintained its leadership position. In 1992-93 its share of the world market attained over 40 per cent, i.e. more than the share of the region in the world economy. North American managers and administrators are used to working with consultants and would turn to them in many instances where their counterparts in other regions would try to cope with the problems at hand with their organizations' own technical resources. No wonder that most innovations in consulting concepts and methods have their origin in North America.

This market will maintain its leadership position in both quantitative and qualitative terms, and will contribute significantly to developments in the profession worldwide. It will, however, become less predominant. American consultants will be increasingly looking for international work opportunities. They will have to make a great effort to improve their understanding of other countries' economies and cultures. Foreign consultants will be increasingly present, and probably quite successful, in the North American market.

Management consulting in Europe

Western Europe on the one hand, and Central and Eastern Europe on the other hand, are two distinctly different markets, although the first steps to their *rapprochement* have been made.

In *Western Europe*, the consulting market can be estimated at some 27-30 per cent of the world market. Its fast development in the last 20 years has been fuelled by the dynamism of European economies and by regional economic integration efforts. The gestation and the establishment of the European Union (EU) have become factors of tremendous importance to the development of consulting. Many barriers to trade in services that still persist in other countries have been removed, or are about to be removed, within the EU. The integration process, including significant changes in the competitive environment, has created many demands for the assistance of consultants.

However, despite progress in regional integration the European consulting market continues to be fragmented because of persisting differences in business practices, languages, taste and local preferences. Most business people in France prefer to communicate and collaborate with a French consultant, not an Irish or a Danish one, and so on. Yet European integration is an irreversible process and consultants will increasingly be able to regard the whole Union, with its current and prospective members, as their market. Sensitivity to national values and local cultures will remain important, perhaps more important than many of the architects of Europe have foreseen.

In *Central and Eastern European countries*, the demand for information and professional advice on management and business exploded in conjunction with the return to a market economy, advancing privatization, and total restructuring and modernization of the economies inherited from the command-economy era. Since the beginning of the 1990s this has been the principal growth market for management consultants, their new frontier. Yet by current international standards this market is still small because of limited resources, modest experience with the use of consultants and an acute shortage of experienced local consulting professionals.

The emerging local consulting profession has been very dynamic in several countries of the region. It has attracted many individuals from research institutes, universities, governments and state-owned enterprises. These people are able to learn quickly, especially if they speak foreign languages and can interact with foreign consultants and business firms. Some of them tend to overestimate their real competence and underestimate the value of experience.

Western European and American consulting firms have been active in the region, with mixed results. Some consultants have rightly taken a long-term perspective, appreciating the imperfections of the current market and understanding that patience, service quality and adaptation to local conditions will be key factors of future successes. Others have looked for easy earnings without bothering to find out about the local clients' real needs, preferences, biases and sophistication.

When foreign consultants started operating in Central and Eastern Europe they were received as missionaries of free and modern business. It did not take long for quite a few of them to spoil their image and be seen as smart money makers. Therefore consultants who are seriously interested in the technically challenging and potentially very large Central and Eastern European market should adopt a highly professional approach, drawing lessons from mistakes made by many colleagues at the outset.

In Central and Eastern Europe, management consulting is rapidly turning into post-privatization consulting. Many new owners start realizing that privatization is a historical achievement and opens a new era of creative entrepreneurship, but provides no guarantee whatsoever that every enterprise will be well managed, dynamic and profitable. Consultants can seize this opportunity to offer their expertise and know-how.

Finally, economic integration with the Western European economy is a major programme objective of the region's business and political leaders. In preparing for it, management consultants can play a key role, and obtain many interesting contracts.

Management consulting in Japan

In Japan, business and government agencies tend to use external advisers to a lesser degree than their North American and Western European colleagues. This explains the relatively smaller size of the current market and the local profession in comparison with other developed countries.

As regards the future, Eiji Mizutani has suggested that in Japan consulting will grow for the following reasons:

- clients are faced with fundamental changes in the business environment;
- more companies are coming to accept the value of outside advice;
- companies are beginning to reduce staff and are thus left with smaller internal resources;
- a growing number of new and smaller companies are entering the marketplace;
- consultants will be called upon to build experience and skills in strategic management;

- consulting has come to be recognized as a good career for top talent out of the universities and among mid-level executives;
- clients will expect consultants to help them with a "scrap and build" methodology to overhaul operations.[2]

To foreign consultants, gaining access to the Japanese market will continue to be difficult on account of traditions, cultural differences, communication problems and other visible or hidden barriers.

The developing world

In the developing countries, services provided by both international and local management consultants have been regarded as one of the inputs in development — a way of injecting needed managerial and business know-how in order to accelerate economic and social development. The bulk of consulting services used to be provided as a part of various development projects and programmes, and funded by international or national technical assistance agencies. Technical assistance brought many foreign consultants to developing countries and also provided a vehicle for the training of local consultants.

In the 1990s, the developing countries can no longer be thought of as homogeneous consulting markets. In technical and business terms, the consulting needs and opportunities in the rapidly industrializing countries are already very similar to those in the economically developed world. In contrast, the consulting markets and the profession in the less developed countries have lagged behind, and are still struggling with the basic difficulties caused by economic stagnation, low growth rates, resource shortages and a deteriorating environment.

This, however, does not imply that management consultants should write off the developing countries' markets. There is scope for expanding and strengthening the local consulting profession using both technical assistance and private business opportunities. The use of foreign consultants will continue to be relatively expensive and should be increasingly confined to technically difficult development projects and to assisting local consultants. The bulk of the economies, including small and medium-sized enterprises and the social sectors, constitute a promising market for consultants who have grown up in local conditions, internalized the local cultures and become fully committed to their countries' development.

34.3 Increasing professionalism in management consulting

In thinking about the consulting profession's future, it would be short-sighted to see only the changing markets and new business opportunities. It is equally important to aim at improvements in the professional side of the service.

Since the Second World War, and especially since the 1960s, the growth of consulting has been spectacular, to approach US$30 billion of annual revenues worldwide in the 1990s. However, this figure is indicative of business growth, not professional development. Although there have been ups and downs, as a business sector consulting has performed brilliantly. Services such as new management know-how, systems, information technology, human resource development or organizational change have been selling extremely well not only because there has been real demand for them, but also because consulting firms of various sizes and profiles have been successful in marketing their services and actually delivering the goods.

Because of these undisputable commercial successes some observers of the consulting scene presume that there cannot really be any serious problem with professional standards and quality. Clients choose freely and if they pay the price, the consulting firm has passed the market test. Its service has been certified by the market as wanted, relevant, useful and of satisfying quality. Why, then, should someone outside the market-place worry about quality standards, ethics, education, the organization of the profession and similar issues? Haven't the successful consulting firms taken care of these issues by themselves?

There are four major reasons why the professional side of consulting will require increased attention in the future.

The first reason is the need to protect the clients. We know well that consulting services are intangible, complex and difficult to assess. In professional services in general, the market test can never play the same role as in the case of mass consumption goods. Yet even goods such as detergents or ice-cream have to undergo tests and meet strict norms defining minimum quality and environmental protection criteria before being granted access to the market-place. In buying complex business and other technical services, clients will increasingly need and request at least basic assurance of competence, honesty, reliability, ability to complete the job, quality and fair pricing. The market by itself does not provide such an assurance. The issue is not how to protect large multinational clients who have already developed sufficient internal competences for selecting and using professional advisers; the issue is how to protect the myriad of smaller and medium-sized clients who need a consultant from time to time and can be easily put off by one unfortunate experience.

The second reason is the need to protect the management consultants themselves. Their image has been tarnished by firms and individuals who have been shameless in selling services and making promises beyond their capabilities. Many clients have paid for services of dubious value. A consultant who feels and behaves as a professional does not want to be held responsible for unprofessional behaviour of others. Yet this is what has been happening: in clients' circles and among the general public there has been a tendency to throw all consultants into the same bag, and regard all of them as people who want to make easy money and cannot be trusted.

The third reason is the need to restore the unity and the balance between the professional and the business side of consulting. Without this unity, consulting risks losing its rationale and identity. In a sense, management and business consulting has become a victim of its own success. The impressive growth of consulting in the last three decades has not been without a price. Rapid expansion, deregulation, tough competition between consulting firms and with firms in other professions, the proliferation of new consultancies due to easy entry, the merger-mania and the shortening of initial training and indoctrination have affected professional standards. To many consultancies, business objectives have become more important than professional objectives. To get more business has become more important than to deliver a perfect service. These changes in consulting have been very similar to those in other, relatively better-established and better-organized professions. Mark Stevens wrote that for generations accountants considered themselves "as professionals who happened to be in business", while in the 1980s this view was reversed and since then they see themselves as "businessmen who happen to be professionals".[3] The same could well have been written about consultants.

The fourth reason is the management consultants' interaction with other professions, including trends such as growing competition for clients or the clients' interest in obtaining harmonized services from advisers belonging to different professions. To survive and maintain their identity in cooperating and competing with other professional service sectors, management consultants must excel in quality, integrity, a comprehensive and dynamic view of the business, and a deep understanding of clients' human concerns.

In Chapter 6 we said that it is probably not too important to decide whether management consulting can at this very moment be regarded as a fully developed and regular profession. What is important are trends, and efforts to enhance positive trends. In the management consulting sector, initiative to detect and enhance positive trends (and indeed arrest negative trends) can be pursued at three levels: an individual firm's level, the profession level and the user (client) level.

The role and responsibility of a consulting firm and its management can hardly be overstressed. The tone has been set by several industry leaders, who have been able to define and consistently apply their own high standards of professional conduct and performance. A large professional firm with a distinct organizational culture and an excellent reputation may find it easy to promote its own standards. Yet nothing but a temptation to gain easy business prevents a small firm, and a sole practitioner, from thinking and acting in the same way. The absence of generally accepted sectoral standards and the modest impact of some professional associations are not an excuse for low standards in any firm.

Turning to the profession level, there is no doubt that consulting can and needs to become better organized in most countries, and internationally. Consultants' voluntary associations should become more visible and aim to increase their impact. Probably there is no need for "one big voice", with a mandate to regulate the whole profession, to use a term that has become popular in the United States. There are differences among consulting firms as regards their technical profiles, conception of professional service, and expectations from their membership in voluntary professional organizations. There is no need to force all firms and individuals to be members of the same professional body. Yet there are common issues and common interests of the profession as a whole. For this reason, the organizations of the profession must find an acceptable formula for communicating with each other and working together in order to represent, defend and educate the profession as a whole. An alternative is government intervention: if the profession proves incapable of self-regulation, governments may decide to step in and start determining what consultants must not do and what behavioural rules they must observe.

The client circles can also make a significant contribution to the professionalization of consulting. In most countries, the market for consulting services has already turned into a buyer's market. Clients can learn how to separate the wheat from the chaff or, as the German consulting association BDU likes to put it, how to identify and ostracize "black sheep". Individual clients can help by stressing professional standards, insisting on high-quality service and rejecting consultants of dubious profiles and reputation. Employers' and industry associations can help by cooperating with consultants' associations and by teaching their own members how to become more competent and more demanding in choosing and using professional services.

---

[1] See *Business Week*, 18 Nov. 1994.

[2] Eiji Mizutani in an address to the World Conference on the Future of Management Consultancy, Rome, May 1993.

[3] M. Stevens: *The Big Six: The selling out of America's top accounting firms* (New York, Simon and Schuster, 1991), p. 22.

APPENDICES

THE CLIENT'S TEN COMMANDMENTS

If you are a user of management consulting services, or a potential user, you may wish to glance through this appendix. The *Ten Commandments* summarize, in telegraphic form, the critical points (not a sequence of steps) of which you need to be aware. Consulting produces good results if consultants are competent in serving clients and clients in using consultants.

---

1. Learn about consulting and consultants!
2. Define your problem!
3. Define your purpose!
4. Choose your consultant!
5. Develop a joint programme!
6. Cooperate actively with your consultant!
7. Involve the consultant in implementation!
8. Monitor progress!
9. Evaluate the results and the consultant!
10. Beware of dependence on consultants!

Now, let us look at the meaning of each Commandment.

1. Learn about consulting and consultants!

Management consulting is a young but dynamic and rapidly developing profession. You can be sure that you will find a consultant for any business or management problem that comes to your mind. But who are these consultants? How do they work? Are they really as good as one often hears? You want to get replies to these questions. Don't wait until the last moment before recruiting a consultant! Find out about consulting and consultants, and try to become a well-informed client who knows the management and business consulting scene!

● This book is also intended for clients. It describes how consultants operate (especially Parts I and II, and selected chapters in Part III), market services (Chapter 25), charge for services (Chapter 26), manage assignments (Chapter 27), and assure quality (Chapter 28). Of course, you may like to see other publications on consulting (Appendix 11).

- There are some special publications on the selection and use of consultants. The ILO has published a companion volume to this book under the title *How to select and use consultants: A client's guide.*

- Reading a book is not enough. Speak with business friends, screen management and business periodicals, attend meetings of management and/or consultants' associations, ask for information from these associations, be alert to news on consulting.

- Criticizing consultants is very fashionable. Make sure that you are informed about such criticism, but don't judge the real value of consulting on the basis of a few caustic articles.

- It is essential to know who is who. Try to collect information on consultants (firms and individuals) who may interest you: what is their speciality and approach, for whom have they worked, what is their reputation, are their fees within your reach?

2. Define your problem!

The purpose of consulting is to help clients in solving their management and business problems. If you have no problem, you do not need a consultant. Therefore you should be convinced that your organization does have a problem which warrants a consulting assignment.

- Define your problem as precisely as possible. What is or could go wrong? What do you want to improve? Why do you need a consultant — are you sure that you and your own people cannot solve the problem?

- Look for new opportunities. Rather than correcting your past shortcomings and errors, a consultant may help you to develop new business, tackle new markets, mobilize new resources and increase your competitive edge.

- If the idea of using a consultant comes from members of your staff who seek your approval, ask them to be explicit and precise in defining the problem and the reasons. Do not accept any superficial and vague justification!

- Keep the definition of your problem open: the consultant will in any case make his or her own diagnosis, and may show that your original definition was biased, narrow or incomplete. The final definition of the problem must be supported by both the client and the consultant.

3. Define your purpose!

The task of the consultancy will be to solve your problem, but you should look at your problem from a wider perspective. What will be the purpose of resolving the problem? What do you want to achieve? What will your organization gain?

Your purposes should be formulated as specific objectives of the consultancy: action (operational) objectives, and learning objectives.

●   Remember that consultants can intervene in various ways. Consider what you want from the consultant in planning and implementing changes in your organization. Information that you lack? Expert advice on your decisions? A new information system? An improved organizational climate? Increased production and sales? Higher profitability? Each of these choices will require a different intervention method and a different volume of consulting services. Your action objectives will reflect your choice.

●   Your learning objectives are equally if not more important. It has been said many times that effective consulting helps clients to learn from their own and the consultant's experience. Define what you want to learn and how you would like to learn during the assignment. This will be your learning objective.

●   Write your objectives down, trying to be as precise as possible. Be flexible and be prepared to redefine these objectives after having spoken with your consultant or received his or her proposals, and even after having started the work. Your consultant may help to redefine your objectives in your own interest.

4. Choose your consultant!

To choose the right consultant is essential, but it is not an easy matter. It requires information, an effective selection procedure, skill in assessing consultants — and patience. Some risk is always involved — but a proper approach to selection will minimize this risk. There are horses for courses, and your aim is to get the right consultant for your organization and the kind of problem you have. You will have to understand and trust each other and enjoy working together. Remember: it is you who is choosing the consultant, not the consultant who is choosing you!

●   Take the choice of a consultant very seriously. Never recruit "someone who just happens to be around" and is easily available, or who has just sent you a flattering letter or an elegant publicity brochure, unless you are sure that he or she is the ideal choice.

●   Use short-lists of consultants, carefully screen candidates to be put on the short-list, get information on their capabilities, clients and past assignments, check leads and references given to you by business and social friends, your own colleagues, consultants' and management associations and any other source.

●   Try to apply a rigorous (though not rigid and bureaucratic) selection procedure including rating and evaluation of consultants' proposals and qualifications. Make the choice as objective as possible and minimize the risk of errors. Improve the procedure on the basis of experience.

- Never give a major assignment to an unknown consultant. If possible, test new consultants on smaller and shorter jobs. Don't pay an unknown consultant an advance for future work.

- Be sure that you choose not only a consulting firm, but also individual consultants employed by this firm (who may be different people from those who came to propose the assignment to you). The consultants have to match personalities in your organization as well as your technical problem.

- If your consultant is sponsored by a technical assistance project or fund, make sure that you have a final say in selection. The consultant will work for you, not for the sponsor. A free consulting service may turn out to cost you a lot if you are not in charge!

5. Develop a joint programme!

The consultant whom you have chosen may be the best one, but he or she is not your employee, and his or her presence and intervention will create an unusual situation in your organization. Careful planning and preparation of the assignment is a necessity.

- Review the proposals received in detail with the consultant, ask questions, suggest improvements in the approach and the work plan.

- Clarify the consultant's role and your own, the style of consulting to be used and responsibilities for all phases of the assignment. Who will do what? How will you and your people cooperate with the consultant? Are you sure that the consultant will not do work that your people can do (this can reduce cost and speed up execution)?

- Reach an agreement on the programme of work to be implemented, the time-table and deadlines to be observed, measurable and controllable results to be attained, reports to be submitted to you and control sessions to be held at critical points of the assignment.

- Settle the financial side clearly and unambiguously: the fee formula and level, the reimbursable expenses, the conditions, form and frequency of payments.

- Sign a contract with the consultant in a form that is customary in your business environment. Use a written contract. Confine the use of verbal agreements to smaller jobs and to consultants whom you know well and trust totally.

6. Cooperate actively with your consultant!

The modern concept of management consulting emphasizes the client's active participation at all stages of the assignment. Both the consultant's and the client's best brains are needed to make the assignment a success. But your involvement does not occur automatically — a real effort is required, especially since a consulting assignment is an additional job to the normal work which goes on in your organization.

- Tell your people about the consultant's presence; introduce the consultant to everyone who should meet him or her.

- Make the right people available at the right time. You will gain nothing by assigning second-rate staff to work with a highly competent adviser.

- Provide readily all information related to the assignment and needed by the consultant (confidential information not required for the assignment does not have to be shared).

- Look for ways in which the design of the assignment can be improved, your participation increased and the consultant's efficiency enhanced — he or she works for you and the ultimate benefit will be yours.

- However, cooperating in the assignment does not mean irritating the consultant, holding his hand, always looking over his shoulder, delaying decisions on his proposals and not letting him proceed with the job. If this is your attitude, don't use consultants.

7. Involve the consultant in implementation!

A universal problem faced by consultants and clients alike is that too many assignments end short of implementation. The report looks all right — but can it be implemented? Can the new scheme work? Are we able to make it work? Will our purpose be achieved? Certain consultants are only too happy to leave the client without implementing the proposals. However, the true professionals do care about implementation and are sorry if they cannot participate in it and learn from it.

- Make it your principle that your consultant will be involved in implementation.

- Choose a degree and form of the consultant's involvement that suit your organization. Several alternatives will be available in most cases.

- If cost is what worries you, choose a light involvement: you implement, but the consultant helps to debug the new scheme and is available if problems arise.

- In any event, avoid implementation by the consultant without the active participation of your staff.

8. Monitor progress!

There are many reasons why the real course of a consulting assignment may deviate from the path originally agreed. Because it is your assignment, and you are keen to get results, it is in your interest to monitor progress very closely and take corrective measures before it is too late.

- Your monitoring will reveal whether the consultant:
  - understands your organization;
  - is taking the right technical direction;

- is behaving as a real professional (with integrity, tact, commitment, efficiency);
- is providing inputs of the right quality and quantity;
- is not facing unexpected obstacles;
- has no frictions and conflicts with your staff;
- is likely to accomplish the agreed objectives.

● Monitor your own performance:
  - are you respecting your commitments?
  - can you keep pace with the consultant?
  - are your people helping the consultant, ignoring him or her, or making difficulties?
● Pay special attention to the collaborative spirit in which the assignment should be taking place!
● Don't underestimate the financial aspects of delivery:
  - is the consultant billing you regularly?
  - are the bills clear and correct?
  - are you paying without delay?
  - will the assignment remain within agreed financial limits?
● Conclusions from monitoring ought to be reviewed with the consultant and joint decisions taken on needed adjustments.

9. Evaluate the results and the consultant!

Many assignments end in a bizarre way. The consultant leaves the organization, a report is submitted and accepted, bills are paid and everyone seems to be happy. Yet the client cannot really say whether or not the assignment was worth while, and whether the benefits obtained justified the costs. No lessons are drawn for future assignments, and for the possibility of using the same consultant again.

● It is in your interest to evaluate every assignment on the basis of facts and figures, not of superficial impressions and hearsay ("the consultant was a very nice guy, everyone liked him around here").
● Evaluate the results obtained. What has changed? Will the changes be lasting? How much will they cost us? What problems remain unsolved?
● Evaluate the consultant. Has he delivered as promised? What could we learn from him? Was working with her an exciting experience? Would we use her again?
● Write your evaluation down. The consultant may contact you again and other people in your organization will want to know how or she he performed when working with you. Such information must be available to your colleagues and successors!

- Evaluate your own approach. Have you done well in this assignment? Have you become more skilful in working with consultants? Are you making effective use of them? Where do you need to improve?

10. Beware of dependence on consultants!

You and your staff may have appreciated and enjoyed the presence of a professional consultant in your organization. Yet the purpose of consulting reaches beyond making professional expertise available to your organization for dealing with current problems. Every assignment should increase your abilities and your independence in dealing with future problems. Dependence on consultants would be a symptom of a very unhealthy state of affairs!

- Don't delegate to consultants any decisions that are your responsibility and that you have to take.

- Don't get used to always having a consultant around to whom you hand over every complicated matter.

- Don't turn to consultants with the same task again: you and your staff should have learned how to tackle such a task.

- Develop internal consulting capabilities for dealing with issues for which an external expert is not necessary or which require an intimate inside knowledge of your organization.

- Don't put all your eggs in one basket — diversify your sources of external expertise! But stay in touch with consultants whose performance was excellent.

* * *

The *Ten Commandments* did not teach you how to use consultants, but stressed critical points in choosing consultants and in working with them. If you want to learn more about consulting, read about it and speak with people who have used consultants. And try it out — first on a smaller assignment, but one dealing with a real, not a fictitious, problem.

When you and your organization become real experts in working with consultants, you may find it useful to define your own policy for using management consultants and other professional services. The *Ten Commandments* provide some guidance on this, but you will certainly be able to establish a policy that reflects your unique needs and experience.

ASSOCIATIONS OF MANAGEMENT CONSULTANTS IN SELECTED COUNTRIES

1. National associations of consultants

Australia

Institute of Management Consultants in
Australia (IMCA)
PO Box 105
Burnside
South Australia 5066

Austria

Fachverband Unternehmensberatung und
Datenverarbeitung (FDU)
Wiedner Hauptstrasse 63
1045 Wien

Vereinigung Oesterreichischer Betriebs-
und Organisationsberater (VOB)
Strauchgasse 3
1010 Wien

Bangladesh

Bangladesh Association of Management
Consultants
98 Malibagh (DIT Road)
Dhaka 1219

Belgium

Association belge des conseils en
organisation et gestion (ASCOBEL)
1-5 avenue de la Joyeuse Entrée
1040 Bruxelles

Brazil

Associação Brasileira de Consultores de
Organização (ABCO)
Rua da Lapa 180, COB
20021 Rio de Janeiro

Instituto Brasileiro dos Consultores de
Organização (IBCO)
Av. Paulista 326
7° andar — cj. 77
CEP 01310 São Paulo

Bulgaria

Bulgarian Association of Management
Consultants (BAMC)
c/o Atlas Consult
PO Box 708
1000 Sofia

Canada

Canadian Association of Management
Consultants (CAMC)
Suite 805
121 Bloor Street East
Toronto, Ontario M4W 3M5

Institute of Certified Management
Consultants of Canada
Suite 805
121 Bloor Street East
Toronto, Ontario M4W 3M5

Management consulting

China

China Enterprise Management
    Association (CEMA)
San Li He
Beijing

Consulting Association of Shanghai (CAS)
81 Wu Xin Road
Shanghai

Croatia

Croatian Management Consulting
    Association (CROCA)
Krsnjavoga 1
41000 Zagreb

Cyprus

Cyprus Management Consultants
    Association
9 Androcleous Street
1st floor, Office 104
Nicosia

Czech Republic

Asociace pro poradenství v podnikání
    (APP)
[Association for Consulting to Business]
Veletržní 21
17000 Praha 7

Denmark

Den Danske Sammenslutning af
    Konsulenter Virksomhedsledelse
    (DSKV)
c/o Schobel & Marholt/AIM
Dyregardsvej 2
2740 Skovlunde

Foreningen af Managementkonsulenter
    (FMK)
Kristianagade 7
2100 København OE

Finland

Liikkeenjohdon Konsultit (LJK)
Pohjantie 12A
02100 Espoo 10

France

Chambre syndicale des sociétés de
    conseils (SYNTEC)
3 rue Léon Bonnat
75016 Paris

Office professionel de qualification des
    conseils en management
3 rue Léon Bonnat
75016 Paris

Germany

Bundesverband Deutscher
    Unternehmensberater EV (BDU)
Friedrich-Wilhelm-Strasse 2
53113 Bonn

Greece

Hellenic Association of Management
    Consulting Firms (SESSMA)
25 Filellinon Street
105 57 Athens

Hong Kong

The Hong Kong Management Association
Management House, 3rd floor
Canal Road
Hong Kong

Hungary

Vezetési Tanacsadok Magyarorszagi
    Szovetsege (VTMS)
[Association of Management Consultants
    in Hungary]
szt. István Krt. 11
1055 Budapest

Iceland

Felag Islenskra Rekstrarradgjafa (FIRR)
c/o Icelandic Management Association
PO Box 760
Reykjavik

India

Institute of Management Consultants of
  India
Centre One, 11th floor, Unit 2, World
  Trade Centre
Cuffe Parade
Bombay 400 005

Indonesia

Ikatan Nasional Konsultan Indonesia
Jl. Bendungan Hilir Raya No. 29
Jakarta 10210

Ireland

Association of Management Consulting
  Organisations (AMCO)
Confederation House
Kildare Street
Dublin 2

Italy

Associazione fra Società e Studi di
  Consulenza di Direzione ed
  Organizzazione Aziendale (ASSCO)
Via San Paolo 10
20121 Milano

Associazione Professionale dei Consulenti
  di Direzione ed Organizzazione
  Aziendale (APCO)
Corso Venezia 49
20121 Milano

Japan

ZEN-NOH-REN (All Japan Federation of
  Management Organizations)
c/o Japan Productivity Center
3-1-1 Shibuya
Shibuya-ku
Tokyo 150

Association of Management Consultants
  in Japan
Shuwashibakoen Sanchome Building
3-1-38 Shiba Park
Minato-ku
Tokyo 105

Chusho Kigyo Shindan Kyokai [Smaller
  Enterprise Consultants Association]
Ginza Section of MITI, 6-15-1 Ginza
Chuo-ku
Tokyo 104

Latvia

Association of Latvian Business
  Consultants
Taunlela 24
Riga, LV 1050

Lithuania

Lithuanian Association of Business
  Consultants
Labdarin 5
2001 Vilnius

Malaysia

Institute of Management Consultants
10th floor, MUI Plaza Letter Box No. 63
Jalan P. Ramlee
Kuala Lumpur 50250

Mexico

Asociación Mexicana de Empresas de
  Consultoría (AMEC)
calz. Legaria 252
México City 17, DF

Netherlands

Orde Van Organisatiekundigen
  en-Adviseurs
Koningslaan 34
1075 AD Amsterdam

Raad Van Organisatie Adviesbureau
  (ROA)
Van Stolkweg 34
PO Box 84200
2500 AE The Hague

New Zealand

Institute of Management Consultants New
  Zealand Incorporated
PO Box 2347
Auckland 1

Management consulting

Nigeria

Institute of Management Consultants
14 Kagoro Close
PO Box 9194
Kaduna

Nigerian Association of Management
  Consultants
c/o Centre for Management Development
PO Box 7648, Ikorodu Road
Lagos

Norway

Norsk Forening av Radgivere i
  Bedriftsledelse (NFRB)
c/o Hartmark-Iras
PO Box 50
1324 Lysaker

Pakistan

National Association of Consultants of
  Pakistan (NACOP)
PO Box 8901
103-B SMCH Society
Karachi

Philippines

Institute of Management Consultants of
  the Philippines
15th Floor, Jakai Building
Ayala Avenue
Makati, Metro Manila

Poland

Stowarzyszenie Doradcov Gospodarczych
  w Polsce (SDG)
[Association of Economic Consultants in
  Poland]
Gorskiego 1, Apt. 3
00 033 Warsaw

Portugal

Associação Portuguesa de Projectistas e
  Consultores (APPC)
Avenida Antonio Augusto Aguiar 126-7°
1000 Lisboa

Romania

Associata Consultantilor in Management
  Din Romania (AMCOR)
10 L. Pătrăşcanu
74671 Bucarest

Russia

Association of Consultants in Economics
  and Management
c/o VNESHCONSULT
Podsosenskii pereulok 20/12
Moscow 103062

Singapore

Institute of Management Consultants
c/o 9 Penang Road # 13-20 Park Mall
Singapore 0923

Slovakia

Slovenská asociácia pre poradenstvo v
  riadeniu
[Slovak Association for Management
  Consulting]
Prokopova 15
851 01 Bratislava

Slovenia

Association of Management Consultants
  of Slovenia (AMCOS)
Slovenska 58
61000 Ljubljana

South Africa

Institute of Management Consultants of
  Southern Africa
PO Box 784-305
Sandton 2146

Spain

Asociación Española de Empresas de
  Ingeniería y Consultoría
  (TECNIBERIA)
Velásquez 94, Aptdo. 14863
28006 Madrid

Sweden

Swedish Association of Management
Consultants (SAMC)
PO Box 7470
10392 Stockholm

Switzerland

Association suisse des conseils en
organisation et gestion (ASCO)
Mühlebachstrasse 28
8008 Zürich

Turkey

Management Consultancies Association of
Turkey (MCAT)
Kocabas Ishani n 111 K.2
Mecidiyeköy
Istanbul

United Kingdom

Institute of Management Consultants
5th Floor, 32/33 Hatton Garden
London EC1N 8DL

Management Consultancies Association
(MCA)
11 West Halkin Street
London SW1X 8JL

United States

Academy of Management
Managerial Consultation Division
c/o Joe Weiss
Management Department, Bentley College
Waltham, MA 02254

American Institute of Certified Public
Accountants (AICPA)
Management Consulting Services Division
Harborside Financial Center
201 Plaza Three
Jersey City, NJ, 07311-3881

Association of Internal Management
Consultants (AIMC)
PO Box 304
East Bloomfield, NY 14443

Association of Management Consulting
Firms (ACME) (Division of CCO)
521 Fifth Avenue
New York, NY 10175-3598

Council of Consulting Organisations, Inc.
(CCO)
521 Fifth Avenue
New York, NY 10175-3598

Institute of Management Consultants
(IMC) (Division of CCO)
521 Fifth Avenue
New York, NY 10175-3598

2. International associations (consulting and related professions)

Africa

Federation of African Consultants
(FEAC/FECA)
PO Box 1387
01 Abidjan

Europe

European Federation of Engineering
Consultancy Associations (EFCA)
79 avenue de Cortenbergh
1040 Bruxelles

European Federation of Management
Consulting Associations (FEACO)
1-5 avenue de la Joyeuse Entrée
1040 Bruxelles

European Foundation for Management
Development (EFMD)
40 rue Washington
1050 Bruxelles

Fédération des experts comptables
européens (FEE)
83 rue de la Loi
1040 Bruxelles

Latin America

Federación Latinoamericana de
Asociaciones de Consultores (FELAC)
Suipacha 552, Piso 4°, Of.1
1008 Buenos Aires
Argentina

Management consulting

Interregional

International Council of Management
  Consulting Institutes (ICMCI)
32/33 Hatton Garden
London EC1N 8DL
United Kingdom

International Federation of Accountants
540 Madison Avenue
New York, NY 10022
United States

International Federation of Consulting
  Engineers (FIDIC)
PO Box 86
1000 Lausanne 12 Chailly
Switzerland

PROFESSIONAL CODES (EXAMPLES)

Code of Professional Conduct of the European Federation of Management Consulting Associations (FEACO)

Code of professional conduct

1. A consultancy shall at all times maintain the highest ethical standard in the professional work undertaken, and in matters relating to a client's affairs act solely in the interests of the client (1).

Where a consultancy is a subsidiary of a parent body which is not in the public practice of management consultancy, all advice will be untied and independent of any influence of that parent body (2).

2. It shall be regarded as unprofessional conduct for a consultancy:

- To disclose or permit to be disclosed confidential information concerning the client's business and staff (3) (4) (5).

- To accept work for which it is not qualified (6).

- To enter into any arrangement which would detract from the objectivity and impartiality of the advice given to the client (7).

- Not to agree with the client in advance on the terms of remuneration and the basis of calculation thereof (8).

- To do anything likely to lower the status of Management Consultancy as a profession (9).

Guidelines for national associations on the interpretation of the code of professional conduct

(1)   A consultant who delivers advice must be able to do so with complete freedom and be protected by a *clause de conscience* from the management of the consultancy firm.

(2)   Whenever a consulting company is legally or financially under control of a non-consulting body, there should be a written undertaking to guarantee that no pressure will be exerted which may prejudice the opinion or the advice of the consultancy.

(3)   Information received by a consultant from employees within the client organization shall be respected.

(4)   Information received from a client source will never be used by the consultancy for any purpose outside the scope of the agreed assignment' (for example: recruitment of people from the staff of the client).

(5)   This includes the acceptance without the prior agreement of all parties of an assignment which gives rise to a conflict of competitive interest with an existing or recent client in an area, such as a strategy study or marketing study, where the knowledge gained at one client would be of current commercial value to the new client.

(6)   A client must be informed and his acceptance sought by a formal agreement where the assistance of specialists not linked directly with the consultancy is required on an assignment.

(7)   It would be considered a breach of this rule for a consultancy:

   (a)   To accept or permit any member of staff to accept from a third party any trade commission, discount or consideration of any kind in connection with the supply of goods or services to the client.

   (b)   To recommend to a client goods or services in which the consultancy or the consultant has direct or indirect interest without disclosing this interest to the client.

   (c)   To enter into any relationship with members of the staff of the client which could alter the impartiality of the consultant's attitude and advice.

   (d)   To pay a commission or any form of remuneration to a third party not on his staff for the introduction of a client except in exceptional circumstances where it is obvious that the objectivity and impartiality of the consultant will be preserved. In this case the commission should be disclosed to the client who will not object as the impartiality is preserved.

(8)   Generally the remuneration shall be calculated on a fixed fee or time-based fee rate agreed in advance. However, an arrangement between a consultancy and a client or a prospective client whereby the consultancy gives prior agreement to make the fee contingent on certain results is permitted where this is accepted practice, such as staff selection, mergers and acquisitions and search for licenses. In circumstances where a contingent fee basis might operate in a manner which could prejudice the independence of the consultants undertaking the assignment or might prove difficult to calculate in practice or might prejudice the long-term relationship with the client, it must not be used.

(9)   It would be considered a breach of this rule for a consultancy:

   (a)   To issue promotional material including advertising which is likely to mislead or give the public a false impression of the consultancies' capabilities, or could be construed as claiming advantages for one member of a national association over its other members or contains remarks or implications which could be interpreted as being derogatory of any other member of the national association.

(b) To accept an assignment, the scope of which is so limited that the consultant is aware that the client will receive either ineffective advice, or advice so incomplete as to require him to seek further advice, without being aware at the onset of the assignment that this will be the case.

Code of Professional Conduct of the Institute of Management Consultants (United Kingdom and Ireland)

Introduction

The objective of the Institute of Management Consultants is the advancement of the profession of management consultancy through the establishment and maintenance of the highest standards of performance and conduct by its members, and by the promotion of the knowledge and skills required for that purpose.

Professional standards

A management consultant is an independent and qualified person who provides a professional service to business, public and other undertakings, by:

- identifying and investigating problems concerned with strategy, policy, markets, organization, procedures and methods;

- formulating recommendations for appropriate action by factual investigation and analysis with due regard for broader management and business implications;

- discussing and agreeing with the client the most appropriate course of action;

- providing assistance where required by the client to implement his recommendations.

In rendering such services to all levels of management, consultants carry a heavy burden of responsibility and an obligation to maintain the highest standards of integrity and competence.

Recognizing this responsibility, the Institute embodies within its Code of Professional Conduct those duties and obligations required of all members which will ensure the highest standards of performance, and thereby enhance the reputation and public recognition of the profession, of the Institute and of its members.

Members of the Institute have basic responsibilities as management consultants to:

- exercise independence of thought and action;

- hold affairs of their clients in strict confidence;

- deal with management problems in perspective and give well-balanced advice;
- strive continuously to improve their professional skills and to maintain a high quality of advice;
- advance the professional standards of management consulting;
- uphold the honour and dignity of the profession;
- maintain high standards of personal conduct.

To honour these obligations all members agree, in writing, to comply with the Institute's Code of Professional Conduct. This distinguishes management consultants who are members of the Institute.

Format of the Code

The Institute's Code of Professional Conduct is structured on three basic principles dealing with:

(i)   high standards of service to the client

(ii) independence, objectivity and integrity

(iii) responsibility to the profession.

These principles are underpinned by detailed rules, which are specific injunctions, and practical notes, which either lay down conditions under which certain activities are permitted or indicate good practice and how best to observe the relevant Principle or Rule.

The Council of the Institute may, from time to time, issue further Principles, Rules or Notes which will be promulgated in the Institute's publications before being incorporated into a revised edition of the Code. Members are expected to abide by all such new provisions from the date of their publication.

The Principles, Rules and Notes of the Code apply not only to the member personally but also to acts carried out through a partner, co-director, employee or other agent acting on behalf of, or under the control of, the member.

Definitions used in the Code

Member:	A Fellow, Member, Associate Member or Affiliate of the Institute.
Client:	The person, firm or organization with whom the member makes an agreement or contract for the provision of services.
His:	Shall apply to members of both sexes.
Declaration:	A written statement referring to and disclosing the facts relevant to the situations covered by particular Rules of the Code.
Independent:	In a position always to express freely one's own opinion without any control or influence from others outside the (consulting) organization, and without the need to consider the impact of such opinion on one's own interests.
Institute:	The Institute of Management Consultants.

Disciplinary action

A member is liable to disciplinary action if his conduct is found, by the Disciplinary Committee of the Institute, to be in contravention of the Code, or to bring discredit to the profession or to the Institute.

In accordance with the By-laws, a member may be required to make a declaration in answer to enquiries from the Institute concerning his professional conduct. A member failing to make such a declaration may be found in breach of the Principle to which the Rule or Note relates.

Principle 1: High standards of service to the client

A member shall carry out the duties which he has undertaken diligently, conscientiously and with due regard to his client's interest.

Rules

1.1 A member will only accept an engagement for which he is suitably qualified.

1.2 Before accepting an assignment a member shall clearly define the terms and conditions of the assignment including the scope, nature and period of the service to be provided, the allocation of responsibilities, and the basis for remuneration (see Notes 1.2.1 and 1.2.2).

1.3 A member will regard his client's requirements and interests as paramount at all times.

1.4 A member shall only subcontract work with the prior agreement of the client (see Note 1.4.1).

1.5 A member will hold as strictly confidential all information concerning the affairs of clients unless the client has released such information for public use, or has given specific permission for its disclosure.

1.6 A member will refrain from inviting any employee of a client advised by the member to consider alternative employment (an advertisement in the press is not considered to be an invitation to any particular person).

1.7 A member will develop recommendations specifically for the solution of each client's problems; such solutions shall be realistic and practicable and clearly understandable by the client.

1.8 To ensure efficient performance of each assignment, a member will exercise good management through careful planning, frequent progress reviews and effective controls.

Notes

1.2.1 Before undertaking or continuing with any work, a member should ensure that his resources are adequate and properly directed to carry it out.

1.2.2 The terms of an assignment should always be evidenced in writing.

1.4.1 When subcontractors are employed, the principal consultant will take responsibility for the quality of the work produced and for compliance with the requirements of the Code. Members are referred to the Institute's guidelines on subcontracting agreements.

Principle 2: Independence, objectivity, integrity

A member shall avoid any action or situation inconsistent with his professional obligations or which in any way might be seen to impair his integrity.

Rules

2.1 A member will maintain a fully independent position with the client at all times, making certain that advice and recommendations are based upon thorough impartial consideration of all pertinent facts and circumstances and on opinions developed from reliable relevant experience.

2.2 A member will declare at the earliest opportunity any special relationships, circumstances or business interests which might influence or impair his judgement or objectivity on a particular assignment (see Notes 2.2.1, 2.2.2 and 2.2.3).

2.3 A member shall not serve a client under terms or conditions which might impair his independence, objectivity or integrity; he will reserve the right to withdraw if conditions beyond his control develop to interfere with the successful conduct of the assignment. He will not practise during a period when his judgement is or might be impaired through any cause.

2.4 A member shall not take discounts, commissions or gifts as an inducement to show favour to any person or body.

2.5 A member will advise the client of any significant reservations he may have about the client's expectation of benefits from an engagement. He will not accept an engagement in which he cannot serve the client effectively.

2.6 A member will not indicate any short-term benefits at the expense of the long-term welfare of the client, without advising the client of the implications.

2.7 A member will discuss and agree with the client any significant changes in the objectives, scope, approach, anticipated benefits or other aspects of the engagement which might arise during the course of carrying it out.

2.8 A member who, in circumstances not specifically covered in these Rules, finds that his professional or personal interest conflict so as to risk a breach of the Principle shall, as the circumstances may require, either withdraw from the situation, or remove the source of conflict, or declare it and obtain in writing the agreement of the parties concerned to the continuance of his assignment (see Note 2.8.1).

Notes

2.2.1 Rule 2.2 requires the prior disclosure of all relevant personal, financial or other business interests which could not be inferred from the description of the services offered. In particular this relates to:

— any directorship or controlling interest in any business in competition, with the client;

— any financial interest in goods or services recommended or supplied to the client;

— any personal relationship with any individual in the client's employ;

— any personal investment in the client organization or in its parent or any subsidiary companies.

2.2.2 A member shall not use any confidential information about a client's affairs, elicited during the course of his assignment, for his own personal benefit or for the benefit of others outside the client organization. There shall be no insider dealing or trading as legally defined or understood.

2.2.3 If any such business or financial interest arises during the course of an assignment, Rule 2.8 shall apply.

2.8.1 It should be noted that the Institute of Management Consultants may, depending on the circumstances, be one of the "parties concerned". For example, if a member is under pressure to act in a way which would bring him into non-compliance with the Code of Professional Conduct, in addition to any other declaration which it might be appropriate to make, he should declare the facts to the Institute.

Principle 3: Responsibility to the profession

A member shall at all times conduct himself in a manner which will enhance the standing and public regard of the profession.

Rules

3.1 A member recognizes that he has a responsibility to the profession as well as to himself and his clients, to ensure that his knowledge and skills are kept up to date, and will take appropriate action to this end.

3.2 A member will not knowingly, without permission, use copyright material, or a client's proprietary data, or materials or techniques that others have developed but have not released for public use.

3.3 A member shall have proper regard for the professional obligations and qualifications of those from whom he receives or to whom he gives authority, responsibility or employment, or with whom he is professionally associated (see Notes 3.3.1 and 3.3.2).

3.4 A member shall only initiate or accept a joint assignment with a member of another professional body if he is satisfied (and can satisfy the client and if required the Institute) that such an assignment would be conducted to the standards represented by this Code of Professional Conduct.

3.5 A member referring a client to another management consultant will not misrepresent the qualifications of the other management consultant, nor will he make any commitments for the other management consultant.

3.6 A member will not accept an assignment for a client knowing that another management consultant is serving the client in a similar capacity unless he is assured, and can satisfy himself, that any potential conflict between the two assignments is recognized by, and has the consent of, the client (see Note 3.6.1).

3.7 When asked by a client to review the work of another professional, a member will exercise the objectivity, integrity and sensitivity required in all technical and advisory conclusions communicated to the client.

3.8 A member will negotiate agreements and charges for professional services only in a manner approved as ethical and professional by the Institute (see Note 3.8.1).

3.9 A member shall not attempt to obtain work by giving financial inducements to clients or client staff (see Note 3.9.1).

3.10 A member, in publicizing his work or making representations to a client, shall ensure that the information given:

— is factual and relevant;

— is neither misleading nor unfair to others;

— is not otherwise discreditable to the profession (see Note 3.10.1).

3.11 A member shall be a fit and proper person to carry on the profession of management consultancy (see Note 3.11.1).

3.12 A member shall not wilfully give the Institute false, inaccurate, misleading or incomplete information.

Notes

3.3.1 Under Rule 3.3, a member will provide all possible opportunities for management consultants he employs to exercise their professional skills as widely as possible within the interests of the client, and will, as opportunities arise, assist them to accept progressively greater responsibility in accordance with their ability and experience.

3.3.2 In a similar way a member will encourage the management consultants he employs to maintain and advance their competence by participating in continuing professional development.

3.6.1 Legal and "fair trading" obligations should take precedence in both public and private sector work.

3.8.1 Members are referred to the Institute's "Guidelines on Charging for Management Consulting Services".

3.9.1 Payment for legitimate marketing activity may be made, and national laws and customs should be respected.

3.10.1 Accepted methods of making his experience and/or availability known include:

— publication of his work (with the consent of the client);
— direct approaches to potential clients;
— entries in any relevant directory;
— advertisement (in printed publication, or on radio or television);
— public speaking engagements.

Members are referred to the Institute's Guidelines on the Promotion of Management Consulting Services.

3.11.1 A member shall at all times be of good reputation and character. Particular matters for concern might include:

— conviction of a criminal offence or committal under bankruptcy proceedings;
— censure or disciplining by a court or regulatory authority;
— unethical or improper behaviour towards employees or the general public.

OUTLINE OF A MANAGEMENT SURVEY

This appendix provides an overview of the main subject areas covered by a diagnostic or management survey of a company. The check-lists suggest the subjects to cover, not a sequence of steps. This sequence will have to be decided with regard to the nature of the client organization, the kind of information that is already available, and the main functional area in which the assignment will be carried out.

In functional areas the consultant undertaking a general management survey will look only for facts that are needed to understand the nature of the client organization, appraise the level of performance, discover underused resources and define possible improvements. The consultant will refrain from detailed analysis, with the exception perhaps of the area on which the assignment is to concentrate. Where possible and meaningful, the consultant will use comparisons (with other organizations, industry standards, foreign countries, etc.).

The paragraphs below are restricted to a summary view of each area. Further suggestions can be found in Chapters 12-22 dealing with consulting in various areas of management. Figure A1 on the following page shows the ten subject areas covered. A different structuring of the survey is possible, however. For example, in an organization involved in an extensive investment programme this would be treated as a separate subject area.

Many consulting firms have developed their own internal guides to diagnosing organizations, which they regard as their proprietary know-how.

Subject area 1: General characteristics of the client organization

Under this heading the consultant will examine key information on the nature, purpose, role and major characteristics of the client organization. The check-list indicates the scope of the subject. The consultant will be particularly interested in factors and events which have shaped the history of the client organization and may be the origin of various deeply rooted organizational traditions, business practices and behavioural patterns.

Figure A1   Subject areas of a comprehensive management survey

(1)	General characteristics of the client organization
(2)	Environmental factors
(3)	Objectives and strategies – overall

(4)	(5)	(6)	(7)	(8)
Finance	Marketing	Production (operations)	Research and development	Human resources

———————————— Objectives, policies, plans ————————————

———————————— Structure, activities ————————————

———————————— Performance ————————————

(9)	Management systems and practices
(10)	Performance – overall

Check-list 1: General characteristics

Subject	Specification
Activity	Type (sector), purpose Main functions, products, services National or multinational profile Complexity and sophistication of products and processes
History	When and how established Growth pattern Key events (acquisitions, mergers, technological breakthroughs, impact of wars or recessions) Key personalities in history of firm
Importance	Volume of activity Volume and structure of resources Position and market share in country, sector, region, local community, internationally Main competitors
Ownership	Pattern (private, public, cooperative) Legal form (partnership, limited company, state enterprise or agency)
Influences	Main owners Centres of control, role of board of directors Social and political influences and pressure groups Membership of employers' and sector organizations
Location	Where located Number and size of units Distances, communications

Subject area 2: Environmental factors

The client organization has to be seen in the context of its socio-economic environment, with which it interacts in many ways. The check-list given below is very broad. In reality, it will be exceptional for the consultant to review all aspects; in most cases only selected environmental considerations will apply. The subjects included in the check-list will be studied from the viewpoint of the needs and opportunities of the client organization and not in a general, all-embracing way.

Some of the environmental factors will be variables that the client organization cannot influence. There are, however, assignments that may include proposals for changes in the environment — for example, consumer taste and demand for the client organization's products may be influenced by customer education and advertising.

Check-list 2: Environmental factors

Subject	Specification
Economic	Broad economic setting Development level and trends Country's economic wealth Structure and state of market State of given industry in the country Financial system, availability of money
Natural resources	Raw materials Fuel and energy Water Land Climate
Human resources	Labour market Education Technical and business skills Training facilities
Socio-cultural	Structure of society (classes, ethnic groups, minorities, income distribution, purchasing power) Consumer taste Social, cultural and religious traditions Social organizations (including workers' and employers' organizations), role, influence
Government	Profile, source of power, stability Economic policy, including regional development Business, investment and export promotion policy Planning, regulation and control of economy Taxation Government services and facilities Local government (functions in economic development)
Political	Political system and life, stability Impact of politics on management
Legal	Labour law Company or commercial law, etc.
Business service infrastructure	Accounting, audit Management consulting Legal advice Insurance Banking services
Physical	Immediate physical environment Transport and communication facilities Telecommunications Utilities and technical services Housing facilities Pollution: environmental protection
Technological capabilities	National and sectoral research base Research and development policies Technological universities

Subject area 3: Objectives and strategies (overall)

The study of the client's business objectives, strategies, policies and plans is a core element in management surveys; it provides orientation to a more detailed analysis of various functions and activity areas, and a basis for appraising performance. The consultant examines both the methodology used (the system whereby objectives, strategies and policies are established and plans worked out) and the particular targets and other objectives established and pursued by management. Special attention is paid to conflicting objectives, strategies and policies, and to blank areas in which the client operates without objectives and plans.

Check-list 3: Objectives and strategies (overall)

Subject	Specification
Approach and methodology	Methods of defining purpose and objectives
	System of strategic, operational and contingency planning
	Areas managed without objectives and plans
Purpose and objectives	Assessment of purpose (mission) and specific organizational objectives as defined by management
Strategic choices	Assessment of major choices (overall and by areas of business)
Investment	Policies and plans, main projects

Subject area 4: Finance

This is a key area of any management survey because the financial strength and results of business organizations reflect the potential and results of almost all other areas and functions.

The *financial appraisal*, as the survey in this area is frequently called, concentrates on analysis of the client's financial reports for the preceding three to five years as a means of assessing strengths and weaknesses, measuring past performance, examining the use of funds available, and establishing upward or downward trends. The findings of the financial appraisal are used to orient further investigation and remedial activities in other functions and areas of management.

What sort of thing should a consultant look for in studying a set of financial reports? First, there is the overall picture presented by the current year's figures. Is the company making enough profit? How strong is it in financial terms? Is it taking or giving too much credit? Are the stocks too high? Is the cash flow satisfactory? Secondly, there is the picture that emerges from studying trends over a period of years. Is the company becoming more profitable? Is it expanding too fast? Is productivity rising or falling? Is liquidity improving or deteriorating?

In both these pictures it is necessary to distinguish between two conflicting aspects of the company's operations — profitability and solvency. A business can be highly profitable yet financially weak. Another may be financially strong but not making enough profit. The method used to interpret financial statements is to calculate certain *ratios*. Cash figures alone are almost meaningless; an increase in profit from $10,000 to $15,000 may be good or bad, depending on the amount of extra resources used in generating the extra profit. Many different ratios can be developed from a set of financial reports, but some of them are of little value or are simply variations of each other. Guidelines on the application and interpretation of ratios are provided in many publications on accounting and financial management.

A correct interpretation of the static picture presented by one year's figures requires considerable skill and care. For instance, if the fixed assets of land and buildings are undervalued in current market terms, a false impression may be given in the profit ratios. The comparison of one business with another should not be undertaken without the utmost care and unless the consultant is thoroughly familiar with both businesses. Different methods may be used to evaluate assets and calculate depreciation, policies on whether to capitalize expenditure or write it off against income may be different, the treatment of research and development costs may vary, changing price levels may invalidate attempts to compare and so on.

The main value of analysing ratios lies in studying the trend within one company over a period of years. Since this approach means comparing like with like, there is little risk of misinterpretation of the main trends.

Check-list 4: Finance

Subject	Specification
Financial management	Strategy and policy
	Position in corporate structure
	Records and reports — timeliness, reliability, quality
	Relationships with banks and financial agencies
Balance sheet and income (profit and loss) account	Comparative analysis
	Key ratios
	Financial performance, health and stability
Sources and application of funds	Sources and cost of funds
	Movement and uses of funds
	Cash flow
	Financial reserves
Financial planning and forecasting	Systems and techniques used
	Assessment of projections made
Auditors' reports	Existence, quality
	Comments made by auditors

Subject area 5: Marketing

In organizations that sell their products or services the marketing function provides an essential link with the environment and strongly influences other functions. The consultant tries to get a picture of the available market and of the product-market strategy followed by the client. He or she will examine the effectiveness of marketing strategy and activity, and their impact on production, research and development, purchasing and other functions. Various components of the marketing function, such as the organization of sales, advertising, the location and turnover of stocks, warehousing, transport, etc., will be briefly reviewed if appropriate.

Check-list 5: Marketing

Subject	Specification
Marketing management	Concept, strategy applied Staffing (numbers, competence) Position in corporate structure
Markets (local and export)	Size, trends Own share Competitors (number, importance, strategy) Market research Backlog of orders
Customers (clients)	Size and structure of customer base Principal customers
Pricing	Strategy and policy Comparison with competitors
Sales	Distribution channels Organization and techniques Sales force (size, competence, motivation) Reliability of delivery Stocks (volume, location, turnover) Selling expenses (volume, trend)
Customer services	After-sales services Technical services (information, training, systems design, consulting, etc.) Learning from customers
Advertising	Importance, cost Techniques, agents Impact

Subject area 6: Production (operations)

It is difficult to describe briefly the activities and problems that may interest the consultant in the very large and diversified area of production and/or operations. More than in other areas, the consultant's problem will be how to recognize essential information in the vast amount of data that production offers.

In essence, the consultant will concentrate on two issues:

- a general examination of the organization of production and the layout of production departments, main material and product flows, relations between marketing and production, purchasing and production, and research and development and production;

- an examination of key indicators of effectiveness of production activities (capacity utilization, lead time of main products, volume and distribution of work in progress, equipment breakdown and stoppages, utilization of working time or production workers, waste, quality of production, various losses in the production area).

In non-productive organizations (services, social organizations, government departments) the consultant will review, in an analogous way, the services or other operations that constitute the organization's main "products".

The consultant will aim to view production and other processes in their totality, paying particular attention to smooth process operation, and to waste and other losses caused by organizational boundaries and poor coordination.

Check-list 6: Production (operations)

Subject	Specification
Production (operations) management	Concept Production strategy applied Staffing (numbers, competence) Position in corporate structure
Production units	Number, location Specialization Linkages
Production capacity	Volume Utilization Bottlenecks Free and spare capacity
Technology	Type Level, sophistication
Land and buildings	Owned or rented Location, access Age, condition, suitability Cost of operation
Plant and machinery	Types, quantities Age, condition, breakdowns Technical sophistication (automation, precision, speed, etc.) Suitability Maintenance (system, level) Special equipment
Production organization	Material and product flows (process diagrams) Work in progress (volume, location, control) Logistics and materials handling New forms of organization
Control and support functions	Planning, scheduling, coordination, records Operational control (system, level) Industrial engineering (work study, value analysis, etc.) Staff capabilities (engineers, technicians)
Quality management	System applied Level attained New trends
Purchasing	Organization Procedures, practices

Check-list 6 *(cont.)*

	Main suppliers, reliability
	Subcontractors
Production workers	Categories
	Skills, experience
	Remuneration, motivation
	Supervisory staff
Safety and health	Accidents
	Preventive measures
Efficiency of production system	Cost of main products
	Labour productivity
	Flexibility
	Losses (stoppages, waste of material and energy, pilferage, etc.)
Impact on environment	Corporate policy
	Current problems and needed improvements

Subject area 7: Research and development

The first question on research and development (R & D) will concern its role in the development and strategy of the client organization. If the organization is research oriented and operates in a technically advanced industry (such as electronics, telecommunications or petrochemicals), the management of its research function may have a considerably greater impact on overall results than does production management. The consultant will examine relations in the total cycle of research — development — manufacturing — marketing, paying particular attention to R & D expenditure and its utilization, to the relationship of R & D management to general management of the firm, to the pace and problems of the transfer of R & D results to production, to the competence of key professional staff and to the main achievements of the R & D department.

Even in organizations having little or no internal research and development, some relationship to external research and development may exist, e.g. licences will be purchased, or new production technologies bought in the form of equipment.

The organization of investment (capital building) activities linked to the application of R & D results may require particular attention in organizations involved in extensive expansion or reconstruction.

Check-list 7: Research and development

Subject	Specification
R & D management	Strategy and policy definition
	Plan, implementation
	Structure

Check-list 7 *(cont.)*

	Position in corporate structure
	Personalities
R & D staff	Numbers
	Qualifications, experience
	Achievements
	Motivation
Innovation potential	Product design, backlog of new designs
	Laboratories
	Prototype workshops
	Testing equipment, pilot plant
	Information and library
Collaboration	Type of arrangements
with other	Partners
organizations	Licence agreements (and similar)
Use of R & D	Results, application
	Pace of innovation
	Impact on business
	Special competitive advantage

Subject area 8: Human resources

The critical issue in the human resource area is the impact of personnel policy (i.e. criteria applied to selection, recruitment, staff development, promotion and remuneration) on the performance and development prospects of the client organization. Although this may be difficult during a short survey, the consultant tries to get a true picture of how and by whom personnel decisions are made and how this affects the morale and motivation of people. Career planning and development, personnel performance appraisal and the role of staff training and development will then be briefly examined. In the field of remuneration and motivation, both financial instruments (wage policy, profit sharing) and other motivational factors (challenging work opportunities, employment security, social services) will be reviewed and their impact on the performance of the organization assessed.

The consultant should in any case become acquainted with the basic principles of labour-management relations practices in the client organization.

Check-list 8: Human resources

Subject	Specification
Human resource management	Concept and policies
	Human resource planning
	Staffing of personnel department
	Position in corporate structure

Check-list 8 *(cont.)*

Staff structure	Age, sex Competence, skills (by categories) Minorities, foreign workers Employment conditions (permanent, temporary, seasonal) Turnover Absenteeism
Recruitment and selection	Recruitment practices Selection practices
Training and development	Career prospects Expenditure on staff development Organization Approaches and methods Job rotation, etc. Staff appraisal
Remuneration and motivation	Wage and salary systems Wage levels and differentials Payment by results Profit-sharing and similar schemes Social benefits Non-financial incentives
Labour-management relations	Nature, practices Impact on management and performance

Subject area 9: Management system and practices

Step by step, the consultant will be extending and deepening his knowledge and understanding of the client organization's management. He will try to determine the relationship between the problems he has discovered and the ways in which decisions on important matters are taken and implemented. Special attention will be paid to the profiles and management styles of key personalities, and to various questions usually embraced by the term "organizational culture".

Check-list 9: Management systems and practices

Subject	Specification
Managers	Key personalities (professional and personal profiles, attitudes to change, motivation)
Organizational structure	Form of structure, history Departments, divisions (specialization, role, relative importance) Relations between line and staff Centralization vs. decentralization Existence, quality and use of charts and manuals
Decision making	Practice applied to main sorts of decision

Check-list 9 *(cont.)*

Coordination	Methods, areas Coordination of key functions
Communication	Networks and channels (formal and informal) Methods
Internal information, planning and control system	Systems used, impact Management information system Activity and performance plans Budgetary and cost control Reporting; reports and records analysis
Modern techniques	Policy, effectiveness Preferred techniques Computer/information technology applications Computer literacy of management and staff Communication technology, etc.
Organizational culture	Values and traditions Habits and rituals Prevailing management style Employee participation
Networking	Linkages and interdependencies with other organizations
Use of external expert services	Policy, importance Experience with management consultants and other advisers

Subject area 10: Performance (overall)

The examination of the client's (i) resources, (ii) objectives, strategies, policies and plans, and (iii) main activities and comparative results in particular functional areas, enables the consultant to make some judgement on the overall performance of the client organization, assess whether this performance has been satisfactory, think of probable future trends and opportunities, and point out possible and needed improvements.

Check-list 10: Performance (overall)

Subject	Specification
Performance indicators	Growth, productivity, profitability, cash-flow, return on investment, market value of shares, employment generation and stability, and other key indicators Principal strengths and weaknesses
Competitive advantage	Special resources, achievements and capabilities Comparison with key competitors
Position in sector	Position attained (leadership, etc.) and image achieved with customers and general public

Check-list 10 *(cont.)*

Trends	Past, current, expected changes Factors and forces likely to affect future performance (positive and negative influences)
Implementing change	Policies Abilities, approaches used Results achieved
Performance assessment	Practices and their impact (frequency, criteria, depth of analysis, conclusions drawn)
Performance improvement	Restructuring, re-engineering, benchmarking or other initiatives Approaches and methods used Results achieved
Image	In customers' circles and general public, among youth, etc.

TERMS OF A CONSULTING CONTRACT

This appendix supplements section 7.6 on consulting contracts. These contracts come in many different forms and degrees of detail. It is useful to be aware of differences in national legislation and practice concerning contracting in general, and contracts for the provision of professional services in particular. In international contracts, the client and the consultant have to agree on the applicable law, which is usually the law of the client organization's home country. In exceptional and justified cases the consultant and the client may agree to apply the law of the consultant's country.

The consultant may be requested to accept the client's standard form and conditions of contract. Normally this is the case if the assignment is part of a programme financed by a technical assistance agency or a development bank, and if the work is for public sector clients.

In other cases, the consultant will be able to use his or her own form of contract, or develop a contract in agreement with the client. To support their members, some consultants' associations have prepared standard contract clauses, or guidelines for contract terms and conditions, reflecting the profession's experience.

In any event, it is strongly recommended to consult a lawyer on the contract form to be used and on unusual contract clauses suggested either by the client or the consultant.

The comments that follow are structured in accordance with the check-list in box 7.5 on page 164 ("What to cover in contracting").

1. Contracting parties

It should be made clear not only who signs the contract (and its cancellation, amendments, etc.), but also who will make operational decisions on work progress, changes in the work plan and staffing, and results. In reality, there are several categories of "client" in most organizations, as pointed out in section 3.3. Technical assistance contracts are often signed by the funding agency, but the real client is the organization receiving assistance. What will be its roles and rights in preparing and implementing the contract?

2. Scope of the assignment

This section describes the work to be performed, the objectives to be achieved, the timetable and the volume of work. Although it is the core section of the contract, its importance is often underestimated. Many consultants feel that their objective should be to sign the contract even if the scope of work has not been fully clarified and could be viewed differently by the consultant or the client. Their credo is: Why bother with detailed work descriptions and plans if we know well that eventually the client will want something else? While flexibility is the consultant's major virtue, a lack of precision in outlining what should be done and achieved has made the life of many consultants and clients difficult.

3. Work products and reports

This section describes the so called "deliverables", i.e. specific documents and reports that the consultant will be transmitting to the client during and at the end of the assignment. Here, too, a great deal of misunderstanding can be avoided by trying to be as specific as possible in describing what the client will receive. What is "a report"? What do we mean by "complete documentation on a training programme for sales managers"?

Unnecessary written reports should not be requested. They take up both the consultant's and the client's time without changing anything in the course of the assignment. Conversely, the need for frequent and short progress review meetings is not fully appreciated in many contracts.

4. Consultant and client inputs

Consultant inputs in the assignment are those that have to be provided within the given contract framework. This includes names (and curricula vitae) of operating consultants, names of partners and other seniors responsible for managing and back-stopping the assignment, management systems and other proprietary know-how to be provided, and other inputs. It should be clearly stated which inputs will be provided within the agreed fee and which will only be available against additional payment. Any such additional inputs will require the client's prior approval.

Furthermore, there should be no ambiguity as regards changes in the agreed inputs — when and under what conditions would the consulting firm be authorized to assign different staff, and when and how would the client be able to ask the consultant to replace the staff assigned to the project. If the client has selected not only a consulting firm, but also particular persons within this firm, the client's view should also prevail in any such changes.

Client inputs, such as time spent on the assignment by managerial and technical personnel, or administrative support, are often taken for granted and vaguely defined. In implementing assignments, many consultants do not really insist on timely and full provision of inputs promised by clients. This practice increases the duration and costs of many assignments and causes a great deal of disenchantment. The client is not available and the consultant proceeds alone with the work . . . only to find out that the client is not happy with the results and will not accept them.

5. Fees and expenses

Chapter 26 provides enough comments on desirable and undesirable fee-setting and billing practices. In drafting a contract, the fee formula applied, the estimated or agreed total fee, the conditions whereby fees may be adjusted, and any expenses that will be charged separately, should be clearly set out.

6. Billing and payment procedure

This procedure is also amply described in Chapter 26. The contract should set out the conditions to be met in requesting advance, interim and final payments, such as the reports that have to be submitted and accepted, the time records to be provided, or the way for presenting bills.

7. Professional responsibilities

As a rule, the consultant will refer to the consulting association's or his firm's code of ethics and professional conduct (and attach such a code to the contract text). If necessary, the contract may also include special clauses on questions such as the conflict of interest to be avoided or activities from which the consultant agrees to refrain.

8. Copyright

Increasingly, consultants use methodologies and training materials covered by copyright. The contract will set the conditions under which these materials are available to the client (limited use within the client firm, no reproduction, fee to be paid for use, and similar).

Copyright concerning the materials produced as part of the assignment is handled in various ways and is a matter of negotiation. Some clients insist that any copyright for work produced for their money belongs to them. Other clients want to be able to use the materials at their own discretion within the limits of their organizations, but agree that copyright should stay with the consultant (especially if the material is not a joint product of the consultant's and the client's work).

9. Liability

As pointed out in section 6.5, legal liability is a relatively new phenomenon in consulting contracts and in many contract texts there is no reference to any liability. Yet liability questions should be given due consideration and the consultant may wish, or be obliged to, take out a liability insurance. This is especially the case if the advice to be provided will have a major impact on the client's business decisions, or if the consultant is designing and delivering systems whose functioning will strongly influence the client's operations (typically in information technology consulting).

10. Use of subcontractors

The use of subcontractors by the consulting firm may be authorized in some contracts and the client may choose to set the conditions for such use.

11. Termination or revision

First, the contract will describe the steps to be taken upon the completion of the assignment, including the settlement of all commitments by both parties and the submission and acceptance of all reports and documentation.

Second, the contract may stipulate that the client can terminate the contract at any point without giving a reason. There may, however, be a mandatory notice (say, one week in a simple management advisory assignment, but 30-60 days in a major engineering consultancy), and/or the client may have to pay the consultant an indemnity (e.g. fees for one month of work or 20 per cent of the remaining fees). If the client wishes to terminate the contract owing to poor performance of the consultant, a precise procedure should be followed (giving the reasons in writing, asking for a reply and immediate action, etc.) and the notice may be shorter.

Third, the consultant must also have a possibility to withdraw from the contract under certain circumstances, e.g. if the client is not paying or has suspended operations for a defined period of time. The contract would stipulate the procedure to be observed by the consultant. If the client has been declared bankrupt, the consultant can normally terminate the contract without notice.

Turning to revisions, the contract may determine the dates and conditions for periodic revisions to reflect changed circumstances and client needs, and the procedure for unplanned revisions suggested by either party.

12. Arbitration

As a rule, consulting contracts use arbitration for settling disputes that cannot be handled amicably. The contracting parties agree on the rules of arbitration and the body to which the case would be referred.

13. Signatures and dates

It should be made clear which client's and consultant's representatives are duly authorized to sign contracts and their amendments, bills and any other formal correspondence, and legally binding commitments concerning the approval and the execution of the contract.

* * *

Further information is available in:

- M. Kubr: *How to select and use consultants: A client's guide*, Management Development Series, No. 31 (Geneva, ILO, 1993);

- World Bank: *Sample form of contract for consultants' services* (Washington, DC, 1989); and *Consultants' services: Lump sum remuneration* (Washington, DC, June 1995);

- European Union: *General conditions for CEC public service contracts applicable in the PHARE programme* (Brussels, n.d.);

- International Federation of Consulting Engineers (FIDIC): *The White Book Guide, with other notes and documents for consultancy agreements* (Lausanne, 1991).

CASE HISTORY OF CONSULTING
TO A GROWING SMALL BUSINESS
(Island Paradise Sportswear)

This case-study has been written to illustrate the role of consultants in the growth and development of a small business. It is based on real company data, although some details, including the name of the company, have been changed.

The company's background

Island Paradise Sportswear is a small business located in Brisbane, Australia. It is a manufacturer of women's fashion swimwear, sportswear and leisure wear. It has been in business for 20 years and in that time sales have grown steadily.

The company was started by Peter and Kate Marshall. They met while crewing a charter yacht in the Caribbean. They married and started a business in Barbados designing and manufacturing swimwear for wealthy tourists. The factory was an old house perched on the water's edge amongst the coconut trees. Upon returning to Australia the following year they decided to apply the same ideas that had worked in the West Indies to Australia. There seemed to be an opportunity in the expanding leisure industry while maintaining the lifestyle they preferred.

Business was initially based in a small suburban apartment near the beach. A few people would come into the flat to work each day and extra production would be done by outworkers (machinists working at home). From the beginning Kate was responsible for swimwear design and exerted a strong force in the business. Peter had several years of accounting training and experience behind him, and looked after the general accounts and business affairs of the fledgling operation.

After the first few months John McMahon bought a minority shareholding in the business and became responsible for sales. With the additional partner, a review of the formal structure of the business was necessary. The Marshalls sought advice from a consulting accountant who advised a change from a partnership to a company structure both for tax reasons and to gain the limited liability status afforded by a company.

In common with many new small businesses the accountant, Henry Jones, was their principal external adviser for many years. He had helped the fledgling business with tax returns in its initial two years, but had little involvement apart from that.

The change in structure was the opportunity to gain a more intimate knowledge of the business. He had several meetings with Peter and inspected the operations before finalizing the new structure.

Peter thought he could turn his hand to any sort of business. They had financed the start-up of the business with some savings and a small overdraft facility at the bank. The bank had required only a rudimentary business plan and a cash-flow budget, together with some security for the overdraft, so no formal planning or market research was undertaken in the early years of the company.

However, a lack of knowledge of the garment industry in Australia, together with severe undercapitalization and a lack of clear planning, caused many early problems and the business could have folded on numerous occasions. It survived only because of Peter's determination not to fail and not to work for anyone else, and Kate's ambitious nature.

The easy lifestyle of the past soon disappeared and running the business became a seven-day-a-week job. After several seasons, sales to a number of local stores and boutiques had become established to the point that significant production expansion was warranted. An established garment manufacturing concern was purchased, enabling the company to move away from the previous home-based operations and the manufacturing and business activities to be centralized and consolidated. Once again the chief business adviser at this point was Henry Jones, the company's external accountant, as a substantial refinancing was required. He helped to prepare the business plan for the new financing. A production consultant was hired for a short assignment to help with the initial factory rearrangement. He prepared a new production strategy and then worked directly in the production room for a few weeks while the new systems were established.

With the move to bigger premises the product range was expanded beyond swimwear to include evening wear, denims, tennis clothes, uniforms and school wear. The sales effort to other areas of the country was also extended.

However, after four years of operation in the new premises the company was barely breaking even and was slowly drifting into financial danger. Although the new products were moderately successful nationally and generated a large turnover, overall the erratic and uncontrolled diversification was not a success. The company had no experience and no strategic advantage in the new lines and the principal product, swimwear, was suffering as a result. Peter had begun to spend less time in the company, leaving John McMahon in charge of day-to-day operations. John had considerable sales ability, but was a poor manager. There was no planning or even sales targeting, which made production planning very difficult.

The first management consultancy

In an annual review of the operations the accountant pointed out the poor performance of the company and suggested that a management consulting associate of his, Jim Scott, analyse its strategy and operations. Initially the budget for the consultant was small, insufficient for a full commission, so Jim suggested some decision-making processes in which he could be involved in key strategy sessions, providing the analytical framework, with the company being responsible for much of the data-gathering and background research.

Jim first spent several weeks in the company, getting to know its operations and the people involved. He was particularly interested to compare the different versions of the operations of the company from its key personnel. Peter and Kate were very clear about their positions. Peter had made a conscious decision to reduce his day-to-day involvement in the company and pursue other interests. They both could see John's limitations as a manager, but appreciated his sales ability and his promises of better days just around the corner. However, they could not really understand why the company was still only marginally profitable while the sales volume was increasing. John was suspicious of Jim's motives and defensive when interviewed by him. Only with considerable coaxing would he show Jim some key sales data and company information.

Jim was careful to interview the other managers and employees individually, as informally as possible. At every opportunity he emphasized his independent advisory role and that he was not there to sack people. He had gained Peter's permission to use company staff to help gather together data about the company and its operations. He used this data and the results of his interviews to form an initial picture of the company prior to leading the strategy development sessions. These took place over several weekends at a place away from the factory. The three partners were involved in the strategy sessions, together with the company's marketing manager, production supervisor and finance controller.

At the first session Jim introduced the general strategic approach and facilitated the discussion, but observed the others as much as possible. It was only towards the end of the session that he gave his own opinions. The initial process identified the lack of a clear focus as a core problem, causing or accompanying:

- poor market position in markets for all of their products;

- poor coordination between sales targets and production programming;

- confusing and often inconsistent management decisions;

- lack of capital for expansion;

- productivity that was lower than the industry standard.

After the second session an analysis of the profitability of different product lines revealed that swimwear was the only profitable line, and the decision was made to immediately concentrate on it as the core product again. This was a bold decision, since it involved an immediate halving of turnover and some production and design disruptions. Both the management consultant and the consulting accountant were involved in establishing management and accounting control systems during this period.

John McMahon was unhappy with the decision to re-focus the product lines and left the company. After discussions with Jim, Peter resolved to return to full-time involvement in the company and wound down his external activities.

Detailed change strategy after the refocus decision concentrated on the financial structure of the company to cope with future growth, and the management and organizational structure.

After a period of four months the company had:

- developed its first mission statement and business plan;

- established more explicit and clear lines of authority and decision-making, with Peter Marshall resuming full-time management of the company as managing director;

- instituted more formal sales management and sales targeting procedures, involving some basic in-house market research and data collection on broad target markets and alternative distribution outlets, and linking these with detailed production planning and financial budgets;

- resolved to find further investors to give the company the capital structure it needed to sustain any growth.

Henry Jones, the consulting accountant, had some prominent sportspeople as clients who were seeking investments in which they could play some semi-active role. Two of them invested in the company and became board members. The management consultant also accepted a board position at this time, bringing the total size of the board to five.

Further developments

The re-focusing exercise was generally successful. The profitability of the operations improved, and marketing and strategic advantages were realized. Island Paradise found a marketing advantage over larger competitors by being able to present themselves as swimwear specialists, in contrast to many competing manufacturers, for whom swimwear was one line amongst many. The company was able to sell to the big retail chains in this way.

By the early 1980s, several years after the refocusing exercise, the company had established itself as a specialist swimwear manufacturer, supplying 6-7 per cent of the Australian market for women's swimwear. The industry was a fragmented one, with a large number of small and medium-sized companies and a low market share for the top firms. Island Paradise produced approximately 120,000 units per annum, making it much smaller than the larger of its close competitors, which were up to three times bigger in terms of turnover.

Sales were throughout Australia, with a slight concentration on the local market in Queensland, which had a strong beach culture and growing tourist industry, and on the major population centre in Sydney. Up to 10 per cent of the company's output was exported internationally, mostly via agents in New Zealand, Hawaii and Singapore. The export history of the company had been patchy, with the local market generally taking precedence.

Although the company was located outside the major market centres, it had been able to turn its relatively small size and relative isolation somewhat to its advantage. It was competing successfully against larger companies by keeping a low profile, thus not prompting a price war, and targeting specialized markets, namely the higher-end fashion market for younger purchasers, using special materials, while still offering some product lines to the cheaper discount and teenage markets.

At this time the company had a positive net worth of approximately Aus$150,000 and annual profits of approximately Aus$120,000. Its manufacturing operations in the city were at full capacity and it was necessary to subcontract the production of some standard items to other factories. A small amount of production (about 5 per cent) was subcontracted to a Malaysian manufacturer. Only basic items were subcontracted for manufacture by others, because of the problems of quality control when using specialized designs or materials.

Reacting to a changed business climate

In the mid-1980s a series of changes in the operating environment of the company prompted a thorough investigation of its strategy. Jim Scott, the management consultant, had now been involved with the company for some time and led a strategic review of the company, with the objective of setting its course for the rest of the decade.

The approach used for this review was similar to the first refocusing exercise, although this time Jim's firm undertook much of the detailed background and analytical work. His firm had grown somewhat in the intervening period and now had the staff available to do this type of work, while the Island Paradise staff were now too busy to devote sufficient time to it.

The main changes identified were those in the market for swimsuits, in the competitive position of the industry and, most importantly, in the import tariff and quota framework then supporting the industry.

A market research company was engaged to supplement the company's knowledge of the market with detail about purchaser characteristics. The demand for women's swimwear had shown a rapid increase until the early 1970s and then had steadied, growing at a modest annual rate since. The market could be conveniently segmented according to price and outlet, user characteristics and materials used.

At the top end of the market was expensive signature merchandise, carrying a designer label, accounting for approximately 2.5 per cent of the market and mostly sold in boutiques and the speciality areas of department stores. Mainstream swimwear accounted for approximately 85 per cent of the market and was sold in department stores, speciality chains and boutiques. Discount chain merchandise accounted for the remainder of the market and was sold through discount stores. There had been the beginnings of a major shake-up in the Australian retail industry at this time, with retailing power becoming concentrated into a small number of large and diversified retailing chains. Island Paradise did not have a signature label and generally produced for the upper end of the mainstream market. Less than 10 per cent of its production was sold to discount chains.

There were three main user groups. For the young fashion group (14-25 years old) key factors were price and style, with brand not considered important. The sportswear group (18-35 years old) is fashion oriented but more conservative, valuing brand, material and quality. The fashion group (over 25 years old) valued brand and fit and would buy more expensive garments. There was no growth in the younger market segments, and the older market segments were becoming proportionately larger as the population age distribution profile shifted. Island Paradise had products covering all three main user segments.

Materials used in the upper end of the markets were more specialized and required particular skills. Island Paradise used these materials exclusively and had well-developed production expertise in them.

While the growth in the swimwear market had been flat, there had been rapid growth in the market for aerobics and exercise clothing. This market had many of the characteristics of the swimwear market, using similar materials and with similar fit and styling requirements. Island Paradise had no spare production capacity to produce any garments for this market.

In 1983 a new government was elected in Australia, with clearly stated policies of structural and economic reform. The textile industry generally had been heavily protected by a tariff and quota system. The incoming government flagged its intention to substantially reduce protection levels in a series of staged reductions.

The role of offshore production and the long-term direction for the company thus became central points in the strategy review. The impending tariff reduction would also open the local market to imported garments from low labour cost countries.

Jim Scott's report was initially presented to Peter and Kate Marshall as the senior management of the company. Any changes would have to have their full support. A subsequent presentation was made to the board. Recommendations were discussed with them and a decision to proceed obtained.

The company's strengths and weaknesses

The strategic review identified the following resources and strengths for the company:

- profitable operations with some ability to borrow further funds from shareholders;
- an established manufacturing facility;
- an experienced senior management team, proven design expertise, and an established and productive workforce capable of specialized manufacture;
- established purchasing and distribution systems for the local market; and
- a well-developed expertise in producing a high-quality product.

The review also identified the following weaknesses and vulnerabilities:

- a highly seasonal cash flow, with consequent additional finance costs;
- a highly geared company with limited further borrowing capacity on its own account;
- the current factory operating at full capacity with no room for expansion;
- total reliance on one person (Kate Marshall) for all design work;

- no succession plan for any key staff who may leave (the production manager was past normal retiring age) and a management team too small to afford a manager in training or designer in training; and

- no established export distribution system and few international contacts apart from current agents and distributors.

The distinctive competences of the company were identified as being in design and styling, including the ability to successfully make and market a garment that many purchasers have trouble in getting to fit well or feel they look good in. All research indicated that styling and fit were considered to be very important by purchasers. One area of specialization that put the company ahead of others was the ability to produce good-quality garments in fabrics that were difficult to sew.

Alternative strategies

A series of alternative strategies were identified by the review. The criterion for evaluating them was the objective to maintain steady growth in company operations and earnings, but to limit the size and structure so that it could be controlled by the existing owners and core management.

The main alternative strategies identified were:

A. No product diversification (concentrate on swimwear)

A1. Geographical focus

This alternative would involve focusing on areas where high-volume sales could be expected. The company would concentrate on selling only to the major population centres in Australia with a strong beach culture. The objective would be to reduce marketing costs for a fixed sales volume.

The principal advantage of this strategy was that sales volume would be tailored to suit existing production capacity. Because selling and distribution costs are substantial for the company (10-12 per cent of revenue), reductions in this area would make a significant contribution to profits. The present management size and financial structure would not need to be changed.

However, the strategy would increase market risk. By excluding certain markets on a geographical basis, the total targeted market size would decrease, making the company more vulnerable to changes in any one segment. Also, with this no-growth, cost-cutting strategy, there would be the danger of a reduction in management efficiency, and a complacency which would become increasingly difficult to turn around.

A2. Market segmentation

This alternative would involve reducing the range of products produced to concentrate on the most profitable lines, but continuing the geographical expansion, selling to areas not yet serviced by the company. The effect of this would be to generally move the product range of the company up market to more expensive lines. It is essentially a moderate-growth, revenue-maximizing strategy.

The advantages of this strategy would be to reduce competition with major market suppliers which operate at the lower-priced end of the market. It would reduce the market risk on any one geographical market and allow production growth to be controlled at a medium rate. The strategy would also capitalize on the reputation and expertise of the company for producing garments of good styling, fit and quality.

The disadvantages are that it would increase marketing, travelling and distribution costs. Production increases would have to be managed carefully from the Brisbane office, or the company would have to move to larger premises to maintain the quality of the finished product. However, the production increases required would be neither large, nor immediate, since much of the top-end market growth would occur as lower market segments would cease to be serviced by the company. The existing management and marketing infrastructure would be sufficient for this strategy, and it would be attractive for the long-term stability of the company.

A3. Product-range enlargement and geographical expansion

This is essentially a high-growth strategy, with the objective of covering all principal market segments for swimsuits in all principal geographical areas. It would involve an increased sales force, an immediate increase in production capacity, or increasing use of imported products, and increased production efficiency to lower unit production costs.

This strategy would give the company a good base for later expansion into general fashion. It would help to reduce the company's dependence on particular people, since it will be able to afford to hire more design and management expertise.

However, for this strategy to be successful, the company would need to marshal the financial, managerial and production resources to be able to meet head-on competition from much larger firms. Island Paradise would find it more difficult to maintain and capitalize on its reputation and image in the more diversified markets.

A4. Export

Either of the latter two alternatives above could incorporate a substantial component of sales outside Australia. This would most probably involve much more offshore production, either in countries in which the swimsuits were marketed or, more likely, in countries with lower production costs.

The initial steps for this would involve the immediate hiring of two new managers: a production controller to ensure product quality and an international marketing manager. The review established that the marginal cost of hiring these two new people equated to additional sales of 30,000 items as a break-even quantity.

This would boost company expertise in critical areas, spread the market risk further and help to solve the domestic production shortfall of the company. However, the costs were reasonably substantial and some financial risk was seen with this strategy.

B. Some product diversification (out of swimwear)

B1. Non-seasonal garments

The production, marketing and cash flow of swimwear are highly seasonal, and the review investigated the feasibility of reducing the adverse effects of this on the company. There were some advantages found in product diversification where use was made of the special expertise and reputation of the company. One such product was exercise clothing using lycra fabric.

The review found no competitive advantage for the company in general fashion, a field in which there is enormous competition, with certain segments being dominated by very large firms with which Island Paradise would find it hard to compete. Returns would consequently be very low and the risks to the company very high.

B2. Non-garment products

The marketing of some non-garment products fitting in with the Island Paradise image was possible through existing distribution channels. The most likely products would be those associated with swimwear, for example, sunglasses and sun cream. These would present an opportunity to promote the beach image of the company and use existing market outlets.

Undertaken on a small scale, and in products closely allied to the company's existing lines, this could represent a useful range of complementary products.

Recommended strategy

The review concluded that Island Paradise was in the business of manu-facturing and marketing fashion products that are difficult for consumers to get to fit well and to look good, or "high consumer anxiety" products. A company that has the ability to perform this function well can charge a premium for its products and Island Paradise is such a company.

The implications of this for the objectives and strategies of the company were clear. The review found that its main emphasis should be on swimsuits and not on general fashion, where the company had no particular expertise. There should be no major product diversification out of swimsuits (B), unless the product has similar requirements for styling and fit. Similarly, there was seen to be no advantage in covering the whole swimwear market (A3). The company did not have the ability to compete on price terms alone, which it would have to do at the lower end of the market. It could not easily marshal the funds or justify the expenditure to gain an overall market position. Neither would it be able to meet the additional production requirements without substantial new investment in production capacity, and this new production would be for products with a low contribution margin. Island Paradise clearly belonged in particular market segments where the premium for the distinctive attributes of its product was highest.

Therefore a product segmentation strategy (A2) was adopted. It was also decided that the risk involved in extending the export operations of the company (A4) was justified and that international markets would be pursued with more purpose than had previously been the case.

Having chosen the strategy, the review identified detailed financial, organizational and staff requirements that would be required to implement it. The technical expertise in garment production had been clearly identified as essential to the overall success of the company. This aspect could sustain local production as competitive even in the face of new competition from lower labour cost countries. Many of the key workers had been engaged on a subcontract or casual basis. It was thought that this did not tie them into the company sufficiently, and the entire workforce was placed in salaried positions and a bonus scheme introduced based on a measure of product quality.

The overall findings of the strategic review were presented to the workforce in several meetings led by Peter. Feedback was sought, at the meetings and informally in small-group discussions, on its conclusions and the most effective ways to achieve the objectives. The objectives and main strategies of the company were then formalized in a short document, which was made available to the staff.

A strategy implementation group including Peter, Jim, two of the senior managers and three workforce representatives was established to coordinate any changes.

One suggestion from the meetings to gain productivity was the introduction of computerized cutting machines. A small subgroup including the production manager and some cutters and pattern graders was formed to investigate the best way to introduce this new technology.

The expansion required additional development and working capital. A medium-term fund-raising strategy was devised by the consultant and the accountant. It involved a combination of a reduction in dividends to boost retained earnings, shareholder loans and new shareholder capital raised over an 18-month period, to fund first the export expansion and then a shift to new premises. The new premises effectively increased production capacity by half and allowed room for later expansion.

The new strategy adopted by Island Paradise was successful. It allowed the company to build on its strengths in production and design, to establish itself firmly in the high and middle fashion sectors of the swimsuit market locally and expand into export markets to generate steady growth for the company. While the expanded production facility in Brisbane retained the manufacture of specialized and high-value lines, the subcontract production with the Malaysian manufacturer of some standard product lines, including the new aerobics clothing range, was expanded and made more regular.

A stable consultant-client relationship

The early relationship with the company formed by the consultant endured. He is instrumental in leading an annual review of the strategy of the company and suggests further work or analysis, sometimes using other specialized consultants where needed. The company now directly employs 60 people in Australia, and a similar number indirectly in other countries through its subcontracting operations. Its sales and profits have grown steadily, with an annual turnover of Aus$4-5 million. It remains an established firm in the industry.

CASE HISTORY OF PROCESS CONSULTING
(Apex Manufacturing Company)

In his book *Process consultation*,[1] Edgar Schein provides a case history of the Apex Manufacturing Company to explain the progressive steps and procedures of an assignment using the process-consulting approach.

1. Initial contact with the client and defining relationships

The contact client from the Apex Manufacturing Company was a divisional manager one level below the president. The company is a large manufacturing concern, organized into several divisions. The contact client indicated that there were communication problems in the top management group resulting from a recent reorganization. Because the company expected to grow rapidly in the next several years, they felt they should work on this kind of problem now.

He spoke openly about his concern that the president needed help in handling certain key people, shared his worries that the president and his key subordinates were not in good communication, and indicated that recent company history suggested the need for some stabilizing force in the organization. I asked him whether the president knew he had come to me and what the president's feelings were about bringing in a consultant. The contact client indicated that the president as well as other key executives were all in favour of bringing someone in to work with them. All saw the need for some outside help.

Eventually, after many months of working with the president and his six key subordinates, I arrived at a point where all of them saw me as a potentially useful communication link. They asked me quite sincerely to report to each one the feelings or reactions of others whenever I learned anything I felt should be passed on. At the same time they were quite open with me about each other, knowing that I might well pass on any opinions or reactions they voiced to me. They did not want me to treat everything as confidential because they trusted me and each other enough.

This case was of great interest because of my own feeling that my having to serve as carrier of this type of information was not an ideal role for me, and reflected an insufficient ability on their part to tell each other things directly. Hence I took two courses of action. First, I tried as much as possible to train each man to tell others in the group directly what he thought about an issue. At the same time. I intervened directly in their process by passing on information and opinions if I felt this would aid the working situation.

A simple yet critical event will illustrate what I mean. Two members, Pete and Joe, did not always communicate freely with each other, partly because they felt some rivalry. Pete had completed a study and written a report which was to be discussed by the whole group. Three days before the report was due, I visited the company and stopped in at Pete's office to discuss the report with him and ask how things were going. He said they were fine, but frankly he was puzzled about why Joe hadn't come to him to look at some of the back-up data pertaining to Joe's function. Pete felt this was just another bit of evidence that Joe did not really respect Pete very much.

An hour or so later I was working with Joe, and raised the issue of the report. Joe and his staff were very busy preparing for the meeting but nothing was said about looking at the back-up data. When I asked why they had not done anything about the data, Joe said that he was sure it was private and would not be released by Pete. Joe wanted badly to see it, but felt sure that Pete had deliberately not offered it. I decided there was no harm in intervening at this point by reporting to Joe how Pete was feeling. Joe expressed considerable surprise; and later in the day, he went to Pete, who gave him a warm welcome and turned over to him three volumes of the data which Joe had been wanting to see and which Pete had wanted very much to share with him. I had to judge carefully whether I would hurt either Pete or Joe by revealing Pete's feelings. In this case I decided the potential gains outweighed the risks.

Getting back to setting the proper expectations on the part of the company, I have to make it very plain that I will not function as an expert resource on human-relations problems, but that I will try to help the group solve those problems by providing alternatives and by helping them to think through the consequences of various alternatives. I also need to stress my expectation that I will gather data primarily by observing people in action, not by interviewing and other survey methods (though these methods would be used whenever appropriate). Finally, I have to point out that I will not be very active, but will comment on what is happening or give feedback on observations only as I feel it will be helpful to the group.

The fact that I will be relatively inactive is often a problem for the group because of their expectation that once they have hired a consultant they are entitled to sit back and just listen to him tell them things. To have the consultant then spend hours sitting in the group and saying very little not only violates this expectation but also creates some anxiety about what he is observing. The more I can reassure the group early in the game that I am not gathering personal data of a potentially damaging nature, the smoother the subsequent observations will go.

In summary, part of the early exploration with the contact client and any associates whom he involves is intended to establish the formal and psychological contract which will govern the consultation. I feel there should be no formal contract beyond an agreement on a per diem fee and a potential number of days to be devoted to working with the client system. Each party should be free to terminate or change the level of involvement at any time. At the psychological contract level, it is important to get out into the open as many misconceptions as possible, and to try to be as clear as possible about my own style of work, aims, methods, and so on.

2. Method of work

The method of work chosen should be *as congruent as possible with the values underlying process consultation*. Thus, observation, informal interviewing, and group discussions would be congruent with:

(1) the idea that the consultant does not already have pat answers or standard "expert" solutions; and

(2) the idea that the consultant should be maximally available for questioning and two-way communication.

If the consultant uses methods like questionnaires or surveys, he himself remains an unknown quantity to the respondent. As long as he remains unknown, the respondent cannot really trust him, and hence cannot really answer questions completely honestly. The method of work chosen, therefore, should make the consultant maximally visible and maximally available for interaction.

Often I choose to start a consultation project with some interviewing, but the purpose of the interview is not so much to gather data as to establish a relationship with each of the people who will later be observed. The interview is designed to *reveal myself* as much as it is designed to *learn something about the other person*. I will consider the use of questionnaires only after I am well enough known by the organization to be reasonably sure that people would trust me enough to give direct and frank answers to questions.

In the Apex Company, the exploratory meeting led to the decision to attend one of the regular meetings of the executive committee. At this time I was to meet the president and the other key executives to discuss further what could and should be done. At this meeting, I found a lively interest in the idea of having an outsider help the group and the organization to become more effective. I also found that the group was willing to enter an open-ended relationship. I explained as much as I could my philosophy of process consultation and suggested that a good way of getting further acquainted would be to set up a series of individual interviews with each member of the group. At the same time, I suggested that I sit in on the weekly half-day meetings of the executive committee. The interviews would then occur after several of these meetings.

At the initial meeting of the group, I was able to observe a number of key events. For example, the president, Alex, was very informal but very powerful. I got the impression initially (and confirmed it subsequently) that the relationship of all the group members to the president would be the key issue, with relationships to each other being relatively less important. I also got the impression that Alex was a very confident individual who would tolerate my presence only as long as he saw some value in it; he would have little difficulty in confronting me and terminating the relationship if my presence ceased to have value.

It was also impressive, and turned out to be indicative of a managerial style, that Alex did not feel the need to see me alone. He was satisfied from the outset to deal with me inside the group. Near the end of the initial meeting, I requested a private talk with him to satisfy myself that we understood the psychological contract we were entering into. He was surprisingly uncomfortable in this one-to-one relationship, had little that he wished to impart to me, and did not show much interest in my view of the relationship. I wanted the private conversation in order to test his reaction to taking some personal feedback on his own behaviour as the consultation progressed. He said he would welcome this and indicated little or no concern over it. As I was to learn later, this reflected a very strong sense of his own power and identity. He felt he knew himself very well and was not a bit threatened by feedback.

Part of the initial mandate was to help the group to relate to the president. In the interviews which I conducted with group members, I concentrated quite heavily on what kind of things went well in the relationship; what kind of things went poorly; how relationship problems with the president were related to job performance; in what way the group members would like to see the relationship change, and so on. I did not have a formal interview schedule, but rather, held an informal discussion with each member around issues of the sort I have just mentioned.

Intervention by the consultant

In the Apex Company, I found that the treasurer consistently made the operating managers uncomfortable by presenting financial information in an unintentionally threatening way. He wanted to be helpful, and he felt everyone needed the information he had to offer, but it often had the appearance of an indictment of one of the other managers; his costs were too high, his inventory control had slipped, he was too high over budget, etc. Furthermore, this information was often revealed for the first time in the meeting, so that the operating manager concerned had no forewarning and no opportunity to find out why things had gone out of line. The result was often a fruitless argument about the validity of the figures, a great deal of defensiveness on the part of the operating manager, and irritation on the part of the president because the managers could not deal more effectively with the treasurer.

As I observed this process occurring repeatedly over several weeks, I decided that merely drawing attention to the pattern would not really solve the problem because everyone appeared to be operating with constructive intent. What the group needed was an alternative way to think about the use of financial control information. I therefore wrote a memo on control systems (see section 5) and circulated it to the group.

When this came up for discussion at a later meeting I was in a better position to make my observations about the group, since a clear alternative had been presented. My feeling was that I could not have successfully presented this theory orally because of the amount of heat the issue always generated, and because the group members were highly active individuals who would have wanted to discuss each point separately, making it difficult to get the whole message across.

In working with the Apex group I found the written "theory memo" a convenient and effective means of communication. With other groups I have found different patterns to be workable. For example, if the group gets away for a half-day of work on group process, I may insert a half-hour in the middle (or at the end) of the session to present whatever theory elements I consider to be relevant. The topics are usually not selected until I observe the particular "hang-ups" which exist in the group. I therefore have to be prepared to give, on short notice, an input on any of a variety of issues.

A final method of theory input is to make reprints of relevant articles available to the group at selected times. Often I know of some good piece of theory which pertains to what the group is working on. If I suggest that such an article should be circulated, I also try to persuade the group to commit some of its agenda time to a discussion of the article.

The key criterion for the choice of theory input is that the theory must be relevant to what the group already senses is a problem. There is little to be gained by giving "important" theory if the group has no data of its own to link to the theory. On the other hand, once the group has confronted an issue in its own process, I am always amazed at how ready the members are to look at and learn from general theory.

Agenda-setting interventions may strike the reader as a rather low-key, low-potency kind of intervention. Yet it is surprising to me how often working groups arrive at an impasse on simple agenda-setting issues. In a way, their inability to select the right agenda for their meetings, and their inability to discuss the agenda in a constructive way, is symbolic of other difficulties which are harder to pinpoint. If the group can begin to work on its agenda, the door is often opened to other process discussions. Let me provide some examples of how this approach works.

In the Apex Company I sat in for several months on the weekly executive-committee meeting, which included the president and his key subordinates. I quickly became aware that the group was very loose in its manner of operation: people spoke when they felt like it, issues were explored fully, conflict was fairly openly confronted, and members felt free to contribute. This kind of climate seemed constructive, but it created a major difficulty for the group. No matter how few items were put on the agenda, the group was never able to finish its work. The list of backlog items grew longer and the frustration of group members intensified in proportion to this backlog. The group responded by trying to work harder. They scheduled more meetings and attempted to get more done at each meeting, but with little success. Remarks about the ineffectiveness of groups, too many meetings, and so on, became more and more frequent.

My diagnosis was that the group was overloaded. Their agenda was too large, they tried to process too many items at any given meeting, and the agenda was a mixture of operational and policy issues without recognition by the group that such items required different allocations of time. I suggested to the group that they seemed overloaded and should discuss how to develop their agenda for their meetings. The suggestion was adopted after a half-hour or so of sharing feelings. It was then decided, with my help, to sort the agenda items into several categories, and to devote some meetings entirely to operational issues while others would be exclusively policy meetings. The operations meetings would be run more tightly in order to process these items efficiently. The policy questions would be dealt with in depth.

Once the group had made this separation and realized that it could function differently at different meetings, it then decided to meet once a month for an entire day. During this day they would take up one or two large questions and explore them in depth. The group accepted my suggestion to hold such discussions away from the office in a pleasant, less hectic environment.

By rearranging the agenda, the group succeeded in rearranging its whole pattern of operations. This rearrangement also resulted in a redefinition of my role. The president decided that I should phase out my attendance at the operational meetings, but should plan to take a more active role in the monthly one-day meetings. He would set time aside for presentation of any theory I might wish to make, and for process analysis of the meetings. He had previously been reluctant to take time for process work in the earlier meeting pattern, but now welcomed it.

The full-day meetings changed the climate of the group dramatically. For one thing, it was easier to establish close informal relationships with other members during breaks and meals. Because there was enough time, people felt they could really work through their conflicts instead of having to leave them hanging. It was my impression that as acquaintance level rose, so did the level of trust in the group. Members began to feel free to share more personal reactions with each other. This sense of freedom made everyone more relaxed and readier to let down personal barriers and report accurate information. There was less need for defensive distortion or withholding.

After about one year the group decided quite spontaneously to try some direct confrontive feedback. We were at one of the typical monthly all-day meetings. The president announced that he thought each group member should tell the others what he felt to be the strengths and weaknesses of the several individuals. He asked me to help in designing a format for this discussion. I first asked the group members whether they did in fact want to attempt this type of confrontation. The response was sincerely positive, so we decided to go ahead.

The format I suggested was based upon my prior observation of group members. I had noticed that whenever anyone commented on anyone else, there was a strong tendency to answer back and to lock in on the first comment made. Hence, further feedback tended to be cut off. To deal with this problem I suggested that the group discuss one person at a time, and that a ground rule be established that the person being described was not to comment or respond until all the members had had a chance to give all of their feedback. This way he would be forced to continue to listen. The ground rule was accepted, and I was given the role of monitoring the group to ensure that the process operated as the group intended it to.

For the next several hours the group then went into a very detailed and searching analysis of each member's managerial and interpersonal style, including that of the president. I encouraged members to discuss both the positives and the negatives they saw in the person. I also played a key role in forcing people to make their comments specific and concrete. I demanded examples, insisted on clarification, and generally asked the kind of question which I thought might be on the listener's mind as he tried to understand the feedback. I also added my own feedback on points I had observed in that member's behaviour. At first it was not easy for the group either to give or receive feedback, but as the day wore on, the group learned to be more effective.

The total exercise of confrontation was considered highly successful, both at the time and some months later. It deepened relationships, exposed some chronic problems which now could be worked on, and gave each member much food for thought in terms of his own self-development. It should be noted that the group chose to do this spontaneously after many months of meetings organized around work topics. I am not sure they could have handled the feedback task effectively had they been urged to try sooner, even though I could see the need for this type of meeting some time before the initiative came from the group.

In this case, my intervention tended to help the group move from chaotic meetings toward a differentiated, organized pattern. In the end, the group spent more time in meetings than before, but they minded it less because the meetings were more productive. The group also learned how to manage its own agenda and how to guide its own processes.

Feedback systems to groups and individuals

After getting to know the top-management group through several group meetings, I suggested that it might be useful to interview and give feedback to the next level below the vice-president. There was some concern on the part of the senior group that there might be a morale problem at this level. Initially I was asked merely to do an interview survey and report back to the top group. I declined this approach for reasons already mentioned: gathering data to report to a higher group would violate process-consulting assumptions because it would not involve the sources of the data in analysing their own process. I suggested instead that I conduct the interviews with the ground rule that all my conclusions would first be reported back to the interviewee group, and that I would tell top management only those items which the group felt should be reported.[2] The group would first have to sort the items and decide which things they could handle by themselves and which should be reported up the line of authority because they were under higher management control. The real value of the feedback should accrue to the group which initially provided the data; they should become involved in examining the issues they had brought up, and consider what they themselves might do about them.

The above-mentioned procedure was agreed upon by the top management. One vice-president sent a memorandum to all members who would be involved in the interview programme, informing them of the procedure, his commitment to it, and his hope that they would participate. I then followed up with individual appointments with each person concerned. At this initial appointment I recounted the origin of the idea, assured the interviewee that his individual responses would be entirely confidential, told him that I would summarize the data by department, and told him that he would see the group report and discuss it before any feedback went to his boss or higher management.

In the interview I asked each person to describe his job, tell what he found to be the major pluses and minuses in the job, describe what relationships he had to other groups, and how he felt about a series of specific job factors such as challenge, autonomy, supervision, facilities, salary and benefits, and so on. I later summarized the interviews in a report in which I tried to highlight what I saw to be common problem areas.

All the respondents were then invited to a group meeting at which I passed out the summaries, and explained that the purpose of the meeting was to examine the data, deleting or elaborating where necessary, and to determine which problem areas might be worked on by the group itself. We then went over the summary item by item, permitting as much discussion as any given item warranted.

The group meeting had its greatest utility in exposing the interviewees, in a systematic way, to interpersonal and group issues. For many of them, what they had thought to be private gripes turned out to be organizational problems which they could do something about. The attitude "let top management solve all our problems" tended to be replaced with a viewpoint which differentiated between intra-group problems, inter-group problems, and those which were higher management's responsibility. The interviewees not only gained more insight into organizational psychology, but also responded positively to being involved in the process of data gathering itself. It symbolized to them top management's interest in them and concern for solving organizational problems. Reactions such as these are typical of other groups with whom I have tried the same approach.

Following the group meeting, the revised summary was then given to top management, in some cases individually, in others, in a group. My own preference is to give it first individually, to provide for maximum opportunity to explain all the points, and then to follow up with a group discussion of the implications of the data revealed in the interviews. Where the direct supervisor of the group is involved, I have often supplemented the group report with an individual report, which extracts all the comments made by interviewees concerning the strengths and weaknesses of the supervisor's style of management. These focused feedback items have usually proved of great value to the manager, but they should be provided only if the manager initially *asked for this type of feedback.*

In giving either individual or group feedback from the interview summary, my role is to ensure understanding of the data and to stimulate acceptance of it, so that remedial action of some sort can be effectively undertaken. Once the expectation has been built that top management will do something, there is great risk of lowering morale if the report is merely read, without being acted upon in some manner. Incidentally, it is the process consultant's job to ensure that top management *makes this commitment initially* and that high-level officials understand that when the interviews are completed there will be some demands for action. If management merely wants information (without willingness to do something about the information), the process consultant should not do the interviews in the first place. The danger is too great that management will not like what it hears and will suppress the whole effort; such a course will only lead to a deterioration of morale.

The results of interviews (or questionnaires) do not necessarily have to go beyond the group which is interested in them. One of the simplest and most helpful things a group can do to enhance its own functioning is to have the consultant interview the members individually and report back to the group as a whole a summary of its own members' feelings. It is a way of hauling crucial data out into the open without the risk of personal exposure of any individual if he feels the data collected about him are damaging or that the analysis of such data will result in conclusions that are overcritical of his performance.

The giving of individual feedback can be illustrated from several cases. In the Apex Company I met with each of the vice-presidents whose groups had been interviewed and gave them a list of comments which had been made about their respective managerial styles. I knew each man well and felt that he would be able to accept the kind of comments which were made. In each case we scheduled at least a one-hour session, so we could talk in detail about any items which were unclear and/or threatening.

These discussions usually become counselling sessions to help the individual overcome some of the negative effects which were implied in the feedback data. Since I knew that I would be having sessions such as these, I urged each interviewee to talk at length about the style of his boss and what he did or did not like about it. In cases where the boss was an effective manager, I found a tendency for subordinates to make only a few vague generalizations which I knew would be useless as helpful feedback. By probing for specific incidents or descriptions, it was possible to identify just what the boss did which subordinates liked or did not like.

Making suggestions

The consultant must make it quite clear that he does not propose any particular solution as the best one. However frustrating it might be to the client, the process consultant must work to create a situation where *the client's ability to generate his own solutions is enhanced*. The consultant wants to increase problem-solving ability, not to solve any particular problem.

In my experience there has been only one class of exceptions to the above "rule". If the client wants to set up some meetings specifically for the purpose of working on organizational or interpersonal problems, or wants to design a data-gathering method, then the consultant indeed does have some relevant expertise which he should bring to bear. From his own experience he knows better than the client the pros and cons of interviews or questionnaires: he knows better what questions to ask, how to organize the data, and how to organize feedback meetings; he knows better the right sequence of events leading up to a good discussion of interpersonal process in a committee. In such matters, therefore, I am quite direct and positive in suggesting procedures, who should be involved in them, who should be told what, and how the whole project should be handled.

For example, I recall that in the Apex Company the president decided at one of their all-day meetings to try to give feedback to all the members. He asked me to suggest a procedure for doing this. In this instance I was not at all reluctant to suggest, with as much force and logic as I could command, a particular procedure which I thought would work well. Similarly, when it was proposed to interview all the members of a department, I suggested exactly how this procedure should be set up; I explained that all the members had to be briefed by the department manager, that a group feedback meeting would have to be held, and so on. I have not been at all hesitant in refusing to design a questionnaire study if I thought it was inappropriate, or to schedule a meeting on interpersonal process if I thought the group was not ready.

In conclusion, the process consultant should not withhold his expertise on matters of the learning process itself; but he should be very careful not to confuse being an expert *on how to help an organization to learn* with being an expert *on the actual management problems* which the organization is trying to solve. The same logic applies to the evaluation of individuals; I will under no circumstances evaluate an individual's ability to manage or solve work-related problems; but I will evaluate an individual's readiness to participate in an interview survey of his group or a feedback meeting. If I feel that his presence might undermine some other goals which the organization is trying to accomplish, I will seek a solution which will bypass this individual. These are often difficult judgements to make, but the process consultant cannot evade them if he defines *the overall health of the organization* as his basic target. However, he must always attempt to be fair both to the individual and the organization. If no course of action can be found without hurting either, then the whole project should probably be postponed.

3. Evaluation of results

Considerable value change and skill growth occurred over the course of the first year. During this time I spent a great deal of time in two major activities: (1) sitting in on various meetings of the top-management group; and (2) conducting interview and feedback surveys of various key groups, as managers decided they wanted such interviews done. In addition, there were periods of individual counselling, usually resulting from data revealed in the interviews.

I have already given examples of the kind of specific activities which occurred in the group meetings, interviews and feedback sessions. It was clear that with increasing experience, the group was learning to tune in on its own internal processes (skill), was beginning to pay more attention to these and to give over more meeting time to analysis of interpersonal feelings and events (value change), and was able to manage its own agenda and do its diagnosis without my presence (skill). The group first discovered this from having to conduct some of its all-day meetings in my absence. Where such meetings used to be devoted entirely to work content, the group found that even in my absence they could discuss interpersonal process with profit. The members themselves described this change as one of "climate". The group felt more open and effective; members felt they could trust each other more;

information was flowing more freely; less time was being wasted on oblique communications or political infighting.

During the second year, my involvement was considerably reduced, though I worked on some specific projects. The company had set up a committee to develop a management development programme. I was asked to sit in with this committee and help in the development of a programme. After a number of meetings, it became clear to me that the kind of programme the group needed was one in which the content was not too heavily predetermined. The problems of different managers were sufficiently different to require that a formula should be found for discussing the whole range of problems. One of the reflections of the value change which had taken place in the managers was their recognition that they should be prime participants in any programme which they might invent. If a programme was not exciting or beneficial enough to warrant the committee's time, it could hardly be imposed on the rest of the organization.

We developed a model which involved a series of small-group meetings at each of which the group would set its own agenda. After every third meeting or so, a larger management group would be convened for a lecture and discussion period on some highly relevant topic. Once the first group (the committee plus others at the vice-president level) had completed six to eight meetings, each member of the original group would become the chairman for a group at the next lower level of the organization. These ten or so next-level groups would then meet for six to eight sessions around agenda items developed by themselves. In the meantime the lecture series would continue. After each series of meetings at a given organizational level, the model would be reassessed and either changed or continued at the next lower level with the previous members again becoming group chairmen.

My role in this whole enterprise was, first, to help the group to invent the idea; second, to meet with the original group as a facilitator of the group's efforts to become productive; third, to serve as a resource on topics to be covered and lecturers to be used in the lecture series; and, fourth, to appear as an occasional lecturer in the lecture series or as a source of input at a small group meeting. As this procedure took form, my involvement was gradually reduced, though I still met with the original committee to review the overall concept.

In recent months I have met occasionally with individual members of the original group and with the group as a whole. My function during these meetings is to be a sounding-board, to contribute points of view which might not be represented among the members, and to help the group to assess its own level of functioning. I have been able to provide the group with some perspective on its own growth as a group because I could more easily see changes in values and skills. It has also been possible for the group to enlist my help with specific interpersonal problems. A measure of the growth of the group has been its ability to decide when and how to use my help, and to make those decisions validly from my point of view in terms of where I felt I could constructively help.

4. Disengagement: Reducing involvement with the client system

The process of disengagement has, in most of my experiences, been characterized by the following features where:

(1) reduced involvement is a mutually agreed upon decision rather than a unilateral decision by consultant or client;

(2) involvement does not generally drop to zero but may continue at a very low level;

(3) the door is always open from my point of view for further work with the client if the client desires it.

In most of my consulting relationships there has come a time when either I felt that nothing more could be accomplished and/or some members of the client system felt the need to continue on their own. To facilitate a reduction of involvement, I usually check at intervals of several months to see whether the client feels that the pattern should remain as is or should be altered. In some cases where I have felt that a sufficient amount has been accomplished, I have found that the client did not feel the same way and wanted the relationship to continue on a day-a-week basis. In other cases, I have been confronted by the client, as with the Apex Company, with the statement that my continued attendance in the operational group meetings was no longer desirable from his point of view. As the president put it, I was beginning to sound too much like a regular member to be of much use. I concurred in the decision and reduced my involvement to periodic all-day meetings of the group, though the initiative for inviting me remained entirely with the group. Had I not concurred, we would have negotiated until a mutually satisfactory arrangement had been agreed upon. I have sometimes been in the situation of arguing that I should remain fully involved even when the client has wanted to reduce involvement, and in many cases I have been able to obtain the client's concurrence.

The negotiation which surrounds a reduction of involvement is in fact a good opportunity for the consultant to diagnose the state of the client system. The kind of arguments which are brought up in support of continuing (or terminating) provide a solid basis for determining how much value and skill change has occurred. The reader may feel that since the client is paying for services, he certainly has the right to make unilateral decisions about whether or not to continue these services. My point would be that if the consultation process has even partially achieved its goals, there should arise sufficient trust between consultant and client to enable both to make the decision on rational grounds. Here again, it is important that the consultant should not be economically dependent upon any one client, or his own diagnostic ability may become biased by his need to continue to earn fees.

5. Memo on control systems

In this study with the Apex Company the following memo was prepared, distributed and later discussed in a meeting:

Some ideas why internal auditing is seen as non-helpful or as a source of tension

(1) Auditors often feel primary loyalty to the auditing group rather than the company as a whole; they tend, at times, to feel themselves outside of the organization. Managers, on the other hand, feel primary loyalty to the organization.

(2) Auditors are typically rewarded for finding things wrong, less so for helping people get their work done. Managers, on the other hand, are rewarded for getting the job done, whether things were wrong or not.

(3) Auditors tend to be (a) *perfectionists*, and (b) *focused on particular problems in depth*. Managers, on the other hand, tend to be (a) *"satisfiers"* rather than maximizers (they tend to look for workable rather than perfect or ideal solutions), and (b) *generalists*, focusing on getting many imperfect things to work together towards getting a job done, rather than perfecting any one part of the job.

(4) The auditor's job tempts him to *evaluate* the line operation and to propose solutions. The manager, on the other hand, wants *descriptive (non-evaluative) feedback* and to design his own solutions.

Some possible dysfunctional consequences of tension between line organization and auditing function

(1) Members of the line organization tend to pay attention to doing well, primarily in those areas which the auditor measures, whether those are important to the organizational mission or not.

(2) Members of the line organization try hard to hide problems and imperfections.

(3) Management tends to use information about subordinates in an unintentionally punishing way by immediate inquiries which give subordinates the feeling of having the boss on their back, even while they are already correcting the problem.

(4) Members of the line organization are tempted to falsify and distort information to avoid punishment for being "found out", and to avoid having their boss "swoop down" on them.

(5) Detailed information gathered by the auditing function tends to be passed too far up the line both in the auditing function and the line organization, making information available to people who are too far removed from the problem to know how to evaluate the information.

Some tentative principles for the handling of auditing

(1) *Line involvement.* The more the line organization is involved actively in decisions concerning (a) which areas of performance are to be audited, and (b) how the information is to be gathered and to whom it is to be given, the more helpful and effective the auditing function will be.

(2) *Horizontal rather than vertical reporting.* The more the auditing information is made available, first to the man with the problem (horizontal reporting), then to his immediate boss only if the problem is not corrected, and then only to higher levels in either the line or the auditing group if the problem is still not corrected, the more likely it is that auditing will be effective (because line organizations will be less motivated to hide or falsify information and less likely to feel punished).

(3) *Reward for helping rather than policing.* The more the managers in the auditing group reward their subordinates for being *helpful* (based on whether they are being perceived as helpful by the line) rather than being *efficient in finding problem areas*, the more effective the auditing function will be. (Auditing people tend to be undertrained in how to use audit information in a helpful way; an appropriate reward system should be bolstered by training in how to give help.)

(4) *Useful feedback.* The more the auditing information is *relevant* to important operational problems, *timely* in being fed back as soon after problem discovery as possible, and *descriptive rather than evaluative*, the more useful it will be to the line organization.

---

[1] E. H. Schein: *Process consultation: Its role in organization development* (Reading, Massachusetts, Addison-Wesley, 1969). Reprinted with the kind permission of the author and the publisher. See also idem: *Process consultation*, Vol. II: *Lessons for managers and consultants* (Reading, Massachusetts, Addison-Wesley, 1987).

[2] This procedure was brought to Edgar Schein's attention by R. Beckhard. See also R. Beckhard: *Organization development: Strategies and models* (Reading, Massachusetts, Addison-Wesley, 1969).

CASE HISTORY OF SENIOR MANAGEMENT TEAM DEVELOPMENT

This case history shows how a management consultant helped the senior management team of a European subsidiary of a large multinational company to spend more time on strategic management, improve its performance as a management team and achieve better business results. The method used was based on the *action-learning* approach in which the consultant helps the managers or experts in the team to use their own knowledge and skills to resolve the problems faced by the organization.

The client organization

The client was the sales division of the corporation. The division had responsibility for sales in the United Kingdom and Ireland, and was based near London. The division employed 80 people and was led by a general manager with eight managers reporting directly to him.

In the six months prior to the consultant's assignment the management team of this division had found themselves repeatedly in an unpleasant situation. On several occasions, they were asked by the corporation's European headquarters to make savings and reduce expenditure, a course of action which they believed to be harmful to their business. They were, however, not able to resist the pressure because they were unable to objectively demonstrate what they believed to be true, namely that although the current results were not satisfactory, there was about to be a market upturn. Reducing crucial sales effort in the way suggested by the European headquarters would, they believed, weaken the sales division at a time when it was just about to take a number of significant orders. They decided that they did not want to be put in a similar situation again and that the way to avoid this in future was to be able to "prove" their case.

Need for a consultancy

The personnel manager suggested to the general manager that they invite a management consultant who was already known to them to come and discuss the issue. In the discussions that followed, the consultant helped to identify three priority problems that the team needed to address.

First, there was an ongoing problem within the sales group concerning the role of the salesperson vis-à-vis product/applications engineering specialists at various stages of the sales cycle. This had become more apparent as the whole sales process had become more "technical".

Second, there was a lack of good information about customers. In addition, most of the information that was available was only in the memories of individual salespeople.

Third, there were communication and relationship problems within the management team, which was reflected down through the organization.

The consultant proposed a three-stage approach to the problem, starting with a two-and-a-half day residential workshop designed to:

- reach agreement on key operational and strategic drivers and performance indicators and put in place systems to manage these;
- identify the problems that needed to be resolved and agree actions to be taken;
- improve teamwork through assessing the interpersonal relationships within the team and agreeing how these could be made more collaborative and constructive.

For the second stage, the consultant proposed a six-month action-learning programme in which the management team would work as a problem-solving team and the consultant would act as their adviser and facilitator. The development forum would be the team's monthly meetings.

Finally, stage three would be a one-day review to assess what has been achieved and agree the way ahead.

The consultant was contracted on the basis of a lump-sum fee for preparatory work and a daily rate to be paid for the time actually worked during the assignment.

Stage 1 — The management workshop

Nine members of the management team attended the introductory workshop in June 1991. The workshop opened with a presentation by the general manager, setting out the issues and goals for the programme. The group then went on to review and agree their goals for the business over the next two years and beyond. This was followed by an exercise in which the team worked in two subgroups to define (a) the roles of the senior managers in the division, and (b) the specific actions that would need to be taken in order to ensure the success of the business. The views of the two groups were then brought together and approved in a plenary session.

In the next step the workshop separated the tasks that are *operational* (concerned with the day-to-day operations and profitability of the business) and *strategic* (those things concerned with the future health of the business). The division's organizational structure and reporting relationships were then discussed in order to agree on the most suitable structure for achieving the business goals. No changes in the structure or the reporting relationships were considered necessary at this time and all senior managers were "confirmed" in their roles. (It should be noted that this is not always the case; therefore prior to the workshop the consultant should warn the general manager that changes in the organization's structure may be proposed during the workshops so that he or she can plan a response). Operational responsibilities and strategic coordination roles were then allocated.

The team then went on to examine their interpersonal relationships. This was done using a number of psychological profiles to provide personal feedback and a view of the cultural style of the organization as seen by senior management. This activity was particularly valuable as it created the opportunity for open discussion within the team on their views of each other. For example, the general manager was seen by most collaborators as "analytical". A typical comment was: "You would rather work with your notebook to solve a problem than talk to us". Another team member was seen by colleagues as "long on promises but short on delivery", and so on. This frank but constructive discussion enabled the team to understand their perception of themselves and the existing organizational culture. This they defined as "judicious competing", a style which was not conducive to the sort of participative management style they wished to adopt, and in fact was the cause of many of their problems.

In particular, the discussions on the existing culture of the organization helped the team to understand:

- why it was spending most of its time on operational rather than strategic issues;
- why the division had no forum for discussing strategic issues since the agendas for all current meetings were oriented towards operations; and
- why, although the division actually had management tools such as a business plan, a manpower plan and a performance review system, the currently prevailing reactive management style precluded the team from using these tools effectively to manage the business. These tools were seen as something for the headquarters rather than for themselves.

The debate allowed the team to understand that their reactive management style was the main reason why they had not been in a position to argue their case with head office over the proposed cost reductions. They were managing the current task (the present), not the strategy for growth and development (the future).

The next step was to agree the measurement criteria for assessing responsibility for operational and strategic decisions. This was done working in small groups on the understanding that the final measurement criteria would have to be agreed by each senior manager with the colleagues directly reporting to him or her back in the workplace before being submitted for approval to the team.

The last part of the workshop was concerned with identifying the key problems that the group felt needed to be resolved if they were to achieve their business and personal goals. The following issues were identified:

(1) A lack of clear differentiation between the roles of various product sales managers. This role confusion resulted in poaching, protectionism, defensiveness, poor communication, reactive pressures, etc.

(2) A strong focus on short-term issues implied that the group was very narrowly driven towards the current sales figures and immediate corporate requirements.

The group needed to use the business plans that it was currently producing for headquarters to manage its business if it wished to control its own destiny.

(3) There was considerable scope for improving the way in which the group managed its people. There were quite a few good "people management" tools available in the organization and the team actually used many of them, including annual performance appraisal, team briefing, etc. The problem was that these things were done because the corporation wanted the division to do so, not because the division's managers believed in their usefulness. Hence there was a need to formulate and practise an improved people management policy in order to focus and motivate people to achieving the division's goals.

After some debate it was decided that the group would work as three teams to analyse these issues, and terms of reference were agreed. The actual projects were as follows:

Project 1 — Defining the staff managers' role;
Project 2 — Planning for our business future;
Project 3 — Developing a coherent people management philosophy.

The final step was to agree the management procedures that would be used to achieve the desired goals. The team chose to continue to make use of their regular weekly meetings to handle the operational issues, and to turn one of these meetings every month into a strategic meeting. It was also agreed that the consultant would be invited to act as facilitator at the strategic meetings for the first six months.

Stage 2 — Regular monthly meetings and implementation of proposals

At the first strategic meeting, which was held one month after the workshop, the team produced an agenda listing the issues to be covered and their proper timing, i.e. budgeting in July, organization and management review in November, performance appraisal in December, etc. In addition to these items, the agenda also provided for reporting on the three projects plus any other important issues. The team decided to rotate the chairmanship, thus ensuring everyone's involvement and interest.

The early meetings concentrated mainly on the findings of the project teams. The findings of the groups led to a number of significant changes over the following six months:

- The monthly sales meeting structure was changed. Previously there had been two separate meetings. These were brought together and a new "open forum" section introduced through which specialists could be invited to address the sales teams.

- A more effective form of team-based performance management was introduced, organized through the functional team meetings.

- The effectiveness of the weekly staff management meetings improved significantly once the strategic issues had been removed to a separate forum.

- Communication within the management team improved as a result of role clarification and improved performance indicators. This also led to greater staff empowerment at the operating level.

- The business planning project, which consisted of a detailed profiling of existing and potential customers and the use of this information in a customer management programme, led to a very significant increase in awareness of customer potential and sales efficiency; this enabled a much more effective use of resources in customer targeting.

Stage 3 — Review and results assessment

The meetings continued on a monthly basis until July 1992 at which time the stage 3 review was held. This had been postponed to enable the management team to reach certain agreed milestones, including the findings of the annual attitude survey. The team identified the following results which they believed they had achieved as a result of the programme:

(1) Morale at all levels in the organization is greatly improved. The annual attitude survey showed a 70 per cent plus satisfaction level across all categories, 50 per cent higher than a year ago.

(2) Overall profitability has improved. The company had its best year ever in 1992.

(3) The management team is working much more effectively together.

(4) The strategic processes are under control. The group now has its own business plans and is using them to drive their business decisions. The general manager believes that this has enabled them to focus their sales effort, and that this has been the principal factor of their current commercial success.

(5) The improved communication procedures have significantly improved staff motivation and morale.

(6) The total customer satisfaction teams have been focused so that they are now making a significant contribution to the efficiency of the operation. Two teams reached the European final for most significant product/service improvement in 1991-92.

(7) The division now has a much more open and two-way relationship with its European bosses, and is seen by them as the most "go-ahead" sales operation in Europe.

In practice the team became much more effective at managing the business. All members improved their personal management skills mainly through applying the corporate people management procedures more effectively. The strategic forum with its rotating leadership has helped team members to work together better. Two years after the completion of the consultancy the division was operating very successfully. Its former general manager was promoted and is currently heading up a much larger division of the corporation based in the United States. A new general manager is finding his feet.

Conclusion

The consultant's role in the process was to help the team members to help themselves. He adopted a facilitator's role, encouraging the team members to discuss openly each other's performance, agree and monitor accountabilities, face up to business challenges and interpersonal issues, and so on. The consultant also provided a certain amount of technical advice in terms of guidance on sources of information, and the like. This case study is an example of a consultancy intervention using the action-learning approach. It was successful because the team wanted to change. All the consultant did was to help them to focus the change and stay on the right track. The team members did the rest. Many assignments are not as successful as this one, basically because the management teams involved do not really want to change.

Nevertheless, action learning is not a panacea. It is only applicable in situations where those involved possess the necessary technical knowledge, but need to be empowered to use it.

PERSON-TO-PERSON
COMMUNICATION IN CONSULTING

This appendix is intended to provide an overview of some of the essentials required in consulting practice, emphasizing that the person-to-person form of communication should be viewed not simply as an art and a skill, but as a downright necessity. Mastery of person-to-person communication adds to the stature of the consultant and sets him or her on the path to becoming a senior and highly respected practitioner.

1. General issues and problems

Person-to-person communication is vitally important for two reasons: first, because it is the means of linking the consultant and the client; and, second, because of its role in bridging the concepts and practices of change between the management and the staff within the client organization.

A review of management consulting practices suggests that on assignments approximately 30 per cent of the time is spent on problem analysis and related matters on an individual basis, whereas 70 per cent is spent in communicating with others. Thus, for the consultant and the client, communication represents a large slice of the available time and effort.

Listening is considered to be the single most important component (accounting for 45 per cent of the total communication time). Next in importance comes speaking (30 per cent), reading (16 per cent), and writing (9 per cent).[1] A quick glance at these figures reveals that three-quarters of management's time involves person-to-person communication — listening and speaking. Considering that the consultant has to provide functional expertise coupled with its application, it is inevitable that considerable emphasis should be placed on training in this form of communication. In training programmes for consultants up to 20 per cent of the total time is devoted to this task.

Finally, it stands to reason that ease of communication facilitates comprehension and acceptance of new ideas which is, after all, the main purpose of the consulting assignment.

Communication is the vehicle for transmitting knowledge and introducing attitude change. Person-to-person communication is its most effective form and essential for counselling work. It is the basis for the preparation of written reports, which usually do no more than confirm agreements previously reached.

Communication is also the source of power for three accelerators creating the greatest impact on the management scene today, i.e. changes in technology, changes in management concepts and methods, and the interaction of different cultures. Person-to-person communication is the final link in the chain required to bring them into effect. Additionally, such communication is a vital part of the synergy phenomenon, which explains why the collaborative efforts of members of a team are often more effective than the individual efforts of those same people.

Edgar Schein has summarized the factors affecting an individual's ability to "build, maintain, improve and, if need be, repair face-to-face relationships", in the following nine points:

(1) self-insight and a sense of one's own identity;

(2) cross-cultural sensitivity — the ability to decipher other people's values;

(3) cultural/moral humility — the ability to see one's own values as not necessarily better or worse than another's values;

(4) a proactive problem-solving orientation — the conviction that interpersonal and cross-cultural problems can be solved;

(5) personal flexibility — the ability to adopt different responses and approaches as needed by situational contingencies;

(6) negotiation skills — the ability to explore differences creatively, to locate some common ground and to solve the problem;

(7) interpersonal and cross-cultural tact — the ability to solve problems with people without insulting them, demeaning them, or destroying their "face";

(8) repair strategies and skills — the ability to resurrect, to revitalize, and to rebuild damaged or broken face-to-face relationships;

(9) patience.[2]

The consultant should be aware that person-to-person communication possesses direct advantages and disadvantages compared with other forms of communication. Major advantages include *immediacy* and *association*. Immediacy offers opportunities to raise questions and provide answers on relevant issues as needs arise. Association permits a clearer understanding of spoken words by associating them with accompanying gestures, intonation and emphasis, and so provides appropriate interpretation. Such interpretation is necessary because the 500 most frequently used words of the English language possess more than 14,000 different meanings (an average of more than 28 per word), which leaves a good deal of room for possible misunderstanding. Similar problems have to be faced in any language.

One major drawback to this form of communication is that permanent records are not usually maintained, and residual interpretation may not be a faithful reproduction of original messages owing to problems created by distortion, omission, addition, and so on. To reduce errors of this nature, the following considerations should be kept in mind:

- brevity (keep the message to a minimum);
- relevance (don't confuse the audience);
- draw conclusions (don't rely on inferences being properly made);
- consider audience level (communicate to express, not impress);
- use own natural style to best advantage (you cannot pretend to be what you are not, but you should, at least, perform to the best of your ability).

Critical elements in the communication process are represented in figure A2 (overleaf). References to the model shown can be found in most literature on this subject. Critical areas, from a consultant's point of view, occur throughout the system and are noted in the figure. They are discussed in the next section.

2. Using communication techniques in consulting

In consulting, person-to-person communication deals with either the reception or the presentation of information. During the life-cycle of an assignment composed of a *beginning*, a *middle* and an *end*, the emphasis for the consultant usually switches from reception to presentation of information. In the initial stages the consultant is mostly fully absorbed obtaining relevant information, and the presentations at this time are usually confined to explaining his or her presence in the organization and the purpose of the assignment.

Reception techniques at the beginning stage

Reception techniques applied at the *beginning* stage involve listening and observing, which have to do with receptivity and assimilation. They might be thought of as "passive" exercises; but this would be entirely wrong, since full concentration is called for, and expected, during this crucial stage. Most people can absorb four times more information than can be delivered verbally; thus there is the ever-present danger of distraction.

Measures to facilitate information gathering include:

- soliciting permission to write down important facts (especially figures);
- using the pregnant pause, i.e. when the speaker stops talking, don't hurry to speak yourself, but look as if you are expecting further information — when it comes it may be most revealing;
- encourage elaboration of points by asking "Anything else?", or "Yes, go on, please!";
- ask for examples to illustrate generalities that are offered;

Figure A2 Critical elements in reception and transmission of person-to-person communication

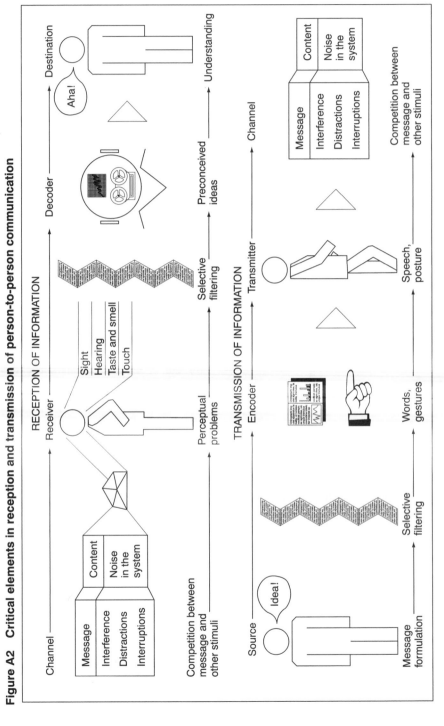

- try not to be involved in speculation, or answering questions in the fact-finding stage; advise that you will certainly give your opinion at a later stage but that you would first prefer to hear all other impressions;

- if necessary answer a question with a question, e.g. to a question put to you, reply with, "Why do you ask that?", or "Behind all good questions usually lies an answer — I would like to know your answer to your own question". Because so much time is involved in listening and observing, and the consultant may be impatient to proceed as rapidly as possible, it is quite possible that bad habits will develop. Some elementary precautions that might be taken to prevent this are indicated in table A1.

Table A1.   Precautions to facilitate the listening process

Bad habits	Possible remedies
Becoming distracted	Try to analyse individual statements and evaluate them (award theoretical marks, e.g. 7 out of 10)
Taking too many notes	Select key points and write digest-style telegram notes
Making snap decisions	Record pertinent data Draw your conclusions after the meeting or interview
Lack of concentration	Try to anticipate the next idea, sentence or phrase
Selective listening	Look for new or hidden meanings
Interrupting the speaker	Wait until there is a natural break in the delivery

Case-building during the middle stage

In the *middle* stage of the communication process a large percentage of time becomes allocated to building a case for the proposed changes and preparing the necessary supporting documents and material. There can be insufficient time allowed for preparation, but only rarely can too much time be allocated; material which is not used can always be discarded.

Preparation involves the development of a structure for the presentation of conclusions and proposals, whether it be for formal or informal presentation. There is no guarantee that your presentation will be heard in its entirety, so prepare summaries for delivery at its commencement, during its course, and on its conclusion so that early-leavers and latecomers (who may be important persons) can be provided with some idea of the total scope of your case.

An outline of your presentation may be in note form, on cards, and so on, but should be available. If time and conditions permit, it is advisable to use audiovisual aids. Rehearsal will improve performance, and opportunities should be taken, whenever possible, to practise before a critical audience.

Delivering the presentation: The end stage

The *end* stage of the process usually revolves around presentations by the consultant. Critical elements to be kept in mind at this stage are:

- introduce the presentation with a summary outline of what is to follow;
- at the conclusion of discrete sections of your delivery, reference to the outline might usefully be repeated, e.g. "Let's see where we are, up to this stage";
- if you are delivering a tightly knit presentation, advise that questions will be handled only after the presentation has been completed or at set times during your delivery; in many cases you will probably have answered likely queries during the course of your presentation, and continuity of delivery and timing will not suffer;
- unless specifically warranted, do not commence with an apology: there is always a chance that it might not be accepted; confidence and a positive approach are priority personal qualities required to induce change;
- most people have an "image" of what they expect to see in a consultant in much the same way as they view doctors, lawyers, engineers and other professionals; by and large, neat but "neutral" clothing styles and a highly organized presentation are expected, and anything else may detract from the presentation;
- when handling questions, answer them one at a time; if objections are raised, deal with them as recommended in section 4.4;
- always make due acknowledgements to persons who have assisted you in your work — it may be necessary to make this a "thank you" to the whole organization;
- if delivering from a written, fully prepared text, try to read each sentence to yourself, pause, look at your audience and say it aloud; pause, glance at the next sentence again silently and then repeat it aloud to your audience while looking at them; with practice, a flowing style can be developed which will convert a script-reading session into an imposing delivery;
- if the consultant is convinced that his or her proposal will supply the changes necessary to assist the organization, he or she must have the strength and the will to fight for the case; this does not mean that the consultant should seek to humiliate any opposition if there is room for compromise; however, he or she should resist it by every possible means.

Consultants bring a wealth of education and experience in communication with them to the profession. A young consultant should have his or her particular style observed and analysed by experienced colleagues, and subsequently try to capitalize on acknowledged strengths and take appropriate steps to remedy weaknesses.

Selected literature on person-to-person communication in consulting is listed in Appendix 11.

---

[1] H. and Z. Roodman: *Management by communication* (Toronto, Methuen Publications 1973), p. 146.

[2] Reproduced with acknowledgement from E. H. Schein: "Improving face-to-face relationships", in *Sloan Management Review* (Cambridge, Massachusetts), Winter 1981, pp. 43-52.

CONSULTANT REPORT WRITING

The reports written by consultants for their clients are mentioned in various chapters of the book according to the occasions and purposes that call for them. This appendix will review the essential factors in the writing and production of all reports used in consulting.

1. Reports in perspective

In consulting work, written communication complements oral communication, but in some cases the written report will become the main or the unique communication channel. In addition to summarizing and conveying information and stimulating the client to act, reports to clients have other important functions. They contribute by their quality and presentation to the impact the consultant makes during the assignment. They also affect the consultant's general reputation. When the personal contacts between consultant and client are limited (for example, if the client obtains written proposals from several consultants and will select one on the basis of these proposals), persuasion may be a vital feature of a report.

An excellent consulting report meets three basic criteria:

- First, it is reader-friendly. Its structure, style, terminology, arguments used and any other features are selected with regard to the client's background, needs and preferences. The basic question is: "What sort of report will render the best service to the client and will be easily read and understood by the client?" and not: "What sort of report do we like to produce in our firm?" Obviously, in many cases the client will have no particular preference and will leave the choice to the consultant. Yet the question must be asked, and discussing it directly with the client may be very helpful.

- Second, a report should be easy for the consultant to write. Ease of writing leads to ease of reading. In addition, it saves time and money for the client, who is going to pay for the time spent by the consultant on report writing, and use his or her own time studying the report. In an extreme case, a poorly drafted report may put off the client and achieve the contrary of what was intended.

● Third, and most importantly, the aim of every report is to convey a particular message. This message (or purpose) needs to be clarified before drafting the report. This course of action will help to structure the report, choose a convenient style, and organize facts and information in support of the message to the client.

As a check, you should ask yourself about the necessity and purpose of any report you intend to produce:

— Why is the report necessary?

— What is its message?

— What will it achieve?

— Is there a better way of achieving this purpose?

— Is now the time for it?

— Who is likely to read it and make use of it?

It is not a bad thing to try drafting an introduction, starting with "The purpose of this report is . . ." If there is any difficulty in finishing the sentence, there is some doubt about the need for the report. The length of time since the last report does not matter, as long as the assignment has progressed satisfactorily in the meantime and the client knows it. The questions mentioned above should be asked even if the report appears to be mandatory because its submission has been agreed in the consulting contract. The situation may have changed, the timing may be wrong, there may no longer be any need for a particular sort of report, and so on.

As a matter of principle, consulting reports do not repeat information obtained from the client or well known to him or her, and general information on the background situation, with the exception of information which directly justifies conclusions or documents the work performed. The essence of information is *news*. Thus, the information content of reports should consist of:

— facts discovered for the first time by the consultant;

— newly discovered significance of known facts;

— newly found connections between known effects and hitherto unknown causes;

— solutions to the client's problems, and their justification;

— facts showing to the client that he or she needs to take action, and any other facts commanding the client's attention.

2. Structuring the report

The contents need to be arranged in *the best sequence* for the nature and purpose of the report and for the desired reaction to it. This may be difficult. The author may be tempted to describe the whole assignment and the whole analytical and thinking process of the consulting team, but the client is looking for results and proposals that will be tangible improvements to the business. Although the author may hope the reader will start at the beginning and read through to the end, there is no guarantee of this. This is one of the hazards of written communication. Persuasion requires careful build-up through a reasoned sequence — which the reader may not choose to follow.

A solution to this may be in a well-presented *summary* at the beginning of the report, which is confined to the principal message of the report and key supporting information. Many busy executives will read the summary for overall guidance to the structure and the main conclusions of the report even if they do not read all chapters. Based on the executive summary, they may choose to look at certain parts of the report more carefully.

A *table of contents* is essential (except in very short reports); it is regrettable that many reports do not have one. The best place for the table of contents is at the very beginning of the report, i.e. preceding an introduction, a preface, a summary, or any other sections. In some countries (e.g. France) it has been customary to give a table of contents at the very end.

The whole report should be carefully planned. It will contain certain main ideas and topics, some of which will have subdivisions. It may help to write headings and sketch the subject-matter on separate sheets or cards. The sheets may then be sorted into the best order for deciding the outline and for drafting.

Marshalling the body of a report into a logical structure is aided by having a formal system of numbers and/or letters for main headings, subheadings and so on. The wording after each number may be printed in a different style. A decimal system may be used, as in the example on the left, or numbers and letters, as in the example on the right:

1. *Main heading*	1. *Main heading*
1.1. Subheading	1. Subheading
1.1.1. Sub-subheading	A. Sub-subheading
	(i) listed item
	(ii) listed item

The advantage of such a scheme is that it makes the writer think about priorities and determine which topics are genuine subdivisions of others. It promotes the orderly organization of the structure and points the way to economy of layout and avoidance of repetition.

For example, a report covering three subject areas, Buying, Stores and Production, deals with three statements about them: Findings, Conclusions and Recommendations. Which of the three layouts overleaf may be the best?

For any particular report one of these may prove easiest, but if "Findings" tell the client nothing new, there is no point in belabouring them. "Conclusions" usually lead straight into "Recommendations". It could even be that the whole report needs to be written as for section 4 in the third column overleaf, the recommendations themselves being written so as to make the findings and conclusions quite clear. A consulting report is not a research paper, but carries a message that should stimulate and orient action.

1. *Findings*	1. *Buying*	1. *Buying*
1.1 Buying	1.1 Findings	1.1 Findings
1.2 Stores	1.2 Conclusions	1.2 Conclusions
1.3 Production	1.3 Recommendations	
2. *Conclusions*	2. *Stores*	2. *Stores*
2.1 Buying	2.1 Findings	2.1 Findings
2.2 Stores	2.2 Conclusions	2.2 Conclusions
2.3 Production	2.3 Recommendations	
3. *Recommendations*	3. *Production*	3. *Production*
3.1 Buying	3.1 Findings	3.1 Findings
3.2 Stores	3.2 Conclusions	3.2 Conclusions
3.3 Production	3.3 Recommendations	
		4. *Recommendations*
		4.1 Buying
		4.2 Stores
		4.3 Production

Everything depends on priorities, weights, balance and purposes; a scheme of marshalling helps to sort them out.

Appendices are useful for taking out of the body of a report detailed descriptions, listings, tables, charts, diagrams, etc., that would break up the continuity of reading and would be difficult to fit in. The body of the report is essentially for reading and quick examination of summary data. Appendices can include items which, though they make a contribution, require a more lengthy examination. It does not help to make a case if the reader is suddenly confronted with several pages of closely tabulated figures. Small tables or diagrams, however, are not disturbing. They break the text monotony, convey selected or summarized information, and should be maintained in the main text.

If a report included, for example, the complete specification of an office system, this would almost certainly be in an appendix. Such an appendix may later become part of a general manual of procedures for the client, while the report may remain confidential.

Acknowledgements have to be made, especially in final assignment reports. This will require tact. If names are mentioned there must be no omissions: every genuine helper likes to see his or her name on the list. At the same time, to include someone who has been more of a hindrance than a help — and knows it — may cause mixed feelings all round. If the list would be too long, it is better to leave it out and settle for general thanks and the remark that "it would be an impossible task to mention everyone who . . .".

3. Drafting the report

Executives are flooded with reports, and hate long and badly written ones. It is useful, therefore, to observe certain principles, which have been summarized in box A1.

Box A1   Principles of clear writing

1. Keep the report as short as possible.

2. Consider your reader, his or her outlook and experience.

3. Write to express, not to impress.

4. Write naturally: style that flows smoothly and does not draw attention to itself is the most effective.

5. Try to keep sentences short; vary their length but let the average be around 20 words.

6. Avoid clumsy sentences and carefully blend short and long words.

7. Use familiar words, avoiding rare or far-fetched ones.

8. Avoid jargon unless it is sure to be familiar to the reader and you know what it means.

9. Avoid unnecessary words that give an impression of padding.

10. Use terms the reader can picture: call a crane a crane, not "a lifting facility".

11. Put action into your verbs; use the force of the active voice; use the passive voice to vary the style.

12. Keep every item of a report relevant to the purpose.

13. Ensure that the contents include all the points necessary to the purpose.

14. Keep a proper balance, giving space and emphasis to each item according to its importance.

15. Keep a serious "tone" as befits a serious purpose; do not tempt the reader to read between the lines; if you do you are at the mercy of his or her imagination.

16. Be careful in the use of numbers: figures tend to draw attention to themselves; decide when absolute values have more significance than percentages and ratios, and vice versa; when quoting figures from other sources, be exact; when estimating, consider the order of accuracy and round off.

17. If you quote from other sources give precise and complete references.

Source: Some of the principles are adapted from R. Gunning: *The technique of clear writing* (New York, McGraw-Hill, 1952).

When the author has the time, the first complete draft should be put aside for a day or two, after which anything wrong is more easily seen and revised. When it looks right to the author, someone else should read it. An operating consultant's draft will normally be read by the project manager or supervisor, who usually has a knack of finding things that a less experienced consultant never suspected. There are, however, some dangers at this point: any report can always be improved, and the temptation to work on it until it is "perfect" may be hard to resist. As with most things, there is a point of diminishing returns.

When drafting the report, the consultant may find out that the report outline originally chosen is not the best one. There is no point in sticking to an inconvenient outline. However, if the client agreed to that outline beforehand, he or she should also be asked to agree to a modified outline to avoid a possible misunderstanding.

If the report is a collective piece of work and the co-authors are known to have different personal styles, final editing should be foreseen. Consistency and homo-geneity (of style, layout, terminology, length of sections, etc.) are key characteristics of excellent reports.

4. Typing and printing the report

The report must look professional in every respect. Its cover and binding should give an excellent impression without looking luxurious. Inside, the layout of the text should allow a generous margin for binding and notes made by the reader, be impeccably printed on a laser printer or similar, and free from extraneous marks or alterations. Any graphs, charts and diagrams must be well drawn and in every respect up to the standard of the typescript.

The consulting firm may have its own standard format that not only distinguishes its reports but caters for filing and control in its reports library. Within the covers, the body of the report may also have a standard layout for division and subdivision of the contents, which can be used if it is not in conflict with the purpose and spirit of a particular report.

The final draft prepared for reproduction should leave the secretary/typist in no doubt as to precisely what is required. The author should take the trouble to lay out the text as it should appear in the final version. The author is also completely responsible for ensuring that no mistakes remain.

The production of reports is greatly improved by judicious use of word processing (see Chapter 31). Most consultants prepare their reports, or their inputs in collective reports, on their personal computers, often directly at clients' premises. All contributors must strictly adhere to a common format. Corrections and amendments can then be made easily by the report author or editor.

A client may wish to receive the report on a diskette or through E-mail in addition to, or instead of, getting printed copies. Systems compatibility should be kept in mind because flawless conversions of documents are rare.

Selected literature on report writing is listed in Appendix 11.

SELECTED BIBLIOGRAPHY
FOR MANAGEMENT CONSULTANTS

Part I.   Management consulting in perspective

Albert, K. J.: *How to be your own management consultant* (New York, McGraw-Hill, 1978); 256 pp.

American Institute of Certified Public Accountants (AICPA): *Consulting services manual* (Jersey City, New Jersey, 1993).

Argyris, Ch.: *Intervention theory and method: A behavioural science view* (Reading, Massachusetts, Addison-Wesley, 1970); 374 pp.

————: *On organizational learning* (Oxford, Blackwell, 1992); 452 pp.

Asian Productivity Organization (APO): *Consulting skills in Asian context: A report of an APO symposium on consulting skills* (Tokyo, 1992); 188 pp.

Barcus, S. W.; Wilkinson, J. W.: *Handbook of management consulting services* (New York, McGraw-Hill, 1986); 440 pp.

Bell, Ch. R.; Nadler, L. (eds.): *The client-consultant handbook* (Houston, Texas, Gulf Publishing Co., 1979); 278 pp.

Bellman, G. M.: *Getting things done when you are not in charge* (San Francisco, California, Berrett-Koehler, 1992); 278 pp.

————: *The consultant's calling: Bringing who you are to what you do* (San Francisco, California, Jossey-Bass, 1990); 238 pp.

Bentley, T. J. (ed.): *The management services handbook* (London, Holt, Rinehart and Winston, 1984); 527 pp.

Bermont, H.: *How to become a successful consultant in your own field* (Washington, DC, Bermont Books, 1978); 157 pp.

————: *Psychological strategies for success in consulting* (Washington, DC, The Consultants Library, 1983); 68 pp.

Block, P.: *Flawless consulting: A guide to getting your expertise used* (Austin, Texas, Learning Concepts, 1981); 215 pp.

Cockman, P.; Evans, B.; Reynolds, P.: *Client-centred consulting: A practical guide for internal advisers and trainers* (London, McGraw-Hill, 1992); 203 pp.

Cody, T. G.: *Management consulting: A game without chips* (Fitzwilliam, New Hampshire, Consultants News, 1986);180 pp.

Cohen, W. A.: *How to make it big as a consultant* (New York, Amacom, 1985); 304 pp.

Cypert, S. A.: *Following the money: The inside story of accounting's first mega-merger* (New York, Amacom, 1991); 279 pp.

Fuchs, J. H.: *Making the most of management consulting services* (New York, Amacom, 1975); 214 pp.

——: *Management consultants in action* (New York, Hawthorn Books, 1975); 216 pp.

Gallessich, J.: *The profession and practice of consultation* (San Francisco, California, Jossey-Bass, 1982); 490 pp.

Garratt, S.: *How to be a consultant* (Aldershot, Gower, 1991); 160 pp.

Golembiewski, T. (ed.): *The handbook of organizational consultation* (New York, Marcel Dekker, 1992).

Goodman, P. S.: *Change in organizations* (San Francisco, California, Jossey-Bass, 1982); 446 pp.

Goodstein, L. D.: *Consulting with human service systems* (Reading, Massachusetts, Addison-Wesley, 1978); 172 pp.

Greiner, L. E.; Metzger, R. O.: *Consulting to management* (Englewood Cliffs, New Jersey, Prentice-Hall, 1983); 368 pp.

Guttmann, H. P.: *The international consultant* (New York, Wiley, revised ed., 1987); 185 pp.

Hersey, P.; Blanchard, K. H.: *Management of organizational behaviour: Utilizing human resources* (Englewood Cliffs, New Jersey, Prentice-Hall, 1982); 345 pp.

Holtz, H.: *How to succeed as an independent consultant* (New York, Wiley, 1983); 395 pp.

Hunt, A.: *The management consultant* (New York, Ronald Press, 1977); 159 pp.

Johnson, B. L.: *Private consulting: How to turn experience into employment dollars* (Englewood Cliffs, New Jersey, Prentice-Hall, 1982); 147 pp.

Kadushin, A.: *Consultation in social work* (New York, Columbia University Press, 1977); 236 pp.

Kelley, R. E.: *Consulting: The complete guide to a profitable career* (New York, Charles Scribner's Sons, revised ed., 1986); 282 pp.

Kishel, G. F.; Kishel, P. G.: *Cashing in on the consulting boom* (New York, Wiley, 1985); 180 pp.

Klein, H. J.: *Other people's business: A primer on management consultants* (New York, Mason-Charter, 1977); 202 pp.

Kubr, M.: *How to select and use consultants: A client's guide*, Management Development Series No. 31 (Geneva, ILO, 1993); 205 pp.

Leavitt, H. J.: *Managerial psychology* (Chicago, Illinois, University of Chicago Press, 1978); 386 pp.

Lippitt, G. L.; Lippitt, R.: *The consulting process in action* (San Diego, California, University Associates, 2nd ed., 1986); 213 pp.

Margerison, Ch. J.: *Managerial consulting skills: A practical guide* (Aldershot, Hampshire, Gower, 1988); 200 pp.

Markham, C.: *Practical consulting* (London, Chartered Accountants' Hall, 1987); 217 pp.

———: *The top consultant: Developing your skills for greater effectiveness* (London, Kogan Page, 1993); 231 pp.

Management consulting 1990: The state of the profession (Fitzwilliam, New Hampshire, Kennedy Publications, 1990); 127 pp.

Metzger, R. O.: *Profitable consulting: Guiding America's managers into the next century* (Reading, Massachusetts, Addison-Wesley, 1988); 191 pp.

Moore, G. L.: *The politics of management consulting* (New York, Praeger, 1984); 176 pp.

Nadler, G.; Hibino, S.: *Breakthrough Thinking: The seven principles of creative problem solving* (Rocklin, California, Prima Publishing, 1994); 416 pp.

Rassam, C.; Oates, D.: *Management consultancy: The inside story* (London, Mercury, 1991); 214 pp.

Schein, E. H.: *Organizational psychology* (Englewood Cliffs, New Jersey, Prentice-Hall, 1980); 274 pp.

———: *Process consultation: Its role in organization development* (Reading, Massachusetts, Addison-Wesley, 1969); 150 pp.

———: *Process consultation: Lessons for managers and consultants*, Vol. II (Reading, Massachusetts, Addison-Wesley, 1987); 288 pp.

Sinha, D. P. (ed.): *Consultants and consulting styles* (New Delhi, Visions Books, 1979); 248 pp.

Smith, B.: *The country consultant* (Fitzwilliam, New Hampshire, Consultants News, 1982); 300 pp.

Steele, F.: *Consulting for organizational change* (Amherst, Massachusetts, University of Massachusetts Press, 1975); 202 pp.

———: *The role of the internal consultant* (Boston, Massachusetts, CBI Publishing Co., 1982); 158 pp.

Stevens, M.: *The Big Eight* (New York, Macmillan, 1981); 270 pp.

———: *The Big Six: The selling out of America's top accounting firms* (New York, Simon & Schuster, 1991); 271 pp.

Stryker, S.: *Guide to successful consulting (with forms, letters and check-lists)* (Englewood Cliffs, New Jersey, Prentice-Hall, 1984); 272 pp.

Tisdall, P.: *Agents of change: The development and practice of management consulting* (London, Heinemann, 1983); 163 pp.

United Nations: *Management consulting: A survey of the industry and its largest firms* (New York, 1993); 93 pp.

Van Doren, G. H.; Nadler, S. D: *Management advisory services manual* (Boston, Massachusetts, Warren, Gorham & Lamont, 1987).

Viney, N.: *Bluff your way in consultancy* (London, Ravette Books, 1986); 62 pp.

Weinberg, G. M.: *The secrets of consulting* (New York, Dorset, 1986); 228 pp.

Weiss, A.: *Million dollar consulting: The professional's guide to growing a practice* (New York, McGraw-Hill, 1992); 274 pp.

Wolf, W. B.: *Management and consulting: An introduction to James O. McKinsey* (Ithaca, New York, Cornell University Press, 1978); 112 pp.

Chapter 4.   Consulting and change

Beckhart, R.; Harris, R. T.: *Organizational transitions: Managing complex change* (Reading, Massachusetts, Addison-Wesley, 1977); 110 pp.

Blake, R.; Mouton, J. S.: *Solving costly organizational conflicts* (San Francisco, California, Jossey-Bass, 1984); 327 pp.

Camp, R.: *Benchmarking: The search for industry best practices that lead to superior performance* (White Plains, New York, Quality Resources, 1989).

Carnal, C.: *Managing change* (London, Routledge, 1991); 101 pp.

Grundy, T.: *Implementing strategic change: A practical guide for business* (London, Kogan Page, 1993); 250 pp.

Hammer, M.; Champy, J.: *Reengineering the corporation: A manifesto for business revolution* (New York, HarperBusiness, 1993); 223 pp.

Huczynski, A. A.; Buchanan, D. A.: *Organizational behaviour: An introductory text* (London, Prentice-Hall, 1991); 615 pp.

Imai, M.: *Kaizen: The key to Japan's competitive success* (New York, Random House, 1986).

Kanter, R. M.; Stein, B. A.; Jick, T. D.: *The challenge of organizational change: How people experience and manage it* (New York, The Free Press, 1992).

Lippitt, G. L.: *Organization renewal: A holistic approach to organization development* (Englewood Cliffs, New Jersey, Prentice-Hall, 1982); 418 pp.

McNair, C. J.; Leibfried, K. H. J.: *Benchmarking: A tool for continuous improvement* (New York, Harper Collins, 1992); 344 pp.

Senge, P. M.: *The fifth discipline: The art and practice of the learning organization* (New York, Doubleday Currency, 1990).

Stewart, V.: *Change: The challenge for management* (Maidenhead, Berkshire, McGraw-Hill, 1983); 166 pp.

Zairi, M.: *Competitive benchmarking: An executive guide* (Letchworth, Hertfordshire, Technical Communications, 1992); 62 pp.

Chapter 5.   Consulting and culture

Bate, P.: *Strategies for cultural change* (Oxford, Butterworth-Heinemann, 1994); 300 pp.

Deal, T. E.; Kennedy, A. A.: *Corporate cultures: The rites and rituals of corporate life* (Reading, Massachusetts, Addison-Wesley, 1982); 232 pp.

Economist Intelligence Unit (EIU): *Managing cultural differences for competitive advantage* (London, 1993); 133 pp.

Hampden-Turner, C.: *Corporate culture* (London, Economist Books, 1990); 240 pp.

Harris, P. R.; Moran, R. T.: *Managing cultural differences* (Houston, Texas, Gulf Publishing Co., 1979); 418 pp.

Hofstede, G.: *Cultures and organizations: Software of the mind* (New York, McGraw-Hill, 1991); 279 pp.

Lippitt, G. L.; Hoopes D. S. (eds.): *Helping across cultures* (Washington, DC, International Consultants Foundation, 1978); 76 pp.

Mizutani, E.: *Strategic cross-cultural management: Its human resource aspect* (Tokyo, International Leadership Development Institute, 1994); 142 pp.

Moran, R. T.; Harris, P. R.: *Managing cultural synergy* (Houston, Texas, Gulf Publishing Co., 1982); 399 pp.

Schein, E. H.: *Organizational culture and leadership* (San Francisco, California, Jossey-Bass, 2nd ed., 1992); 423 pp.

Part II.   The consulting process

Bancroft, G.; O'Sullivan, G.: *Quantitative methods for accounting and business studies* (London, McGraw-Hill, 1993); 380 pp.

Barish, N. N.; Kaplan, S.: *Economic analysis for engineering and managerial decision making* (New York, McGraw-Hill, 1978); 791 pp.

Bennett, R.: *Management research: Guide for institutions and professionals* (Geneva, ILO, 1983); 245 pp.

Bentley, T. J. (ed.): *The management services handbook* (London, Holt, Rinehart and Winston, 1984); 527 pp.

Block, P.: *Flawless consulting: A guide to getting your expertise used* (Austin, Texas, Learning Concepts, 1981); 215 pp.

Bowlin, O. D., et al.: *Guide to financial analysis* (New York, McGraw-Hill, 1980); 335 pp.

Buffa, E. S.; Dyer, J. S.: *Essentials of management science; Operations research* (New York, Wiley, 1978); 528 pp.

Clark, J. J.; Clark, M. T.: *A statistics primer for managers* (New York, The Free Press, 1983); 258 pp.

Clover, V. T.; Balsey, H. L.: *Business research methods* (Columbus, Ohio, Grid Publishing Co., 1979); 385 pp.

Consultants News: *25 "best" proposals by management consulting firms* (Fitzwilliam, New Hampshire, 1984); 510 pp.

Dunham, R. B.; Smith, F. J.: *Organizational surveys: An internal assessment of organizational health* (Glenview, Illinois, Scott, Foresman and Co., 1979); 179 pp.

EIU: *Global benchmarking for competitive edge* (London, 1993); 117 pp.

Emory, C. W.: *Business research methods* (Homewoood, Illinois, Irwin, 1976); 483 pp.

Fédération Internationale des Ingénieurs-Conseils (FIDIC): *The White Book guide (with other notes on documents for consultancy agreements)* (Lausanne, 1991); 115 pp.

Francis, D.: *Effective problem solving: A structured approach* (London, Routledge, 1991); 128 pp.

Greenberg, L.: *A practical guide to productivity measurement* (Washington, DC, Bureau of National Affairs, 1973); 77 pp.

Greiner, L. E.; Metzger, R. O.: *Consulting to management* (Englewood Cliffs, New Jersey, Prentice-Hall, 1983); 368 pp.

Harnett, D. L.: *Statistical methods* (Reading, Massachusetts, Addison-Wesley, 1982); 730 pp.

Harrison, I. W.: *Capital investment appraisal* (London, McGraw-Hill, 1973); 90 pp.

Holtz, H.: *Government contracts: Proposalmanship and winning strategies* (New York, Plenum Press, 1979); 288 pp.

International Labour Office (ILO): *How to read a balance sheet* (Geneva, 2nd (revised) ed., 1985); 213 pp.

Kanawaty, G. (ed.): *Introduction to work study* (Geneva, ILO, 4th (revised) ed., 1992); 523 pp.

Kepner, C. H.; Tregoe, B. B.: *The new rational manager* (Princeton, New Jersey, Kepner-Tregoe, 1981); 224 pp.

Kervin, J. B: *Methods for business research* (New York, Harper, 1992); 750 pp.

Kubr, M.; Prokopenko, J.: *Diagnosing management training and development needs: Concepts and techniques*, Management Development Series, No. 27 (Geneva, ILO, 1989); 304 pp.

Lopez, F. M.: *Personnel interviewing: Theory and practice* (New York, McGraw-Hill, 1971); 356 pp.

Margerison, Ch.: *Managerial problem solving* (Bradford, West Yorkshire, MCB Publications, 1982); 166 pp.

Maynard, H. B.: *Industrial engineering handbook* (New York, McGraw-Hill, 1971); 1,980 pp.

McNair, C. J.; Leibfried, K. H. J.: *Benchmarking: A tool for continuous improvement* (New York, Harper, 1992); 344 pp.

Nadler, G.; Hibino, S.: *Breakthrough Thinking: The seven principles of creative problem solving* (Rocklin, California, Prima Publishing, 2nd (revised) ed., 1994); 416 pp.

———; ———; Farrell, J.: *Creative solution finding* (Rocklin, California, Prima Publishing, 1995); 498 pp.

Nierenberg, G. I.: *The art of negotiating* (New York, Pocket Books, 1984); 254 pp.

Oxenfeldt, A. R.: *Cost-benefit analysis for executive decision making: The danger of plain common sense* (New York, Amacom, 1979); 432 pp.

Payne, T. A.: *Quantitative techniques for management: A practical approach* (Hemel Hempstead, Prentice-Hall, 1981); 452 pp.

Platt, C. J.: *Survey of company reports: An analysis of current practices in presenting information* (Farnborough, Hampshire, Wieton Publications, 1978); 125 pp.

Rawlinson, J. G.: *Creative thinking and brainstorming* (Farnborough, Hampshire, Gower, 1981); 128 pp.

Reeves, T. K.; Harper, D.: *Surveys at work: A practitioner's guide* (Maidenhead, Berkshire, McGraw-Hill, 1982); 259 pp.

Shenson, H. L.: *How to strategically negotiate the consulting contract* (Washington, DC, Bermont Books, 1980); 107 pp.

Silverman, J. M., et al.: *Action-planning workshops for development management* (Washington, DC, World Bank, 1986); 74 pp.

Warren, R.: *How to understand and use company accounts* (London, Business Books, 1983); 221 pp.

Weisbord, M. R.: *Organizational diagnosis* (Reading, Massachusetts, Addison-Wesley, 1978); 180 pp.

Westwick, C. A.: *How to use management ratios* (Aldershot, Hampshire, Gower, 1973); 284 pp.

White, D. J.: *Decision methodology* (London, Wiley, 1975); 274 pp.

Part III.   Consulting in various areas of management

Chapter 12.   Consulting in general and strategic management

American Management Association (AMA): *Managing a dynamic organization* (New York, 1993); 93 pp.

Ansoff, H. I.: *Strategic management* (London, Macmillan, 1979); 236 pp.

Bacon, J.: *Corporate boards and corporate governance* (New York, The Conference Board, 1993); 37 pp.

Baden-Fuller, D.; Stopford, J. M.: *Rejuvenating the mature business* (London and New York, Routledge, 1992); 232 pp.

Bennis, W.: *Why leaders can't lead: The unconscious conspiracy continues* (San Francisco, California, Jossey-Bass, 1989); 169 pp.

Burke, R.: *Project management: Planning and control* (Chichester, Sussex, Wiley, 2nd ed., 1993); 390 pp.

Campbell, A., et al.: *A sense of mission* (London, Hutchinson, 1990); 288 pp.

Chakravarthy, B.; Lorange, P.: *Managing the strategy process: A framework for a multibusiness firm* (Englewood Cliffs, New Jersey, Prentice Hall, 1991); 432 pp.

Deal, T. E.; Kennedy, A. A.: *Corporate cultures: The rites and rituals of corporate life* (Reading, Massachusetts, Addison-Wesley, 1982); 232 pp.

Drucker, P.: *Innovation and entrepreneurship: Practice and principles* (New York, Harper and Row, 1985); 277 pp.

————: *Management* (New York, Harper and Row, 1973); 840 pp.

Drucker, P. F.: *Managing for the future* (Oxford, Butterworth-Heinemann, 1992); 278 pp.

————: *The practice of management* (London, Pan Books, 1970); 480 pp.

Economist Intelligence Unit (EIU): *Best practices: Management* (London, 1993); 105 pp.

————: *Do you need a mission statement?* (London, 1990); 147 pp.

————: *The successful corporation of the year 2000* (London, 1994).

Gilder, G.: *The spirit of enterprise* (New York, Simon and Schuster, 1984); 272 pp.

Goldstein, A. S.: *Corporate comeback: Managing turnarounds and troubled companies* (New York, Wiley, 1988); 230 pp.

Goodman, S. T.: *How to manage a turnaround* (New York, The Free Press, 1984); 279 pp.

Hamel, G.; Prahalad, C. K.: *Competing for the future* (Boston, Massachusetts, Harvard Business School Press, 1994); 327 pp.

Hammer, M.; Champy, J.: *Reengineering the corporation: A manifesto for business revolution* (New York, HarperBusiness, 1993); 223 pp.

Handy, Ch.: *The empty raincoat: Making sense of the future* (London, Hutchinson, 1994); 280 pp.

————: *Gods of management: The changing work of organizations* (London, Souvenir Press, 1986); 240 pp.

————: *Understanding organizations* (London, Penguin Books, 3rd ed., 1985); 487 pp.

Harrison, F. L.: *Advanced project management: A structured approach* (New York, Wiley, 1992); 315 pp.

Harvey-Jones, J.: *Making it happen: Reflections on leadership* (London, Collins, 1988); 266 pp.

Horton, T. R.: *The CEO paradox: The privilege and accountability of leadership* (New York, Amacom Books, 1992); 192 pp.

Irons, K.: *Managing service companies: Strategies for success* (Wokingham, Berkshire, Addison-Wesley, 1994); 258 pp.

Johannson, H. J., et al.: *Business process reengineering: Breakpoint strategies for market dominance* (Chichester, Sussex, Wiley, 1994).

Kanter, R. M.: *The change masters* (New York, Simon & Schuster, 1983).

————: *When giants learn to dance* (New York, Simon & Schuster, 1989).

Katzenbach, R.; Smith, D. K.: *The wisdom of teams: Creating the high-performance organization* (New York, Harper Business, 1994); 336 pp.

Keen, P. G. W.; Knapp, E. M.: *Every manager's guide to business processes: A glossary of key terms and concepts for today's business leader* (Boston, Massachusetts, Harvard Business School Press, 1995); 240 pp.

Khandwalla, P. N.: *Innovative corporate turnarounds* (London, Sage, 1992); 279 pp.

Kotter, J. P.: *The general managers* (New York, The Free Press, 1982); 221 pp.

Kurogane, K. (ed.): *Cross-functional management: Principles and practical applications* (Tokyo, APO, 1993); 253 pp.

Lank, A. G.; Neubauer, F.; Parikh, J.: *Intuition: The new frontier of management* (Oxford, Blackwell, 1994); 265 pp.

Lawler, E. E.: *High involvement management: Participative strategies for improving organizational performance* (San Francisco, California, Jossey-Bass, 1986).

Leavitt, H. J.: *Corporate pathfinders* (Chicago, Illinois, Irwin, 1986).

Lorange, P., et al.: *Implementing strategic processes: Change, learning and cooperation* (Oxford, Blackwell, 1993).

————: *Planning and control: Issues in the strategy process* (Oxford, Blackwell, 1993); 246 pp.

McNair, C. J.; Leibfried, K. H. J.: *Benchmarking: A tool for continuous improvement* (New York, Harper Collins, 1992); 344 pp.

Mintzberg, H.: *Power in and around organizations* (Englewood Cliffs, New Jersey, Prentice-Hall, 1983); 700 pp.

————: *Structures in fives: Designing effective organizations* (Englewood Cliffs, New Jersey, Prentice-Hall, 1983); 312 pp.

————: *The rise and fall of strategic management* (New York, The Free Press, 1993); 288 pp.

North, K.: *Environmental business management: An introduction*, Management Development Series, No. 30 (Geneva, ILO, 1992); 194 pp.

Ohmae, K.: *The mind of the strategist* (New York, McGraw-Hill, 1982).

O'Toole, J.: *Vanguard management* (New York, Doubleday, 1985); 432 pp.

Peters, T.: *Thriving on chaos: Handbook for a management revolution* (London, MacMillan, 1988); 561 pp.

————: *Liberation management: Necessary disorganization for the nanosecond nineties* (New York, Knopf, 1992); 834 pp.

————; Austin, N.: *A passion for excellence: The leadership difference* (New York, Random House, 1985); 437 pp.

————; Waterman, R. H.: *In search of excellence* (New York, Warner Books, 1982); 360 pp.

Pinchot, G.: *Intrapreneuring: Why you don't have to leave the corporation to become an entrepreneur* (New York, Harper and Row, 1985); 368 pp.

Porter, M. E.: *Competitive advantage: Creating and sustaining superior performance* (New York, The Free Press, 1985); 557 pp.

————: *The competitive advantage of nations* (New York, The Free Press, 1990).

————: *Competitive strategy: Techniques for analysing industries and competitors* (New York, The Free Press, 1980).

Rock, M. L. (ed.): *The mergers and acquisitions handbook* (New York, McGraw-Hill, 1987); 518 pp.

Sinatra, A., et al.: *The management of corporate acquisitions: International perspectives* (London, Macmillan, 1994); 526 pp.

Solomon, R. C.: *Ethics and excellence: Cooperation and integrity in business* (New York, Oxford University Press, 1992); 305 pp.

Steiner, G. A.; Miner, J. B.: *Management policy and strategy* (New York, Macmillan, 1982); 357 pp.

Steiner, G. A.: *The new CEO* (New York, Macmillan, 1983); 133 pp.

Sui-Lun, W.: *Strategic information systems in Japan: Creating competitive advantages* (Tokyo, APO, 1993); 86 pp.

Watson, G. H.: *Strategic benchmarking: How to rate your company's performance against the world's best* (New York, Wiley, 1993); 270 pp.

Yamanouchi, T.: *A new study of technology management* (Tokyo, APO, 1995); 308 pp.

Zairi, M.: *Competitive benchmarking: An executive guide* (Letchworth, Hertfordshire, Technical Communications, 1992); 62 pp.

Chapter 13. Consulting in financial management

Andersen, T. J.: *Euromarket instruments: A guide to the world's largest debt market* (New York, New York Institute of Finance, 1990); 308 pp.

Ansell, J.; Wharton, F. (eds.): *Risk: Analysis assessment and management* (Chichester, Sussex, Wiley, 1992); 230 pp.

Auerbach, R. D.: *Money, banking and financial markets* (New York, Macmillan, 1985); 650 pp.

Bean, D. G.: *Financial strategy in the acquisition decision* (Farnborough, Hampshire, Gower, 1975); 175 pp.

Bierman, H.; Smidt, S.: *The capital budgeting decision* (London, Macmillan, 1975); 482 pp.

Bradley, J. W.; Korn, D. H.: *Acquisition and corporate development* (Lexington, Massachusetts, Lexington Books, 1981); 252 pp.

Clark, J. J., et al.: *Capital budgeting: Planning and control of capital expenditures* (Englewood Cliffs, New Jersey, Prentice-Hall, 1979); 468 pp.

Cobham, D.: *Markets and dealers: The economics of the London financial markets* (London, Longman, 1993); 183 pp.

Eckl, S., et al.: *Financial engineering* (Oxford, Basil Blackwell, 1990); 243 pp.

Edwards, A. D. P.: *The exporter's and importer's handbook on foreign currency* (London, Macmillan, 1990); 126 pp.

Ensor, R.; Muller, P.: *The essentials of treasury management* (London, Euromoney Publications, 1981); 259 pp.

Franks, J.; Broyles, J.: *Modern managerial finance* (New York, Wiley, 1979); 376 pp.

Glautier, M. W. E.; Underdown, B.: *Accounting theory and practice* (London, Pitman, 1976); 741 pp.

Grass, M. (ed.): *Control of working capital* (Farnborough, Hampshire, Gower, 1972); 151 pp.

Gray, J.; Johnston, K. S.: *Accounting and management action* (New York, McGraw-Hill, 1973); 574 pp.

Grundy, T.: *Corporate strategy and financial decisions* (London, Kogan Page, 1992).

Heywood, J.: *Foreign exchange and the corporate treasurer* (London, A. and C. Black, 1978); 163 pp.

Holmes, G.; Sugden, A.: *Interpreting company reports and accounts* (London, Woodhead Faulkner, 4th (revised) ed., 1992); 232 pp.

Horngren, C. T.: *Cost accounting: A managerial emphasis* (Englewood Cliffs, New Jersey, Prentice-Hall, 1982); 997 pp.

Hovers, J.: *Expansion through acquisition* (London, Business Books, 1973); 178 pp.

Hull, J.: *Options, futures and other derivative securities* (Englewood Cliffs, New Jersey, Prentice Hall, 1993); 492 pp.

Johnson, H. T.; Kaplan, R. S.: *Relevance lost: The rise and fall of management accounting* (Boston, Massachusetts, Harvard Business School Press, 1987).

Johnson, H. T.: *Relevance regained: From top-down control to bottom-up empowerment* (New York, The Free Press, 1992); 228 pp.

Kettell, B.: *The finance of international business* (London, Graham and Trotman, 1979); 275 pp.

Levy, H.; Sarnat, M.: *Capital investment and financial decisions* (New York, Prentice Hall, 4th ed., 1990); 711 pp.

Manson, B.: *The practitioner's guide to interest rate risk management* (London, Graham & Trotman, 1992).

McCarthy, G. D.; Healey, R. E.: *Valuing a company: Practices and procedures* (New York, Ronald Press, 1971); 521 pp.

Mehta, D. R.: *Working capital management* (Englewood Cliffs, New Jersey, Prentice-Hall, 1974); 182 pp.

Merrett, A. J.; Sykes, A.: *The finance and analysis of capital projects* (London, Longman, 1973); 573 pp.

Nobes, C.: *International classification of financial reporting* (London, Routledge, 2nd ed., 1992); 153 pp.

Pocock, M. A.; Taylor, A. H.: *Handbook of financial planning and control* (Farnborough, Hampshire, Gower, 1981); 423 pp.

Redhead, K.; Hughes, S.: *Financial risk management* (London, Gower Press, 1988).

Rodríguez, R. M.; Carter, E. E.: *International financial management* (Englewood, Cliffs, New Jersey, Prentice-Hall, 1979); 686 pp.

Shapiro, A. C.: *Multinational financial management* (Boston, Massachusetts, Allyn and Bacon, 4th ed., 1992); 729 pp.

Smith, G. V.: *Corporate valuation: A business and professional guide* (New York, Wiley, 1988); 224 pp.

Tennent, M.: *Practical liquidity management* (Farnborough, Hampshire, Gower, 1976); 201 pp.

Van Horn, J.: *Financial management and policy* (Englewood Cliffs, New Jersey, Prentice-Hall, 1980); 809 pp.

Walker, T.: *A guide for using the foreign exchange market* (New York, Wiley, 1981); 372 pp.

Weston, J. F.; Brigham, E. F.: *Managerial finance* (Hinsdale, Illinois, Dryden Press, 1978); 1030 pp.

Chapter 14. Consulting in marketing and distribution management

Best, A.: *When consumers complain* (New York, Columbia University Press, 1981); 232 pp.

Blattberg, R. C., et al.: *The marketing information revolution* (Boston, Massachusetts, Harvard Business School Press, 1994); 368 pp.

Cespedes, F. V.: *Concurrent marketing: Integrating product, sales, and service* (Boston, Massachusetts, Harvard Business School Press, 1995); 336 pp.

Churchill, G. A.: *Marketing research: Methodological foundations* (Chicago, The Dryden Press, 4th ed., 1987); 900 pp.

Clancy, K. J.; Shulman, R. S.: *Marketing myths that are killing business* (New York, McGraw-Hill, 1993).

Elliot, K.; Christopher, M.: *Research methods in marketing* (London, Holt, Rinehart and Winston, 1973); 250 pp.

Enis, B. M.; Cox, K. K.: *Marketing classics: A selection of influential articles* (Boston, Massachusetts, Allyn and Bacon, 1981); 533 pp.

Gattorna, J.: *Handbook of physical distribution management* (Aldershot, Hampshire, Gower, 1983); 528 pp.

Green, P. E.; Tull, D. S.: *Research for marketing decisions* (Englewood Cliffs, New Jersey, Prentice-Hall, 1978); 67 pp.

Gronroos, C.: *Strategic management and marketing in the service sector* (Helsinki, Swedish School of Economics and Business Administration, 1982).

Halliburton, Ch.; Hunerberg, R.: *European marketing: Readings and cases* (Wokingham, Berkshire, Addison-Wesley, 1993); 490 pp.

Kotler, P.: *Marketing essentials* (Englewood Cliffs, New Jersey, Prentice-Hall, 1984); 556 pp.

————: *Marketing management: Analysis, planning and control* (Englewood Cliffs, New Jersey, Prentice-Hall, 1984).

————: *Principles of marketing* (Englewood Cliffs, New Jersey, Prentice-Hall, 1983); 640 pp.

Levitt, T.: *The marketing imagination* (New York, The Free Press, 1983); 203 pp.

McCarthy, E. J.: *Basic marketing: A managerial approach* (Homewood, Illinois, Irwin, 1981); 762 pp.

Nash, E. L.: *The direct marketing handbook* (New York, McGraw-Hill, 1984); 946 pp.

Ogilvy, D.: *Ogilvy on advertising* (New York, Crown, 1983); 224 pp.

Robeson, J. F.; House, R. G.: *The distribution handbook* (New York, The Free Press, 1985); 970 pp.

Sammon, W. L., et al.: *Business competitor intelligence: Methods for collecting, organizing and using information* (New York, Wiley, 1984); 357 pp.

Seibert, J. C.: *Concepts of marketing management* (New York, Harper and Row, 1973); 570 pp.

Shapiro, B. P.; Sviokla, J. J: *Seeking customers* (Boston, Massachusetts, Harvard Business School Press, 1993); 340 pp.

Staudt, T.; Taylor, D. A.: *A managerial introduction to marketing* (Englewood Cliffs, New Jersey, Prentice-Hall, 1970); 576 pp.

Toyne, B.; Walters, P. G. P.: *Global marketing management: A strategic perspective* (Needham, Massachusetts, Allyn and Bacon, 1989); 747 pp.

Willemin, J. H.: *The handbook of professional service management* (Lund, Studentlitteratur, 1984); 275 pp.

Chapter 15.   Consulting in production management

Adam, E. E.; Ebert, R. J.: *Production and operations management: Concepts, models and behavior* (Englewood Cliffs, New Jersey, Prentice Hall, 5th ed., 1992); 729 pp.

Aguayo, R.: *Dr. Deming: The man who taught the Japanese about quality* (London, Mercury, 1990); 284 pp.

APO: *Top management forum: Industrial organizations in the 1990s — Management of linkages* (Tokyo, 1994); 146 pp.

Apple, J. M.: *Plant layout and materials handling* (London, Wiley, 3rd. ed., 1977).

Banks, J.: *Principles of quality control* (London, Wiley, 1989).

Berry, W. L., et al.: *Manufacturing planning and control systems* ((Homewood, Illinois, Irwin, 3rd ed., 1992); 844 pp.

Biegel, J. E.: *Production control, a quantitative approach* (Englewood Cliffs, New Jersey, Prentice-Hall, 1971); 295 pp.

Biemans, F. P. M.: *Manufacturing planning and control: A reference model* (Amsterdam, Elsevier, 1990).

Birchdale, D.: *Job design: A planning and implementation guide for managers* (Epping, Essex, Gower, 1975); 141 pp.

Buffa, E. S.: *Meeting the competitive challenge: Manufacturing strategies for US companies* (Homewood, Illinois, Irwin, 1984); 190 pp.

Buffa, E. S.; Sarin, R. K.: *Modern production-operations management* (New York, Wiley, 1987); 816 pp.

Brown, J. K. (ed.): *Manufacturing: New concepts and new technology to meet new competition* (New York, The Conference Board, 1984); 47 pp.

Butera, F.; Thurman, J. E. (eds.): *Automation and work design* (Amsterdam, North-Holland, 1984); 758 pp.

Clarly, K.; Fujimoto, T.: *Product development performance* (Boston, Massachusetts, Harvard Business School Press, 1991).

Collard, R.: *Total quality* (London, Institute of Personnel Management, 2nd ed., 1993).

Crosby, P.: *Quality is free* (New York, New American Library, 1980); 270 pp.

Davenport, T. H.: *Process innovation: Reengineering work through information technology* (Boston, Massachusetts, Harvard Business School Press, 1993); 337 pp.

Economist Intelligence Unit (EIU): *Best practices: Environment* (London, 1993); 157 pp.

Edosomwan, J. (ed.): *People and product management in manufacturing* (Amsterdam, Elsevier, 1990); 334 pp.

Feigenbaum, A. V.: *Total quality control* (New York, McGraw-Hill, 1983).

Greene, J.: *Production and inventory control handbook* (New York, McGraw-Hill, 1970); 800 pp.

Hutchinson, D.: *Quality circles handbook* (New York, Nichols, 1985); 272 pp.

Ishikawa, K.: *Guide to quality control* (Tokyo, APO, 1986); 225 pp.

Juran, J. M.: *Juran on leadership for quality* (New York, The Free Press (Macmillan), 1989); 376 pp.

Juran, J. M., et al.: *Quality control handbook* (New York, McGraw-Hill, 3rd ed., 1974); ca. 1600 pp.

Kanawaty, G. (ed.): *Introduction to work study* (Geneva, ILO, 4th (revised) ed., 1992); 524 pp.

————: *Managing and developing new forms of work organization*, Management Development Series, No. 16 (Geneva, ILO, 2nd (revised) ed., 1981); 206 pp.

Larson, S.: *Inventory systems and control handbook* (Englewood Cliffs, New Jersey, Prentice-Hall, 1976); 288 pp.

Lawlor, A.: *Productivity improvement manual* (Aldershot, Hampshire, Gower, 1985); 306 pp.

Luck, D. J.: *Product policy and strategy* (Englewood Cliffs, New Jersey, Prentice-Hall, 1972); 118 pp.

Maskell B. H.: *Performance measurement for world class manufacturing: A model for American companies* (Cambridge, Massachusetts, Productivity Press, 1991); 408 pp.

Mayer, R. R.: *Production and operations management* (New York, McGraw-Hill, 1975); 660 pp.

Maynard, H.: *Handbook of modern manufacturing management* (New York, McGraw-Hill, 1971); 1,100 pp.

————: *Industrial engineering handbook* (New York, McGraw-Hill, 1971); 1980 pp.

Mizuno, S.: *Company-wide total quality control* (Tokyo, APO, 1988).

————; Akao Y. (eds.): *QFD: The customer-driven approach to quality planning and deployment* (Tokyo, APO, 1994); 363 pp.

Munro-Faure, L.; Munro-Faure, M.: *Implementing total quality management* (London, Financial Times/Pitman, 1992); 304 pp.

Muther, R.: *Practical plant layout* (New York, McGraw-Hill, 1955); 370 pp.

North, K.: *Environmental business management: An introduction*, Management Development Series, No. 30 (Geneva, ILO, 1992); 194 pp.

Ohno, T.: *Toyota production system: Beyond large-scale production* (Cambridge, Massachusetts, Productivity Press, 1988); 142 pp.

Osada, T.: *The 5 S's: Five keys to a total quality environment* (Tokyo, APO, 1991); 159 pp.

Pisano, G. P.; Hayes, R. H.: *Manufacturing renaissance* (Boston, Massachusetts, Harvard Business School Press, 1995); 384 pp.

Riggs, J. L.: *Production systems: Planning, analysis and control* (New York, Wiley, 1979); 604 pp.

Robson, M.: *Quality circles: A practical guide* (Aldershot, Hampshire, Gower, 1982); 204 pp.

Salvendy, G.: *Handbook of human factors* (New York, Wiley, 1984).

Schonberger, R. J.: *World class manufacturing, the lessons of simplicity applied* (New York, The Free Press, 1986); 256 pp.

Senju, S. (ed.): *TQC and TPM* (Tokyo, APO, 1992); 158 pp.

————; Nakamura, Z.: *Economic engineering for executives: A common-sense approach to business decisions* (Tokyo, APO, 1990); 159 pp.

Shen, G. C.: *Productivity measurement and analysis* (Tokyo, APO, 1985); 59 pp.

Sink, D. S.: *Productivity management: Measurement and evaluation, control and improvement* (New York, Wiley, 1985); 518 pp.

Skinner, W.: *Manufacturing: The formidable competitive weapon* (New York, Wiley, 1985); 330 pp.

Spenley, P.: *World class performance through total quality* (London, Chapman & Hall, 1992); 171 pp.

Susman, G. I. (ed.): *Integrating design and manufacturing for competitive advantage* (New York, Oxford University Press, 1992); 325 pp.

Tersine, R. J.: *Materials management and inventory systems* (New York, Elsevier North-Holland, 1976); 425 pp.

Thomas, A. B.: *Stock control in manufacturing industries* (Farnborough, Hampshire, Gower, 1980); 221 pp.

Thurman, J. E., et al.: *On business and work: Towards new frontiers* (Geneva, ILO, 1992).

Underwood, L.: *Intelligent manufacturing* (Wokingham, Berkshire, Addison-Wesley, 1994); 220 pp.

Vollmann, T. E., et al.: *Manufacturing, planning and control systems* (Homewood, Illinois, Dow Jones-Irwin, 3rd ed., 1992).

Vollmann, T. E., et al.: *The new performance challenge: Measuring operations for world class competition* (Homewood, Illinois, Dow Jones-Irwin, 1990).

Walters, R. W., et al.: *Job enrichment for results: Strategies for successful implementation* (Reading, Massachusetts, Addison-Wesley, 1975); 307 pp.

Warner, M., et al.: *New technology and manufacturing management, strategic choices for flexible production systems* (New York, Wiley, 1990).

Wheelwright, S. G.; Clark, K. B.: *Revolutionizing product development* (New York, The Free Press, 1992).

————; Clark, I.; Hayes, R. A.: *Dynamic manufacturing* (New York, The Free Press, 1988).

Womack, J., et al.: *The machine that changed the world* (New York, Rawson Associates, 1990).

Chapter 16.   Consulting in human resource management

American Society for Training and Development (ASTD): *Trainer's guide to management development* (Baltimore, Maryland, 1990).

APO: *Asian dynamism through human resource development* (Tokyo, 1993); 554 pp.

Anderson, A. H.: *Successful training practice: A manager's guide to personnel development*, Human Resource Management in Action series (Cambridge, Massachusetts, Blackwell, 1993).

Argyris, Ch.: *On organizational learning* (Oxford, Blackwell, 1992); 452 pp.

————: *A handbook of personnel management practice* (London, Kogan Page, 4th ed., 1991); 976 pp.

Armstrong, M.; Murlis, H.: *Reward management: A handbook of salary administration* (London, Kogan Page, 1988); 563 pp.

Arthur, D.: *Recruiting, interviewing, selecting and orienting new employees* (New York, American Management Association, 2nd ed., 1991); 333 pp.

Black, J. S., et al.: *Global assignments: Successfully expatriating and repatriating international managers* (San Francisco, California, Jossey-Bass, 1992).

Boydell, T.: *Management self-development: A guide for managers, organizations and institutions*, Management Development Series, No. 21 (Geneva, ILO, 1985); 267 pp.

Brewster, C.: *The management of expatriates* (London, Kogan Page, 1991).

Brewster, Ch.; Tyson, S. (eds.): *International comparisons in human resource management* (London, Pitman, 1991); 268 pp.

————; Hegewisch, A. (eds.): *The European human resource management guide* (London, Academic Press, 1992).

————; ————; (eds.): *Policy and practice in European human resource management: The evidence and analysis* (London, Routledge, 1994).

Business International: *Managing manpower in Europe* (Geneva, 1982); 192 pp.

Byrne, J. A.: *The headhunters: A provocative look at the corporate search business* (London, Kogan Page, 1987); 254 pp.

Courtis, J.: *Cost effective recruitment* (London, Institute of Personnel Management, 1976); 92 pp.

Craig, R. L. (ed.): *Training and development handbook: A guide to human resource development* (Berkshire, Massachusetts, McGraw-Hill, 3rd ed., 1987).

Decenzo, D. A.; Robbins, S. P.: *Personnel/human resource management* (Englewood Cliffs, New Jersey, Prentice-Hall, 3rd. ed., 1988).

Dowling, P.; Schuler, R. S.: *International dimensions of human resource management* (Boston, Massachusetts, Kent, 1990).

Edwards, S., et al.: *Manpower planning; Strategy and techniques in an organizational context* (Chichester, Sussex, Wiley, 1983); 208 pp.

Eichel, E.; Bender, H. E.: *Performance appraisal: A study of current techniques* (New York, American Management Association, 1984); 64 pp.

EIU: *Managing people in Europe: The HR challenge of leaner companies* (London, 1994).

————: *The talent-intensive organization: Optimising your company's human resource strategies* (London, 1993); 190 pp.

Fombrun, C. J., et al.: *Strategic human resource management* (New York, Wiley, 1984); 499 pp.

Gladstone, A.: (ed.): *Labour relations in a changing environment* (Berlin, De Gruyter, 1992).

————: *The manager's guide to international labour standards*, Management Development Series, No. 23 (Geneva, ILO, 1986); 89 pp.

Glueck, W. F.: *Personnel: A diagnostic approach* (Plano, Texas, Business Publications, 1982).

Gorlin, H.; Schein, L.: *Innovations in managing human resources* (New York, The Conference Board, 1984); 38 pp.

Hall, L.; Torrington, D.: *Personnel Management: A new approach* (New York, Prentice-Hall, 1991); 620 pp.

Hamner, W. C.; Schmidt, F. L. (eds.): *Contemporary problems in personnel* (Chicago, St. Clair Press, 1977); 510 pp.

Hansen, C. P.; Conrad, K. A.: *Handbook of psychological assessment in business* (New York, Quorum Books, 1991); 352 pp.

Henderson, R. I.: *Compensation management: Rewarding performance* (Englewood Cliffs, New Jersey, Prentice-Hall, 1988); 592 pp.

Herriot, P. (ed.): *Assessment and selection in organizations: Methods and practice for recruitment and appraisal* (New York, Wiley, 1990).

Hill, N. C.: *Counselling at the workplace* (New York, McGraw-Hill, 1981); 282 pp.

Hyman, R.; Ferner, A. (eds.): *New frontiers in European industrial relations* (Oxford, Blackwell, 1994); 410 pp.

ILO: *Job evaluation* (Geneva, 1986); 203 pp.

————: *Payment by results* (Geneva, 1984); 164 pp.

Inohara, H.: *Human resource development in Japanese companies* (Tokyo, APO, 1990); 293 pp.

Institute of Management: *Management development to the millenium: The Cannon and Taylor working party reports* (London, 1994); 102 pp.

Joanes-Parker, J.; Perry, R. H. (eds.): *The executive search collaboration: A guide for human resources professionals and their search firms* (Quorum Books, 1990).

Kennedy's pocket guide to working with executive recruiters (Fitzwilliam, New Hampshire, Kennedy Publications, 1994); 160 pp.

King, P.: *Performance planning and appraisal: A how-to-book for managers* (New York, McGraw-Hill, 1989); 170 pp.

Kubr, M.; Prokopenko, J.: *Diagnosing management training and development needs: Concepts and techniques*, Management Development Series, No. 27 (Geneva, ILO, 1989); 304 pp.

Loughran, C. S.: *Negotiating a labor contract: A management handbook* (Washington, DC, Bureau of National Affairs, 2nd ed., 1992); 473 pp.

McBeath, C.; Rands, D.: *Salary administration* (London, Business Books, 1976); 320 pp.

McKinnon, R.: *Headhunters* (London, Scope Books, 1987); 172 pp.

Mizutani, E.: *Strategic cross-cultural management: Its human resource aspect* (Tokyo, International Leadership Development Institute, 1994); 142 pp.

Nadler, L.: *Corporate human resources development: A management tool* (New York, Van Nostrand Reinhold, 1980); 199 pp.

————; Nader, Z.: *The handbook of human resource development* (New York, 2nd ed., Wiley, 1990); 950 pp.

Odiorne, G. S.: *Strategic management of human resources: A portfolio approach* (San Francisco, California, Jossey-Bass, 1984); 356 pp.

Perry, R. H.: *How to answer a headhunter's call: A complete guide to executive search* (New York, Amacom, 1984); 249 pp.

Pfeffer, J.: *Competitive advantage through people: Unleashing the power of the workforce* (Boston, Massachusetts, Harvard Business School Press, 1994); 304 pp.

Pigors, P.; Myers, C. A.: *Personnel administration: A point of view and a method* (London, McGraw-Hill, 1981); 588 pp.

Plumbley, P. R.: *Recruitment and selection* (London, Institute of Personnel Management, 1985); 176 pp.

Senge, P. M.: *The fifth discipline: The art and practice of the learning organization* (New York, Doubleday, 1990).

Schein, E. H.: *Career dynamics: Matching individual and organizational needs* (Reading, Massachusetts, Addison-Wesley, 1978); 276 pp.

Schmitt, N.; Borman, W. C., and Associates (eds.): *Personnel selection in organizations* (San Francisco, California, Jossey-Bass, 1993); 553 pp.

Schuler, R. S.; Hube, V. L.: *Personnel and human resource management* (St. Paul, Minnesota, West Publishing, 5th ed., 1993).

Sparrow, P.; Hiltrop, J.-M.: *European human resource management in transition* (London, Prentice-Hall, 1994); 695 pp.

Stewart, V.; Stewart, A.: *Practical performance appraisal* (Farnborough, Hampshire, Gower, 1978); 192 pp.

Storey, J. (ed.): *New perspectives on human resource management* (London, Routledge, 1989); 208 pp.

Taylor, A. R.: *How to select and use an executive search firm* (New York, McGraw-Hill, 1984); 173 pp.

Thomason, G.: *A textbook of personnel management* (London, Institute of Personnel Management, 1981); 619 pp.

Toplis, J., et al.: *Psychological testing: A manager's guide* (London, Institute of Personnel Management, 2nd ed., 1991); 169 pp.

Towers, B. (ed.): *Handbook of human resource management* (Oxford, Blackwell, 1992); 400 pp.

Tracey, W. R. (ed.): *Human resources management and development handbook* (New York, Amacom, 1985); 1550 pp.

Truell, G. F.: *Coaching and counselling: Key skills for managers* (Buffalo, New York, PAT Publications, 1981); 77 pp.

Truelove, S. (ed.): *Handbook of training and development* (Oxford, Blackwell, 1992); 312 pp.

Wexley, K. N.; Hinrichs, J.: *Developing human resources* (Washington, DC, BNA Books, 1991); 273 pp.

Willis, L.; Daisley, J.: *Developing women through training: A practical handbook* (Maidenhead, McGraw-Hill, 1991); 200 pp.

Zemke, R.; Kramlinger, T.: *Figuring things out: A trainer's guide to needs and task analysis* (Reading, Massachusetts, Addison-Wesley, 1982); 348 pp.

Chapter 17.   Consulting in information technology

Daniels, C. N.: *Information technology: The management challenge* (Wokingham, Berkshire, Addison-Wesley, 1994); 190 pp.

Diebold, J.: *Managing information* (New York, Amacom, 1985); 144 pp.

Ein-Dor, P.; Jones, C. R.: *Information systems management: Analytical tools and techniques* (Amsterdam, North-Holland, 1985); 230 pp.

EIU: *The management challenge of information technology* (London, 1991); 110 pp.

Greene, Ch. B.: *Benchmarking the information technology function* (New York, The Conference Board, 1993); 23 pp.

Hirschheim, R.; Lacity, M. C.: *Information systems outsourcing: Myths, metaphors and realities* (New York, Wiley, 1993); 269 pp.

Lucas, H. C.: *Information systems: Concepts for management* (New York, McGraw-Hill, 1982); 515 pp.

Institute of Certified Management Consultants of Canada (ICMC): *Management practices in information technology* (Toronto, Ontario, 1993).

Keen, P. G. W.: *Shaping the future: Business design through information technology* (Boston, Massachusetts, Harvard Business School Press, 1991); 288 pp.

————: *Every manager's guide to information technology: A glossary of key terms and concepts for today's business leader* (Boston, Massachusetts, Harvard Business School Press, 2nd ed., 1995); 304 pp.

McGee, J. V., et al.: *Managing information strategically* (New York, Wiley, 1993); 240 pp.

Simon, A. R.: *How to be a successful computer consultant* (New York, 2nd ed., McGraw-Hill, 1990); 259 pp.

Walton, R. E.: *Up and running: Integrating information technology and the organization* (Boston, Massachusetts, Harvard Business School Press, 1991); 231 pp.

Wiig, K.: *Expert systems: A manager's guide*, Management Development Series, No. 28 (Geneva, ILO, 1990); 182 pp.

Williams; M.: *Annual review of information science and technology* (Medford, Learned Information, 1993); 495 pp.

Chapter 18. Consulting in small enterprise management

American Institute of Certified Public Accountants (AICPA): *Assisting a financially troubled business* (New York, 1992); 46 pp.

————: *Assisting closely held businesses to plan for succession* (New York, 1992): 31 pp.

APO: *Productivity through consultancy in small industrial enterprises* (Tokyo, 1974); 500 pp.

Baumback, C. M.: *Basic small business management* (Englewood Cliffs, New Jersey, Prentice-Hall, 1983); 540 pp.

Bork, D.: *Family business, risky business: How to make it work* (New York, Amacom, 1986); 180 pp.

Choo, J. A. L.: *Modernizing small-scale industries and businesses* (Tokyo, APO, 1992); 83 pp.

Clark, S. A.: *Beating the odds: 10 smart steps to small business success* (New York, Amacom Books, 1992); 283 pp.

Coleman, B.: *The small business survival guide* (London, Norton, 1984); 350 pp.

Daily Telegraph: *How to set up and run your own business* (London, 1984); 207 pp.

Dickson, D. E. N. (ed.): *Improve your business: Handbook* (129 pp.) and *Workbook* (83 pp.) (Geneva, ILO, 4th impression, 1994).

Harper, M.: *Small business in the third world: Guidelines for practical assistance* (Chichester, Sussex, Wiley, 1984); 211 pp.

Jones, S.; Cohen, M. B. (eds.): *The emerging business: Managing for growth* (New York, Wiley, 1983); 425 pp.

Kline, J. B., et al.: *Managing the small business* (Homewood, Illinois, Irwin, 1982); 466 pp.

Kuriloff, A. H., et al.: *Starting and managing the small business* (London, McGraw-Hill, 1993); 720 pp.

Neck, P.; Nelson, R. (eds.): *Small enterprise development: Policies and programmes*, Management Development Series, No. 14 (Geneva, ILO, 2nd (revised) ed., 1987); 282 pp.

Peace Corps: *Guidelines for management consulting programmes for small-scale enterprise* (Washington, DC, 1981); 212 pp.

Reeb, W. L.; Winters S. L.: *Small business consulting* (New York, American Institute of Certified Public Accountants (AICPA), 1991).

Rosenblatt, P. C., et al.: *The family in business* (San Francisco, California, Jossey-Bass, 1985); 321 pp.

Schumacher, E. F. S.: *Small is beautiful: A study of economics as if people mattered* (London, Abacus, 1973); 250 pp.

Shook, C.; Shook, R. L.: *Franchising: The business strategy that changed the world* (Englewood Cliffs, New Jersey, Prentice-Hall, 1993); 260 pp.

Steinhoff, D.; Burgess, J. F.: *Small business management fundamentals* (London, McGraw-Hill, 6th ed., 1993); 570 pp.

Stillman, R. J.: *Small business management: How to start and stay in business* (Boston, Massachusetts, Little, Brown, 1983); 275 pp.

Woodcock, C. (ed.): *The Guardian guide to running a small business* (London, Kogan Page, 1984); 248 pp.

Chapter 19.   Consulting for micro-enterprises

Bogaert, MVdB.sj: *Training village entrepreneurs, guidelines for development workers* (Delhi, Skills for Progress, 1986); 136 pp.

Buzzard, S.; Edgcomb, E.: *Monitoring and evaluating small business projects: A step-by-step guide* (New York, SEEP, 1987); 262 pp.

Chambers, R.: *Challenging the professions: Frontiers for rural development* (London, IT Publications, 1993); 80 pp.

De Soto, H.: *The other path* (New York, Harper and Row, 1989).

Devereux, S.; Pares, H.: *Credit and savings for development: A manual for the poor* (Oxford, Oxfam, 1987); 90 pp.

Edgcomb, E.; Cawley, J.: *An institutional guide for enterprise development organizations* (New York, PACT Publications, 1993); 312 pp.

Gajanayake, S.; Gajanayake, J.: *Community empowerment: A participatory training manual on community project development* (New York, PACT Publications, 1993); 160 pp.

Harper, M.: *Consultancy for small business* (London, IT Publications, 1976); 254 pp.

————: *Entrepreneurship for the poor* (London, IT Publications, 1984); 135 pp.

Kraus-Harper, U.; Harper, M.: *Getting down to business, a training manual for businesswomen* (London, IT Publications, 1991); 160 pp.

Levitsky, J. (ed.): *Microenterprises in developing countries* (London, IT Publications, 1989); 274 pp.

May, N.: *No short cuts: A starter resource for women's group fieldworkers* (London, Change, 1992); 60 pp.

Millard, E.: *Financial management of a small handicraft business* (London, IT Publications/Oxfam, 1987); 38 pp.

————: *Export marketing for a small handicraft business* (London, IT Publications/Oxfam, 1992); 140 pp.

OEF International: *Marketing strategies, training activities for third world women entrepreneurs* (Washington, DC, 1986); 96 pp.

Rolfe, C., et al.: *Refugee enterprise, it can be done* (London, IT Publications, 1989); 150 pp.

Small-scale enterprise, Policy document No. 3 (The Hague, Ministry of Foreign Affairs, 1992); 106 pp.

Technonet Asia: *Achievement motivation training: Trainer's guide and handbook of exercises* (Singapore, 1984); 315 pp.

Theis, J.; Grady, H. M.: *Participatory rapid appraisal for community development workers* (Delhi, Skills for Progress, 1986); 136 pp.

Chapter 20. Consulting for the public sector

Abramson, R.; Halset, W.: *Planning for improved enterprise performance: A guide for managers and consultants*, Management Development Series, No. 15 (Geneva, ILO, 1979); 178 pp.

Ahmed, Z. U. (ed.): *Financial profitability and losses in public enterprises* (Ljubljana, International Centre for Public Enterprises in Developing Countries, 1982); 167 pp.

APO: *Improving productivity in civil service: A symposium report* (Tokyo, 1993); 139 pp.

Borcherding, T. E. (ed.): *Budgets and bureaucrats: The source of government growth* (Durham, North Carolina, 1977).

Drucker, P. F.: *Managing the non-profit organization: Principles and practices* (New York, Harper, 1992).

————: *Post-capitalist society* (New York, Harper, 1993).

Gowan, V. Q.: *Consulting to government* (Cambridge, Massachusetts, Infoscan, 1979); 368 pp.

Hodgetts, J. E.: *The Canadian public service* (Toronto, University of Toronto Press, 1973).

International Association of Schools and Institutes of Administration (IASIA): *Excellence in public management: Facing the challenge*, Report of the 1993 IASIA Annual Conference (Brussels, 1994)

Kolderic, T. (ed.): *An equitable and competitive public sector* (Minneapolis, Hubert H. Humphery Institute of Public Affairs, University of Minnesota, 1984).

Lane, J. E.: *The public sector: Concepts, models and approaches* (London, Sage Publications, 1992); 240 pp.

Organization for Economic Cooperation and Development (OECD): *Public management developments: Survey 1993* (Paris, 1993); 191 pp.

Osborne, D.; Gaebler, T.: *Reinventing government: How the entrepreneurial spirit is transforming the public sector* (Reading, Massachusetts, Addison-Wesley, 1992); 405 pp.

Salamon, L. M. (ed.): *Beyond privatization: The tools of government action* (Washington, DC, Urban Institute Press, 1989).

Savas, E. S.: *Structural adjustment and public service productivity* (Geneva, ILO, 1993; MAN DEV/63, mimeo.)

The Government's use of external consultants (London, HMSO, 1994); 188 pp.

Wilson, J. Q.: *Bureaucracy* (New York, Basic Books, 1989).

Chapter 21.   Consulting in privatization

Asian Development Bank (ADB): *Privatization: Policies, methods and procedures* (Manila, 1985); 380 pp.

Central and Eastern European Privatization Network (CEEPN): *Preparing enterprises for privatization: Business valuation* (Ljubljana, 1992); 156 pp.

Češka, R., et al.: *Small privatization in Central and Eastern Europe* (Ljubljana, Central and Eastern European Privatization Network, 1993); 52 pp.

Copeland, T., et al.: *Valuation: Measuring and managing the value of companies* (New York, Wiley, 2nd ed., 1991).

Eckert, J. K. (ed.): *Property appraisal and assessment administration* (Chicago, International Association of Assessing Officers, 1990).

Ellerman, D. P. (ed.): *Management and employee buy-outs as a technique of privatization* (Ljubljana, Central and Eastern European Privatization Network, 1993); 211 pp.

European Bank for Reconstruction and Development (EBRD): *Management and employee buy-outs in central and eastern Europe — an introduction* (London, 1993); 99 pp.

Feldman, R. A.; Mehra, R.: *Auctions: Theory and possible applications to economies in transition* (Washington, DC, International Monetary Fund, 1993, mimeo.); 26 pp.

Gray, C. V.: *Evolving legal frameworks for private sector development in Central and Eastern Europe* (Washington, DC, The World Bank, 1993).

Kikeri, S., et al.: *Privatization: The lessons of experience* (Washington, DC, The World Bank, 1992); 86 pp.

Lord, R. (ed.): *Privatization yearbook 1993* (London, Whitaker, 1993).

Prokopenko, J. (ed.): *Management for privatization: Lessons from industry and public service*, Management Development Series No. 32 (Geneva, ILO, 1995); 300 pp.

Savas, E. A.: *Privatizing the public sector: The key to better government* (Chatham, New Jersey, Chatham House Publishers, 1987).

Smith, G. V.: *Corporate valuation: A business and professional guide* (New York, Wiley, 1988); 224 pp.

State Committee of the Russian Federation for the Management of State: *The privatization manual* (Moscow, 1993); 2 vols.

Treuhandanstalt: *Privatization: Together into the social market economy* (Cologne, Deutscher Instituts-Verlag, 1992); 301 pp.

United Nations: *Methods and practices of privatization* (New York, 1993); 210 pp.

Chapter 22. Consulting in productivity and performance improvement

APO: *Improving productivity in civil service: A symposium report* (Tokyo, 1993); 139 pp.

EIU: *Making quality work: Lessons from Europe's leading companies* (London, 1992); 269 pp.

——: *Global benchmarking for competitive edge* (London, 1993); 117 pp.

McNair, C. J.; Leibfried, K. H. J.: *Benchmarking: A tool for continuous improvement* (New York, Harper, 1992); 344 pp.

Munro-Faure, L.; Munro-Faure, M.: *Implementing total quality management* (London, Financial Times/Pitman, 1992); 304 pp.

Osada, T.: *The 5 S's: Five keys to a total quality environment* (Tokyo, APO, 1991); 211 pp.

Prokopenko, J.: *Productivity management: A practical handbook* (Geneva, ILO, 1987); 287 pp.

Ross, J. E.: *Managing productivity* (Reston, Virginia, Reston Publishing Co., 1977); 190 pp.

Senju, S., et al.: *Profitability analysis: Japanese approach* (Tokyo, APO, 1989); 215 pp.

—— (ed.): *TQC and TPM* (Tokyo, APO, 1992); 158 pp.

Part IV. Managing a consulting firm

Greenbaum, T. L.: *The consultant's manual: A complete guide to building a successful consulting practice* (New York, Wiley, 1990); 228 pp.

Greiner, L. E.; Metzger, R. O.: *Consulting to management* (Englewood Cliffs, New Jersey, Prentice-Hall, 1983); 368 pp.

Hicks, T. G.; Mueller, J. F.: *Standard handbook of consulting engineering practice* (New York, McGraw-Hill, 1986).

Kubr, M. (ed.): *Managing a management development institution*, Management Development Series, No. 18 (Geneva, ILO, 1982); 277 pp.

Lambert, T.: *High income consulting: How to build and market your professional practice* (London, Nicholas Brealy Publishing); 316 pp.

Lant, J. L.: *The consultant's kit: Establishing and operating your successful business* (Cambridge, Massachusetts, JLA Publications, 1981); 203 pp.

Maister, D. H.: *Managing the professional service firm* (New York, The Free Press, 1993); 376 pp.

Management consulting 1990: The state of the profession (Fitzwilliam, New Hampshire, Kennedy Publications, 1990); 127 pp.

Metzger, R. O.: *Developing a consulting practice* (New York, Sage Publications, 1993); 138 pp.

Chapter 23. Fundamentals of consulting firm management

Maister, D. H.: *Managing the professional service firm* (New York, The Free Press, 1993); 376 pp.

Millar, V. E.: *On the management of professional service firms: Ten myths debunked* (Fitzwilliam, New Hampshire, Kennedy Publications, 1991); 50 pp.

Chapter 24. The consulting firm's strategy

Holtz, H.: *The consultant's guide to hidden profits: The 101 most overlooked strategies for increased earnings and growth* (New York, Wiley, 1992); 230 pp.

Maister, D. H.: *Managing the professional service firm* (New York, The Free Press, 1993); 376 pp.

Management consulting 1990: The state of the profession (Fitzwilliam, New Hampshire, Kennedy Publications, 1990); 127 pp.

Shenson, H. L.: *Shenson on consulting: Success strategies from the consultant's consultant* (New York, Wiley, 1990); 200 pp.

Webb, S. G.: *Marketing and strategic planning for professional service firms* (New York, Amacom, 1982); 304 pp.

Chapter 25. Marketing of management consulting

Braun, I.: *Building a successful professional practice with advertising* (New York, Amacom, 1981); 289 pp.

Carlson, R. K.: *Personal selling strategies for consultants and professionals: The perfect sales equation* (New York, Wiley, 1993); 209 pp.

Connor, R. A.; Davidson, J. P.: *Marketing your consulting and professional services* (New York, Wiley, 1985); 219 pp.

Consultants News: *Public relations for management consultants: A practical compendium* (Fitzwilliam, New Hampshire, 1980); 83 pp.

————: *The news release idea book for management consultants* (Fitzwilliam, New Hampshire, 1981); 296 pp.

————: *25 "best" proposals by management consulting firms* (Fitzwilliam, New Hampshire, 1984); 510 pp.

Davidson III, R. L.: *Contracting your services* (New York, Wiley, 1990); 256 pp.

Forsyth, P.: *Marketing professional services: A handbook* (London, Pitman, 1992); 270 pp.

Hameroff, E. J.; Nichols, S. S.: *How to guarantee professional success: 715 tested, proven techniques for promoting your practice* (Washington, DC, The Consultant's Library, 1982); 183 pp.

Karlson, D.: *Marketing your consulting or professional services* (Los Altos, California, Crisp Publications, 1988); 107 pp.

Kennedy, J. H. (ed.): *Public relations for management consultants* (Fitzwilliam, New Hampshire, Consultants News, 1981); 83 pp.

————: *How management consulting firms are using advertising today* (Fitzwilliam, New Hampshire, Kennedy Publications, 1994).

Kotler, P.; Bloom, P. N.: *Marketing professional services* (Englewood Cliffs, New Jersey, Prentice-Hall, 1984); 296 pp.

Maister, D. H.: *Managing the professional service firm* (New York, The Free Press, 1993); 376 pp.

McCaffrey, M.: *Personal marketing strategies* (Englewood Cliffs, New Jersey, Prentice-Hall, 1983); 219 pp.

Schrello, D.: *The complete marketing handbook for consultants*, 2 vols. (Long Beach, California, Schrello Direct Marketing, 1994); 590 pp.

Wheatley, E. W.: *Marketing professional services* (Englewood Cliffs, New Jersey, Prentice-Hall, 1983); 205 pp.

Wilson, A.: *Practice development for professional firms* (London, McGraw-Hill, 1984); 232 pp.

Chapter 26.   Costs and fees

Consultants News: *Fees and expense policies/statements of 24 management consulting firms* (Fitzwilliam, New Hampshire, 1984); 55 pp.

Reed, R. C.: *Win-win billing strategies: Alternatives that satisfy your clients and you* (Chicago, Illinois, American Bar Association, 1992); 244 pp.

Shenson, H. L.: *The contract and fee-setting guide for consultants and professionals* (New York, Wiley, 1990); 263 pp.

Chapter 27.   Assignment management

American Institute of Certified Public Accountants (AICPA): *Developing a consulting services control and management program* (Jersey City, New Jersey, 1993).

Barcus, S. W.; Wilkinson, J. W. (eds.): *Handbook of management consulting services* (New York, McGraw-Hill, 1986); 439 pp.

Van Doren, G. H.; Nadler, S. D.: *Management advisory services manual* (Boston, Massachusetts, Warren Gorham and Lamont, 1987).

Chapter 28.   Quality management and assurance

European Committee for Standardization (ECS): *Quality Systems BS5750: Part 1: 1987, ISO9001 — 1987, EN29001 — 1987* (Brussels, 1987); 10 pp.

Collard, R.: *Total quality* (London, Institute of Personnel Management, 2nd ed., 1993).

Feigenbaum, A. V.: *Total quality control* (New York, McGraw-Hill, 1983).

Flood, R. L.: *Beyond TQM* (Chichester, Sussex, Wiley, 1993); 303 pp.

Fox, M. J.: *Quality assurance management* (London, Chapman and Hall, 1993); 377 pp.

Hart, C.: *Extraordinary guarantees: A new way to build quality throughout your company and ensure satisfaction for your customers* (New York, Amacom, 1993).

Institute of Management Consultants (IMC): *Quality assurance briefing notes 1-6* (London, 1992-93); each 4 pp.

————: *Model quality manual for XYZ consultancy* (London, 1993); 34 pp.

Juran, J. M.: *Juran on leadership for quality* (New York, The Free Press (Macmillan), 1989); 376 pp.

Maister, D. H.: *Managing the professional service firm* (New York, The Free Press, 1993); 376 pp.

Management Consultancies Association (MCA): *Quality assurance ISO9001 1987/EN29001 1987/BS5750 Part 1 1987 Guidelines for management consultancy* (London, 1990); 9 pp.

————: *Quality assurance practice notes for management consultance* (London, 1990); 60 pp.

Mastenbroek, W. F. G.: *Managing for quality in the service sector* (Oxford, Blackwell, 1991).

Munro-Faure, L., et al.: *Implementing total quality management* (London, Financial Times/Pitman Publishing, 1992); 304 pp.

————: *Achieving quality standards — A step-by-step guide to BS5750/ISO9000* (London, Institute of Management/Pitman Publishing, 1993); 210 pp.

Spenley, P.: *World class performance through total quality* (London, Chapman and Hall, 1992); 171 pp.

Tunks, R.: *Fast track to quality* (New York, McGraw-Hill, 1992); 292 pp.

Chapter 29.   Operational and financial control

AICPA: *Consulting services manual* (Jersey City, New Jersey, 1993).

Altman, M. A.; Weil, R. I.: *Managing your accounting and consulting practice* (New York, Matthew Bender, 1978).

Association of Management Consulting Firms (ACME): *1993 Survey of European key management information* (New York, 1993); 53 pp.

————: *Survey of United States key management information* (New York, 1993); 138 pp.

ILO: *How to read a balance sheet* (Geneva, 2nd (revised) ed., 1985); 213 pp.

Maister, D. H.: *Managing the professional service firm* (New York, The Free Press, 1993); 376 pp.

Thomsett, M. C.: *Fundamentals of bookkeeping and accounting for the successful consultant* (Washington, DC, Bermont Books, 1980); 134 pp.

Chapter 30.   Structuring consulting firms

AICPA: *Consulting services manual* (Jersey City, New Jersey, 1993).

Bakewell, K. G. B.: *How to organize information* (Aldershot, Hampshire, Gower, 1984); 225 pp.

Daniells, L. M.: *Business information sources* (Berkeley, California, University of California Press, 1985); 673 pp.

Pyeatt, N.: *The consultant's legal guide* (Washington, DC, Bermont Books, 1980); 145 pp.

Reed, S. G.: *Small libraries: A handbook for successful management* (Jefferson, North Carolina, McFarland, 1991); 142 pp.

Saint Clair, G.; Williamson, J.: *Managing the new one-person library* (London, Bowker Saur, 2nd ed., 1992); 170 pp.

Vernon, K. D. C.: *Information services in management and business* (London, Butterworth, 2nd ed., 1984); 346 pp.

————— (ed.): *Library and information services of management development institutions: A practical guide*, Management Development Series, No. 24 (Geneva, ILO, 1986).

Chapter 31.   Information technology in consulting firms

Barcus, S. W.; Wilkinson, J. W. (eds.): *Handbook of management consulting services* (New York, McGraw-Hill, 1986); 439 pp.

Holtz, H.: *The consultant's edge: Using the computer as a marketing tool* (New York, Wiley, 1985); 364 pp.

Simon, A. R.: *How to be a successful computer consultant* (New York, McGraw-Hill, 2nd ed., 1990); 259 pp.

Part V.   Developing management consultants and the consulting profession

Chapter 32.   Careers and compensation in consulting

ACME: *Professional profile of management consultants: A body of expertise, skills, and attributes* (New York, 1989); 40 pp.

IMC: *A body of knowledge for the accreditation of management consultants* (New York, 1979); 75 pp.

Maister, D. H.: *Managing the professional service firm* (New York, The Free Press, 1993); 376 pp.

Margerison, Ch. J.: *Managerial consulting skills: A practical guide* (Aldershot, Hampshire, Gower, 1988); 200 pp.

Speicher, K.; Stamp, S.: *Management consulting 1996* (Boston, Massachusetts, Harvard Business School Press, 1995); 178 pp.

Chapter 33.   Training and development of consultants

AICPA: *University education for management consulting* (New York, 1978); 144 pp.

Andolsen, A. A. (ed.): *Management consulting: A model course* (New York, ACME, 1988); 95 pp.

APO: *Consulting skills in Asian context: A report of an APO symposium on consulting skills* (Tokyo, 1992); 188 pp.

Bellman, G. M.: *The consultant's calling: Bringing who you are to what you do* (San Francisco, California, Jossey-Bass, 1990); 238 pp.

Boydell, T.: *Management self-development: A guide for managers, organizations and institutions*, Management Development Series, No. 21 (Geneva, ILO, 1985); 267 pp.

Katz, A. S.: *Professional personnel policies development guidebook* (Reading, Massachusetts, Addison-Wesley, 1982); 256 pp.

King, P.: *Performance planning and appraisals: A how-to book for managers* (New York, McGraw-Hill, 1984); 160 pp.

Kubr, M.; Prokopenko, J.: *Diagnosing management training and development needs: Concepts and techniques*, Management Development Series, No. 27 (Geneva, ILO, 1989); 304 pp.

Markham, C.: *The top consultant: Developing your skills for greater effectiveness* (London, Kogan Page, 1993); 231 pp.

Nadler, L. (ed.): *The handbook of human resource development* (New York, Wiley, 1984); 845 pp.

Phillips, K.; Shaw, P.: *A consultancy approach for trainers* (Aldershot, Hampshire, Gower, 1989); 166 pp.

Tracey, W. R. (ed.): *Human resource management and development handbook* (New York, Amacom, 1985); 1550 pp.

Truell, G. F.: *Coaching and counselling: Key skills for managers* (Buffalo, New York, PAT Publications, 1981); 77 pp.

Chapter 34.   Preparing for the future

APO: *Consulting skills in Asian context* (Tokyo, 1991); 188 pp.

General Agreement on Tariffs and Trade (GATT): *GATS: The general agreement on trade in services and related instruments* (Geneva, 1994); 55 pp.

Management consulting 1990: The state of the profession (Fitzwilliam, New Hampshire, Kennedy Publications, 1990); 127 pp.

World Bank: *The consulting profession in developing countries*, World Bank Discussion Paper (Washington, DC, 1992); 85 pp.

Appendices

Appendix 1 (on choosing and using consultants)

ACME: *How to select and use management consultants* (New York, 1987); 33 pp.

Bennett, R.: *Choosing and using management consultants* (London, Kogan Page, 1990); 301 pp.

Cannon, J. T.: *No miracles for hire: How to get real value from your consultant* (New York, American Management Association, 1990); 287 pp.

Easton, T. A.; Conant, R. W.: *Using consultants: A consumer's guide for managers* (Chicago, Illinois, Probus Publishing, 1985); 200 pp.

EIU: *Choosing and using a management consultant* (London, 1993); 322 pp.

————: *Executive search in Europe: Choosing and using a headhunter* (London, 1993); 290 pp.

Fuchs, J. H.: *Making the most of management consulting services* (New York, Amacom, 1975); 214 pp.

Golightly, H. O.: *Consultants: Selecting, using and evaluating business consultants* (Danbury, Connecticut, Watts, Franklin, 1985); 256 pp.

Holtz, H.: *Utilising consultants successfully: A guide for management in business, government, the arts and professions* (Westport, Connecticut, Quorum Books, 1985); 221 pp.

————: *Choosing and using a consultant: A manager's guide to consulting services* (New York, Wiley, 1989); 208 pp.

Kubr, M.: *How to select and use consultants: A client's guide*, Management Development Series, No. 31 (Geneva, ILO, 1993); 205 pp.

McGonagle, J. J. Jr.: *Managing the consultant: A corporate guide* (Radnor, Pennsylvania, Chilton, 1981); 210 pp.

Shenson, H. L.: *How to select and manage consultants: A guide to getting what you pay for* (Lexington, Massachusetts, Lexington Books, 1990); 241 pp.

Taylor, A. R.: *How to select and use an executive search firm* (New York, McGraw-Hill, 1984); 173 pp.

Transport and General Workers Union: *Management consultants: Friends or enemies?* (London, 1983); 30 pp.

Ucko, T. J.: *Selecting and working with consultants: A guide for clients* (Los Altos, California, 1990; 76 pp.

Appendices 9 and 10 (on communication and report writing)

Alexander Hamilton Institute: *Executive's guide to effective writing* (New York, 1980); 109 pp.

Axtell, R. E.: *Do's and taboos of public speaking: How to get those butterflies flying in formation* (New York, Wiley, 1992); 200 pp.

———— (ed.): *Do's and taboos around the world: A guide to international behaviour* (New York, Wiley, 2nd ed., 1990); 200 pp.

Calero, H.; Oskam, B.: *Negotiate for what you want: Talking your way to success in business, community affairs and personal encounters* (Wellingborough, Northamptonshire, Thorsons Publishers, 1988); 333 pp.

Casse, P.: *The one-hour negotiator* (Oxford, Butterworth-Heinemann, 1992); 117 pp.

Gowers, E.: *The complete plain words* (London, HMSO, 3rd (revised) ed., 1986); 288 pp.

Gunning, R.: *The technique of clear writing* (New York, McGraw-Hill, 1968).

Holcombe, M. W.; Stein, J. K.: *Presentations for decision makers* (New York, Van Nostrand Reinhold, 2nd ed., 1990); 222 pp.

Honey, P.: *Face to face: A practical guide to interactive skills* (London, Institute of Personnel Management, 1976); 150 pp.

Kennedy, G.: *Everything is negotiable* (London, Business Books, revised ed., 1989); 284 pp.

Munter, M.: *Guide to managerial communication* (Englewood Cliffs, New Jersey, Prentice-Hall, 1982); 170 pp.

Nierenberg, G. I.: *The art of negotiating* (New York, Pocket Books, 1984); 254 pp.

Leech, T.: *How to prepare, stage, and deliver winning presentations* (New York, Amacom, 1985); 417 pp.

Poe, R. W.: *The McGraw-Hill guide to effective business reports* (New York, McGraw-Hill, 1982); 209 pp.

Schneider, A. E., et al.: *Organizational communications* (New York, McGraw-Hill, 1975); 367 pp.

Simpkin, R.; Jones, R.: *Business and the language barrier* (London, Business Books, 1976); 291 pp.

Strunk, W.: *The elements of style* (New York, Macmillan, 1959); 70 pp.

Sussams, J. E.: *How to write effective reports* (Aldershot, Hampshire, Gower, 1983); 109 pp.

Swets, P. W.: *The art of talking so that people will listen* (Englewood Cliffs, New Jersey, Prentice-Hall, 1983).

Yager, J.: *Business protocol: How to survive and succeed in business* (New York, Wiley, 1991); 246 pp.

Zinsser, W.: *On writing well: An informal guide to writing non-fiction* (New York, Harper and Row, 1980); 187 pp.

Periodicals

Consult (London, Institute of Management Consultants).

Consultants News (Fitzwilliam, New Hampshire, Kennedy Publications).

Consultation (New York, Human Sciences Press).

Consulting (Suresnes, France, M. M. Editions).

Journal of Management Consulting (Milwaukee, Wisconsin, Journal of Management Consulting, Inc.).

Management Consultancy (London, VNU Business Publications).

Management Consultant International (Dublin, Lafferty Publications).

Management Consultants News (Chorleywood, Hertfordshire, Prime Marketing Publications).

Directories

Consultants and Consulting Organizations Directory 1990, 2 vols. (Detroit, Michigan, Gale Research, 10th ed., 1989).

Directory of Executive Recruiters 1992 (Fitzwilliam, New Hampshire, Kennedy Publications, 1992); 822 pp.

Directory of Key Executive Search Firms in Europe (Geneva, Consultex, 1992); 43 pp.

Directory of Management Consultants (Fitzwilliam, New Hampshire, Kennedy Publications, 1993); 840 pp.

Directory of Management Consultants in the UK 1991 (London, Task Force Pro Libra, 1991); 497 pp.

Directory of Outplacement Firms 1995-96 (Fitzwilliam, New Hampshire, Kennedy Publications, 1994).

EIU: *Executive search in Europe: Choosing and using a headhunter* (London, 1993); 290 pp.

European Consultants Directory (Detroit, Michigan, Gale Research Co., 1992).

European Directory of Management Consultants 1995 (London, A.P. Information Services, 1995).

FEACO directory (Brussels, European Federation of Management Consulting Associations, 1991).

Le guide professionnel des sociétés de conseil (Suresnes, France, M.M. Editions, 7th ed., 1996).

Bibliographies

ACME 1988 annotated bibliography of selected resource materials (New York, Association of Management Consulting Firms, 1988); 84 pp.

Regional and country surveys
(all by ALPHA Publications, Beaconsfield, Buckinghamshire, UK)

Management consultancy services in Japan (1989).

Management consultancy services in the USA (1990).

Management consultancy services in Western Europe (1994).

INDEX